HANDBOOKS

D0027086

MONTANA

W. C. McRAE & JUDY JEWELL

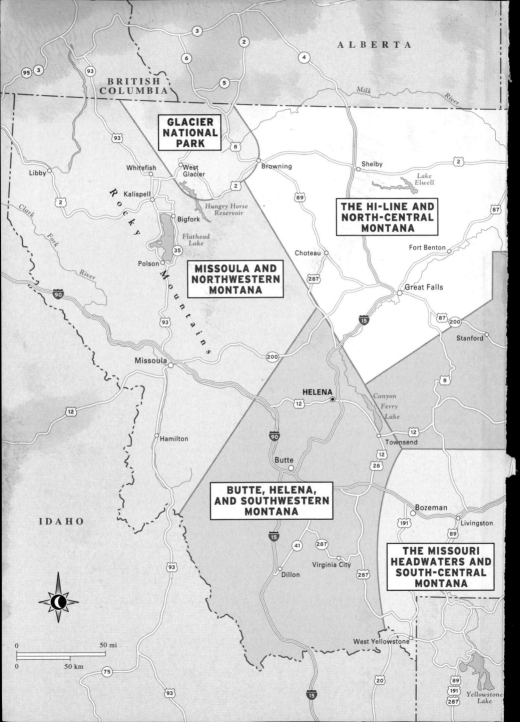

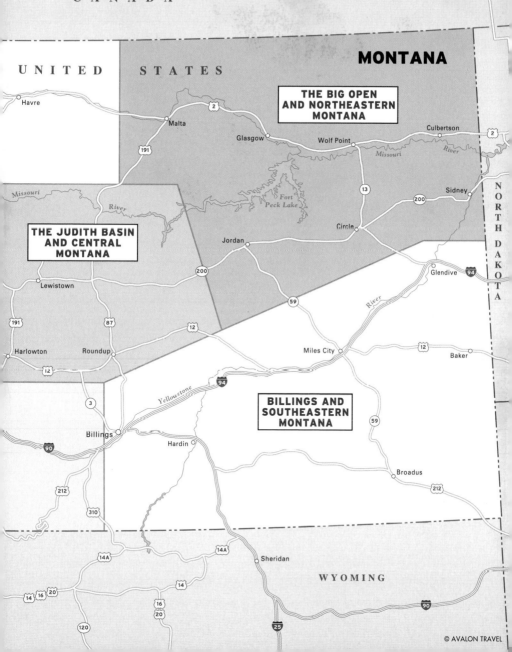

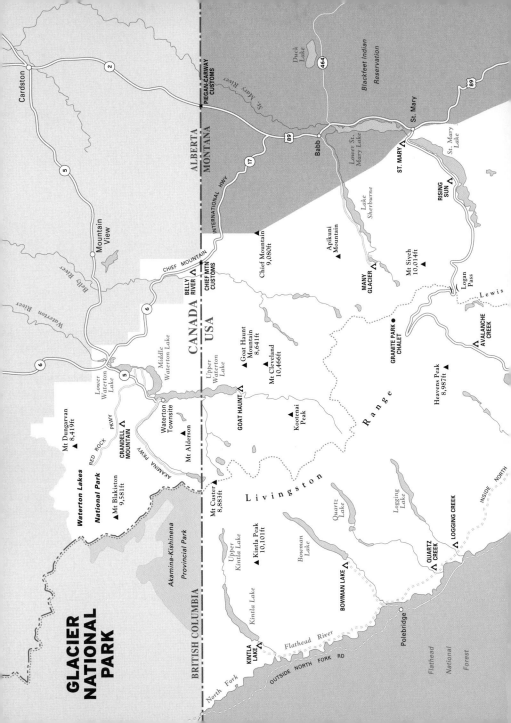

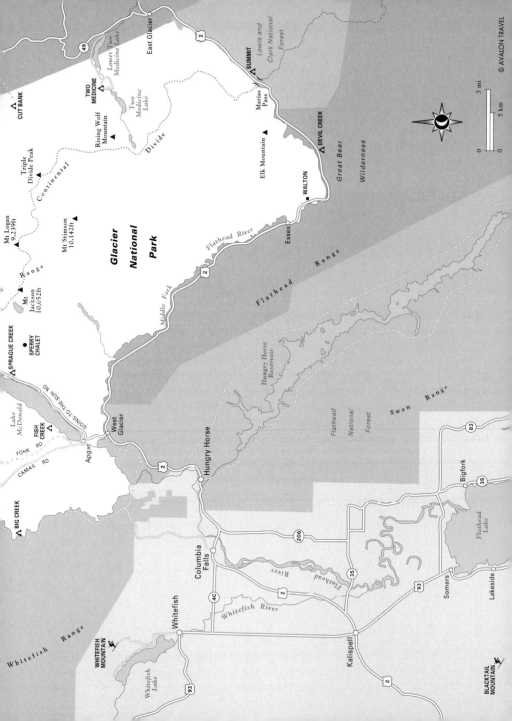

© AVALON TRAVEL

5 mi

5 km

East Glacier

Lower Two Medicine Lake

TWO MEDICINE

CUT BANK

Rising Wolf Mountain

Two Medicine Lake

Divide

Triple Divide Peak

Continental

SUMMIT

Lewis and Clark National Forest

Marias Pass

DEVIL CREEK

Elk Mountain

Great Bear Wilderness

WALTON

Mt Logan 9,239ft

Mt Stimson 10,142ft

Glacier National Park

Range

Mt Jackson 10,052ft

SPRAGUE CREEK

SPERRY CHALET

Flathead River

Essex

Flathead Range

Middle Fork

Lake McDonald

GOING-TO-THE-SUN RD

FISH CREEK

West Glacier

FOHK RD

Apgar

CAMAS RD

BIG CREEK

Hungry Horse

Hungry Horse Reservoir

Flathead National Forest

Swan Range

83

Bigfork

35

Flathead Lake

Columbia Falls

206

35

93

Somers

Lakeside

Whitefish Range

40

2

Flathead River

WHITEFISH MOUNTAIN

Whitefish

93

Whitefish River

Whitefish Lake

Kalispell

2

BLACKTAIL MOUNTAIN

49

2

Contents

Discover Montana

There is a grandness to Montana that surpasses mere size and encompasses something more of the spirit. With its soaring Rocky Mountain peaks rising above high plains carved by mighty rivers, Montana seems a place of legend, a marvel of vastness, wilderness, and epic history at the very crown of the continent. One might even say that Montana is more than a state – Montana is a state of mind.

For such a remote place, Montana has been a traveler's destination for centuries. During summers, Native American hunting parties journeyed into Montana, returning to their mountain homes with stories of a rich, mysterious land full of buffalo and holy sites. Cattle drivers, following the seasons northward, summered in Montana and returned south with tales of abundant game, endless grasslands, and high adventure. Immigrant farmers and ranchers were drawn to the expanses of Montana and brought the newcomer's conviction of fresh beginnings and wry aspirations. Nowadays, Montana attracts writers and artists who find in the state a "sense of place" both nurturing and hostile to the people who endure here.

Montana is often described as if it were two states – an eastern prairie and a western mountain range – but more than a common government links these regions. A visitor first notices the space: A sense of monumentality unites Montana, whether it's the glaciated peaks of the west or the

eroded badlands of the east. It's called Big Sky Country; out here nature limbers up, stretches past the horizons, and takes up room.

But as much as space, the people define Montana. Today's Montanans derive from many strains: immigrant farmer, sheepherder, Native American, miner, logger, shopkeeper, rancher. They were all people who came to a hard land and stayed, making from Montana a living only of sorts, but always a home. Montanans are self-reliant and quick to see humor, with personalities so expansive that so few really do fill the state.

History is not very old here. Montanans are still experiencing their past, not as Western history, but as Western ethic. We invite you to experience this: Stop to investigate Montana's towns and cities, its streams and parks. Follow a hunch, dawdle along a side road. The land fairly explodes with small epiphanies of beauty. Take the long way around to a spot where a moment of history can be relived, where a lazy picnic can be shared, or where the obscure and the out-of-the-way can be found for its own sake.

Planning Your Trip

▶ WHERE TO GO

Montana is a very big state, and unless you have weeks to spend on the road, you simply won't be able to see and experience all that the state has to offer. On a shorter trip, choose a corner or two to explore. Region by region, here are the state's highlights.

Missoula and Northwestern Montana

Missoula is a friendly student-oriented city that's home to the University of Montana, legions of writers, and a dynamic arts community. To the south, the narrow Bitterroot Valley is a recreational wonderland. The Bitterroot River is renowned for trout fishing. Overlooking the rugged Mission Mountains, the National Bison Range preserves a wild herd of the American Bison, hunted nearly to extinction in other parts of the West.

Flathead Lake is one of the state's most popular destinations. This is an ideal place for a quiet vacation of water sports and fishing. Bigfork, on the lake's east side, is one of the artiest small towns in Montana, with some of the best restaurants in the state. Whitefish sits at the base of the large destination ski resort Whitefish Mountain Resort. The two combine to create a lively recreational scene, both in winter and summer.

Glacier National Park

The single most scenic destination in Montana, this park protects a wilderness of lakes, towering glacier-scarred peaks, and fragile alpine meadows. Lake McDonald glimmers at the base of the fantastically carved peaks. You'd be hard-pressed to find a more scenic drive in North America than Going-to-the-Sun

South Central Montana's Livingston

Glacier National Park's Lake McDonald

Road, which climbs from the lake to cross the Continental Divide. Waterton Lakes National Park, adjoining Glacier Park in Canada, continues this wonderful mountain and lake scenery. It's the backcountry that makes Glacier Park so thrilling. Be sure to get out of the car and explore.

Butte, Helena, and Southwestern Montana

This is the region of Montana's first gold rush and its early mining history. Ghost towns such as Bannack and Virginia City tell the fascinating story of vigilantes and the early gold-mining frontier. Helena, the state capital, is a gold camp that managed to evolve into an endearing small city filled with fantastic period architecture. Butte, once known as the "Richest Hill on Earth," has more history per square inch than anywhere else in Montana. For recreation and beauty it's hard to beat the Big Hole Valley, and there's history at the

Big Hole Battlefield, where Chief Joseph and his Nez Percé defeated the U.S. cavalry. Dillon is a charming town at the center of a huge ranching valley. Fishing is excellent, and there's marvelous wildlife viewing at Red Rock Lakes, home to rare trumpeter swans.

The Missouri Headwaters and South-Central Montana

In this mountainous region, all roads lead to Yellowstone National Park, the nation's oldest and largest. Three of the park's entrances are in Montana. Be sure to stop and spend time in Bozeman, a charming small university town filled with art galleries and great restaurants. Livingston is another well-preserved town that's been transformed by its community of famous, cutting-edge visual and literary artists.

Big Sky, the state's most upscale ski resort, and the ski area at Red Lodge make this a great winter destination. In summer, hikers take to the mountains in Absaroka-Beartooth

The wide-open spaces of the Big Open are well-suited for ranch work.

a mandatory stop for fans of the Corps of Discovery. The Bighorn River, in the Crow Reservation, is one of Montana's best trout fishing rivers. You don't have to be an angler to be amazed by the river's mighty Bighorn Canyon and the Yellowtail Dam.

The Judith Basin and Central Montana

Rolling prairies and isolated mountain ranges make this one of Montana's most lovely, low-key destinations. Lewistown is a friendly town with a beautiful old downtown little changed since the 1910s. In mid-August, the state's premier cowboy poetry event is held here. Harlowton is another well-preserved railroad town along the Musselshell River and Highway 12, one of the most scenic routes across the state. The Charles M. Bair Family Museum in Martinsdale preserves an eclectic, fascinating collection of art and antiques in a rambling ranch home—sort of a Little Versailles on the Prairie. White Sulphur Springs offers hot springs cures and mineral baths, and just down the valley the wild Smith River entices white-water rafters and anglers to explore a remote river canyon.

Wilderness, which boasts Montana's highest peaks and oddities, including grasshopper glaciers. Anglers come from around the world to toss a fly in the fabled trout waters of the Madison, Gallatin, and Yellowstone Rivers.

Billings and Southeastern Montana

One absolute must-see in this part of the state is the Little Bighorn Battlefield National Monument. The clash of Custer's troops with the warriors of the Sioux and Cheyenne Nations is one of those defining moments in history, and the battlefield is one of the West's most haunted places. Near Glendive, Makoshika State Park is a badlands preserve with hiking trails through a wildly eroded landscape. Miles City's Range Riders Museum is one of the state's best community museums. East of Billings, Pompey's Pillar is a sandstone bluff with carvings made by members of the Lewis and Clark Expedition over 200 years ago. It's

The Big Open and Northeastern Montana

As its name indicates, this part of Montana is full of wide-open spaces. If you're looking for unadulterated Western experience, stop in little towns such as Malta or Jordan for an eyeful of cowboy and cowgirl culture.

If you're passing through on a summer weekend, check to see if there's a rodeo in the area. The Wolf Point Wild Horse Stampede is one of the state's most famous. Massive Fort Peck Dam is one of the world's largest, backing up the Missouri River for 150 miles. Surrounding it is the C. M. Russell National Wildlife Refuge, the largest in the contiguous United States and home to a wealth of fossils (these are some of the richest dinosaur digs in the world). Migratory birds make stopovers at Medicine Lake, a series of prairie wetlands in extreme northeast Montana. Fort Union Trading Post National Historic Site, near the confluence of the Missouri and Yellowstone Rivers, is a wonderful re-creation of an 1840s fur-trading fort.

The Hi-Line and North-Central Montana

This mostly flat agricultural area brushes up against the front range of the Rocky Mountains. Great Falls is home to the new Lewis and Clark National Historic Trail Interpretive Center, which retells the story of the Corps of Discovery's 1804–1806 journey from St. Louis to the Pacific and back. Also in Great Falls, the C. M. Russell Museum preserves a large collection of this amazing artist's works. Havre's raucous pioneer days are revealed in the Havre Beneath the Streets tours, which show the businesses and communities that thrived below the city's streets in the 1890s. Near Choteau, Egg Mountain contains outcrops of fossilized dinosaur eggs. View these egg fossils at the Old Trail Museum and schedule a tour of a dino dig at the Two Medicine Dinosaur Center. Just west of Choteau, the Rocky Mountain Front rears up, a beautiful and remote area where the prairie meets the mountains.

► WHEN TO GO

Most travelers come to Montana in the summertime, when it's easy to get around and towns are busy with events such as rodeos, powwows, and arts fairs. Even at the peak of the summer season, crowds usually aren't a big problem. Even if there are a lot of tourists, there's even more Montana.

Skiers, both downhill and cross-country, should definitely consider traveling here in the winter. Of course, that's when the ski towns are in full swing, but there are many pleasures to be had from a quiet winter visit on cross-country skis or snowshoes to Glacier National Park.

Make note that fall is hunting season and that during the spring and early summer, many mountain roads and trails will still be blocked by snow.

Remember that Montana is a big state—it takes a good two days just to drive across it on the interstate—and allow yourself ample time to explore. A week will give you a good amount of time either to touch on a few areas of the state or to really explore one region.

the Tongue River, near Ashland

Explore Montana

▶ MONTANA'S BEST ROAD TRIP

Montana is a big state, but for those who don't mind doing some driving, it's possible (indeed, exhilarating) to do a wide-ranging tour. Expect this Tour de Montana to take the better part of two weeks. If you really want to explore any particular area, add more time.

Northwestern Montana and Glacier National Park

Start your trip in Missoula, northwestern Montana's cultural hub and an easy place to land. From there, a trip north up the Mission Valley, home of the Flathead Reservation, brings you to Flathead Lake, the largest freshwater lake in the West. Stay in tiny Polson, bustling Bigfork, or Whitefish, the region's recreational capital, then head east for a tour of Glacier National Park.

Your best bet is to drive through the park on the Going-to-the-Sun Road. Even a relatively deliberate drive along this road can take all day, so plan to either spend at least one night in a park lodge or in one of its eastside border towns, St. Mary or East Glacier.

North-Central Montana

From Glacier National Park's eastern edge

along the Clark Fork River, Missoula

TRAILING T. REX: FOSSIL STOPS

Montana may be a ways from the center of life in the modern United States, but 70 million years ago, Montana was a happening place. At the time, Montana was at the shore of a vast shallow sea, where ancient dinosaurs prowled the shoreline forests. These plants and animals eventually met their fates and are preserved in Montana's incredibly rich fossil beds. If you have a fossil or dinosaur enthusiast in your family, this itinerary, which would take a week or 10 days in its entirety, would provide lots of memories.

SOUTHEASTERN MONTANA
If you enter Montana from the southeast corner, travel about 80 miles south of I-94 on Highway 7 to **Ekalaka**, one of the most isolated towns in all of Montana. This Old West community is home to the **Carter County Museum**, which contains the only known remains of *Pachcephalosaurus*, discovered locally by the high school science teacher, a noted amateur paleontologist.

NORTHEASTERN MONTANA
From Ekalaka, travel northwest on Highway 333 about 60 miles to **Miles City** and then another 86 miles northwest on Highway 59 to **Jordan,** the remote capital of the Big Open. In the Missouri River badlands north of Jordan are some of the richest fossil beds in the nation: A complete skeleton of a *T. rex* is in the small community museum. As you drive Highway 543 north about 25 miles to **Hell Creek State Park,** on the banks of Fort Peck Reservoir, you'll drop through geologic time; the Hell Creek Formation is the geologic layer with the greatest concentration of Cretaceous-era remains.

From Jordan, head east on Highway 200 for 36 miles, then turn north and follow Highway 24 for 60 miles to **Fort Peck,** where the Fort Peck In-

terpretive Center displays the fossil remains of ancient life uncovered while this enormous Missouri River dam was constructed in the 1930s.

From Fort Peck, head a few miles north on Highway 24 to Highway 2, then continue about 70 miles west to **Malta.** The **Judith River Dinosaur Institute,** near Malta, offers a variety of hands-on programs at fossil excavations along the Missouri. While these multiday camps can't accommodate drop-in enthusiasts, with a little planning they would be the perfect focus for a family or group excited to learn extraction techniques and lab skills.

NORTH-CENTRAL MONTANA
A few hours to the west (take Highway 2 west to Havre, then Highway 87 south to Great Falls, then to **Choteau**), along the Rocky Mountain Front, are the dinosaur nests of **Egg Mountain,** where paleontologists unearthed the ancient nesting grounds of *Maiasaura*. Displays of fossilized *Maiasaura* eggs are found at the excellent **Old Trail Museum** in Choteau, and the **Two Medicine Dinosaur Center** leads tours and offers dino dig programs to the local fossil beds. Multiday paleontology workshops are also offered through the center.

SOUTH-CENTRAL MONTANA
Highway 89 will take you the long, slow, interesting way from Choteau to **Livingston** (about 220 miles; stop for the night in White Sulphur Springs if you need a rest), which is a quick 26 miles east of **Bozeman** on I-90. Jack Horner, from Montana State University in Bozeman, has been the driving force behind the surge in Montana dinosaur excavation and interpretation in recent years, and the fossil highlights of his long career can be seen at the **Museum of the Rockies** in Bozeman.

just south of St. Mary, you can see the striking Rocky Mountain Front as you travel south along Highway 89. It's about 140 miles from St. Mary to Great Falls, where visits to the Lewis and Clark National Historic Trail Interpretive Center and the C. M. Russell Museum will easily fill a day or two.

Central Montana
Then it's just over 100 miles east on Highway 87 to Lewistown, which is small enough to give you the flavor of eastern Montana life. Lewistown is surrounded by places to hike, fish, or explore (including ghost towns and the Missouri River badlands).

the view from Beartooth Highway in South-Central Montana

Southeastern Montana

Head southeast to the "big" city life in Billings. Spend the night if you like (there's a vibrant bar and brewpub scene here), or continue about 60 miles southeast from Billings on I-90 to the Little Bighorn National Monument and the spectacular Bighorn Canyon.

South-Central Montana

Turn back west on I-90, and at Laurel turn south on Highway 310 for about 10 miles, then southwest on Highway 212 for about 30 miles to Red Lodge, at the base of the Beartooth Highway. Plan to spend a day driving this winding road up to Yellowstone National Park, where you can stay as long as you like and never run out of places to explore. Though it's only 120 miles from Red Lodge to Gardiner via the Beartooth Highway (Highway 212), it's an all-day drive. When it's time to leave Yellowstone, travel north on Highway 89 through Gardiner 53 miles

to Livingston, which is a quirky hybrid of old and new West, with atmospheric old bars and high-end art galleries sharing Main Street. Just 26 miles west of Livingston on I-90 is Bozeman, home of Montana State University and the Museum of the Rockies (a dinosaur lover's must-see).

Stay on I-90 west as far as Three Forks (30 miles west of Bozeman), where at the Missouri headwaters, Lewis and Clark had to make some tough travel-planning choices. (As do you—if you're running short on time, take I-90 west 173 miles back to Missoula.)

Southwestern Montana

To continue an exploration of Montana's heritage, head south 61 miles on Highway 87 to Virginia and Nevada Cities, where frontier-era buildings have been preserved, and there's a visceral sense of the ruggedness of gold-rush towns. For a true ghost town that's remarkably well preserved, don't miss Bannack, just south of Highway 278, west

Southwestern Montana's Big Hole Valley

of Dillon and about 80 miles from Virginia City, on the edge of the expansive Big Hole Valley. From the Big Hole, follow Highways 278 and 43 west over Chief Joseph Pass, and stop along Highway 43 about 60 miles west of Bannack to visit the Big Hole National Battlefield, where the Nez Percé, fleeing their Oregon homeland, were attacked by the U.S. Army.

Once you reach the Bitterroot Valley, it's an easy day's drive (about 100 miles north along Highway 93) back to Missoula.

▶ A LEWIS AND CLARK EXPEDITION

When Lewis and Clark led the Corps of Discovery across Montana, they had little idea what they'd find there. They hoped for an easy passage from the upper Missouri River to the Columbia River; they knew they would encounter Native Americans, and in fact were counting on help from the local tribes. They knew they'd see all sorts of unfamiliar flora and fauna, and they were trained to document and preserve these species. But they found geography that was much more convoluted than they'd imagined, Indians who provided more help than they'd thought would be needed, and a richness of plant and animal life that is reflected in almost every journal entry.

Lewis and Clark took five months—from April 25, 1805, to September 10, 1805—to cross Montana, but you'll probably want to do it in a week or two. And while you may not need to report your discoveries to the president, as Lewis and Clark did, you'll surely return home with plenty to share with family and friends.

Missouri Headwaters State Park, in the Jefferson River Valley

The trip from Virgelle to Fort Benton can either be on back roads or on Highway 87. A real highlight of a Lewis and Clark pilgrimage is to take a boat trip through the wild and scenic stretch of the Missouri where the corps saw "seens of visionary inchantment." Road travelers can drive the Missouri Breaks Backcountry Byway.

The great waterfalls of the Missouri meant many days of portaging for the corps members; for travelers, Great Falls, 36 miles southwest of Fort Benton via Highway 87, is the site of the excellent Lewis and Clark National Historic Trail Interpretive Center.

Upper Missouri Valley

From Great Falls, it's 90 miles south on I-15 to Helena. East of town are the Upper Missouri Lakes, formed by a series of dams. Behind Holter Dam are the "remarkable clifts" that Lewis called Gates of the Mountains, which modern travelers can visit on guided boat tours.

Along the Missouri and Milk Rivers

Start, as they did, in the eastern part of the state, along the Missouri River at Fort Union, a fascinating re-creation of an 1840s frontier trading post at the confluence of the Missouri and Yellowstone Rivers, and head west along Highway 2, following the Missouri to Fort Peck, about 120 miles west of the North Dakota line. Spend the first night at Fort Peck, with its enormous reservoir, dinosaur museum, and 1930s New Deal architecture, including a well-preserved hotel from the town's dam-building heyday. West and north of Fort Peck, Highway 2 follows the Milk River, named by Meriwether Lewis for the color of its water. From Fort Peck to Havre is about 160 miles, then it's another 50 miles south on Highway 87 to Virgelle, where you'll rejoin the Missouri and head about 25 miles south to Fort Benton.

Jefferson River Valley

From Helena, continue some 66 miles upstream (southeast on Highway 287) through Townsend to Three Forks, where the Madison, Jefferson, and Gallatin Rivers merge to form the Missouri. Perched on a bluff at Missouri Headwaters State Park, you'll realize how difficult it was for the explorers to pick the correct stream to follow to the Continental Divide. (It was the Jefferson.)

The easiest way up the Jefferson now is to take I-90 about 30 miles west of Three Forks to Whitehall, then turn south and travel another 30 miles on Highway 41 to Twin Bridges. About 15 miles southwest of Twin Bridges, on Highway 41, you'll see Beaverhead Rock, the landform that told Sacagawea that she was near the place where she'd grown up. Another 15 miles down Highway 41 is Dillon, a good base for exploring this part of the state.

SOAK IT UP: HOT SPRINGS OF MONTANA

Hot water gurgles up all over the state, and it's exploited to one degree or another by a wide variety of resorts, from the rustic to the chic. Be sure to bring a swimsuit – these aren't clothing-optional spots! A breakneck tour of the state's hot springs can be done in a few days, but chances are you'd rather relax and make this into a weeklong trip.

NORTHWESTERN MONTANA

The town of **Hot Springs** is a good place to kick off your tour. It's pretty down-home, so it'll get you used to a slower pace right off the bat. Here you can stay at the **Symes Hotel,** swim in the outdoor pool, and bathe in an old-fashioned tub filled with sulfurous water. Don't rush out of town before stopping at **Wild Horse Hot Springs,** where the private plunges and steam rooms take rusticity to a new – and surprisingly heavenly – level.

Head southeast to Paradise for a swim at **Quinn's Hot Springs,** and then farther on to the Bitterroot Valley, where you'll find **Lolo Hot Springs.** This is a good place to spend the night; you can think of Lewis and Clark and their crew cleaning up here after months on the road. The next day, continue south to Sula to the **Lost Trail Hot Springs** with its nice outdoor pool, indoor hot tub and saunas, lodge, cabins, and campground.

SOUTHWESTERN MONTANA

Moving on from the Bitterroot Valley to the Big Hole, **Jackson Hot Springs** is the main thing going in Jackson, and it is another good place to spend a night. But don't miss **Elkhorn Hot Springs** in Polaris, another rustic place with cabins and a lodge.

Traveling northeast you'll find **Fairmont Hot Springs** near Anaconda, which has large pools and full resort facilities. Stay here if you like the more luxurious style, or travel about 35 miles north on I-15 to visit **Boulder Hot Springs,** a huge and partially renovated old hotel with a nice outdoor pool and indoor plunges.

CENTRAL MONTANA

One hundred miles east of Boulder on Highway 12 you'll find **White Sulphur Springs** and the

Spa Hot Springs Motel, with an outdoor swimming pool, indoor soaking pool, therapeutic treatments, and motel.

SOUTH-CENTRAL MONTANA

From White Sulphur Springs, it's another Montana-sized jaunt of 100 miles down Highway 89 to **Pray** and the state's crown jewel of hot springs, **Chico Hot Springs,** home of a huge outdoor pool, a cool old lodge, and tons of atmosphere. Plan to stay here for at least one night and then head back north.

You can also visit the pools and day spa at **Bozeman Hot Springs** in Bozeman. From the "Four Corners" intersection right near Bozeman Hot Springs, head about 25 miles west on Highway 84 to **Norris Hot Springs,** a charming pool filled with the "water of the gods."

One last stop, for those travelers who have ample budgets, is **Potosi Hot Springs,** up the road from Norris, past the tiny town of **Pony.** If your wallet's too thin to take in Potosi, drag your wrinkled body out of that pool at Norris and get moving toward home!

soaking it up at Chico Hot Springs

HISTORIC HOTELS

Travelers have been journeying to Montana for a couple of centuries, and if you count the Native Americans who traveled to the plains to hunt, for quite a bit longer. Though the native hunters didn't build hotels, the travelers who came after Lewis and Clark became increasingly used to comfortable accommodations, and by the early 1900s most towns had hotels – and many of these historic hotels are still in operation. An itinerary based on historic hotels and B&Bs in historic homes will bring you close to the history of the Old West and take you to out-of-the-way destinations that were once important travel centers.

NORTHEASTERN MONTANA

Coming into the state from the east on Highway 2, stop at the **Fort Peck Hotel,** about 120 miles from the state line, built in the 1930s to house guests at one of the nation's largest New Deal projects, the Fort Peck Dam. The old hotel has been upgraded in recent years, but the rambling old structure perfectly captures the spirit of the 1930s.

NORTH-CENTRAL MONTANA

Some of the most unique accommodations in Montana are the homesteaders' homes, pioneer hotel rooms, and sheep wagons at **Virgelle,** a ghost town that has come back to life as a departure point for canoe trips down the Wild and Scenic Missouri River. A variety of lodgings are offered by the Virgelle Mercantile and Missouri River Canoe Company (in a town as small as Virgelle, businesspeople must diversify!); the owner has collected deserted homes from the prairies and brought them here, rebuilding them in all their frontier glory.

If homesteading isn't in your blood, then the **Grand Union Hotel** in **Fort Benton,** south of Virgelle, might be more your style. When it was built as one of the most luxurious hotels in Montana in 1882, Fort Benton was the uppermost point of navigation on the Missouri River, and the Grand Union Hotel welcomed guests off steamboats from St. Louis. This opulent hotel has been completely updated and refurbished and offers excellent meals.

On the way to Glacier National Park, stop by the tiny community of **Dupuyer** to stay at **Inn Dupuyer.** This bed-and-breakfast has built a larger structure around a century-old two-story log cabin. Guests have the benefit of a modern dining room and bathroom facilities while spending the night in the homey comfort of a historic log home.

GLACIER NATIONAL PARK

Glacier National Park has many famous lodges, but savvy travelers and railroad diehards make their way to Essex (on the southern border of the park) to spend the night at the **Izaak Walton Inn,** built as a railway workers' hotel in the 1930s. This old lodging is wonderfully atmospheric and is a magical destination in winter for cross-country skiing – and the fishing ain't bad either.

NORTHWESTERN MONTANA

South of Bigfork (a good spot for lunch), the **Double Arrow Lodge,** about 120 miles from Essex, is a well-loved lakeside lodge and cabin resort from the 1930s, stretching along the shores of beautiful **Seeley Lake.** The old resort has just the right degree of rustic homeyness, and food in the lodge restaurant is notable.

SOUTHWESTERN MONTANA

To reach the next night's lodging, make your way to **Philipsburg.** The biggest news in Philipsburg in, well, 120 years is the reopening of the **Broadway Hotel.** This handsome old lodging has reopened its doors after a complete updating and refurbishing of its rooms and is a fun and comfortable place to begin exploration of the region's rich mining history.

In **Boulder,** history of a different kind is on display at **Boulder Hot Springs.** For centuries, Native Americans came for R&R in these hot mineral waters, and when white entrepreneurs moved in during the 1880s, a glamorous European-style hot-springs spa and hotel sprang up – one of the earliest tourist destinations in the state. If you're looking for a unique and colorful spot to soak away travel aches and pains, this is it.

the 1930s Izaak Walton Inn

SOUTH-CENTRAL MONTANA

In **Three Forks,** where the three branches of the Missouri join, the imposing **Sacajawea Hotel** offers very comfortable lodgings and fine dining in a beautifully renovated lodge.

Continuing east, the **Grand Hotel** in **Big Timber,** while not exactly big-city grand, is pretty special for this little town. The handsome brick building has extracomfortable rooms upstairs and the town's best restaurant downstairs. Naturally, there's also a good bar where you can get to know the mix of locals and travelers who end up here at the end of the day.

Just 22 miles east of Big Timber, **Reed Point** offers one of Montana's most unique hotels, the aptly named **Hotel Montana.** This century-old hotel is in a sleepy little river town that comes alive once a year for the annual Great Montana Sheep Drive (this is not a misprint). Also known as the Running of the Sheep, the September event honors the sheepherders and ranchers who founded the town. This beautifully renovated, slightly fabulous hotel bespeaks these days of the Wild and Woolly West.

SOUTHEASTERN MONTANA

It's about 200 miles of interstate driving east from Reed Point to **Miles City**. Miles City once boasted fine hotels where ranchers and livestock buyers met to trade stories and cattle, but only one of these old hotels is still in business. The **Olive Hotel** is no longer the gem it once was – 'round about 1890 – but it's still a perfectly comfortable place to stay, and there's no better place to use as base camp to explore the fantastic old bars of downtown Miles City.

Horse Prairie Valley

If you want to muddle around in the south-western corner of the state for as long as the corps did, you really couldn't find a lovelier place. A trip along southwestern Montana's back roads (try Highway 324, which joins I-15 about 20 miles south of Dillon) will take you to Horse Prairie Valley, where the corps met a band of Shoshone Indians and their chief, Sacagawea's brother, and to Lemhi Pass and the Continental Divide.

Bitterroot Valley

Of course, it wasn't a quick trip over the divide and to the Pacific for the Corps of Discovery. They struggled in the mountains here and ulti-mately headed north down the Bitterroot River to leave the area west of Lolo (present-day Highway 12). As you head north on Highway 93 through the 100-mile-long Bitterroot Valley, don't miss Travelers' Rest, south of Lolo, and the newly discovered corps latrine, which pro-vides rare physical evidence (don't worry, it's not *that* graphic) of the explorers' visit.

▶ FISHING SOUTHWEST MONTANA

Montana is well known as a fishing paradise, and some of the nation's best streams are in the southwestern part of the state. Be sure to pick up a fishing license (available at any fly shop) and check the fishing regulations. Don't be surprised to find that almost every-body here is a catch-and-release fly angler, even in places where that's not mandated. The state maintains many fishing access areas near bridges and stream banks; any special regulations or precautions are posted at these fishing sites. Most fishing access areas are also de facto campgrounds. Though the following itinerary is broken down day by day, it's ideal to allow at least two days at each spot to become acquainted with the local stream habitats.

Day 1

Pack your fly rod and waders and head south from Missoula along Highway 93 to the Bitterroot Valley, where the many fishing ac-cess sites make it easy to get to the river. Fish the Bitterroot for rainbow, brown, and west-slope cutthroat trout as well as some brook-ies and bull trout. It's easy to camp in the Bitterroot National Forest or to find a place to stay in one of the several small towns

in the valley. Hamilton, 50 miles south of Missoula, is the biggest, and a popular base.

Days 2-3

Just south of Conner, the river divides into east and west forks. Continue south along Highway 93, which follows the East Fork of the Bitterroot as far as Sula. Stay on 93 as the river bends east, and head to the Continental Divide at Lost Trail Pass, about 50 miles south of Hamilton. Turn west onto Highway 43 and head down into the Big Hole, a beau-tiful vast high valley. Plan to spend a night in Jackson, about 50 miles east of the pass, at the Jackson Hot Springs (it's your only choice in this small town, but a good one) and fish the Big Hole River. In the Big Hole you'll find the expected assortment of trout, but also a few arctic grayling. From Jackson, follow the river's wide arc along the northern edge of the valley (highways 278 and 43 and I-15 form this 160-mile loop of the Big Hole), through Wisdom, Wise River, Divide, Silver Star, and Melrose, all tiny towns with few amenities. If you're really taking your time, this trip could take a few days. On the south-eastern rim of the Big Hole and conveniently located on I-15, Dillon makes a good base.

Hamilton, 50 miles south of Missoula, is a good base for fishing.

Day 4

From Dillon, catch Highway 41 along the Beaverhead River and follow it 29 miles to Twin Bridges (home of the R. L. Winston Rod Company), where the Beaverhead and the Big Hole join to form the Jefferson River.

Days 5-6

After exploring these streams, head 43 miles east on Highway 287 past Virginia and Nevada Cities to Ennis, a Madison River town that has staked its claim on fly-fishing. Fish the Madison upstream of Ennis, then head 45 miles north on Highway 287 to Three Forks, where the Madison, Jefferson, and Gallatin Rivers meet at the Missouri Headwaters State Park. This is a powerful place to visit and a decent enough place to cast a line. In Three Forks, longtime fishing guide Bud Lilly has turned an old rooming house into, well, a fixed-up old rooming house for anglers.

Day 7

From Three Forks, travel east on I-90 for 24 miles, then turn south at Belgrade (Highway 85, which becomes Highway 191) to fish the Gallatin all the way south to West Yellowstone (some 90 miles), where you find the upper reaches of the Madison River. Enter Yellowstone National Park for the Firehole, the Gibbon, and the Yellowstone.

Day 8

Follow the Yellowstone downstream, north along Highway 89, into Montana's Paradise Valley, where a night at Chico Hot Springs is always a treat, especially if you've been camping for a while. It's about 75 miles from West Yellowstone.

The Yellowstone is the longest undammed river in the lower 48 states.

Days 9-10

Take a couple days (or as long as you like) to fish the 23-mile stretch of the Yellowstone between Chico and Livingston, which is 26 miles east of Bozeman on I-90. Though Highway 89 follows the Yellowstone, the East River Road, which parallels 89 on the east side of the river, is a good option. By then it'll probably be time to dry out those waders and head home.

MISSOULA AND NORTHWESTERN MONTANA

By common perception, the northwestern part of the state is wet, forested, and populous. But in fact, the main city, Missoula, has only 64,000 inhabitants, receives no more than 13 inches of rain in an average year, and is only particularly well-forested in the Rattlesnake corridor. Much of this corner of the state has been voraciously logged, and the climate is too harsh for seedling trees to easily reforest the clear-cut areas.

The other common perception about northwestern Montana is that it's a recreationalist's dream come true. That it is: Not only is it the gateway to Glacier National Park, but there are fishing areas, hiking trails, and public campgrounds galore, particularly in the national forests.

For many visitors, this is archetypal Montana; these beautiful lakes and soaring mountain peaks are what you came here for. However, you're not alone. The last decade has seen burgeoning growth in this area, particularly in the Flathead Valley, so be prepared to share this corner of Montana with quite a few others.

Northwestern Montana's topography is characterized by a series of forested mountain ranges (the Cabinets, Missions, Bitterroots, Flatheads, Salish, Whitefish, Purcells, and Swans), running generally northwest to southeast, and the valleys that separate them. Although this is a mountainous area, it's not particularly high by Montana standards; Montana's lowest spot (1,892 feet) is where the Clark Fork River enters Idaho near Troy in the state's northwest corner.

Missoula is at the mouth of Hell Gate Canyon, the Clark Fork River's path between Mt. Jumbo (to the north, with the "L" for Lolo

HIGHLIGHTS

(Hiawatha Mountain Bike Trail: This 15-mile trail along a former railroad runs gently downhill from its start at Lookout Pass, and passes over trestles and through tunnels. Most riders catch a shuttle for the return trip (page 43).

(National Bison Range: Obviously bison are the main attraction, but come prepared to see bighorn sheep, pronghorn, elk, mule deer, white-tailed deer, and mountain goats as well. Even if all the animals are in hiding, thve land, the sky, and the light are beautiful here (page 60).

(St. Ignatius Mission: Built in 1854, the St. Ignatius Mission was the second Catholic mission in Montana. Inside the more modern (1891) brick church, lovely murals painted by the mission cook very sweetly illustrate scenes from the Bible (page 61).

(Jewel Basin Hiking Area: Unlike many wilderness areas, the trails here are relatively easy to reach and suitable for day hikes. Lakes stud the basin; the meadows are strewn with Indian paintbrush, bear grass, fireweed, and showy daisies; and there are great views of Flathead Lake (page 71).

(Conrad Mansion: This 1895 Kalispell mansion is considered one of the best examples of late-19th-century Pacific Northwest architecture (page 81).

(Danny On Trail: Even in summer, a gondola travels up and down Big Mountain. But if you really want to take time to examine the

LOOK FOR **(** TO FIND RECOMMENDED SIGHTS, ACTIVITIES, DINING, AND LODGING.

wildflowers – and in late summer, pick huckleberries – hike this trail from the base of the ski area to the top of the gondola. Hike up, and you can ride down for free. Or pay to ride up, and hike back down (page 91).

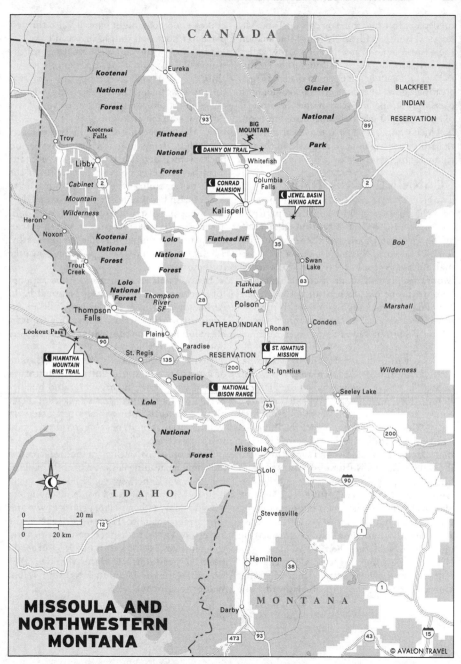

CANADA

Kootenai

National

Forest

Eureka

Glacier

National

Park

BLACKFEET

INDIAN

RESERVATION

93

BIG
MOUNTAIN

89

Troy

Kootenai
Falls

Flathead

National

Forest

Cabinet

Mountain

Wilderness

Libby

DANNY ON TRAIL

Whitefish

Columbia
Falls

CONRAD
MANSION

Kalispell

JEWEL BASIN
HIKING AREA

2

2

Heron

Noxon

Kootenai

National

Forest

Lolo

National

Forest

Flathead NF

35

Bob

Swan
Lake

Trout
Creek

Lolo
National
Forest

Thompson
River
SF

28

Flathead
Lake

Polson

83

Marshall

Thompson
Falls

Lookout Pass

90

HIAWATHA
MOUNTAIN
BIKE TRAIL

Plains

St. Regis

135

Paradise

Superior

FLATHEAD INDIAN

RESERVATION

200

ST. IGNATIUS
MISSION

St. Ignatius

Ronan

Condon

Wilderness

Seeley Lake

NATIONAL
BISON RANGE

93

Lolo

Lolo

National

Forest

Missoula

200

Lolo

90

IDAHO

Stevensville

1

0   20 mi

0   20 km

12

Hamilton

38

1

MONTANA

Darby

1

15

MISSOULA AND NORTHWESTERN MONTANA

473

93

43

© AVALON TRAVEL

spelled out in white stone on the hills) and Mt. Sentinel (south, with an "M" for Montana) on the eastern edge of town. The narrow valley immediately broadens as four other sizable river valleys join it and open up the landscape, creating a bowl-like setting that makes for both pleasingly temperate weather and the dreaded phenomenon of winter temperature inversion, in which warm, moist air, often laden with particulate matter, is trapped and held in the valley by high pressure.

PLANNING YOUR TIME

Travelers entering the region from the west on I-90 should consider spending part of a day on the **Hiawatha Mountain Bike Trail,** at the far western edge of the state, just off I-90. Otherwise, Missoula makes a good formal jumping-off spot for a tour of northwest Montana. Plan to spend a couple of nights here, with one day devoted to both sightseeing and informal hanging-out in this pleasant town. It's also possible to spend a full day touring the Bitterroot Valley, returning to Missoula for the night.

Once you've had your fill of Missoula, head north into the Mission Valley. If you're in luck, it'll be powwow time on the Flathead Reservation, but if not, there's plenty of Native American history and culture to take in. (For a tour with a tribal guide, contact the **People's Center** in Pablo.) Plan to devote an early morning or an evening around sunset to watching wildlife at the **National Bison Range.** If birds are more your thing, check out the wetlands at the **Ninepipes Refuge.** The **Mission Mountains** have many good hiking trails and lovely lakes, but be sure to get a tribal recreation permit at any local store before setting out into the wilderness here.

Even with some lingering along the way, Polson is an easy day's drive from Missoula, and this town at the foot of Flathead Lake makes a good overnight base. It's also the best place to find a boat tour of Flathead Lake.

For those who want a slower pace and the simplest, least glitzy spa experience imaginable, take a detour to the tiny town of **Hot Springs** and spend the day checking out various plunges and pools. It's most relaxing if you just stay here for the night.

At the northern edge of Flathead Lake, **Bigfork** is as bustling as Hot Springs is laid back. Remember, this is bustling in Montana terms—it'll never be New York. This is the place to remember where you put that extra wad of cash because it's easy to be tempted by shopping and restaurants. But even on a budget, Bigfork is still entertaining, with plenty of inexpensive camping and free hiking nearby. The **Jewel Basin** is a good place for a day hike in these parts.

In **Kalispell** you can stock up on supplies for a trip into nearby Glacier National Park. Although it seems at first glance to be an entirely utilitarian town, Kalispell's **Conrad Mansion** and **Hockaday Museum of Art** are both worth visiting.

Just a few miles north, **Whitefish** is more of a party town. With **Whitefish Mountain** loaded with snow in the winter and huckleberries in the summer, this is a place for recreation. It's worth noting that Amtrak stops in Whitefish, making it possible to ride the train to a ski vacation.

If you only have one day in the area, chances are you'll be heading either across I-90 or along Highway 93. Either way, you're bound to spend time in Missoula; if that's not quite enough to fill your day, either make a short Lewis and Clark pilgrimage to **Travelers' Rest** in the Bitterroot Valley, perhaps combined with a trip to **Lolo Hot Springs** or a hike to **Peterson Lake,** or head north into the Mission Valley for a hike in the **Mission Mountain Tribal Wilderness Area.**

Missoula

Missoula, tucked in a fertile valley and filled with students, loggers, truck drivers, and writers, is the hub of western Montana. The Missoula Valley has always been a crossroads, first for Indians, then for white settlers, and nowadays for Montana's major highways. It remains a great focus and jumping-off point for the traveler.

The city (pop. 64,000, elev. 3,205 feet) takes its sense of confluence seriously. Practically within the city limits, the Clark Fork is joined by the Blackfoot and Bitterroot Rivers and several smaller streams. As home to the University of Montana, Missoula is a center of learning and one of the state's major cultural centers; it has preserved much of its historic architectural character and offers good restaurants and a full-bodied nightlife. Missoula's nickname, the Garden City, is apt. As a locale, it's about as temperate, fertile, and hospitable as possible in Montana.

But Missoula is more than a picturesque university town. The university and artistic population is notoriously bohemian and political, while the working core of the city is, in Montana terms, decidedly blue-collar. Depending on the perspective, Missoula is either a working-class town with a radical university imposed on it or a liberal-arts college town infiltrated by the proletariat. But the juxtaposition works: scratch a logger and find a poet.

For many visitors, Missoula, or something like it, is the very image of what they expect of all Montana. However, Montanans from the rest of the state mistrust Missoula. To them the town is Montana with an attitude. Much of the east versus west dichotomy of Montana is really shorthand for ambivalence about Missoula and the progressive politics and lifestyles that emerge from it. Throughout the rest of Montana the university is disdainfully referred to as "the dance school."

For a traveler, Missoula is an agreeable home base for excursions into the wonders of western Montana. However, for a visitor with a little time and a taste for artistic and political ferment, Missoula can become addictive. The city's saloons and salons are filled with testimonials of those who planned to pass through but have yet to leave.

HISTORY

With five valleys nearly converging here, it's no surprise that the area has long been used as a thoroughfare. Salish Indians from the Bitterroot and Mission Valleys traveled through Hell Gate Canyon to reach buffalo hunting grounds east of the mountains. They were regularly attacked by the Blackfeet as they entered the canyon, thus giving the passage a formidable reputation. In fact, *Missoula* is from a Salish word that has been variously translated as "by the cold chilling waters," "river of awe," or simply an exclamation of surprise and horror.

Early white settlers seemed to agree. As the story goes, French trappers were horrified when they came across the remains of all the Salish who never made it through the canyon, and called it *Porte de l'Enfer,* which became Hell Gate in English.

The first whites on record to explore the Missoula area were Meriwether Lewis and a brigade of his men on their return trip from the Pacific. Lewis and his group camped at the confluence of the Rattlesnake and Clark Fork Rivers in July 1806 and headed through Hell Gate Canyon without incident.

The Hell Gate Treaty of 1855 opened Missoula and much of western Montana to white settlement. The treaty council took place about seven miles west of Missoula on present-day Highway 263, where a state monument can now be found.

Missoula's growth was spurred by the arrival of the Northern Pacific Railway in 1883. Timber was also important to the town's development. In 1886, A. B. Hammond built what was reputedly the world's largest lumber mill at Bonner, seven miles east of Missoula. It produced timbers for railroads and mines as well as construction lumber.

NORTHWESTERN MONTANA

FLORA AND FAUNA OF NORTHWESTERN MONTANA

Northwestern Montana is the most lushly vegetated part of the state, and its forests, rivers, and wetlands provide homes to a wide variety of birds, fish, and large mammals.

FLORA

Thanks to the warm wet weather blowing over the mountains of Washington and Oregon from the Pacific Ocean, northwestern Montana's forests resemble those of the Pacific Coast with their abundance of conifers, including Douglas fir, western red cedar, and western hemlock. Ponderosa pine, lodgepole pine, and western white pine are other Pacific trees that are important to the landscape and economy of western Montana. There's also a good sprinkling of trees more characteristic of the Rockies, such as Engelmann spruce, western larch, and subalpine fir.

The **bitterroot**, the state flower, was an important food for the Flathead Indians. It is most abundant in the valley that bears its name, where it flowers early in the summer. Subalpine wildflowers bloom wildly on the mountainsides once the snow has melted. Look for glacier lilies, bear grass, Indian paintbrush, and lupine. Shrubs tend to grow at lower elevations than the wildflower meadows. **Huckleberry** bushes run amok in the open areas of northwestern Montana. Look to meadows, old burns, and clear-cuts for the most intense growth. Berries begin to ripen at lower elevations toward the end of July, moving upward as the summer progresses. When in huckleberry country, keep an eye out for bears, which love to feast on the tasty fruit.

Oregon grape and kinnikinnick (whose bark was smoked like tobacco by the Indians) are other common shrubby plants in northwestern Montana forests.

FAUNA

Grizzly bears live in some of the more isolated areas of northwestern Montana, including the Cabinet and Mission Mountains Wilderness Areas. Black bears are more widespread. Don't mess with either type.

Bighorn sheep can be spotted on steep hillsides throughout the state's northwestern corner. There's a special bighorn-viewing area on Highway 200 just east of Thompson Falls and a de facto one along Highway 2 west of Libby. Bighorns also live on the National Bison Range in Moiese, which is just about the only place

---

When other Montana cities vied for the state capital and prison, Missoula alone attempted to land the university. It was established as the University of Montana in Missoula in 1895. Since then it has become a major cultural force, as well as one of the city's major employers.

SIGHTS

Most of Missoula's historic downtown is located on the north side of the Clark Fork. The historic residential areas are across the river, near the university.

Downtown

The old business district was located near the river, along the Mullan Road (now Front Street), where C. P. Higgins and Frank Worden built a sawmill, flour mill, and store along the banks of the Clark Fork. Most of these buildings burned in 1884, and when the city rebuilt, the influence of the incoming Northern Pacific Railway pulled the downtown northward from the Clark Fork along Higgins Avenue.

Many of these buildings remain. The **Missoula Mercantile Building** (now Macy's), at the corner of Front and Higgins, was built between 1882 and 1891. The Merc, as it was known, was established in 1866 and was the city's primary mercantile establishment for more than a century. Note the cast-iron facade along Higgins Avenue.

North on Higgins is the **Higgins Block** (1889), containing well-preserved late-19th-century commercial architecture. On the corner, beneath a prominent cupola, is a gingerbread bank in the Queen Anne style. Farther

in western Montana you'll see **buffalo,** except those kept in private herds as ranch stock or a tourist attraction. Elks, white-tailed and mule deer, moose, and mountain goats are among the other ungulates, or hoofed animals, that inhabit northwestern Montana.

Mountain lions once had a reputation for being rather elusive, but over the past few years they've been reported to roam the streets of Columbia Falls and send joggers up trees in Missoula's Greenough Park.

There's an astounding variety of **birdlife** in northwestern Montana: bald eagles, ospreys, woodpeckers, dippers, Clark's nutcrackers, western tanagers, great blue herons, hawks, owls, vultures, blue grouse, ruffed grouse, magpies, and hummingbirds. There is a host of waterfowl and shorebirds around Ninepipe and Pablo Wildlife Refuges in the Mission Valley. Loons nest in several lakes near Eureka and in the Swan Valley.

There are three major **trout** species in northwestern Montana: cutthroat, bull, and rainbow. The westslope cutthroat is Montana's state fish, and while not officially endangered, it is the object of some concern. Catch-and-release fishing is generally recommended – and in some places

mandatory – for cutthroat. Bull trout live primarily in the Flathead River system, but their populations have also declined dramatically. In order to protect them from further decline, they are off-limits to anglers on all streams west of the Continental Divide. Rainbow trout are widespread and are especially prolific in the Kootenai River, where they're native.

Kokanee salmon were introduced to the Flathead system in the 1930s and flourished there for about 50 years. In recent years, Flathead populations of this landlocked salmon have declined precipitously, most likely because of competition with mysis shrimp. Kokanee are still plentiful in other lakes, including Lake Mary Ronan (west of Flathead Lake) and Lake Koocanusa.

Dams and development have altered the riparian ecology in northwestern Montana. Native fish, including bull trout, westslope cutthroat, and whitefish, having faced the dams and competition from nonnative species such as lake trout and kokanee salmon, are now seriously threatened by habitat degradation caused by logging. In clear-cut areas, soil and debris erode into streams, muddying the water and disturbing the delicate chemistry the fish need.

along the same block are other old stores, now housing trendy businesses. One vintage interior worth visiting, **Butterfly Herbs,** has an espresso bar in the back.

The **County Courthouse** (200 W. Broadway) was constructed in 1910. This large, three-story edifice is noteworthy for its murals. These scenes from Montana history were painted by Edgar Paxson, who was called *Cot-lo-see* (He Who Sees Everything) by admiring Indians.

Missoula's two **train stations** are imposing and handsome. The **Northern Pacific Depot** was built in 1889 at the north end of Higgins Avenue. Missoula's bustling **Farmer's Market** takes place in the park in front of the depot on Saturday mornings and Tuesday evenings in summer—the market is a great spot for people-watching and loading up on coffee, baked

goods, and the local bounty of fruit and vegetables. The Spanish-style **Milwaukee Road Depot** was built in 1910 under the Higgins Avenue Bridge on the south side of the Clark Fork. Neither is in operation as a rail depot.

Carousel for Missoula

A major source of civic pride is the Carousel for Missoula (406/728-0447, 11 A.M.–7 P.M. daily June–Aug., 11 A.M.–5:30 P.M. daily Sept.–May, $1.50 adult, $0.50 child), which stands in Caras Park near the river just west of the Higgins Bridge. All the horses were hand-carved—making this the first hand-carved carousel assembled in the United States in more than 60 years—and each horse has a highly personal, sometimes touching, story associated with it. The fund-raising, carving, and

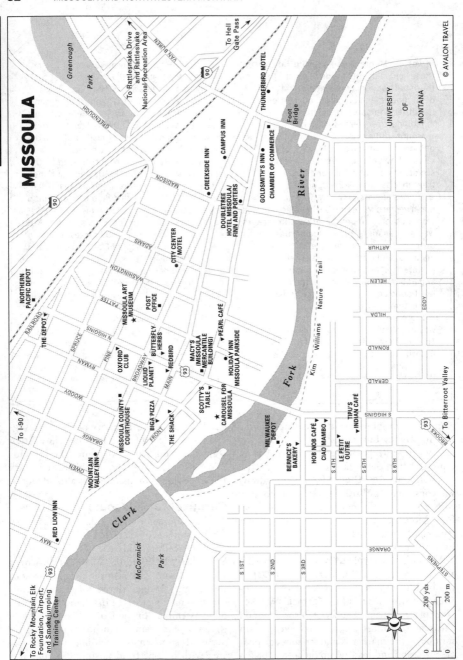

NORTHWESTERN MONTANA

MISSOULA

To Rattlesnake Drive
and Rattlesnake
National Recreation Area

To Hell
Gate Pass

Greenough
Park

GREENOUGH

VAN BUREN

THUNDERBIRD MOTEL ■

Foot
Bridge

● CAMPUS INN

MADISON

● CREEKSIDE INN

GOLDSMITH'S INN ●
CHAMBER OF COMMERCE ■

DOUBLETREE
HOTEL MISSOULA/
FINN AND PORTERS

River

UNIVERSITY
OF
MONTANA

© AVALON TRAVEL

NORTHERN
PACIFIC DEPOT ■

ADAMS

● CITY CENTER
MOTEL

WASHINGTON

RAILROAD

THE DEPOT ▼

PATTEE

MISSOULA ART
MUSEUM ★

N HIGGINS

POST
OFFICE ■

Fork

ARTHUR

HELEN

HILDA

EDDY

SPRUCE

PINE

BUTTERFLY
HERBS ▼

▼ PEARL CAFÉ

RYMAN

OXFORD
CLUB ▼

BROADWAY

▼ REDBIRD

MACY'S
(MISSOULA
MERCANTILE
BUILDING) ■

RONALD

LIQUID
PLANET ▼

MAIN

▼ HOLIDAY INN
MISSOULA PARKSIDE

Nature Trail

GERALD

WOODY

BIGA PIZZA ▼

MISSOULA COUNTY
COURTHOUSE ■

FRONT

SCOTTY'S
TABLE ▼

★
CAROUSEL FOR
MISSOULA

Kim Williams

S HIGGINS

ORANGE

THE SHACK ▼

MOUNTAIN
VALLEY INN ●

OWEN

MILWAUKEE
DEPOT ■

TIPU'S
▼ INDIAN CAFÉ

BROOKS

93 To Bitterroot Valley

To I-90

BERNICE'S
BAKERY ●

HOB NOB CAFÉ ▼
CIAO MAMBO ▼

LE PETIT
OUTRE ▼

S 4TH

S 5TH

S 6TH

Clark

RED LION INN ●

MAY

McCormick

Park

Fork

ORANGE

STEPHENS

S 1ST

S 2ND

S 3RD

93

To Rocky Mountain Elk
Foundation, Airport,
and Smokejumping
Training Center

0   200 yds
0   200 m

construction process really hit a community chord, and almost any local will regale you with stories about the carousel and the meanings of each horse. Next to the carousel, the fantastic **Dragon Hollow playground** was also built by community volunteers.

Missoula Art Museum

The Missoula Art Museum (335 N. Pattee, 406/728-0447, 11 A.M.–5 P.M. Tues.–Sat., free) has a fine home in the city's old Carnegie Library. The museum houses an excellent small permanent collection featuring some top-notch Montana artists and displays traveling art exhibits.

University of Montana

The University of Montana (406/243-0211, www.umt.edu) is located on the south side of the Clark Fork, at the mouth of the river's Hell Gate Canyon. A green and leafy campus built around a central oval, it's a pleasant place to explore, as is the university district, an area of grand and historic old homes.

The university, established by the Montana Legislature in 1895, has developed into an academically broad-based institution with a strong liberal-arts emphasis. Its schools of journalism and forestry are nationally recognized, as is its graduate program in creative writing.

The earliest remaining building on campus is the **University Hall,** built in 1899. Besides containing the university president's office, the building's central tower houses a carillon. At noon each day, students are serenaded by a 15-minute recital of bell music.

Behind University Hall is **Mansfield Library,** named for one of Montana's former senators, Mike Mansfield, and his wife, Maureen. Across a grassy mall from the library is the **University Center** (UC), a modern three-story building constructed around a central atrium. It's a good place to hang out and watch student behavior. At the second-floor food court, a wide variety of quick and inexpensive food is available. On the ground floor is the UC Bookstore (406/243-4921), a good all-purpose bookstore and art-supply source.

Hiking the trail up to the M is a popular activity for U of M students.

One of the university's newer additions is the **Montana Theatre** (406/243-4581), which houses two stages for live theater.

For a bird's-eye, or rather a mountain-goat's-eye, view of the university and the city, climb up Mt. Sentinel to the university's big red-and-white M. It's a 40-minute hike from the trailhead at the north end of the UC parking lot.

The University District

One of Missoula's most pleasant neighborhoods, the university district contains some interesting architectural specimens. Some of the old homes have been turned into fraternity or sorority houses, but others remain private homes. None are open to the public, but a stroll or drive through the area is a pleasant way to learn that Missoula took its early-20th-century affluence seriously. The grandest homes face Gerald Avenue, parallel and one block east of South Higgins. See especially the neoclassical mansion at 1005 Gerald (built 1902–1903), once the home of John R. Toole, a prominent early Montana politician and industrialist, and

THE UNUSUAL EVOLUTION OF FORT MISSOULA

Fort Missoula was built in 1877 in response to the flight of the Nez Percé from their homeland and white settlers' fear of the increasingly recalcitrant Flathead Indians. However, the threat of Indian attack never really materialized, and troops at the fort saw real action only once, at the Battle of the Big Hole. There, troops from Fort Missoula attempted an ambush of Chief Joseph's retreating Nez Percé and were disastrously defeated.

Thereafter, the story of Fort Missoula ceases to sound much like that of an embattled frontier outpost and begins to take on more curious dimensions. In 1888 the Twenty-fifth Infantry Corps, an all-black regiment under the authority of white officers, was garrisoned at the fort. In 1896 bicycle enthusiast Lieutenant James Moss established the Twenty-fifth Infantry Bicycle Corps, which sought to test the potential of the bicycle as a military conveyance. The lieutenant, in comparing the bicycle to the horse, reasoned that the bike "doesn't require as much care. It needs no forage; it moves much faster over fair roads, it is not as conspicuous.... It is noiseless and raises but little dust."

In order to prove to General Nelson Miles that the bicycle was a viable means of troop transport, Moss and 20 men left Missoula on bicycles the following year, bound for St. Louis – 1,900 miles overland. The trip, made on mud trails and sandy paths, took only 41 days. The army higher-ups were not impressed, however, and the Bicycle Corps returned to Missoula by train.

During World War I the fort served as an army training center, and during the Depression it was the regional headquarters for the Civilian Conservation Corps. During World War II, 1,200 Italian seamen and 650 American men of Japanese descent were detained at the fort, and following the war it served as a prison for court-martialed military personnel.

Fort Missoula was closed as a military post in 1947. The fort presently houses government offices and a historical museum. Its grounds are used for such benign events as dog shows.

the university president's house at 1325 Gerald, built around 1930.

South of the university, Missoula's **Vietnam Veterans' Memorial** is in a rose garden at Brooks and Franklin.

Rocky Mountain Elk Foundation

Hunters and other wildlife enthusiasts will want to stop by the Rocky Mountain Elk Foundation (5705 Grant Creek, 406/523-4500, www.rmef.org, 8 A.M.–5 P.M. Mon.–Fri., 10 A.M.–4 P.M. Sat.). The large display area has a mix of wildlife art and mounted animals, including some truly impressive elk. There's also a theater with wildlife films, a gift shop, and a nature trail. The elk foundation is a nonprofit organization, mostly composed of hunters concerned with wildlife habitat conservation. Along with their conservation work, they are strong proponents of responsible hunting and publish a good free brochure of tips for hunters.

Fort Missoula

When Chief Joseph and the Nez Percé retreated across Montana in 1877, Missoula citizens asked the federal government for protection from the Indians, and Fort Missoula was hastily established just southwest of town. During the Second World War the fort was used as a detention center for Italian workers, including merchant seamen, World's Fair employees, and the crew of an Italian luxury liner seized in the Panama Canal.

Two original buildings (a stone powder magazine and an officers' quarters) remain from the 1877 fort site and are now part of the **Fort Missoula Historical Museum** (406/728-3476, www.fortmissoulamuseum.org, Mon.–Sat. 10 A.M.–5 P.M. and Sun. noon–5 P.M. summer, Tues.–Sun. noon–5 P.M. winter, $3 adult, $2 senior, $1 student), which contains exhibits of local history. Other buildings of interest have been relocated to the fort, including an old church, a schoolhouse, and a Forest Service lookout tower. The wide boulevards, green lawns, and white military buildings now evoke a real sense of history. To get there, take Highway 93 south to Reserve Street, turn right, and follow signs at the junction with South Avenue.

Smokejumpers Center

Undeniably unique to Missoula and a source of pride to natives is the Forest Service Smokejumpers Center (5765 W. Broadway, 406/329-4934, 8:30 A.M.–5 P.M. Mon.–Fri. June–Aug., free). Here, firefighters are trained in the science of fighting forest fires as well as the art of parachuting into forest wildfires. The center is open to visitors daily during the summer and features exhibits, films, a diorama, and a tour of the parachuting base. The center is just past Missoula International Airport, south of Highway 93.

RECREATION

Hiking

Many of the in-town hikes are on paths shared by bicyclists. A casual walker can just wander down to the river and pick up the paths that run on either bank in the downtown area. Heading east, the **Kim Williams Trail** follows the south bank of the Clark Fork out of town.

For those who want more of a challenge, head over to the university and follow the zig-zag trail up Mt. Sentinel to the M. It takes about 40 minutes, and a little huffing and puffing, to get there, but on a clear day there are great views of Missoula and Hell Gate Canyon.

Head north from I-90 on Van Buren, which quickly becomes Rattlesnake Drive, and travel about four miles to the **Rattlesnake National Recreation Area and Wilderness.** Here you'll find as much of a wilderness hike as you're likely to find in any city. Missoula's outdoor stores sell trail maps.

Bicycling

Missoula is a great place to travel by bike, and bicycle tourists should definitely stop by the **Adventure Cycling Association** headquarters

(150 E. Pine, 406/721-1776, www.adventure-cycling.org). They distribute a small bicycle-touring map of Missoula as well as a host of other maps for routes stretching across the nation. Two major bike routes cross in Missoula: the north-south **Great Parks Route** and the east-west **Transamerica Route.** Adventure Cycling also operates bicycle tours and is a clearinghouse for information on cycle touring. There's always the opportunity for casual or obsessive bike talk at their offices.

The **Rattlesnake National Recreation Area,** a corridor through the Rattlesnake Wilderness, is a mountain biker's dream, but be sure to avoid cycling in the adjacent wilderness area; maps are available at local outdoor stores.

Mt. Sentinel's summit can be reached by riding south on Pattee Canyon Drive to the un-marked, gated Crazy Canyon Road and climbing to the top of the 5,158-foot peak. A less strenuous fat-tire ride is on the path along the Clark Fork, perhaps venturing east of downtown into the **Kim Williams Nature Area,** named for the late National Public Radio commentator whose voice represented all things Missoulian to many listeners across the country.

Rent a bike at the **Open Road** (517 S. Orange St., 406/549-2453) or **Missoula Bicycle Works** (708 S. Higgins Ave., 406/721-6525).

Fishing

Fishing in Missoula can be as unpremeditated as throwing a line into the Clark Fork from a bridge in the middle of town. The Clark Fork, which was horribly polluted until cleanup measures were taken in the 1970s, is now home to some trout.

Excellent fishing spots abound within an hour's drive of town. The **Clark Fork, Blackfoot,** and **Bitterroot Rivers** harbor rainbow, brown, cutthroat, and bull trout. Like the Clark Fork, the Blackfoot has had some environmental hurdles to overcome in recent years, but local anglers say it's on its way back. **Rock Creek** is reached by traveling 26 miles east of Missoula on I-90 to exit 126. Rock Creek has been designated a blue-ribbon trout stream, although it is not necessarily an easy stream to

© JUDY JEWELL

Kayakers play in the Clark Fork River just downstream from the Higgins Street Bridge in downtown Missoula.

fish. Catch-and-release fishing is enforced along the middle stretch of the creek, and fishing with bait is prohibited, except by children.

Campsites along Rock Creek range from **Ekstrom's Stage Station** (406/825-3183), a full-service tent and RV campground (complete with flush toilets, hot showers, a store, and swimming pool) 0.5 mile from I-90 on Rock Creek Road, to **Siria** (www.fs.fed.us/r1/lolo/) a small bare-bones Forest Service campground with no drinking water, 29 bumpy miles up Rock Creek Road.

For fishing supplies, stop by **Kingfisher Fly Shop** (926 E. Broadway, 406/721-6141) or **Grizzly Hackle** (215 W. Front, 406/721-8996). Both shops run guide services; daylong trips run about $400.

Kayaking

The many rivers of western Montana offer wonderful opportunities for kayak and raft trips. Actually, you don't even need to leave downtown Missoula to play in a kayak; check out the "play wave" that has been constructed

in the Clark Fork River just downstream of the Higgins Street Bridge by Caras Park.

The friendly and experienced **10,000 Waves Raft and Kayak Adventures** (1311 E. Broadway, 406/549-6670 or 800/537-8315, www.10000-waves.com) is one of the best of the local outfitters and offers trips on the Bitterroot, Blackfoot, and Clark Fork through both Hell Gate Canyon and Alberton Gorge. Trips are available on regular inflatable rafts, hard-shell or inflatable kayaks, or the new "sit-on-tops." Raft trips are the least expensive, starting at $52 for a half-day excursion; full-day trips, which include lunch, begin at $82. A variety of kayak lessons and clinics are also offered.

Skiing

Montana Snowbowl (406/549-9696 or 800/728-2695, www.montanasnowbowl.com) has more than 30 runs, reaching up to three miles long, and a 2,600-foot vertical drop. It's about 12 miles out of town, reached by taking the Reserve Street exit from I-90 and driving north on Grant Creek Road to Snowbowl Road. Lift tickets at Snowbowl are $36 for adults, $15 for children, with student, senior, and half-day rates available. Both skis and snowboards can be rented, and lessons are available.

In the Garnet Range, east of Missoula, the **Garnet Resource Area** (406/329-3914, $3 adult) is a Bureau of Land Management (BLM)-operated ghost mining town with 55 miles of cross-country ski and snowmobile trails. From State Highway 200, about 30 miles east of Missoula, turn south between mile markers 22 and 23. Or follow I-90 to Bearmouth 26 miles and turn north five miles on Highway 10 to Bear Gulch Road. Follow the signs for Garnet.

Closer to town, there's challenging cross-country skiing up Pattee Canyon, and the **Rattlesnake National Recreation Area and Wilderness** (RNRAW) has miles of trails; many are suitable for skiing. Consult the RNRAW map, available at outdoors stores, for possibilities.

Golfing
Nine-hole public golf courses include the **Highlands Golf Club** (102 Ben Hogan Dr., 406/721-4653), featuring the historic Greenough Mansion as its clubhouse and restaurant, and the course on the **University of Montana** campus (406/728-8629). **Larchmont Golf Course** (3200 Old Fort Rd., 406/721-4416) has 18 holes.

Swimming
Missoula is a good place to get some exercise after a long car trip. The university's indoor **Grizzly Pool** (406/243-2763) has regularly scheduled public hours and is a good option for lap swimmers. An indoor water park at **McCormick Park** (600 Cregg Ln., 406/721-7275), at the west end of the Orange Street Bridge, has two waterslides and places for both lap swimmers and water play. Splash Montana, at **Playfair** (3001 Bancroft, 406/542-9283), behind Sentinel High School, is an outdoor pool with features for both kids and adults.

ACCOMMODATIONS
Because Missoula is a real crossroads, a great number and variety of lodgings are available. Unless there's a big football game, graduation, or some other major event going on at the university, you'll have little trouble finding something. There are many inexpensive and somewhat marginal motels along Broadway near downtown Missoula; be forewarned that many of these can be the sites of weekend parties. Also, no matter where you stay, bring earplugs; trains do run through town.

Under $50
During the winter and on summer weekends, **Gelandesprung Lodge** (406/549-9777 or 800/728-2695, www.montanasnowbowl.com, $36 shared bath, $48 private bath), at Montana Snowbowl, offers reasonably priced rooms in a European-style slope-side lodge, with use of the lodge's hot tub and common kitchen.

Missoula has several motel strips with plenty of inexpensive options. Most convenient to downtown and the university are the older places along East and West Broadway. The Highway 93 strip south of town offers more up-to-date lodgings but is farther from the center of things (unless your focus is the Bitterroot Valley).

The **City Center Motel** (338 E. Broadway, 406/543-3193, $43 and up) has a decidedly budget ambience but is a fine place to stay, with in-room refrigerators and microwaves.

$50-100
West of downtown, next to the hospital, the (**Mountain Valley Inn** (420 W. Broadway, 406/728-4500 or 800/249-9174, http://mvi-missoula.com, $64 and up) is nicer than most of the other places in this price range. It's an easy walk to downtown restaurants.

On the east end of downtown, the **Creekside Inn** (630 E. Broadway, 406/549-2387 or 800/850-5131, $62 and up) is a basic but comfortable motel that allows pets (with a $25 refundable deposit) and has an outdoor pool. It's just across Broadway from one of the town's top hotels (the DoubleTree) and it's an easy walk to downtown, the university, or the riverside paths. Almost next door, the **Campus Inn** (744 E. Broadway, 406/549-5134 or 800/232-8013, www.campusinnmissoula.com, $72 and up) is reasonably well-maintained but not fancy. Just to the east is the **Thunderbird Motel** (1009 E. Broadway, 406/543-7251 or 800/952-2500, www.thunderbirdmotel.net), another good bet for visitors who aren't looking for frills.

On the Highway 93 strip south of downtown, the standard **Super 8 Brooks Street** (3901 Brooks, 406/251-2255 or 888/900-9010, $56 and up) is a good launching pad for trips to the Bitterroot Valley.

Over $100

The **C'mon Inn** (2775 Expo Pkwy., 406/543-4600 or 888/989-5569, www.cmoninn.com, $109 and up) is a very attractive newer log-design motel a few miles from town at I-90 exit 101 with an indoor pool, waterfall, rustic decor lounge area, hot tubs, an exercise room, and a popular Ping-Pong table.

The sprawling **Red Lion Inn** (700 W. Broadway, 406/728-3300 or 800/733-5466, www.redlion.com, $109 and up) is in a good location near downtown; it has a pool, a hot tub, a restaurant, and a meeting room. Rates include a good continental breakfast; pets are allowed.

Once the home of the university's second president, (**Goldsmith's Inn** (809 E. Front, 406/721-6732, www.goldsmithsinn.com, $129–165) is Missoula's topflight bed-and-breakfast. Relocated to the north bank of the Clark Fork and renovated to its original 1911 splendor, Goldsmith's boasts a total of seven rooms: four suites with private sitting areas (one suite has a private deck and hot tub) and three queen rooms. All rooms have private bathrooms and include breakfast. The dining room at Goldsmith's is open to the public; a summer breakfast on the deck overlooking the river is a Missoula tradition. During the off-season prices drop to about $90, making it an excellent value.

The university district and downtown also has some of Missoula's nicest and most expensive lodgings. The (**Doubletree Hotel Missoula/Edgewater** (100 Madison, 406/728-3100 or 800/222-8733, www.missoulaedgewater.doubletree.com, $156 and up) is right on the Clark Fork across from the university. Facilities include a pool and hot tub, and some rooms are accessible for guests with disabilities. This is a quiet and sophisticated place to stay, with a good restaurant.

Right downtown and also on the river is the **Holiday Inn Missoula Parkside** (2005 S. Pattee, 406/721-8550 or 800/399-0408, www.himissoula.com, $152 and up). The hotel, which was recently remodeled, offers an indoor pool, hot tub, sauna, and fitness center. Rooms come with irons and ironing boards, flat-screen TVs, and free movie channels.

Although its airport location is far from central, the **Wingate Inn** (5252 Airway Blvd., 406/541-8000, www.wingateinnmissoula.com, $125 and up) is popular with families because of the two waterslides that empty into its relatively large indoor pool.

The historic **Gibson Mansion B&B** (823 39th St., 406/251-1345 or 866/251-1345, www.gibsonmansion.com, $115–135), located in a residential neighborhood not far from the university, is a very comfortable Missoula home base, with sumptuous breakfasts.

Campgrounds

Missoula's private campgrounds are all close to I-90. The sprawling **Missoula KOA** (3450 Tina Ave., 406/549-0881 or 800/562-5366, www.missoulakoa.com, all year, $32–63 RV, $26–31 tent, $45–52 cabin), complete with swimming pool and hot tub, is off I-90 at exit 101 (Reserve Street). **Jim and Mary's RV Park** (9800 Hwy. 93 N., 406/549-4416, www.jimandmarys.com, all year, $27–29 RV) is a Good Sam campground with no tent sites; it's on the way out of town toward the Flathead Valley and Glacier National Park. The **Jellystone RV Park** (9900 Jellystone Ave., 406/543-9400 or 800/318-9644, www.campjellystonemt.com, May–Oct., $34–36 RV, $29 tent, $52 cabins) is off I-90's exit 96 and has big pull-through sites, a pool, and a good play area.

The Department of Fish, Wildlife, and Parks (406/542-5500, http://fwp.mt.gov) operates a couple of campgrounds a little farther from town. **Chief Looking Glass** (year round, $12) is on the Bitterroot River 14 miles south of Missoula on Highway 93 (to milepost 77), then one mile east on the county road. **Beavertail Hill** (May–Sept., $15) is 0.25 mile south of the Beavertail Hill exit off I-90 (milepost 130, 26 miles southeast of Missoula).

FOOD

There are reasons to linger over Missoula's abundance of good restaurants. For the traveler coming to Missoula from the east, this may be the first ethnic food seen in days. For the traveler heading into eastern Montana, Missoula may be the last place to enjoy a choice beyond fast food and steak. Every franchise imaginable is found along the Highway 93 strip. However, for those with a hankering for something local, Missoula shouldn't disappoint.

Casual Meals

From downtown motels, it's an easy walk across the Higgins Street Bridge for a morning muffin and coffee at **Bernice's Bakery** (190 S. 3rd St. W., 406/728-1358, 6 A.M.–8 P.M. daily). Only a block away, **Le Petit Outre** (129 S. 4th St. W., 406/543-3311, 7 A.M.–6 P.M. Mon.–Fri., 8 A.M. 5 P.M. Sat.) has only a couple of tables out front for seating, but offers a wonderful selection of brioche, panini, and European-style breads to go.

If it's juice and coffee that you're after, **Butterfly Herbs** (232 N. Higgins, 406/728-8780, 8 A.M.–5 P.M. daily) houses a juice and espresso bar in an impressive old downtown storefront. **Liquid Planet** (223 N. Higgins, 406/541-4541, 7 A.M.–11 P.M. daily) combines a coffee shop and a wine store in one location—crepes and pastries make this a popular late-night hangout.

The Shack (222 W. Main, 406/549-9903, 7 A.M.–3 P.M. Sun.–Tues., 7 A.M.–9 P.M. Wed.–Sat., breakfast and lunch under $10, dinner under $20) has been one of Missoula's favorite breakfast and lunch stops since the 1950s. It's going stronger than ever and is now open for dinner.

The retro-hip **Hob Nob Cafe** (531 S. Higgins Ave., 406/542-3188, 7 A.M.–4 P.M. Mon.–Fri., 8 A.M.–4 P.M. Sun., $6–9) is a good place for a big breakfast among friendly Missoulians. The food is largely organically grown and the delicious breads homemade.

For just about the only East Indian food you'll find in Montana, visit **Tipu's Indian Café** (115 ½ 4th St. W., 406/542-0622, 11:30 A.M.–9:30 P.M. daily, lunch buffet $8, dinner $9–16). It's tucked away down a little alley and serves tasty vegetarian curry dinners with rice and dal and a lunch buffet. The chai is worth a special stop.

Follow up an Indian dinner by walking around the corner to the **Big Dipper** (631 S. Higgins, 406/543-5722, noon–10 P.M., $2–4.50) for a scoop of cardamom ice cream (don't worry, there are many more conventional flavors).

Missoula's favorite pizza-of-the-moment place is found at **Biga Pizza** (241 W. Main St., 406/728-2579, 11 A.M.–10 P.M. daily, sandwich $8, pizza $12–18), where the ingredients are locally grown when possible, leading to some innovative (and delicious) pizzas, such as winter squash with leeks or caramelized cauliflower, sausage and cheddar, and great salads.

For a rollicking Italian-American atmosphere that's popular with families, **Ciao Mambo** (541 S. Higgins, 406/543-0377, 5–10 P.M. nightly summer, 5–9 P.M. nightly winter, $10–18) can't be beat. No reservations are accepted, so expect to stand in line for a while before settling in to a giant plate of spicy spaghetti arrabbiata.

If you're hungry, thirsty, or looking to gamble away your money any time of the day or night, the **Oxford Club** (337 N. Higgins, 406/549-0117, 24 hours, $4–13) is there to serve you. Although not for the fainthearted or the easily appalled, the Ox is a Missoula fixture. Late at night, this is local color at its most opaque.

The **Good Food Store** (1600 S. 3rd St. W., 406/541-3663, 7 A.M.–10 P.M. daily) is Missoula's best source for natural and health foods.

Fine Dining

A couple of restaurants on South Higgins, just a block from the river, offer good dinners.

At **【 Scotty's Table** (131 S. Higgins, 406/549-2790, 11 A.M.–10 P.M. Tues.–Sat., 5–10 P.M. Sun., entrées $22–26), in the basement of the historic Wilma Theater, a casual bistro-style ambience complements the rather sophisticated fresh seasonal food. Here you'll find innovative twists on standard dishes and sauces, such as a flank steak made with bison meat, and an aioli with cumin, stone-ground mustard, and edamame beans.

The other outstanding restaurant, **【 Red Bird** (111 N. Higgins, 406/549-2906, 5–9:30 P.M. Tues.–Sat., dinner entrées $22–35, wine bar small plates $9–20), right downtown tucked off the main lobby of the historic Florence Hotel, also uses local ingredients whenever possible, and buys whole animals to make tasty cured meats and sausages in-house. The food is great, and the restaurant's architecture is stunning. Even if you're not up for a somewhat spendy dinner, stop in at the restaurant's wine bar and have a sandwich or small plate (try creamy herb-flecked gnocchi or duck and pear pâté).

Also delightful is the **Pearl Café and Bakery** (211 E. Front St., 406/541-0231, 5–10 P.M. Mon.–Sat., entrées $19–35), with a gentle French influence on the bison steaks and grilled salmon.

A longtime local favorite is **The Depot** (201 W. Railroad, 406/728-7007, 5:30–10 P.M. nightly, $12–35) offers steaks, fresh fish, and seafood in conjunction with a vaunted salad bar.

Don't let its setting in the Doubletree Hotel put you off: **Finn and Porter** (100 Madison St., 406/728-3100, 6 A.M.–10 P.M. daily, dinner $20–50) serves good steak dinners in a lovely riverside setting.

NIGHTLIFE

Nowhere does Missoula's unique mix of population become more apparent than in its many bustling watering holes. Some bars are of interest because of their historic character; others because of the characters they attract. Remember that bar life in Montana is primarily social in nature. Bars are where people meet up. There is no stigma attached to not drinking alcohol. Even if you don't care for a drink, go

along for the friendly welcome. Be prepared, however, for lots of unrepentant gambling and a certain loss of ambience to the chattering of electronic gaming devices.

The downtown area is chockablock with curious old bars. The **Missoula Club** (139 W. Main, 406/728-3740) is a peanut-shells-on-the-floor, grill-in-the-back sports bar with fixtures unchanged since the 1940s. Don't attempt to resist their grilled hamburgers. They are, in their simplicity, the stuff of legend.

Also legendary, but for different reasons, is the **Oxford Club** at Pine and North Higgins. Although not always edifying, it has character by the bottleful and a certain attraction for writers. Watch the creative writing students who eye the bar's sullen denizens, waiting for epiphanies.

More standard youthful hangouts are the **Rhino** (158 Ryman, 406/721-6061) and the **Top Hat** (134 W. Front, 406/728-9865). The latter offers live music (blues and swing, mostly) in an atmosphere heavy with Missoula's peculiar indolent funkiness. Missoula's music club scene is found at **Sean Kelly's** (130 W. Pine, 406/542-1471), where there's jazz, Celtic, and a bit of everything, including a good selection of Irish whiskeys. The **Union Club** (208 E. Main, 406/728-7980) is another popular downtown spot for live music.

If you're searching for the gay bar in town, descend the steps at 225 Ryman Avenue (406/543-9174) to the **AmVets Bar** (yes, the AmVets).

Red's White Sox Bar (217 Ryman, 406/728-9881) is a safe haven for Chisox fans and others willing to stand up for a favorite team. (Missoula has a rookie-league baseball team, the Ospreys.) Another old-time bar that's a comfortable place to play pool and mingle in a mixed locals-and-students atmosphere is the **Silver Dollar** (307 W. Railroad St., 406/728-9826).

If you want to go out and sample Missoula nightlife but aren't into the bar scene, go to **Break Espresso** (432 N. Higgins, 406/728-7300), a coffee shop that stays open late and is a magnet for caffeine-propelled studying and hanging out.

EVENTS

Summertime Saturday mornings (and Tuesday evenings) bring the **Farmer's Market** to the Circle Square, at the northern end of Higgins Street next to the old Northern Pacific rail depot.

Early each April, the university hosts an excellent **wildlife film festival** (406/728-9380, www.wildlifefilms.org).

A Native American **powwow** is held annually, usually in May, in the university field house. The chamber of commerce (406/543-6623) can provide exact dates and times.

The 221-mile bicycle **Tour of Swan River Valley** is an annual springtime event, usually held in late May. Register well in advance for the TOSRV ride; it's sponsored by Missoulians on Bicycles (406/543-4489, www.missoulabike.org).

The **International Choral Festival** (406/721-7985, www.choralfestival.org) is a midsummer event drawing choirs from all over the world for a series of free concerts. The festival is held once every three years; 2009 is a festival year.

The **Western Montana Fair** is held in Missoula during the third week of August. It's time to take in a rodeo, a delectable Montalado (a Montana-style enchilada), the llama pavilion, and perhaps a few carnival rides.

SHOPPING

For many travelers, Missoula will either be one of the first or one of the last places visited in Montana. Missoula's shops offer the visitor either a last chance to stock up on vital comestibles and to drink that final espresso, or the first opportunity in days to assuage deprivations incurred farther inland.

Butterfly Herbs (232 N. Higgins, 406/728-8780) offers tea, coffee, herbs, spices, soaps, and in fact a little of everything. The store is a well-preserved specimen from the end of the 19th century. The back of the store is a good espresso bar and café.

Local artist Monte Dolack's whimsical nature-oriented paintings, posters, and cards have gained a wide following. Visit the

Monte Dolack Gallery at 139 West Front (406/549-3248).

The **Bird's Nest** (219 N. Higgins, 406/721-1125) is a center for new and secondhand regional books, and **Fact and Fiction** (220 N. Higgins, 406/721-2881) is a good general bookstore.

Because of Missoula's access to the outdoors, recreation stores are important to the visitor. A good source of equipment, for both sale and rent, is the **Trail Head** (221 E. Front St., 406/543-6966). The staff are usually able to offer good advice on local trails and conditions. **Pipestone Mountaineering** (129 W. Front St., 406/721-1670) is another good place to gear up for the outdoors.

Find genuinely fashionable women's clothing at **Nolita** (531 N. Higgins, 406/728-6556).

SERVICES

The **police station** (406/523-4777) is at 435 Ryman.

The main Missoula **post office** (406/329-2200) is at 1100 W. Kent, but the downtown **Hell Gate Station** (200 E. Broadway, 406/329-2222) may prove to be more convenient.

St. Patrick's Hospital (500 W. Broadway, 406/543-7271) is located right downtown.

The **First Interstate Bank** (101 E. Front, 406/721-4200) is the main bank in town and the place to go to exchange foreign currency.

INFORMATION

The Missoula **Chamber of Commerce** (825 E. Front St., 406/543-6623, www.missoulachamber.com) has racks brimming with brochures on Missoula and the surrounding area. The Missoula Convention and Visitors Bureau (800/526-3465, www.missoulacvb.org) has a good website.

The regional **U.S. Forest Service** office (200 E. Broadway, 406/329-3511) sells national forest maps. This is also a good place for general information on hiking and camping in national forests.

The regional office of the **Department of Fish, Wildlife, and Parks** (3201 Spurgin Rd., 406/542-5500) is a source of advice on fishing and hunting and can provide a list of public campgrounds.

The **public library** is at 301 E. Main Street (406/721-2665). What you don't find on their shelves may well be in the stacks of the **university library** (406/243-6860). Of particular interest there is the Mansfield Collection, located on the third level down. U.S. Senator Mike Mansfield left his papers to the University of Montana, and they're housed here along with a great collection of regional history.

TRANSPORTATION
Air
Missoula International Airport (555 Hwy. 10 W., 406/728-4381, www.msoairport.com) is just northwest of town. Alaska/Horizon, Frontier, Northwest, United, and SkyWest (Delta) Airlines fly into Missoula. Shuttle service (406/543-9416) is available from the airport into town, and many hotels provide shuttles. Hertz, Budget, National, and Avis all have rental cars at the airport. Nearby (with service to the airport), find Thrifty, Enterprise, Dollar, and Alamo.

Bus
The **Greyhound** station is at 1660 W. Broadway (406/549-2339). Greyhound buses run three times daily along the interstate. Smaller bus lines operate out of the same terminal (same telephone number). **Rimrock Trailways** (800/255-7655) goes to Whitefish and Billings.

Mountain Line Transit (1221 Shakespeare, 406/721-3333, www.mountainline.com, Mon.–Sat. until early evening, $0.85) operates the city buses, which are all equipped with bike racks. Most buses leave from the downtown transit center, behind the courthouse on East Pine between Ryman and Woody Streets. There's a nice indoor waiting area stocked with bus schedules and served by a Break Espresso outlet.

Taxi
Taxi service is provided by **Yellow Cab** (406/543-6644) and **Green Taxi** (406/728-8294), which uses hybrid vehicles.

The Lower Clark Fork

It's easy to rush past this western edge of Montana, and in truth there aren't that many ways to penetrate this densely forested mountainous region. But a bike ride along the Hiawatha Trail, a dip in the pools at Quinn's Hot Springs, or a sighting of mountain sheep outside Thompson Falls may prove to be a highlight of a trip to Montana.

ALONG I-90
Forest-rimmed, hilly, and as wild as an interstate ever gets, I-90 follows the Clark Fork and St. Regis Rivers most of the way between the Idaho border and Missoula. From the state line east to Frenchtown, just west of Missoula, I-90 follows the Mullan Road, built by John Mullan and his crew in the 1860s as a military road from Fort Benton to Walla Walla, Washington.

Pull off I-90 at Haugan (exit 16) to visit the **Savenac Historic Site,** a tree nursery started

along the Mullan Road in 1909. A year later a three-million-acre fire destroyed the new nursery and much else. After the fire, forest rangers stole pine cones from squirrel caches (replacing them with nuts) and replanted the pine seeds. The nursery eventually flourished, providing seedlings to reforest national forests all over the west.

Like De Borgia to the west, St. Regis was named for the Jesuit missionary St. Regis De Borgia. **St. Regis** is where the St. Regis River flows into the Clark Fork. The St. Regis parallels I-90 to the west of town, and the Clark Fork to the east. At the town of St. Regis the Clark Fork turns sharply to the north. Highway 135 follows it along the lovely stretch to Highway 200.

Superior was a mining boomtown. Gold was discovered on a stream called Cayuse Creek in 1869, and over the next year, 10,000

THE MULLAN ROAD

It took John Mullan and his crew from 1858 until 1862 to build a military wagon road from Fort Benton to Walla Walla, Washington. This was a particularly vital stretch of road because Fort Benton marked the farthest point that steamboats could travel up the Missouri River, and Walla Walla provided access to the Columbia River. His route has held up well; I-90 follows its course from Deer Lodge to the Idaho line.

John Mullan also has the distinction of having written the first travel guide to Montana. In 1865 he authored the *Miners' and Travelers' Guide to Oregon, Washington, Idaho, Montana, Wyoming and Colorado*. As may be expected, the Montana portion follows the Mullan Road.

Oct., trail pass $9 adult, $5 child). The centerpiece of the trail is the 8,771-foot Taft Tunnel, built in 1909 and cut through solid rock from the Montana side of Lookout Pass through to Idaho. As the track descends into Idaho, it winds through another ten tunnels and over nine wooden trestles before reaching the valley floor.

Bikers need headlights to traverse the trail, and hikers will want to bring along strong flashlights. Be prepared to get a little wet and chilly in the tunnel. Even though the grade never exceeds 1.7 percent, vertigo-inducing trestles stand along sheer cliffs and over steep rocky canyons. Whether you're on foot or on a bike, you'll have your heart in your mouth on several occasions.

To reach the beginning of the trail and Taft Tunnel, take exit 5 (Taft Area) from I-90. Turn south and follow Rainy Creek Road for two miles, and take the road toward East Portal at the Y junction. The parking area is immediately ahead, and just beyond is the gate to the tunnel. The trail follows the contours of Loop Creek until it meets the Moon Pass Road, which leads to Wallace in 20 miles via Placer Creek Road. An additional 31 miles of trail, heading east to St. Regis, are in the works.

A shuttle service ferries cyclists back to Lookout Pass. Plan a full day for this trip, and reserve a spot on the shuttle in advance by calling the Lookout Pass Ski Area (208/744-1301, $9 adults, $6 children). Mountain bike rentals are available at the ski area (exit 0 from I-90) for $28–32; you can also rent a tagalong bike or a trailer for kids.

people swarmed to the mining camp. In some areas, such as Louisville, Chinese miners moved into the abandoned shacks and gleaned the remaining gold. Mining booms came intermittently over the next few decades but pretty much ended in 1910, when a huge forest fire destroyed the Keystone Mine and most everything else for miles around.

Alberton is alongside a notorious gorge in the Clark Fork River (see *Other Recreation* below) and was originally a railroad town. It was a division point for the Milwaukee Road, whose depot has been restored and is visible from I-90.

Frenchtown was settled by French Canadians as the Mullan Road was being built. It's now a mill town and a bedroom community of Missoula.

◖ Hiawatha Mountain Bike Trail

A rails-to-trails project converted 15 miles of Chicago, Milwaukee, and St. Paul Railroad track, tunnel, and trestle into the exhilarating Hiawatha Mountain Bike Trail (208/744-1301, www.ridethehiawatha.com, late May–early

Other Recreation

Recreation at **Lookout Pass,** on the Montana-Idaho border, turns from biking to skiing in the winter, when an average of 400 inches of generally powdery snow falls at the ski area here (208/744-1301, www.skilookout.com). Lookout has a small downhill ski area (with free lessons for kids!) and good cross-country trails. Weekend adult lift tickets cost $30 for a full day, $25 after 12:30 P.M.; midweek the rates drop by three dollars. Many special rates

CAMELS IN THE ROCKIES

Camels in the Rockies? Well, why not? They're strong, they don't drink too much...so thought the U.S. Army in the 1860s, when some innovative military man began importing camels to use as pack animals. Although perhaps more efficient than the customary mules, camels weren't so easy to boss around. Apparently they were harder to recognize, too; several of the camels on the Mullan Road were shot after being mistaken for moose.

are available for seniors, college students, military, and juniors; kids under six are free.

Alberton Gorge (or Cyr Canyon) is a 20-mile stretch of white water on the Clark Fork River. There are plenty of fishing-access sites along the Clark Fork that can be used to put in and take out boats. It's an especially challenging run when the river is high; only experienced paddlers should attempt it before August. Even when the water level drops, it's not a trip for beginners, although Missoula-based **Lewis and Clark Trail Adventures** (406/728-7609 or 800/366-6246, www.trailadventures.com, half-day trip $50 adults, $40 children; full day $70 adults, $55 children) runs regular raft trips through Alberton Gorge, as does **10,000 Waves** (406/549-6670 or 800/537-8315, www.10000-waves.com, half-day trip $52 adults, $50 children; full day $82 adults, $70 children). Those who aren't tempted by the white water may choose to fish this section of the Clark Fork for brown, cutthroat, rainbow, and bull trout.

Accommodations

Most eastbound I-90 travelers press on to Missoula once they cross into the state, but there are several quite passable lodgings along the interstate. Just west of the state line in the Idaho town of Mullan, the **Lookout Motel** (208/744-1601, $25–40) has clean, basic rooms with no phones.

Down the road from Lookout, there is a string of small towns with (mostly) small unremarkable motels. You'll know the town of Haugan is coming well in advance from the many billboards heralding the **World Famous 50,000 Silver Dollar Bar** (exit 16, 406/678-4242 or 800/531-1968, $50–75). The sprawling Silver Dollar complex has a bar, casino, gift shop, and restaurant at its heart, and it's a good place to stop for roadside refueling or a break from the road.

The highway-side but still quite woodsy **Black Diamond Guest Ranch** (121 E. Frontage Rd., 406/678-4000, www.blackdiamondguestranch.com, cabins $50–70) has lodging in 100-year-old cabins (rustic, but with bathrooms and basic kitchens), camping in large canvas-walled tents ($8 per person, showers extra) and RVs ($10–25), and trail rides. Pets are permitted.

In St. Regis, the **Super 8** (exit 33, 406/649-2422, $60–80) is a reliable spot that permits pets.

Down the road in Superior, the **Budget Host Big Sky Motel** (exit 47, 406/822-4831 or 800/283-4678, www.thebigsky.net/budgethost, $48 s, $54 d) has spacious rooms and is a good bet for a pleasant stay.

In downtown Alberton, the **Ghost Rails Inn** (exit 75 or 77, 406/722-4990 or 888/271-9317, www.ghostrailsinn.com, late March–Dec., $60–90) has been transformed from a funky old wood-frame hotel built in 1909 to house railroad crews into a tidy B&B inn, just down the street from a used-book treasure trove, the Montana Valley Bookstore. When Missoula's motels are booked full, this is a very attractive alternative.

Camping

Several Lolo National Forest campgrounds (www.fs.fed.us/r1/lolo) are convenient to I-90. **Cabin City** Forest Service campground (Memorial Day–Labor Day, $7) is a little more than two miles off I-90 at exit 22, just east of De Borgia. Unless you hit a busy weekend, it's relatively peaceful. The campsites are set in a lodgepole pine forest, and there's a 0.75-mile nature hike down to Twelvemile Creek.

© PAUL LEVY

The World Famous 50,000 Silver Dollar Bar is a convenient place to stop along I-90.

The **Slowey** (mid-May–late Sept., $10) campground is between exits 37 and 43. **Quartz Flat** (mid-May–late Sept., $10) is at the rest stop east of Superior, near mile marker 58. It's convenient but exposed to I-90's lights and noise.

AROUND PARADISE

Paradise, on Highway 200, may have originally been "Pair-o-Dice" after a roadhouse on the road along the Clark Fork, but Paradise isn't such a bad name in itself. There's the river, the mountains, Montana's banana belt, and not much else—but hey, who needs it?

The neighboring town of Plains was originally called "Horse Plains." Its moderate climate made it a favorite spot for Indians and their horses to spend the winters. You can still see the old **Horse Plains Jail,** at the corner of Blake and McGowan a block north of Highway 200, and the **Wild Horse Plains School House,** a log building dating from 1878 on the west end of town next to the highway.

Accommodations

◖ **Quinn's Hot Spring Resort** (406/826-3150 or 888/646-9287, www.quinnshotsprings.com,

$120–245), in a woodsy area three miles south of Highway 200 on Highway 135, has a clutch of newer cabins, a lodge, and a good restaurant. The temperature of the outdoor swimming pool is adjusted according to the weather; adults pay $8 (included in lodging fee) for a dip, $6 for children (must be potty trained).

Camping

Highway 135 follows the Clark Fork River from I-90 at St. Regis to Highway 200 just east of Paradise. **Cascade Campground** (www.fs.fed.us /r1/lolo, late May–late Sept., $10) is a small, basic roadside Forest Service campground. It's on Highway 135 six miles south of Highway 200. There's a surprising amount of roadside noise generated by Highway 135, but the setting is nice; there is a hike up to a waterfall, the Clark Fork River is just across the road, and if it's chilly, the hot springs resort is less than four miles up the highway.

THOMPSON FALLS

David Thompson, who established his Saleesh House here in 1809, is the namesake of Thompson Falls (pop. 1,345, elev. 2,463 feet).

Thompson, an English-born explorer, astronomer, and geographer for both the Hudson's Bay and North West Companies, traveled down the Kootenai River from Canada and into Montana in 1807. Over the next few years he set up trading posts along the Kootenai and Clark Fork Rivers and became the first white man to travel the entire length of the Columbia River, which he mapped from mouth to source. Thompson spoke several Indian languages and won the trust and respect of local Indians.

The falls here were dammed in 1916, backing up a two-mile-long reservoir behind the dam. There are two more dams downstream from this one, making the Clark Fork more like a lake than a river for much of its course from Thompson Falls to the Idaho state line.

Sights

Thompson Falls Island, at the foot of Gallatin Street, is a day-use park that's closed to automobiles. It's full of bluffs and rocky rises and is a good place to hike around and watch the birds, including the ospreys nesting on the bridge.

The **Old Jail Museum** (109 S. Madison St., 406/827-4002, mid-May–Labor Day, Mon.–Fri. noon–4 P.M.) is indeed housed in the old jail, behind the police station.

East of Thompson Falls, the **KooKooSint Mountain Sheep Viewing Area** is a roadside pullout with several informative signs. (*KooKooSint* is the name given to David Thompson by the local Indians. It means "Man Who Looks at Stars.") Bighorn sheep were eaten by the Flathead Indians and by Thompson, who found them a welcome addition to his sparse winter diet. You're most likely to see sheep here in the spring, when they're at lower elevations eating the new grass, or during late November or December, when they descend to feed in the valleys and mate. Open south-facing slopes provide a winter habitat. The lambs are born in early May on the high ridges, and the sheep summer in the mountains. Mountain sheep have spongy hooves with hard edges to lend traction and support, allowing them to traverse steep slopes easily and quickly.

Recreation

Several looped hiking trails lead to small lakes in the Lolo National Forest north of Thompson Falls. Reach the **Four Lakes Creek** trailhead by driving north on Thompson River Road (which intersects Highway 200 five miles east of town) about six miles, turn left onto the West Fork Thompson River Road, and follow it, bearing left as it becomes Four Lakes Creek Road (Forest Service Road 7669), some eight miles to the trailhead. A Lolo National Forest map will detail the trails.

Fishing access to the Thompson River is easy; a road runs along it almost the entire way from Highway 200 north to Highway 2. Expect to pull mostly rainbow trout, and perhaps some brown trout, from the stretch near Highway 200.

Accommodations

Falls Motel (112 Gallatin, 406/827-3559 or 800/521-2184, www.thompsonfallslodging.com, $55–90) is a friendly place near good strolling on Thompson Falls Island. The motel has a hot tub in a pleasant little solarium; dogs are permitted for a $10 fee. Just west of town and set back from the highway, the spacious **Rimrock Lodge** (4946 Hwy. 200, 406/827-3536, http://rimrocklodgemontana.com, $75–90) has good views of the Clark Fork River, a popular restaurant and lounge, and a bowling alley. Ask at the desk about the nature trail looping the motel grounds. Pets are permitted.

More riverfront lodgings are on the west side of the bridge over the Clark Fork, a mile west of town. Here you'll find the attractive **Riverfront Motel and Cabins** (4907 Hwy. 200, 406/827-3460, $50–125), which also has spaces for RVs.

Camping

Thompson Falls State Recreation Area (406/752-5501, http://fwp.mt.gov, May–Sept., $12) is a mile west of Thompson Falls, just off Highway 200 on the Clark Fork. The riverside spots have running water but no other amenities. **Copper King** and **Clark Memorial** (www.fs.fed.us/r1/lolo, late May–late Sept., $5) are Forest Service campgrounds with no running water located up Thompson River Road (catch this road five miles east of town). Copper King is four miles off Highway 200; Clark Memorial is another 1.5 miles up the road.

Food

The **Rimrock Lodge** (406/427-3536, 6 A.M.–9 P.M., mostly $5–12) serves breakfast, lunch, and dinner and has good river views. Downtown, the **Thompson Grill** (611 Main St., 406/827-4900, 7:30 A.M.–9 P.M. Mon.–Sat., $6–25) is a popular spot for burgers and good milkshakes. On Friday and Saturday nights, dinners are fancier and more leisurely.

NORTH OF THOMPSON FALLS ON HIGHWAY 200

Highway 200 runs along the Clark Fork River north and west of Thompson Falls to the Idaho border; thanks to the 190-foot-high Noxon Dam, for a large part of this stretch the river is known as Noxon Reservoir. The towns of **Trout Creek** and **Noxon** each have a few places to stay.

If you're in the mood to drive back roads, **Vermillion Falls** is 12 miles from Trout Creek on Vermillion River Road. A couple of miles farther along the road, find **Willow Creek Campground,** a small, free, and primitive (no water) Forest Service campground.

In Trout Creek, the **Lakeside Motel** (2957 Hwy. 200, 406/827-4458, www.lakeside-resort-motels.com, $75 and up) has motel rooms and cabins. **North Shore Campground** (www.fs.fed.us/r1/kootenai, mid-Apr.–Nov., $7) is on Noxon Reservoir about two miles west of Trout Creek.

Although Noxon has a couple of budget motels, for something beyond a bed and a ceiling, try the **(Bighorn Lodge B&B** (406/847-4676 or 888/347-8477, www.bighornlodgemontana.com, $95 s, $150 d). In addition to comfortable rooms (there's also a guest house that rents for $350) and full breakfasts, the folks at the Bighorn provide guests with canoes, kayaks, and bikes, and can arrange guided horseback rides and fishing trips.

The Bitterroot Valley

Probably nowhere else in Montana provides such a diverse and satisfying unity of attractions as the Bitterroot Valley. First of all, let's make it clear that the Bitterroot is stunningly beautiful. The Bitterroot River, flanked by groves of cottonwood, winds through a wide fertile valley of farms and pastureland. The heavily wooded humped arch of the west-lying Bitterroot Mountains rears back to reveal precipitous canyons and jagged peaks. The Sapphire Range to the east is characterized by relatively low forested peaks. Historic, quiet old towns slumber in a purposeful way: There are comings and goings, but no commotion.

Opportunities for recreation are almost limitless. The Bitterroot River provides great fishing, and the streams flowing out of the Sapphire Mountains have better fishing than the Bitterroot drainages, which debouch from alpine lakes in rounded valleys scooped out

by glaciers, then fall quickly through narrow canyons gashed through the resistant mylonite rock. The Bitterroot National Forest offers thousands of acres of wilderness, with more than 1,600 miles of maintained trails to dramatic peaks, pristine lakes, and wildlife viewing. Across the valley to the east the Sapphire Range offers gem hunting and more wildlife habitat. Proximity to Missoula lends sophistication to the services in the Bitterroot, but suburban sprawl also engulfs the lower valley with residential subdivisions.

HISTORY

The Flathead Indians came to the Bitterroot from the west, and although they made regular trips to the plains to hunt buffalo, they made ample use of the valley's roots, huckleberries, and fish.

In 1805 Lewis and Clark passed down the

THE BITTERROOT VALLEY

camping spot called Travelers' Rest. From here the corps followed Lolo Creek up and over Lolo Pass, and down more hospitable drainages to the Columbia. The following year they retraced their trail to Travelers' Rest. Clark and half the corps returned up the Bitterroot to cross over Gibbon Pass into the Big Hole.

Lewis is responsible for the name of the plant that gives this valley its name. While local Indians found the roots of the bitterroot both tasty and fortifying, Lewis pronounced it bitter and nauseating. His name now identifies the plant in Latin: *Lewisia rediviva.*

The Bitterroot Valley, with its fertile bottomland and protected climate, attracted farmers from the beginning. The discovery of gold in nearby valleys and the establishment of mining boomtowns created a demand for foodstuffs. As farmers moved into the area, they began to pressure the government to remove the Flathead from the valley, and in 1872 James Garfield, who later became the 20th president, was sent to transfer the Indians north to the Mission Valley.

Five years later the Nez Percé passed through the Bitterroot on their tragic flight across the Northwest. Under the leadership of Chief Joseph, the band of about 700 Indians and nearly 2,000 horses traveled from Idaho down Lolo Creek and up the Bitterroot toward Crow country, fleeing the army infantry. Chief Joseph vowed to the army and the Bitterroot settlers to march peaceably through the settled areas of the Bitterroot in return for unmolested passage. The offer was not accepted officially, and the Nez Percé simply skirted a hastily constructed barricade at Fort Fizzle and proceeded up the Bitterroot. No shots were fired as they passed through the valley. Once over the Continental Divide in the Big Hole, however, Col. John Gibbon and 183 men ambushed the Nez Percé at the Battle of the Big Hole.

Agriculture

Farming really took hold in the Bitterroot after the Northern Pacific extended a spur line to Hamilton. One of the largest enterprises in the valley was Marcus Daly's Bitterroot Stock

Bitterroot Valley from the south, over Lost Trail Pass. The Corps of Discovery had already crossed the Continental Divide at Lemhi only to discover that although the Salmon River in Idaho flowed into the Columbia drainage, it did so as the aptly named "River of No Return." The Salmon was hopelessly impassable. The corps climbed up into Montana again, this time to follow the Bitterroot down to the area near Lolo Creek, where they established a favorite

HOW ARCHAEOLOGISTS LOCATED TRAVELERS' REST

Before his great journey, Meriwether Lewis studied all the things an explorer must know, including a little bit of doctoring. His physician mentor was Dr. Benjamin Rush, who gave Lewis a stash of pills to use as a cure-all. Dr. Rush's Thunderbolts were essentially very strong mercury-laced purgatives.

While at Travelers' Rest, a couple of the Corps of Discovery members report, "Goodrich and McNeal are both very unwell with the pox which they contracted last winter with the Chinook women") and were administered the pills. They presumably spent a good bit of their time at the camp latrine, relieving themselves of whatever had ailed them, along with a good dose of mercury. When archaeologists surveyed the area in 2002 they noted a trench-like depression in the ground. They assayed the soil in and around the trench for mercury, which was present in the trench but not in surrounding areas.

Researchers also located the corps' camp kitchen, situated as military protocol would have it, 300 feet from the latrine. Here, using equipment that detects geological disruptions, archaeologists found changes in the magnetic properties of the soil. They also found fire-cracked rocks and traces of charcoal that would have resulted from large military-style cooking fires rather than the smaller fires used by the Indians who frequented the area.

Travelers' Rest has become one of the few sites with physical proof of Lewis and Clark's visit.

Farm. The copper magnate from Butte preferred the Bitterroot as a summer home, and he built a magnificent mansion on his 26,000-acre holding. Considering the fact that Daly modeled his farm on an Irish manor, it's no surprise that racehorses were the most noted of the farm's products.

In the early years of the 20th century the Bitterroot was home to an elaborate irrigation scheme that turned the valley into a huge apple orchard. The Big Ditch, as it was functionally named, provided water to the eastside bench land, which was divided into subdivisions of 10 acres each. At the height of apple euphoria, 22,000 acres of the Bitterroot were in fruit production. The soil and climate didn't quite live up to the exaggerated promises of the developers, and by the 1950s apple production ceased to be a significant element of the area's economy.

While agriculture remains important in the Bitterroot, much of the farmland in the lower valley has now been subdivided into small "ranchettes." This part of the valley has largely been converted into a bedroom community of Missoula.

RECREATION

The Bitterroot National Forest contains 1.6 million acres, with nearly 750,000 of these protected as wilderness. Forest Service roads provide entrance for mountain bikers or off-road vehicle enthusiasts, while 950 miles of maintained trails give hikers access to some of the most tortured geology and pristine landscapes in the Rockies.

Fishing

All the larger streams that feed into the Bitterroot River harbor rainbow, cutthroat, and brook trout, and some of the higher lakes in the Bitterroots, such as the Big Creek Lakes, are known for good fishing.

For the angler, though, the real news is the Bitterroot. The river seems largely untainted by the effects of a century's worth of forestry, farming, suburban sprawl, and irrigation. In fact, even in the busy heart of the valley, the cottonwoods and willows that line the shore shield the angler from the realities of Bitterroot development. The trout here are both numerous and large. Rainbows and browns fill the majority of creeks, but cutthroat and the elusive

A BIT ABOUT THE BITTERROOT

While the bitterroot lily, Montana's state flower, grows throughout most of the western part of the state, the Bitterroot Valley is, unsurprisingly, a good place to plan a sighting.

Legend holds that the plant sprang from the tears of a Flathead mother whose family was starving. The sun, hearing the mother's sorrow, sent a bird as a messenger to turn her tears into a plant whose roots were nutritious (albeit as bitter as the mother's sorrow) but whose beauty would reflect the devotion of the grieving woman.

The roots of these beautiful light-pink flowers were a staple of the Indian diet. They were eaten fresh in season and also dried for use in the winter or when traveling. The Flathead boiled or steamed the roots, then mixed them with berries, marrow, or meat. Although the snow-white meat of the roots can be bitter to the point of causing nausea, the Flathead found that if they were gathered before flowering, or dried sufficiently, the bitterness was much reduced.

Elaborate rituals accompanied the bitterroot's harvest. Among the Flatheads, one old woman led other female gatherers out in the search. When the party reached the first bitterroot, the leader would stick her elk-horn digger at the base of the plant. After the others planted their diggers, a prayer was offered, and the first plant was uprooted. Only after the prayer was offered was the season open; to dig before the ceremony was to invite a small harvest. The following day the first root was given to the chief, and a daylong feast ensued.

bull are also apprehended. The lower part of the river near Missoula is where the lunkers are most likely lurking (and, rumor has it, largemouth bass), while farther south, up Connor way, is where the trout are thickest.

The state has established 10 fishing-access sites on the river, and there's also easy access from bridges. At no place is the Bitterroot far from the road, although remember to ask for permission before crossing private land. Boat rentals are available in Hamilton, and organized float and fishing trips are offered by the region's many outfitters.

THE LOWER BITTERROOT

From **Hamilton** (pop. 3,965, elev. 3,600 feet) north to Missoula, the Bitterroot passes through the towns of **Corvallis, Victor, Stevensville, Florence,** and **Lolo**. Excluding the lodges of typically nomadic Indians, this part of the valley is the oldest continuously inhabited area in Montana, and it shows. Interesting old Victorian farmhouses are scattered among the fields, and isolated apple trees from once substantial orchards can still be seen in meadows. Main streets have changed little since they were built. Despite the crags of the Bitterroot Range rising to the west, here the Bitterroot feels lived-in and comfortable.

The visitor should leave Highway 93 as soon as possible (at Florence at the Missoula end and at Hamilton from the south) and instead take the East Side Highway, MT 269. While 93 is undeniably a faster road, it's also very busy. The East Side Highway affords the best views of the Bitterroots and goes through the pretty towns of Corvallis and Stevensville.

Travelers' Rest

Although it had long been known that the Corps of Discovery camped in the Bitterroot Valley near present-day Lolo during their westward trip in 1805 and the following spring, on their way east the exact location of this campground was a matter of some speculation. In 2002, archaeologists were able to pin down the precise location of Travelers' Rest (Hwy. 12, 406/273-4253, www.travelersrest.org, 8 A.M.–8 P.M. daily Memorial Day–Labor Day, 9 A.M.–4 P.M. Mon.–Fri., noon–4 P.M. Sat.–Sun. Labor Day–Memorial Day, $2

© JUDY JEWELL

St. Mary's Mission, in Stevensville, was built in 1866 by Father Anthony Ravalli.

non–Montana residents), and the site was quickly developed as a state park. Although the area really just looks like a grassy field in a pretty rural setting, it is somehow poignant to think of the Corps of Discovery resting here.

When they left this camp on July 2, 1806, Lewis and Clark parted ways, with Lewis and his small crew heading through Hellgate Pass and into Blackfoot territory, and Clark and his group heading back to the Beaverhead, where their boats had been left the previous year, and down the Yellowstone River. The groups planned to meet up at the mouth of the Yellowstone but had no way of knowing whether that would actually happen.

Lewis and Clark buffs should also head 25 miles west of the town of Lolo to the **Lolo Trail Center** (Hwy. 12, 406/273-2201, www.lolotrailcenter.com), a good private museum in the Lolo Hot Springs Complex. Although those who aren't enthralled with the Corps of Discovery will see this as just a big boring gift shop, Lewis and Clark pilgrims will want to spend time (and perhaps a few bucks) here.

St. Mary's Mission and Fort Owen

In 1841 St. Mary's Mission was founded in the Bitterroot Valley after repeated requests for Catholicism from the Flathead and Nez Percé of the area. Father Pierre-Jean De Smet, the missionary dispatched to found St. Mary's, was also Montana's first agriculturalist. He planted oats, wheat, and potatoes at the mission. This was probably also an initial attempt to make the Indians into farmers. Troubles arose between the missionaries and the Flathead, and in 1850 St. Mary's was sold to John Owen, who made it into a trading post.

St. Mary's Mission (4th St., Stevensville, 406/777-5734, www.saintmarysmission.org, 10 A.M.–4 P.M. daily mid-Apr.–mid-Oct., tours $5 adults, $2 students) at Stevensville was rebuilt in 1866 by Father Anthony Ravalli out of the original hewn logs of the 1841 structure. The interior of the one-room chapel, with its wood-burning stove and wainscoting, is pretty much as Father Ravalli left it. Also on the grounds are the mission pharmacy, Father Ravalli's cabin, and a graveyard. While Father Ravalli's grave is meant to be the draw here, more curious is the sign indicating INDIAN GRAVES before an open field. St. Mary's Mission is on 4th Street two blocks west of Main.

What's left of **Fort Owen** (Hwy. 269, Stevensville, 406/542-5500, http://fwp.mt.gov) is just east of Highway 93 between the highway and the town of Stevensville cutoff (follow signs for Fort Owen State Park). The original 1850 structure evolved from the log palisade of a frontier trader into an adobe-brick fortress with turrets and walkways after Owen became the federal Indian agent to the Flathead. Of the original buildings, one barracks remains and serves as a museum with interpretive exhibits.

Daly Mansion

Marcus Daly bought his Bitterroot Stock Farm in 1889 and built the Marcus Daly Mansion (406/363-6004, www.dalymansion.org, 10 A.M.–5 P.M. daily Apr.–Oct., $8 adult, $7 senior, $5 youth 6–17) in 1897. After his death, the house was enlarged in 1910 to its present Georgian revival splendor. Built primarily as a summer home for the Daly family, Riverside, as the mansion was known, looks over the Bitterroot Valley to the rugged peaks in Blodgett Canyon that vie with the Bitterroots for splendor. The house remained in private hands until 1987, when it was acquired by the state.

Riverside is probably the most beautiful estate in Montana. A tree-lined boulevard leads to 50 acres of grounds, which contain an arboretum of specimen trees, a swimming pool, a playhouse, and a tennis court. The 24,213-square-foot mansion contains 42 rooms, 24 of which are bedrooms and 15 are baths. Some of the original furniture and most of the old fixtures remain. The grounds alone are worth a strolling tour.

The mansion is located four miles south of Corvallis and two miles north of Hamilton on MT 269. After leaving the highway, follow a boulevard about one mile until you reach the grounds.

Marcus Daly's most famous racehorse was Tammany. In keeping with the Daly tradition, Tammany did not simply have a stable, but a brick edifice called Tammany Castle. To see what upscale horses lived in at the end of the 19th century, go one mile east of Hamilton on MT 269, and look to the south about 100 yards. The stable is not open to the public.

Hamilton

Hamilton is unique because it didn't just spring up as opportunity (or the railroad) allowed. Rather, it sprang fully formed from the brow of copper magnate Marcus Daly, who, after designing his model Irish manor, decided to establish a model town nearby. In 1890 Daly brought in planners who laid down a city complete with free plots for churches, ready-designed banks, shops, schools, and rather glorious homes. As a result, Hamilton wears its age gracefully. Stop to picnic or let the kids loose in one of its parks. An easy stop for either activity is a small playground only one block west of Highway 93 on Bedford, two blocks south of Main. There's a more substantial park where Madison Street bumps up against the Bitterroot River.

Hamilton contains several handsome old homes and public buildings. The **Ravalli County Museum** (205 Bedford St., 406/363-3338, 10 A.M.–4 P.M. Mon., Thurs., and Fri., 9 A.M.–1 P.M. Sat., 1–4 P.M. Sun.) is housed in the Old Ravalli County Court House, built in 1900. This stone-and-brick landmark bears a resemblance to the University of Montana's Main Hall. The museum has a good collection of Flathead Indian artifacts, pioneer-era memorabilia, and an exhibit on wood ticks. Like the courthouse, the **City Hall** (175 S. 3rd) is on the National Register of Historic Places.

Hamilton is also known for the Rocky Mountain Research Laboratory (903 S. 4th St., 406/363-9275), where research on Rocky Mountain spotted fever was conducted. The fever, which is spread by ticks and is debilitating, if not fatal, to humans and livestock, is endemic to parts of the Bitterroot. The discovery of a treatment opened infested and otherwise uninhabitable areas of the valley. The laboratory, which is being expanded to handle

© JUDY JEWELL

Hamilton, the Bitterroot Valley's largest town, is at the base of the mountains.

extremely dangerous pathogens, is now involved in studying ways to combat bioterrorism and emerging infections such as staph.

Hiking

Any creek worth mentioning in the Bitterroots has a trail up it, and nearly all are worth considering for a hike. (A few trails burned in the huge Bitterroot fires of 2000, but most were spared.) But if you have only a day to spend in the lower Bitterroots, consider one of the following.

A largely overlooked long day hike (or unstressful overnight trip) that's close to Missoula leads up the Sweeney Creek drainage to **Peterson Lake.** Forest Service roads (turn west on Forest Service Road 1315 two miles south of Florence) will take the hiker most of the way up the canyon wall to a trailhead. After a couple of miles of easy traversing, the trail drops to alpine lakes, with the car having done most of the climbing.

Another popular ascent of intermediate challenge involves climbing **St. Mary's Peak.** Again, this hike boasts a trailhead midway up the mountain, and one of the great views that

the peak affords is onto the local lookout tower. From Highway 93, go two miles south of the Stevensville turnoff. A brown sign promising St. Mary's Peak points up the switchbacks of Forest Service Road 739. The trailhead is about 10 miles from the highway, and it's a 4.5-mile hike to the lookout.

Between Victor and Hamilton, at the crossroads hamlet of Corvallis, turn west to reach the **Mill Creek** trail. It's about three miles in along a great trail to a waterfall; if you want to make a backpacking trip out of it, keep going for another 11 miles to a high mountain lake. This trail was damaged by the 2000 fires but has had lots of work since then.

Also damaged by the massive 2000 Bitterroot fire was the trail up lovely Blodgett Canyon, west of Hamilton. It's now a good place to see wildlife and regenerating plant life. Hike the 1.5-mile (one way) **Blodgett Overlook Trail** for an overview. There are also good views of the valley on the drive to the trailhead. From Hamilton, head west on Main Street to Blodgett Creek Road (Forest Rd. 736), then turn left onto Forest Road 735; the trailhead is about five miles from town. To hike up the canyon itself, follow Blodgett Camp Road and make a right onto Forest Road 746; follow the trail 1.5 miles to a nice pool or eight miles to Blodgett Lake.

The **Lee Metcalf National Wildlife Refuge** is a good place for short hikes along the Bitterroot River. This riverside refuge is full of ospreys, eagles, and whatever migrating birds need a place to spend the night. White-tailed deer and coyotes also live here. In the summer, after nesting season, a two-mile loop trail is open through the refuge. Two shorter trails are open year-round, and picnics are encouraged. From the East Side Highway (Hwy. 269), watch for the binocular signs indicating a sanctioned wildlife-viewing area, either just south of Florence or just north of Stevensville.

Other Recreation

Take a dip in the big outdoor pool at **Lolo Hot Springs** (406/273-2290, 10 A.M.–10 P.M. daily summer, 10 A.M.–8 P.M. daily winter, $7 adults, $5 children under 12), on Highway 12 about 12 miles northeast of the state line. Lewis and Clark camped and bathed here. Nowadays, these hot springs are popular with skiers returning from a long day in cross-country heaven at Lolo Pass. Lolo Hot Springs also offers wintertime **snowmobile rentals** for $165 per day.

A paved **bike path** between Lolo and Florence parallels Highway 93 and is a grand alternative to cycling on the busy highway.

There are **public golf courses** in Stevensville and Hamilton. The Stevensville course, just north of town on Wildfowl Lane (406/777-3636) has nine holes; the Hamilton Golf Club, on Golf Course Road southeast of town (406/363-4251), has an 18-hole course.

Cross-country skiing is pretty much the order of the season after snowfall and is as casual as just parking the car and putting on your skis. All of the Bitterroot canyons are good bets, and they are even more pleasant covered with snow, as they tend to be pretty rocky and rugged in summer. The real treasure for cross-country skiers, though, is Lolo Pass. Snow simply dumps along the pass all winter, but the

Highway Department keeps the road open. Lolo Pass is 37 miles east of Lolo on Highway 12. It's very popular, but it's still possible to strike out and get away from the crowds.

Downtown Hamilton is home to **Simple Yoga** (220 W. Main St., 406/544-2101), with several classes every weekday.

Outfitters

If the thought of all that nature in the Bitterroot makes you a little jumpy or just lonely, consider hiring an outfitter to ease that transition into the wilderness. After seeing the piles of fliers at the chamber of commerce, you'll wonder if there's anyone in the Bitterroot who is *not* an outfitter or who at least doesn't run a "guest ranch." The following are just highlights of what's available, but an inquiring letter to the chamber will be sure to result in cascades of mail.

Bill Abbot and his guides at **Trout Fishing Only** (406/363-2408, www.abbotsmontanafishing.com) will row you into good fishing waters, then tell you what to do when you get there. They offer day trips and overnighters on the Bitterroot, Beaverhead, and Big Hole Rivers, and will arrange lodging and lunches. **Bitterroot Anglers** (3000 College St., Stevensville, 406/375-1901, http://bitterrootanglers.com) specializes in overnight float trips with camping alongside the Bitterroot ($330 per person per day).

Highway 93 has nearly as many fly shops as mini-marts, and store personnel will, in the way of cagey anglers, offer a few tips.

Accommodations

Hamilton has the largest choice of motels in the Bitterroot Valley, where the best choice for budget lodging is the **City Center Motel** (415 W. Main St., 406/363-1651, $50 and up), at the quiet end of Main Street. Pets can be accommodated here, and some rooms have full kitchens.

In downtown Stevensville, the old community hospital has been turned into the attractive **◖ Stevensville Hotel** (107 E. 3rd St., 406/777-3087 or 888/816-2875, www.stevensvillehotel.com, $65–125). The rooms are decorated with antique furniture and with art from the owners' travels in the South Pacific (they spent many years living and traveling on their sailboat). A newly constructed annex is a couple of blocks from the main hotel and includes rooms with kitchens. Pets are permitted in a few rooms here.

The **Best Western Hamilton Inn** (409 1st St., 406/363-2142 or 800/426-4586, $75 and up) offers more standard rooms and a free continental breakfast. Similar amenities, plus an attached casino and pet rooms, are at the **TownHouse Inn** (1113 N. 1st St., 406/363-6600, www.townpump.com, $85 and up).

For a different twist in lodging, consider staying at **Lolo Hot Springs** (38500 Hwy. 12, 406/273-2294 or 877/541-5117, www.lolo-hotsprings.com, $55–65 camping cabins, $85 and up deluxe cabins), which is 25 miles up Highway 12 along Lolo Creek, or the adjacent **Lolo Trail Center** (406/273-2201, www.lolotrailcenter.com, $90 and up), where accommodations are in comfortable motel rooms without phones or TVs.

A well-run Bitterroot Valley B&B is **Deer Crossing B&B** (396 Hayes Creek Rd., 406/363-2232 or 800/763-2232, www.deer-crossingmontana.com, $100–149), south of Hamilton. Rooms are in a large log house or one of two cabins; dogs are permitted with advance notice.

Camping

The U.S. Forest Service maintains several campsites in the Bitterroots. Most require a fair amount of determination to make use of. Some are essentially trailheads into Bitterroot canyons, and others demand long dusty drives on county roads, but some are handy enough for the more casual traveler to consider.

Lolo Creek Campground (www.fs.fed.us/r1/lolo, late May–Sept., $10) is 15 miles west of Lolo on Highway 12, and for the angler, right on Lolo Creek. An even more enticing fishing and camping site is the state's **Chief Looking Glass Fishing-Access Site** (http://fwp.mt.gov, May–Nov., $12), which is a developed campsite as well. Look for the fishing-access sign on Highway 93 at milepost 77, about

midway between Lolo and Stevensville. Then turn east one mile to the river.

Charles Waters (www.fs.fed.us/r1/bitterroot, Apr.–Oct., $10) is a developed site at the trailhead up Bass Creek, with access to hiking up the canyon and fishing in the stream. Watch for the Forest Service sign for Bass Creek Trail four miles south of Florence or four miles north of Stevensville on Highway 93. It's about three miles in to the campsite.

There are more amenities at some of the area's private campgrounds. Two nice places are on the river south of Hamilton; both have tent areas as well as RV spaces: **Angler's Roost** (406/363-1268, $16 tent, $26 RV full hookup), three miles south of Hamilton, and **Bitterroot Family Campground** (406/363-2430 or 800/453-2430), eight miles south of Hamilton, with similar prices.

Food

The hungry traveler will not want for opportunities to fill up in the Bitterroot. There are so many cafés and restaurants along the road that one imagines that Bitterroot residents do little but journey from coffee klatch to lunch and back again. The traveler can't go far wrong with most Bitterroot eateries, and there are a few worth planning ahead for.

Some Missoulians claim that their city's best restaurant is actually in Lolo: **Guy's Lolo Creek Steakhouse** (6600 Hwy. 12, 406/273-2622, 5–10 P.M. Tues.–Sun., $11–27, reservations not accepted) is at the very northern edge of the Bitterroot Valley, practically in the Missoula suburbs. Be prepared to wait for a while to be seated, admiring the beautiful log building, which was constructed with 135- to 150-year-old logs, many felled and bucked by Guy. The steaks are cooked over an open-pit wood fire, and those who haven't been dreaming of the perfect Montana steak can satisfy themselves with fish, chicken, or what the restaurant refers to as "rabbit food."

Glen's Mountain View Cafe (Florence, 406/273-2534, 9 A.M.–8 P.M. summer, 9 A.M.–3:30 P.M. winter, lunch $5–9), a little log building right on Highway 93, is known for its extraordinary pastries. Not that the rest of the menu is lacking (Glen's raises its own beef), but the pies are reckoned to be the best in the area.

Find a good lunch in Stevensville at **Food Fetish** (308 Main St., 406/777-2133, lunch Wed.–Fri., dinner Wed.–Sat., brunch Sun., $5–10 lunch, $10–20 dinner), where you can go as simple as a French dip or as elegant as grilled Copper River salmon.

In Victor, eat your beef at the **Victor Steakhouse** (2426 Meridian Rd., 406/642-3300, 11 A.M.–8 P.M. daily, $8–20). Atmosphere is provided by the mounted animal heads observing you devour the excellent steaks. Also in Victor, the **Hamilton Public House** (104 Main St., 406/642-6644, 11 A.M.–10 P.M., $6–10) dispenses pub grub, a nice selection of beers, and Celtic music.

The Banque (225 W. Main St., 406/363-1955, 4:30–9 P.M. daily, $10–25) in Hamilton offers well-prepared food in a historic Marcus Daly–built bank building.

The Bitterroot's best burgers are in Hamilton at down-home **Nap's** (220 N. 2nd St., 406/363-0136, 11 A.M.–8 P.M. daily, $4–14). At 🄒 **The Spice of Life** (163 S. 2nd St., 406/363-4433, 5–9 P.M. Wed.–Sat., $8–20), you'll find good salads, an eclectic dinner menu with often-spicy Caribbean, Thai, Japanese, and Italian influences, and a homey bistro setting with live music Wednesday evenings.

Bradley O's (1131 Hwy. 93 S., 406/375-1110, 5–9 P.M. nightly, $8–40), six miles south of Hamilton, is the sort of restaurant that the Bitterroot does best: steak (certified Angus) and seafood in a simple setting.

For atmosphere, head west of town to the **Grubstake** (1017 Grubstake Rd., 406/363-3068, hours vary seasonally, call for reservations and directions), where the polygonal restaurant is perched on a mountaintop with great views and occasional glimpses of wildlife. The food is also good: Sunday, Monday, and Tuesday nights are devoted to barbequed ribs and chicken ($14).

Taste some good local beer at **Bitterroot Brewing** (101 Marcus St., 406/363-7468), where the tasting room is open weekdays 11:30 A.M.–8 P.M., Saturday noon–6 P.M., and Sunday 2–6 P.M. Tasty English-style ales and pub food such as fish tacos ($5–10) are the specialty at this friendly microbrewery located behind the Safeway and across the railroad tracks.

Information and Services

The **Bitterroot Valley Chamber of Commerce** (105 E. Main St., 406/363-2400, www.bitterrootvalleychamber.com) is just east of the stoplight in Hamilton.

The **Bitterroot National Forest Headquarters** (406/363-7100, www.fs.fed.us/r1/bitterroot) is in Hamilton at 1801 N. 1st Street. The **Stevensville Ranger District Office** (406/777-5461) is at 88 Main Street.

The **Hamilton Public Library** (406/363-1670) is at 306 State Street. Hamilton also supports a good general bookstore, **Chapter One** (252 Main St., 406/363-5220), a friendly place that serves as a de facto community center.

The **Marcus Daly Memorial Hospital** (406/363-2211) is at 1200 Westwood Drive in Hamilton.

THE UPPER BITTERROOT

The Bitterroot Valley narrows upstream from Hamilton, and the character of the countryside changes as it passes **Darby, Lake Como,** and **Sula**. The river flows faster here, and the mountains encroach. With rocky ramparts closing in, the Bitterroot ceases to be a broad valley dotted with farms and subdivisions and becomes a wooded canyon. People scramble for logging jobs or work for the Forest Service or at the local Job Corps center. For the traveler, recreation is the draw in the upper Bitterroot.

Darby marks the southern edge of old Lake Missoula, which existed in the bad old days when the entire Missoula Valley system was alternately underwater and drained as the ice age saw necessary. At **Connor,** just south of Darby, the Bitterroot River divides into the West Fork and the East Fork. The highway also divides. Highway 93 follows the East Fork up Lost Trail Pass over the Continental Divide south into Idaho or east into the Big Hole Valley. The West Fork proceeds up Highway 473 into deep canyons, first along a paved road, then along an improved road to Painted Rocks Lake.

At **Sula** on Highway 93, the East Fork opens onto pastureland. All of a sudden it's cattle country, a last reprise of the Bitterroot Valley before it disappears into the heights of the Continental Divide.

History

Lewis and Clark straggled off Lost Trail Pass in September 1805 after being foiled on their way to the Columbia by the chasms of the Salmon River. They crept back into Montana via the Bitterroot and almost immediately met a lodge of Flathead Indians. At present-day Sula, the Corps of Discovery found 400 Flathead and 500 horses encamped and quickly made friends. Remember the landscape; the enormous painting in the Montana House of Representatives in Helena depicts this meeting.

The valley at the junction of the East Fork and Camp Creek later became known as Ross's Hole. Alexander Ross was a Canadian trapper who nearly died of cold here with his family in 1824.

The Nez Percé passed through Ross's Hole in 1877 on their way to the Battle of the Big Hole, just over the Continental Divide. While the tribal leaders felt they had escaped the pursuing army, others, with "medicine powers," began to foresee the coming ambush. By this time, the army force, under the command of General Gibbon, had caught up with the fleeing Indians, who unwisely had taken a break from their flight from Idaho once they had reached Montana.

Recreation

The upper Bitterroot has reserved some of the best recreation for those willing to drive the extra miles to get there. You can grow hoarse talking about the hiking possibilities in the Bitterroot Range, but probably the most astonishing ascent of the entire range is the climb up **Trapper Peak.** At 10,157 feet it's the highest mountain in the Bitterroots, but it's

only a moderately difficult eight-mile round-trip day hike. The trailhead is reached by following West Fork Road, MT 473, at Connor. Once you pass the Trapper Peak Civilian Jobs Corps Center, go almost seven miles to the signs pointing to the Trapper Peak trailhead. Switchbacks take you most of the way up the back of the mountain, but there's enough slogging left to satisfy more energetic hikers. If you do only one ascent in the Bitterroots, this should be it.

If a day on the mountain isn't possible for you, then enjoy the other end of Trapper Peak at **Lake Como.** This lake just west of Darby is nestled in a valley rimmed by the most unrestrained peaks in the Bitterroots. It should be no surprise that other people know of Lake Como (the Italian Lake Como is its namesake and chief rival in beauty), and don't expect to be the only camper at the lake. There's good trout fishing but too many speedboats to make it a bucolic getaway. There's an easy eight-mile loop trail around the lake. Watch for Lake Como signs five miles north of Darby.

Another good but slightly longer day hike will take the curious to **Overwhich Falls,** which drops 200 feet along the wall of the Continental Divide near Lost Trail Pass. It's about six miles in, but after following the switchbacks up to the trailhead, it's fairly easy going. From the Indian Trees Forest Service Campground, follow the signs for Road 729 to Porcupine Saddle. From the trailhead, the trail follows Shields Creek to the falls.

Just across the road from Lost Trail Hot Springs, **Nee-Me-Poo Trail** traces the route of the Nez Percé on their 1877 flight from the U.S. Army. This section of the trail heads uphill through an open ponderosa pine forest past views down the Bitterroot Valley to Gibbons Pass, six miles from the road. It's a pleasant hike with a day pack filled with trail mix and water, but it's hard to hike this route without imagining what it would be like to walk it with family, friends, coworkers, and neighbors of all ages, pursued by the U.S. Army.

A good West Fork hike starts from the Sam Billings Campground and sticks pretty close to aptly named **Boulder Creek** for the four-mile trip to Boulder Lake.

Painted Rocks Lake is a reservoir on the West Fork of the Bitterroot that receives a lot fewer visitors than Lake Como and offers better fishing, although irrigation usually draws it down during the late summer and fall. There are Indian pictographs on the rocks to the west of the lake. Painted Rocks Lake is 23 miles southwest of the junction of highways 473 and 93. South of the lake, down West Fork Road, the still-standing Alta Ranger Station was the nation's first ranger station.

The Bitterroot upstream, south of Darby, becomes a stream with fast action. The river is never far out of sight, and access is easy if you maintain the courtesy of asking permission to cross private property. One fishing-access site warrants mention: The **Hannon Memorial Fishing Access Site** at Connor allows the angler to fish both the East and the West Forks of the Bitterroot as they converge. Camping is allowed.

If you don't mind a slightly funky atmosphere, stop by **Lost Trail Hot Springs** (406/821-3574, $6 adults, $4 children), seven miles south of Sula, for a swim in the large, pleasantly warm pool; indoors there's a hot tub and sauna.

Lost Trail Powder Mountain (406/821-3211, www.losttrail.com, Thurs.–Sun. Dec.–Apr., $31 adult, $21 child, $5 one ride) straddles the Idaho-Montana border on Highway 93. Although it's a relatively small ski area with lots of intermediate runs, a few double chairlifts, and a vertical drop of only 1,200 feet, there's usually good powder here.

Accommodations

Darby is a rough-hewn little town that seems only a few steps from its early logging days. Although there are some swanky houses on the edges of town, in-town motels are pretty simple.

To stay in miniature log cabins, go to the **Travellers Rest Cabins** (601 N. Main St., 406/821-3282, $50–60); each cabin has a single and a double bed. In the same price range is the 1940s-era **Wilderness Motel** (308 S. Main St., 406/821-3405, $40–70) with several kitchenettes and a bunkhouse that can sleep six.

Another midrange place to stay if you don't mind somewhat dilapidated cabins is the **Lost Trail Hot Springs Resort** (8321 Hwy. 93 S., 406/821-3574, www.losttrailhotsprings.com, $65 lodge room, $80 cabin) in Sula. Along with the hot mineral water and an on-site bar and restaurant, there are easy-access recreational opportunities such as mountain biking, hiking, cross-country skiing, horseback riding, and fishing,. Pets are accepted with a fairly stiff fee and stringent requirements. Lost Trail Hot Springs is six miles south of Sula on Highway 93, and six miles north of Lost Trail Pass.

Resorts and Luxury Cabins

If you don't want to stay in a motel on Darby's Main Street or pitch your tent in a Forest Service campground, head a few miles up the West Fork Road to one of Montana's most exclusive resorts, owned by the CEO of Intel. Perched above the valley, the **Triple Creek Guest Ranch** (5551 West Fork Rd., 406/821-4664, www.triplecreekranch.com, $650–2,495 per couple per night includes all meals, house wine, and ranch activities) offers accommodations in luxurious cabins and houses, gourmet meals, and fine wine. There are hot tubs aplenty, a well-kept heated swimming pool, tennis courts, horseback riding, fishing (all gear provided), and hiking trails heading out from the ranch property. Many guests come here to sample the various activities rather than concentrate strictly on fishing or riding, and an activities director helps them plan their days. Those who can't quite leave their work (and with these high-powered guests, that's pretty common) should note that, although there's no cell phone coverage here, there are phones in the room and Wi-Fi in the lodge. Although no minimum stay is imposed, there's enough to keep most people busy for nearly a week. The Triple Creek is very much geared toward couples and is an adults-only place; no children under 16 are allowed.

If those prices aren't in your budget but you hanker for a relaxing Montana mountain getaway, consider the **Nez Percé Ranch** (7206 Nez Perce Rd., Darby, 406/349-2100, www.nezperceranch.com, $1,200 per week). This comfortable resort offers self-catering accommodations (bring your own food and cook it yourself) along the Bitterroot River in three large log cabins. The ranch sits on 100 forested acres with a half-mile of private fishing access. Each cabin has two bedrooms, a full kitchen, and a porch with a barbecue. If there are openings, you can reserve a cabin for a three-night minimum at $225 per night.

Rye Creek Lodge (458 Rye Creek Rd., 406/821-3366 or 888/821-3366, www.ryecreeklodge.com, $250–500) is a luxury cabin resort south of Darby. Each cabin has a private hot tub, a kitchen, and laundry facilities; most have two bedrooms.

Camping

The Forest Service maintains several campgrounds in the upper Bitterroot (www.fs.fed.us/r1/bitterroot, late May–late Sept.), mostly off the beaten path. A couple are handy for casual campers who don't want to get too far off the highway. **Indian Trees** ($10) is six miles south of Sula, right next to Lost Trail Hot Springs at a location where Flathead women once spiked ponderosa pines to extract sap, which was used as a sweetener.

Lewis and Clark camped at **Spring Gulch** ($12), and so can you. The campground is right on the East Fork River, five miles north of Sula on Highway 93. Right behind the **Sula Store** (7060 Hwy. 93 S., 406/821-3364, $13 tents, $18–20 RVs, $40–90 cabins) are campsites and cabins (complete with bedding, but the cheapest require a short walk to the bathhouse) at the beginning of the canyon leading from Ross's Hole.

There are several Forest Service campgrounds up the West Fork Road; **Sam Billings** is a lovely free spot (no water) near the Boulder Creek trailhead, and there's another campground past Painted Rocks Lake at Alta ($8).

Food

With the exception of the Triple Creek Ranch, which feeds its clients quite well, don't expect to find fine dining in the Upper Bitterroot. There are a few cafés in Darby, and the country store in Sula has a small restaurant.

Information

Bitterroot National Forest **ranger stations** can be found in **Sula** (7338 Hwy. 93 S., 406/821-3201) and **Darby** (712 N. Main, 406/821-3913).

Flathead Reservation and Mission Valley

The Flathead Reservation measures about 65 by 35 miles east to west and is managed by the Confederated Salish and Kootenai Tribes, with headquarters at Pablo. Of about 6,950 tribal members, some 4,500 live on or near the reservation. The Flathead population is centered at Arlee; most of the Kootenai tribal members live near Elmo.

The Mission Mountains Tribal Wilderness is the first place in the United States where an Indian nation has designated tribal lands as a wilderness preserve. It covers the west side of the range's peaks; to the east it's the Flathead National Forest, with access from Highway 83 in the Swan Valley. Any hiking or camping in

the Mission Mountains Tribal Wilderness requires a tribal conservation permit, available at many local stores. A three-day conservation permit costs $8 for non-Montanans; if you intend to fish on tribal land, which includes the southern half of Flathead Lake, get the $17 combined-use/fishing permit.

HISTORY

Salish-speaking Indians originally lived near the Pacific Coast, where most Salish-speakers still reside. Legend has it that an argument developed as to whether flying ducks quacked with their wings or with their bills. The ones who voted for the wings ended up moving to the Bitterroot Valley and eventually became known as the Flathead Salish. When they arrived in the Bitterroot Valley, the Pend d'Oreille who were living there moved north, apparently as a gesture of friendliness, to the area around present-day Paradise and Plains.

Until the Blackfeet moved onto the Montana plains in the mid-1700s, the Flathead Salish spent a great deal of time on the eastern plains hunting buffalo. Travel to the west was more limited, generally just far enough to fish for salmon west of Lolo Pass. Camas, bitterroot, and serviceberries were other dietary staples that the Flathead still gather.

Lewis and Clark and early white settlers found the Flathead to be friendly and helpful. The Flathead continued good relations with white settlers, with much intermarriage.

The 1855 Hell Gate Treaty formed the Flathead Reservation, but Victor, head chief of the Salish, refused to move his people from their home in the Bitterroot Valley. By the 1870s the influx of white settlers into the valley made the government attempt to foist a new treaty onto the Flathead. Charlo, Victor's son and the new head chief of the tribe, held firm against moving to the reservation in the Jocko-Mission Valley, but he and his people did what they could to accommodate the white homesteaders. Maintaining a good relationship with whites was important enough to Chief Charlo that he refused to help his friend Chief Joseph of the Nez Percé on his flight east. He told Joseph that if the Nez Percé caused any harm to the settlers in the Bitterroot Valley, the Nez Percé could expect the Flathead to defend the whites.

Charlo never signed the reservation treaty. However, in 1872, Arlee, a Flathead war chief, did sign it, and he thus won recognition from the U.S. government as head chief of the Flathead tribe. Charlo stayed behind in the Bitterroots until 1891, when he told the government agents who were pressuring him to move, "I will go—I and my children. My young men are becoming bad; they have no place to hunt. I do not want the land you promise. I do not believe your promises. All I want is enough ground for my grave."

During the early years of the Flathead Reservation, Indians lived in both log cabins and, weather permitting, in tepees. Many took up farming, with several successful farms eventually dotting the valley. The 1887 Dawes Act allotted parcels of reservation land to individual Indians in an effort to make them understand the concept of owning the land. Unallotted land was often dealt to the U.S. government and then thrown open to white homesteaders. The Dawes Act was repealed in 1934, when tribal rather than individual identity was emphasized in the Tribal Reorganization Act. Under these provisions, the Confederated Salish and Kootenai Tribes were incorporated. By that time, much of the land within the confines of the Flathead Reservation was owned by non-Indians, as it remains today.

ST. IGNATIUS AND VICINITY

St. Ignatius is a reservation town at the feet of some stunningly jagged peaks. It's home to the Salish Cultural Committee (406/745-4572) and a longhouse, located near the St. Ignatius Mission, used by the tribe for spiritual and ceremonial events. There's a full day's worth of sightseeing in the vicinity of St. Ignatius.

🄲 National Bison Range

It may sound a little boring, driving around in your car for two hours on a one-way road, staring out the window for a glimpse of shaggy critters, but it's not. The National Bison Range (406/644-2211, http://bisonrange.fws.gov, $5 per vehicle) has two driving tours, and it's worth taking a couple of hours to go on the long one. Stop in at the visitors center and find out where the herds have been spotted recently. Bison are the main attraction, but expect to see bighorn sheep, pronghorn, elk, mule deer, white-tailed deer, and mountain goats as well. Even if all the animals are in hiding, the land, the sky, and the light are beautiful here. As with most wildlife viewing, it's best to visit early in the morning or around dusk.

The National Bison Range was established in 1908 in response to concern that the buffalo had been slaughtered to the point of extinction.

Part of the original herd was purchased from the Conrad family of Kalispell, who were early buffalo ranchers. The animals are now flourishing here, and a bison roundup is held in early October at the Bison Range.

The Bison Range is on a parcel of land carved from the Flathead Reservation by Highway 212 near Moiese. If you're approaching from Highway 93, catch Highway 212 between St. Ignatius and Ronan. If you're on Highway 200, there's a turnoff to Highway 212 near Dixon. From the north, turn off Highway 93 at St. Ignatius.

If there's no time for a tour, at least be sure to keep your eyes peeled as you drive Highway 93 north of Ravalli. Sometimes the bison come down off their mountain to water just a hundred yards or so from the highway.

Dixon

Dixon, a small town on Highway 200 west of Ravalli at the southwestern edge of the National Bison Range, is noted for its bar. The **Dixon Bar** has the longest-standing liquor license in the state of Montana, and in October 1970 had the distinction of having three poems about it appear on one page of *The New Yorker* magazine. Stop by and ask the bartender to let you read them.

⬛ St. Ignatius Mission

In 1854 St. Ignatius became the site of the second Catholic mission in Montana. Father Adrian Hoecken, a Jesuit priest, originally established the mission in Idaho, but it was moved to the Mission Valley at the behest of the Pend d'Oreille Indians. A boys' school, a mill, and a press (which printed a dictionary of the Pend d'Oreille language) eventually grew up around the mission.

One of the Jesuits' original log buildings, a chapel that doubled as living quarters for the priests, still stands beside the brick church, which was built in 1891. The church deserves as much of a look as the wooden chapel; there are striking murals inside, painted by Brother Joseph Carignano, the mission cook. While these murals may not initially impress those who

GLACIAL LAKE MISSOULA

Glacial ice dammed the Clark Fork River in northern Idaho approximately 15,000 years ago, forming Glacial Lake Missoula, which filled the valleys of western Montana. River water ultimately floated the ice dam like an ice cube in a glass of water, and the lake drained with spectacular force, coursing across eastern Washington and forming the Columbia River Gorge. The ice dam on the Clark Fork settled back down into the riverbed and once again plugged the outlet. The lake filled again, drained again, and was reformed at least 41 times over the course of about 2,500 years. Each cycle was shorter, and the lake didn't fill as deep. The record of these successive fillings and drainings can still be seen as a series of faint, perfectly horizontal lines on the sides of Mt. Jumbo and Mt. Sentinel above Missoula.

compare them to those at St. Paul's Cathedral or Chartres, they clearly succeeded in illustrating the life of Jesus and in imparting biblical stories to the Indians. Sunday mass is still held weekly at 9:15 A.M. Good Friday and Easter services at the mission church have developed into a uniquely Flathead Catholic ceremony.

Recreation

To explore the **Mission Mountains Tribal Wilderness,** first pick up an $8 tribal recreation permit, available at Allard's Trading Post and other local stores. A map of the Flathead National Forest or the Flathead Reservation is another essential.

St. Mary's Lake is less than 10 miles from St. Ignatius on St. Mary's Lake Road. (Find the road just southeast of the mission and follow it as it turns into a fairly bumpy, dusty gravel road, turns left, and heads into the hills.) There are several places to pitch a tent around the lake, and it's worth taking along fishing gear and a tribal fishing permit; there are some lunker trout around here. Just over a mile up the road is the first of the **Twin Lakes,** which are a little more isolated and quieter than St. Mary's. No motorboats are allowed on the Twin Lakes; St. Mary's does permit them.

Drop in for a yoga class at **Working Wellness** (203 Main St., St. Ignatius, 406/370-5445, www.workingwellness.com).

Accommodations

Established with cyclists and backpackers in mind, **St. Ignatius Campground and Hostel** (406/745-3959, http://camp-hostel.com) is a friendly, if somewhat eccentric, place on the northern outskirts of St. Ignatius. Lodging is bunk style ($14) in the "earthship," an environmentally friendly, passive solar-heated building constructed of recycled tires and cans. Showers and toilets are in a separate bathhouse, where visitors can use a laundry room. There's also a pleasant camping area, open both to tenters and RVs (full hookups), and a couple of tepees ($10 s, $14 d).

Free camping behind the senior center in Charlo is provided by the Lions Club. It's a convenient place to stay if you want to get an early jump on bird and animal watching.

The **Sunset Motel** (333 Mountain View, St. Ignatius, 406/745-3900, $65) is a simple but comfortable motel just above Hwy. 93 in St. Ignatius. Pets are allowed here.

Up against the Mission Mountains, **Cheff's Guest Ranch** (4274 Eagle Pass Rd., 406/644-2557, www.cheffguestranch.com) offers accommodations on a working cattle and horse ranch outside of Charlo. Weeklong packages ($950 per person) include all meals, lodging, and horseback riding. A couple of cabins are equipped with kitchens and can be rented by the night ($140) or week ($780) and lodge rooms arc available on a B&B basis ($80). Cheff's also run pack trips and short horseback rides $40 for 2 hours).

Shopping

Doug Allard's Trading Post has a wide selection of beadwork done on the Flathead Reservation. Expect to find some great beaded earrings and hair ornaments, as well as less apparently traditional beaded cigarette-lighter covers. There's also a chance for a close view of some buffalo here; Allard has a small herd paddocked near the trading post. A couple of miles north of Allard's, the **Four Winds Trading Post** (406/745-4336) specializes in moccasins, Indian artifacts, and toy trains. Preston Miller, proprietor of Four Winds, also collects historic buildings from around the Mission Valley and has moved several to the trading post.

Events

Arlee, 15 miles south of St. Ignatius on Highway 93, is the site of the **Fourth of July Powwow,** held annually by the Confederated Salish and Kootenai Tribes. It's a major event, not to be missed if you're anywhere in the area at the time. Expect to see both traditional and fancy dancing to the accompaniment of amazing drumming. Groups of drummers, as well as individual dancers, compete for prize money. In another area of the powwow, the sounds of hand drums signal stick games, which are ritualistic and high-stakes gambling competitions. For those not up to the complications and $100 ante of a stick game, poker and blackjack games are set up in small shacks.

Jewelry, crafts, and cassette tapes of popular drum groups are for sale at several booths. There's also plenty of food, including fry bread and "Indian tacos." The powwow grounds are the site of an encampment during this long weekend. Tepees, tents, and campers crowd into the dusty field, and the celebration goes on late into the night. The powwow grounds are right in Arlee, just east of Highway 93.

Admission is free, non-Indians are welcome, and drugs and alcohol are strictly prohibited.

RONAN AND VICINITY

Ronan was named for Peter Ronan, an Indian agent. The area around Ronan was part of the Flathead Reservation until 1910.

The **Garden of the Rockies** pioneer museum (1071 Terrace Lake Rd., 406/676-5210) is four blocks west of the Highway 93 stoplight. There are mock-ups of a doctor's office, barbershop, schoolroom, kitchen, bedroom, and living room. Expect a friendly volunteer to give you a personalized tour; perhaps you'll get a demonstration of a favorite object, such as a hand-pumped vacuum cleaner.

Pablo, five miles north of Ronan, is the headquarters of the Confederated Salish and Kootenai Tribes and home of **Salish-Kootenai College** (406/275-4800, www.skc.edu), which offers programs in general studies, Native American studies, nursing, and a range of human services and vocational fields. The college library is a good place to read up on the Salish and Kootenai tribes.

Ninepipe National Wildlife Refuge

This wetland waterfowl refuge is north of the National Bison Range between highways 93 and 212. The large reservoir and many smaller lakes are rimmed with marshlands, making it difficult to hike from many of the roadside viewing points. The best views are generally from the road that goes along the northern edge of the reservoir off Highway 212. The many pothole lakes around the refuge were dug out as glaciers moved across the land some 12,000 years ago.

Ninepipe is in the path of a major migratory flyway in the Rocky Mountain Trench. Prime bird-watching occurs in September. Canada geese, mergansers, mallards, redheads, great blue herons, grebes, double-crested cormorants, American wigeons, pintails, whistling swans, California gulls, ring-billed gulls, pheasants, bald eagles, and American avocets are some of the birds you might spot here.

Check at the headquarters of the National Bison Range for information on the birds and regulations. A tribal fishing permit is required before throwing a line into the reservoir. No hunting is permitted on the refuge, and it is closed during waterfowl-hunting season (in the fall) and nesting season (March through mid-July).

Pablo National Wildlife Refuge, off Highway 93 about a dozen miles north of the Ninepipe Refuge, is a similar waterfowl sanctuary and is governed by similar regulations.

Ninepipes Museum of Early Montana

Located in the motel complex adjacent to the wildlife refuge, this museum (41000 N. Hwy. 93, 406/644-3435, www.ninepipes.com, 9 A.M.–5:30 P.M. daily June–Oct., 11 A.M.–5 P.M. Wed.–Sun., Apr.–May, $4 adult, $3 student, $2 child 6–12) celebrates the history and culture of the Flathead Reservation and the early history of all of Montana.

The People's Center

This tribal gallery and gift shop (406/883-5544, www.peoplescenter.org, 9 A.M.–6 P.M. daily April–Sept., 9 A.M.–5 P.M. Mon.–Fri. Oct.–March), located in Pablo, also runs Native Ed-Ventures tours and educational programs led by tribal members.

Accommodations

The **Ninepipes Lodge** (41000 N. Hwy. 93, 406/644-2588, www.ninepipes.com, $75) is the area's most attractive motel. It's located across from the bird refuge five miles south of Ronan.

Arts and Entertainment

The **Red Poppy** (1 Eisenhower St. SW, Ronan, noon–6 P.M. Mon.–Sat.) is a fine arts and music cultural center across from True Value in Ronan. Along with art, music, and movement classes, the Red Poppy hosts an occasional concert.

HOT SPRINGS AND VICINITY

The western part of the Flathead Reservation has a couple of commercial hot springs in and around the very modest and unresortlike town of Hot Springs. Several massage therapists have practices in town, so it's easy to get *very* relaxed here.

Locals mix with day trippers up from Missoula at Camas Hot Springs, a series of outdoor pools on the northeast edge of town developed by the Confederated Salish and Kootenai Tribes. Two soaking pools, one large and one small, are near a path leading to hot seeps welling up from the ground. Admission is

$5 for the whole day, and no-frills RV camping is available. Another tribe-run site is **Rose's Plunge,** at the Camas Recreation Center. **Wild Horse Hot Springs** (406/741-3777, 11 A.M.–8 P.M., $5), six miles off Highway 28 from Hot Springs, is a place to relax in a private room with a plunge, a steam room, a shower, and a toilet. The plunge is like a cement baby pool with hot water. It's not a posh place, but it somehow has the feeling of a refuge, a place where chills and bone weariness melt away and you're left with your pores open to the rolling hills and golden light of the surrounding reservation. RV camping is available out back, but most people just come for a soak.

If you do want to spend the night within an easy sniff of the waters, **Symes Hot Springs Hotel and Mineral Baths** (104 Wall St., 406/741-2361, www.symeshotsprings.com, $50–115) has rooms with bathtubs plumbed with the local sulfurous brew; there are also newer outdoor soaking and swimming pools. This downtown Hot Springs hotel is a mix between an old-fashioned therapeutic spa and a New Age retreat, with a pretty good restaurant, helpful staff, and relaxed, friendly clientele.

Economy rooms are equipped with a toilet and sink off the bedroom; to bathe you go downstairs to a long row of huge clawfoot tubs, each enclosed in its own wooden cubicle, and draw yourself a bath. Showers are also available, and more expensive rooms ($68 and up) have their own tubs. If you're here for the real treatment, there's a massage therapist on site.

Another Hot Springs original is **Alameda's Hot Springs Retreat** (308 N. Springs St., 406/741-2283, $50–75), which has hot tubs, massages, and rooms (all with private toilet but some with shared shower facilities) in an old-fashioned motel. Pets are allowed both here and at Symes.

Flathead Lake

When western Montanans go away for a weekend, there's a pretty good chance they're headed to Flathead Lake. At 28 miles long, 7–8 miles wide, and more than 300 feet deep, it's the largest natural freshwater lake west of the Mississippi. The lakeshore is dotted with campgrounds and summer cabins, many owned by the same families for years.

Flathead Lake fills a trench carved by glaciers during the Pleistocene Epoch. A terminal moraine at the foot of the lake divides the Flathead Valley from the Mission Valley to the south.

Three upper forks of the Flathead River join above Kalispell to pour into Flathead Lake. The North Fork originates in southeastern British Columbia, the Middle Fork rises in the northern part of the Bob Marshall Wilderness (near the southern edge of Glacier National Park), and the South Fork flows from the southeastern region of the Bob Marshall Wilderness via Hungry Horse Reservoir.

Steamboats ran on Flathead Lake in the late 1800s and early 1900s. Their route was from Demersville (a now-defunct town on the Flathead River, halfway between Kalispell and Flathead Lake) down to Polson.

The first white settlers on the eastern banks of the lake arrived in 1891 and quickly hit on the idea of growing cherries there. Homesteading started in earnest around 1910, when reservation land became available to non-Indians under the Dawes Act. Fruit orchards were established all along the eastern shore of the lake. Although they're subject to periodic killing frosts, Flathead Lake's cherry trees are productive enough to supply farm stands and roadside vendors around the region.

POLSON

Polson (pop. 4,308, elev. 2,938 feet) is tucked into a glacial moraine at the foot of Flathead Lake, where the lower Flathead River drains from the lake and flows toward its junction with the Clark Fork around Paradise. Highway 93 takes

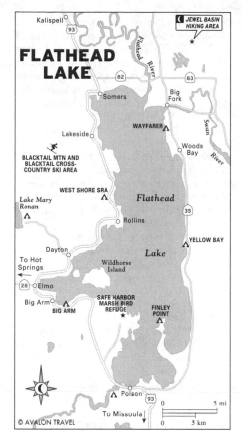

FLATHEAD
LAKE

Kalispell
93

Somers

Big
Fork

JEWEL BASIN
HIKING AREA

Lakeside

WAYFARER

Woods
Bay

BLACKTAIL MTN AND
BLACKTAIL CROSS-
COUNTRY SKI AREA

WEST SHORE SRA
Lake Mary
Ronan

Flathead

Rollins

35

YELLOW BAY

Dayton

To Hot
Springs

Lake

Wildhorse
Island

28   Elmo

Big Arm   SAFE HARBOR
MARSH BIRD
BIG ARM   REFUGE

FINLEY
POINT

Polson
93

To Missoula

0   5 mi

0   5 km

© AVALON TRAVEL

a turn here and becomes an east-west road for its extremely busy run through Polson. It's the seat of Lake County and the business center of Flathead Lake and the upper Mission Valley.

Parks

There's plenty of public shoreline, and several parks make appealing sitting, swimming, fishing, or boat-launching spots: **Boettcher Park** is toward the eastern edge of town, **Sacajawea Park** is right downtown off Kootenai Avenue, and **Riverside Park** is on the east end of the bridge over the river.

Lake Cruises

Lake cruises on the *KwaTaqNuk Princess*

(406/883-3636, www.kwataqnuk.com, mid-June–Sept.) run several times daily during the summer, leaving from the KwaTaqNuk Resort marina. A three-hour tour departs daily at 1:30 P.M. ($23 adult, $21 senior, $13 child, $57 family) and makes a loop around Wild Horse Island. Ninety-minute cruises depart at 10:30 A.M. and 7:30 P.M. ($17 adult, $15 senior, $10 child, $40 family).

Polson-Flathead Historical Museum

This museum (704 Main St., 406/883-3049, 9 A.M.–5 P.M. Mon.–Sat., 10 A.M.–3 P.M. Sun., Memorial Day–Labor Day, $2 donation requested) is a dark jumbled place that houses a stuffed steer named Rudolf, a Lewis and Clark puppet display, and a 7.5-foot sturgeon caught in Flathead Lake in 1955 and reputed to have been the Flathead Monster.

Miracle of America Museum

The Miracle of America Museum (58176 Hwy. 93, 406/883-6804, 8 A.M.–8 P.M. daily summer; 8 A.M.–5 P.M. Mon.–Sat., 1:30–5 P.M. Sun. winter; $4 adult, $1 child) is marked by a large log towboat in the parking lot. Inside this sprawling and big-hearted "Smithsonian of the West," the intrepid museumgoer will find a unique homage to cleanliness: a collection of antique vacuum cleaners. Music lovers will thrill to the sound of the violano, a coin-operated violin-piano combination; the State Fiddlers' Hall of Fame is also housed here. There's simply *a lot* of everything here, from old motorcycles to vintage tractor seats.

Kerr Dam

The Kerr Dam, a 204-foot-tall concrete arch dam on the lower Flathead River eight miles southwest of Polson, controls the water level of the lake and the lower river. It was built during the Depression and opened in 1939. It is operated by the Montana Power Company, which leases the land from the Confederated Salish and Kootenai Tribes. The lease payments, which amount to $9.4 million annually, are a major part of the tribes' economy. Reach it by

THE FLATHEAD MONSTER

Is there a monster lurking deep in Flathead Lake? Sightings have been reported for well over 100 years, and in 1955 it was even reported to have been caught. Although the creature in question turned out to be a 7.5-foot, 181-pound white sturgeon, it is preserved in the Polson-Flathead Historical Museum.

The capture of the sturgeon did not put an end to monster sightings. Read detailed incident reports at www.monsterwatch.itgo.com.

heading west on 7th Avenue to Highway 354 and following the signs. (This makes a nice bike ride if you don't mind rolling hills with one steep climb.) A long flight of steps leads to a vista over the dam before the road goes down to the power station.

Safe Harbor Marsh Preserve

The Nature Conservancy (406/443-0303) maintains a bird refuge north of Polson at Safe Harbor Marsh. Reach it by turning off Highway 93 just north of town onto Rocky Point Road. More than 130 species of birds and waterfowl have been observed here.

Recreation

All manner of watercraft, including sea kayaks and canoes, can be rented from **Absolute Water Sports** (406/883-3900 or 800/358-8046, www.absolutewatersportrentals.com) at the KwaTaqNuk Resort marina.

The lower Flathead River, considered to be Montana's warmest river, has spectacular badlands scenery and some thrilling rapids just below Kerr Dam. The **Buffalo Rapids** are a challenging stretch of white water for experienced rafters. Those with less-than-expert white-water skills should get on the river at the Buffalo Bridge, about 10 miles below Kerr Dam, or sign on with the **Flathead Raft Company** (50362 Hwy. 93 N., 406/883-5838

or 800/654-4359, www.flatheadraftco.com, half-day trips $42 adult, $36 senior, $34 child 8–12), which has a branch at Riverside Park in Polson that operates tours of the lower Flathead River, including Buffalo Rapids. The raft company also offers white-water kayak instruction and trips and sea kayak tours of Flathead Lake (half-day $79 adult, $69 child).

Polson's 18-hole **golf course** (111 Bay View Drive, 406/883-8230) is east of downtown on the lake side of Highway 93.

Because the southern half of Flathead Lake is on the Flathead Reservation, **anglers** need a tribal permit, which can be purchased at tribal headquarters in Pablo or at the Ace Hardware or Wal-Mart in Polson. Although the number of kokanee salmon in the lake has decreased sharply in recent years, there are still lake trout (many topping 20 pounds), whitefish, and some cutthroat trout throughout the lake, as well as largemouth bass and perch in warm shallow spots, such as Polson Bay. Fishing Flathead Lake requires some thought about water depth and temperature—the big guys live deep. Although the lower Flathead River doesn't have much in the way of trout, there are plenty of big pike.

There are **cross-country ski trails** about five miles north of Polson, west of Highway 93.

Entertainment and Events

The former golf course clubhouse is now the **John Dowdall Theatre**, home to the Port Polson Players (406/883-9212), a summer theater. The season starts in July, with plays at 8 P.M. Wednesday through Saturday evenings and at 2 P.M. Sunday.

Accommodations

$50-100: Several older motels are along Highway 93 just east of Polson's city center. Note that because they're *on* 93, there's going to be a bit of road noise. A good moderately priced choice is the **Cherry Hill Motel** (1810 Hwy. 93, 406/883-2737, $60) with duplex units on a bluff overlooking the lake; these rooms are a little bit removed from the road. The **Bayview Inn** (406/883-3120 or 800/237-

© JUDY JEWELL

Polson is at the southern edge of Flathead Lake.

2965, www.bayview-inn.com, $70 s, $78 d) has great views of Flathead Lake and the Mission Mountains and substantially lower rates during the off-season. Pets are welcome here.

Over $100: The large **Best Western KwaTaqNuk Resort** (406/883-3636 or 800/ 528-1234, www.kwataqnuk.com, $107 and up), a casino and hotel owned by the Confederated Salish and Kootenai Tribes, is the only real lakeside hotel in town. The KwaTaqNuk has both indoor and outdoor pools adjacent to the marina.

Port Polson Inn (502 Hwy. 93, 406/883-5385 or 800/654-0682, www.bestvalueinn .com, $114), just across the road from the lake, has indoor and outdoor hot tubs, an exercise room and sauna, kitchenettes, and free continental breakfast. It's not a fancy place, but it has a good location and is well kept up.

Camping

Campers may want to check out the **Polson KOA** (406/883-2151 or 800/562-2130, www.polsonkoa.com, RV with hookups $35–55), located about 0.5 mile north of the bridge, just west

of Highway 93. If you want to camp close to Polson and you'd like a nice setting with some amenities, this is the place to be. Farther north of town you'll find lakeside state parks.

Food

Some of the Flathead Valley's best meals come from **Isabel's** (203 Hwy. 93, 406/883-0987, breakfast, lunch, and dinner Mon.–Sat., dinner Mon.–Fri. winter, breakfast and lunch $7–9), housed in an nicely restored old homestead with a colorful cowgirl motif. Simple dinners are served Monday through Thursday ($10); Friday nights bring fancier food.

Another good place that won't bust the budget is **Hot Spot Thai** (1407 Hwy. 93, 406/883-4444, 11:30 a.m.–2 p.m. Mon.–Fri. and 5–9 p.m. Mon.–Sat., $8–12). They have a deck with lake (and highway) views.

Down by the lake at Boettcher Park, the **Boardwalk Cafe** (30 Country Club Shores, 406/883-1088, 11 a.m.–5 p.m. Wed.–Sun. mid-May–Aug., closed on rainy days, about $5) is a newly freshened-up local institution where, during the summer months, you can eat fish and chips or a burger at an outside table (no indoor seating).

Both beer drinkers and soda lovers should go a few blocks out of their way to find **Glacier Brewing Co.** (6 10th Ave. E., 406/883-2595, 2–8 p.m. daily). In addition to microbrews such as Port Polson Pilsner and Slurry Bomber Stout, Glacier brews up a fine root beer and a good (though extrasweet) cherry cream soda.

Information and Services

St. Joseph Medical Center (6 13th Ave. E., 406/883-5377) has 24-hour emergency service. The **post office** is at 219 1st Street East.

The **Polson Chamber of Commerce** (406/883-5969, www.polsonchamber.com) has an office at 418 Main Street.

The **public library** (2 1st Ave. E., 406/883-8225) has several cases of books on Montana, a good variety of magazines, and lovely views onto Flathead Lake. Across the hall in the same building, find **Sandpiper Gallery** (406/883-5956), with its displays of regional arts and crafts.

WEST SIDE OF FLATHEAD LAKE

While driving along this side of Flathead Lake, you have a good view across the water to the Mission Mountains. There's more of an open feeling to this side of the lake than the east side—off to the west the rolling Salish Mountains mellow the light and lend a glow to the surrounding land and sky.

Wild Horse Island

There are indeed wild horses on this island near the Big Arm of Flathead Lake. There's also a thriving herd of bighorn sheep and a wealth of birdlife, including ospreys, bald eagles, red-tailed hawks, and Canada geese. The island exists because its rock base resisted the plowing action of the glacier that scooped out Flathead Lake. It was used as a sort of safe house for the local Flathead and Pend d'Oreille horses when Blackfeet came on raids.

Private concerns took over the island for many years, but it became a state park in 1977, and in 1983 the Bureau of Land Management began turning horses loose there. In 1940 two bighorn sheep were transplanted there as a tourist attraction. The herd grew to beyond what the island could support, and many sheep died of starvation before the Montana Department of Fish, Wildlife, and Parks began moving Wild Horse Island bighorns to other areas of the state.

Wild Horse Island (406/849-5256, http://fwp.mt.gov) is a day-use park; camping and fires (including camp stoves) are prohibited, and there are still some private landholdings to avoid. You'll need a boat to get here (available at Sunny Shores Marina, 406/849-5622). The *KwaTaqNuk Princess* cruises from Polson around Wild Horse Island every day of the summer at 1:30 P.M., but it doesn't dock.

Camping

Big Arm State Recreation Area (406/752-5501 or 406/751-4577 for yurt reservations, http://fwp.mt.gov, day use year-round, $5 per vehicle non–Montana resident, camping May–Sept., $15 camping, $40 yurt) is 14

miles north of Polson on Highway 93. This campground has showers, a rarity in the public campgrounds of Montana. It's a good spot if you want to swim or boat, but the campsites are packed close together, making it a little uncomfortable for just plain camping. Don't expect to find peace and solitude here, but it's a lovely lakeside spot, so it's understandable that families flock here.

Between Dayton and Lakeside on Highway 93, **West Shore State Recreation Area** (same rates as above, no yurts or showers) is another state campground on Flathead Lake.

Elmo

Hub of the Flathead Reservation's Kootenai population, Elmo is the site of the **Standing Arrow Powwow** during the third weekend of July. Although not as large as the powwow held in Arlee, it's a good opportunity to see dancing, drumming, and stick games. The **Kootenai Culture Committee** (406/849-5541), the powwow's sponsor, has its headquarters in Elmo.

Dayton

The **Mission Mountain Winery** (406/849-5524, 10 A.M.–5 P.M. daily May–Oct.) has some vineyards, a winery, and a tasting room in Dayton. The quality of Mission Mountain's wines has improved dramatically in recent years, and it's worth stopping in for a taste of Monster Red, a merlot-cabernet blend.

Lake Mary Ronan

Six miles off Highway 93 near Dayton, Lake Mary Ronan is a popular place to fish, especially for kokanee salmon, which flourish here as they used to in Flathead Lake. Because the lake is not on reservation land, only a state fishing permit is needed. There are several fairly rustic resorts on the lake, all with cabins, tent and RV camping, boat rentals, and restaurants, and all able to accommodate pets in at least a few cabins. Come here to kick back, *not* to be catered to and pampered (unless you import your own pamperer).

Lake Mary Ronan Resort (406/849-5483 or 888/845-7702, www.lakemaryronanlodge.com,

$65–200 cabins, $10 tents, $20 RVs), eight miles from Highway 93 near the end of the lake road, has cabins and a trailer home with bedding and kitchens (but no cooking gear) and a few campsites.

Just six miles from the highway, **Mountain Meadows Resort** (406/849-5459, www.lakemaryronan.com, $50–70) has cabins with and without bathrooms and what may be the state's most rustic golf course with "weeds that have been cut real short"—it's sort of, but not totally, a joke.

Camp Tuffit (406/849-5220, www.camp-tuffit.com, $24–99) has the venerable feel of your aunt's backyard: very pretty, well manicured, with green grass and Adirondack chairs. Most accommodations are in very simple rustic housekeeping cabins (you use the common bathhouse) but there are a few larger, somewhat more modern houses. Boats go for $19–38 per day. Although there isn't really any tent camping here, there are a few RV spaces.

Lake Mary Ronan State Park (http://fwp.mt.gov, May–Sept., $5 non-Montanans), a very nice campground near Mountain Meadows Resort, is the lake's best bet for tent campers.

Rollins

So you picked up a bottle of wine in Dayton. Now stop at **M & S Meats** in Rollins (406/844-3414) for some buffalo jerky to add to your Montana gift basket. If you'd rather not tote around M & S's renowned buffalo meat and sausage, they'll ship a gift basket for you.

Lakeside

One of Montana's newest ski resorts, **Blacktail Mountain** (406/844-0999, www.blacktailmountain.com, $34 adult, $24 teen, $15 child 8–12) is up the road from Lakeside. With three chairlifts (no high-speed quads) serving 24 runs and few crowds, it's a nice low-key place with terrain that's accommodating to beginning and intermediate skiers and boarders. Unlike most ski areas, the lodge and parking areas are at the top of the mountain, meaning that skiers can hit the slopes right away in the morning, rather than starting the day in a lift line. Half-day

rates and a variety of special deals are available, as are rentals and lessons.

Blacktail Cross-Country Ski Area is off Blacktail Road about eight miles from Lakeside. The trails (you can download a map from www.blacktailmountain.com) range from easy to difficult and are at an elevation of about 5,500 feet, which means a fairly long skiing season and a chance to get above the clouds. If you have two vehicles, park one at the lower parking lot and use it to shuttle back to the upper lot at the end of your ski tour. Only upper lot parking is necessary if you plan to ski the easiest (and the only groomed) trail of the network. Do not ski on the road: There is logging truck traffic on it, even in winter.

There are several motels in pretty Lakeside. The **Bayshore Resort Motel** (616 Lakeside Blvd., 406/844-3131 or 800/844-3132, www.bayshoreresortmotel.com, $110–175) has a prime setting with adequate, but not fancy, kitchenette rooms and small apartments right on Flathead Lake. In addition to lodging, the resort offers charter fishing, and canoe and sailboat rentals are available right next door.

At the northern end of town, the **Sunrise Vista Inn** (7005 Hwy. 93 S., 406/844-0231, May–Sept., $80 and up) has a dock and access to a stretch of beach.

For something rather private and exclusive, consider staying at **Flathead Lake Suites** (829 Angel Point Rd., 406/844-2204 or 800/214-2204, www.angelpoint.com, $700–800 per week per couple). Located on a peninsula jutting out into Flathead Lake with 312 feet of shoreline, the three large suites (actually part of an enormous private home) come with complete kitchen, dining and sitting area, large two-room baths, and private entrances. Guests have full run of the extensive property, including a dock, fishing platform, canoe, rowboat, patio, barbecue area, beach pavilion, and gazebo.

Just off Hwy. 93, **Tamarack Brewing** (105 Blacktail Rd., 406/844-0244, 11 A.M.–midnight daily, $7–12) serves microbrews and good food. Grab a spot on the creekside patio and sip a Yard Sale ale.

Just west of the highway, **Bluestone Grill**

and Tap (306 Stoner Loop Rd., 406/884-2583, 5–9 P.M. nightly, $18–24) specializes in modern American comfort foods, including a popular meatloaf laced with buffalo meat.

Somers

The tidy modern kitchenette cabins at **Somers Bay Log Cabin Lodging** (5496 Hwy. 93 S., 406/857-3881 or 888/443-3881, www.somersbaycabins.com, $129–189) are just south of town, across the highway from the lake.

Right next door, (**Mackinaw's Grill** (5480 Hwy. 93 S., 406/857-3889, dinner from 5 P.M. nightly, $15–28) is one of the very best places to eat along Flathead Lake. This massive three-story log lodge serves mesquite-grilled fresh fish flown in from the Pacific, great steaks and prime rib, and a wide selection of stir-fries, pasta, and continental-influenced dishes. Service is prompt and professional while retaining Montana friendliness; the wine list is quite good and well-priced. Views from the dining room are stunning; there's a lively bar on the main floor.

Another popular local place in a cool historic building is **Tiebucker's Pub & Eatery** (75 Somers Rd., 406/857-3335, 5–9 P.M. Tues.–Sat., open until 10 P.M. in summer, $8–23), located in the former Great Northern Railroad depot. In addition to the pub, which offers Montana microbrews and sandwiches, the dining room specializes in Italian grilled and barbecued meats, including ribs, as well as fresh fish, steamer clams, and steaks.

Right behind Tiebucker's is the southern terminus of a **rails-to-trails bike and walking path,** which goes four miles north, mostly rather close to Highway 93.

Lake cruises depart from a dock across from the Montana Grill. To reserve a daytime or sunset cruise on the 65-foot *Far West,* call 406/857-3203; you can also arrange a sailboat cruise at the same number.

Somers Bay is a good place to paddle a canoe. The water here is relatively shallow and warmer than the rest of the lake, and the lakeshore is dotted with old wharves and buildings, islands, and birds (keep an eye out for ospreys diving into the lake).

EAST SIDE OF FLATHEAD LAKE

Except for the touristy town of Bigfork at the northeastern edge, the east side of Flathead Lake is even less developed than the west side. Toward the southern end of the lake, cherry orchards are both a business and an attraction around Flathead Lake. Cherries are usually harvested beginning the third week of July.

The University of Montana runs the **Flathead Lake Biological Station** (406/982-3301, www.umt.edu/flbs) at Yellow Bay. Limnology, the study of the life of lakes, ponds, and streams, especially research on water quality and plankton, is a major focus here. Summer classes in freshwater biology and ecology are offered for credit and for audit. If your interest is more casual, drop by the station. Students are often pleased to discuss their research, and there are newsletters and bulletin boards to browse.

Camping

The campgrounds off Highway 35 can be quite pleasant during off-peak times, and crowded and noisy during summer weekends. **Finley Point State Recreation Area** (406/887-2715, http://fwp.mt.gov, May–Sept., $15–18) is four miles off Highway 35 on cherry-tree-studded Finley Point. The **Yellow Bay State Recreation Area** (406/752-5501, May–Sept., $15) and campground is right next to the University of Montana's Biological Station.

BIGFORK

Bigfork is situated on a bay where the Swan River empties into Flathead Lake. It's an exceptionally lovely site that's turned into the kind of upscale resort community that was once foreign to the state. Certainly no other town in northwestern Montana is so devoted to art galleries, fine restaurants, high-end boutiques—and real estate offices.

The year-round population of about 1,500 can rise exponentially during the summer. High summer is theater season in Bigfork, with its accompanying tour buses and crowds. If the prospect of crowded sidewalks seems a

OSPREYS

Several ospreys maintain nests along the north shore of Flathead Lake. As you drive along Highway 82 between Bigfork and Somers, notice the large nests made of cow dung and sticks perched atop telephone poles.

Fledgling bird-watchers may initially confuse an osprey with another fish-eating bird, the bald eagle. An osprey is smaller than an eagle and has a white belly (an eagle's belly is dark). A feet-first plunge into water is the osprey's distinctive fishing style.

Ospreys winter in Mexico from about late September to mid-April. It's thought that mates winter separately but reunite at the site of the previous year's nest. Eggs hatch in late May or early June. Canada geese may compete for osprey nests.

little daunting, consider visiting Bigfork in the off-season, when it's more pleasant to wander through the galleries and bookshops.

Bigfork was founded in 1902, about the time the hydroelectric plant at the mouth of the Swan River was built to supply electricity for Kalispell. The electric company is still here, and the bridge is the best place to stand and ponder how it works. (Water from the Swan River is diverted to a higher level, then dropped through turbines to generate power.)

Recreation

In keeping with its role as a resort village, Bigfork has one of the best golf courses in the West. The 27-hole **Eagle Bend Golf Club** (406/837-3700; reserve well in advance), just off Holt Drive west of Highway 35, has received high ratings from *Golf Digest* magazine and from Montana golfers. Eagle Bend also houses the **Montana Athletic Club** (850 Holt Dr., 406/837-2582), which includes racquetball, squash, aerobics, an indoor pool, and a weight room.

Boat tours of Flathead Lake leave regularly from Bigfork. Tour the lake and Wild Horse Island with **Pointer Scenic Cruises** (406/837-5617), a nine-passenger charter boat. To arrange a **sailboat tour** of Flathead Lake aboard a classy 1920s-era racing sloop, call Flathead Lake Lodge (406/837-5569).

Right in town, the two-mile **Swan River Nature Trail** offers a bit of peace and quiet to those who'd rather hike or mountain bike while their traveling companions shop in downtown Bigfork. Catch the trail near the corner of Grand and Electric avenues.

Rent a bike from **Mountain Mike's** (417 Bridge St., 406/837-2453)—Mike can also tell you where to ride or even take you on a guided bike tour.

Some of the state's wildest water is found in the mile or so of the Swan River immediately before the Bigfork dam. Kayakers love it, but it's not for the inexperienced.

◖ Jewel Basin Hiking Area

The Jewel Basin Hiking Area was set aside as an easily reached wilderness-like area. There are 35 miles of trails that make day-hike loops or longer backpack trips. To get there from Bigfork, take Echo Lake Road off Highway 83. (It can also be reached from the west side of Hungry Horse Reservoir.) Pick up an extremely helpful map at Forest Service offices in Bigfork, Hungry Horse, or Kalispell.

Hikes take you through wildflower meadows and thickets of subalpine fir. Climbing in from the west, you'll first have expansive views of the Flathead Valley and Lake, then pass over a ridge and realize that Jewel Basin is indeed a basin. It's hard to say which are the jewels—the lakes that stud the basin or the Indian paintbrush, bear grass, fireweed, and showy daisies strewn throughout the meadows. Some of the lakes are stocked with trout.

Entertainment

Bigfork is known throughout the state for its summer theater productions: The **Bigfork Summer Playhouse** (526 Electric Ave., 406/837-4886, www.bigforksummerplayhouse.com, Mon.–Sat. summer) mounts classic Broadway musicals such as *The King and I* and the occasional farce, such as *Urinetown.* Along with the town's lovely setting the theater is largely what fueled Bigfork's growth as a tourist destination.

Bigfork makes a big deal of holidays. Christmas brings lots of lights and conifer boughs, then there's Easter, cherry blossoms in early May, a white-water festival in mid-May, the playhouse's opening night on the Fourth of July, and the Festival of the Arts in early August—it's hard to arrive in Bigfork when there's not *something* going on.

Galleries

Several arts-and-crafts galleries are in downtown Bigfork. The **Bigfork Art and Cultural Center** (525 Electric Ave., 406/837-6927) shares a building with the public library. **Art Fusion** (471 Electric Ave., 406/837-3526), which shows the work of some of the state's top artists, is always worth a stop. The **Bridge Street Gallery** (382 Bridge St., 406/837-3059) also sells the work of local artists.

Gary Riecke's studio (452 Electric Ave., 406/837-5335), across from the Bigfork Inn, features Western and wildlife art. Sculptor **Bob Stayton** (470 Electric Ave., 406/837-3790) also displays the work of some 20 other artists.

Accommodations

Lodging is expensive in Bigfork (although during the spring, fall, and winter, prices can drop by nearly 50 percent at many lodgings). The town is a little too highfalutin to have a good selection of budget motels. In fact, the only place that comes close to fitting that bill is the **Timbers Motel** (8540 Hwy. 35, 406/837-6200 or 800/821-4546, www.timbersmotel.com, $99 and up), located slightly out of Bigfork proper, above Bigfork Bay and Highway 35. There's a pool, sauna, and outdoor hot tub; pets are welcome with a $10 fee. The setting, back off the highway among trees, is rather snug and comfortable.

The centrally located **Grand Hotel Bigfork** (425 Grand Dr., 406/837-7377, www.grandhotelbigfork.com, $149) is another good bet. The six upstairs rooms all have private balconies; downstairs is a deli.

Marina Cay (180 Vista Lane, 406/837-5861 or 800/433-6516, www.marinacay.com, rooms $119–195, condos $215–359) is a large, attractive resort complex right on the bay that contains the majority of the rooms available in Bigfork. Facilities include several restaurants and bars, a marina with boat rentals and other recreational outings, lounge-side pool, and a couple of hot tubs.

For a more intimate place to stay right in the heart of downtown Bigfork, the **Swan River Inn** (360 Grand Ave., 406/837-2220, $145 and up) has comfortable and carefully decorated B&B suites overlooking Bigfork Bay and a good restaurant downstairs.

Right on the edge of town, where the Swan River flows into Bigfork Bay, the **☾ Bridge Street Cottages** (309 Bridge St., 406/837-2785 or 888/264-4974, www.bridgestreetcottages.com, studios $185, one-bedroom cottages $250–325) are just close enough to town, but not smack-dab in the middle of it. Most are one-bedroom cottages with full kitchens, but there are also a few studios with refrigerators and coffeemakers. These cottages are good places to stay if you want to settle in for a while; weekly and monthly rates are available.

Five miles south of town in Woods Bay, the **☾ Mountain Lake Lodge** (1950 Sylvan Dr., 406/837-3800 or 877/823-4923, www.mountainlakelodge.com, $195–285) is a classy lodge-style motel with spacious rooms, an outdoor pool, two on-site restaurants, and great views.

A few miles south of town, just across the road from the lake, the **Islander Inn** (39 Orchard Lane, 406/837-5472, www.sleepeatdrink.com, $119–179) has accommodations in bungalows, each one named after a different island—from Bali to Zanzibar to Wild Horse—and decorated in the style of that place. These colorful cottages have basic cooking facilities (most have microwaves and refrigerators, while a couple have full kitchens), and well-behaved dogs are allowed in some units with a stiff deposit and $20 nightly surcharge. During the off-season, room rates drop dramatically.

Guest Ranches

One of Montana's most famous and exclusive guest ranches, **⟨ Averill's Flathead Lake Lodge** (406/837-4391, www.flatheadlakelodge.com) is a well-established full-service dude ranch that runs $3,143 per week per adult (includes all meals and activities; children and teens have lower rates). The ranch is located right on the shores of Flathead Lake, just south of Bigfork, so if you're looking for a family ranch vacation that mixes swimming, fishing, tennis, and windsurfing with the traditional horseback riding and campfire singalongs, this is it.

Camping

Save an easy $100 by making **Wayfarers State Recreation Area** (406/837-4196, http://fwp.mt.gov, May–Sept., $15) your base in Bigfork. This campground is just across Highway 35 from the main road into town. Because there are only 30 sites here, plan your arrival strategically, especially on holiday weekends.

Food

You can eat very well in Bigfork; people drive for miles to dine here. Dinner reservations are mandatory at most restaurants. Many are closed in the winter.

La Provence (408 Bridge St., 406/837-2930, 11 A.M.–2 P.M. Tues.–Sat., $6–7; 5–9 P.M. Mon.–Sat., $18–35) is a good place for a leisurely lunch on the patio. At dinnertime, the French chef-owner lets loose with Mediterranean-meets-Montana cuisine like venison tenderloin with a fig confit and bordeaux sauce.

The **Garden Bar** (451 Electric Ave., 406/837-9914, 11 A.M.–2 A.M. $8–12) is a casual place to drop in for a beer. The bar is chatty and friendly, and the tables out back provide a quiet place to sit and read in the afternoon.

The **Bigfork Inn** (604 Electric Ave., 406/837-6680, dinner from 5 P.M. nightly, brunch 10 A.M.–2 P.M. Sun., $15–26) is one of Bigfork's originals, the place that put Bigfork on the culinary map several decades ago. Open for dinner only, the menu is eclectic, with steaks, pasta,

three types of schnitzel, and a showcase duck with local bing cherry and black currant sauce. Overlooking Bigfork Harbor is **Swan River Inn** (360 Grand Ave., 406/837-2220, 9 A.M.–10 P.M. Tues.–Sun. summer, 5–10 P.M. Tues.–Sun. winter, $16–26.). The specialties here are pasta or sandwiches for lunch, or steaks, lamb, chicken, and more pasta for dinner. On pleasant afternoons the bayside deck is a great place to relax and have a leisurely meal.

Another well-regarded dinner restaurant in downtown Bigfork is **Showthyme!** (548 Electric Ave., 406/837-0707, dinner from 5 P.M. nightly), located in an old brick bank building next door to the Bigfork Playhouse. Food here is subtle, refined, and often innovative. Vegetarian and pasta dishes are featured; dinners run $14–28, and there's outside seating in good weather. If there's no time for a full dinner before the theater, stop by **The Vault** (small plates $8–12) for Asian-inspired small plates; it's at the same location as Showthyme!

Upstairs in the little mall on Electric Ave., **Invite** (459 Electric Ave. 406/837-2786, noon–10 P.M. daily, $19–35) has a good variety of fish along with steaks and elk chops; it's one of the few places you'll find walleye on the menu (especially prepared with a gourmet touch).

South of town at the Mountain Lake Lodge, **Terra** (1950 Sylvan Dr., 406/837-3800, breakfast and dinner daily, dinner $18–32) is a lovely place to sit outside in nice weather; the menu ranges from classy treatments of buffalo and elk to a Jamaican-inspired shrimp-and-scallop pasta.

Head about five miles south of town to find **The Raven** (39 Orchard Lane, 406/837-2836, 11:30 A.M.–2 A.M. daily summer, 4 P.M.–midnight winter, $4–15), a lakeside restaurant with a great deck and a sort of Jimmy Buffet parrothead appeal. The decor is Caribbean, and dinner specialties come from around the world; sushi is served several nights a week and is a favorite.

Information

The **chamber of commerce** (8155 Hwy. 35, 406/837-5888, www.bigfork.org) is next to the Lakehills Shopping Center.

The **library** is at 525 Electric Avenue, with the Art and Cultural Center. **Electric Avenue Books** (490 Electric Ave., 406/837-6072) is a good general bookstore with a congenial atmosphere. It's a pleasant place for a bookstore lover to pass an hour or so on an inclement day. **Bay Books and Prints** (350 Grand Ave., 406/837-4646) specializes in books on Montana. Charlie Russell and Lewis and Clark buffs will find it especially hard to leave without a book or two. Most of the books are used, with a good selection of rare and out-of-print titles. The place closes up during the winter.

The Swan and Blackfoot Valleys

The Swan Valley is not as large and broad as the valleys to the west, but with two rivers and many lakes, the Swan Range shooting out to the east, and the Mission Mountains stacking up high in the southwest, it is quite beautiful. Being between the Bob Marshall and Mission Mountains Wilderness Areas, it is a popular vacation spot for Montanans, but it doesn't draw the crowds that you'll find around Flathead Lake, Bigfork, or Glacier National Park.

Even an amateur geologist can pick out the signs of the glaciers that formed the Swan Valley. Drive down Highway 83 and look up at the jagged peaks and high cirques of the Mission and Swan Ranges. Visit the Mt. Morrell Lookout and see some of the glaciers that remain on the Mission Range. Notice the distinctive pothole lakes southeast of Salmon Lake. And the big lakes—Seeley, Salmon, Alva, Placid, and Inez—all were created when glaciers melted 10,000 years ago.

Wildlife viewing is a special attraction of the Swan Valley and its many lakes. Although a canoe is probably the best vehicle for nature watching around the lakes and rivers here, keep your eyes open while you're driving or biking Highway 83; there are several designated wildlife-viewing areas, mostly featuring waterbirds.

Toward the southern end of the valley, Salmon Lake, Seeley Lake, and Lake Alva are nesting sites for loons. These large, white-necklaced, solid-boned birds are known for their eerie wails and their diving abilities. (Loons have been reported to dive as deep as 200 feet, although typical dives are much more shallow.) During the loons' nesting period (May through mid-June), it is important to stay well away from the nests, especially while fishing on the lakes. The presence of humans can cause the loons to abandon their nests.

Recreation

The lakes and easy access to mountains and wilderness are the main recreational attractions of the Swan Valley, but there's more here than boating, fishing, hiking, hunting, and horseback riding.

Highway 83 through the Swan River Valley is the stage for a popular bicycle tour held every spring. The **Tour of the Swan River Valley** (TOSRV West, www.missoulabike.org) starts in Missoula, heads up the Swan Valley, and comes back down through the Mission Valley. Even with summer traffic, Highway 83 is a good cycling road with plenty of rest stops and campsites.

The Swan Valley has surprisingly good cross-country skiing in the winter. It's high enough to have snow when it's raining in nearby Missoula.

Anglers stand a chance of hooking bull trout and kokanee salmon in Swan Lake, and Lindbergh and Holland lakes are also worth fishing for these two species, as well as for cutthroat and rainbow trout.

SWAN LAKE

The **Swan River National Wildlife Refuge** is a nesting area for bald eagles, blue herons, and other birds. Canada geese, whistling swans, and mallards winter here. Other animals that can be spotted in this marsh, grassland, and river habitat include elk, moose, deer, beavers, river otters, muskrats, and grizzly and black bears. The refuge is on the Swan River in the northern part of the Swan Valley, near the town of Swan Lake.

Accommodations

These lodgings are actually quite close to Bigfork, and are good laid-back alternatives to staying in that more expensive town. The attractive (C **Laughing Horse Lodge** (71284 Hwy. 83, 406/886-2080, www.laughinghorselodge.com, $75–145) has newer log cabin–style units furnished with massive log beds (but with no telephones, alarm clocks, or TVs). The lodge is run as a dog-friendly B&B, and rates include a good breakfast. The restaurant here is worth a stop, even if you're not sleeping over, and kayaks and bikes are available for rent.

Up a steep rutted road from Highway 83 north of Swan Lake are the **Swan Lake Guest Cabins** (406/837-1137 or 888/837-1557, $100–175), with newly constructed, nicely detailed log cabins. The cabins, tucked into the woods, all come with propane grills and comfy porch swings. Dogs are allowed.

Camping

At the north end of Swan Lake, the **Swan Lake Recreation Area** (406/837-7500, www.fs.fed.us/r1/flathead, mid-May–Sept., $14) includes a Forest Service campground on the east side of the highway and a day-use area with a swimming beach and a boat launch on the west side. **Point Pleasant State Forest Campground** (406/754-2301, June–Oct.) is a small, free campground seven miles south of Swan Lake.

HOLLAND LAKE AND CONDON

All of the Swan Valley is lovely, but perhaps no single spot captures the essence of this narrow, lake-filled valley flanked by sawtooth peaks as well as Holland Lake. In addition, the lake is graced with a charming old-fashioned resort that has played home to generations of visitors.

Recreation

Holland Lake is the trailhead for a popular trail into the **Bob Marshall Wilderness Area.** It's about 10 miles from road's end to the wilderness boundary, and most people entering this way go around Upper Holland Lake and up over Gordon Pass toward the South Fork of the Flathead River.

Across Highway 83 from Holland Lake, several roads lead west from Condon toward the **Mission Mountains Wilderness Area.** The Lindbergh Lake road leads to a campground (free, no water) and several trailheads. Lindbergh Lake is named for Charles Lindbergh, who camped here not long after his transatlantic flight. Hikers should pick up either a Flathead National Forest map (south half) or a more detailed Mission Mountains Wilderness map. Both are available at the ranger station in Bigfork. Be aware that the Mission Mountains are home to some grizzly bears.

Accommodations

(C **Holland Lake Lodge** (406/754-2282 or 877/925-6343, www.hollandlakelodge.com) is four miles off the highway at the end of Holland Lake Road. It's a down-home woodsy kind of place, with rooms in the main lodge or in cabins scattered along the lakefront. The Holland Lake Lodge may not have the luxury of the new guest ranches that new money is bringing into Montana, but there's a veneer of charm and rustic comfort that only decades of history can produce at this lodge, which has been in business since 1924. Meals in the restaurant are very good, especially in high season. You'll want to kill some time in the friendly bar and lounging area.

During the summer, lodge rates include lodging, all meals, and a daily hour-long canoe or kayak rental for $125 per person per night ($185 single occupancy) in lodge rooms, $145 per person per night in cabins (per-person rates go down if you pack more than two people into the rooms, and children are given a substantial discount). All-inclusive multiday packages can also be arranged.

During the winter the lodge maintains

cross-country ski trails and rents skis and snowmobiles. If you visit in the middle of February, you may have the opportunity to rub up against the unique subculture of dogsled racing. This is the turnaround point in a 500-mile dogsled race that starts and finishes in Helena.

The **Swan Valley Centre Cabins** (milepost 42 on Hwy. 83, 406/754-2397 or 866/754-2397, $65–95) are fairly rustic, but a good deal. Each of the three cabins is equipped with a kitchen and, for that ultimate backwoods touch, a TV with no reception. (Well, they're TV/VCR combos, and the on-site general store will lend you movies to watch.)

A more convenient choice is the attractive, log-sided **Swan River Lodge** (406/745-2688, www.theswanriverlodge.com, $60 and up) on Highway 83 near milepost 46. Although it's really just a basic motel, it's an exceptionally nice one.

Camping

Holland Lake (406/837-7500, www.fs.fed.us/r1/flathead, mid-May–Sept., $14) is the site of one of the prettiest, and sometimes one of the most crowded, Forest Service campgrounds in the area. It's south of Condon and east of Highway 83 on Holland Lake Road. The lake contains cutthroat, bull, and rainbow trout, and kokanee salmon.

Holland Lake is a popular departure point for horse trips into the Bob Marshall Wilderness Area, and in addition to the regular Forest Service campground there's a campground for horse packers a little farther down the road from the campground. **Owl Creek Packers' Camp** charges a few dollars for a corral fee. At the road's end there are short hiking trails for the casual day hiker as well as trails leading into the Bob Marshall Wilderness Area. The hike in to Holland Falls is not difficult (three miles round-trip).

Food

The dining room at **Holland Lake Lodge** is open to the public, and it's well worth a visit. During the summer, when a professional chef is in residence, the dinners ($14–30) are particularly inspired and feature both steaks and more continental fare like roast duck. But even the simpler lunch menu and winter fare have some treats; the "Gut Bomb" is a locally renowned burger.

The **Swan Valley Cafe** (6799 Hwy. 83, 406/754-3663, 7 A.M.–3 P.M. Mon.–Wed., 7 A.M.–8 P.M. Thurs.–Fri., 8 A.M.–8 P.M. Sat., 8 A.M.–3 P.M. Sun., $5–22), just north of milepost 42, is a reliable place that offers vegetarian meals along with the burgers and steaks.

BOB MARSHALL WILDERNESS AREA

In 1964 the Bob Marshall Wilderness Area was created when 950,000 acres were set aside; in 1978 the Scapegoat Wilderness was added to the south and the Great Bear Wilderness to the north of the Bob Marshall. The three contiguous areas include 1.5 million acres, falling roughly east of the Swan Valley. The designated wilderness areas are heavily used during the summer and fall. Backpacking and horse packing are the main summer activities, while hunting predominates in the fall, starting in mid-September.

The Chinese Wall is an impressive and popular destination in the "Bob." To the west the earth's crust has thrust upward and forced the eastern part to slide underneath it for a distance of about 20 miles. Haystack Mountain provides a good view of the Chinese Wall from the west.

Great Northern Mountain (8,705 feet) is the highest spot in the Great Bear Wilderness. The Middle Fork of the Flathead runs through the Great Bear.

Access to the Wilderness

Napa Point Road starts near the headquarters of the Swan River State Forest and provides access to the **Inspiration Pass** trailhead. It's a challenging but fairly lightly used trail. Sup Creek Campground near the trailhead is a good place to spend the night before embarking on the full-day hike to Sunburst Lake.

Smith Creek Pass also receives less traffic than many of the other trails that lead into the wilderness. To reach the trailhead, take Falls Creek Road (across from the Condon Work Center on Highway 83) four miles to Smith Creek Road. Make a sharp right and drive another mile to the trailhead. The climb up the west side of the pass is not easy, and coming down the east side can be even tougher.

Gordon Pass, starting from Holland Lake, is well maintained and heavily used by horse packers and hikers. Big Salmon Lake is a popular destination. Trails come at it from every direction, but the shortest route is from Holland Lake.

Pyramid Pass, with a trailhead near Seeley Lake, leads to the headwaters of the South Fork of the Flathead River, which starts as Danaher Creek deep in the Bob and flows toward the southern tip of Hungry Horse Reservoir. Reach the trailhead by taking Cottonwood Lakes Road (just north of the town of Seeley Lake) to Morrell Road (No. 467). Turn left on Morrell Road and travel six miles to Pyramid Pass Road (No. 4381, Upper Trail Creek Road). Turn right and drive six miles to the trailhead. Pyramid Pass is a steep climb and receives medium to heavy use by backpackers and horse packers.

From the south, reach the **North Fork of the Blackfoot** trailhead by taking Highway 200 to five miles east of Ovando and turning up the North Fork of Blackfoot Road. Drive four miles to North Fork Trailhead Road, and take it seven miles to the trailhead. It's a fairly heavily used trail, with both foot and horse traffic.

Many outfitters run trips into the Bob; horse-packing guides from the **Seven Lazy P** (406/466-2044, www.sevenlazyp.com), based in Choteau, have excellent reputations.

SEELEY LAKE AND VICINITY

Seeley Lake is the only place in the Swan Valley with full services. Because of the many moderately priced motels and comfortable, long-established lodges and resorts, Seeley Lake has a long tradition of hosting summer family reunions and weddings. With the lake's water recreation and access to hiking, good restaurants, golf, and just plain relaxation, there's something for everyone to do here.

Clearwater Canoe Trail

The Clearwater Canoe Trail is really a floating and hiking loop trail. There's a three-mile canoe segment from an access point off Highway 83 four miles north of the town of Seeley Lake, then a one-mile hike back to the put-in spot. The meandering Clearwater River is a good place to watch birds. Keep an eye out for loons. Canoe rentals are available at the nearby Tamaracks Resort.

Other Recreation

Morrell Lake and **Morrell Falls** are on a national recreation trail north of Seeley Lake via Cottonwood Lakes Road to the east of Highway 83. It's an easy two-mile hike in to the falls (actually a 100-foot-tall lower fall topped by a series of smaller falls and cascades). **Morrell Mountain Lookout** is about 18 miles from the highway via Cottonwood Lakes Road (follow it for nine miles) and Road 4365 (follow it for another nine miles). It's a rough drive in a passenger car, and it's wise to check with the ranger station (406/677-2233) for current road conditions. The lookout has views of the Mission Mountains, the Swan Range, and the Blackfoot and Clearwater Valleys.

The **Mission Mountains Wilderness Area** falls on the eastern part of the mountains' divide; the western part is the Mission Mountains Tribal Wilderness and is managed by the Confederated Kootenai and Salish Tribes. The wilderness managed by the Forest Service has about 45 miles of trails. There are several trails into the Mission Mountains Wilderness Area: Glacier Creek, Cold Lakes, Piper Creek, Fatty Creek, Beaver Creek, Lindbergh Lake, Jim Lakes, Hemlock Creek, Meadow Lake, and Elk Point. Maps of the Mission Mountains Wilderness or the southern half of the Flathead National Forest are available at the ranger station in Bigfork.

Seeley Lake is a good place to **fish** for bass, and it's also stocked with rainbow trout. To the south, Salmon Lake has rainbow and cutthroat trout and kokanee salmon.

Seeley Lake gets pretty snowy in the winter. Most local lodgings are proud to point out that you can ski or snowmobile from your door into a million acres of wilderness. Find an extensive network of groomed **cross-country ski trails** one mile east of Seeley Lake, up Morrell Creek Road. These trail loops double as **mountain bike trails** in the summer. The **Double Arrow Lodge** maintains trails on its property and runs an outfitting service (406/677-2411 or 406/677-2317).

Accommodations

$50–100: The friendly **Seeley Lake Motor Lodge** (406/677-2335 or 800/237-9978, www.seeleylakemotorlodge.com, $50–81), on Highway 83, is one of the better deals on Seeley Lake, located convenient to recreation and to services in the little town center.

The nicely remodeled **Whitetail Cabins** (3806 Hwy. 83, 406/677-2024, www.whitetailcabins.com, $75 and up) are just above the highway north of town; these kitchenette cabins are one of the best deals in the valley.

North of the town of Seeley Lake, on the lake, the **Montana Pines Motel** (mile marker 16 on Hwy. 83, 406/677-2775 or 800/867-5678, $60 and up) is a motel complex built on the original town site of Seeley. The Elkhorn Restaurant is adjacent to the motel, right near the highway.

Over $100: The most attractive and upscale resort in the Seeley-Swan is the ❰ **Double Arrow Resort** (406/677-2777 or 800/468-0777, www.doublearrowresort.com, $150 and up), a gem of a Swan Valley hideout. The lodge and cabins sit on a bluff overlooking a stream and a meadow filled alternately with golfers and browsing deer; the old lodge and dining room, built in the 1930s, are extremely welcoming and idyllic; you'll want to curl up with a book or watch the sunset from the veranda. The food here is also top-notch. Choose from a room in the lodge, a homey cabin, or a larger log lodge that'll sleep up to eight. During the off-season rooms are deeply discounted. Breakfast (with the best coffee for miles around) and use of a large indoor pool, hot tub, and tennis courts are included. None of the rooms have a TV or telephone.

The Double Arrow is also a good base for recreation. The nine-hole course is a real beauty, shaded by ponderosa pines and cleft by a chattering stream. The resort offers a full range of horseback activities, as well as mountain bike, canoe, and fishing gear rentals. In winter the Double Arrow is the center of a series of cross-country trails and also rents snowmobiles; you can even arrange for horse-drawn sleigh rides.

The rustic log cabins at the **Lodges on Seeley Lake** (Boy Scout Road, 406/677-2376 or 800/900-9016, www.lodgesonseeleylake.com, $120–303), just west of Seeley Lake town site, were favorites of local writer Norman Maclean. These 1930s-era cabins have been joined by a handful of modern ones, and there's a central lodge with games and easy chairs. Cabins all have fireplaces as well as full kitchen and bathroom facilities, and canoes, rowboats, and bikes are available for guests' use.

On the north shores of Seeley Lakes is **Tamaracks Resort** (milepost 17 on Hwy. 83, 406/677-2433 or 800/447-7216, www.tamaracks.com, $119–450). The resort consists of a central lodge and lakefront cabins with kitchens (the least-expensive cabins sleep two people; the top-of-the-line cabin sleeps 10). The resort is right on Seeley Lake, and canoes, fishing boats, and mountain bikes are available for rent. There's also an area for RV and tent campers.

Camping

There are three national forest campgrounds around Seeley Lake: **Big Larch** (406/677-2233, www.fs.fed.us/r1/lolo, mid-May–mid-Nov., $10) is closest to the highway on the east side of the lake; **River Point** and **Seeley Lake** (both Memorial Day–Labor Day, $10) are farther around the southern and western sides of the lake, respectively. Several miles south of Seeley Lake, the state park campgrounds at **Placid Lake** (406/542-5500, http://fwp.mt.gov, May–Nov., $15) and **Salmon Lake** (May–Sept., $15) are often less crowded than their northern counterparts.

Food

In these parts, the **Seasons Restaurant at Double Arrow Resort** (406/677-2777,

$18–28), two miles south of Seeley Lake, is the best place to eat. The menu specializes in continental cuisine, featuring dishes such as a bacon-wrapped filet mignon of buffalo topped with chipotle butter or duck glazed with cherries and soy sauce. It's a pleasure to eat here, and not just because the food is good; the dining room, overlooking the Seeley Valley, is beautiful and the service top-notch.

For a good hand-cut steak, delicious potatoes, and authentic Montana atmosphere, go to **Lindey's Prime Steak House** (406/677-9229, $16–28), located on the lake in the town site.

Information

Find the **chamber of commerce** (406/677-2880, www.seeleylakechamber.com) downtown across from the Chicken Coop restaurant. The **Seeley Lake Ranger Station** (406/677-2233) is about three miles north of town at the northern end of Seeley Lake.

BLACKFOOT VALLEY

The Blackfoot River is well-known to local anglers and floaters. It's a lovely undammed river noted for its variety of fish habitats and its 30 miles of "recreation corridor," which allow easy public access to the river. Read Norman Maclean's classic, *A River Runs Through It*, to get a feel for the place.

Blackfoot-Clearwater Wildlife Management Area

The Blackfoot-Clearwater Wildlife Management Area, east of Highway 83 and north of Highway 200, includes the southern part of Salmon Lake as well as the lower Clearwater River. Near the junction of the two highways the land is prairie, but the northeastern corner of the area rises into forested mountains. The entire area is closed December 1–May 15, but open to hunters and anglers at other times of the year (within the restrictions of hunting season). There are plenty of deer and elk here, as well as black bears, grouse, and waterfowl.

Garnet Ghost Town

Garnet Ghost Town (406/329-3914) is an abandoned mining town where about 30 buildings have been preserved. In the winter it's a great place for cross-country skiing. To reach Garnet, take Highway 200 about 24 miles east of Missoula and turn south at Greenough Hill. The rough Garnet access road is 11 miles from the turnoff.

Recreation

Fishing, especially for brown trout, has long been a major preoccupation in the Blackfoot Valley. Although past mining and ongoing heavy logging have deteriorated conditions, rehabilitation efforts have begun to pay off. On the Blackfoot and its tributaries, catch-and-release is required for cutthroat and bull trout (actually, you're not supposed to intentionally catch bull trout at all). For the more prevalent brown and rainbow trout, check current regulations.

The **Clearwater Bridge** is a fishing-access site on Sunset Hill Road (which intersects Highway 200 just east of Greenough Hill). Farther down Sunset Hill Road is another fishing-access site. To reach the **Scotty Brown Bridge,** turn down the gravel road seven miles east of Clearwater Junction on Highway 200. It's marked with a fishing-access site sign, and the road leads to several fishing and camping sites.

Blackfoot River Road has two junctions with Highway 200, one just north of the McNamara Bridge (14 miles east of Missoula) and the other at the Roundup Bridge (28 miles east of Missoula). There are several fishing-access sites along this road, most with undeveloped campsites nearby.

During the winter, the recreational focus shifts to **snowmobiling.** There are more than 200 miles of groomed trails, many of them springing from a hub in Lincoln.

Guest Ranches

Ovando's 🄲 **Lake Upsata Guest Ranch** (201 Lower Lakeside Ln., 406/793-5890 or 800/594-7687, www.upsata.com, $110) is a beautifully located guest ranch that offers more than the usual horseback rides and campfires, although these traditional activities are by no means neglected. The lodge and the eight guest units (each individual log cabin comes with two beds, private baths, and a stocked refrigerator) share a great view of a small private lake backed up against the Swan Mountains. Swimming, canoeing, kayaking, and fishing in Lake Upsata are each right outside your cabin door. Much of the time the ranch is booked by family and business groups; B&B-style lodgings are available for $110 per night for people who are just passing through. Summer backcountry pack trips run $265 per day; hunting and float trips are also available.

In Ovando, **White Tail Ranch** (406/793-5043 or 888/987-2624, www.whitetail-ranch.com, from $160 per person per day, $1,500 per person per week) offers all meals, horseback riding, and a full range of ranch activities, such as nature walks, mountain biking, and nightly campfires.

Food

For food in this stretch of the Blackfoot, there's a collection of truck stops at Clearwater Junction, where highways 83 and 200 meet, although the restaurants at Seeley Lake are just 15 miles north. In Ovando, **Trixi's Antler Saloon** has a reputation as a *real* Montana bar, the kind that posts a sign bidding customers to leave their guns outside.

Camping

Many fishing-access sites have good campgrounds. The **Johnsrud Fishing Access Site** is about one mile off Highway 200, 11 miles east of Bonner. Continuing east on the gravel road that leads to Johnsrud will bring you to several more fishing-access sites with campgrounds, including **Thibodeau, Corrick's Riverbend,** and **Ninemile Prairie.**

Outfitters

The Ovando area offers good west-side access to the Scapegoat and Bob Marshall Wilderness

Areas. For an outfitted pack trip into these stunningly beautiful areas, contact the folks at Lake Upsata Guest Ranch (see above), who have a good crew of wranglers leading backcountry trips. **WTR Outfitters** (406/793-5666 or 800/987-5666, www.wtroutfitters.com) is another well-established outfitting business.

LINCOLN

There was a gold strike here at roughly the same time in 1865 that President Lincoln was assassinated—hence the name of the gold-laced Lincoln Gulch and of the valley's major town. For years, that was how the history of Lincoln, Montana, went. Then Ted Kaczynski turned out to be more than the local hermit. Since he was arrested as the Unabomber in 1996, Lincoln has become a vaguely familiar name to many Americans.

There's not too much to Lincoln today (no, you can't visit Ted's cabin—it was taken into evidence years ago), but you'll be happy to see the town's motels and cafés if you're caught in bad weather or grow weary on the Highway 200 slog between Missoula and Great Falls.

If you find yourself in Lincoln in the winter and you're looking for something to do, try dogsledding. **Montana Mush** (406/362-4004) offers a chance to ride through the southern edge of the Scapegoat Wilderness on a dogsled.

Accommodations and Food

Lincoln has several motels; none of them are fancy or expensive, but most are serviceable and have friendly proprietors. **Leeper's Motel** (406/362-4333, $60–80) has units in a grove of trees just back from Highway 200.

There's not much in the way of restaurants, but Lincoln has a sprinkling of cafés plus the old and venerable **Lambkin's** (406/362-4271, 6:30 A.M.–8 P.M. Mon.–Thurs., 6:30 A.M.–9 P.M. Fri., 7 A.M.–9 P.M. Sat., $8–15), a good place for such standard fare as chicken-fried steak.

North of Flathead Lake

KALISPELL

Drive around northwestern Montana for a while, and by the time you pull into Kalispell you'll feel that you're in a real city. Kalispell is the commercial center for the booming "resortification" of northwestern Montana, although like too many other Montana towns, the locals seem to measure success by the length and relentlessness of suburban commercial strips.

Kalispell is on the Flathead River near where the Stillwater and Whitefish Rivers converge with it (elev. 2,930 feet), about seven miles above Flathead Lake. It's at the upper end of the Flathead Valley, and the mountains visible to the north are part of the Whitefish Range; to the east, the Swan Range rises. Between Kalispell and Flathead Lake, the Flathead River is as convoluted as the folds of a brain.

In the days before the railroad, Flathead Lake steamers made it up as far as Demersville, a now nonexistent town located four miles southeast of Kalispell.

When transcontinental railroad building was underway, Charles Conrad, a Fort Benton freight kingpin, got a hot tip from the head of the Great Northern Railway, Jim Hill, to move west to the Flathead area. Conrad did, and in 1891 the Great Northern arrived. The existing towns of Demersville and Ashley (0.5 mile west of present-day Kalispell) picked up and moved to form a new town, Kalispell. Conrad prospered and became a uniquely Montanan model citizen, keeping his own buffalo herd on what is now known as Buffalo Hill, just north of downtown.

◖ Conrad Mansion

The Conrad Mansion (330 Woodland Ave., 406/755-2166, www.conradmansion.com, 10 A.M.–5 P.M. Tues.–Sun. May 15–Oct. 15; $8 adults, $3 children) was built in 1895 and for most of the next 80 years was home to members of the Conrad family. None of the original architecture was changed during this time. When the home was donated to the city

of Kalispell in 1975, the interior and exterior were renovated, and the mansion is now considered one of the best examples of Pacific Northwest late-19th-century architecture.

Other Sights

Woodland Park (2nd St. E. north of Woodland Ave.) is a lovely city park, with rose gardens, a duck pond and lagoon, a large swimming pool, and a track. It was originally part of Charles Conrad's estate.

The **Hockaday Museum of Art** (302 2nd Ave. E., 406/755-5268, www.hockadayartmuseum.org, 10 A.M.–6 P.M. Tues.–Fri., 10 A.M.–5 P.M. Sat., noon–4 P.M. Sun. summer, 10 A.M.–5 P.M. Tues.–Sat. winter, $5 adult, $4 senior, $2 students) hangs some striking and innovative contemporary art as well as more traditional Western art. Anyone who thinks that conceptual art is solely an urban phenomenon should stop in and see what's going on in the studios of Twodot and Bozeman. There's a small crafts shop in the gallery, which is housed in the old brick Carnegie Library building. The center also sponsors Arts in the Park weekend in July.

At the **Central School Museum** (124 2nd Ave. E., 406/756-8381, www.yourmuseum.org, 10 A.M.–5 P.M. Mon.–Sat. June–Sept., 10 A.M.–5 P.M. Tues.–Fri. Oct.–May, $5 adult, $4 senior), sometimes called "The M," historical exhibits, including a history of the Forest Service in Montana, are housed in an 1894 school building.

On Highway 2, 13 miles west of Kalispell, stop near milepost 108 to see the **Indian pictographs** on the cliffs on the north side of the road.

Recreation

The 27-hole **Buffalo Hill Golf Course** (1176 N. Main St., 406/756-4530) is one of northwestern Montana's most challenging greens. Also just north of town is **Big Mountain Golf Club** (3230 Hwy. 93 N., 406/751-1950).

Lone Pine State Park is five miles southwest

Many small Montana towns, including Kalispell, benefited from the Carnegie library fund.

of town off Foys Lake Road (get there from Hwy. 2 via Meridian Rd.). It's set up on a hill, and hiking trails lead to overlooks with a good view of Kalispell and Glacier National Park.

The large **city pool** is in the middle of Woodland Park (406/758-7812). **The Summit** (205 Sunnyview Ln., 406/751-4100), a fitness center on Buffalo Hill just north of the city center, has a large indoor pool and fitness equipment.

Events

The **Northwest Montana Fair** (406/758-5810) is held at the fairgrounds in Kalispell in mid-August every year.

If you're in town during the concert season (fall through spring), catch the **Glacier Symphony and Chorale** (406/257-3241, www.glaciersymphonychorale.org), which performs at the high school auditorium; they also play a summer pops concert in Bigfork.

Accommodations

During the summer, Kalispell's lodgings fill up quickly with people on their way to and from Glacier National Park. Most chains have a presence here, as well as a host of somewhat scruffy budget motels (look for these on Highway 2 east of downtown.) In winter, expect much lower rates, sometimes as much as half the summer rates listed here.

$50-100: The **White Birch Motel** (17 Shady Ln., 406/752-4008 or 888/275-2275, $60–90) is away from the busy downtown intersections; the more expensive rooms have kitchenettes while the others have refrigerators and microwaves. The White Birch, which sits on seven acres just east of Kalispell, also has tent and RV camping.

As budget motels go, the **Aero Inn** (1830 Hwy. 93 S., 406/755-3798 or 800/843-6114, www.aeroinn.com, $95 and up) is a pretty good bet. Kitchenettes are available, pets are permitted in smoking rooms, and there's a free continental breakfast.

Over $100: The 🦫 **Kalispell Grand Hotel** (100 Main St., 406/755-8100 or 800/858-7422, www.kalispellgrand.com, $92–140) is a nicely renovated hotel right in downtown Kalispell. While the lobby and sitting areas preserve a

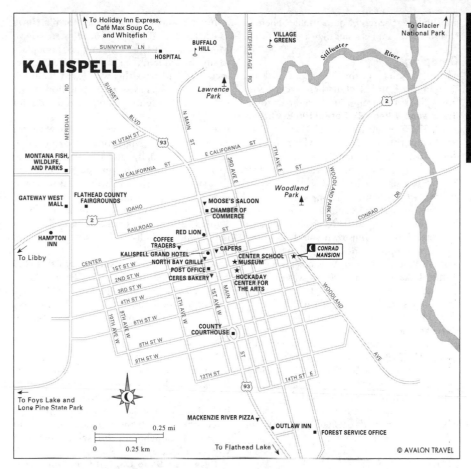

KALISPELL

comfortable late-19th-century glamour, the guest rooms are very nicely furnished and fully modern, with large gleaming bathrooms. Pets are accepted, and there's free parking, free continental breakfast, and afternoon cookies.

The **Red Lion Hotel Kalispell** (20 N. Main, 406/751-5050 or 800/325-4000, http://redlion.rdln.com, $159 and up) is also right downtown on the edge of a large shopping mall. The lobby here has a Western lodge look, and the rooms are spacious.

The large and recently renovated **Outlaw Inn** (1701 Hwy. 93 S., 406/755-6100 or 800/325-4000, www.outlawhotel.com, $100) has two

indoor pools, a casino and restaurant adjoining, a health club, and small convention facilities.

One of Kalispell's newer hotels is the very large and extracomfortable **Hampton Inn** (1140 Hwy. 2 W., 406/755-7900 or 800/426-7866, $145 and up). Facilities include a fitness center, indoor pool, and hot tub, and rates include a rather lavish continental breakfast.

Another new hotel, tucked behind a big-box home supply store on the leading edge of Kalispell's northern sprawl, is the surprisingly nice **Holiday Inn Express** (275 Treeline Rd., 406/755-7405, www.impressguest.com, $150). The rooms are trim and elegant, and the pool and exercise rooms quite usable. There's a stiff surcharge for pets, but they are permitted.

Camping

There's not much in the way of peaceful tent camping in Kalispell, but there are a handful of RV-style campgrounds right in town: **Greenwood Village RV Park** (1100 E. Oregon, 406/257-7719, Apr.–Oct.); **Glacier Pine RV Campground** (120 Swan Mountain Dr., 406/752-2760, year-round), one mile east of Kalispell on Highway 35; and **Rocky Mountain Hi** (825 Helena Flats Rd., 406/755-9573, year-round), which is located four miles east of Kalispell on Highway 2 and has some tent sites. Expect RV camping rates to run around $25.

A little farther from town you'll find more tent-friendly options, including Whitefish Lake State Park, just outside of Whitefish. To get to **Ashley Lake** (406/863-5400, www.fs.fed.us/r1/flathead, mid-May–mid-Sept., free, no water), go 16 miles west of Kalispell on Highway 2, then 13 miles north on the county road that starts around milepost 105. Still farther west of Kalispell (32 miles) is the **McGregor Lake** (406/293-7773, www.fs.fed.us/r1/kootenai, mid-May–Labor Day, $12) Forest Service campground. Even though it's just off Highway 2, it's not a bad spot, and it has a few relatively private tent sites. Lake trout are the big fish here, but kokanee salmon, cutthroat and brook trout, and yellow perch are also caught.

Food

If a full breakfast isn't necessary, head to the **Coffee Traders** (326 W. Center St., 406/756-2326, 7 A.M.–5 P.M. Mon.–Fri., 7 A.M.–3 P.M. Sat., 8 A.M.–3 P.M. Sun.) for espresso drinks and scones. Right downtown, **(Ceres Bakery** (318 Main St., 406/755-8552, 7 A.M.–6 P.M. Mon.–Fri., 7 A.M.–3 P.M. Sat.) makes the region's best (well, the only) artisanal bread and pastries.

South of downtown, one bright spot on the ugly Highway 93 strip is **MacKenzie River Pizza** (1645 Hwy. 93 S., 406/756-0600, lunch and dinner daily, $7–17), the Kalispell branch of the Montana chain that consistently puts out some of the state's best pizza.

If you're staying downtown, **Norm's News** (34 Main St., 406/756-5466, 9 A.M.–5 P.M. Mon.–Sat., 11 A.M.–4 P.M. Sun., $5) is a place to stop in and join the group of retired gentlemen who gather at this well-loved Kalispell institution. Norm's is a combination newsstand and soda fountain and a good place for a burger and shake.

Kalispell's most renowned tavern, **Moose's Saloon** (173 N. Main St., 406/755-2338, 11 A.M.–2 A.M. daily, under $10), is a place to spend an evening throwing peanut shells on the floor while drinking beer and listening to local musicians. Legend has it that this is where Evel Knievel came up with the idea to blast across Hells Canyon on his motorcycle. Pizza is the food of choice at Moose's; sandwiches are also good.

Right downtown, the **North Bay Grille** (139 1st Ave. W., 406/755-4441, 11:30 A.M.–2 A.M. Mon.–Sat., 4 P.M.–midnight Sun., $14–33) is an elegant and trendy spot with the emphasis on fairly traditional preparations of steak, seafood, and pasta.

Kalispell's best dinner restaurant is **(Capers** (121 Main St., 406/755-7687, dinner from 5 P.M. Tues.–Sat., reservations recommended, $12–30), a chef-owned spot with a commitment to organic foods and high-quality meat, including grilled buffalo tenderloin topped with a huckleberry-port barbeque sauce. The wine list is also well thought out, with some really good wines available by the glass.

Cafe Max Soup Co. (20 Commons Way, 406/257-7687, 11 A.M.–7 P.M. Mon.–Fri., 11 A.M.–5 P.M. Sat., about $5), tucked into a mini-mall just off Hwy. 93 north of town (find it behind the car wash with the large cow's head logo), serves about a dozen homemade soups every day, as well as good sandwiches and salads. Ingredients are fresh and often organic, and the soups, such as Cuban black bean with pulled pork and rice, make a substantial and tasty lunch.

Information

The **chamber of commerce** is located downtown (15 Depot Loop, 406/758-2800,

© JUDY JEWELL

Styled similarly to the lodges in Glacier National Park, the Whitefish train depot serves Amtrak and also houses a historical museum.

www.kalispellchamber.com). The **Flathead National Forest Headquarters** (650 Wolfpack Way, 406/758-5200) has a variety of pamphlets and fliers, and a few books for sale.

Services
The **Kalispell Regional Medical Center** (310 Sunnyview Ln., 406/752-5111) is the biggest and most complete hospital you'll find until you get to Missoula. It's off Highway 93 just north of downtown.

Transportation
Glacier Park International Airport, eight miles northeast of Kalispell on Highway 2, is served by United, Delta, Alaska/Horizon, and Northwest.

At the airport you'll find **Avis** (406/257-2727 or 800/331-1212), **Budget** (406/755-7500 or 800/527-0700), **Hertz** (406/758-2220 or 800/654-3131), and **National** (406/257-7144 or 800/227-7368). **Dollar, Enterprise,** and **Thrifty** are all near the airport.

Rimrock Trailways (station at the Sawbuck Casino, 1301 Hwy. 93 S., 406/245-5392 or 800/255-7655) provides bus transportation to Missoula and the I-90 Greyhound line.
Amtrak serves Whitefish, just 14 miles north.

WHITEFISH AND VICINITY
Whitefish (pop. about 7,700) calls itself the "recreation capital of Montana." It's a likely enough claim, what with the town's 3,033-foot setting at the base of a major ski mountain some 40 miles from Glacier National Park. To orient yourself in Whitefish, it may help to realize that Highway 93, usually a north-south road, turns to the west as it passes through Whitefish.

Fur trading and logging brought the first white settlers to this area, but it took the railroad to bring about permanent and stable settlements. In 1893 Whitefish became a division point for the Great Northern Railway. Railroad workers flooded into town, and the bars followed. In 1904 Whitefish supported 14 saloons. Central Avenue was a muddy rut then; the Cadillac Hotel, at the corner of Central and Railway, had a wooden boardwalk built on stilts to avoid the mud.

Success as a tourist destination has brought changes to this town that pulled tree stumps out of its muddy city streets for so long that it earned the nickname "Stumptown." Whitefish Mountain (formerly known as Big Mountain) has become a major ski area, and many of those skiers are returning for summertime visits or to start their own businesses here.

Sights
Most people come here for the proximity to Big Mountain and Glacier National Park. In fact, that's why most of the local people ended up here. It's the sort of place a skier or avid outdoors person moves to.

Surprisingly enough, Whitefish has a **Frank Lloyd Wright building,** but only the most fervid architectural buff would find it particularly interesting. It's on Central Avenue between 3rd and 4th Streets and looks like any old one-story

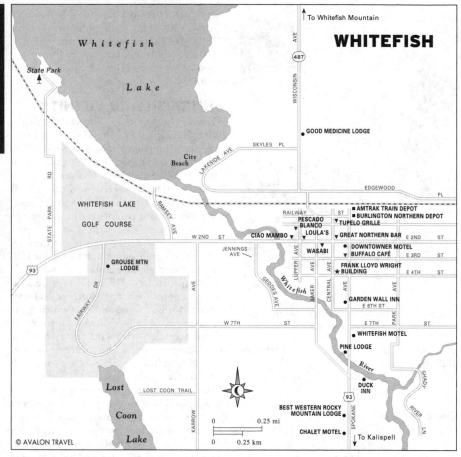

modern office building, currently housing insurance offices and opticians.

The old **Great Northern Depot** is styled along the same lines as the Glacier Park chalet hotels. It is currently used by Burlington Northern Santa Fe and Amtrak, and also houses the **Stumptown Historical Museum** (500 Depot St., 406/862-0067, www.stumptownhistoricalsociety.org, 10 A.M.–4 P.M. Mon.–Sat., free). It's definitely worth a stop for a browse.

Recreation

The best local hiking is on Whitefish Mountain (see *Whitefish Mountain Resort* below), but several hiking trails originate from various points around Tally Lake, about 20 miles west of town via Highway 93 and Forest Service Road 113. From the Tally Lake campground, the **Tally Lake Overlook** is a 1.2-mile hike. The **Boney Gulch Trail** is a steep three-mile trail. Its trailhead is on Road 913 about three miles from the campground. For the less driven hiker, the **Stove Pipe Canyon Trail** is just one mile long and goes into a canyon that is true to its name. This trail starts off Road 2924 on the west side of the lake.

The Forest Service irregularly maintains cross-country ski trails at **Round Meadows,** about 10 miles northwest of town. Take Highway 93 north to Star Meadows Road. A trail map is available from the ranger station in Whitefish or the Forest Service office in Kalispell. The elevation here is relatively low (approximately 3,300 feet), and good skiing is generally limited to late December through early March. Once the snow melts, mountain bikers take to the trails here.

Dogsledding is another winter sport to consider if you want a day away from the skis. **Dog Sled Adventures** (406/881-2275) operates out of Olney about 20 miles north of Whitefish. A good day trip is the 12-mile loop through the Stillwater State Forest.

Glacier Cyclery (326 E. 2nd St., 406/862-6446) rents bikes and trailers and serves as a staging area for bicycle tourists, who can arrange to have their bikes shipped to the store in advance of bike trips in the area. The staff can provide you with a bike map of the area and suggest rides; they also sell Flathead National Forest maps with good mountain-bike roads highlighted. During the summer, Glacier Cyclery stables a fleet of mountain bikes on Big Mountain.

The best bets for summer **swimming** in Whitefish are **City Beach** or the beach at **Whitefish Lake State Recreation Area** ($5 for day use). Boat tours of the lake start at City Beach.

Whitefish Lake Golf Course (406/862-4000) is one of the best in the state. This country club–like 36-hole course is on Highway 93 West, across from the Grouse Mountain Lodge.

Drive north to fish in **Upper Stillwater Lake,** off Highway 93 just north of Olney. The lake reportedly has bull, cutthroat, rainbow, brook trout, perch, and northern pike in it. There's a small undeveloped lakeside campground.

For guided fishing trips, call or stop by **Lakestream Fly Fishing Shop** (334 Central Ave., 406/862-1298).

Whitefish Sea Kayaking (321 Columbia Ave., 406/862-3513) rents boats and leads tours of Whitefish and Flathead lakes. Of course, there's plenty of white water over near Glacier

Park; see that chapter for outfitters running the various forks of the Flathead River.

Entertainment

Although it may seem that Whitefish is wholly devoted to outdoor recreation, there are several artists and other culture mavens in town. The **Whitefish Theatre Company** (1 Central Ave., 406/862-5371) is housed in an attractive arts center and draws enough support to produce plays almost year-round.

Accommodations

Most of Whitefish's accommodations are either along the long, busy Highway 93 strip south of town (also called Spokane Avenue) or up at Whitefish Mountain Ski Resort (see the *Whitefish Mountain Resort* section for more information). Quality is quite high, as are prices, and be sure to reserve early. Summer high-season rates are listed here; there's usually a significant reduction in the off-season.

Whitefish Motel (620 8th St., 406/862-3507, $75 and up) is a modest courtyard motel with in-room kitchens. It's off the main drag and just about the only place in town costing less than $100 during the busy summer season. In the winter, long-term rentals are offered.

Over $100: The **₵ Good Medicine Lodge** (537 Wisconsin Ave., 406/862-5488 or 800/860-5488, www.goodmedicinelodge.com, $100–240) is especially attractive—a cross between a small inn and a B&B. While a big breakfast buffet is provided and there are pleasant common rooms, the atmosphere is low-key, and you don't feel as if you need to whisper as you pad around. Rooms have vaulted wooden ceilings, upscale-rustic decor, and great views. Some rooms are wheelchair accessible, all rooms have telephones, and there's a hot tub and a guest laundry. The lodge is located in an older residential neighborhood on the way to Whitefish Mountain.

Also on the road to Whitefish Mountain, **Hidden Moose Lodge** (1735 E. Lakeshore Dr., 406/862-6516 or 888/733-6667, www.hiddenmooselodge.com, $139 and up) is an attractive newer log lodge with B&B accommodations in upscale Western-themed rooms. Each room is equipped with a TV and DVD player, telephone, refrigerator, and deck. The common areas, including the great room and an outdoor deck and hot tub, are all striking and good places to hang out and enjoy the complimentary evening drink.

For comfort in a conveniently located, historic, and beautifully restored home, the **(Garden Wall Inn** (504 Spokane Ave., 406/862-3440 or 888/530-1700, www.gardenwallinn.com, $135–185) is a good choice. The home was built in the 1920s, with strong arts-and-crafts influences; fabrics, tiles, wall coverings, and art have been carefully selected to evoke the era. Most of the furniture is native to 1920s Montana, which lends a specifically regional atmosphere to the graciously decorated rooms. Modern considerations haven't been neglected, however, and all rooms have private baths. A four-person suite is available for $235. Both the owner and the innkeeper have trained as professional chefs, and the breakfasts are renowned. The innkeepers are also avid outdoors people and will help plan excursions.

The **(Duck Inn** (1305 Columbia Ave., 406/862-3825 or 800/344-2377, www.duckinn.com, $129–199) is a small inn overlooking the river, with fireplaces, themed rooms, a substantial complimentary breakfast, and an intimate and friendly ambience.

If you're heading to Montana hoping to stay in your own log cabin, then consider the **North Forty Resort** (3765 Hwy. 4 W., 406/862-7740 or 800/775-1740, www.northfortyresort.com, $189–249) between Whitefish and Columbia Falls, making it a good base for trips to Glacier National Park. The 22 recently constructed deluxe cabins are located in a quiet pine-shaded grove, and all have full kitchens, baths, and fireplaces. The furniture is hand-crafted in Montana. All cabins sleep at least five, and some sleep up to eight. Hot tubs and a sauna are also available. Pets are allowed in some cabins.

Gaynor's Resorts (406/862-3208, $225–325) has two separate settings: cabins on the family ranch (1992 KM Ranch Rd.) or cabins

in the woods (6544 Farm to Market Rd.). The cabins in both places all sleep at least six people and are beautifully designed and maintained. Trail rides are available for an extra fee.

More standard, though very nice, motel accommodations are at the **Pine Lodge** (920 Spokane St., 406/862-7600 or 800/305-7463, www.thepinelodge.com, $140 and up), an attractive motel with a fairly large indoor-outdoor pool (a swimming channel connects the two pools, and the indoor one has a current generator for those who want the sensation of swimming upstream), hot tub, exercise room, and some rooms with kitchenettes and fireplaces.

The **Downtowner Motel** (224 Spokane Ave., 406/862-2535, www.downtownermotel.cc, $110) is the only lodging in the heart of downtown Whitefish and has an outdoor hot tub, a sauna, and a pretty good exercise room. The motel isn't deluxe, but it's a short walk from good restaurants, shops, and bars.

Best Western Rocky Mountain Lodge (6510 Hwy. 93 S., 406/862-2569 or 800/862-2569, www.rockymtnlodge.com, $140–190) is one of the newest Whitefish accommodations, with a grand lobby, continental breakfast, pool, hot tub, exercise room, and guest laundry. Available are attractive minisuites with fireplace, whirlpool tub, microwave, refrigerator, and wet bar. Rooms in the adjoining annex are a bit less expensive ($112) and not as plush. **Holiday Inn Express** (6390 Hwy. 93 S., 406/862-4020 or 800/888-4479, www.hiexpress.com/whitefishmt, $171 and up) is notable for its indoor pool with a 90-foot waterslide and two outdoor hot tubs.

The **Chalet Motel** (6430 Hwy. 93 S., 406/862-5581 or 800/543-8064, www.whitefishlodging.com, $140) offers an indoor pool, sauna, and hot tub. Although it's a perfectly acceptable place, it's a little tired.

The Grouse Mountain Lodge (1205 Hwy. 93 W., 406/862-3000 or 800/321-8822, www.grousemountainlodge.com, $205 and up) is a large recreation, convention, lodging, and restaurant complex located across from the golf course. Guests have access to a pool, a sauna, hot tubs, tennis courts, high-speed Internet, and rooms looking out onto a golf course rather than a highway strip.

To rent a condo on Whitefish Lake, call **Bay Point on the Lake** (406/862-2331 or 800/327-2108, www.baypoint.org, $155 and up). Rates for these comfortable and quiet lodgings vary seasonally, and there are eight different room configurations with three different luxury levels available, so it's best to call and discuss your needs. For a vacation home rental, contact **Five Star Rentals & Property Management** (406/862-5994, www.fivestarrentals.com).

Guest Ranches: At the **Bar W Guest Ranch** (2875 Hwy. 93 W., 406/863-9099 or 866/828-2900, $85–250 B&B rate or $1,575 and up per person double occupancy for five days, six nights all-inclusive) you'll feel a little removed from the town of Whitefish, even though it's less than 10 miles away. Here you'll be immersed in the Western life, with plenty of horseback riding, which is the ranch's main attraction. A variety of packages are offered, including the "Cowgirl Up" women's weeks; the ranch's by-the-night B&B rate does not include riding.

Camping

Whitefish Lake State Park (406/862-3991, http://fwp.mt.gov, May–Sept., $15) is about two miles west of town off Highway 93. Pick this as your place to stay if you're after convenience, if you want to spend some time near civilization, if you want to eat out or shop in Whitefish, or if you want a handy launching spot for a trip to Glacier National Park. It's a crowded place, even for a state park campground, and trains rattle and toot their way through all night long, but it's a good place to meet friendly people. There's a boat launch and a swimming beach popular with local kids. The campground has running water, flush toilets, and showers.

Out of town, **Tally Lake** (800/416-6992, www.fs.fed.us/r1/flathead, Memorial Day–Labor Day) has a Forest Service campground six miles west of Whitefish on Highway 93, then 15 miles west on Forest Service Road 113.

Food

Whitefish is a great place to eat breakfast. The **(Buffalo Cafe** (514 3rd St. E., 406/862-2833, 6:30 A.M.–9 P.M. Tues.–Sat., 8 A.M.–2 P.M. Sun., $5–8 for breakfast and lunch) is populated with an easy mix of locals and tourists. The breakfast menu features about half a dozen variations on huevos rancheros and at least as many omelets, and it's all really yummy! When we visited in the spring of 2008, the Buff was remodeling in order to serve dinners.

Other good breakfast spots are **Loula's** (300 2nd St. E, 406/862-5614, 7 A.M.–4 P.M. daily summer, 7 A.M.–3 P.M. daily winter, $4.50–8.50), which is perhaps best loved for its berry pies, and **Mama Blanca's** (306 2nd St. E., 406/862-3640, 6 A.M.–11 P.M. daily, $4–16), serving delicious Latin American food with elements from Puerto Rican, Cuban, and Dominican cuisine.

If you're heading south of town and want some coffee for the road, stop at **Montana Coffee Traders** (5810 Hwy. 93 S., 406/862-7633, 8:30 A.M.–5:30 P.M. Mon.–Sat.). Their downtown shop (110 Central Ave., 406/862-7667) is more a place to linger.

Third St. Market (corner of 3rd and Spokane, 406/862-5054) is the local health-food store. Many of the towns in this part of Montana have small health-food stores, but this one is more of a complete food store and community rendezvous than most.

The **(Great Northern Bar and Grill** (27 Central Ave., 406/862-2816, 11 A.M.–2 A.M. daily, mostly around $6) is a friendly, low-key bar with sports on the TV in the front and sandwiches and spaghetti served at the tables in the back. It's open for lunch and dinner, and usually has live music in the bar on weekend nights. The local brew, Black Star, is made in the brewery across the street and served on tap here.

The **(Tupelo Grille** (17 Central Ave., 406/862-6136, 5:30–10 P.M. daily, $17–30) has become a local favorite. It focuses on Southern specialties, such as shrimp and grits, and Cajun food. Don't miss dessert here; the bread pudding deserves all the raves it gets.

The most flat-out-fun dinner restaurant in Whitefish is the casual and noisy **Ciao Mambo** (234 E. 2nd St., 406/863-9600, 5–10 P.M. Mon.–Sat., until 9 P.M. on winter weekdays, $10–18), with a brassy New York Italian atmosphere, delicious food in that same tradition, and a wine list worthy of *Wine Spectator*'s notice. For real entertainment, eat at the bar that surrounds the kitchen area.

Another great choice is, believe it or not, a sushi restaurant. **Wasabi** (419 E 2nd St., 406/863-9283, dinner from 5 P.M. Tues.–Sun., $8–25) has delicious fresh fish and a soothing, elegant atmosphere.

Check out **Pescado Blanco** (235 1st St., 406/862-5285, 5–9 P.M. nightly, $13–18) for Mexican dinners that veer well away from cheesy Mexican-American platefuls served at most Montana Mexican restaurants. Here you'll find something more like Montana-Mexican fusion, such as bison enchiladas.

The **Bulldog Saloon** (144 Central Ave., 406/862-5601, 11 A.M.–11 P.M. for food; bar open until 2 A.M., $5–8) is a good bar to hang out in and maybe munch a burger. **Casey's** (101 Central Ave., 406/862-8150), a casino bar, is housed in Whitefish's oldest building. It was built in 1903, when Whitefish was a rollicking railroad town, and after a day on the slopes, many still find it an excellent place to rollick. For something more of this century and a little more refined, the **Craggy Range** (10 Central Ave., 406/862-7550, kitchen open 11:30 A.M.–10 P.M. daily, entrées mostly $12–20) has standard bar food and good pasta and dinner entrées.

If you're staying on Whitefish Mountain, or feel like a steep drive, the ski lodges at the base of the slopes have quite good food; the Cafe Kandahar is the one that's worth a special trip. (See the *Whitefish Mountain Resort* section for more information.)

Information and Services
The **Whitefish Chamber of Commerce** (520 E. 2nd Ave., 406/862-3501, www.whitefish-chamber.org) dispenses an array of brochures and maps.

The **Whitefish Ranger Station** (406/863-5400) is on Highway 93 near the turnoff for the Whitefish Lake State Recreation Area (and next door to Grouse Mountain Lodge).

Whitefish has a lovely **library** near the train depot at 9 Spokane Avenue (406/862-6657). The local bookstore, **Bookworks** (244 Spokane Ave., 406/862-4980), is an excellent place to pick up regional literature, field guides, or a good novel to read in your motel room.

Transportation
Amtrak stops at the North Central Avenue Depot (406/862-2268, www.amtrak.com) on its way across the top of the country. The Empire Builder runs between Chicago and Seattle or Portland and stops in Whitefish daily. The eastbound train comes through around 7:30 A.M., the westbound at approximately 9 P.M.

Rimrock Trailways stops at the Amtrak station at 11:25 A.M. daily on its run up from Missoula; after a quick stop it heads south again.

The **Duck Inn** (1305 Columbia Ave., 406/862-3825 or 800/344-2377) doubles as a rental car agency. Rentals are also available at **Budget Rent-a-Car** (803 Spokane Ave., 406/862-8170 or 800/248-7604).

WHITEFISH MOUNTAIN RESORT
With about 300 inches of snow a year, 12 lifts (including three high-speed quads) serving 94 trails, and the pleasant Amtrak-accessible town of Whitefish at the bottom of the hill, it's easy to see why people come from all over to ski Whitefish Mountain (406/862-1900, www.skiwhitefish.com, early Dec.–early Apr., $56 adults, $46 seniors and youth 13–18, $30 ages 7–12), which until 2007 was known as Big Mountain. The elevation at the summit is 7,000 feet, the base is at 4,600 feet, the vertical drop is 2,300 feet, and there are lights for night skiing ($15 for everyone). An entire resort community has built up around the ski area, with several hotels and condominiums, a handful of restaurants, a grocery store, a day care center, and ski shops.

Even during the summer, there's plenty of reason to make the steep, tortuous drive—or bike ride, for the ambitious and low-geared— to Whitefish Mountain.

The Forest Service has an information center in the basement of the Summit House, and on Tuesday afternoons in the summer, hosts an environmental lecture series.

Mountain biking is a big summer activity at Whitefish Mountain. Bikes are available for rent at the resort, and there are 20 miles of single-track on the mountain. An all-day lift ticket for a person and a bike costs $24; a one-ride ticket is $12.

The **Whitefish Mountain Nordic Center** ($12 trail pass) is just below the main parking lot. Its 10-mile trail network is rather challenging for both winter skiing (including skating) and summer mountain biking.

((Danny On Trail

The Danny On Trail leads from the main parking lot 3.8 miles up to the summit. There are plenty of huckleberries on the trail late in the summer, and spur trails offer wildflower meadows and vistas of the Flathead Valley. For $12 ($10 seniors, $8 children) you can buy a ride up on the gondola and either hike or ride back down. The thrifty will appreciate the free ride down on the lift that's available to those who make the hike up. The entire trail is usually clear of snow from July through mid-September.

Walk in the Treetops

Perhaps the coolest summer activity on the mountain is the three-hour Walk in the Treetops (406/862-2900, 9:30 A.M. and 1 P.M. daily, some 5 P.M. tours late June–early Sept., $54, reservations required), which starts with a shuttle or one-mile bike ride, then segues into a naturalist-led hike through the forest canopy on a boardwalk suspended up to 60 feet above the ground. Though walking across a fairly narrow plank suspended far above ground sounds like some terrifying character-building exercise, the solid cable-rigged railings and the securely tied safety harness on each participant make this adventure accessible to all but the

most acrophobic. After a few minutes of getting used to the height, the treetops begin to seem like a great place to view not only the nearby lakes and mountains, but a wide variety of bird life, such as western tanagers, red tail and kestrel hawks, pine grosbeaks, and kinglets. Squirrels, pine martins, moose, deer, and coyotes may also be spotted. Participants must be at least 10 years old and 54 inches tall.

Accommodations

If you plan to stay at Whitefish Mountain, you'll generally pay for the convenience of skiing to and from your door, but there are frequent deals, especially for groups. The lodges at Whitefish Mountain are also open in summer, and rates are generally about 25 percent lower than the high-season winter prices listed here.

Many, but not all, of the accommodations on the mountain are run by the ski area; for this broad selection of rooms and condos, the easiest way to arrange for lodgings is to call Whitefish Mountain's central reservation number (800/858-4152) and discuss your needs with the reservations clerk, or check the options at their website (www.whitefishmountain.com). Of the lodgings offered by the ski area, **Hibernation House** ($95) is the economy choice, especially if you're traveling or your own or with one other person. This is a bed-and-breakfast hotel; breakfast is included in the rates. At the **Edelweiss Condominiums** ($155 and up) all of the studio units have kitchens and fireplaces. **Anapurna Properties** ($150 and up) offers a wide range of condos and private homes with indoor pools and hot tubs.

The mountain's upscale hotel isn't handled by the ski area's central reservations. ((**Kandahar Lodge** (3824 Big Mountain Rd., 406/862-6098 or 800/862-6094, www.kandaharlodge.com, $188 and up) is Whitefish Mountain's fanciest, with an excellent restaurant and alpine lodge decor; suites with kitchens are available.

About three miles down the hill from the lift area is **Ptarmigan Village** (3000 Big Mountain Rd., 406/862-3594 or 800/552-3952, www.ptarmiganvillage.com, $125 and up), with studio condos, indoor and outdoor pools, hot tubs, and a sauna. This is a good pick if you don't fancy being right in the hub of the ski area; it's in a woodsy setting and is much less bustling than the area up the mountain. It's operated independently of the ski area.

Food
The best dining is at **Cafe Kandahar** (406/862-6247, 7:30–10:30 A.M. and 5:30–9:30 P.M. daily, $20–32, dinner reservations recommended) for serious cuisine with French and creole influences. The atmosphere is far more casual at the **Hell Roaring Saloon & Eatery** (406/862-6364, 11 A.M.–11 P.M. daily during ski season, 5:30–10 P.M. summer, $8–22), in the chalet at the base of the lifts, with good Southwestern-influenced food and a lively bar.

COLUMBIA FALLS
There are no falls in Columbia Falls (pop. 3,827, elev. 2,960 feet). When it was time to name the town, *Columbia* was the initial choice. Since that name had already been taken, *Falls* was tacked on just because it sounded good.

When Columbia Falls was established in the 1890s, it was supposed to have become a division point for the Great Northern Railway. Kalispell, then Whitefish, became the actual division points, leaving Columbia Falls built to a rather grander scale than its activity would warrant.

For the traveler, Columbia Falls is a handy jumping-off point for both Hungry Horse Reservoir and Glacier National Park. There are several motels and enough stores to do some last-minute stocking up before heading into the mountains.

Recreation
Test the 10 slides and hot tub at **Big Sky Waterpark** (7211 Hwy. 2 E., 406/892-5025, 11 A.M.–7 P.M. daily Memorial Day–Labor Day, $23 adults and teens, $18 children and seniors), at the junction of highways 2 and 20.

The **Meadow Lake Resort** (100 St. Andrews Dr., 406/892-8700) has an 18-hole golf course open to the public.

If you're looking for a guided hiking vacation in northwestern Montana, **Great Northern Llama Co.** (600 Blackmer Ln., 406/755-9044, www.llama-treks.com) offers trips into the Flathead National Forest featuring ridgetop hiking in the company of pack llamas. Prices for a fully outfitted four-day trip (including tents, food, and camping gear) are $950 per adult and $850 per child.

Accommodations
Glacier Inn Motel (1401 2nd Ave. E., 406/892-4341, $70) is a simple but convenient family-run motel.

The **Western Inn Glacier Mountain Shadow Resort** (406/892-7686, $90 and up), located at the junction of highways 2 and 206, shows its spirit by offering a discount to Harley riders and tepees for bicycle tourists ($20). Pets are permitted.

One of the finest B&Bs in these parts is **Bad Rock Country Bed & Breakfast** (406/892-2829 or 888/892-2829, www.bad-rock.com, $125–250), just south of Columbia Falls off Highway 206. In addition to the rooms in the main house (including a two-room family suite), behind the house are four modern, stylishly simple log cabin suites (no kitchens), constructed with squared logs and filled with rustic pine furniture and gas fireplaces. All rooms have private baths and queen or king beds, breakfast is ample and delicious, and the hospitality is top-notch. The B&B is located in a 30-acre meadow with views onto the mountains leading to Glacier Park; from the hot tub the lighted runs of Whitefish Mountain are visible at night.

North of town, just past the Blankenship turnoff to the North Fork area of Glacier Park, **Moss Mountain Inn** (4655 North Fork Road, 406/387-4605, www.mossmountaininn.com, June–Sept., $129–149) is a showcase for sustainability and good organic food, much of it grown in the B&B's garden. The small inn has three suites decorated with Caribbean and Indonesian art and a spacious solarium. During the winter the inn operates as a writers' retreat.

Meadow Lake Resort (100 St. Andrews Dr., 406/892-8700 or 800/321-4653, www.meadowlake.com, $189 and up), which includes a small hotel and condominiums, borders an 18-hole championship golf course. There are tennis courts, a fitness center, an outdoor swimming pool, and a year-round outdoor hot tub on the grounds. During the winter the resort runs a shuttle to and from the Whitefish Mountain ski area. The restaurant here is one of the area's best.

Camping
The Forest Service's **Big Creek Campground** (www.fs.fed.us/r1/flathead, $12) is 21 miles north of Columbia Falls on Road 210, where Big Creek runs into the North Fork of the Flathead River. During the summer it's one of the quieter spots around, as well as one of the least expensive.

Food
The old-fashioned **Pines Cafe** (30 9th St. W., 406/892-7696, 6 A.M.–5 P.M. daily, about $7), a handy stop along Highway 2 in downtown Columbia Falls, has been taken over by Whitefish's Montana Coffee Traders. Stop here for good breakfasts, lunches, baked goods, and espresso drinks.

The **Nite Owl** and the **Back Room** (522 9th St. W., 406/892-3131 or 406/892-9944, 5 A.M.–11 P.M. daily, $5–17) is a casual bar, café, and dinner house complex that serves really good pizza, chicken, and ribs. It doesn't look like much, but ponder the always-full parking lot and rest assured that this is the best inexpensive food in Columbia Falls.

Information and Services
The Columbia Falls **Chamber of Commerce** (406/892-2072, www.columbiafallschamber.com) is at 233 13th Street East.

HUNGRY HORSE
There's obviously a story surrounding the name of Hungry Horse, the next town east of Columbia Falls. During the severe winter of 1900, two draft horses used for logging in the area, Tex and Jerry, wandered off. When they were found about a month later, they were all scraggly and hungry.

Although there'd been settlements in the area since the end of the 19th century, the Hungry Horse post office wasn't established until 1948, when the federal government began planning to dam the South Fork of the Flathead River. The dam was completed in 1952.

Sights
Fans of dam technology will want to tour the visitors information center at the **Hungry Horse Dam** (406/387-5241) four miles south of town. The 564-foot-high concrete dam holds back the 34-mile-long Hungry Horse Reservoir. Guided tours of the dam are offered during summer.

A road circles the reservoir and provides access to trails into the surrounding national forest and wilderness areas. Jewel Basin Hiking Area lies to the west of the reservoir, the Great Bear Wilderness is to the east, and the Bob Marshall Wilderness is to the south. Great Northern Mountain, east of the reservoir, rises to an elevation of 8,720 feet. The South Fork of the Flathead River flows into the southern end of the reservoir. You'll see guest ranches around the reservoir, and there's no dearth of public campgrounds.

Hungry Horse Reservoir is a good place to fish for cutthroat and bull trout; most people fish from boats, and the best fishing is during the late summer and fall.

Don't want to ogle the dam? How about visiting the **House of Mystery** (7800 Hwy. 2 E., 406/892-1210, www.montanavortex.com, 10 A.M.–5 P.M. daily Apr. and Sept., 10 A.M.–6 P.M. daily May–Aug., $8 adult, $6 child), where laws of physics go awry, or the **A-Mazing Ventures Fun Center** (406/387-5902, 9:30 A.M.–dark, Memorial Day–Labor Day), with a giant maze and bumper boats, both on Highway 2. Divert the kids as you pass by.

Great Bear Wilderness Area
The Great Bear Wilderness Area comprises 285,771 acres just south of Glacier National

Park, north of the Bob Marshall, on the west side of the Continental Divide. An airstrip at Schafer Meadows is an unusual feature of this wilderness area, and it's possible to fly in; call **Red Eagle Aviation** (406/755-2376) for details.

Trailheads from the Spotted Bear Ranger Station lead to Lodgepole Creek and the Spotted Bear River. Just about every trail in the wilderness complex will go into the valley of the South Fork of the Flathead River. The headwaters of the Middle Fork of the Flathead River are in the Great Bear Wilderness.

Accommodations

The Hungry Horse Ranger District (406/387-3800, www.fs.fed.us/r1/flathead) rents out several rustic cabins ($30–50) and a rather remote lookout ($20).

Other than camping, about the least expensive lodging you'll find in this area is at the **Crooked Tree Motel** (406/387-5531, $70–140), west of Hungry Horse on Highway 2. Some rooms have kitchenettes, and there's also an indoor pool and RV park.

Between Hungry Horse and Coram, find the **Tamarack Lodge** (406/387-4420 or 877/387-4420, www.historictamaracklodge.com, $99–275), where the log lodge dates back to 1907. Rooms are also available in cabins and a motel. Lodge rooms ($135) include a B&B-style breakfast.

Even though its name is a little odd, the **Mini Golden Inns Motel** (8955 Hwy. 2 E., 406/387-4313 or 800/891-6464, www.hungryhorselodging.com, $100 and up) is a surprisingly pleasant place to stay along this busy highway, with many wheelchair-accessible rooms. Pets are allowed.

Located 55 miles south of Highway 2, the **Spotted Bear Ranch** (800/223-4333, www.spottedbear.com) is an upscale lodge catering mostly to anglers and hunters. A three-day fishing vacation here costs $2,100 per person, including all meals and guide service.

Camping

There are eight Forest Service campgrounds (406/387-3800, www.fs.fed.us/r1/flathead,

$10–12) around Hungry Horse Reservoir. It's necessary to bring your own drinking water to all of them; even those that once had piped water have had their services cut back.

Lost Johnny Camp is eight miles down Road 895 from Hungry Horse; **Lost Johnny Point** is one mile farther. **Lid Creek** is 15 miles from Hungry Horse; **Lakeview** is 24 miles; **Handkerchief Lake** is 35 miles from Hungry Horse on Road 895, then another two miles on Road 897. There's a trail from Handkerchief Lake up to the Jewel Basin Hiking Area. **Spotted Bear** is at the south end of the reservoir, 55 miles from Martin City on Road 38 (and about the same distance from Hungry Horse). **Elk Island** (accessible only by boat), **Murray Bay,** and **Emery Bay** are along the east side of the reservoir. Emery Bay is the closest spot to Martin City; it's seven miles down Road 38.

Food

The huckleberry is the culinary specialty of Hungry Horse. The **Huckleberry Patch** (8858 Hwy. 2 E., 406/387-5000) is a convenient place to load up on gifts of huckleberry preserves and to toss down a slice of huckleberry pie or a huckleberry milkshake in the café. It's also easy enough to pick your own berries. They start ripening around mid-July, and almost any trip off Highway 2 into the hills will lead to good picking—but watch out for bears; they feast on berries to prepare for hibernation.

Information

The *Hungry Horse News* is the newspaper of record in these parts, definitely worth picking up if you want to read a weekly paper loaded with stories of mountain lions in the streets, bear maulings and bee stings in Glacier Park, and numerous DUI violations.

The Forest Service has two **ranger stations** in the area. One is in Hungry Horse (406/387-3800) and the other, which is staffed May through October only, is at Spotted Bear, at the southern end of Hungry Horse Reservoir (406/758-5376).

The Northwestern Corner

The Kootenai (pronounced KOOT-nee) National Forest is the defining physical feature of this far corner of the state. It has a Pacific quality, and its lush, forested hillsides are drained by the Kootenai, the Clark Fork, and a host of smaller rivers and streams.

Western red cedar, western hemlock, western white pine, whitebark pine, lodgepole pine, ponderosa pine, alpine larch, western larch, mountain hemlock, grand fir, subalpine fir, Douglas fir, Engelmann spruce, juniper, cottonwood, quaking aspen, alder, and paper birch are all native to northwestern Montana. Years of forest management, however, have changed the composition of the new-growth forests to increase their timber yields. Timber managers often replant only a single fast-growing species, changing the forest from a diverse system with dozens of different species to a monocrop similar in composition to a potato patch.

Logging can increase erosion and decreases water quality, threatening fish habitats, but logged areas do support both plant and animal life. Wildflowers bloom in clear-cuts, huckleberries and elderberries invade, and deer and elk populations flourish in open areas created by timber cutting. There are also moose in the forested areas here, and some bighorn sheep and mountain goats reside on the hillsides.

HISTORY

The Kootenai Indians moved from the north to the Tobacco Plains area around present-day Eureka and along the Kootenai River around the 1500s. After the Blackfeet arrived on the plains in the 1700s, the Kootenai largely restricted their travel to the west side of the Rockies. Many of the Kootenai people in Montana now live on the Flathead Reservation (mostly around Elmo).

David Thompson was the first white man in the area. He explored the Kootenai River in 1808 and portaged around Kootenai Falls. Thompson sent Finan McDonald to the area near Libby to establish a trading post for the North West Company. Trappers and fur traders followed in the wake of Thompson and McDonald, but it took gold and silver to bring a significant number of white settlers to the region. Placer mining started in 1869 and continued for about 20 years.

Even with trapping and mining activity, this corner of Montana was an isolated place until the Great Northern Railway came through in 1893. The railroad truly opened the north to development. Not only was there an easy way to get into the area, but there was also a way to haul away the abundant natural resources, particularly the trees. The growth of the timber industry was thus linked to the railroad.

Although much of the economic focus here has been on forestry, mines still operate around Libby and Troy. Improved methods of extracting minerals and rising prices fuel interest in both small and large-scale operations.

BULL RIVER ROAD AND THE CABINET MOUNTAINS WILDERNESS

Bull River Road (Highway 56) runs from Highway 200 (just west of Noxon) to Troy. The Bull River and several lakes are along the road, and the Cabinet Mountains Wilderness is just to the east. Fishing is good in the river (but not spectacular in Bull Lake, which does not feed the river). There's a good chance that wildlife will be somewhere along this road almost any time you drive it. You'll probably see deer, and there are also plenty of elk and moose in the area.

Highway 56 was an Indian trail; it was also used by smugglers bringing Chinese laborers down from Canada to work on the construction of the Northern Pacific Railway.

Ross Creek Cedar Grove

Ross Creek Cedar Grove is about four miles off Highway 56 just south of Bull Lake (17 miles north of Highway 200). The gravel road has a steep section and isn't suitable for large RVs. The western red cedar forest here is a Pacific rainforest, which is a little unusual for Montana. It gets 50 inches of rain a year, so don't be surprised if you take the mile-long nature hike in a shower. The raised boardwalk trail on the interpretive hike protects the forest floor and makes it easy to hike in the rain. There are trails up the Middle Fork and the South Fork of Ross Creek starting from the parking lot of the cedar grove. Bring your cross-country skis here in the winter for a lovely easy tour through the big trees.

Indian history records that Bull Lake was formed when a landslide blocked a stream and destroyed a camp. There is still some evidence of such a slide at the foot of the lake.

Cabinet Mountains Wilderness

In the Kootenai National Forest, the Cabinet Mountains Wilderness comprises nearly 95,000 acres. It can be reached from Highway 56 or Highway 200. Snowshoe Peak is the high point in the wilderness at 8,738 feet. There is good hiking here, and some rock-climbing on the peaks.

To reach the four-mile-long trail to **St. Paul Lake,** a 4,715-foot-high lake in a cirque beneath St. Paul Peak, go up East Fork Road off Bull River Road. About one mile up East Fork Road is a Forest Service sign noting directions and distances to several trailheads. The St. Paul Lake trailhead is four miles from this point, up a gravel road that's easy to drive in a passenger car until the final short descent to the trailhead, which requires some caution. The trail passes through some old-growth western red cedar and western hemlock before it reaches the lake.

Camping

The **Bull River Campground** (406/295-4693, www.fs.fed.us/r1/Kootenai, mid-Apr.–Nov., $10) is situated by the Cabinet Mountains where Bull River runs into the Clark Fork.

There's also camping on the road to the Ross Creek Cedar Grove. **Bad Medicine Campground** (406/295-4693, www.fs.fed.us/ r1/Kootenai, Apr.–Nov., $10) is two miles off

Highway 56 overlooking Bull Lake. There is a boat launch at this cedar-scented site.

TROY AND VICINITY

At 1,892 feet, Troy is the lowest point in Montana. It's a town of about 950 on the west bank of the Kootenai River, which flows northwest from Troy into Idaho. The Purcell Mountains to the north of Troy were completely blanketed by ice age glaciers, which ground the mountains into soft peaks. To the south, glaciers carved valleys and cirques in the Cabinet Mountains but did not cover them so completely as to smooth them out.

The Yaak River drains the Purcell Mountains in the far northwest corner of the state and flows into the Kootenai River just west of Troy. The Yaak has gained a certain literary fame thanks to writer Rick Bass, whose *Winter Notes* and *The Book of Yaak* chronicle snow, woodcutting, and isolation. The road between Yaak and Rexford has both densely forested areas and massive clear-cuts.

Sights

Troy's **historical museum** (406/295-1064) is housed in an old railroad building on Highway 2. A short nature trail runs behind the museum.

Recreation

Pulpit Mountain Trail, a national recreation trail, is a five-mile (one-way) hike just north of Troy. It passes an old fire lookout on Pulpit Mountain and has good views of the Cabinet Mountains. The easiest way to walk the trail is to start from the trailhead on Lynx Creek Road and hike to where the trail comes out on Rabbit Creek Road.

To reach the **Northwest Peak Scenic Area,** turn up Pete Creek Road just west of Yaak. This is an isolated area of the state, and it's rare to see many other hikers on the trails. One of the more popular trails leads to Northwest Peak. It's a two-mile hike to the peak, which has grand views and a deserted lookout. Call the Troy ranger station (406/295-4693) for trail information.

You can cross-country ski the 4.5-mile Hellroaring Creek trail, 29 miles northwest of Troy on the Yaak River Road. This is also a popular snowmobiling area.

Accommodations

There are a couple of inexpensive motels along Highway 2 in Troy, both of which seem to cater to long-term renters. Libby, just a few miles east, has better choices.

For a remote getaway, head up to Yaak, where the **Yaak River Lodge** (27744 Yaak River Rd., 406/295-5463, $40 per person bunkhouse, $125–175 suites) is popular with hunters and other outdoors people. The **Dirty Shame Saloon** (29453 Yaak River Rd., 406/295-5439, $35) also has a few simple cabins for rent.

Camping

Yaak River Campground (406/295-4693, www.fs.fed.us/r1/Kootenai, $9), seven miles west of Troy on Highway 2, is a good entrance or exit campground to the state. There are plenty of paths down to the river. There are several other Forest Service campgrounds in the area. Head up the Yaak River to **Yaak Falls Campground** (free, no water) set by a cascade eight miles up from Highway 2. **Whitetail Campground** ($7) is on a quiet stretch of the Yaak River; it's not a bad place for a swim. **Pete Creek** ($7) is an exceptionally pretty campground set on a bluff above Pete Creek, just west of the town of Yaak.

Food

Head off the highway and down Kootenai Street to the **Northwest Music Hot Club Coffee House** (302A E. Kootenai St., 406/295-5541), a combination music store (selling a wide variety of stringed instruments), café, and live entertainment venue. Friday nights almost always bring performers to the stage at this friendly spot. This is a great place to stop for coffee, lunch, or a new ukulele, and it's an easy place to make a friend in Troy.

Odie's Big Sky Cafe (1410 E. Missoula Ave., 406/295-2233, 8 A.M.–8 P.M. daily, $5–15), at the west end of town on Highway 2, is the most popular place to eat in town.

If you're a brave traveler hankering for a lively bar, wander down by the railroad tracks, where the **Home Bar** (228 E. Yaak Ave.) and several others accommodate locals and the occasional passerby (especially those who arrive on a Harley).

It would be a shame to drive all the way up to Yaak and not stop in at the **Dirty Shame Saloon** (29453 Yaak River Rd., 406/295-5439, breakfast, lunch, and dinner daily, $5 breakfast specials, $8–11 dinner specials), where the food is way better than you might expect and local color is abundant.

Information

The **ranger station** (12858 Hwy. 2, 406/295-4693) is on the west edge of town; visitor information is dispensed at the historical museum.

LIBBY

Libby (pop. 2,662, elev. 2,066 feet) spills along the Kootenai River Valley, with the Cabinet Mountains to the south, the Purcell Mountains to the northwest, and the Salish Mountains to the northeast. Although it's not an obvious tourist town, it's easy to spend a day or two in the area, especially if you're hiking, fishing, or—in the autumn—watching the local eagles.

History

David Thompson's reconnoitering in 1808 resulted in a small influx of fur traders during the first half of the 1800s, but little development occurred until gold was found in 1865. A mining town was thrown up by Libby Creek in the 1880s, and it moved to wherever the gold seemed to be. Sometimes the development was called New Town; other times, Old Town seemed the more appropriate name. The name of a prospector's daughter ultimately won out. Libby ended up in its present location when the railroad came through in 1892.

Trees were initially harvested for mine timbers, then for railroad bridges and ties. Ultimately the timber industry eclipsed both

© PAUL LEVY

Libby is known as the City of Eagles for its large population of bald eagles.

mining and the railroad and has become Libby's increasingly unreliable mainstay.

Mining, however, continued until 1990, when W. R. Grace and Co. shut down its vermiculite mining and processing operation in Libby. Mixed in with the vermiculite was a mineral called tremolite, a rare and toxic form of asbestos. Tragically, the miners and many townspeople have suffered from the effects of asbestos poisoning. Many have died from asbestos-related cancers, and even more are ill. Even though W. R. Grace and Co. *and* the U.S. government knew about the asbestos, nothing was done to stop the dust that contaminated the town. In 2000, after the *Seattle Post-Intelligencer* and other journalists began running stories on the asbestosis, the Environmental Protection Agency (EPA) started paying attention. About this time, Grace bought back the mine, which they'd sold years before, banned EPA officials from it, and backed off from promises to clean it up. In 2001 W. R. Grace and Co. filed for bankruptcy, claiming it could not handle the deluge

of personal-injury lawsuits. By the summer of 2001 about 5,500 Libby residents had been tested for asbestosis. Nearly 20 percent of those tested had lung abnormalities. Many homes were contaminated, thanks to the free vermiculite insulation that was available for years in big piles outside the processing site. The EPA has now cleaned up the major source areas around town, including the school athletic field. The cleanup efforts are ongoing and now focus on smaller areas on private property.

Sights

The **Heritage Museum** (1367 Hwy. 2 S., 406/293-7521, 10 a.m.–5 p.m. Mon.–Sat., 1–5 p.m. Sun., June–Aug., free) is a large polygonal log building with a dark interior filled with display cases brimming with Libby's old musical instruments (including two ukelins, one pianoette, two mandolin harps, and the sheet music for "Let Me Call You Sweetheart"), household implements, and logging equipment. There are special displays on the region's wildlife, logging, and mining.

Of the several historical buildings in downtown Libby, the oldest is what is now the dentist's office at 209 West 2nd Street. It was built in 1899 and was originally the Libby hospital. The ballpark across the street was once the site of an Indian camp. One place that's changed a bit over the years is the white-and-red apartment building on East 1st Street across from the train depot. It was once known as Helen Hunter's Place and was Libby's first brothel in 1906.

If you're out to relive Libby's history, it may be more profitable to pan for gold on Libby Creek than to watch vaudeville or go glassy-eyed over displays of old kitchenware. Gold was discovered in Libby Creek in 1865 and was mined fairly intensively around the end of the 19th century. There's still some gold there, though. The original dredging equipment got only 85–90 percent of what gold was in the creek. What's left is most likely to be found near the bottom of gravel piles left by early miners. The Forest Service has an area set aside for gold panning on Libby Creek; it's important not to search outside the designated area because mining claims are staked close by.

To reach the **Libby Creek Gold Panning Area** (406/293-7773, www.fs.fed.us/r1/kootenai), turn from Highway 2 onto Bear Creek Road (seven miles south of Libby) and drive 18 miles to the small parking area beside Libby Creek. (Or take Libby Creek Road, 12 miles down Highway 2 from Libby, and follow it just over 10 miles to the panning zone.) Howard Lake Campground is one mile south of the gold-panning area. If you tire of prospecting, follow Libby Creek Road (the road that goes west at the Howard Lake junction) to its end and take an easy two-mile round-trip hike along Libby Creek past an old miner's cabin.

Kootenai Falls

For a look at the cascading, 200-foot-high Kootenai Falls from the highway, there's a turnout on Highway 2 about five miles west of Libby. This is one of the few waterfalls on a major Northwest river that hasn't had its power harnessed for electrical generators. A trail leads from the casual campground by the highway pullout, across a bridge over the railroad tracks, and down to viewpoints of the cascades. Continue west on the trail to a swinging footbridge downstream from the falls. Bighorn sheep are often seen just east of here grazing on the cliffs across the river.

Recreation

The 23-mile **Skyline National Recreation Trail** (406/293-7773, www.fs.fed.us/r1/kootenai) starts at the west fork of Quartz Creek, northwest of Libby, and ends in the Yaak Valley. It's a good place for an overnight backpacking trip, with lots of camping spots and wildlife.

The Kootenai River is popular with rafters and canoeists. The Canoe Gulch Ranger Station on Highway 37 is a good put-in spot, and boats can be taken out in town just below the California Avenue Bridge. The trip is a little too challenging for inexperienced river runners, and it's important to remember that Kootenai Falls, five miles downstream from Libby, are not passable.

There are large rainbow trout living below Libby Dam (a 33-pound trout was caught here), but those who fish this part of the Kootenai River should pay close attention to the water level; release of water from the dam can cause quick rises. Fishing is best when the water level drops. For water-release schedules, call Libby Dam's River Discharge Information (406/293-3421). **Kootenai Anglers** (13546 N. Hwy 37, 406/293-7578) is the local fly shop and guide service.

Stone Hill, near Lake Koocanusa on Highway 37, is a very popular rock-climbing area, especially in the spring. More than 200 routes are accessible from the roadside near the Libby Dam visitors center.

The downhill ski area at 5,952-foot **Turner Mountain** (406/293-4317, www.skiturner.com, weekends and holidays, $28 adult, $23 child), 22 miles up Pipe Creek Road from Libby, has a 2,100-foot vertical drop on trails that are generally ungroomed and mostly for expert skiers (70 percent are black diamond runs) and are accessed via the world's longest T-bar.

There are groomed **cross-country ski trails** at **Bear Creek** (go seven miles south of Libby on Hwy. 2, then right onto Bear Creek Rd. 278 for about 2.5 miles) and **Flatiron Mountain** (22 miles out Pipe Creek Rd. to Rainbow Lake Rd.). Few of the logging roads around Libby are plowed in the winter. Stop by the ranger station to find out which roads have been set aside for skiers. Snowmobilers should check with the Forest Service to see which roads are designated for snowmobile use.

Events

Logger Days (406/293-8585) are held in mid-July every year. Libby's **Nordicfest** (406/293-6430), held the second weekend of September, features Scandinavian food, crafts, music, and dancing.

Accommodations

Get a bird's-eye view of this country from the **Big Creek Baldy Mountain Fire Lookout** (877/444-6777, www.reserveusa.com, $30). It's about 26 miles from Libby via Pipe Creek

Road. The cabin, which is atop a 41-foot tower, is equipped with everything but sleeping bags, food, and water.

A host of inexpensive motels line Highway 2 in Libby. **Venture Motor Inn** (443 Hwy. 2 W., 406/293-7711 or 800/221-0166, www.ventureinnlibby.com, $70 and up) is the nicest place to stay in town. It has a heated pool, hot tub, and restaurant, and just out back is Fireman's Park, a good place for a morning walk. Another good bet is the **Caboose** (714 W. 9th St., 406/293-6201 or 800/627-0206, www.mtwilderness.com, $60 and up); there's no pool here but everything else you might need. **Sandman Motel** (688 Hwy. 2 W., 406/293-8831, www.sandmanmotel.us, $45) is set back off the road just a bit. It has an outdoor hot tub and some rooms with microwaves and refrigerators. Pets are permitted at all of these motels.

Camping

There's camping in **Fireman's Park,** behind the Libby Chamber of Commerce building. It's a bit too much in the thick of things for tent camping, and there are no hookups, but the convenience and the price ($5 RVs, $2 tents) are enticing. There are several public campgrounds on Lake Koocanusa, not far from town.

Food

Expect hearty American food from Libby's restaurants, and you won't be disappointed. For breakfast be sure to stop by the **Libby Cafe** (411 Mineral Ave., 406/293-3523, 6:30 A.M.–3:30 P.M. daily, $7–13) for a huckleberry muffin or huckleberry pancakes.

Fiesta Bonita (30270 Hwy. 2 W., 406/293-6687, 11 A.M.–8 P.M. daily, $8–17) is a popular, and pretty good, Mexican restaurant.

If you're still searching for the ultimate Montana steak, don't pass up the **M-K Steak House** (9948 Hwy. 2 S., 406/293-5686, 5–9 P.M., $12–24), about 10 miles east of town on Highway 2. This is the place the locals go for a special night out.

For a bar with live music on the weekends, try the **Pastime** (216 Mineral Ave., 406/293-9925), which has been around since 1916, when it was known as the Pastime Pool Hall. Note the original carvings behind the bar.

The **Red Dog Saloon** (406/293-8347, evenings and weekend afternoons, pizza $12–18) is seven miles up Pipe Creek Road in Libby, on the way to Turner Mountain. It's a little ways off the main drag, but haven't you been craving a pizza with whole-wheat crust? It's a friendly local hangout for both food and drinks.

Information and Services

Visitor information is proffered on Highway 2 near the Venture Inn (406/293-4167, www.libbychamber.org). The **Kootenai National Forest Headquarters** is at 1101 Highway 2 West (406/293-6211). Another ranger station is at **Canoe Gulch,** 13 miles north of Libby on Highway 37, near Libby Dam.

Saint John's Lutheran Hospital is at 350 Louisiana Avenue (406/293-0100).

Transportation

Amtrak (100 Mineral Ave., 800/872-7245) stops ever so briefly in Libby; the eastbound train comes through at 5:30 A.M., the westbound at 11 P.M., and the station is generally unstaffed.

LAKE KOOCANUSA

Ninety-mile-long Lake Koocanusa, framed by the Purcell and Salish Mountains, was formed in 1972 when the Libby Dam backed up the Kootenai River from just above Libby all the way north into Canada.

Libby Dam now provides hydroelectric power to much of the Northwest and stores water in Lake Koocanusa to prevent flooding downstream. Water is released from the dam to supply the 17 dams downstream on the Columbia River. The dam is a straight-axis, concrete gravity dam: It holds back Lake Koocanusa by its own weight. The Libby Dam has an attractive visitors center (406/293-5577, June–Sept. 9:30 A.M.–6 P.M.), 17 miles north of Libby, for guided tours of the dam and powerhouse. There's also a boat launch and picnic area.

Paved roads circle a good portion of Lake

© PAUL LEVY

The massive Libby Dam holds back the Kootenai River, creating Lake Koocanusa.

Koocanusa. Highway 37 runs along the east side; Forest Service Road 228 follows the western shore. There are only a couple of places to cross the lake. Libby Dam has a bridge, and Montana's highest and longest bridge spans the lake just south of Rexford.

The name Koocanusa, derived from Kootenai, Canada, and U.S.A., was coined by a resident of Rexford, a town largely flooded by the lake. Part of the town simply picked up and moved to higher ground, a grand tradition among dam-flooded sites.

Recreation

There is good fishing around Libby Dam, most notably for kokanee salmon. Bald eagles are onto this one too and can be spotted here in the fall, swooping down for spawning kokanee. Late October through mid-November is the peak season for eagle viewing. Arrive early in the morning and you may see 40 or 50 eagles just downstream from the dam.

Just up the road from the visitors center is a trail (approximately two miles) to Alexander Mountain, continuing on 1.5 miles to Fleetwood Point. The short trail to Little North Falls (off Road 228) is wheelchair accessible.

Camping

Campsites are abundant around Lake Koocanusa. On the west side, six miles above Libby Dam, is **McGillivray**, a large Forest Service campground and recreation area. There's a boat launch and a swimming area on the lake at McGillivray, but they can only be used when the lake is filled with water, generally any time after early July. If McGillivray is too crowded, check the sign at the entrance for smaller and less developed campgrounds in the area.

It's possible to reserve a campsite in advance at **Rexford Beach Campground** (800/280-2267, www.reserveusa.com). **Tetrault Lake** and **Sophie Lake,** north of Rexford near Lake Koocanusa, both have Forest Service campgrounds.

Rocky Gorge and **Peak Gulch** are Forest Service campgrounds on the lake on Highway 37 south of the Lake Koocanusa Bridge.

Mariners' Haven (406/296-3252) is a private campground near Rexford with tepee rentals, a grocery store, and a marina.

Information

The **Canoe Gulch Ranger Station** (Hwy. 37 just south of junction with Rd. 228, 406/293-7773 or 406/293-5758 for a recording) has information on recreation around Lake Koocanusa.

EUREKA

Eureka (pop. 1,028, elev. 2,577 feet) is located on the Tobacco River, so named because that was a crop grown by the area's Kootenai Indians (though some sources contend that missionaries attempted to grow tobacco here and that the name comes from their failed efforts).

The northern part of Highway 93 was originally an Indian trail and was used later by fur traders and pack trains traveling between Missoula and Vancouver, Canada.

The Tobacco Valley, Plains, and the Paradise Valley all claim the title of "banana belt of Montana." Farming supplements timber around Eureka; in fact, coming in from the big timber country to the west, Eureka looks strikingly agricultural.

Sights

Downtown Eureka, though not large or flashy, is quite appealing, and it's easy to while away an hour or two exploring the shops and cafés on Dewey Avenue or strolling along the two-mile Riverwalk.

Eureka doesn't just have the standard small-town historical museum; rather it has a full-blown **historical village** near the south end of downtown. Most of the buildings there were salvaged from the town of Rexford. The old Rexford general store now houses a museum, which boasts, among the old books and papers, an ancient permanent-wave machine for hair. Another oddity here are larch balls, which form when larch trees drop their needles into a stream and the currents and eddies form the needles into a ball.

Murphy Lake, 14 miles southeast of Eureka on Highway 93, is home to a loon

Downtown Eureka has its artsy side.

population as well as a host of other animals, including horned grebes, bald eagles, herons, ospreys, white-tailed and mule deer, and beavers. Be sure to respect the privacy of nesting loons, which are protected during nesting season by boating restrictions on the southern end of the lake.

Recreation

Ten Lakes Scenic Area is adjacent to the Canadian border near Eureka and has been nominated for wilderness-area designation. To reach the Ten Lakes area, turn off Highway 93 at Grave Creek (about 10 miles south of Eureka) and follow the road for 30 miles, almost to its end. Several hiking trails start at the end of the road (just beyond Little Therriault Lake) and lead to many of the lakes in the area.

Paradise and **Bluebird Lakes** are the closest, about two miles in, with an elevation gain of about 1,000 feet. A pamphlet with a rough trail map is available at the Murphy Lake Ranger Station south of Eureka. Pick up a map of the Kootenai National Forest for clearer detail.

In the winter, Grave Creek Road and several spur roads are groomed for cross-country skiing and snowmobiling. To access 4.5 miles of easy snowmobile-free cross-country skiing, park at the **Birch Creek Recreation Area** adjacent to the Murphy Lake ranger station.

Accommodations

On the north edge of town, **Ksanka Inn** (Hwy. 93 and Hwy. 37, 406/296-3127, www.ksanka.com, $50) is a 24-hour store, deli, and bakery as well as a motel.

A little nicer is the **Riverstone Family Lodge** (6370 Hwy. 93 N., 866/345-0026, www.riverstonefamilylodge.com, $109 and up), with recently built duplex cabins (rent one side or both) in a pretty setting about five miles north of town.

Camping

North of Eureka, the Ten Lakes Scenic Area has two campgrounds, **Big Therriault Lake** and **Little Therriault Lake** (www.fs.fed.us/r1/Kootenai, $5). To the south, camp at **Murphy Lake** ($7).

Food

Heaven's Peak (312 Dewey Ave., 406/297-7771) is a friendly natural foods store. Stop in at the very popular **Cafe Jax** (207 Dewey Ave., 406/297-9084, 7 A.M.–3 P.M. Mon.–Sat., 8 A.M.–4 P.M. Sun., $6–9) for a hearty breakfast or a milkshake.

Information and Services

The **Eureka Ranger Station** (949 Hwy. 93, 406/296-7188) is on the north edge of town. There's also a ranger station at Murphy Lake, south of Eureka (406/882-4835).

GLACIER NATIONAL PARK

Glacier National Park (406/888-7800, www .nps.gov/glac, $25 per vehicle, $15 Nov.–Apr., $12 per person for bicyclists, motorcyclists, and foot travelers, $10 Nov.–Apr., separate fee for Canada's Waterton Lakes National Park) contains more than 1,500 square miles of extraordinarily scenic wilderness. Towering glacier-pocked summits bend over mirrorlike lakes. Wildlife, including bears, bald eagles, moose, and ptarmigans, inhabits the park's thick forests, stream sides, and rocky promontories; more than 60 species of mammals and 200 species of birds make their homes in Glacier. Easily one of the most spectacular drives in the country is Going-to-the-Sun Road, which climbs from lakes and forest up the face of the Rockies to a fragile alpine meadow almost 7,000 feet above sea level.

Glacier is a park for the outdoor-minded; as much as possible, you'll want to leave the car behind. More than 700 miles of hiking trails link backcountry peaks and lakes. In winter the park's roads double as cross-country ski trails.

Sometimes called the "Crown of the Continent" for its staggeringly rugged skyline, Glacier and its Canadian cousin Waterton Lakes National Park (403/859-2224, www.pc.gc.ca/pn-np/ab/waterton/, C$6.80 per day adult, C$5.80 senior, C$3.40 youth 6–16, C$17.10 family) form one of the crown jewels of the national park system.

PLANNING YOUR TIME

It takes several days even to begin to skim the surface of Glacier National Park, but in reality many people have only a day to spend here.

HIGHLIGHTS

◖ Cross-Country Skiing Around the Izaak Walton Inn: The Izaak Walton Inn is a great spot any time of year, but it's especially magical as a wintertime base for cross-country skiing (page 114).

◖ Going-to-the-Sun Road: It's hard to visit Glacier Park without traveling the Going-to-the-Sun Road, and if you ride the park shuttle you'll really get to ogle the details of the marvelously engineered road through a showcase of geology. Plus the road gives you access to great hiking trails (page 120).

◖ Logan Pass: Take the park shuttle bus to this pass, the high point of the Going-to-the-Sun Road, and avoid the parking nightmare. Drop by the visitor center here, and if there are any naturalist hikes getting ready to leave, make sure to join in. Otherwise, enjoy the alpine scenery (page 124).

◖ Highline Trail: After a visit to Logan Pass, spend a few hours on this trail, with its above-the-timberline views and chattering marmots. Go as far as you'd like, then turn around and return the way you came. If you go far enough, you can hook up with other trails and construct a fine backpacking trip (page 125).

◖ Glacier Park Lodge: Like all the park's lodges, Glacier Park Lodge has a spectacular lobby, and it's not necessary to book a room here in order to visit and enjoy the architecture (page 127).

◖ Grinnell Glacier: Quick! See a glacier while you still have a chance. Take a day hike from Many Glacier to reach Grinnell Glacier (page 132).

LOOK FOR ◖ TO FIND RECOMMENDED SIGHTS, ACTIVITIES, DINING, AND LODGING.

◖ Upper Waterton Lake: Don't neglect a visit to Waterton Lakes National Park in Canada, just north of the border. Take a boat ride on Upper Waterton Lake to reach prime hiking trails. It's also OK just to ride the boat and never hike a step (page 136).

GLACIER NATIONAL PARK

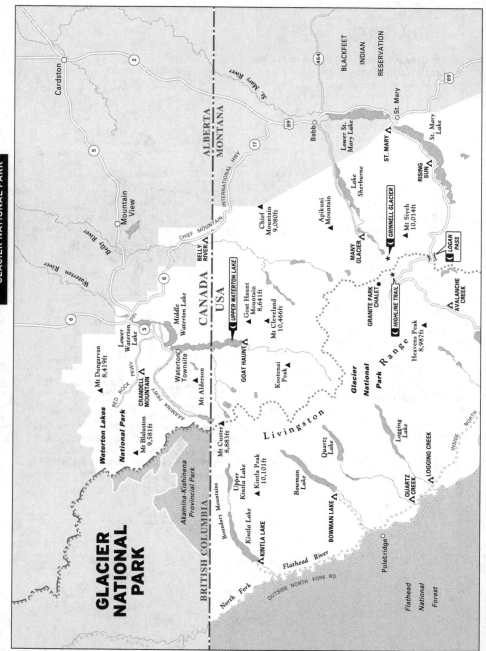

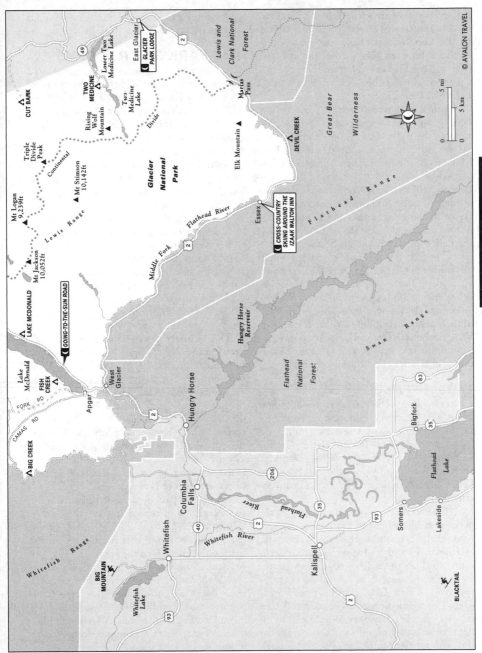

GLACIER NATIONAL PARK

If that's the case, structure your day around a drive or shuttle ride on the spectacular **Going-to-the-Sun Road,** but be sure to get out of the car for at least one hike (if you stop at Logan Pass, you can hike in an alpine meadow or take a jaunt on the Highline Trail) and to visit the Lake McDonald Lodge.

With a few more days to play around here, you can explore the several distinctive areas of the park: the isolation and big lakes up the North Fork; the forests around Lake McDonald; the comparative spareness of the east side; the incredible closeness of the mountains, the glaciers, and—sometimes—the bears at Many Glacier; and the distinctly Canadian flavor of Waterton Lakes. Add another day or two and head along the southern edge of the park for a visit to the Izaak Walton Inn in Essex. In fact, if you choose to make a winter pilgrimage to Glacier, the Izaak Walton makes a cozy base for several days of cross-country skiing in and around the park.

Longer visits almost invariably mean more hiking, perhaps including a backpacking trip. Visitors who plan far in advance (or those lucky last-minute few) may be able to arrange a stay in one of Glacier's backcountry chalets.

Entrance Points

The two main park entrances are at Apgar (near West Glacier) on the western edge, and St. Mary on the east. These two points are linked by Going-to-the-Sun Road. On the western edge north of Apgar is the Polebridge entrance, which provides access to Bowman Lake and trails in the park's remote northwestern corner.

Other entrances on the eastern edge of the park, Two Medicine and Many Glacier, have roads that dip just a short way into the park. Highways 49 and 89 form the main north-south road on the eastern edge of the park; from this highway about four miles north of the town of East Glacier, a short road leads in to Two Medicine Lake. The road to Many Glacier splits off Highway 89 at the town of Babb and travels nine miles to its terminus near the Swiftcurrent Motor Inn. Continue north

on Highway 89 to cross the border into Canada and visit Waterton Lakes National Park.

THE PARK'S EARLY DAYS

Under pressure from the railroads, miners, and settlers, the Blackfeet sold the eastern slope of what is now Glacier National Park in 1895 for $1.5 million, thus opening up the area for business. Copper mining was a bust here, as was oil exploration. Tourism—amply advertised by the Great Northern Railway, which in 1891 completed its service through Marias Pass just south of the park—was left as the area's economic mainstay. Conservationists, in league with powerful railroad interests, sought to establish the area as a national park. In 1910 President Taft signed the bill creating Glacier National Park.

Between 1910 and 1917 the Great Northern spent $1.5 million developing tourist facilities. It built a series of huge lodges, chalets, and tent camps, each a day's horseback ride away. The Great Northern's recommended itinerary of hikes, fishing, and trail rides required a full week to "do" the park.

This leisurely, genteel, and recreation-oriented era was challenged in 1933 when the Civilian Conservation Corps finished the Going-to-the-Sun Road, thus introducing the automobile to Glacier. The volume and pace of traffic in the park increased: In 1925 only 40,000 people visited Glacier; 210,000 visitors traveled through in 1936, many simply to experience the Going-to-the-Sun Road. The old Great Northern facilities fell into disuse, and strip towns grew up on the outskirts of the park to service the needs of motorists. Fragile ecosystems in the park began to deteriorate under the weight of increased traffic. Tourism in Glacier reached a nadir during the late 1960s, when a survey found that the average tourist spent only 25 hours in the park.

Glacier Park's backcountry is still not on the typical tourist's itinerary, and many people still zoom over Going-to-the-Sun Road on a cross-country road-trip blitz. But increased environmental awareness since the 1970s has multiplied the number of people who linger among Glacier's unique topography and wildlife haunts.

FLORA AND FAUNA

Glacier National Park rises from a high-plains ecosystem on the east to alpine tundra along the Continental Divide and back down to Pacific forests, all within 25 miles. It's an amazingly concentrated venue for viewing many of Montana's wide-ranging animals and plants.

FLORA

Plants, more than animals, reflect the quick-changing and numerous ecosystems in the park. Skirting Lake McDonald and other westside lakes are forests of red cedar, Douglas fir, and hemlock. Watch for skunk cabbages and bracken ferns in marshy lowlands. Farther up mountain slopes are extensive stands of lodgepole and deciduous cone-bearing larch, indicating an ongoing history of forest fires.

Along the Continental Divide are expanses of alpine tundra. The midsummer wildflower display, including lemon-yellow glacier lilies, dark blue gentians, pink heathers, and the greenish white spires of bear grass, is spectacular. Examine rocky outcrops for colorful lichens.

The east side of the park is much drier, with aspen commingling with the dominating conifers. Wildflowers include red and white geraniums, Indian paintbrush, gaillardia, and pasqueflowers.

FAUNA

Grizzly bears are the most talked-about animal in the park, but they are much less numerous than the smaller black bears. Both species deserve respect. Recognize grizzly bears by the huge shoulder muscles, which form a substantial hump just behind the neck. Generally a mottled brown color, grizzlies also have a dish-shaped face. Black bears aren't always black but are often brown or cinnamon-colored. At 200 pounds, they are one-third the size of their grizzly brethren.

Mountain goats haunt the peaks and escarpments of Glacier Park. Near Logan Pass, they gather at natural salt licks in the cliffs above the road. Bighorn sheep, a few wolves, white-tailed deer, and moose are other large residents. Near streams, watch for beavers and river otters. Hoary marmots abound along hiking trails, and ground squirrels nose into pant legs and lunch bags at every picnic area.

Ospreys and bald eagles are the park's principal birds of prey. Watch for water ouzels, or "dippers," near streams; they're not drowning themselves, but diving and bouncing around underwater looking for food. A hatch of ptarmigans sauntering across the road often brings traffic to a halt.

ACCOMMODATIONS

The enormous lodges built by the Great Northern Railway still stand at East Glacier, Waterton, and Many Glacier, and they have become near trademarks for the park. These old lodges, along with the Swiss chalet–style Lake McDonald Lodge, are tremendously evocative and charming, but rooms aren't cheap, and for the money the amenities aren't great. That said, you simply must stay in at least one of these old landmarks. (But don't try to bring a dog along; no pets are allowed in park lodgings.) See specific areas in the following sections for accommodations details; see *Information* below for central reservations numbers.

There are good campsites at each entry to the park and at lakeside recreation areas.

Motels abound just outside the park boundaries, particularly near the west entrance.

In the backcountry, the Sperry and Granite Park Chalets are accessible only by trail and require reservations far in advance.

BACKCOUNTRY TRAVEL

Although most travelers stick to scenic drives and day hikes, Glacier's backcountry makes up over 95 percent of the park, and many visitors come back year after year to explore these remote trails. In fact, backcountry travel has increased in recent years, causing environmental impacts that have necessitated more regulations.

Prepare well for such an outing; you'll need a backcountry permit allowing you to camp at designated backcountry campgrounds

BEAR GRASS

Bear grass covers the slopes of Glacier National Park in July and August. Not every summer brings a bumper crop, however, and that has less to do with the weather than it does with the plant's life cycle. An individual bear grass plant blooms only once every seven years. Some years the torch-like stalks are abundant; other years there's a mere scattering.

Bear grass, which is relatively resistant to fire, is often the first plant to grow after a fire, sprouting from rhizomes just below the surface of the ground. Like many other native plants, it needs periodic burns to produce strong new growth.

Native Americans used the long, tough leaves of the plant (a member of the lily family) for trading, especially with Pacific Coast tribes, who wove the leaves into clothing and watertight baskets. Some tribes also roasted and ate the root.

Although bears don't eat bear grass, elk and mountain goats do.

© JUDY JEWELL

Bear grass is a highlight of Glacier's summer wildflower display.

(backcountry information line 406/888-7857 mid-Mar.–Oct., $5 per person per night, $2.50 youth 8–15, plus $30 per trip reservation fee, reservations accepted starting Apr. 16). During the initial planning stages of a backpacking trip, be sure to visit the park website. Here you'll find a backcountry application and detailed strategies for getting a permit for your ideal trip, a map detailing all backcountry campgrounds and noting which sites can be reserved, and lots of good information about backcountry safety.

Although waiting until you're at the park to get a permit will save you the $30 reservation fee, it may severely limit your choices of where you can camp. Backcountry permits are available at the following locations:

- Apgar Backcountry Permit Center (daily May–Oct.; during off-season, permits are available at Park Headquarters on weekdays and at the Apgar Visitor Center on weekends)

- St. Mary Visitor Center (daily late May–mid-Sept.)

- Many Glacier and Two Medicine Ranger Stations (daily late May–mid-Sept.)

- Polebridge Ranger Station (daily early June–mid-Sept.)

- Waterton Lakes National Park Visitor Reception Centre (daily early June–mid-Sept., payment by credit card only—no cash). Waterton staff are only authorized to issue trips that start at Chief Mountain or Goat Haunt.

Most hikers visit the backcountry in July and August; depending on the amount of snowfall the previous winter, even early July hikers can expect to encounter snow on the trails or dangerous high-water stream crossings.

A guide service, Glacier Guides (406/387-5555 or 800/521-7238, www.glacierguides.com), is permitted to lead trips in Glacier's backcountry.

INFORMATION

The park service distributes a free **Vacation Planner** at the park gates and neighboring tourist centers; it's also posted on the park's website. It contains a good overview of current information on rates, programs, recreation, and services. Another helpful source is the commercial site at www.americanparknetwork.com.

For reservations at any of Glacier's and Waterton's lodges or motels, call 406/892-2525 or visit www.glacierparkinc.com, the website of Glacier Park Inc. (GPI, the official concessionaire in charge of lodging and transportation in the park). Sperry and Granite Park Chalets are operated by Belton Chalets (888/345-2649, www.sperrychalet.com, www.graniteparkchalet.com).

Although the park is open daily year-round, most park services only operate from late May through September.

Classes

The **Glacier Institute** (406/755-1211, www.glacierinstitute.org) offers classes and seminars, Elderhostel programs (academic college classes for seniors), and daylong explorations year-round in and around the park. Workshops focus on many aspects of natural history as well as outdoor skills, including Wilderness First Responder, first aid, and EMT classes.

For spur-of-the-moment education about the park, take a hike with a ranger: Several hikes of varying intensity are offered daily in each area of the park during the summer.

GETTING THERE

Kalispell offers the closest airline service to the park. **Amtrak's Empire Builder** (800/872-7245, www.amtrak.com) provides train service, with daily stops at East Glacier (summer only), Belton (West Glacier), and Essex, on Highway 2 near the southern tip of the park.

Intercity bus lines can get you as close as Whitefish on the west and Great Falls to the east.

From Kalispell, you can also arrange a shuttle to the park by contacting **Airport Shuttle Service** (406/752-2842) or **Kalispell Taxi** (406/752-4022) or **Wild Horse Limousine** (406/756-2290 or 800/841-2391, www.wildhorselimo.com, $139 to Apgar). Rental cars

are available in Kalispell, Whitefish, and Great Falls.

GETTING AROUND

The spectacular road through the park, the Going-to-the-Sun Road, is closed by snow during the winter months, and spring and fall are devoted to road repair. The road is generally open from mid-June to late September. Be sure to gas up before entering the park; there are no gas stations in the park. Highway 2, which skirts the southern border of the park, is open year-round, as is the Outside North Fork Road leading to Polebridge.

Park Shuttle

Since the summer of 2007, the park has operated a free shuttle bus along the Going-to-the-Sun Road (buses every 15–30 minutes 6:45 A.M.–11:45 P.M. July 1–Labor Day). Although you are still allowed to drive along the road, the shuttle is a great option if you're out for sightseeing or hiking. Three shuttle routes—Apgar, Lake McDonald, and St. Mary Valley—combine to make stops at all visitor centers, campgrounds, and trailheads.

Since 2004, Going-to-the-Sun Road has been the site of extensive road repairs (it's a high-elevation road built during the era of Model T Fords, and it direly needed attention). The shuttle is one way to avoid some of the construction hassle and to avoid the environmental impact of heavy auto traffic.

Commercial Van Tours

The park's 1930s-era red rolltop buses, operated by GPI, take visitors on tours of the park with stops at all of Glacier's lodges and inns. In nice weather the canvas tops roll back to create a sort of convertible. A variety of tours are offered (406/892-2525, www.glacierparkinc.com, $65 for an 8-hour tour). These buses are favorites of many longtime parkgoers; after several years of being out of service for repairs, the fleet is up and running again.

Glacier Park Inc. also runs van shuttles connecting the St. Mary Visitor Center (and the free Going-to-the-Sun Road shuttle) with

GOING-TO-THE-SUN ROAD REPAIRS

When Glacier National Park was first developed as a tourist destination, it was at the behest of the Great Northern Railway, which built the park hotels and ferried visitors in and out of the park on their trains. Because there were no roads, parkgoers got around on horseback. The backcountry chalets were originally used by these horseback travelers.

Rather than keep the park as a rather high-end getaway for wealthy urbanites, the park's first superintendent, William Logan, supported the idea of building a road across the park. This was in the early 1920s, when automobile travel was just becoming commonplace, and cars were relatively small and narrow.

Even building a road to accommodate Model T traffic was a terrific feat. Especially around the Garden Wall, the cliffs are sheer and the access difficult. It took 11 years to build the road, which stretches 50 miles across the park with one big switchback called "the Loop".

The Going-to-the-Sun Road has held up pretty well, given the harsh climate and its cliff-hanging architecture, but it has been subject to considerable wear and tear.

A big push to repair the road began in 2004 with work concentrated along the 11-mile stretch of road that traverses through alpine terrain, where the terrain is steep, the pavement is narrow, and there is little to no shoulder. Repair work is at its peak in late spring (until mid-June) and early fall (after mid-September). Between mid-June and mid-September, traffic delays of 30 minutes or so occur during peak visitor hours. Expect longer delays during the early morning, evening, and night.

The repair project is expected to continue until about 2012. In **summer 2009**, roadwork is scheduled to occur west of Logan Pass between Haystack Creek and Big Bend. Weather permitting, the entire road will be open for public vehicle traffic from Friday, June 19, to Monday, September 21, 2009.

In **summer 2010,** roadwork is scheduled to occur west of Logan Pass between Big Bend and Logan Pass. Weather permitting, the entire road will be open for public vehicle traffic from Friday, June 18, to Monday, September 20, 2009.

Repairs will preserve the historic quality of the road, including its RV-prohibitive width. For project updates and road reports, visit www.nps.gov/glac.

Many Glacier, Two Medicine, East Glacier, and Waterton. These are not free—it's $8 from Many Glacier to St. Mary.

From East Glacier, **Sun Tours** (406/226-9220 or 800/786-9220, www.glaciersun-tours.com) offers interpretive tours of the park from a Native American perspective. Tours highlight Blackfeet culture and history and how that culture and history relate to the park's natural features.

Vehicle Restrictions

Because Going-to-the-Sun Road is narrow and tortuous by modern standards, there is a limit on the size of vehicles allowed between Avalanche Campground on the western side of the Continental Divide and Sun Point to the east. All vehicles (including towed campers) must measure less than 21 feet in length and less than eight feet in width (including mirrors). Vehicles taller than 10 feet may have trouble traveling westbound from Logan Pass to the Loop because of rock overhangs.

Bicycles are not allowed on Going-to-the-Sun Road from 11 A.M. to 4 P.M. between June 15 and Labor Day. Contact the National Park Service for other cycling restrictions.

PETS

Although pets are permitted on leashes in park campgrounds and parking areas, they are not allowed on the trails, in the backcountry, or in any park buildings. They must not be left unattended.

West Glacier and the Flathead River Middle Fork

The Middle Fork of the Flathead River runs out of the Bob Marshall and Great Bear Wilderness Areas and along the southwest border of the park to West Glacier. Along the edge of the park, the tiny town of **Essex** is home to a classic old hotel.

SIGHTS

Save up your money for a **helicopter ride** over the park. **Glacier Heli-Tours** (406/387-4141 or 800/879-9310, $90 and up), located across the highway from the Vista Motel, is a reliable operator.

Head about 35 miles southeast on Highway 2 to visit the **goat lick,** a mineral-laden cliff that provides goats with salt. A parking area near milepost 182 vents onto a short trail to the overlook. Spring is the big mineral-licking season; evenings in early June are certain to keep visitors entranced with billy, nanny, and kid goats. Binoculars help.

The relatively gentle **Marias Pass** marks the Continental Divide on Highway 2, between Essex and East Glacier. Salish tribes living west of the Continental Divide traditionally traveled over this pass on yearly trips to hunt buffalo. After the Blackfeet Indians moved to prairies east of the park in the late 1700s, they consolidated their hold over the entire area; Marias Pass became the scene of bloody battles when Salish hunting parties encountered Blackfeet warriors.

When James J. Hill was planning the route of the Great Northern Railway, he heard rumors of a lost pass over the Continental Divide. In the winter of 1889, railroad surveyor John J. Stevens found Marias Pass and deemed it navigable by rail.

RECREATION
Hiking

Most of the hikes in this part of Glacier are long backpacking trips on little-used trails into wild country. Animals, including bears, abound in these woods and stream bottoms. Glacier National Park maps show trails along every creek. Those planning to hike in the area should seek up-to-date trail information and permits, which are required for overnight hikes, from the backcountry permit station at Apgar.

A couple of shorter hikes originate at the unstaffed Walton Ranger Station, near Essex. Hike to **Ole Creek** and follow the trail as far as you like. The same trailhead provides access to the **Scalplock Lookout,** four unrelentingly steep miles to great views.

Leave the highway about two miles east of the goat lick to find a trail into the Great Bear Wilderness Area.

Rafting

Several white-water companies are based in West Glacier. Float trips on the Middle Fork of the Flathead account for most of their scheduled outings, though arrangements can be made to float the South Fork (in the Bob Marshall Wilderness Area) or the North Fork (in the northwest corner of Glacier Park). Half-day and full-day trips along the lower stretch of the Middle Fork are good family floats, with great scenery and some white water. The river's upper stretch is a wild four- to six-day trip (around $900).

Glacier Raft Co. (406/888-5454 or 800/235-6781, www.glacierraftco.com) gets good recommendations from local folks. It and other operators offer similar trips and prices: **Glacier Wilderness Guides** (406/387-5555 or 800/521-7238, www.glacierguides.com); **Great Northern Whitewater** (406/387-5340 or 800/735- 7897, www.gnwhitewater.com); **Wild River Adventures** (406/387-9453 or 800/700-7056, www.riverwild.com). Daylong floats run $77–85; half days are $45–50. Each of these companies will provide longer trips, with the option of adding hikes and horseback rides to the river run.

The Middle Fork is a Wild and Scenic River, and this official designation is particularly apt in its upper reaches in the Bob Marshall and Great

MOOSE NEWS

There's never any doubt when you've seen a moose. With its big rack, its long legs, and its sheer size, the moose is one of North America's most distinctive animals. No matter how comical it may look, nor how much it makes you think of Bullwinkle, a moose, which stands about six feet high at the shoulder and weighs about a thousand pounds, is not to be taken lightly.

The word *moose* comes from the animal's Algonquian Indian name, which means "twig-eater." And that's what you'll usually see them doing, because it takes a big bundle of twigs to satisfy a moose's hunger. During the summer they more often browse for food underwater and can be seen standing in marshes or shallow lakes, dipping their faces in and out of the water. You may also see a moose taking a swim across a lake. Curiously, moose do not have teeth in the front of their upper jaw; they use their thick sturdy tongues and lips to pull the leaves from a branch, then crush the food with their six pairs of molars and six pairs of premolars.

Because of the way a moose's eyes are set toward the sides of its head, the animal has a rather large blind spot to its front. This is most likely why it has the reputation of being nearsighted. Its eyes move independently (one can roll forward while the other goes back)... go ahead, try doing that yourself!

Only male moose have antlers. Also, bull moose have light brown hair above the eyes and black faces, while a cow moose's face is uniformly light brown.

Moose live across western Montana and are commonly seen in the North Fork area of Glacier National Park and just outside of West Yellowstone.

No matter how adorable or goofy a moose looks, remember that it's a wild animal, and a very large wild animal at that. They have the reputation of being fearless and unpredictable. Males can be particularly aggressive, and females are very protective of their young. Check out www.mooseworld.com for more details.

Bear Wilderness Areas. It's possible to fly in to float this wilderness river; the Schaefer Meadows airstrip is near the river in the Bob Marshall.

The wilderness stretches of the river are not easy, and they can be dangerous for novices. Even the lower reaches are better floated in a raft or kayak than a canoe, and anyone with questionable skills should sign on with an outfitter. Early summer is the best time to float the Middle Fork; water levels are high, but not at flood stage, and some of the chill has gone out of the air.

Fishing

The stretch of the Middle Fork of the Flathead paralleling Highway 2 isn't a particularly noteworthy fishing stream, but its upper reaches in the Great Bear Wilderness are loaded with trout. These aren't official fishing waters of the national park, so a Montana fishing license is required. The raft companies listed above serve double duty as fishing guides.

Bicycling

During the summer, the Forest Service roads and ski trails around Essex are suitable for mountain biking, and the **Izaak Walton Inn** (406/888-5700) in Essex has bikes for rent.

◖ Cross-Country Skiing Around the Izaak Walton Inn

Ski trails around the Izaak Walton Inn in Essex are free to hotel guests; nonguests can pay a few dollars for a day pass. More than 20 miles of trails are groomed regularly, and though most of them are geared toward novice or intermediate skiers, a few runs are studded with face-plant opportunities, even for good skiers. If there's fresh powder, leave the trails for a while and practice making graceful turns down the sides of Dickey Bowl. (It's right behind the trail system.) Most trails are also OK for snowshoers. It's worth venturing away from the inn's trail system into Glacier National Park for at least one day of skiing. Guests who'd rather not go it alone can

© JUDY JEWELL

GLACIER NATIONAL PARK

Lodge your family in a caboose at the Izaak Walton Inn.

sign on to a guided tour. Après-ski at the Izaak Walton means a visit to the inn's sauna, then hanging out in the lobby to watch the trains go by. There's usually enough snow for skiing from Thanksgiving through mid-April.

Other Cross-Country Skiing Trails

Trail networks are also maintained by the **Glacier Wilderness Resort** and the **Glacier Highland Motel.** The Glacier Highland's seven miles of trails start right behind this West Glacier motel; stop in the office to get a map.

The 13 miles of trails near the Glacier Wilderness Resort are between West Glacier and Essex. Skiers follow old sections of Highway 2 and climb to Garry Lookout.

Go to Marias Pass for excellent skiing at the Continental Divide; it's as gentle as a major pass can be, with terrain suitable for beginners and intermediates.

Golfing

Glacier View Golf Club (406/888-5471) is just north of Highway 2 at West Glacier. It's a public 18-hole course looking onto the mountains.

ACCOMMODATIONS

Most of the motels around West Glacier are small, family-run places. It's no surprise that they fill up quickly during the summer. The lodgings in Apgar Village, at the park's west entrance, are just a couple of miles from West Glacier.

$50-100

The view from the **Vista Motel** (406/888-5311 or 800/837-7101, www.glaciervistamotel.com, mid-May–mid-Sept., $67–140) is grand. Perched on a bluff overlooking Highway 2 and the peaks of Glacier, this is a hard one to miss on the drive in from Kalispell. The view *is* the best thing about this place (the Vista is showing its now-considerable age), and that, plus convenience, friendliness, and a heated pool, makes it a good bet.

The **West Glacier Motel** (200 Going-to-the-Sun Road, 406/888-5662, www.westglacier.com, mid-May–late Sept., rooms $82 and up, cabins $141 and up) is just off Highway 2 in the cluster of businesses near the park entrance. Its woodsy location on the Flathead River provides easy access to fishing and float trips, which can be arranged by management. Rooms have a budget ambiance, if not price.

Over $100

For years it was impossible to stay at the Swiss-style **⟨⟨ Belton Chalet** (406/888-5000 or 888/235-8665, www.beltonchalet.com, $145 and up), built in 1910 when the park opened, closed for years, and renovated and reopened in 2000. The rooms still have an old-fashioned charm, which means no TVs or phones; one modern touch is the addition of spa services, quite nice after a night on the train or a day of hiking. A three-bedroom cottage ($299) is great for larger groups. This is where early park visitors debarked from the train, and Amtrak still stops here daily. During the winter season, from early October to late May, only cottage rentals are available ($99–225).

The **Great Northern Resort** (406/387-5340 or 800/735-7897, $260–295) offers several chalets, each chalet containing a kitchenette, fireplace, and barbecue and two or three bedrooms. The owners also operate a white-water raft outfitting service and can arrange horseback riding and fishing trips. During spring and fall, rates drop to as low as $99; in peak summer season a three-night stay is required.

Those who aren't bent on barreling right down Going-to-the-Sun Road would be wise to look 30 miles southeast to the **⟨⟨ Izaak Walton Inn** (406/888-5700, www.izaakwaltoninn.com) in Essex. The hotel was built by the Great Northern in 1939 to house railroad workers. (Essex was, and still is, an important railroad post; it's where extra engines are added to help trains over Marias Pass.) It's now popular with park visitors and has gained a cultlike standing among railroad buffs and cross-country skiers.

And well it should. The Izaak Walton is truly one of Montana's best getaways. Amtrak's Empire Builder stops a stone's throw from the half-timbered hotel, and groomed ski trails run for miles. Energetic skiers can take a guided tour in the park or can drive to the unplowed Going-to-the-Sun Road or to East Glacier for a ski trip to Two Medicine Lake. Cross-country skis and snowshoes are available for rent. In summer the lodge is open to hikers, anglers (this isn't called the Izaak Walton for nothing), and mountain bikers (bikes also for rent).

Even if you don't have time or the inclination to head into the wilderness, the Izaak Walton has atmosphere to spare; you'll love curling up in the lobby by the fireplace or having a drink in the friendly downstairs bar. Most guests eat at the lodge restaurant.

Rooms in the lodge all have private baths and are $137–255 during high season (June 16–Sept. 15 and Dec. 16–March 31). The Izaak Walton has also renovated some cabooses and plunked them down on a hillside across the tracks. The cabooses sleep four, have kitchenettes (which can save you some money on restaurant meals if you're willing to schlep groceries to Essex), and cost $690 for a three-night stay. (Be sure to ask about the cancellation policy; it's extremely strict.) None of the rooms have TVs, radios, or telephones, but there is a Finnish sauna. If you arrive via Amtrak, the Izaak Walton also has cars for rent.

Camping

All of West Glacier's campgrounds are private RV enterprises ($12–30 per night). You can find a Forest Service campground, **Big Creek** (406/387-3800, www.fs.fed.us/r1/flathead, $12), about 20 miles northwest of town, at the north end of Camas Creek Road. There are also many coveted campsites in Glacier Park itself.

Lake Five Resort (540 Belton Stage Rd., 406/387-5601, www.lakefiveresort.com, RV site $40–45, tepees $50–60, cabins from $110) is on Belton Stage Road a little way north of Highway 2. It's a pleasant Montana-style lakeside resort complete with cabins, boat rentals, and lake swimming. The season runs mid-May through mid-September.

North American RV Park and Campground (406/387-5800 or 800/704-4266, www.northamericanrvpark.com, mid-Apr.–mid-Sept.), between Coram and West Glacier, rents a few clean and cozy yurts ($30–40) and small camping cabins ($50); for both of these options, be prepared to trek to the bathhouse. The park also has plenty of room for RVs ($25–35).

Tent campers and RVers alike will be glad for the **West Glacier KOA** (355 Half Moon Flats Rd., 406/387-5341 or 800/562-3313, www.westglacierkoa.com, tent $29, RV $29–47, cabin $62–72) and will find it handy (two miles west of the park entrance), well-equipped, and large. Even bigger and closer to the park, **Glacier Campground** (12070 Hwy. 2 W., 406/387-5689, www.glaciercampground.com, tent $19, RV $20–27, cabin $35–45) is noted for its evening barbecues and a generally high activity level on the sprawling forested campground. The season for both the KOA and Glacier Campground runs May through September.

FOOD

Stop in for a good meal in a lovely atmosphere at the Belton Chalet's (**Grill Dining Room** (406/888-5000, dinner nightly, $20–30). Here you can dine on buffalo meatloaf doused with chipotle gravy. Lighter meals (that same tasty meatloaf, made into a sandwich, about $10) and a variety of microbrews are available from the adjoining **Belton Taproom.**

A good bet in an unlikely spot (at Glacier Campground) is the **West Glacier Cafe** (12070 Hwy. 2 W., 406/387-4134, dinner Wed.–Sun.), run by a culinary-school teacher and one of her students. All meals are made from scratch using fresh food; try a grilled pizza.

The food at the **Izaak Walton Inn** (406/888-5700, all meals daily, dinner $11–25) is immensely satisfying after a day of cross-country skiing, and it has just enough of a comfort-food factor to keep you eating more. Expect such homey entrées as chicken and dumplings; grilled pork medallions with huckleberry barbecue sauce provide a satisfying nod to gourmet sensibilities here. The dining room looks right out onto the tracks, and railroad workers mix with Essex neighbors, railroad buffs, and cross-country skiers in the dining room. It's a great place to stop for a meal, and it'll make most diners want to sign up for a hotel room.

TRANSPORTATION

Amtrak stops daily at West Glacier's Belton Station (8:23 P.M. westbound and 8:16 A.M. eastbound) and Essex Station (7:41 P.M. westbound and 8:55 A.M. eastbound).

Car rentals are available at **Glacier Highland Resort** (406/888-5427 or 800/766-0811), just across from the depot.

North Fork of the Flathead River

The northwestern border of Glacier National Park is formed by the North Fork of the Flathead River. Dirt roads inside and outside the park run up the valley to the small settlement of Polebridge; the inside road, open only in summer, is especially spectacular in a scary way. Since early in the park's history, the hamlet of **Polebridge** has been a quiet neighbor just outside Glacier's boundary. Many residents of Polebridge have fought development that would bring them fully into the tourist hubbub. There's no electricity running up the North Fork, and Polebridge has some of Montana's finest outhouses.

Don't look for naturalist-led day hikes or bus tours of this northwest corner of Glacier; it's the park's least developed valley, although perhaps also its most threatened. Curiously, the Inside North Fork Road is the park's oldest, built in 1901 when oil was struck near Kintla Lake.

Threats of road building, logging, dams, mineral exploration, and general development continue in the non–national park areas of the North Fork. In early 2008, oil giant BP dropped a controversial plan by to extract coal-bed methane from a site just over the border in Canada after lots of activism by North Forkers and politicking by Montana's senators Max Baucus and Jon Tester.

SIGHTS

McGee Meadows

Five miles up Camas Creek Road from Apgar, McGee Meadows is a marshy magnet for wildlife. Moose are particularly fond of such boggy areas and may be spotted by quiet evening visitors. The road here is relatively high and exposed, yielding good views of the park's mountains. To the west there are a couple of hiking trails from Camas Creek Road into the Apgar Mountains. Howe Ridge is to the east, and ridge runners must hike up from the Inside North Fork Road; the trail past shallow Howe Lake crosses moose and beaver habitat.

Bowman Lake

Bowman Lake is one of the park's prettiest and least visited. (There's a reason for this—it's at the end of a long, rough, narrow dirt road.) Long and thin and surrounded by mountains, this is a good spot for photography and reflection. Hiking trails start at the Bowman Lake campground and head seven miles along the lakeshore to the head of the lake (then up to Brown Pass and other trails), or up into the mountains that come right down to the lake. The six-mile trail to Numa Lookout combines the two: It starts along the lake then climbs nearly 3,000 feet to the lookout. The campground here is usually pretty uncrowded; RVs are not recommended, and it's a good place to follow bear-country precautions.

Stargazing

Spend a night up the North Fork and look at the stars. With no electric lights to compete, they're particularly bright. The local café and saloon in Polebridge is called the Northern Lights, which are commonly visible.

RECREATION

Hiking

A flat seven-mile trail edges Bowman Lake's northwest shore and is a good up-and-back walk for a family. Extend the trip by continuing past the lake on a relatively gentle creekside climb to **Brown Pass.** (It's another seven miles between the backcountry campground at

the head of Bowman Lake and the Brown Pass campground.) From the pass, hikers can cross the divide and continue east to Goat Haunt, on Waterton Lake, or take the high road back west to Kintla Lake.

Or try this variation: Start at **Kintla Lake,** hike 32 miles east to Goat Haunt, and then head south to a terminus at Logan Pass. Cut this trip shorter by taking the boat from Goat Haunt up to Waterton. The country between Upper Kintla Lake and Brown Pass is phenomenal, and one of the places a hiker is most likely to see black bears or grizzlies. The Hole-in-the-Wall Campground, one mile west of the Continental Divide along this trail, may be the park's finest and is certainly one of the most remote.

The **Numa Lookout** trail, five uphill miles to Numa Ridge, is a good place to walk slowly with an eye out for wildlife and good views of Bowman Lake and the Livingston Range. Catch the trail at Bowman Lake Campground.

Also starting at the foot of Bowman Lake, a trail skirts Numa Ridge and runs almost six miles to tiny **Akokala Lake.**

Fishing and Boating

Fish the lakes up the North Fork for magnificent scenery and an occasional cutthroat trout. Most anglers take to boats on Bowman Lake, which is open to motorboats with engines below 10 horsepower; no motorized boats are allowed in Kintla Lake. Canoeists will go nuts over both of these lakes—they're long, with miles of animal-sheltering shoreline to explore.

Cross-Country Skiing

The broad North Fork Valley is just as beautiful, and even more isolated, when it's covered with snow. Skiing is generally good here because cold temperatures keep the snow powdery. And it can get *cold*; a -35°F morning at the North Fork Hostel may sharply reduce outhouse visits, and early morning ski tours may not start quite so early.

Two ski trails start at the Polebridge Ranger Station: one, suitable for beginners, heads three miles north to Big Prairie; the other follows the six-mile-long unplowed road to Bowman Lake.

Stop in at the ranger station before heading out; they'll tell you whether it's safe to ski onto Bowman Lake.

ACCOMMODATIONS AND FOOD

There isn't much to say about lodgings in the North Fork, except that Polebridge's ☾ **North Fork Hostel and Square Peg Ranch** (406/888-5241 or 406/253-4321, www.nfhostel.com, closed March, $15 dorm bed, $45 cabin, $80 log home) is a great place for a budget traveler or anyone with a relaxed sense of sociability. Lights and kitchen appliances are powered by propane, wood stoves provide the heat, guests come prepared with sleeping bags and food, and the outhouse is plastered with reading material. The hostel rents mountain bikes, canoes, skis, and snowshoes, and sometimes can, with advance notice, arrange a $50 shuttle from the Amtrak stop in West Glacier. The **Northern Lights Saloon and Café** is nearby and offers light meals and drinks.

The other place to stay in town, the **Polebridge Mercantile** (406/888-5105, cabins $30–35, tepees $20), is not much more expensive and no fancier than the hostel. Anyplace else, these propane-powered cabins would be the really *cool* place in town to stay, but here they've got strong competition from the hostel. Either way, bring a sleeping bag or bedding and basic cooking utensils; don't even bother with a hair dryer or travel iron. The **bakery** in the Mercantile is a great place for specialty breads, pastries, sandwiches, and coffee.

During the summer, the café next to the mercantile is worth a stop for its conviviality and good food. The **Northern Lights** (406/888-5669, dinner nightly Memorial Day–Labor Day, dinner about $10–12) pours beer as well as coffee and is a comfortable Polebridge hangout: It's the only restaurant for miles around, which means it can get crowded—in midsummer, come prepared for a wait.

Camping

Bowman Lake Campground ($15 in summer, $10 primitive camping mid-Sept.–Nov., no reservations) is the largest and most popular in the North Fork. Hiking trails wander off in all directions, including an easy one along the lakeshore. The campground at **Kintla Lake** ($15 summer, $10 primitive camping in May and mid-Sept.–Nov., no reservations) is small, with only 13 sites and fewer trails to choose from, but equally desirable. Both of these campgrounds are fairly developed national park campgrounds, although they don't have the parking-lot quality of those in the more traveled areas of Glacier.

Other roadside campgrounds a notch down in development are **Big Creek** (406/387-3800, www.fs.fed.us/r1/flathead, $12), a Forest Service campground on the Outside North Fork Road near the Camas Creek entrance to the park, and **Logging Creek** and **Quartz Creek**, Glacier National Park campgrounds ($10 July–Nov.) on Inside North Fork Road between Apgar and Polebridge. These are primitive campgrounds; bring your own water.

PRACTICALITIES
Information

The periodically staffed **Polebridge Ranger Station** is right near the no-longer-pole-constructed bridge over the North Fork. Stop here for backcountry permits, trail information, or a chat about the local wolf packs.

Transportation

Drive in from the park on Camas Creek or Inside North Fork roads; the Inside North Fork is rougher, but there are some campgrounds along it. From Columbia Falls, the Outside North Fork Road, with good views of the Livingston Range, leads to Polebridge. Blankenship Road connects the Outside North Fork Road with West Glacier. In the winter, Outside North Fork Road and Blankenship Road are plowed.

Lake McDonald Valley

The forests surrounding Lake McDonald are Glacier National Park at its most Pacific. Western red cedar and western hemlock form the climax forest; Douglas fir, larch, pine, and spruce add diversity.

The oldest rocks on the west side of the park are around the head of Lake McDonald. These slatelike rocks were laid down under seawater. Up the Going-to-the-Sun Road, greenish mudstone of the Appekunny Formation developed in shallower water. Farther east and higher on the slopes, the rocks of the Grinnell Formation were originally mudflats. They turned red when exposure to the air oxidized their ferrous minerals.

Once the road begins climbing, it moves into the Empire Formation, grayish-green rocks deposited underwater, and then to the Helena (Siyeh) limestone, which comes into view near the Loop. The Helena Formation is dotted with stromatolites, cabbage-like fossil traces of blue-green algae.

Lake McDonald Valley has all the earmarks of glacial action; it's long, straight, and U-shaped. The lake is 10 miles long, one mile wide, and more than 400 feet deep. Dozens of hiking trails take in everything from damp old-growth forests to alpine meadows.

SIGHTS
Apgar

Just inside the park entrance at West Glacier, Apgar Village greets visitors with an information center, gift shop, motels, a campground, cafés, and lovely Lake McDonald. The National Park Service purchased much of the town in 1930, but part of it is still privately owned.

◖ Going-to-the-Sun Road

It took practically 20 years to build this road; when it opened for travel in 1933, it was an instant hit. The road, which starts its 52-mile run over the spine of the Rockies at Apgar, is a spectacular drive, even when clogged with

traffic. Glacier may be a hiker's park at heart, but for those without the capacity or the time for trail walking, the Going-to-the-Sun Road provides a good view of the park's muscles and bones. The free park shuttle allows motorists to actually enjoy the views rather than concentrating on the road.

From Lake McDonald the road follows McDonald Creek to the east and slightly uphill. The grade increases after Logan Creek, and it becomes genuinely steep as it approaches the Loop, a big switchback that brings the road under the Garden Wall, which it follows to the Continental Divide at Logan Pass. Approaching the pass from the west, it's easy to follow the changes in vegetation and geology: The lush coniferous forests near Lake McDonald give way to shrubs and scattered pines, and distinctive green and red mudstone and buff-colored limestone replace the dark shalelike rocks near the lake.

Lake McDonald

In 1895 an early homesteader, George Snyder, built a small hotel by Lake McDonald, 15 years before the area became a national park. John Lewis, a Columbia Falls furrier, took over Snyder's hotel, built the present lodge in 1914, and decorated it with hunting trophies (most of which still stare down from timbered beams and balconies). The artist Charlie Russell had a cabin nearby, and it has long been rumored that the pictographs around the lodge's fireplace are his work.

One needn't be a hotel guest to lounge in the **Lake McDonald Lodge** lobby or in the chairs overlooking the lake, and it's a comfortable stop after a day of hiking.

Lake McDonald has long been the territory of tourist cruise boats (406/257-2426, www.glacierparkboats.com, 11 A.M., 1:30, 3:30, 5:30, and 7 P.M. daily, adults $14, children $7). Tours are an hour long; the evening tour is especially popular, and sunsets can be phenomenal.

Evening programs by park naturalists

© JUDY JEWELL

McDonald Creek runs along Glacier National Park's Going-to-the-Sun Road.

are scheduled nightly at Lake McDonald Lodge, Apgar Campground, and Fish Creek Campground. These are usually quite interesting, and they're free.

RECREATION
Hiking

A forested trail starts at Fish Creek Campground and follows a ridge along the **west bank of Lake McDonald,** eventually looping around the muddy head of the lake and ending up at the lodge. It's 6.7 miles from the campground to the lodge; a mile-long walk from the campground goes to **Rocky Point,** yielding good views of the lake and the mountains.

Hike from the Lake McDonald Lodge up to **Sperry Chalet** (6.2 miles one-way) or three steep miles farther to **Lake Ellen Wilson** or, on another spur, to **Sperry Glacier.** The trail continues on another 10 miles from Lake Ellen Wilson (which has a backcountry campground) over Gunsight Pass and returns to Going-to-the-Sun Road at the Jackson Glacier viewpoint, five miles east of Logan Pass. From this point,

it's another long day's hike over Piegan Pass and down the other side of the Continental Divide to the Many Glacier Hotel.

From the same trailhead near the lodge, paths branch off to shallow **Fish Lake** (six miles round-trip), the **Mt. Brown Lookout** (a steep, arduous 10-mile round-trip), and Snyder Lake (4.5 miles in to a campground beside an emerald lake nestled in the mountains).

One of the park's easiest and most popular hikes takes in the western red cedar and hemlock forest near Avalanche Campground. The 0.7-mile-long, wheelchair-accessible **Trail of the Cedars** follows a boardwalk over the floor of the old-growth forest, past Avalanche Gorge, and returns via the campground. It's a splendid trail, even with crowds; solitude seekers will like it even better in the winter, when cross-country skiers may share the trail with moose.

The trail to **Avalanche Lake** starts near Avalanche Campground and the Trail of the Cedars and follows Avalanche Creek two miles through forest to the lake. Waterfalls draining Sperry Glacier tumble over the 1,500-foot wall, which encloses a cirque, and pour the glacial water into Avalanche Lake.

Bicycling

Because of heavy traffic and slim shoulders, bicycle travel along Going-to-the-Sun Road is restricted during the busy summer months. From June 15 to Labor Day, bikes are prohibited on the road between Apgar and Sprague Creek Campground, and between Logan Creek and Logan Pass, 11 A.M.–4 P.M. Logan Creek, at the base of the Loop, is about 10 miles from Sprague Creek Campground and about six miles from Avalanche Campground. Between Apgar and Logan Creek the road stays in the McDonald Creek Valley, climbing some but not dramatically. Shortly after it crosses Logan Creek, the road really takes off uphill. Expect the ride between Logan Creek and Logan Pass to take three hours, and expect to feel more exhilarated than exhausted upon reaching the summit.

Cyclists who'd rather not dodge the cars on Going-to-the-Sun Road can bike the paved trail between Apgar and the park entrance.

GLACIER NATIONAL PARK

Also starting in Apgar, Camas Creek Road heads up toward the North Fork area, and it is paved for the first 12 miles.

Boating and Fishing

Rent boats at the Apgar dock. Canoes and rowboats are $14 per hour, motorboats are $22. There's fishing tackle for rent at the boat dock, but the savvy angler won't bother with the few planted cutthroat or the lake trout that migrated over to Lake McDonald from Flathead Lake.

Horseback Riding

Swan Mountain Outfitters (877/888-5557) runs horseback rides in the park. Rides leave from corrals at **Apgar** (406/888-5010) and **Lake McDonald** (across the road from the lodge, 406/888-5121), and range from a $32 one-hour amble to a $135 daylong ride to Sperry Chalet. Call for specific destinations and departure times.

Cross-Country Skiing

In the winter, Going-to-the-Sun Road is plowed to the head of Lake McDonald. From the parking area there, it's possible to ski as far up the road as stamina permits. The skiing is technically easy, and there's usually some wildlife around. Pull off the main drag and follow the **Sacred Dancing Cascade** hiking trail or ski up to the **Trail of the Cedars.**

For a longer trip (about 12 miles), ski up Camas Creek Road, take a right at McGee Meadow, and return on the **Inside North Fork Road.** A final detour through the Fish Creek Campground to **Rocky Point** adds a couple of miles and a good view of Lake McDonald.

ACCOMMODATIONS
$50-100

The only moderately priced rooms in the area are in the woods alongside McDonald Creek at the **Apgar Village Lodge** (406/888-5484, www.westglacier.com, mid-May–Sept.), with older motel rooms (the cheapest ones without TVs or alarm clocks) running $78–108 and cabins for $94–250.

Hike seven miles from Logan Pass along

the Highline Trail to the backcountry **(Granite Park Chalet** (888/345-2649, www.graniteparkchalet.com, July–mid-Sept., $80 first person, $68 each additional person in room, $15 optional linen fee; reserve well in advance), built in 1914 and perched on an igneous outcropping at the north end of Garden Wall. Four trails lead to the chalet; the most popular is the stunningly beautiful, nearly level Highline Trail, which follows the base of the Garden Wall from Logan Pass. (Hikers with a fear of heights should note that in some places the Highline Trail hugs the edge of a cliff.) Other trails come in from the loop on Going-to-the-Sun Road (four miles), over Swiftcurrent Pass from Many Glacier (eight miles), and from Goat Haunt at the head of Waterton Lake (an approximately 23-mile backpacking trip via the northern extension of the Highline Trail).

Hikers generally bring their own sleeping bags, food, and water, although it is possible to rent bedding and purchase premade meals—be sure to do this via the website in advance of your trip. In lieu of electricity, there's a propane stove and a few propane lights. Guests may use the kitchen area to prepare their own food, and though there's no running water, guests are provided with filtered water to drink. It's also possible to spend an extra $15 for bed linens if you don't want to bring a sleeping bag.

Over $100

(Lake McDonald Lodge (406/892-2525, www.glacierparkinc.com, late May–late Sept., $114–160, reservations required) is perhaps the most charming of Glacier's lodges. It retains rugged, hunting-lodge touches, such as grizzly bear hides draped over the balcony railings, animal heads posted on massive timbered columns above the lobby, and a walk-in fireplace bordered by pictographs (rumored to have been drawn by Charlie Russell). The rooms aren't as comfortable as the lobby, however, and they're pretty spendy ($160). An adjoining motel and cabins are somewhat less expensive.

In Apgar Village, the **Village Inn** (406/892-

2525, www.glacierparkinc.com, late May–mid-Sept., $120–185) is also operated by Glacier Park Inc. The lakeside motel rooms are adequate, although nowhere near as charming as the Lake McDonald Lodge. Families may opt for a two-bedroom suite that sleeps six.

With a gorgeous setting and classic rustic mountain architecture, (**Sperry Chalet** (406/387-5654 or 888/345-2649, www.sperrychalet.com, mid-July–early Sept., $170 for one person, $115 for each additional person in room, includes meals, reservations essential), perched on a rocky ledge 6,560 feet above sea level that's popular with the local mountain goats, offers full-service backcountry lodging midway on a trail between Lake McDonald Lodge and Logan Pass; it's a 6.7-mile hike from Lake McDonald Lodge. Accommodations are rustic, with no heat, electricity, or running water, but come with three meals a day. Bedding is also provided, so there's no need to pack in a sleeping bag. Reservations must be made well in advance.

Camping

The **Apgar Campground** (early May–mid-Oct., $20; Apr. and mid-Oct.–Nov., primitive camping $10; winter camping free with park pass) is the park's largest and most bustling, although sites are laid out to provide a reasonable amount of privacy. Depending on how you look at it, it's either conveniently or annoyingly close to Apgar Village. Lake McDonald is a short walk away.

Just slightly off the beaten path, **Fish Creek Campground** (877/444-6777, www.recreation.gov, June–Labor Day, $23, reservations available with additional $9–10 fee) is a triple-looped jumble of trailers. It's off Camas Creek Road on the northwestern shore of Lake McDonald. Fish Creek is a handy base for day trips around the Lake McDonald area and up the North Fork of the Flathead River. If you get up early, there's seclusion enough for a bracing naked plunge into the lake (no showers at any park campgrounds).

Sprague Creek Campground (mid-May–mid-Sept., $20), on Going-to-the-Sun Road

about a mile west of Lake McDonald Lodge, is appealing to some because of its small size and by not permitting towed RVs, but it's actually less private and secluded than Apgar or Fish Creek. It is, however, a handy jumping-off point for bicyclists heading up the Going-to-the-Sun Road.

For a no-frills hike-in chalet, try the extremely popular Granite Park Chalet (see *Accommodations* section).

FOOD

The well-detailed **Russell's Fireside Dining Room**(Lake McDonald Lodge, 406/892-2525, 6:30–10 A.M., 11:30 A.M.–2 P.M., and 5–9:30 P.M. daily late May–late Sept., dinner $10–23, no reservations accepted) has a faux-hunting-lodge theme that strongly influences the dinner menu (think wild game). Even if you just stop in for a bowl of chili or a salad, the ambience (more than the passably decent food) makes it worth a visit. If the dining room seems to be just too expensive or too much of a production, the lodge's cozy **Stockade Lounge** (406/892-2525, 11:30 A.M.–midnight, under $10) is a good bet for a buffalo burger and a beer.

Across from the lodge, **Jammer Joe's Grill and Pizzeria** (11 A.M.–9:30 P.M. mid-June–early Sept., $6–12) serves good beer and tolerable food that's less expensive than the lodge dining room.

Don't turn up your nose at **Eddie's Cafe** (406/888-5361, 7 A.M.–9 P.M. daily early June–mid-Sept., $7–20); it's a good place to pick up lunch (sack lunches $9) before heading out on a hike. Desserts and ice cream are especially tempting here.

Camp stores at Apgar and the Lake McDonald Lodge complex stock essential groceries.

INFORMATION

The **Apgar Visitor Center** (406/888-7800) has park rangers on duty 8 A.M.–7 P.M. (shorter hours during the spring and fall, weekends during the winter) to answer questions and suggest hikes; pick up backcountry permits at the nearby permit office (406/888-5819).

TRANSPORTATION

Park shuttles depart from the Apgar Transit Center (6:45 A.M.–11:45 P.M., free), which serves as the transfer point between two of the three shuttle routes. The Apgar Route provides local access to Apgar Village, Fish Creek Campground, Apgar Campground, and the transit center. The Lake McDonald Route travels between the Apgar Transit Center and Logan Pass, making several stops along the way. At Logan Pass riders can transfer to the St. Mary Valley Route to continue along the Going-to-the-Sun Road. Although these are not interpretive tours (see *Commercial Van Tours* in the chapter introduction for these), shuttle rides provide a great way to get to and from hiking trails.

Logan Pass to St. Mary

From the Highline Trail at Logan Pass to Two Dog Flats around St. Mary Lake, the scenery on the east face of Glacier National Park is just as spectacular as, and more exposed than, that on the west side of the Continental Divide. Geology is suddenly lucid as red Grinnell rocks and the green rocks of the Appekunny Formation glow in the morning light bouncing off St. Mary Lake.

East of the pass, drying winds blow across stands of aspen and cottonwoods to the plains, which suddenly replace the mountains a few miles east of St. Mary.

SIGHTS
◖ Logan Pass

At 6,680 feet, Logan Pass is an alpine–arctic tundra environment. Just uphill from the visitors center, tiny wildflowers poke up through the July snow, the native grasses are stunningly green, and the glacier-cut mountains are close at hand. In a landscape so big, it's a surprise when your eye is drawn to tiny wildflowers, but they're captivating for their toughness. The nodding yellow glacier lily, which often pokes up through the snow, is emblematic of Logan Pass.

Even though the landscape here is shaped by a harsh climate, it's not able to withstand flower-picking or trampling by hordes of hikers. To learn more about alpine ecology, stop in for a naturalist's talk at the Logan Pass visitors center. Talks occur throughout the day from early June through Labor Day. The visitors center stays open as long as the road is passable, usually from June through September.

Glaciers started on either side of the Continental Divide at Logan Pass and eventually ran backward into each other. Rather than leaving a spiky arête (sharp ridge) like the Garden Wall (chiseled away on both sides), the wall was entirely eroded.

St. Mary Lake

Even nonhikers will want to stop at the **Sun Point** trailhead and walk a few yards to the "peak finder." Of the nine peaks visible from Sun Point, **Going-to-the-Sun Mountain** stands out at 9,942 feet. The mountain, whose name was taken for the road, recalls Napi, the Blackfoot Old Man, who left his home in the sun to help the Blackfeet. Once he had finished his work on earth, he returned home via this mountain.

Boat tours (406/257-2426, www.glacier-parkboats.com, 10 A.M., noon, 2, and 4 P.M. daily, 1.5-hour cruise, adults $20, children $14; 6:30 P.M. daily one-hour cruise, adults $14, children $7) of St. Mary Lake set out several times a day from the dock across from the Rising Sun complex. The 6:30 P.M. sunset cruise is popular, but unlike the daytime rides it's not accompanied by a park naturalist. Passengers on the 10 A.M. boat can enjoy an optional two-hour walk to St. Mary Falls with a guide and return later.

HIKES AROUND LOGAN PASS
Hidden Lake Overlook

Glacier's most popular trail is the boardwalk from Logan Pass to **Hidden Lake Overlook,**

© JUDY JEWELL

Catch the spectacular Highline Trail at Logan Pass.

a three-mile round-trip hike through delicate alpine meadows, home to marmots, ptarmigan, and mountain goats. The weather can be blustery up here, even in midsummer, and the 500-foot climb to more than 7,000 feet above sea level can be surprisingly fatiguing.

🄲 Highline Trail

For a fairly level trail that goes on for miles, the Highline Trail can't be beat. It's the main route to Granite Park chalet (7.6 miles), and it can be frustratingly crowded, but the above-timberline views, bear-grass meadows, and chattering marmots are absorbing enough to eclipse the other hikers. (Do note that there are some high ledges to traverse here; people hiking with young children and those with a fear of heights might want to give this trail a pass.)

HIKES AROUND ST. MARY LAKE
Sun Point

Walk out to Sun Point for a view of St. Mary Lake and the surrounding mountains. For visitors who aren't up to a long backcountry hike,

Sun Point is a good place to stretch your legs without exhausting yourself and get a dramatic view of the scenery. This was the site of the most elaborate of the Glacier's chalets; it fell into disuse and was dismantled in the late 1940s once Going-to-the-Sun Road became the focus of trips to the park. From Sun Point the trail skirts the lakeshore for less than a mile to **Baring Falls.**

Sunrift Gorge

Sunrift Gorge is on Baring Creek just above the falls; cap off the Sun Point walk by taking the spur trail and climbing to the gorge. Or, follow the lead of most gorge viewers and park in the Sunrift Gorge pullout and walk 50 yards up the path to the narrow chasm, formed not by erosion but by a vertical slip of the rock.

Siyeh Pass and Preston Park

Those in search of a *real* hike will want to continue past Sunrift Gorge to Siyeh Pass and Preston Park. This is no easy amble; the trail shoots up once it leaves Baring Creek, and Siyeh is Glacier's highest pass. As one would expect, persevering hikers are rewarded with great views and a delicate alpine environment. After passing alpine larch trees and wildflower meadows at Preston Park, the Siyeh Bend cut-off trail heads back to Going-to-the-Sun Road, making this a 12-mile hike. (Actually, most people do this hike in the opposite direction, which is easier uphill, but yields less-spectacular views.) Park naturalists lead 10.5-mile hikes from Siyeh Bend on Going-to-the-Sun Road about once a week during the summer (starting at 8:30 A.M., about 8 hours); it's one of the park's best naturalist-led hikes.

Gunsight Lake

An eight-mile hike to Gunsight Lake starts at either Sun Point, or more commonly at the Jackson Glacier Overlook west of St. Mary Lake on Going-to-the-Sun Road. There's a campground at Gunsight Lake; Gunsight Pass is another *steep* two miles up the trail. From the pass, the trail drops down to Lake Ellen Wilson and Sperry Chalet, and ultimately reaches the road again at Lake McDonald Lodge. The whole 18-mile Gunsight Pass route takes most hikers two days. Besides the inevitable switchbacks and vistas, expect to see mountain goats along this trail.

OTHER RECREATION
Boating, Windsurfing, and Fishing

Although boats are permitted on St. Mary Lake, there's no place to rent them. Windsurfers sometimes take advantage of the ever-present breeze here, generally wearing wet suits because the lake never seems to lose its chilly edge.

Anglers generally prefer boat fishing to bank fishing on St. Mary Lake, which is not really known for good fishing but does have some whitefish, rainbow, and brook trout. Hikers are rewarded by better fishing at Red Eagle Lake, south of the park entrance, or at Gunsight Lake.

Cross-Country Skiing

Loop trails around **Red Eagle Valley,** near the eastern park entrance, offer several miles of skiing for beginning and intermediate skiers. For those who want more of a challenge, the trail to Red Eagle Lake is a 14-mile round-trip along Red Eagle Creek.

ACCOMMODATIONS

Rising Sun Motor Inn (406/892-2525, www.glacierparkinc.com, $107–124) near St. Mary Lake has uninspiring motel rooms and cabins (they call them "cottages," but they're pretty basic) with the familiar steep tariffs and lack of amenities, such as TVs, telephones, and air conditioning, of other park lodging.

At the St. Mary crossroads, the **St. Mary Lodge and Resort** (406/732-4431 or 800/368-3689, www.stmarylodgeandresort.com, $119–450) includes the newer and more luxurious **Great Bear Lodge** as well as the older St. Mary Lodge buildings and several cabins with kitchens. These places are *not* Glacier Park Inc. enterprises. The views don't suffer for being just outside the park boundaries, and the accommodations are every bit as comfortable as, and a touch cheaper than, those inside the park.

Camping

The **Rising Sun Campground** (late May–mid-Sept., $20) isn't particularly appealing in itself—83 shrubby, often hot sites—but it's just across the road from St. Mary Lake; there's a hiking trail heading up Rose Creek to Otokomi Lake, and there are pay showers in the nearby cabin complex.

Just inside the park boundary, the rather drab **St. Mary Campground** (800/365-2267, www.recreation.gov, late May–late Sept., $23; Apr.–late May and late Sept.–Oct., primitive camping $10; Nov.–Mar., no fee) is about twice as large as Rising Sun but is not so well positioned for boaters and hikers. However, it is possible to reserve a site in advance.

There's a **KOA** (406/732-4122, www.goglacier.com, May–Sept., $28 tent, $35–48 RV) in St. Mary with tent sites tucked among riverside trees.

FOOD

Hungry travelers should note that between Lake McDonald and St. Mary, Rising Sun is the only place to buy food. The **Two Dog Flats Grill**

(406/892-2525, 6:30–10 A.M., 11:30 A.M.–2 P.M., and 5–9:30 P.M. daily mid-June–late Sept., $11–20) serves decent café breakfasts, lunches, and dinners with a little Tex-Mex twist.

There's a better meal waiting in St. Mary. The best bet is the **(Park Cafe** (406/732-4482, 8 A.M.–9 P.M. daily May–Sept., dinners around $15), where the hip, friendly staff serves good food (including excellent vegetarian fare) and delicious pies at the junction of Highway 89 and Going-to-the-Sun Road. At lunch, try a curried vegetable burrito.

Up the road, between St. Mary and Babb, it's hard to miss the brightly painted **(Two Sisters Cafe** (406/732-5535, 8 A.M.–10 P.M. daily June–Sept., $8–22), another fun and funky place with good food, including some of the best burgers and sweet-potato fries you'll find anywhere.

The **Snowgoose Grille** (406/732-4431, 7 A.M.–9 P.M. mid-May–Sept., dinner entrées $12–28) at St. Mary Lodge is more elegant than the other places in the area and features good salads and pasta dishes, buffalo rib eye, and other entrées that occasionally transcend the expected steak, trout, and chicken dishes.

INFORMATION

Rangers at the **Logan Pass Visitor Center** (9 A.M.–7 P.M. late June–Labor Day, 9:30 A.M.–4:30 P.M. Labor Day–Sept. 30) keep the fireplace stoked on chilly days and dispense maps, backcountry permits, and advice. More-detailed maps and books on the park's trails, geology, and history are available from the **Glacier Natural History Association** here. The **St. Mary Visitor Center** (7 A.M.–9 P.M. late May–Labor Day, shorter hours in spring and fall) is located just inside the eastern park entrance.

TRANSPORTATION

Free **park shuttles** (every 30 minutes, 7:15 A.M.–8:15 P.M.) leave from the St. Mary Visitor Center to Logan Pass. Glacier Park Inc. (406/892-2525, www.glacierpark-inc.com, several buses daily early June–late Sept., $8 to Many Glacier, no reservations) also runs shuttle buses on the east side of the park, providing transportation to East Glacier, Two Medicine, Cut Bank, Many Glacier, and Waterton.

GLACIER NATIONAL PARK

East Glacier and Vicinity

Although East Glacier is not the best base for a several-day tour of the park, it is a handy entrance point for travelers from the east. Camp or hike at nearby Two Medicine Lakes, with all the scenery and far less company than you'll find at Many Glacier or Lake McDonald.

There's more of a Native American presence here than in many other areas of the park. Even though most of East Glacier is controlled by non-Indians, it is within the Blackfeet Reservation boundaries and is part of an area that is historically and culturally important to the Blackfeet.

For the Native American angle on the park, join one of **Sun Tours'** (406/226-9220 or 800/786-9220, www.glaciersuntours.com) interpretive tours of the park featuring Blackfoot guides.

THE LAND

The Lewis Overthrust came to a halt just west of present-day East Glacier, and its leading edge is visible at Running Eagle Falls near Lower Two Medicine Lake. The hard Precambrian rock of the Lewis Formation rolled on top of a younger, softer shale, which has worn away to form the gentler hilly landscapes east of the overthrust.

Glaciers dug out the bottoms of the three Two Medicine Lakes (upper, middle, and lower). Moraines formed dams, allowing water to fill the troughs. Two Medicine Valley is surrounded by peaks, many adorned with waterfalls and hanging valleys.

EAST GLACIER
(Glacier Park Lodge

Glacier Park Lodge is a spectacular building,

with huge Douglas fir timbers forming the Ionic columns in the Greek revival lobby. Early park visitors typically pulled in on the train from the east and disembarked at East Glacier to spend a night at the lodge before saddling up to ride the circuit of backcountry chalets and tent camps in the company of a guide. For a hearty evocation of such a trip, read Mary Roberts Rinehart's *Through Glacier Park in 1915*. Once Going-to-the-Sun Road was built, auto travel supplanted both the train and the horse, and the spotlight was off the massive lodge.

TWO MEDICINE

Two Medicine boasts some of the park's most spectacular scenery, but it's a ways from the Going-to-the-Sun Road and is often overlooked.

A glacier gouged Lower Two Medicine Lake at the foot of purplish red Rising Wolf Mountain (elev. 9,505 feet). Backcountry chalets built by the Great Northern were the first stop on a horseback circuit popular in the preautomobile days. One such wooden chalet remains as the Two Medicine camp store.

Boat tours of Two Medicine Lake leave the dock at 9 and 10:30 A.M. and 1, 3, and 5 P.M. daily mid-June–early Sept. The 45-minute tour costs $11 for adults and $5.50 for children.

RECREATION
Hiking
It's a short walk from the well-marked bridge over Two Medicine Creek through some conifers and across a rocky creek side to **Running Eagle Falls** (Trick Falls). When there's plenty of water, it appears to be like any other waterfall. The trick comes when water volume decreases late in the summer and water spouts from a hole beneath the main shelf of the falls. Look at the rim of the falls for the fault line marking the eastern edge of the Lewis Overthrust. Running Eagle, or Pitamakan, was a Blackfoot woman who reportedly led warriors over Cut Bank Pass on raids against Flathead and Kootenai tribes to the west.

For a full day's hike, **Upper Two Medicine**

Lake is five miles from the Two Medicine Campground. The trail runs along the south shore of Lower Two Medicine Lake. To shorten the hike, catch the tour boat to the head of the lake.

Hike eight miles up the valley of Cut Bank Creek to **Triple Divide Pass.** The trail starts at the campground and, after a hike and a final scramble from cairn to cairn, reaches the spot where Atlantic, Pacific, and Hudson Bay Creeks issue from the Continental Divide.

Boating
Canoes, rowboats, and motorboats rent for $12–20 per hour at the boat dock on Lower Two Medicine Lake. Although motorboats are permitted, speed is limited to 10 miles per hour.

Fishing
Pick up a tribal permit at the lodge or Two Medicine camp store to fish the Two Medicine River or Lower Two Medicine Lake. Once inside the park boundaries, stop by any visitors center or ranger station and get park fishing regulations (no license is necessary). Brook and rainbow trout lurk in Lower Two Medicine Lake and Cut Bank Creek.

Golfing
The nine holes of the **Glacier Golf Course** (406/892-2525, $18 for nine holes) span Highway 49 just north of the lodge. Because the course is run by GPI, it keeps the same season as the lodge.

Cross-Country Skiing
Once the snow starts piling up in late December, it's easy to strap on skis at East Glacier and glide to Two Medicine Lake. On nice days it's an easy day trip.

ACCOMMODATIONS
Under $50
Step upstairs from the 1920s log **Brownie's Market** (406/226-4426, May–Sept., $15 dorm bed, $31 private room) to find a charmingly decrepit youth hostel with sloping linoleum

floors and lots of old photos and books in the sleeping rooms.

Backpackers Inn (406/226-9392, May–Sept., $10) also offers dorm accommodations (bring your own sleeping bag) in cabins behind Serrano's Mexican Restaurant. The cabins face onto a pleasant grassy yard.

$50-100

Several small motels house guests in detached cabin-like units. All of these places are comfortable, but none are fancy. Cabins at **Sears Motel** (1023 Hwy. 49, 406/226-4432, www.searsmotel.com, mid-May–Sept., $50–60) are run by very friendly folks (and their sheepdog) who also maintain a tent and RV campground and run a rental car business. Ask in advance and they'll pick you up at the train depot. **East Glacier Motel** (1107 Hwy. 49, 406/226-5593, www.eastglacier.com, May–Sept., $77–89) has cheery motel rooms (some with kitchens) and cabins. At **Jacobson's Cottages** (1204 Hwy. 49, 406/226-4422 or 888/226-4422, $50–60) conventionally shaped units are tucked behind the A-frame office, and the proprietor will pick you up at the Amtrak stop.

There's a secluded feeling to the cabins at **Bison Creek Ranch,** two miles west of town on Highway 2 (between mileposts 207 and 208, 406/226-4482 or 888/226-4482, May–Sept., $55–95 including breakfast). The larger cabins have kitchens, and there's also a family-style restaurant (dinner only) on site.

Pretty much all of East Glacier packs up and heads somewhere with less snow and howling wind from October through April. Off-season travelers should look to **Dancing Bears Inn** (406/226-4402, $75–90), off Highway 2. Rates drop in the winter. Dancing Bears is also one of the few motels in town that allows pets.

Over $100

Even if you stay elsewhere, plan to check out the impressive lobby and common rooms at **Glacier Park Lodge** (406/892-2525, www.glacierparkinc.com, late May–Sept., $140–450). There's a heated pool out the back door. (See the *Glacier Park Lodge* section above for more details.)

Bear Creek Guest Ranch (Hwy. 2, mile marker 192, 406/226-4489, www.bearcreekranch.com, $1,895 per adult for one week, $1,395 per child 5–15) is 17 miles west of East Glacier via Highway 2. It's a long-established guest ranch with cabin and lodge accommodations, full meal service, and horseback riding.

Camping

Camp on **Two Medicine Lake** (late May–late Sept., $20; late Sept.–Oct., primitive camping $10), 12 miles from East Glacier via Highway 49. During the peak summer season, campfire presentations by park naturalists and Blackfoot tribal members are held most evenings at 8 P.M.

Head west of East Glacier on Highway 2 to reach Forest Service campgrounds, which often have empty spaces when the national park campgrounds are full. **Summit Campground** (www.fs.fed.us/r1/lewisclark, $12), near the rest area at Marias Pass, is 12 miles from East Glacier. **Devil's Creek Campground** (www.fs.fed.us/r1/flathead, $12) is another six miles southwest on Highway 2.

FOOD

◖ **Serrano's Mexican Restaurant** (29 Dawson Ave., 406/226-9392, 5–10 P.M. nightly mid-May–Sept., less than $15) has good Mexican food and margaritas that taste extraspecial after a long hike. The **Glacier Village Restaurant and Villager Dining Room** (304 Hwy. 2 E., 406/226-4464, 6:30 A.M.–9 P.M. daily June–Sept., dinner $8–19), at the junction of Highways 49 and 2, puts out some tasty dinners. Special care is lavished on desserts.

Next door to Brownie's Grocery and the hostel is the **Whistle Stop Restaurant** (1024 Hwy. 49, 406/226-9292, breakfast, $5–10) with a bakery and great breakfasts (huckleberry French toast).

Don't forget the **Great Northern Steak and Rib House** (406/892-2525, 6:30–10 A.M., 11 A.M.–3 P.M., and 5–9:30 P.M. daily, late May–Sept., dinner $12–22), the Western-themed Glacier Park Lodge dining room with steak and barbecue specialties. Breakfast is a buffet.

GLACIER NATIONAL PARK

INFORMATION AND SERVICES

There's no Glacier National Park visitors center in East Glacier, but the **information desk** at the lodge is staffed by generally helpful people. The **ranger station** at Two Medicine Lake has more specific information on nearby hiking trails.

The **post office** is east of Highway 2, behind the Glacier Park Trading Company. A **Laundromat** and **showers** are two blocks south at the Y Lazy R RV Park behind the Exxon station.

TRANSPORTATION

Amtrak stops at the East Glacier Park station during the summer. The westbound train comes through in the evening; eastbound service is midmorning daily. From September through May the train stops in Browning rather than East Glacier; check exact dates and times with Amtrak (800/872-7245, www.amtrak.com).

Car rentals are available at the Sears Motel (406/226-9293).

Many Glacier

Aside from the Going-to-the-Sun Road, this is the most popular and the most spectacular area of Glacier National Park. The mountains are *right there*, with the knife-edge-thin Garden Wall as a backdrop to the southwest, and a glacier but a day hike away. Many Glacier is spectacular enough to warrant a quick detour just for a snooze on the hotel veranda, but it also makes a good base for several days' worth of hiking, canoeing, and bicycle or horseback riding.

THE LAND

Head up any of the numerous valleys converging on the hotel, and on the way to high cirques and glaciers, observe all four of Glacier's geologic formations. Tan Altyn limestone is exposed in the hotel parking lot. Climb through the green layers of Appekunny mudstone, look for mud cracks and ripple marks in the red Grinnell mud, then scale the buff-colored Helena (or Siyeh) Formation, where large stromatolites abound. High on the Garden Wall, the Purcell diabase is a dark 100-foot-tall layer of igneous rock that shot up through the mud and limestone until it spread into a yielding gap in the sedimentary layers. The molten intrusion seared the adjacent limestone layers, turning them to marble.

Just east of Many Glacier is the edge of the Lewis Overthrust. Chief Mountain, visible from the road between Babb and Waterton Lakes National Park, is the far eastern outpost

of the overthrust of Precambrian rock and the leading edge of the Rocky Mountains. Younger Cretaceous shales, buried by older rocks in most of Glacier Park, take over the valley floor just east of the mountains.

Glaciers filled Swiftcurrent Valley and left their trademark U-shaped valleys running down from the peaks and converging in Many Glacier Valley. Valley floors here are striped with moraines and dotted with glacial lakes, which get colder and more milky-blue as they near their glacial sources. Cirques tucked into the face of the Garden Wall were the starting points for many glaciers, and the Grinnell and Gem glaciers still creep across the shady flank of the arête.

SIGHTS
Park Tours

A five-hour bus tour (406/226-5666 or 406/892-2525, $50, plus C$30 for tea) leaves Many Glacier Hotel every day at 11:30 A.M. and heads up to Canada for tea at the Prince of Wales Hotel, then back to Many Glacier via the Blackfeet Reservation.

Boat Tours

Scenic cruises of **Swiftcurrent** and **Josephine Lakes** leave the hotel boat dock several times daily. Grinnell Glacier, only partially visible from the hotel, comes into view as the boat crosses Josephine Lake. The one-hour tour is

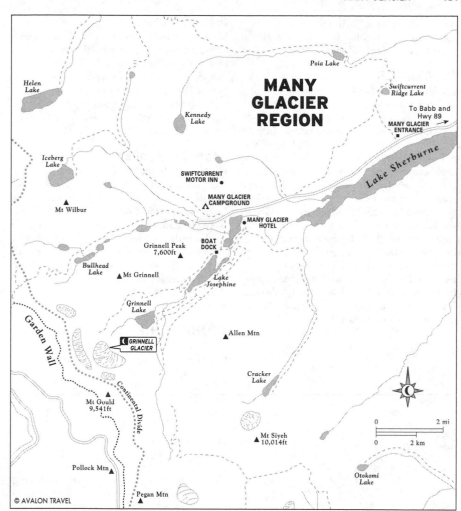

MANY GLACIER REGION

Poia Lake

Helen Lake

Swiftcurrent Ridge Lake

Kennedy Lake

To Babb and Hwy 89
MANY GLACIER ENTRANCE

Iceberg Lake

Lake Sherburne

SWIFTCURRENT MOTOR INN

MANY GLACIER CAMPGROUND

▲ Mt Wilbur

MANY GLACIER HOTEL

BOAT DOCK

Grinnell Peak 7,600ft ▲

Bullhead Lake   ▲ Mt Grinnell

Lake Josephine

Grinnell Lake

GRINNELL GLACIER

▲ Allen Mtn

Garden Wall

Cracker Lake

Continental Divide

▲ Mt Gould 9,541ft

0   2 mi
0   2 km

▲ Mt Siyeh 10,014ft

Pollock Mtn ▲

Otokomi Lake

© AVALON TRAVEL

▲ Pegan Mtn

GLACIER NATIONAL PARK

$18 for adults and $9 for children. It's easy to hop off the boat for a hike or a picnic at Josephine Lake and then catch another boat back to the hotel.

SHORT HIKES
Swiftcurrent Lake
Of the many hikes in the Many Glacier area, the one around **Swiftcurrent Lake** is the simplest, if the least spectacular. It's a good evening stroll

from the lodge or campground—two miles of flat lakeside terrain. The trail occasionally breaks out of the trees for views of the Garden Wall and nearby mountains. Pick up a nature guide at the official trailhead, the picnic area halfway between the lodge and the campground.

Grinnell Lake
Another easy walk combines a boat trip to the far end of Josephine Lake with a two-mile

round-trip hike to Grinnell Lake, a milky aquamarine lake full of icy water and glacial flour from Grinnell Glacier.

DAY HIKES
🅒 Grinnell Glacier

Park naturalists lead several different hikes each day in Many Glacier Valley. Hikers with a modicum of stamina and a passing interest in geology should try to catch the naturalist-led hike to Grinnell Glacier. In combination with a boat shuttle across Swiftcurrent and Josephine Lakes ($18), the all-day hike is eight miles round-trip with a 1,600-foot elevation gain. (Forgo the boat rides and it becomes 11 miles.) Grinnell Glacier reached its peak size during a sort of miniature ice age in the 1800s. Melting since then has left two smaller glaciers: The Salamander clings high on the Garden Wall; Grinnell Glacier proper is below and to the left. A warming trend starting in the 1980s has enlarged the iceberg-laden lake beneath the glacier, making it particularly hazardous to walk onto the glacial ice.

© JUDY JEWELL

An easy hike from Many Glacier Hotel is the trek around Swiftcurrent Lake.

Iceberg Lake

Watch out for bears on the trail to Iceberg Lake, an aptly named glacial lake 4.7 miles from the trailhead in the Swiftcurrent parking lot. The trail crosses alpine meadows before dropping into a cirque holding the milky blue lake. Mountain goats, marmots, and an occasional bear share this path with myriad hikers.

Ptarmigan Falls and Ptarmigan Lake

Take the same initial stretch of trail to reach Ptarmigan Falls (two miles) and Ptarmigan Lake (4.3 miles). The waterfalls and flower-strewn meadows make up for the steepness of the trail. Hikers reaching the lake with boundless energy should go another mile to the 183-foot-long **Ptarmigan Tunnel,** which emerges onto the north face of the Ptarmigan Wall, looking out to the Belly River country.

LONGER HIKES

For an extended jaunt, start at the camp store parking lot and head up Swiftcurrent Creek past **Red Rock Falls,** cross the Continental Divide at **Swiftcurrent Pass,** and join up with the **Highline Trail** on the other side. It's eight miles from the trailhead in the camp store parking lot to the Granite Park chalet (and campground), and another eight miles from the chalet to Logan Pass.

Start at the hotel, pass Josephine and Grinnell lakes, and skirt Mt. Siyeh and Going-to-the-Sun Mountain on the 12-mile route across **Piegan Pass** to **Going-to-the-Sun Road.** Geology, wildflower meadows, waterfalls, mountain goats, and big views are highlights of this hike. There are no backcountry campgrounds along this trail.

OTHER RECREATION
Boating

Rent a canoe or rowboat at the boat dock behind the hotel. Determined canoeists will heft their boats 0.25 mile over the moraine separating Swiftcurrent and Josephine Lakes. The

© JUDY JEWELL

GLACIER NATIONAL PARK

Hike the trail to Grinnell Glacier before it melts!

isolation and views from Josephine Lake are worth the portage.

Motorboats, except for the "scenic cruise boats," are prohibited on Swiftcurrent and Josephine Lakes but are allowed on larger Lake Sherburne.

Horseback Riding

The corral (406/732-4203) behind the Many Glacier Hotel parking lot is the starting point for several regularly scheduled guided horseback rides. All-day rides (about $135) leave each morning to Poia Lake. Shorter rides ($32–80) leave several times a day for Grinnell Lake, Josephine Lake, or Cracker Flats.

Fishing

There are trout in Swiftcurrent Lake, but they're not always eager to swallow a hook. Both Josephine and Grinnell Lakes are home to brook trout; it's worth the extra hike to Grinnell Lake for both the beautiful turquoise lake and the fish. For a change from the trout, head down to Sherburne Lake for northern pike.

ACCOMMODATIONS
$50-100

The **Swiftcurrent Cottages** (406/892-2525, www.glacierparkinc.com, mid-June–mid-Sept., $55–80) are especially popular with families; although the less-expensive cabins lack toilets and kitchens, they evoke pleasant hazy memories of some idealized summer camp or the perfect 1962 family vacation.

Over $100

The ◖ **Many Glacier Hotel** (406/892-2525, early June–late Sept., $135–255 d), a 200-room Swiss-style chalet in an isolated valley on Swiftcurrent Lake, has the loveliest setting in the park, with stunning views from the lobby windows. Geology comes right down to meet you here, and wildlife is often spotted on the slopes across the lake. If you plan to spend a significant amount of time in your room, splurge on the lake view ($160): The view is what makes this place; the rooms themselves evoke 1970s dorm rooms, and the walls are thin.

Less appealing than the lodge or cabins, but sometimes available on short notice, are motel rooms in the **Swiftcurrent Motor Inn** (406/892-2525, mid-June–mid-Sept., $107–124 d). Please note that the Pinetop Motor Inn facilities are among the park's least desirable.

Camping
No reservations are accepted for the **Many Glacier Campground** (late May–late Sept., $20; late Sept.–Oct. primitive camping $10), so campers need to grab a spot early in the day; it's often full shortly after noon.

FOOD
The **Ptarmigan Dining Room** (6:30–10 A.M., 11 A.M.–3 P.M., and 5–9:30 P.M. daily early June–late Sept., dinner $13–22) at the Many Glacier Hotel has a continental Swiss-inspired theme. It's the same meat and fish dispensed to other Glacier Park hotels, but here it's sauced and stuffed rather than grilled or breaded and fried.

In the Swiftcurrent Motor Inn, you'll find the **Italian Gardens Ristorante** (6:30–10 A.M.,

11 A.M.–3 P.M., and 5–9:30 P.M., $7–15), a pretty good casual pizza and pasta place with Montana microbrews, and a camp store.

INFORMATION AND SERVICES
Rangers dispense trail information and backcountry permits from their station near the campground. Find general trail information and specifics on bus tours and hotel activities at the information desk in the **Many Glacier Hotel** lobby.

The most coveted of all services for campers—**showers** and a **Laundromat**—are in the Swiftcurrent cabin complex. Purchase shower tokens at the camp store.

TRANSPORTATION
Many Glacier is 12 miles west of Babb, a crossroads town on the Blackfeet Reservation nine miles north of St. Mary. Travelers relying on public transportation can catch a shuttle at St. Mary to the Many Glacier Hotel and vice versa.

Waterton Lakes National Park

Just across the Canadian border from Glacier is Waterton Lakes National Park (403/859-2224, www.pc.gc.ca/pn-np/ab/waterton, day pass C$6.80 adult, C$5.80 senior, C$3.40 youth 6–16). Although a much smaller park (it covers only 203 square miles), it's worth visiting for spectacular scenery and a distinctly Canadian flavor. The views from Waterton are outstanding—both the look down glacier-dug Waterton Lake and the view of the prairies meeting the mountains. The two parks are known collectively as the Waterton-Glacier International Peace Park, but they are managed separately with separate entry fees.

There's actually a town in Waterton Park, with a handful of year-round residents, several private summer cottages, and a small tourist strip on the Cameron Creek delta. Development has been kept pretty much in check, though; there are no soaring condominium towers and no McDonald's.

All prices quoted for Waterton are in Canadian dollars. Alberta's area code is 403.

As with most of the eastern slopes of the Rockies, the wind can be persistent and strong in Waterton.

HISTORY
Native people camped in the Waterton Valley some 8,500 years ago. By 500 B.C. a plains culture based on buffalo hunting was firmly established. By A.D. 500 the locals picked up and moved to the western slopes of the Rockies and became known as the Kootenai (or, in Canada, the Kootenay). Kootenai hunters continued to travel regularly to the Waterton area for bison until they were forced from the plains by the Blackfeet, who controlled the southern Alberta plains from the early 1700s until the buffalo disappeared a century later.

Oil seepages had been noticed by Indians and early white settlers, and in the early 1900s,

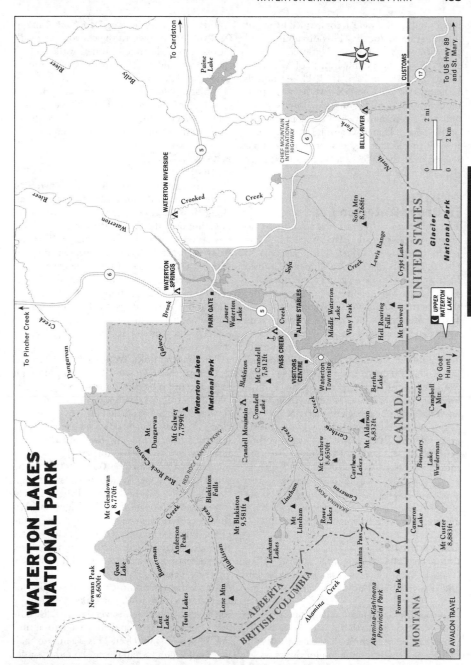

WATERTON LAKES NATIONAL PARK

GLACIER NATIONAL PARK

To Cardston →

Paine Lake

Belly River

To Pincher Creek →

CUSTOMS

To US Hwy 89 and St. Mary →

WATERTON RIVERSIDE

Crooked Creek

CHIEF MOUNTAIN INTERNATIONAL HIGHWAY

Fork

BELLY RIVER

Sofa Mtn 8,268ft

Lewis Range

Crypt Lake

UNITED STATES

Glacier National Park

WATERTON SPRINGS

Waterton River

Brook

PARK GATE

Lower Waterton Lake

Galwey

Dungarvan

ALPINE STABLES

Middle Waterton Lake

Vimy Peak

Hell Roaring Falls

Mt Boswell

UPPER WATERTON LAKE

Sofa Creek

PASS CREEK

VISITORS CENTRE

Waterton Townsite

Bertha Lake

Campbell Mtn.

To Goat Haunt →

CANADA

Waterton Lakes National Park

Blakiston

Mt Crandell 7,812ft

Crandell Lake

Cameron Creek

Carthew

Campbell Creek

RED ROCK CANYON PKWY

Mt Galwey 7,799ft

Mt Dungarvan

Crandell Mountain

Mt Carthew 7,650ft

Mt Alderson 8,832ft

Carthew Lakes

Boundary Lake Werderman

WATERTON LAKES NATIONAL PARK

Mt Glendowan 8,770ft

Red Rock Canyon

Blakiston Falls

Mt Blakiston 9,581ft

Lineham

Mt Lineham

Rowe Lakes

AKAMINA PKWY

Cameron Lake

Newman Peak 8,600ft

Goat Lake

Bauerman

Anderson Peak

Blakiston Creek

Lineham Lakes

Akamina Pass

Mt Custer 8,883ft

MONTANA

Lost Lake

Twin Lakes

Lone Mtn

ALBERTA

BRITISH COLUMBIA

Akamina-Kishinena Provincial Park

Forum Peak

Akamina Creek

© AVALON TRAVEL

0   2 mi
0   2 km

North

5

6

17

5

6

modest oil strikes were accompanied by major machinery and ruckus. This disruption, and the formation of Glacier National Park in 1910, led to the establishment of Waterton Lakes Dominion Park in 1911. Although hunting and commercial fishing were prohibited within park boundaries, building was not, and a community soon developed on the north shore of Upper Waterton Lake. Kootenai Brown, a well-educated mountain man who'd settled near the lakes, was named the park's first superintendent.

SIGHTS
◖ Upper Waterton Lake

The *International* (403/859-2362, www.watertoncruise.com, early May–early Oct., C$32 adult, C$16 teen, C$10 child) has cruised 500-foot-deep glacier-dug Upper Waterton Lake since the Prince of Wales Hotel opened in 1927. The two-hour round-trip boat ride from the Waterton marina to Goat Haunt, Montana, at the southern end of the lake departs several times daily. From the boat you'll get good views of tower cliffs, waterfalls, and one mountain after another. From Memorial Day through Labor Day, hikers can hop off at Goat Haunt (provided they have the ID required to cross the international border), explore the trails there, and take a later boat back to Waterton.

For a short boat ride to a good hiking area, ride the water shuttle to Crypt Landing (403/859-2362, www.watertoncruise.com, mid-May–early Oct., C$16 adult, C$8 child 4–12) and hike 5.4 miles past waterfalls, up a short ladder, and through a tunnel to pop out at Crypt Lake (see *Hiking,* below), then catch an afternoon boat back to Waterton.

Other Sights

Cameron Falls drops from a hanging valley, where a small glacier came in from the side and was swallowed up by the large Waterton Valley glacier.

A paddle-wheeled boat submerged in Emerald Bay beneath the Prince of Wales Hotel can be seen through the clear water. It holds a particular fascination for divers.

Take the nine-mile-long **Red Rock Canyon Parkway** from town to the canyon. At road's end there's a short self-guided walk around the canyon and a picnic area; it's a 20-minute amble to Blakiston Falls.

A **bison paddock** north of the park entrance corrals a small herd of buffalo. There's a quite pretty driving tour through the paddock, which is more interesting than it sounds.

RECREATION
Hiking

Walkers and bicyclists share the **Townsite Trail,** a two-mile tour that you can catch along the lakefront in the town site and take to Cameron Falls. Take off from the park information center and follow the trail up the **Bear's Hump,** a hard rock protrusion that stopped the advance of the huge glacier that filled Waterton Valley during the last ice age. From the top of the hump, you'll have a great view of the lakes and town below. It's less than a mile to the top of the ridge, but the climb is steep and views are often accompanied by stiff winds.

The **Bertha Lake Trail** is a 3.5-mile tromp starting at the town site and heading through montane and subalpine forests to a high cirque lake. Waterton is known for its variety of wildflowers, and they're particularly well-displayed along this trail. For hikers who are not up to the seven-mile round-trip, **Bertha Falls** is just under two miles up the same trail.

Take the tour boat to **Goat Haunt** at the south end of Upper Waterton Lake and from there hike one mile to Rainbow Falls and back, or take off on foot back to the Waterton town site. There's an eight-mile trail up the west side of the lake, although the trail passes mostly through lodgepole pine, Engelmann spruce, and some aspen and birch trees with only a few views over the lake.

Catch the water shuttle to Crypt Landing for the 5.4-mile hike to **Crypt Lake.** On the way to the lake, hikers pass several waterfalls, sidle along steep trails, creep through a natural tunnel, and climb 3,000 feet. This is a hike to challenge both muscles and nerves. It's rather scarier

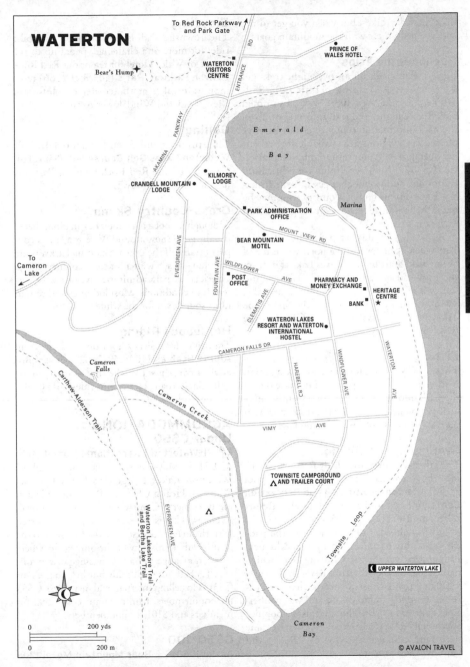

WATERTON

To Red Rock Parkway
and Park Gate

PRINCE OF
WALES HOTEL

Bear's Hump

WATERTON
VISITORS
CENTRE

ENTRANCE RD

ACAMINA PARKWAY

Emerald

Bay

KILMOREY
LODGE

CRANDELL MOUNTAIN
LODGE

PARK ADMINISTRATION
OFFICE

Marina

MOUNT VIEW RD

To
Cameron
Lake

BEAR MOUNTAIN
MOTEL

EVERGREEN AVE

FOUNTAIN AVE

WILDFLOWER AVE

POST
OFFICE

CLEMATIS AVE

PHARMACY AND
MONEY EXCHANGE

BANK

HERITAGE
CENTRE

WATERTON

AVE

WATERON LAKES
RESORT AND WATERTON
INTERNATIONAL
HOSTEL

CAMERON FALLS DR

Cameron
Falls

HAREBELL RD

WINDFLOWER AVE

Carthew-Alderson Trail

Cameron Creek

VIMY   AVE

TOWNSITE CAMPGROUND
AND TRAILER COURT

Waterton Lakeshore Trail
and Bertha Lake Trail

EVERGREEN AVE

Townsite   Loop

UPPER WATERTON LAKE

0   200 yds

0   200 m

Cameron
Bay

© AVALON TRAVEL

GLACIER NATIONAL PARK

than most day hikes, but when you get to the lake you're up there with the mountain goats.

Backcountry Trips

Before setting out on an overnight trek, get a backcountry camping permit (403/859-5140 April–mid-May, 403/859-5133 summer, C$9.80 per night) and trail information from the park information center or administrative office. Reservations are available for wilderness campsites. A nonrefundable reservation fee (C$11.70) is charged, plus a modification fee for any additional changes to your itinerary. Reservations for backcountry trips may be made 90 days in advance beginning April 1 of each year.

A good two-day trip is the 19-mile **Tamarack Tour** toward the northwestern end of the park. Start on the Rowes Lake trail from the trailhead on the Akamina Parkway, and follow it north and west past tiny Lone Lake, Twin Lakes, and Lost Lake to the Snowshoe Trail, which follows Bauerman Creek to the Red Rock Parkway.

Fishing

There's a C$9.80 fee for a seven-day Canadian National Park fishing permit. Purchase one at the park information center or administrative office if you plan to go after the trout, northern pike, or whitefish of the Waterton lakes.

Swimming and Diving

The lakes are a little too chilly for most swimmers, but there's a 60-foot indoor saltwater pool at the **Waterton Health Club and Recreation Center,** located in the Waterton Lakes Resort (Cameron Falls Dr., 403/859-2151).

Divers will want to scout around the paddle-wheel boat submerged in Emerald Bay. Fish gravitate to the rusty rotting boat, which hauled logs on the Waterton River in the early 1900s and was subsequently a floating tearoom, until it fell into disuse and was deliberately scuttled in 1918. Though this is a popular area among divers in the know, it's best to come with both cold-water diving experience and your own equipment.

Bicycling

The Townsite Trail is perfect for an easy bike ride; for more of a challenge, pedal up to the Prince of Wales Hotel for tea or out Red Rock Canyon Parkway. **Pat's** (403/859-2266) rents mountain bikes at the corner of Mountain View Road and Windflower Avenue.

Golfing

The stunning and recently restored 18-hole **Waterton Lakes Golf Course** (403/859-2114, C$36) is on the Red Rock Canyon Parkway just north of Highway 5.

Cross-Country Skiing

Although it's not a big winter destination, there's usually good snow around Waterton, and a couple of trails off the upper Akamina Parkway are maintained each winter for cross-country skiing. Check at the park administrative office for current trail conditions. Most lodgings and restaurants shut down for the winter.

Horseback Riding

Trail rides leave every hour on the hour from **Alpine Stables** (403/859-2462, www.alpinestables.com), just past the edge of town on the golf course road. Hour-long rides cost C$30; daylong rides are C$135.

ACCOMMODATIONS
Under C$50

HI-Waterton International Hostel (403/859-2151, May–Sept.) is part of the plush Waterton Lakes Lodge. It's housed in the Waterton Health Club and Recreation Center, on the corner of Cameron Falls and Windflower Avenues. This is an exceptionally nice hostel, with the benefit of discounted admission to the health club. (This may be the only hostel where you can arrange to have a massage or a manicure!) A bed in a small, tidy bunkroom goes for C$31 (Hostelling International members), C$35 for nonmembers. Family rooms cost C$93 for members and $101 for nonmembers.

C$50-100

At the 1960s-era **Bear Mountain Motel** (208

Mount View Rd., 403/859-2366, www.bearmountainmotel.com, C$89–140), some rooms have kitchenettes, but none have telephones. It's nothing fancy, but it's the only place in this price range in town.

Over C$100

The grand **Prince of Wales Hotel** (406/892-2525 or 403/236-3400, www.glacierparkinc.com, mid-June–mid-Sept., C$265–799), built by the Great Northern Railway in 1926 as a stopover for tour buses shuttling between Glacier National Park and Jasper, Alberta, is perched on a bluff over town. It's run as part of the Glacier Park Inc. hotel system and has a British Isles theme overlaid on the Glacier Park hotel chassis. Big wingback chairs look out from the lobby over Upper Waterton Lake, and the Garden Court dining room looks out onto neither a garden nor a court. Top-end rooms here have an awe-inspiring view onto the lake; many other rooms are cramped.

A congenial alternative to the Prince of Wales

The lobby of the Prince of Wales Hotel overlooks Upper Waterton Lake.

is the **Kilmorey Lodge** (403/859-2334, www.watertoninfo.ab.ca/kilmorey, C$129–252), situated at the base of the hill, just on the edge of town. It's like an overgrown log-cabin B&B, with a homey lounge complete with an oversized atlas of Canada on the coffee table, a tiny bar, and a dining room.

Just across from the Kilmorey, **Crandell Mountain Lodge** (102 Mountview Rd., 403/859-2288 or 866/859-2288, www.crandellmountainlodge.com, open year-round, C$129–209) has 13 country inn–style rooms, including a couple of suites with kitchens.

Waterton Lakes Resort (101 Clematis Ave., 403/859-2150 or 888/985-6343, www.watertonlakeslodge.com, May–Oct., $174–219) offers Waterton's most comfortable accommodations in separate lodges that cluster around a central courtyard. Hotel guests are free to use the health club next door, and there's a good restaurant in the lobby. Some rooms have kitchenettes.

Camping

The wind-tossed **Townsite Campground** (late Apr.–mid-Oct., C$21.50–35.30) is of the parking-lot variety, but many of the 238 sites are close to the lake, and there are showers. It's immediately south of downtown, near the Bertha Lake trailhead and the Falls Theatre on Windflower Drive. Reservations (877/737-3783, www.pccamping.ca) are available for the Townsite Campground.

Belly River Campground (mid-May–mid-Sept., C$14.70) is a cheaper, but not necessarily more appealing, alternative off Chief Mountain International Highway just north of the international border. It's away from the lakes and can be hot. The **Crandell Mountain Campground** (mid-May–early Sept., C$20.60) is a pleasant, though sometimes crowded, spot five miles from town on the Red Rock Canyon Parkway.

FOOD

Midway between downtown and the hilltop Prince of Wales Hotel, the **Lamp Post** (403/859-2334, 7:30 A.M.–10 P.M. daily year-round), Kilmorey Lodge's dining room, strikes a happy medium for a good dinner in

GLACIER NATIONAL PARK

comfortable, attractive surroundings. Lunches are about C$10, and dinners are C$17–39. For a drink, try the intimate bar inside the Kilmorey. After a few dinners in Glacier Park hotels, this may provide a welcome fresh touch. Tucked behind the Kilmorey Lodge, the outdoor **Gazebo Cafe** (403/859-2342, July–Aug., dinner about C$20) is informal and reasonably priced for pasta or salads.

The dining room at the **Prince of Wales** (403/859-2231, 6:30–10 A.M., 11 A.M.–3 P.M., and 5–9:30 P.M., dinner C$20–35) puts a British Isles twist on the standard Glacier Park hotel menu: They serve shepherd's pie at lunch, and dinners include British Columbia salmon. There's also a quite charming **(tearoom** here, serving delicious scones and other pastries 2–4 P.M. Full high tea costs C$36.

INFORMATION AND SERVICES

Just across from the Prince of Wales Hotel, the **Park Information Centre** is open mid-May through mid-October (403/859-2445). The **park administration office** (403/859-2224) is open year-round on Mountain View Road. The in-town **Heritage Centre** (117 Waterton Ave., 403/859-2267) is run by the Waterton Natural History Association. The friendly staff will help plan hikes, meals, and motel stays. A small historical museum and a book shop operate out of the same Waterton Avenue building.

Free interpretive programs are presented each evening in the **Falls Theatre** across from Cameron Falls and in the theater at **Crandell**

Campground. Programs focus on both history and nature studies and usually include slides or a movie.

For **ambulance services,** call 403/859-2636. Reach the **fire department** at 403/859-2113. The **police station** is at the corner of Waterton Avenue and Cameron Falls Drive (403/859-2244).

Most businesses will accept U.S. dollars at the current exchange rate, but dispensing foreign currency in change is restricted. Find bank machines and money exchange at the Tamarack Village Square (403/859-2378).

TRANSPORTATION

The Chief Mountain International Highway (Highway 17) connects Glacier and Waterton National Parks, but both the highway and the customs stations along it close down mid-September to mid-May, forcing drivers to head north from Montana on Highway 89 to Cardston, then west on Highway 5 to Waterton.

Citizens of Canada and the United States will need a government-issued ID to cross the border, and proof of sufficient funds to finance your trip. It is a good idea to bring a passport if you have one.

Waterton Sports and Leisure (403/859-2378), an outdoor supply store in Tamarack Village Square, runs shuttles for hikers.

A tour **boat** runs from the Waterton Marina to Goat Haunt, Montana, at the southern end of Upper Waterton Lake. For more information, see *Upper Waterton Lake* in the *Sights* section.

BUTTE, HELENA, AND SOUTHWESTERN MONTANA

Southwestern Montana is rich in almost every meaning of the word. Early prospectors discovered some of the richest gold deposits ever along the flanks of the Rocky Mountains here. Beginning at Bannack in 1862, then in Virginia City, and then in almost every ravine throughout the area, prospectors found mineral wealth. Gold camps sprang up, the easily panned gold played out, and the settlement moved on.

This early colorful era of Montana's mining history ended when silver replaced gold as the mineral of choice. Silver demanded mills and smelters for extraction, which required costly investment. Soon the ripsnorting life of the prospector was replaced by a corporate payroll, and panning for gold in a lonely stream was traded for a shift underground with a crew of workers.

Whereas the early transitory life of the placer miner left few monuments, corporate mining from the 1880s to the 1930s built cities of worldwide influence. During the 1880s, Butte, "the richest hill on earth," was the largest silver producer in the world. At one time Helena boasted more millionaires per capita than anywhere else in the nation.

The boom that fed this early growth has largely turned bust. Nowadays, residents measure their wealth in the majestic beauty of the mountains, the free-flowing rivers filled with trout, and the potent culture of old cities and towns whose rich culinary heritage is still keenly observed.

Montanans know that some of the best recreation in the state is here. The Jefferson River and its tributaries provide blue-ribbon

SOUTHWESTERN MONTANA

HIGHLIGHTS

◖ Berkeley Pit: Don't think that just because this is a giant pool of toxic water it's not worth a visit. Its vastness and its proximity to uptown Butte will give you a real sense of the scale of open-pit copper mining and how it swallowed up whole neighborhoods. The pit has filled with water since mining ceased here. (page 150).

◖ The M & M: This is the state's most famous bar; the mix of gambling, a 24-hour café, and a clientele of hardened bargoers makes this institution one of Butte's most authentic assets (page 153).

◖ Old Montana Prison Complex: The disturbingly attractive buildings of the prison complex were built by forced convict labor (page 155).

◖ Philipsburg: Downtown Philipsburg's Victorian storefronts are colorful and well-preserved, many with original signage. The area's many ghost towns are also worth visiting (page 161).

◖ Big Hole National Battlefield: In 1877, rather than move onto a reservation, Chief Joseph's band of Nez Percé fled their home. When they paused to rest in the Big Hole, they were ambushed by the U.S. Army. The battlefield is a moving place to visit in a beautiful setting (page 164).

◖ Bannack: The remains of this well-preserved ghost town commemorate the rich 1862 gold strike on Grasshopper Creek, the scene of some of Montana's most violent early history. It's operated as a state park and is free from development (page 172).

◖ Virginia City: Here original and restored buildings from the 1860s and 1870s have been more or less in use ever since they were built; today it's a "working ghost town." Just downstream, **Nevada City** was abandoned in the 1880s and restored in the 1950s when period buildings were brought in from other areas of the state (page 178).

LOOK FOR **◖** TO FIND RECOMMENDED SIGHTS, ACTIVITIES, DINING, AND LODGING.

◖ Montana State Capitol: This imposing structure is domed with a cupola of Butte copper. In the House Chamber hangs one of Charles M. Russell's largest and most acclaimed works (page 190).

◖ Montana Historical Society: Montana's premier museum mixes fine art, history, and changing exhibits. One of the nation's largest public collections of Charles M. Russell's art is here (page 191).

◖ Holter Lake and the Gates of the Mountains: Holter Lake is the most awe-inspiring of the three upper Missouri Lakes. Behind the dam lies the Gates of the Mountains, so named by Meriwether Lewis (page 200).

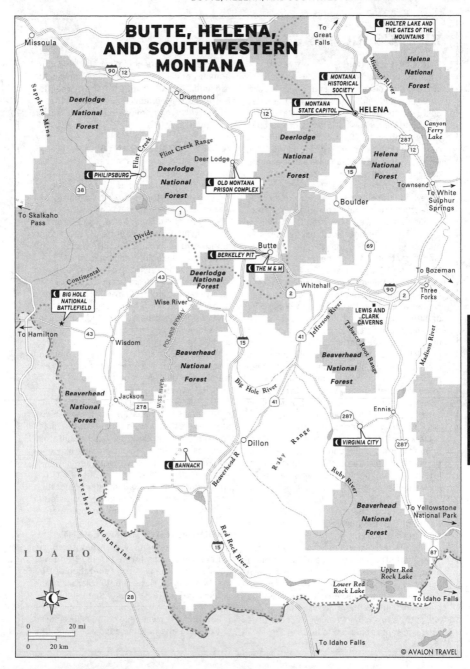

BUTTE, HELENA, AND SOUTHWESTERN MONTANA

Missoula

To Great Falls

HOLTER LAKE AND THE GATES OF THE MOUNTAINS

Missouri River

Helena National Forest

90 12

Sapphire Mtns

Deerlodge National Forest

Drummond

MONTANA HISTORICAL SOCIETY

MONTANA STATE CAPITOL

12

HELENA

Canyon Ferry Lake

287

12

Flint Creek

Flint Creek Range

Deer Lodge

Deerlodge National Forest

Deerlodge National Forest

Helena National Forest

PHILIPSBURG

OLD MONTANA PRISON COMPLEX

Forest

15

38

Townsend

To White Sulphur Springs

To Skalkaho Pass

1

Boulder

Divide

Butte

BERKELEY PIT

69

THE M & M

Continental

Deerlodge National Forest

To Bozeman

43

Whitehall

90

Three Forks

BIG HOLE NATIONAL BATTLEFIELD

Wise River

2

2

POLARIS BYWAY

LEWIS AND CLARK CAVERNS

Jefferson River

To Hamilton

43

Wisdom

15

41

Tobacco Root Range

WISE RIVER

Beaverhead National Forest

Beaverhead National Forest

Madison River

Big Hole River

Beaverhead National Forest

Jackson

278

41

Ennis

Ruby Range

287

Dillon

287

Beaverhead R.

BANNACK

VIRGINIA CITY

Ruby River

Beaverhead National Forest

To Yellowstone National Park

I D A H O

Beaverhead Mountains

15

Red Rock River

87

Upper Red Rock Lake

28

Lower Red Rock Lake

To Idaho Falls

0   20 mi

0   20 km

To Idaho Falls

© AVALON TRAVEL

SOUTHWESTERN MONTANA

BUTTE'S RICH PAST

THE COPPER KINGS

When the first placer miners arrived near Butte in 1864, they discovered pits dug with elk antlers: Apparently Indians also knew of the area's gold deposits. But prospecting for gold requires water, and here, in this basin just under the crest of the Continental Divide, scarcely a stream runs. The gold camp drifted along until 1874, when the first silver claims were made. Abundant quartz in the Butte area contained an unparalleled richness in silver. The rush was on.

News of the silver strikes spread quickly, attracting miners and entrepreneurs from throughout the West. Two stand out: William Clark, a canny businessman, banker, and former miner from the Bannack gold-rush days, gained control of one of the richest mines. In 1876, Marcus Daly arrived in Butte from Colorado, sent by mining investors to scout out the mines of Butte. Both men controlled enough capital to develop the rich mineral deposits of Butte.

Silver doesn't freely occur like gold does. It must be milled out of the rock, usually quartz, in which it is suspended. This shift in method produced far-reaching changes in the Montana mining West. The gold camps inhabited by free-spirited prospectors quickly evolved into industrial towns dominated by the political and corporate interests of mine and smelter owners – and by organized labor.

Clark became the first of the mining kings of Butte by owning not only mines but also the supply stores, transportation systems, real estate, banks, and processing plants necessary for the development of Butte.

Daly was the first industrialist to recognize the potential of the Butte copper deposits. He bought up the now-legendary Anaconda Mine and discovered veins of nearly pure copper 100 feet across; this mine alone produced more than 50 million pounds in 1887. Before anyone else realized the value of copper – copper for electric wire was only just becoming a worthwhile commodity – Daly bought up the mines adjacent to the Anaconda. He built the city of the same name 26 miles west of Butte, where he sent copper ore to be smelted.

Besides investment capital, the third component needed to make Butte boom was the railroad. The Utah and Northern reached Butte in 1881, suddenly linking Butte minerals with a world in the midst of industrialization and modernization.

A CITY OF IMMIGRANTS

Mining on this scale demanded thousands of miners. Beginning in the 1880s, a vast influx of foreign miners flooded into Butte from eastern and northern Europe, from Italy and Ireland, and from Wales and Cornwall. By 1885, 22,000 people lived in Butte. These men and their families brought to Butte the dreams and enthusiasm of immigrants. Butte was opportunity, financial stability, and excitement.

The social and civic life of Butte was a wild tapestry fashioned from bits and pieces of each incorporated culture. Each ethnic group had its own neighborhood and customs. Greyhound coursing, Irish football, cockfights, opium dens and secret Chinese societies, fancy-dress balls, a noted opera house, gambling and prostitution, St. Patrick's Day, and Balkan feasts combined with a dozen other celebrations and cultural traditions – all these mutated into a uniquely energetic way of life in Butte.

But there was also a dark side. Mining is dangerous work. Quite apart from the obvious risk of cave-ins, the dust and fumes in the mines contributed to everything from respiratory diseases to cancer. Above ground, air pollution was absolutely treacherous. In the 1890s, smoke and fumes so darkened the air that streetlights burned night and day. Vegetation ceased to grow, and dogs and cats were found dead in the streets from ambient poisons.

LABOR VERSUS MANAGEMENT

Butte labor was highly organized; the Butte Miners' Union was formed in 1878 and was Local No. 1 of the Western Federation of Miners. Daly and Clark were both tolerant of the unions, and Butte had never seen significant labor-management action.

But when the ownership of the mines moved out of state and became depersonalized, the stage was set for confrontation. Increased rancor characterized the relations of management and labor, but the real battles were fought within the rank and file. Divided between conservative accommodationist members and more radical workers, some of whom organized for the "Wobblies," or the Industrial Workers of the World (IWW), the labor movement in Butte shattered completely. As conditions in the mines worsened and management demanded lower pay, the two union factions adamantly disagreed about what action to take. Violence broke out: In June 1914 the old Union Hall was bombed in Butte, two men were shot, and miner set upon miner.

Finally, in September the governor was forced to declare martial law. Left-wing union leaders were tried and imprisoned, and the elected mayor and sheriff of Butte, both socialists, were removed from office.

This turn of events was music to the ears of management, which chose this moment to break the back of the union: They disavowed both union elements and declared the Butte mines an open shop. Events flared up once more in 1917, when 164 miners died in an underground fire. Workers organized, again with the help of the IWW. Management refused to bargain with the miners, and Butte went out on strike. The Company sent in 200 detectives to infiltrate the movement. One night, masked men forced an IWW leader from his bed, dragged him behind a car to the outskirts of Butte, and hanged him.

The lynching threw Butte into pandemonium. Fearing a renewed shutdown of the mines, the U.S. government declared martial law and sent federal troops into the city. By branding the strikers as antiwar and seditious, the Company and its governmental allies again prevailed. Butte labor remained strongly, but not effectively, organized thereafter.

THE DECLINE OF BUTTE

During the Great Depression, the price of copper fell from $0.18 per pound in 1928 to $0.05 per pound in 1933. The decline of Butte had begun. The old veins were playing out, and the ore was becoming more costly to extract.

Butte struggles on. Denny Washington, a Montana-born industrialist, bought the Anaconda Company properties in 1985 and developed low-overhead, low-labor methods of extracting profits from the rich ore and rich heritage of Butte. His company has since been acquired by the giant URS Corporation.

Copper mine head frames still dominate Butte's skyline.

SOUTHWESTERN MONTANA

trout fishing, white-water rafting, and stream-side campsites. Enormous national forests provide unparalleled camping, hiking, and wildlife-viewing opportunities: The Beaverhead-Deerlodge National Forest alone is larger than many Atlantic states.

The southwestern corner of Montana contains a unique mix of plant and animal life. In an hour a hiker can easily pass from an arid prairie environment of sagebrush and pronghorn, through verdant forests of lodgepole pine, spruce, and fir, and explore alpine tundra life along the many crenellations of the Continental Divide.

Especially notable in this area are the large populations of mountain goats and bighorn sheep along the peaks of the Flint Creek and Anaconda-Pintler Wilderness Areas. Prairie fowl, such as sage grouse, seem out of place when sighted with 10,000-foot peaks in the background.

PLANNING YOUR TIME

For those interested in the history of the Old West, southwestern Montana is an incredibly rich destination; if you're interested in the history of the gold rush, Native America, or frontier ranch life, you could easily spend a week here. That the region is also rich in hot springs, mountain recreation, and fishing just makes the living a bit easier.

The two major destinations in this part of Montana are Helena and Butte, both legendary for the wealth that mining brought to early prospectors and to later industrialists.

Helena is a gracious small city backed up into a narrow Rocky Mountain valley. As the state capital, it deserves a couple of days' visit just to check out the capitol, the excellent **Montana Historical Society Museum,** and the amazing frontier architecture. The massive Queen Anne mansions that line the graceful old streets are evidence of the city's original wealth. A second day in the Helena area should be spent exploring the environs, either gold mine ghost towns or the boat tours through **Gates of the Mountains,** where the first part of the Missouri River carves a canyon through sheer uplifts of limestone.

Butte, as you will discover, is another story. This scruffy, entirely fascinating mining center was once one of the West's largest cities from 1880 to 1930; then the mines closed, leaving this once-thriving city more an open-air museum than an actual urban center. However, there's history galore—and just wandering the streets, having drinks in venerable bars, and a long contemplation on just what an extraction economy *really* amounts to makes this one of Montana's most unique destinations. Stop by the **World Museum of Mining** to marvel at the riches of silver and copper produced by "the richest hill on earth," and visit Chinese opium dens and brothels—now museums—to get a sense of what the Western frontier was really like. Two days in Butte will just begin to scratch the surface if you're a fan of Western history.

Downstream from Butte is **Deer Lodge,** where two completely incongruent sites are well worth a stop. The **Old Montana Prison** is an eerily beautiful structure that served as the state penitentiary from the 1890s to 1979. Tours are fascinating, and if you like the feeling of being "in the pen," stay for a theater production on the outdoor stage. The **Grant-Kohrs Ranch National Historic Site** tells a different tale of Western history—that of an early cattle ranch founded in the 1860s.

West of Deer Lodge and the Clark Fork Valley, in the western foothills of the Flint Creek Mountains, is **Philipsburg,** a beautifully preserved mining town that's little changed since the 1890s. With a newly reopened summer theater—Montana's oldest, built in 1891—good restaurants, and the excellent, newly remodeled **Broadway Hotel** from 1890, Philipsburg is a lovely spot to spend the night. And if by now you've got the mining bug, you can drive west of town to try your luck at mining for jewels at the **Gem Mountain Sapphire Mine.**

South of Philipsburg is the **Big Hole Valley,** a scenic high valley devoted to ranching, fishing, and recreation. A highlight is the **Big Hole National Battlefield** where the Nez Percé under Chief Joseph defeated the U.S.

Army in 1877. History of another sort was made at **Bannack,** where Montana's first gold strike was made in 1862. Bannack went on to become the first territorial capital, and just as suddenly as it boomed came the bust. By 1890 the town was deserted, and it's now one of the West's most complete ghost towns. If all this frontier history has you feeling a bit creaky, spend the night at **Jackson Hot Springs,** where the naturally therapeutic hot mineral waters will soak out your aches and pains.

Early Montana's other big gold rush town was **Virginia City,** another territorial capital but not quite yet a ghost town. Many old businesses are still in operation, and wandering the steep streets is like wandering through an open-air museum of the mining West. Historic homes provide excellent B&B accommodations, while vintage bars provide nightlife spice.

PRACTICALITIES

Information

Travel Montana, the state tourism bureau, provides good free information on events, sights, and lodgings. Southwestern Montana is contained in their **Gold West Country** region (406/846-1943 or 800/879-1159, www.goldwest.visitmt.com).

Getting There

Helena and Butte are both served by major airlines. **Greyhound** travels along I-90, linking Butte to Seattle and Chicago. **Rimrock Stage** runs the I-15 route, linking Great Falls and Helena to Greyhound at Butte.

Driving the local roads can be hazardous in winter; call 406/494-3666 for local **road conditions.** On the Internet, check www.mdt.state.mt.us/travinfo.

Butte

Montana's most representative city, Butte (pop. 32,110, elev. 5,755 feet) is also unique. Touted as "the richest hill on earth," Butte was the nation's largest single source of silver in the late 19th century and the largest source of copper until the 1930s.

This early and extreme wealth gave Butte a singular history and destiny. The town's politicians utterly dominated Montana government for the first 50 years of statehood. It became the state's first industrialized city, and it was also the largest until the 1960s.

Montanans from other parts of the state have always been deeply ambivalent about Butte; its political infighting, religious rivalries, hot temper, and its wealth and self-importance created a statewide atmosphere of distrust. However, many of the things that now seem typically Montanan— the can-do swagger, the spirited politics, the jocular and embracing sociality, its unspoken sense of neighborliness, even its food and drink (and the gusto and quantity in which they're consumed)— reached a zenith in the early days of Butte.

The city's greatest resource was always

its people, the swirling mix of Irish, Poles, Italians, Slavs, Chinese, and others who forged the cosmopolitan collection of neighborhoods known as Butte. Nowadays, Billings makes much of being Montana's largest city and enjoys likening itself to a youthful Denver. Early in the 1900s, though, Butte had nearly as large a population tucked into a steep swale on Silverbow Creek; with its bluster and ethnic diversity, Butte was more like Chicago than any other city in the West.

Butte was a much larger, more vigorous city before the Berkeley Pit left a big hole in its center, but some of the charm and much of the history of the old city still remain: People still self-assuredly bustle, good food and drink are unquestionably an elemental part of daily life, and the old mansions and civic buildings that great wealth built still stand beside the ugly smokestacks, head frames, and piles of tailings.

SIGHTS

For a quick introduction to the sights and history of Butte, take the **Trolley Tour.** The

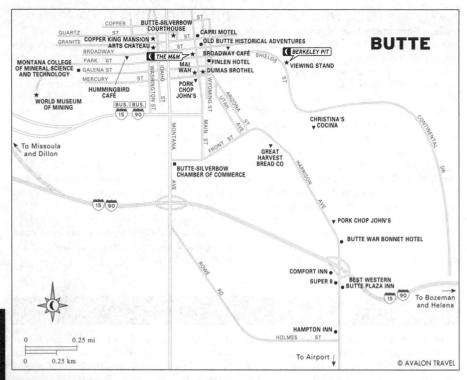

1.5-hour tour leaves the chamber of commerce office (1000 George St., 406/723-3177 or 800/735-6814; 9 and 11 A.M. and 1:30 and 3:30 P.M. Mon.–Sat., 10 A.M., noon, and 2 P.M. Sun., Memorial Day weekend–Sept., $10 adults, $5 children.

A more active way to explore Butte's history is offered by **Old Butte Historical Adventures** (117 N. Main St., 406/498-3424, www.buttetours.info, 10 A.M.–4 P.M. on the hour, $10 adults, $8 seniors, $5 children under 12), offering tours of Butte's underground as well as a couple of tours exploring aboveground historic neighborhoods. Guides are knowledgeable and enthusiastic, and bring the old buildings to life. Especially wonderful is the speakeasy on the underground tour; it was forgotten after Prohibition ended and rediscovered, in great condition, in 2004. Tours are fairly vigorous, so people with difficulty walking up and down hills and steps for an hour and a half should opt for the trolley tour.

World Museum of Mining

Located west of Montana Tech at the end of West Park Street (155 Museum Way, 406/723-7211, www.miningmuseum.org, 9 A.M.–6 P.M. daily, Apr.–Oct., $7 adults, $6 seniors, $5 youth 13–18, $2 children 5–12), the museum complex sits on an old mining claim called the Orphan Girl. Included on the grounds are a head frame, ore carts, a locomotive, and other hardware. The indoor museum contains mining tools, steam engines, ore samples, and an extensive archive of old photos from Butte's boom years.

In the same complex is **Hell Roarin' Gulch,** a replica of a mining camp from 1900. A millinery shop, Chinese herb store, bank, church,

© PAUL LEVY

Uptown Butte is truly uptown.

school, post office, and other period buildings have been faithfully reconstructed.

Montana Tech

Montana Tech, a division of the University of Montana, sits on a bench of Big Butte, the promontory just west of uptown Butte. Established in 1900, the college specializes in teaching mineral science and other professional and technical curricula.

From the ramparts of the campus are great views over the city to the Continental Divide; a statue of 19th-century copper baron Marcus Daly shares the view from the university's entrance on Park Avenue. Visit the **Mineral Museum** (Main Hall, 406/496-4414, 9 A.M.–5 P.M. daily mid-June–mid-Sept., 9 A.M.–4 P.M. Mon.–Fri. mid-Sept.–mid-June, free), where 1,500 mineral specimens, including a 27.5-ounce gold nugget found near Butte in 1989, are displayed. In a separate darkened room is an interesting exhibit of fluorescent minerals.

Uptown

Butte's magnificent homes and commercial and civic buildings attest to its early wealth and importance. Increasingly, vacant buildings and boarded-up windows are more the norm than the exception as the town sadly slumps into a pre–ghost town torpor.

Much of uptown Butte is protected as a national landmark, and many individual buildings are on the National Register of Historic Places; the chamber of commerce provides a brochure with a walking tour of historic buildings. The following are open to the public:

The **Copper King Mansion** (219 W. Granite St., 406/782-7580, www.thecopperkingmansion.com, 9 A.M.–4 P.M. daily May–Sept., 9 A.M.–4 P.M. weekends April and Oct., $7 adults, $3.50 children) was built in 1888 by William Clark at a time when he was one of the world's richest men. This three-story brick High Victorian mansion contains 30 rooms, many with frescoed ceilings, carved staircases, inlaid floors, and Tiffany windows. Clark spent $300,000 on the building and imported many craftsmen from Europe. The third floor boasts a 60-foot-long ballroom and a chapel. Immerse yourself more deeply by spending the night; the mansion is also a B&B.

Clark's son Charles was so taken by a

SOUTHWESTERN MONTANA

château he visited in France that he procured the plans and had it reconstructed in Butte. Now known as the **Arts Chateau** (321 Broadway St., 406/723-7600, www.bsbarts. org, 11 A.M.–5 P.M. Mon.–Sat. May–Sept., $4 adults, $3 seniors, $2 children, $10 families), it serves as Butte's community arts center.

The showpiece of Butte civic architecture is the **Butte-Silver Bow Courthouse** (155 W. Granite St.), built in 1910. A lovely stained-glass dome tops the four-story rotunda, murals decorate the ceilings, and oak fixtures predominate throughout. Butte leaders spent almost twice as much on this courthouse as the state spent on the Montana capitol.

Down on Mercury Street, the **Dumas** building (45 E. Mercury St., 406/494-6908, www. thedumasbrothel.com, 10 A.M.–5 P.M. daily, $8 tour) was Butte's longest-lived brothel, in operation from 1890 until 1982. It's unique in that the building was purpose-built as a brothel: The two-story brick building still has quite a few architectural features peculiar to a house of prostitution, such as windows onto the corridors and bedrooms that the miners more appropriately called cribs. This structure is the only surviving remnant of Butte's once-thriving red-light district. The Dumas is uniquely Butte—be sure to check it out.

Also unusual is **The Mai Wah** (17 W. Mercury St., 406/723-3231, www.maiwah. org, 11 A.M.–5 P.M. Tues.–Sun., Memorial Day–Labor Day; $3 admission, $6 extensive tour), a museum dedicated to telling the story of Chinese miners and workers who pioneered in Butte. The Mai Wah building contained several Chinese-owned businesses; Butte's China Alley, the heart of the old Chinatown, is adjacent.

Visit the cars of your family's past at the **Piccadilly Museum of Transporation** (20 W. Broadway St., 406/723-3034, www.picca-dillymuseum.com, 10 A.M.–5 P.M. Mon.–Sat., Memorial Day–Sept., $3 donation suggested); along with cars there are displays of transportation memorabilia, including license plates, highway signs, and gas station ads.

Another gem of old Butte architecture is the **Mother Lode Theater** (316 W. Park St.,

406/723-3602). This magnificent theater has been refurbished and serves as Butte's performing arts center. Although the theater is not open for regular tours, art events and organizations use the facility, so try to have a look.

Overlooking Butte from the vastness of the Continental Divide is **Our Lady of the Rockies** (406/782-1221 or 800/800-5239, www.ourla-dyoftherockies.com, tours 10 A.M. and 2 P.M. Mon.–Sat., 11 A.M. and 2 P.M. Sun., June–Sept., $12 adults, $10 seniors, $9 teens, $5 children), a 90-foot statue of the Virgin Mary. Completed in 1985, the monument was the result of six years of volunteer community work, including building the access road to the site, 8,510 feet above sea level. There is a viewing point at Continental Drive and Pine. Private vehicles are not allowed on the road up to the statue; you'll need to join a tour bus group (the buses leave from the Butte Plaza Mall, 3100 Harrison Ave.).

Berkeley Pit

Veering from the high to the low, there's the Berkeley Pit, the enormous open-pit copper mine just next to uptown Butte. Because of the high costs of hard-rock underground mining, in 1955 Anaconda began stripping low-grade copper ore from the surface. Eventually the Berkeley Pit reached a depth of 1,800 feet; the gulf from side to side is more than one mile across. Mining has ceased here, and today the pit is filling with water—Montana's deepest body of water. It is also probably its most toxic water, percolating up as it does through abandoned mine shafts. The poisonous water is a threat to passing waterfowl: A flock of endangered trumpeter swans died in the lake one spring. If left undrained, it's only a matter of time before the rising water will enter the Butte water table, causing further havoc. A viewing stand (200 Shields St., 406/723-3177, March–Nov., $2) allows you to look down into the Berkeley Pit and its eerily green water (from dissolved copper and mineral salts).

Recreation
Stodden Park (Sampson and Utah Streets, 406/494-3686) has a swimming pool, picnic

grounds, tennis courts, and a nine-hole golf course.

Fourteen miles north of Butte on I-15 (at the Elk Park exit) is **Sheepshead Mountain Recreation Area:** This fishing and wildlife-viewing facility is completely accessible to wheelchairs. It's a stopover for migrating waterfowl, and moose and elk are frequently sighted.

Rock climbers need only look to I-90 and **Homestake Pass,** where the Boulder batholith's granite juts up from the interstate. Head 25 miles south on I-15, turn east at exit 99, and head to **Humbug Spires Wilderness Study Area** to climb the 600-foot granite outcroppings or merely to hike and gawk.

Spectator Sports

Watch a speed-skating race at Butte's **High Altitude Sports Center** (Continental Dr. interchange on I-90, 406/494-7570), a training center for Olympic athletes. The rink is also open for public skating on weekends November–February (call for schedules).

EVENTS

Butte's biggest annual event is **St. Patrick's Day,** when uptown is decked out with shamrocks and a big parade turns the streets into a sea of green. The parade route then heads pretty much straight through the bar doors or into any of the many restaurants serving special corned beef and cabbage.

The Fourth of July is celebrated in a similarly heady fashion, and there's always a good fireworks display.

Prepare for **Evel Knievel Days** (www.knievelweek.com, end of July) by learning all the verses to *Born to be Wild*. Expect crowds; motorcycle not required.

Another recent addition to the festival calendar is **An Rí Rá** (www.mgcsonline.org), a, Irish cultural festival that focuses more on music, dancing, and language than on drinking, held the second weekend of August.

Butte was chosen to host the **National Folk Festival** in 2008, 2009, and 2010. This mid-July festival includes music, dance, and storytelling performances and a variety of workshops celebrating the cultural roots of the United States.

ACCOMMODATIONS

$50-100

In the historic center of Butte, there are a couple of pleasant older motels. The **Finlen Hotel & Motor Inn** (100 E. Broadway, 406/723-5461 or 800/729-5461, www.finlen.com, $54–72) was once Butte's landmark hotel; although it's now largely taken up with offices and apartments, a couple of floors are reserved for hotel rooms. It's joined by an adjacent motor court and is central for exploring Butte's nooks and crannies. The nearby **Capri Inn** (220 N. Wyoming, 406/723-4391 or 800/342-2774, $55 and up) lacks the charm of the Finlen but is a good budget choice.

Those interested in staying in a grand historic home should check out the **Copper King Mansion B&B** (219 W. Granite St., 406/782-7580, www.copperkingmansion.com, $65–115). In addition to a B&B, the Copper King Mansion—William A. Clark's private Xanadu, built in 1884—also serves as a museum. In fact, travelers stay in the rooms viewed by the public during museum hours. Access to the rooms is structured, so travelers should weigh potential disruptions against their need for seclusion before arranging a stay.

Most of Butte's motels cluster around I-90 exit 127. Of these mostly chain operations, a few stand out. **Butte Comfort Inn** (2777 Harrison Ave., 406/494-8850 or 800/442-4667, www.montana-motels.com, $95 and up) is one of Butte's largest hotels. There's a hot tub, indoor pool, fitness room, generous continental breakfast, and pets are allowed.

The **Butte War Bonnet Hotel** (2100 Cornell Ave., 406/494-7800 or 800/443-1806, www.buttewarbonnet.com, $81 and up) has an indoor pool and hot tub, exercise room, and restaurant and lounge.

At the **C** **Copper King Lodge and Convention Center** (4655 Harrison Ave., 406/494-6666 or 800/332-8600, $81 and up), you'll get an indoor pool, sauna, hot tub, indoor tennis courts, exercise room, guest laundry, and restaurant and lounge, with room service. Pets are permitted.

Over $100

The classiest hotel in town is the **Hampton Inn** (3499 Harrison Ave., 406/494-2250 or 800/426-7866, www.buttehamptoninn.com, $105 and up), with fancy linens, extracomfy beds, and an indoor pool.

Best Western Butte Plaza Inn (2900 Harrison Ave., 406/494-3500 or 800/543-5814, $125 and up) offers an indoor pool, exercise room, sauna, steam room, and hot tub. The hotel is near shopping, and there's a complimentary breakfast buffet daily.

Removed from both uptown and I-90 is **(** Toad Hall Manor B&B** (1 Green Ln., 406/494-2625 or 866/443-8623, www.toadhallmanor.com, $99–165), which takes its name and its aura from *The Wind in the Willows*. The inn (it's a cross between a small hotel and a B&B) overlooks the country club golf course and is as elegant as Butte gets these days.

If you don't mind staying a few miles out of town, consider making **Fairmont Hot Springs** (see nearby *Upper Clark Fork River Valley* below) your base.

Camping

The **Butte KOA** is off I-90's exit 126, two blocks north (406/782-0063). Farther from town, find the Forest Service's (406/494-2147, www.fs.fed.us/r1/b-d) **Lowland** campground to the north of town (Elk Park exit from I-15). The Bureau of Land Management (406/533-7600, www.mt.blm.gov/bdo) runs **Divide Bridge** and **Dickey** campgrounds south of town (Divide exit from I-15).

FOOD

Only in Butte could one even begin to make the argument that there is a historic Montana cuisine. Its large ethnic population and its intense urban character gave restaurants a prominence and an enthusiastic clientele that was unusual in frontier Montana. Butte specialties include the pasty (pronounced PAST-ee), brought over from Cornwall, England, and the pork chop

sandwich. Meals in Butte were traditionally served in courses; the price of dinner included a relish tray, breadsticks, soup and salads, a pasta course, the main dish, and dessert. This evening's worth of food and service is called eating "Old Meaderville" style, for the Meaderville Italian neighborhood that collapsed into the Berkeley Pit, fine restaurants and all.

One of the best restaurants in Montana is the **(** Uptown Cafe** (47 E. Broadway St., 406/723-4735, www.uptowncafe.com, 11 A.M.–2 P.M. Mon.–Fri., 5–10 P.M. nightly, lunch $6–10, dinner $11–30), where the best of Butte tradition meets lively up-to-the-minute sauces and ingredients. The wine list is intriguing, the ambience is light and friendly, and the fare—with lots of fresh seafood, veal, and pasta on the menu, and a nice selection of homemade desserts—is superb. Early dinner specials (until 6:30 P.M.) are a real bargain at $12.50.

Butte's most famous restaurant is **Lydia's** (4915 Harrison Ave., 406/494-2000, 5:30–10 P.M. nightly, $20 and up), which is housed in a modern-era building out on the edge of town. The typical steaks and seafood are joined by Italian food and plenty of old-fashioned but highly creditable side dishes, served in an atmosphere of slightly dated chic. (Be sure to tour the restaurant's stained-glass windows and lamps.)

Back in uptown Butte, **Metals Banque Grill** (8 W. Park St., 406/782-5534, 11 A.M.–11 P.M. daily, $7–23) serves its own beers and ales, as well as a full menu featuring steaks, pasta, and very good Southwestern dishes in an old bank vault.

Don't count out Butte for steaks. **Land of Magic Too** (801 S. Utah, 406/723-4141, 5–9 P.M. daily, $19–26) is an offshoot of Logan's beloved steakhouse.

For something uniquely Butte, try **Pork Chop John's** (8 Mercury St., 406/782-0812, or 2400 Harrison Ave., 406/782-1783, 10:30 A.M.–10:45 P.M., $3). The boneless pork chop sandwich is a Butte original; order it the traditional way, with pickles, onions, and mustard, and think of all the hungry miners who also gained satisfaction here.

Nancy's Pasty Shop (2810 Pine, 406/782-7410) can give you a taste of Butte's other culinary gem ($5). **Joe's Pasty Shop** (1641 Grand, 406/723-9071) is another favorite for pasties. **Park Street Pasties** (800 W. Park St., 406/782-6400) is a newcomer, creating what may be a little pasty war. **Gamer's Café** (15 W. Park, 406/723-5453, 7 A.M.–2 P.M. Mon.–Sat., $2–7), a Butte favorite for hearty meals for more than a century, also serves pasties.

If what you're really hankering after is some good Tex-Mex, head to **Christina's Cocina Cafe** (2201 Silver Bow, 406/782-0346, 11 A.M.–9 P.M. daily, $6–15).

To start the morning in Butte, swing up to the **Great Harvest Bread Company** (1803 Harrison Ave., 406/723-4988, 6 A.M.–6 P.M., $4–7) for muffins or great lunchtime sandwiches.

Broadway Cafe (302 E. Broadway, 406/723-8711, 11 A.M.–11 P.M. Mon.–Fri., 5–11 P.M. Sat., $6–16), housed in a historic building, is Butte's hippest place for espresso, microbrews and wine, or pizza and live music. Another comfortable place to hang out is the sweet and earnest **Hummingbird Cafe** (605 W. Park, 406/723-2044, 7:30 A.M.–3 P.M. Tues.–Fri., 9 A.M.–4 P.M. Sat., $6–7), which uses organic ingredients when possible in its smoothies, juices, soups, and sandwiches.

The artsy **Venus Rising Cafe** (124 S. Main St., 406/491-4476, 7 A.M.–6 P.M. Mon.–Fri., 8 A.M.–2 P.M. Sat.–Sun., lunch $4–5) is a coffee shop with a few wraps and sandwiches; it's sometimes open late on Friday nights for music.

NIGHTLIFE

Within a state that already has a rowdy reputation, Butte bears the sybaritic crown; in the Butte equation, bars are elemental. Remember that in Montana, you don't have to drink alcohol to go out to bars; bars are *what you do.*

A night out on the town in Butte should include the infamous M & M as well as the **Silver Dollar** (133 S. Main St.), **Irish Times Pub** (2 E. Galena), and **Maloney's** (112 N. Main St.).

(The M & M

The M & M (9 N. Main St.) is probably the most famous bar in the state; the mix of gambling, a 24-hour café, and a clientele of hardened bargoers makes this institution one of Butte's most authentic assets. The M & M, which opened in 1890, has had several owners over the years, but its doors had reputedly never been locked. The bar closed down in April 2003, and a locksmith had to be called because the lock mechanism wouldn't turn. Fortunately new owners have taken over, and the M & M is back to its 24-hour activity.

INFORMATION AND SERVICES

The **Butte-Silver Bow Chamber of Commerce** (406/723-3177 or 800/735-6814, www.butteinfo.org) is at 1000 George Street. **St. James Hospital** (406/723-2500) is at 400 South Clark Street.

TRANSPORTATION

Butte's Bert Mooney Airport is served by **SkyWest**.

Also at the airport, south off Harrison Avenue, are car rental agencies: **Avis** (406/494-3131 or 800/331-1212) and **Budget** (406/494-7573 or 800/527-0700). **Enterprise** (3350 Harrison Ave., 406/494-1900 or 800/261-7331) is near the airport.

Greyhound (800/231-2222) and **Rimrock Stage** (800/255-7655) bus lines link Butte to other Montana cities. The bus station is located at 1324 Harrison Avenue (406/723-3287). For a cab, call **Mining City Taxi** (406/723-6511). **The Bus** (406/497-6515), as Butte's small transit system is known, runs during the daytime Mon.–Fri., with a limited Saturday schedule.

The Upper Clark Fork River Valley

Silver Bow Creek drains the Butte Basin before charging almost 1,000 feet down a narrow channel to the wide valley below. Here the creek is renamed the Clark Fork River, and it begins to pick up the many tributaries that eventually make it one of the most important arms of the mighty Columbia.

Early settlers knew this as the Deer Lodge Valley. The state's first ranches grew up when some miners recognized that a quicker and more dependable profit could be made selling agricultural products to the booming mining towns.

Today, this open stretch of the Clark Fork River Valley is the stepping-off point for hikes in the rugged Flint Creek Range. Fishing in the revivified Clark Fork River is both popular and possible; in the not-too-distant past it was neither.

FAIRMONT HOT SPRINGS

This old hot springs spa (1500 Fairmont Rd., 406/797-3241 or 800/332-3272, www.fairmontmontana.com, pool use $8.25 adults, $5 children 10 and under, $4.50 seniors), just off I-90 halfway between Butte and Anaconda, is one of the most popular family resorts and conference hotels in Montana. The hot springs here fill four pools. Two of them (one indoors, one out) are Olympic-sized and heated to 90–100°F; the others run 100–105°F and are meant for soaking weary muscles. There's a separate charge to use the somewhat old-fashioned-looking waterslide; a combined pool and slide pass costs $13.75 for adults and $10.50 for kids. A challenging and well-designed 18-hole golf course is a very big draw (the fifth hole is the state's longest).

Fairmont is a good base for hiking and riding in the Deerlodge National Forest and Anaconda-Pintler Wilderness Area, fishing and water sports at Georgetown Lake, and skiing at Discovery Basin. Cross-country skiers love Fairmont; after a day skiing the trails around nearby Mt. Haggin, a good hot soak takes the ache out of tired muscles.

If soaking doesn't do the trick, the resort's massage therapists can provide a Swedish, saltglow, or hot rock massage ($70 and up).

At Fairmont, a full range of rooming options includes suites and kitchenettes; double rooms start at $145. Don't expect luxury; the rooms are a little worn around the edges. The food is good, considering the variety of clientele they have to please. There are dancing and drinks in the lounge.

Some resorts with Fairmont's amenities and potential would discourage kids, but not here. This is a great place to take active children. Indeed, when schools are out it's a bit raucous, but fun for kids. There are enough supervised activities here that harried parents might even be able to have some time to themselves.

DEER LODGE

Named for a salt lick that was popular with deer during the frontier days, Deer Lodge is the center of a vast valley full of history and recreation.

Deer Lodge's ornate Victorian homes are witness to the prosperity and aspirations of early farmers and ranchers. The fact that early legislatures established the State Home for the Insane in Warm Springs, the State Tuberculosis Sanitarium in Galen, and the State Penitentiary in Deer Lodge is indicative of the valley's political clout.

While the valley prospered as a result of its proximity to Butte and Anaconda markets, the pollution of these two industrial centers was at odds with the farms and ranches. The Works Progress Administration's 1939 *Montana, A State Guide Book* described the waters of Silver Bow Creek just above present-day Fairmont Hot Springs as "muddied with the refuse of Butte mines, though in places it is intensely blue from dissolved copper salts." The Clark Fork was unable to support aquatic life until the 1960s, after 10 years of cleanup. In 1903, after cattle began dying in the fields from poisoned air, the smelter at Anaconda raised its

THE GRANT-KOHRS RANCH NATIONAL HISTORIC SITE

Canadian trader Richard Grant and his sons Johnny and James began trading cattle in the 1850s along the Oregon Trail in Idaho. With cattle fattened on western Montana grasses, the Grants would trade westbound pioneers one fat, healthy cow for two emaciated specimens that had just crossed the plains. It didn't take long for the Grants to amass a huge holding of cattle. In 1862 Johnny Grant established a base ranch in the Deer Lodge Valley, Montana's first. When the gold rush began in the 1860s, cattlemen like the Grants were already in place to sell beef to hungry miners.

When the first influx of prospectors swooped into Bannack in 1862, some disenchanted souls decided to explore the new territory for other options. Among them was a German named Conrad Kohrs. After a stint as Bannack's butcher, he put together his own cattle herd and went off to Deer Lodge Valley. He bought Johnny Grant's ranch and never looked back. Building on Grant's base, Kohrs was the foremost rancher in Montana for almost 40 years.

Johnny Grant's 1862 log home was considered the finest house in the territory, but when Conrad Kohrs took over, he expanded both the house and the ranch; by the 1880s Kohrs was grazing cattle on over a million acres of open-range prairie and meadow across four states and southern Canada. Even after the disastrous winter of 1886, Kohrs was able to ship 8,000–10,000 cattle per year to eastern markets.

Kohrs reduced the size of the ranch in the 1910s, but the Deer Lodge holdings stayed in the family until 1972, when the National Park Service bought the ranch to preserve it as a historic monument. The old 23-room ranch house is wonderfully intact – a delightful mix of Victoriana and frontier living. Kohrs' wife Augusta acquired an impressive array of valuable furniture (especially impressive considering that much of it came to Montana by steamboat and then overland to the Deer Lodge Valley).

The outbuildings contain old tools, horse-drawn conveyances, and period equipment. The old bunkhouse was in many ways the center of the ranch; here, the hired men ate, played cards, and slept while in camp. Their spare rooms and modest environs contrast vividly with life in the Big House.

smokestack 300 feet in order to disperse its smoke higher in the atmosphere.

Between stricter mining regulations and the decline of mining in general, the valley has returned to a degree of its former integrity. A portion of the Clark Fork by Warm Springs offers such great fishing that it is now regulated by the Department of Fish, Wildlife, and Parks.

Grant-Kohrs Ranch National Historic Site

The Grant-Kohrs Ranch (316 Main St., 406/846-3388, www.nps.gov/grko, 8 A.M.–5:30 P.M. daily May 1–Oct. 1, 9 A.M.–5 P.M. the rest of the year, free), the home and outbuildings of Montana's first ranch, provides a fascinating glimpse into the real life of cowboys and ranchers in the early days of Montana (see sidebar). The ranch is maintained as a working ranch; the house is open for guided tours only, and no more than 12 people may tour at once. Admission is on a first-come, first-served basis. Wagon tours ($5 per person, $15 family) are offered hourly Thursday through Monday from mid-June through Labor Day.

(Old Montana Prison Complex

The Old Montana Prison (1106 Main St., 406/846-3111, www.pcmaf.org, 8 A.M.–8 P.M. daily Memorial Day–Labor Day, 10 A.M.–4 P.M. winter, $8 adults, $7 seniors, $4 children covers admission to all local museums) is the core of a series of contiguous historical exhibits. Montana Territory first established a penitentiary in Deer Lodge in 1871, but the

SOUTHWESTERN MONTANA

disturbingly attractive buildings now open to the public were begun in the 1890s. The castellated three-story cell block of red brick was built in 1912. It contains 200 cells, each six by seven feet. W. A. Clark financed the construction of the prison theater in 1919. The oldest structure is the quarried sandstone guard wall, 24 feet high and anchored four feet below ground, built in 1893.

All of these structures (and others) were built by forced convict labor, a practice that was later outlawed. After a violent prison riot and investigation into the deteriorating conditions at the old prison, a new facility was built in 1979. Most of the facility is open for self-guided tours. Check out the gun ports in the shower room, the "galloping gallows" for off-premises executions, and maximum-security's Black Box. The **Montana Law Enforcement Museum** is located in the prison. Here is a memorial to officers slain in the line of duty, as well as curiosities such as Lee Harvey Oswald's handcuffs.

Resist the reaction to find all of this really creepy, and do visit the old prison. The perfectly preserved quarters and facilities tell a grim story of prison life in the recent past, but almost eerily, the handsome architecture and pleasing symmetry of the row upon row of empty cells give the prison a forlorn but intense beauty.

Also in the prison complex is the **Montana Auto Museum,** the world's second-largest antique Ford automobile collection. Edward Towe began his hobby in 1953 with the acquisition of a 1923 Ford Model-T Runabout; the collection now comprises more than 100 automobiles. Some of the standout cars are the 1931 A-400 convertible sedan, a 1955 Thunderbird, and Henry Ford's personal "camper," a modified 1922 Lincoln that served as a picnic basket on wheels when Henry Ford went for weekend getaways.

Other Museums

Across the street is the **Powell County Museum** (1199 Main St., 406/846-1694), which contains dinosaur bones, Indian tools, mining equipment, cowboy gear, and other relics of Powell County's rich history. Nearby is **Yesterday's Playthings** (1017 Main St., 406/846-1133), a doll and toy museum. The collection features 1,000 antique dolls from the private collection of Genevieve Hostetter. The **Frontier Montana Museum** (1153 Main St., 406/846-0026) displays Western memorabilia, with a particular focus on guns and saloon memorabilia. Your ticket to the Old Montana Prison includes admission to all of the above museums as well; these smaller museums close down from Labor Day to Memorial Day.

Historic Downtown

Deer Lodge was home to several early ranchers and settlers whose fine period houses attest to their wealth and ambition; the city's commercial and civic buildings reflect a shared economic self-assuredness. The state's first college buildings, built in 1878, are now used by the local school district.

At the Courthouse Square stand the Powell County Courthouse, a statue and fountain commemorating John Mullan and pioneers who came west along the Mullan Road, and a Milwaukee Road engine originally built to sell to the Soviet Union. There is an abundance of lovely old homes, including the girlhood home of Jeanette Kelly, the original Betty Crocker.

Recreation

The Flint Creek Mountains rise directly west of Deer Lodge. These jagged peaks harbor many high mountain lakes linked with good hiking trails; these are also good trails to explore on mountain bikes. From the **Racetrack** Forest Service campground, a rough road continues eight miles to **Indian Meadows trailhead.** Here, a series of alpine lakes reposes beneath the 9,000-foot Twin Peaks. The lakes are high enough to be undependable as fisheries. To reach Racetrack, turn west at Warm Springs and continue 10 miles on a good road.

Hikes to other high mountain lakes begin at **Tin Cup Lake,** eight miles west of Deer Lodge, off Montana State Prison Road; and west of Rock Creek Lake, about 15 miles

THE BUTTE PASTY

One of Butte's enduring gastronomic standbys is the pasty (PAST-ee), a meat pie native to Wales and Cornwall. Early miners brought the pasty with them from their Celtic homelands. Here, as there, the savory and resilient pasty made a convenient lunch down in the mine. Pasties are still common in Butte, where they remain a popular alternative to their cousin the hamburger. And believe it or not, natives really do argue about who makes the best pasty in Butte.

However, you needn't call Montana for take-out to enjoy pasties at home. The following recipe is as old as the proverbial richest hill on earth, compliments of Butte:

DOUGH

- 1 1/2 cups white flour
- 1/2 tsp. baking powder
- 1/4 tsp. salt
- 1/4 cup butter or shortening
- 1/4 cup cold water

Mix dry ingredients, and cut in butter or shortening with a pastry knife. Add water gradually and stir until a ball of dough is formed. Knead lightly for 10-20 seconds.

FILLING

- 1/2 lb. steak, diced into small cubes
- 1 medium onion, chopped finely
- 1 small turnip, chopped finely
- 1 medium potato, diced
- 2 tbsp. butter

Mix the steak and vegetables. Divide the dough in two, and roll into a circle about the size of a pie pan. Place one half of the meat mixture on half of the dough circle to within one inch of the edge. Sprinkle the meat with salt and pepper, and put 1 tablespoon of butter on the meat. Enclose the meat by folding over the other half of the dough circle. Seal edges with fork tines. Repeat with remaining ingredients.

Place the pasties on a baking sheet and slit a small hole in the top. Bake at 400°F for 45 minutes, occasionally pouring a teaspoon of water in the slit to keep the meat moist. Reduce heat to 350°F and bake for another 15 minutes. Serve warm with lots of gravy. Makes two pasties.

---

northwest of Deer Lodge on Forest Service Road 168. Consult the Deer Lodge National Forest Map and the ranger station (91 N. Frontage Rd., 406/846-1770, www.fs.fed.us/r1/b-d) for more information.

The city **swimming pool** is at 703 5th Street. **Deer Lodge Golf Club** (406/846-1625) welcomes visitors to its nine-hole course just west of town.

Accommodations

Don't expect to find fancy accommodations in Deer Lodge. **Scharf's Motor Inn,** near the old prison (819 Main St., 406/846-2810, $63 and up) has a restaurant, a guest laundry, and allows pets. The **Western Big Sky Inn** (210 Main St., 406/846-2590, $66 and up) has a pool and is convenient to the Grant-Kohrs

Ranch. The **Deer Lodge Inn** (1150 Main St., 406/846-2370 or 877/424-6423, $75 and up) offers a pool and lies right off I-90.

Camp in town along the Clark Fork River at the **KOA** (330 Park St., 406/846-1629).

Food

For the best steaks in this old ranching town, go to the **Broken Arrow Steak House** (317 Main St., 10 A.M.–2 A.M. daily, 406/846-3400). For family dining, try **Scharf's** (819 Main St., 406/846-3300, 7 A.M.–9 P.M. daily), next door to their motel.

Information and Services

The Powell County **Chamber of Commerce** is at 1109 Main Street (406/846-2094, www.powellcountymontana.com).

The **Powell County Memorial Hospital** is at 1101 Texas Street (406/846-2212).

DRUMMOND

Between Deer Lodge and Drummond, the Clark Fork River is squeezed by the Flint Creek Mountains and the Garnet Range into an increasingly narrow valley.

Montana's gold rush began here. In 1860, James and Granville Stuart were panning in Gold Creek when their pans showed color. Word of the gold strike brought in a flood of prospectors from the spent gold rushes in other parts of the West. Gold Creek was never a rich producer, and only a few temporary shacks ever occupied this gold camp. Years later, however, better technology allowed developers to extract the remaining gold with dredges—as the mounds of tailings attest.

Pintler Scenic Route

Montana Highway 1 leaves the Clark Fork Valley at Anaconda to wind through high mountain valleys and past ghost towns and old mining centers. For most of its distance, Highway 1 travels along Flint Creek. Its high north-issuing valley is flanked by the low undramatic ridges of the Sapphire Mountains to the west and the easterly rugged Flint Creek Range. The highway plunges down to join the Clark Fork and I-90 at Drummond. This alternative to the interstate doesn't involve any extra mileage, but it does lead to plentiful scenic and historic sites, including the towns of Anaconda, known chiefly for its smelter but also for its incredible Superfund cleanup, and Philipsburg, a convivial old silver town with a wealth of century-old storefronts, private homes, and civic structures. Located in a steep draw beneath craggy peaks, "P-Burg," as Montanans call it, is one of the most picturesque towns in the state.

Recreation includes skiing at one of Montana's best small ski areas, lake fishing at 5,500 feet, sapphire hunting, and exploring the ghosts of the mining towns that didn't quite make it.

ANACONDA AND VICINITY

Anaconda is the town that Marcus Daly built. As the smelter for Butte's enormous reserves of copper and zinc, Anaconda became a powerful city, nearly edging out Helena as capital of Montana.

To the industrialists who built Butte, its incredible mineral wealth was only half the equation. A *lot* of water was needed to refine the ore. Butte, situated in an arid basin near the Continental Divide, had scarcely enough water for prospectors to successfully pan for gold.

Copper King Marcus Daly decided that, rather than bring the water to the ore, he'd take the ore to a better water source. He went to the Warm Springs Creek Valley, 26 miles west of Butte, to establish a smelter. Daly laid out the town in 1883 and named it "Copperopolis." As unlikely as it now seems, Montana already had a settlement with that name, and the new town was renamed Anaconda (pop. 8,888, elev. 5,331 feet) for Daly's mine in Butte.

The **Washoe Smelter,** towering on a hill above Anaconda, became the largest copper smelter in the world. Daly established the Butte, Anaconda, and Pacific Railroad solely to transport the ore from his Butte mines to the Washoe. The smelter could process 1,000 tons of ore an hour; it employed about 3,500 workers. The immense smokestack that rose above Anaconda became a landmark; at 585 feet high, nearly seven million bricks were used in its construction.

Anaconda was a classic "company town." Daly was inordinately proud of the town that he founded, and he graced it with fine civic buildings. When Montana became a state in 1889, Daly mounted a huge campaign to name Anaconda the new capital. He immediately clashed with W. A. Clark, who favored retaining Helena, the territorial capital. A classic Copper King feud ensued. Daly spent $2.5 million promoting Anaconda and disdaining Helena and Clark. Clark painted a picture of Anaconda as a grimly obedient company town, and he minted copper dollars as exemplars. In 1894 Helena won out, but by fewer than 2,000 votes.

Anaconda was inextricably tied to the fate of Butte. When Butte stumbled, Anaconda also faltered. After years of failing business, ARCO, which had purchased Anaconda in the late 1970s, closed the Washoe Smelter in 1983.

Sights

Anaconda has preserved its historic town center. Stop by the chamber of commerce (306 E. Park) for a map of historic buildings. One of the most imposing buildings is the old **City Hall** (401 E. Commercial, 406/563-2242). Built in 1895, it is made of local materials: pressed brick, Anaconda granite, and copper trim. City and county offices are now housed in the courthouse, along with the historical society and the **Copper Village Museum and Art Center.**

The **Deer Lodge County Courthouse** (406/846-2680), at the south end of Main Street, dominates the town. Built in 1898, it features a rotunda, a copper-clad cupola, curving staircases, and a dumbwaiter to convey books from floor to floor.

An art deco extravaganza, the **Washoe Theatre** (305 Main St., 406/563-6161) is one of Anaconda's most stellar showcases. The hammered metal-leaf decorations are almost overwhelming. The imposing **Hearst Free Library** (401 Main St.) was an 1898 gift to Anaconda from newspaper magnate William Randolph Hearst's mother, Phoebe.

Catch the 1936 **vintage bus** at the chamber of commerce (306 E. Park, 406/563-2400, $5 adults, $1.50 children) for a 90-minute tour of Anaconda. Tours start at 10 A.M. and 2 P.M. Mon.–Sat., mid-May to mid-September.

The **Copper King Express** (800 W. Commercial, 406/563-5458 or 877/563-5458, www.copperkingexpress.com, noon Sat. late May–mid-Sept., $25 adult, $20 senior, $18

student 6–18, $5 under 6) is an excursion train running from its Anaconda roundhouse to Rocker (just west of Butte) through rugged Durant Canyon.

Recreation

The biggest thing to hit Anaconda since the smelter is the Jack Nicklaus–designed **Old Works Golf Course** (406/563-5989, www.oldworks.org). Built by ARCO on a huge Superfund site, the course incorporates many historic features of the erstwhile Old Works Smelting Site, including black slag left over from mining, resulting in a strikingly attractive black and green course. This is a long tough course—seven miles from start to finish, with some exceptional holes. Greens fees are reasonable for such a high-caliber course; summer weekday rates run $33 for nine holes, $43 for 18.

Another former Superfund site, **Warm Springs Ponds** is an almost shockingly good place to go bird-watching or fishing (catch-and-release only). These ponds and wetlands, created from ponds built to catch mining wastes drifting downstream from Butte, are laced with 15 miles of hiking or biking trails and include nesting areas for ospreys and many songbirds. Some of the state's largest trout have been pulled from these ponds. To reach the ponds, take Exit 201 (Warm Springs) from I-90 and head east.

Georgetown Lake, 15 miles west of Anaconda on Highway 1, provides fabled fishing and water sports access, with plenty of campgrounds (see the *Camping* section below). Closer to Anaconda and less crowded with locals are a couple of wildlife-viewing areas.

Mt. Haggin Wildlife Management Area offers stunning views onto local mountains and also the chance to see bashful moose and elk. Mt. Haggin is popular with cross-country skiers in winter and mountain bikers in summer. To reach Mt. Haggin, follow Highway 274 south from Anaconda 14 miles; watch for the sign for **Mule Ranch Vista.** With 54,137 acres under protection, Mt. Haggin is the state's largest wildlife management area.

Accommodations

Right downtown is the **Marcus Daly Motel** (119 W. Park, 406/563-3411 or 800/535-6528, $79 and up); it's both comfortable and convenient, with an attentive owner. Special rates, including ski and golf packages, are available. The **Vagabond Lodge Motel** (1421 E. Park, 406/563-5251 or 800/231-2660, $65–85) is an attractive brick inn across from the city park and within walking distance of the golf course.

Find B&B lodgings at the **Hickory House** (218 Park, 406/563-5481, www.hickoryhouseinn.com, $90–100), a nicely restored former rectory with a lovely garden. The owners also rent a four-bedroom house ($150) near the golf course.

Also consider staying just a few miles down the road at **Fairmont Hot Springs.**

Camping

Lost Creek State Park (406/542-5500, http://fwp.mt.gov/parks, May–Nov.) six miles off Highway 48, two miles east of Anaconda, is a campground in a narrow limestone canyon. A waterfall, interesting geology, and mountain goats and bighorn sheep make this a nice alternative to urban RV sites. **Big Sky RV Park** (200 N. Locust, 406/563-2967) has fishing access on Warm Springs Creek and is near public parks. **Warm Springs Campground** (www.fs.fed.us/r1/b-d, late June–mid-Sept.) is in the Beaverhead-Deerlodge National Forest 11 miles northwest of town on Highway 1, then two miles north on Forest Service Road 170.

Food

Although Butte has many more dining options, it's possible to find both pasties and multicourse meals in Anaconda. **Wind's Bakery** (208 E. Park, 406/563-2362) and **June's Pasty Shop** (407 W. 3rd St., 406/563-2205) offer the local version of the meat-filled pies.

Despite its rather grim exterior, **Barclay II Supper Club** (1300 E. Commercial, 406/563-5541, dinner from 5 P.M. Tues.–Sun., $10–30) is Anaconda's most stylish restaurant, serving large Italian-influenced meals with many courses. A little more up-to-date, with microbrews

(still evolving, we suspect) and grilled steak, fish, and pork is the **Rocky Mountain Brewing Company** (315 E. Commercial, 406/563-3317, 10 A.M.–9 P.M. daily, $7–20), with a brewery and an adjacent restaurant (which is permitted to serve beer until 8 P.M.).

Information and Services

The **Anaconda Chamber of Commerce** is at 306 East Park (406/563-2400, www.anacondamt.org).

The **Community Hospital of Anaconda** is at 401 West Pennsylvania (406/563-8500).

GEORGETOWN LAKE

Georgetown Lake, at the upper reaches of Flint Creek, is one of the state's oldest hydroelectric projects. The lake is incredibly popular with the locals and is visited summer and winter.

Flint Creek was first dammed in 1885 and was further developed in 1891 when the silver mines in Philipsburg demanded a source of electric power. In the 1890s Marcus Daly's Butte, Anaconda, and Pacific Railroad ran weekend trains to the lake for the workers in Butte and Anaconda. A steamboat plied the lake, offering excursion trips.

Today, the preferred pastimes at Georgetown Lake are boating, windsurfing, fishing, and snow-kiting, although many people simply go there to weekend at their cabins.

Discovery Ski Area

Located 20 miles west of Anaconda in the Flint Creek Range, Discovery (406/563-2184, www.skidiscovery.com, $35 adult, $18 senior or child 12 and under) offers a vertical drop of 2,700 feet along 40 runs. Full rental facilities are available, as well as food and beverage services at the ski lodge. Discovery is known both for its ski school and for its lack of crowds. There's no lodging at the ski area, but there are some reasonably priced small places nearby; Fairmont Hot Springs Resort offers package deals combining lodging and skiing.

Accommodations and Food

Camping is easy at Georgetown Lake, with

an abundant mix of private and public campgrounds in the area. At **Denton's Point KOA** (west two miles on S. Shore Rd., 406/563-6030), there's a marina with a bar and restaurant. Just up the road is **Georgetown Lake KOA** (406/563-3402), open all year. Tent campers will prefer the Forest Service's (406/859-3211, www.fs.fed.us/r1/b-d) **Lodgepole Campground** (reservations available at 877/444-6777, www.recreation.gov, late May–late Sept., $10, $8.65 reservation fee) just across from Georgetown Lake. **Flint Creek Campground** (May–Sept.) is a primitive Forest Service campground three miles west of Georgetown Lake just off Highway 1. Remember to bring drinking water, because there is no piped water.

Although most visitors here camp or stay in their family cabins, a couple of Georgetown Lake hotel-restaurant combinations offer good food plus access to the lake and nearby Discovery Basin skiing. The **Seven Gables Resort** (18 S. Hauser, 406/563-5052 or 800/472-6940, http://sevengablesmontana.com, $50 and up) is just off the main highway on the road to Discovery Basin and offers rooms (pets are allowed), a café, and a bar. Another good bet is the **Brown Derby** (13902 Hwy. 1, 406/563-5788, www.brown-derby.com, $50), a nice little motel with a good restaurant across the highway a short ways from the lake.

◖ PHILIPSBURG

Between Georgetown Lake and Philipsburg, Highway 1 follows Flint Creek down precipitous Flint Creek Canyon to the Philipsburg Valley. The terrain eventually becomes more hospitable to ranching, and between Philipsburg and Drummond the landscape becomes increasingly agrarian.

Whether it is the community's isolation or the integrity of its Victorian-era architecture, Philipsburg has recently gained a reputation as a refuge for artists. Philipsburg has an exceedingly handsome Victorian-era town center, and each year sees another old building brought back to life with lots of paint, loving care, and entrepreneurial pride.

decorative moldings in Philipsburg

© BILL MCRAE

History

A lone miner discovered silver ore at Philipsburg (pop. 940, elev. 5,195 feet) in 1864, but he didn't pursue his claim. His barroom oratory about the rich deposits, however, attracted more ambitious miners. In 1866 the rich Hope Mine, Montana's first silver mine, was established, and by the next year the camp boasted 700 inhabitants. The silver deposits were rich enough to attract the Northern Pacific's spur line to Philipsburg in 1887.

The Bimetallic Mining Company entered the town in 1885. At the time it was the state's largest silver mill, and its smokestacks still tower over Philipsburg. Its demand for power led to the creation of Georgetown Lake.

Sights

Philipsburg never really changed much after 1900, and the old town has remained intact. The chamber of commerce passes out a brochure for a walking tour to 32 historic buildings. Lots of antique stores and cafés now line the streets. Downtown's Victorian storefronts

SOUTHWESTERN MONTANA

are especially colorful and well-preserved, many with original signage. The grade school, built in 1894, is the oldest school building in Montana still in use.

Newly reopened is the **Opera House Theatre** (140 S. Sansome St., 406/859-0013), Montana's oldest theater still in operation, built in 1891. The theater presents a three-play summer season of melodramas and vintage stage productions from July 4 through September 1.

The **Granite County Museum and Cultural Center** (155 S. Sansome St., 406/859-3020) houses exhibits on hard-rock mining and ghost towns. This is a good place to learn about the many ghost towns in the neighborhood; ask for directions to Kirkville, Black Pine, or Red Lion.

Four miles southeast of Philipsburg on a gravel road is **Granite,** whose rich mines earned it the nickname "Silver Queen." Granite boomed along with Philipsburg; $30 million of silver was mined there during the 1880s. Granite suffered more grievously when the bottom fell out of the gold market in 1893. Within hours of the mines' closing, 3,000 miners and their families reportedly descended on Philipsburg to withdraw their bank accounts and purchase one-way tickets out. The handsome Miner's Union Hall, a three-story brick structure, is one of the few buildings still standing.

Mining hasn't totally gone bust in Philipsburg. Visitors can stop by the **Sapphire Gallery** (115 E. Broadway, 406/859-3236 or 800/525-0169) and dig through concentrate from nearby mines for sapphires. Very nice sapphire and ruby jewelry is also sold here.

Accommodations

Right downtown, the **(Broadway Hotel** (103 W. Broadway, 406/859-8000, www.broadwaymontana.com, $80–130) is a beautifully restored hotel from 1890, with nine themed rooms, all with private baths, including a suite with its own card room. If you need more space, a couple of pet-friendly guest cottages are near the hotel ($140). A continental breakfast in the hotel's coffee bar is included. This wonderfully updated and comfortable hotel is alone worth the detour to Philipsburg!

The **Inn at Philipsburg** (915 W. Broadway, 406/859-3959, www.theinn-philipsburg.com, $44 and up) also has an RV park and meeting rooms; pets are accepted.

Food

A great addition to town is the **Philipsburg Cafe** (136 W. Broadway, 406/859-7799, 11 A.M.–4 P.M. Wed.–Sun., 6–8:30 P.M. Fri.–Sat., lunch $7–8, dinner $12 Fri., $20 Sat.), serving good lunches (yet another place to try a pasty) and special dinners with a choice between two entrées: Friday nights are pretty homey (spaghetti and meatballs or chicken teriyaki) whereas the several-course Saturday night meals reveal the chef's culinary-school training (skirt steak with mushroom sauce or a lemon-roasted chicken).

If you choose to forgo all nutritional guidelines, then by all means pig out at the **Sweet Palace** (109 E. Broadway, 406/859-3353), a huge candy store. **Doe Brothers** (120 E. Broadway, 406/859-7677, 8 A.M.–8 P.M. daily summer, 8 A.M.–6 P.M. winter, $5–13) strikes a good balance—it's an old-fashioned soda fountain that also serves pasties. The **Gallery Cafe** (127 E. Broadway, 406/859-3534, 8 A.M.–8 P.M., $4–7) serves good food and the atmosphere of a Richard Hugo poem. For a traditional Montana evening meal of steak or prime rib, stop by **Montana John's Silver Mill Saloon** (128 E. Broadway, 406/859-7000, 11 A.M.–3 P.M. Sat.–Sun., 4:30 P.M.–10 P.M. Tues.–Thurs., 4:30 P.M.–11 P.M. Sat.–Sun., $9–36).

Information

Find the Philipsburg **Chamber of Commerce** at 135 South Sansome (406/859-3388, www.philipsburgmt.com). The **Philipsburg Ranger Station** is at 88 Business Loop (406/859-3211, www.fs.fed.us/r1/b-d).

THE SKALKAHO PASS ROAD

Six miles south of Philipsburg, Highway 38 leaves Highway 1 and winds west through the Sapphire Mountains, eventually dropping into the Bitterroot Valley at Hamilton. Travelers should consider this 50-mile drive, partly on gravel roads, for several reasons. The Skalkaho

Pass Road connects two otherwise distant valleys along a route with great scenic value. On the west side of the divide the road is forested and steep, often cliff-hanging. The east half is gentler and runs along the lovely upper reaches of Rock Creek, one of Montana's premier fishing streams.

Anglers will want to leave Highway 38 for Rock Creek Road and follow it to its confluence with the Clark Fork River. The upper reaches of Rock Creek receive a lot less attention than the more developed areas closer to Missoula, but the fishing is as good.

Amateur prospectors can try their hand at sapphire mining along the banks of Rock Creek. The **Gem Mountain Sapphire Mine** (13 miles west of the junction with Hwy. 1, 406/859-4367 or 866/459-4367, www.gem-mtn.com, 9 A.M.–7 P.M. Memorial Day–Labor Day, 9 A.M.–5 P.M. Labor Day–mid-Oct., $14 per bucket) offers buckets of sapphire-rich gravel to process. The sapphires come in several shades (classic blue being one of the rarest) and are relatively easy to find. You can choose to wash the gravel yourself, for the real prospector experience, or buy prewashed concentrated

gravel by the bucket. The gravel is placed on sorting tables, and then it's up to you to spot the gems. The staff members are happy to help—they even offer a faceting and mounting service—and the experience makes a good family outing. There's informal picnicking and camping near the mine along Rock Creek.

West of Skalkaho Pass, 32 miles from Highway 1, Skalkaho Falls roars down under the highway and makes a great place to picnic. Although hiking isn't necessary to enjoy the falls, plenty of hiking trails, both formal and informal, sprout from the road. Trail 313, at the divide, is a good one to follow for a short or long hike. Head north along this trail to Dome-Shaped Mountain, home of mountain goats. The trail also passes by the **Skalkaho Game Preserve,** accessible by a rough dirt road at Skalkaho Pass. Marshes here are favorite summer habitat for elk; patient visitors may also see mule deer, coyotes, and black bears.

Skalkaho Pass Road is closed from mid-October to June. Early or late in the season, call the state highways department (800/226-7623, www.mdt.mt.gov) to be certain the road is open.

The Big Hole River Country

The Big Hole is known as the "Valley of 10,000 Haystacks" for the stacks of loose unbaled hay that the local ranchers persist in using for hay storage; the ranches don't have much truck with laborsaving technology. Time has not forgotten this isolated valley, but neither has it been thinking of the Big Hole very recently.

The Big Hole Valley is some of the highest and flattest land in Montana. Almost all of the farm and ranch land hovers well above 6,000 feet in wide valley swatches 15 miles across.

Lewis and Clark named the three forks of the Jefferson River Wisdom, Philanthropy, and Philosophy. In time, Wisdom River became the less abstract Big Hole River, so named by later ranchers who were impressed with the vast real estate hemmed in by towering peaks. The Big

Hole River flows north, draining a huge high valley lying between the Bitterroot Mountains on the west and the Pioneer Mountains on the east. After bumping into the Anaconda Range, the river does a U-turn and flows south, picking up the east-slope drainage of the Pioneers.

For anglers and floaters, the river's the thing. Fishing in the Big Hole is superlative, and the rafting is challenging. For hunters, this is the best hunting ground for pronghorn in the state, outside of the prairies of eastern Montana. History buffs can hike the trails and war fields of the Battle of the Big Hole, where in 1877 the Nez Percé fought the U.S. Army as the Indians tried to flee incarceration on reservations.

To comprehend the Big Hole's allure, understand that this is still the West. Resorts haven't

© BILL MCRAE

In the Big Hole, hay is still stacked loose, not baled.

yet replaced ranches. You can catch trout elsewhere in Montana, but here you can share a drink and tell your fish stories to a hired hand or cowboy, not a conventioneer.

⬤ BIG HOLE NATIONAL BATTLEFIELD

In 1877, rather than move onto a reservation, Chief Joseph's band of Nez Percé fled their home in northeastern Oregon and Idaho to find refuge with the Crow tribe. When they paused to rest in the Big Hole, they were ambushed by the U.S. Army. The Big Hole National Battlefield, which preserves the site of the battle, is a moving place to visit in a beautiful setting.

The Nez Percé

One of the most famous Indian battles in Montana history involved an Indian tribe that's not indigenous to the state. The Nez Percé homeland was the region where Oregon, Washington, and Idaho meet. There the Nez Percé made their way as seminomadic fishers, hunters, and gatherers. The Nez Percé Nation

was a largely peaceable confederation of loosely knit tribal units, each under a powerful chief.

By the 1850s, white settlement began to displace the Nez Percé. An 1855 treaty confined them to a reservation; because the boundaries included their traditional homeland, and because the treaty also restricted white settlement on their land, they complied.

By 1863, however, more stockmen, miners, and settlers were encroaching on Nez Percé land. A new treaty was drawn up, reducing the reservation to one quarter of its former size. The Nez Percé chiefs whose land was still within the reservation signed the new treaty; those chiefs whose land was being taken away refused. On the pretext that the signature of any Nez Percé chief represented the commitment of the whole tribe, the U.S. government ordered the "nontreaty" Nez Percé onto the new reservation.

While both the Indians and the U.S. Indian Bureau dallied for several years without strict enforcement of the order, increasing pressure from settlers—especially after Custer's rout in 1876—made compliance a priority. In 1877 the U.S. Army was sent in to compel the delinquent Nez Percé onto the reservation.

At this time, a band of young warriors attacked and killed four white settlers in Oregon, whom the Indians believed guilty of earlier murders of Nez Percé elders. Fearing harsh retaliation and foreseeing a dismal future for the tribe, five bands of the nontreaty Nez Percé—about 800 people—fled eastward from the Wallowa Lake area of northeastern Oregon. After two skirmishes in Idaho, where the Indians eluded the army, the Nez Percé realized they had to leave the area completely. They crossed over to Montana, intent on journeying to Crow country on the Yellowstone, where they hoped to reestablish the tribe.

The Battle of the Big Hole

Once in Montana the pace of the exodus slowed, and after pushing up the Bitterroot Valley the Nez Percé camped on the western side of the Big Hole Valley. Here they considered themselves out of reach of the army for a few days. They stopped to cut new travois poles and to ready themselves for more traveling.

The Nez Percé knew that the Washington-based army detachment was two weeks behind them. However, they didn't realize that the Seventh Infantry, under Col. John Gibbon of Fort Shaw, had moved south to ambush them. In the early morning of August 9, 1877, a Nez Percé sentry rode into the advance guard of Colonel Gibbon's forces. He was shot and killed, and the gunfire awoke the rest of the Indian warriors. Mounting a full attack on the Nez Percé as they emerged from their tepees, the infantry killed women, children, braves, and elders indiscriminately.

Indian warriors quickly took up defensive positions, and with sniper fire forced the army back onto the side hill. Both sides sustained heavy losses. The Nez Percé successfully besieged the army troops the rest of that day and night, giving the Nez Percé time to strike their bivouac and flee eastward in search of Crow allies. (The Crow proved to be no allies, and the Nez Percé confronted the army yet again, in the Battle of Canyon Creek.)

The Battlefield

Hike the trails here not just for their history, but for the quiet beauty of this lush meadow flanked by mountains and a swift stream.

The **visitor center** (406/689-3155, www.nps.gov/biho, 9 A.M.–6 P.M. daily Memorial Day–Labor Day, 10 A.M.–5 P.M. the rest of the year, free) provides audiovisual displays that explain the background of the Nez Percé flight and the Big Hole battle. Exhibits include artifacts of the battle and items from the daily life of the early settlers and the Indian tribes who fought here in 1877.

An extensive network of self-guided hiking trails links the sites of the battle. From the parking lot, a 1.5-mile trail leads to the site of the Nez Percé camp; a shorter trail leads to the siege area. Here, for devotees of military strategy, interpretive signs chart the development of the battle in great detail. A somewhat steeper hike leads to the site of the howitzer captured by the Nez Percé, where there are great views over the battlefield and the Big Hole Valley.

For hiking of a different magnitude, the **Nee-Me-Poo Historic Trail** (www.fs.fed.us/npnht) passes through the Big Hole Battlefield. This 1,200-mile trail follows the route of the Nez Percé from Oregon to the Bears Paw Mountains, where the army finally apprehended the fleeing tribe.

Accommodations

There are picnic facilities at the lower parking lot along the river, but camping is not allowed. The closest services are in Wisdom, 10 miles east. **May Creek Forest Service campground** (406/689-3243, www.fs.fed.us/r1/b-d, July–Labor Day, $7) is eight miles west on Highway 43.

THE BIG HOLE

Although the Big Hole River is more than 100 miles long, the term *big hole*—frontier-ese for a deep, wide valley—refers to the river's upper basin. Here, between Jackson and Fishtrap, is fabled ranch country, rivaling only eastern Montana for its eternal flatness and traditional Western ways. Here too is great fishing for the discriminating angler, with rushing streams full of scrappy brook trout and rare arctic grayling, a long-finned species rarely found outside of Alaska and northern Canada. Almost all river access is through private land, so be sure to ask permission from the landowner.

Jackson

Captain Clark and his return party passed through here in 1806 and stopped at the local hot springs. Not content with just a soak, the Corps of Discovery also cooked their dinner in the 138°F water. Now, as then, this little community is known mostly for the springs.

The (**Jackson Hot Springs Lodge,** off Highway 278 (406/834-3151 or 888/438-6938, www.jacksonhotsprings.com, $33–85) operates a Western-style resort at the spot where Lewis and Clark dined. The lodge is right on Jackson's main drag and dominates the town. Even if you don't stay the night, stop for a swim ($5) or a drink at the bar. Open year-round, the lodge caters to summer anglers and tourists but really gears up for winter guests. Nearby are excellent cross-country trails, some groomed and others informal; snowmobilers also use the lodge as a center. Standard accommodations at the resort are in cabin-like motel rooms; rates for these begin at $85 per night. However, there are some tiny cabins with a shared bath that run $33 per night; if you want to stay in one of the budget cabins, you'll have to speak up. A few lodge rooms ($55) are also available, as are sites for tents ($10) and RVs ($25). Good food (three meals a day), drink, and entertainment are provided at the lodge.

A couple of Forest Service campgrounds (406/689-3243, www.fs.fed.us/r1/b-d, early July–Labor Day, $7) are west of Jackson. **Miner Lake** is about 10 miles west of town via Forest Service Road 182, which heads off toward the Bitterroots right at the south end of town. The campground is not well-marked; look off to your left when you're 10 miles out of town and you'll find at least one of the many de facto campsites in the area. To reach the **Twin Lakes** campground, take Road 1290 west from Highway 278 about halfway between Jackson

and Wisdom and travel for about 13 miles. Both campgrounds are pretty places perched on the east slopes of the Bitterroots. The lakes are great canoe spots, but motorboats are not allowed.

Wisdom

This little crossroads—more an outpost than a town—is a trading center for the cattle ranches and hay farms that stretch across the wide valley. Higher civilization is making inroads, however. As a sign of changing times, Wisdom supports watering holes for local ranch hands and a tony art gallery.

The nicest place to stay in Wisdom is the attractive **Nez Perce Motel** (406/689-3254, $50 and up), with some kitchenettes. It's also worth considering staying down the road at Jackson Hot Springs.

Head 10 miles east of town on Road 31 to a small **campground** at the trailhead leading to Sand Lake and Lily Lake. Actually, keep going on the trail system here and you can cross the Pioneers, coming out north of Elkhorn Hot Springs.

The center of life in Wisdom revolves around its bars and restaurants. **Fetty's Bar and Cafe** (406/689-3260, less than $15) is a local institution serving three meals a day. The **Antlers Saloon** is a popular place for a drink; it's not unlike having a beer in a taxidermy shop. Lurid green **Conover's Trading Post** is the community's all-around store and community center.

The really incongruous business in town is the **Wisdom River Gallery** (406/689-3800, 9 A.M.–5 P.M. daily). Here the art of the West rubs cheeks with the life of the West. This fine selection of blue-chip Western art—with some local talent—somehow finds a market in Wisdom. The **Big Hole Crossing Restaurant** serves grilled entrées (7 A.M.–9 P.M. summer, 8 A.M.–8 P.M. winter, breakfast or lunch about $5, dinners top out at $15) in the back of the gallery.

Go 28 miles west of Wisdom on Highway 43 to pick up the **Continental Divide Trail** at Chief Joseph Pass. The Bitterroot Ski Club maintains an extensive network of groomed cross-country ski trails on the north side of

© JUDY JEWELL

Wisdom isn't big, but it has the Antlers Saloon.

Highway 43 at the pass. No dogs are permitted on the groomed trails.

The **Wisdom Ranger Station** can be contacted at 406/689-3243.

Wise River

Between Wisdom and Wise River, the Big Hole Valley narrows. The river enters a canyon and picks up speed. Rainbow and brown trout begin to dominate the waters, in numbers and sizes that excite a national audience of fly-fishers. There are several fishing-access sites as the river enters its canyon: good for anglers, handy for floaters, and perfect for picnickers. At the town of Wise River, the river of the same name enters the Big Hole. A designated scenic byway along Highway 484 begins here.

A couple of lakes in the Anaconda Mountains to the west are of interest to the traveling angler. **Mussigbrod Lake,** 23 miles northwest of Wisdom, has some of the best arctic grayling fishing in the Lower 48. There's also a Forest

Service campground. There's another campground at **Pintler Lake,** 10 miles off Highway 43 up Pintler Creek Road. The lake offers good fishing for rainbow and cutthroat and a scenic base camp for explorations of the surrounding pine forests.

What passes on the map for a town at Wise River is in fact a couple of bars at the junction of the Big Hole and Wise Rivers. Not to sound dismissive—a couple of bars in fact *do* a town make, at least out here in fly-fisher's heaven.

The Wise River Club (406/832-3258) is a taciturn old bar full of broken-down furniture and taxidermy. It's still enough of a local's bar to be at once suspicious and friendly. The restaurant is open for three meals a day. The club's motel has rooms for about $50; there is also limited camping for RVs.

South of Wise River, the road to Elkhorn Hot Springs is dotted with Forest Service **campgrounds.** Most of these spots are right on the Wise River, with good fishing access.

Outfitters and guest ranch resorts provide accommodation options for anglers. The **Complete Fly Fisher** (406/832-3175 or 866/832-3175, www.completeflyfisher.com) offers guided fishing, great cooking, and lodging in cabins or lodge rooms, about $4,300 for a week. The attractive riverside **Big Hole Lodge** (406/832-3252, www.flyfishinglodge. com, $3,150 and up per person per week) offers accommodations to their angler guests.

The **Wise River Ranger Station** can be reached at 406/832-3178.

THE LOWER BIG HOLE RIVER

Downstream south from the community of Divide, the Big Hole, with great fishing up to this point, becomes a blue-ribbon trout fishery. Brown trout are both huge and abundant. Mid-June, when the salmon flies hatch, marks a frantic season for fish and fishers alike. To the misfortune of the trout, there are several good fishing-access sites between Divide and Glen.

Divide

Floaters need to beware of a diversion dam just upstream from Divide. Here, water from the

Big Hole River is pumped over the Continental Divide to Butte at a rate of five million gallons per day. In its day, the pump station was quite an engineering feat; it's on the National Register of Historic Places.

For hikers, often overlooked is the **Humbug Spires Primitive Area,** a day hike into an area of geologic interest. Intense faulting has fractured granite extrusions into steep, sharp needles that resemble menhirs (prehistoric monoliths). About three miles in, the trail reaches a watershed, and there's a good view over the spiny valley. Exit I-15 at Moose Creek Road, three miles south of Divide, and turn east.

Melrose

Near Melrose, the Big Hole leaves its steep-sided canyon and resolutely flows to its appointment with the Beaverhead River. This is a good place to leave I-15 and follow old Highway 10. From Glen, off-road enthusiasts can follow a gravel road along the Big Hole River as it trends east to the Beaverhead. It's a pretty drive, becoming dramatic as it approaches historic Beaverhead Rock from its back side.

Melrose lollygags along the old rail sidings that spawned its early growth, a town caught in the midst of a stretching exercise. This pleasant hamlet is known for its fishing; with several fishing-access sites, an attractive motel, a cabin resort, a café, and bars, it's no wonder that anglers flock here.

Head west out of Melrose up Trapper Creek (Rd. 40), then Canyon Creek (Rd. 41) to the Lion Creek trail, a nine-mile loop from the campground at road's end to Lion Lake and back again. From the lake, a hike up nearby Sharp Mountain will give you a pretty good chance of spotting mountain goats.

As elsewhere on the Big Hole, it's easy to find an outfitter to guide you to the fish. **Sundown Outfitters** (406/835-3474) is associated with the Sunrise Fly Shop and offers big-game hunting in addition to fishing trips.

The **Sportsman Motel** (N. Main St., 406/835-2141, $61–96) is a handsome log motel complex with gas barbecue grills, horse boarding (other pets are allowed too), laundry facilities, and an RV park. Two private cabins ($96) and a two-bedroom log house ($250 per night, three-night minimum) are also available. Head 4.5 miles south of town on the frontage road to **Great Waters** (406/835-2024, www.greatwatersinn.com, $2,490 per week includes all meals and guide), an attractive fishing resort with a guide service and a good restaurant in the lodge. Nonanglers can stay for $150 per night (includes meals).

THE PIONEER MOUNTAINS

Surrounded on three sides by the meanderings of the Big Hole River, the Pioneer Mountains are in fact two different ranges divided down a north-south axis, linked yet separated, sort of like the underside of a coffee bean. These out-of-the-way mountains come to life in the winter; a hot springs resort and a small downhill ski area combine to bring in the locals. In the summer the hills are covered with violet-blue lupine. The Wise River drainage is popular with anglers; there are several large Forest Service campgrounds with fishing access along the river.

Highway 484 bisects the Pioneer Mountains, from Wise River in the north through Polaris to Highway 278 in the south. The Forest Service has designated this route running down the furrow of the coffee bean as the **Pioneer Mountains Scenic Byway.**

Maverick Mountain Ski Area

The legendary heavy snows of southwestern Montana are put to good use at the homey, family-oriented Maverick Ski Area (406/834-3454, www.skimaverick.com, Thurs.–Sun.), where the vertical drop is 2,120 feet. Maverick Lodge offers lessons, rentals, day care, and food; cross-country skiers are welcome. A lift ticket is only $26 per day, $18 for children, or $18 adults on nonholiday Thursdays and Fridays, but there are only 18 runs and one real lift. A shuttle bus leaves from the Wells Fargo Bank parking lot in Dillon at 8:15 A.M. on Saturdays, Sundays, and holidays during ski season ($4).

Many skiers come up for the day from Dillon, but the closest lodging to Maverick is the **Grasshopper Inn** (406/834-3456, $55–75), at the base of the slopes beside the near–ghost town of Polaris. The Grasshopper has motel rooms and a fairly basic restaurant (dinner $8–22).

Elkhorn Hot Springs

This venerable resort (13 miles north of Hwy. 278 on Hwy. 484, 406/834-3434 or 800/722-8978, www.elkhornhotsprings.com) is the other popular lodging for skiers. Cross-country skiers converge here; with 25 miles of cross-country trails managed by the resort, an entire mountain range of informal trails to explore, and a good hot soak to come home to, this is near-heaven (at an elevation of 7,385 feet, literally so). In summer the hot springs are popular for hikers. There are two outdoor mineral pools plus a sauna, and it costs $6 ($4 for kids) for a swim.

Rooms are either in the lodge ($40 and up, bathroom down the hall) or in rustic cabins scattered among the trees. The restaurant in the lodge is open for three meals a day. Cabins, with electricity and wood-burning stoves but no plumbing (an outhouse is shared with neighboring cabins), start at $80 for a double (swimming included). Don't come to Elkhorn expecting a trendy New Age getaway; it's funky and remote, and with that in mind, charming and relaxing.

If you want to stop at Elkhorn for a swim and a soak but would prefer to camp out, the very pretty Forest Service **Grasshopper Creek Campground** (June–mid-Sept., $8) is less than one mile down the road. Pick up the Blue Creek trail just south of the campground and head into the West Pioneers. North of Elkhorn Hot Springs are several more campgrounds and trailheads.

Crystal Park

At this Forest Service–maintained site four miles north of Elkhorn Hot Springs (406/683-3900, $5 per vehicle), rock hounds can dig for quartz crystals. It's a very popular spot, attracting dedicated amateur crystal miners who come with shovels and screens to sift through the dirt for quartz and amethyst. But even ill-equipped novices can scrape through the topsoil for a few minutes and come up with a small crystal or two.

The Southwestern Corner

Montana schoolchildren are taught to recognize the state's western boundary as Abraham Lincoln's long-faced profile. The scruff of Lincoln's beard is Beaverhead County, the state's largest and one of its most varied. The Continental Divide careens along towering snowcapped peaks, which ring in valleys so broad, flat, and covered with sagebrush that ranchers from eastern Montana would feel at home: This is western Montana's prairie province. Some of the oldest and largest ranches in Montana stretched across these high flatlands.

History was quick to find this corner of Montana. High on a forgotten pass between Montana and Idaho is Sacagawea Historical Area, where the Corps of Discovery crossed the Continental Divide. Bannack State Park, Montana's best-preserved ghost town, commemorates the state's first city and first territorial capital. Red Rock Lakes National Wildlife Refuge is one of the nation's most important bird sanctuaries. It is a primary breeding ground for trumpeter swans, which were once feared extinct.

With two million acres of national forest in Beaverhead County alone, and a vast network of streams forming the Missouri's most distant headwaters, southwestern Montana has plenty of room for outdoor recreation. Yet the great fishing, hunting, and hiking opportunities in this lovely corner of Montana are blessedly free of crowds.

SOUTHWESTERN MONTANA

RED ROCK VALLEY

The Red Rock River, the Missouri's most distant headwater, drains a broad valley overlooked by the Continental Divide. This is high country: the valley stretches out prairie-like at elevations above 6,000 feet.

Red Rock Lakes

This remote and beautiful valley, ringed with high but rounded peaks, would probably be ignored by the traveler if it weren't for Red Rock Lakes. At these marshy lakes, biologists discovered trumpeter swans, once feared extinct in the United States, in 1933.

Trumpeter swans formerly ranged over much of the continent. However, during the 19th century, hunters found a vigorous market for quill pens, powder puffs, and swan meat. As the homestead movement changed the environment of eastern Montana, with land falling to the plow and marshes being drained, swan populations plummeted. Biologists found only 66 trumpeters in 1933 at Red Rock Lakes, the last individuals of the species in the country.

The U.S. Department of the Interior established the 40,300-acre **Red Rock Lakes National Wildlife Refuge** (406/276-3536, www.fws.gov/redrocks) in 1935. Currently 600 trumpeters summer here, and as geothermal activity maintains ice-free water temperatures year-round, the winter population swells to 2,000.

The Defenders of Wildlife, a group concerned with wildlife preservation, has called the refuge one of the most beautiful in America. Upper and Lower Red Rock Lakes are nestled beneath the 9,800-foot Centennial Mountains. This isolated corner of Montana is home to a variety of wildlife, including moose, deer, elk, pronghorn, and foxes; 258 bird species have been sighted at the lakes.

To reach the refuge, turn at Monida, just below the Continental Divide on I-15. The reserve is a rattly 28 miles up a gravel road. Wildlife viewing is best between May and November, which is about the only season the road is dependably passable. The reserve can

also be reached in good weather from Idaho on the Red Rock Pass Road, 17 miles from West Yellowstone on Highway 87.

Recreation

Fishing is allowed in most areas of the refuge and provides good sport for trout anglers. Nonmotorized boats are allowed on some areas of the lakes; check with refuge managers. Arctic grayling are caught in streams that feed the lakes. Hunting is permitted in designated areas of the refuge for specific species.

Practicalities

The closest motel is in Lima. Although it is pretty basic, **Mountain View Motel & RV Park** (111 Bailey St., 406/276-3535, $45–55) will give you a bed and a roof. Otherwise, this is camping country. There are two **campgrounds** at the wildlife refuge—one alongside each lake—meaning great views but also a potential mosquito assault.

Yesterday's Cafe (406/276-3308, 7 A.M.–8 P.M. summer, 7 A.M.–7 P.M. winter, $4–10) in Dell serves the area's best home-style cooking in a refurbished country schoolhouse.

HORSE PRAIRIE VALLEY

The Red Rock River meets Horse Prairie Creek at Clark Canyon Reservoir, and the Beaverhead River issues forth. While the reservoir is popular with local boaters and anglers, and old ranches fill the wide valley traditionally known as the Horse Prairie, travelers will want to explore the area to relive some of the most stirring moments of the Lewis and Clark Expedition.

The Shoshone Indians were the first Montana-area natives to acquire horses. They stormed north through the upper Jefferson River drainages to threaten and finally dominate the high plains east of the Rocky Mountain front in the 1750s. The Blackfoot federation, moving south from Canada with guns obtained from the British, halted the Shoshone's expansion. The Shoshone were forced back into Idaho by the 1800s, where Lewis and Clark first encountered them.

TRUMPETER SWANS

Trumpeter swans are North America's largest waterfowl. A mature male weighs in at 26 pounds, and his wings stretch eight feet. These swans are pure white, with black beaks. Sometimes their heads are stained yellowish – a result of diving in iron-rich mud.

Trumpeters mate for life, and their lives are long. Individuals can live for almost 30 years in the wild. The same mated pair often returns to the same nest year after year. Females are called pens, and males are called cobs. Swan young, hatched from eggs weighing 12 ounces, are called cygnets.

The continent's largest population of trumpeters occurs in Alaska, although significant numbers of swans can now be found from the mouth of the Columbia River north along the Pacific Coast. However, Montana's Red Rock Lakes National Wildlife Refuge remains one of the most beautiful places to observe these rare fowl. Take binoculars, because trumpeters are wary of people. Parts of the refuge may be closed to protect nests.

Corps of Discovery

As the Corps of Discovery pushed up the Jefferson River in search of the Missouri headwaters, Sacagawea began to recognize landmarks of her childhood.

Recognizing the need for horses to proceed over the difficult Continental Divide that faced them, Lewis and three men went ahead to scout for the Shoshone, into whose homeland Sacagawea insisted they had entered. Lewis sighted the expedition's first Indian in Montana in the Horse Prairie Valley and continued over Lemhi Pass to encounter a Shoshone lodge near Tendoy, Idaho. After tenuous negotiations for horses, the Shoshone agreed to backtrack with Lewis and his party to meet the rest of the corps.

As the party approached, Sacagawea began to suck her fingers, a sign that she recognized her kin. A Shoshone woman broke rank and ran forward to embrace Sacagawea, recognizing her from her childhood. When Sacagawea was summoned to interpret the dialogue between the whites and the natives, she entered the tent where the men were conversing and immediately recognized her brother Cameahwait, who was now chief of the Shoshone.

Consider for a moment what the negotiations for horses and supplies entailed. Sacagawea translated her brother's Shoshone terms into Minataree, which her husband, Charbonneau, understood. He in turn spoke French to a French-speaking member of the corps, who then translated the terms into English for Lewis and Clark. However circumlocutory, the translations worked. The corps traded for 24 horses, and on August 29, 1805, the entire party climbed over Lemhi Pass and the Continental Divide into Spanish territory.

Lemhi Pass

A drive up the steep, graveled road to Lemhi Pass (elev. 7,373 feet) is a must for any Lewis and Clark buff with a high-clearance vehicle. Turn off Highway 324 onto Lemhi Pass Road and follow the road, sometimes more rock than gravel, for about 20 miles. From the top—the Montana-Idaho border—mountains stretch to the west as far as the eye can see. A sign commemorates the Corps of Discovery's historic ascent and subsequent descent into Idaho.

Just below the crest of the pass on the Montana side, the state has established **Sacagawea Historical Area,** with picnic facilities and a small campground. Here, where a tiny spring gushes out of the rock only yards from the Continental Divide, Lewis thought he had found the "most distant fountain of the waters of the Mighty Missouri." (It's not; that distinction goes to Hellroaring Creek south of the Red Rock Lakes.) The party of four drank from the spring and stood astride it "exultingly," thankful to have lived to put a foot on each side of the "heretofore deemed endless Missouri."

Today's visitor will be unable to resist doing

the same. Bring a picnic; this is an enchanting spot and you'll want to stretch your legs before bumping back down to the valley. A steep Forest Service road continues into Idaho; however, it's not advised for cars. Check with the Salmon Ranger Station (208/756-2215); sometimes the road is closed for logging.

Recreation

There's often good fishing for trout in Clark Canyon Reservoir, although the barren treeless setting and the seemingly always underfilled lake are charm-free. The 5,000-acre lake is popular with boaters from Dillon. The Red Rock River just above the lake is good fishing for cutthroat and rainbow.

Practicalities

Dillon is the closest center for amenities. There are six primitive campgrounds on the shores of the Clark Canyon Reservoir.

❮ BANNACK

Prospectors found rich gold panning along Grasshopper Creek in 1862. Bannack sprang up in response, becoming the first real town in Montana. By the time it became the territorial capital in 1864, Bannack boasted hotels, a governor's mansion, churches, and a Masonic temple.

Montana's vigilante movement was born in Bannack. The first elected sheriff, Henry Plummer, was a smooth operator who ran a gang of road agents—deceptively called the Innocents—on the side. They preyed on miners and travelers until vigilantes prevailed and hanged more than 20 suspected outlaws.

Bannack is now a well-preserved ghost town whose remains commemorate the scene of some of Montana's most violent early history. Bannack State Park is self-guided and undeveloped; visitors are free to explore this fascinating old territorial capital at will and without threat of gift shops.

History

Prospectors gone bust in the Colorado gold boom came north to southwestern Montana

and in 1862 discovered gold at Grasshopper Diggings, about 20 miles west of Dillon. The first of the great Montana booms was on. A sign written in axle grease stood at the confluence of the Beaverhead River and Grasshopper Creek:

TU GRASS HOP PER DIGINS

30 MYLE

KEEP THE TRALE NEX THE BLUFFE.

By winter, a thousand ragtag adventurers, many of them refugees from the Civil War, assembled on the banks of Grasshopper Creek. They named their camp Bannack (symptomatically misspelled) for the native Bannock Indians.

When it came to law and order, which the advent of sudden great wealth demanded, early Montanans just faked it. Henry Plummer was a veteran of the California and Nevada gold rushes, and his urbane good looks and considerable charm won the trust of Bannack (and later Virginia City) voters, who elected him sheriff.

At the same time, Plummer also secretly led a band of road agents of considerable ruthlessness. These ruffians and killers preyed on travelers, authorities, Indians, and anyone else who got in their way. Bannack in 1863 was the West portrayed by Hollywood: gunfights in the street, men gunning each other down over cards, strangers killing strangers for the way they looked. Especially at risk were travelers between Bannack and Virginia City; stage robberies were customary, and cold-blooded murder was frequent.

Even for the Wild West, violence in Bannack was excessive: During the first year of Plummer's stint as sheriff, the Innocents, as he called his gang, killed more than 100 men. Just as many deaths probably went unreported; in a gold camp of several thousand miners, the summer's orgy of lawless killings claimed a significant percentage of the population.

Once Grasshopper Creek froze up and panning ceased for the winter, outraged citizens decided to take the law into their own hands. A secret alliance of men formed a Vigilance

© BILL MCRAE

Bannack, Montana's first capital, is today one of the state's best-preserved ghost towns.

Committee and codified their own set of laws and punishment (invariably death), a secret oath, and their cabalistic secret number 3-7-77, with which they marked their victims (and which is now part of the Montana State Patrol's insignia).

The vigilantes moved quickly. In a period of two weeks, 24 of Plummer's gang were summarily hanged. Plummer's last words were "Give me a good drop."

The experience of lawlessness reinforced the need for a stronger civil authority. In 1864 the miners in Bannack and Alder Gulch sent Judge Sidney Edgerton to petition the U.S. government for territorial status, which the Senate granted and President Lincoln signed on May 26. Bannack became the first territorial capital when Edgerton convened the first legislature here; his house became the first Governor's Mansion.

Bannack's prominence had already begun to fade as the far richer colors of Alder Gulch attracted upward of 10,000 miners by 1864. The territorial capital followed the miners to Virginia City. Little remained of Bannack by 1890.

Bannack State Park

More than 60 structures remain standing at Bannack (406/834-3413, www.bannack.org, 8 A.M.–dusk; $5 per vehicle, $1 bicyclist or walk-in). The streets, homes, hotels, and civic buildings extend along Grasshopper Creek in various states of disrepair. The entire park is self-guided: Explore at will, being careful of dubious stairways and decrepit second stories. The old hotel is rumored to be the most photographed site in Montana. Other buildings of note are the governor's mansion, the Masonic hall, the jail, and the Methodist church. During the summer, guided tours are offered (2 P.M. Mon.–Fri., 10:30 A.M. and 3 P.M. Sat.–Sun.). The third weekend of July is **Bannack Days** at the state park. Events include a black-powder shoot, horse and wagon rides, and a buffalo-steak barbecue.

The **park campground** (406/834-3413) costs $12 per site or $25 to stay in a tepee (call to reserve). To reach Bannack, turn off Highway 278 and follow a county road for three miles. From the south, Bannack can be reached from Highway 324 at Grant, 11 miles along a gravel road.

Dillon

Even if Dillon (pop. 3,752, elev. 5,057 feet) weren't the center of a vast region of broad fertile valleys filled with old ranches and rushing streams brimming with trout; even if Dillon weren't surrounded by national forests and wildlife refuges; and even if Dillon weren't close to the crossroads of Lewis and Clark, Chief Joseph, Henry Plummer, and a territory's worth of early miners and ranchers, Dillon would deserve the traveler's attention.

Dillon is an authentic old trade town that has managed to endure the recent economic malaise of the agricultural West without facing extinction or resorting to survival as a self-parody for tourists. Filled with historic architecture but kept young by the presence of students at the University of Montana–Western, blessed with decent restaurants, and faithful to the old bars that—then, as now—have consoled cowboys, sheepherders, and miners, Dillon is one of Montana's most bewitching small cities and makes an excellent base for day trips to the Big Hole Battlefield, the Pioneer Mountains, Bannack, and Virginia City.

SIGHTS
Historic Dillon

For a city of its size, Dillon has an unexpected array of architectural styles. The Beaverhead County Museum provides a free brochure, *Historical Tour of Dillon,* covering many of the local curiosities.

Some highlights: The **Beaverhead County Courthouse,** at Pacific and Bannack Streets, was built in 1889 and contains a four-faced Seth Thomas clock in its tower. The **Dillon Tribune Building,** at Bannack and Idaho Streets, housed Dillon's first newspaper; the 1888 facade is made entirely of pressed metal. One of the grandest of all the old hotels in Montana is the **Metlen Hotel,** built in 1897 as "one of the best, if not the best, constructed edifices in the state." A little down on its luck today, the Metlen is still an imposing monument to the era of grandiose railroad hotels.

Orr Mansion, at the south end of Idaho Street, is flanked by estates of other early entrepreneurs. William Orr was a California cattleman who brought his herd north to the Beaverhead country in 1862. Success was more or less immediate, and by 1864 Orr began to build his Italianate villa.

At the **Beaverhead County Museum** (15 S. Montana St., 406/683-5027), a towering Alaskan brown bear (mounted, of course) oversees the exhibits of Indian artifacts, early ranching curios, and mining memorabilia.

University of Montana-Western

The 34-acre State Normal School, established to train teachers for Montana's classrooms, was established in Dillon in 1893. The original structure, added to in 1907, forms Old Main, an imposing and distinctive brick edifice incorporating eclectic design elements including Gothic windows and Queen Anne towers.

Recent economic circumscriptions by the state Board of Regents have forced the college to affiliate with the University of Montana in Missoula. UM–Western (710 S. Atlantic St., 406/683-7011) specializes in training prospective teachers for Montana's rural schools, and it also hosts many Elderhostel programs.

Shopping

People come to Dillon from all over western Montana to shop at the **Patagonia Outlet** (34 N. Idaho St., 406/683-2580) for bargain-priced outdoor clothing.

RECREATION

You can't turn around in Dillon without bumping up against great recreation opportunities. Dillon is the natural hub for the entire southwestern corner of Montana, where fishing, hiking, hunting, camping, and exploring the outdoors in general are incarnated in rich abundance.

Biking

Some of Montana's best dirt-road biking is detailed on the Great Divide Mountain Bike

Route, section 2, a map published by Missoula's Adventure Cycling (406/721-1776 or 800/755-2453, www.adv-cycling.org). Order the map, which includes the area between Polaris in the Pioneer Mountains all the way south into Wyoming, from Adventure Cycling.

Fishing

The races and runnels that form the fabric of the Jefferson River are all legendary, highly productive fisheries. The Beaverhead River forms below Clark Canyon Dam; between here and Dillon is some of the most challenging and satisfying trout fly-fishing in Montana. Much of this fast-

flowing river is fished best by floating; during high flows, travelers should consider enlisting the aid of outfitters. Of course, one river does not an anglers' paradise make: the Ruby, Big Hole, and Red Rock Rivers, not to mention the mountain streams that feed them, are all within easy casting distance from Dillon. Don't miss Blacktail Deer Creek, just southeast of Dillon, for more leisurely, streamside fishing for brookies and cutthroat.

Hiking

With the Continental Divide arrayed around the perimeter of southwestern Montana, it's no wonder there's great hiking and camping just about everywhere that's uphill. A Beaverhead National Forest map reveals hikes in every direction, but avid hikers should try to visit a few isolated ranges.

The Snowcrest Range contains rugged and seldom-visited 10,000-foot peaks, with large populations of elk and mountain goats. The mountains divide the Ruby, Red Rock, and Blacktail Deer drainages in a remote area. The Snowcrests are about 20 miles southeast of Dillon along Blacktail Deer Creek Road. Even more remote and rugged are the mountains at the head of **Big Sheep Creek** (turn west at the Dell exit 45 miles south of Dillon and follow signs for Big Sheep Canyon).

Between the Beaverhead Mountains (guardians of the Continental Divide) and the Tendoy Mountains, tributaries of Big Sheep Creek fan out. Trails lead up to glaciated valleys and knife-edge ridges along the Montana-Idaho border. Check with the Forest Service office in Dillon for details.

Outfitters

For horseback rides or pack trips into the Pioneer Mountains, call **Diamond Hitch Outfitters** (406/683-5494 or 800/368-5494). Rates start at about $30 for a short trail ride; dinner rides from Dillon are $60.

Guide Tim Tollett operates a fly shop, **Frontier Anglers** (680 N. Montana, 406/683-5276 or 800/228-5263, www.frontieranglers.com), and leads fishing trips. **Backcountry Angler** (426 S. Atlantic St., 406/683-3462) offers rooms, a fly shop, and guided fishing trips.

Lewis and Clark buffs may want to arrange a tour with the **Great Divide Wildlands Institute** (406/683-4669, www.greatdivide-tours.com). This outfitter specializes in historical tours, sometimes on horseback, to sites along the Corps of Discovery's route.

PRACTICALITIES
Accommodations

For a decent budget motel within walking distance to downtown, try the **Creston Motel** (335 N. Atlantic St., 406/683-2341, $45 and up). Pets are permitted.

The nice-for-the-price **Sundowner Motel** (500 N. Montana St., 406/683-2375 or 800/524-9746, $45 and up), across the street from the local fertilizer plant and four blocks from downtown, has a playground, permits pets in smoking rooms, and serves free morning coffee and donuts.

A homey and comfortable place to stay on the edge of downtown are the rooms rented out by the **Backcountry Angler** (426 S. Atlantic St., 406/683-3462, www.backcountryangler.com, $75 and up). Although the outfitter's fishing clients get first dibs on these suites with kitchens, there are occasional openings for the general public.

The **Best Western Paradise Inn** (650 N. Montana St., 406/683-4214 or 800/528-1234, $77 and up) is relatively plush, with an indoor pool, exercise room, hot tub, and restaurant-casino on the premises. The other very comfortable conventional hotel is out by I-15: The **GuestHouse Inn** (580 Sinclair St., 406/683-3636 or 800/214-8378, www.guesthouseintl.com, $109 and up) has an indoor pool and a breakfast bar.

Guest Ranches and Fishing Lodges

If you want to go native, stay at a guest ranch. **Hildreth Livestock Ranch** (406/681-3111, www.greatdivideadventure.com, $45–60 per person double occupancy, higher during big-game season) is a working Chiangus cattle ranch 50 miles southwest of Dillon that welcomes guests in guest houses on the ranch. Guest houses have full kitchens. Bicyclists are given a special welcome.

At the **Five Rivers Lodge** (406/683-5000, www.fiverriverslodge.com), perched above the Beaverhead River near spring-fed ponds on Highway 41, the emphasis is on fishing, although there are amenities for nonanglers. Guests stay in comfortable rooms, are fed three meals a day, and are accompanied by a guide on fishing expeditions to public streams and private spring creeks and ponds. Rates run $3,095 for five days of fishing and six nights of lodging. Shorter stays and nonfishing discounts are available.

Hidden Valley Guest Ranch (10135 Hwy. 91 S., 800/250-8802, www.hvgr.com, $75–225 d) has lodging in cabins or deluxe tepees and outdoor activities such as hiking, mountain biking, and fishing.

Camping

The **Bureau of Reclamation campground** (www.usbr.gov/gp, free) at Barretts, five miles south of town on the frontage road, sits right on the Beaverhead River as it leaves its canyon. Head 20 miles south of Dillon to **Clark Canyon Reservoir,** where more Bureau of Reclamation campgrounds line the shore and are conveniently, but not annoyingly, close to I-15. Right in town, the **Dillon KOA** (735 W. Park, 406/683-2749, RV $33, tent $25) has a pool, showers, and restrooms. The **Southside RV Park** (exit 62, 104 E. Poindexter St., 406/683-2244, $27) has a lovely location on Blacktail Deer Creek.

Food

Start off a day in Dillon with a jolt of espresso and a homemade scone at **Sweetwater Coffee** (26 E. Bannack St., 406/683-4141, 8 A.M.–6 P.M., lunch $6–7). It's also a good place to have a bite of lunch so that you don't shop the nearby Patagonia outlet on an empty stomach.

Sparky's Garage (420 E. Poindexter St., 406/683-2828, 6:30 A.M.–9 P.M. daily, $5–18), a popular spot for ribs, pulled pork, sweet-potato fries, and tasty cornbread, is near the university.

Don't be afraid to head down the stairs to **Blacktail Station** (26 S. Montana St., 406/683-6611, 5–9 P.M. daily, $8–30), offering steaks, daily pasta specials, and good meal-sized salads. The other downtown stronghold is the **Klondike** (33 E. Bannack, 406/683-2141, 7 A.M.–9 P.M. daily, $9–23), with traditional ranch-country meals.

INFORMATION AND SERVICES

The well-equipped **chamber of commerce** is in the old railroad depot (125 S. Montana St., 406/683-5511).

GETTING THE GOLD OUT

The tremendously rich gold-bearing gravels of Alder Gulch lay beneath a considerable weight of overburden. Shafts and tunnels had to be dug and the gravel hoisted out to the surface. The gravel was then shoveled into a "rocker," where water sloshed away lighter materials while the gold nuggets tumbled into baffles on the bottom of the device. If the claim was near streams, water could be diverted into sluice boxes. Dozens of miners could work along a sluice, sometimes hundreds of feet long. During the first five years of mining operations in Alder Gulch, an estimated $40 million was extracted, and by 1928 the total exceeded $100 million, with gold at $16 an ounce.

After miners removed the richest deposits of gold in Alder Gulch, more advanced technology allowed the processing of low-grade ore and tailings from early mining to extract trace deposits. The large berms of gravel at the little town of Alder reveal the debris of gold-dredging operations from the early 1900s. Although gold-seekers still pan for gold, and mines south of Virginia City produce gold and silver, the talc mines in the Ruby Range are now the area's largest operations.

Barrett Memorial Hospital is at 1260 South Atlantic Street (406/683-3000).

The **Dillon Ranger District,** Beaverhead National Forest, is at 420 Barrett Street (406/683-3900, www.fs.fed.us/r1/b-d). The **Bureau of Land Management** office is at 1005 Selway Drive (406/683-8000, www.mt.blm.gov/dfo).

Transportation

If you're flying to this neck of the woods, check fares on flights into Idaho Falls; it's less than two hours down I-15 and often cheaper than flying into Montana airports.

SOUTHWESTERN MONTANA

Alder Gulch and the Ruby River Valley

In 1863, one year after the first big gold strike in Montana, a group of prospectors led by Bill Fairweather left Bannack for the Yellowstone Valley. En route they were harried by Crow Indians and turned back. After pitching camp in the Gravelly Range, the prospectors decided to pan for tobacco money. Their panning turned up rich color, and the miners realized they had discovered a major gold deposit at Alder Gulch.

They vowed to keep silent about their claims, but after they returned to Bannack, their free-spending ways drew the attention of other prospectors. When they started back to Alder Gulch, hundreds of miners followed them, each hoping to cash in on the presumed new strike. Within a year, 10,000 hopefuls lived in settlements along Alder Gulch.

The settlement that sprang up at Virginia City became the second capital of Montana Territory. Virginia City has survived as other gold camps have not; it's still the governmental seat of Madison County, and among the deserted buildings are shops, hotels, and restaurants that belie its guise of a ghost town.

◖ VIRGINIA CITY

Virginia City (pop. 137, elev. 5,760 feet) is that oxymoronic anomaly, a working ghost town. Five streets of original and restored buildings from the 1860s and 1870s define the town, which led to Virginia City's designation as a national historic landmark in 1962. But the town never died. Virginia City is still the county seat, and behind its false fronts and log-frame structures, cafés and shops serve locals year-round.

Although Bannack came first as a gold camp, Virginia City was Montana's first incorporated town; while the gold at Bannack played out quickly, mining continued at Virginia City. When the second territorial congress convened in 1865, it met at the state's population center, Virginia City, thereby elevating it to territorial capital. It remained so until 1875.

When Montana became a territory in 1864, an official court system was put in place, although vigilantes retaliated against presumed wrongdoers for several more years. Other institutions soon followed: The state's first school district was established in Virginia City in 1866.

Sights

Virginia City is best thought of as an open-air museum of the early mining West. While strolling along the board sidewalks, poke into the old buildings. Those that aren't currently in business have been restored and contain artifacts of Alder Gulch's boom years. Most of the following structures lie along Wallace Street, now Highway 287. Buildings are open early May–early September.

The **Madison County Courthouse,** built in 1876, still serves as the seat of local government. The territorial offices were housed on the second floor of the **Content Corner** building. The **Montana Post Building,** with its display of printing equipment, was home to Montana's first newspaper. Within **Vigilante Barn,** the Montana vigilante movement was supposedly born.

The **Pioneer Bar** is an authentic restoration of a mining-era watering hole. The **Bale of Hay Saloon** contains period mechanical peep shows and is still a good place to get a beer and hear a bar band. The **Masonic Temple,** built of cut stone, still houses lodge meetings. The **Madison County Museum** contains artifacts from the Alder Gulch mining days, including furniture, clothing, and photos, and a collection of barbed wire. The **Thompson-Hickman Memorial Museum and Library** (406/843-5346) contains the preserved clubfoot of a desperado and other vigilante mementos, as well as ore samples and mining equipment.

Other buildings have been restored to serve their original purposes, as barber shops, grocery stores, and other small businesses of an early mining camp and state capital.

© PAUL LEVY

Many of Virginia City's old storefronts still house thriving businesses.

A short walk south on Jackson Street leads to **Alder Gulch Discovery Monument,** which commemorates the original gold strike of 1863. North on Fairweather Street about 0.5 mile to a bluff above town is the **Boothill Cemetery.** Here are buried three road agents who were hanged by vigilantes during their brief tour of duty. Bill Fairweather was buried here until he was reinterred in a new cemetery with more law-abiding neighbors. Fairweather maintained the respect of the citizens of Alder Gulch by riding along Wallace Street scattering gold dust for children and the less fortunate. From Boothill there is also a good view of Alder Gulch.

Tour the area aboard a **1941 fire engine** (406/843-5421 or 800/317-5421, 10:30 A.M.–6 P.M. late May–mid-Sept., $7.50 adults, $4.50 children 12 and under, carry-on kids free); the drivers do a good job of pointing out the sights and telling colorful stories. **Stagecoach** (406/843-5364, 10:30–about 6 P.M. daily summer, $15 adults, $12 children 7–12) rides are also popular; the same folks offer horseback rides in the area and "corral rides" for children ($30 one hour, $10 corral ride).

Montana's oldest summer-stock theater group, the **Virginia City Players** (406/843-5377 or 800/829-2969, www.virginiacityplayers.com, June–early Sept., $15 adults, $8 children), performs at two of Alder Gulch's historic buildings. At the **Opera House** they perform period melodramas and comedies. At the **Gilbert Brewery** (406/843-5218 or 800/829-2969, early May–late Sept., $15), now restored as a bar, Montana's first brewery provides the stage for slightly naughty comedy shows nightly.

Credit for the restoration of Virginia City belongs to Charles and Sue Bovey, who worked hard in the 1940s to preserve the old frontier town. They bought many of the dilapidated buildings and restored them to their original condition. Heirs of the Boveys were forced to sell the properties because of the high cost of insurance and upkeep. After protracted negotiations with buyers as varied as Knott's Berry Farm and the National Park Service, the state of Montana bought Virginia City and maintains it essentially as an open-air museum and park.

SOUTHWESTERN MONTANA

Accommodations

Virginia City is a popular place to stay in the summer. If you can't find a room in town, consider staying in Ennis. The **Fairweather Inn** (315 W. Wallace St., 406/843-5377 or 800/829-2969, www.aldergulchaccommodations.com, $70 with shared bath or $80 with private bath) is a lovingly restored Victorian hotel. Rooms go fast, especially on weekends, so call ahead for reservations. It's open from mid-May to Labor Day only. Virginia City's B&B inns are open year-round in restored and period-furnished National Historic Register homes. The **Stonehouse Inn** (306 E. Idaho, 406/843-5504, www.stonehouse-innbb.com, $85) is on a quiet street just a block away from the main drag; the large stone house was built in 1884 by the local blacksmith. The **Bennett House Country Inn** (115 E. Idaho, 406/843-5220 or 877/843-5220, www.bennetthouseinn.com, $85–95, shared baths) is a tall, trim Victorian house with a cute kitchen-equipped log cabin ($125) out back.

The **Virginia City RV Park** (406/843-5493, www.virginiacityrvpark.com, tent $22, RV $26–30, cabin $65), just east of Virginia City, offers miniature golf and horseshoes for the kids.

Food

During the summer it's easy to find a bite to eat in one of the cafés along Wallace Street. Most places charge $6–9 for lunch, $12–20 for dinner, and they're all pretty casual. Stop by the **City Bakery** (325 W. Wallace St., 406/843-5227) for breakfast rolls, cookies, fancy petit fours, or lovely lavender scones. You'll find City Bakery pastries, good coffee, and a non–Old West atmosphere at the **Metropolitan Market** (213 W. Wallace St., 406/843-5227, 9 A.M.–4 P.M. daily May–Oct.).

At **Lynch's Virginia City Cafe** (210 W. Wallace St., 406/843-5511, 11 A.M.–8 P.M. daily May–Oct.), it's possible to get a buffalo burger instead of beef. Winter visitors will appreciate the **Outlaw Cafe** (118 W. Wallace St., 406/843-5394), which serves three meals a day year-round.

Virginia City's best dinners are at **Ⅽ Bandito's** (312 W. Wallace St., 406/843-5556, 5–10 P.M. nightly Memorial Day–Sept., $18–26). It's in the historic Wells Fargo building, and the interior is as classy as the building itself, with Oriental rugs, white tablecloths, and a nicely refurbished tin ceiling. There's a Southwestern twist to the food here, and weekend evenings often bring live music.

Information

Find the **Virginia City Chamber of Commerce** at 211 West Wallace Street (406/843-5555 or 800/829-2969, www.virginiacitychamber.com).

The **Ruby Valley Hospital** is at 220 East Crofoot, Sheridan (406/842-5453).

NEVADA CITY

Virginia City's sister city one mile downstream grew up in the boom days of placer mining in Alder Gulch. Abandoned by the 1880s, the ghost town was restored in the 1950s by Charles and Sue Bovey, the driving force behind Virginia City's renovation. The Boveys brought in period buildings from other areas of Montana, creating an outdoor museum of early mining in Montana.

During the peak summer season, an $8 admission fee ($6 youth 6–16, free for children under six) is required to tour most of the buildings (a few are outside of the fenced-off fee area).

In addition to restored shops and businesses, the **Alder Gulch Short Line Steam Railroad Museum** (800/829-2969) contains a collection of rolling stock and engines from the early days of railroading. Museum admission includes fare on the narrow-gauge rail line between Nevada and Virginia Cities. Most of the trips are on a gasoline-powered train ($5 one-way, $8 round-trip); real rail buffs should try to come on a weekend during July or August, or during a summer holiday, when the steam-powered Locomotive No. 12 pulls the train ($8 one-way, $12.50 round-trip).

Also of interest is the **Nevada City Music Hall,** which houses an astonishing collection

© PAUL LEVY

Be sure to check out the two-story outhouse in Nevada City.

of old mechanical music machines. Check behind the Nevada City Hotel to glimpse the renowned two-story outhouse.

The **Nevada City Hotel and Cabins** (406/843-5377 or 800/648-7588, mid-May–late Sept., $85–100) was originally a stage station from south of Twin Bridges; it was moved here and restored with an eye to modern comforts. The cabins are original miners' lodgings, now equipped with bathrooms, but still rustic. At **Just an Experience,** just east of town on Highway 287 (406/843-5402 or 866/664-0424, www.justanexperience.com, $75–125), rooms are either in the main house or in rustic kitchenette cabins.

The **Star Bakery Restaurant** (406/843-5525, 7 A.M.–3 P.M. Mon.–Wed., 7 A.M.–8 P.M. Thurs.–Sun. Memorial Day–Labor Day, $4–10) is a charming café for light meals.

RUBY RIVER VALLEY

During the 1860s and 1870s the stage route called the Vigilante Trail ran from Alder Gulch down the Ruby River to Twin Bridges, and then to Bannack or Helena. Thievery along this route

led to the establishment of the vigilantes. Here too, traders and farmers began communities that would outlast the mining boom.

The Ruby River rises in the gentle peaks north of the Red Rock Lakes. Native Americans called the Ruby *Passamari* (Stinking Water) for the sulfur springs along its banks. The Ruby River, later named for the deceptive red garnets that early settlers mistook for rubies, is interred at Ruby Reservoir, where much of its flow is diverted into irrigation canals.

Alder

After low-tech placer mining extracted the richest gold deposits along Alder Gulch, gold dredges were brought in to rework the displaced, lower-grade gravel. The banks of pebbles at Alder are the remains of this process.

Dredging in the Ruby Valley reached its height during World War I, when Harvard University sponsored the operations and pocketed the proceeds. Nearly a hundred years later, the banks of dredged gravel remain unreclaimed and unproductive for commercial mining.

Rock hounds who want to take a stab at

finding some gems in the Ruby Valley can stop along the highway between Nevada City and Alder, where the roadside **Red Rock Mine** offers an opportunity to sift through the gravel for garnets. A bucket of gravel, typically containing many tiny garnets, is $10.

The Northern Pacific built a branch line from Whitehall to Alder in the early 1900s to take out the dredged gold and other precious metals from the nearby hills. Today, talc mines in the Ruby Range are the area's most important mining operations. Watch for the white mounds near railroad sidings.

At Alder, a gravel road leads south seven miles to **Ruby Reservoir.** There is a free campground and, when the lake's not drawn down by irrigation, boating and fishing. Keep an eye out for garnets. A fair gravel road (eventually becoming Forest Service Road 100) continues up the Ruby River, where better fishing and great vistas reward the off-road enthusiast. About 20 miles from Ruby Reservoir is a Forest Service campground, called **Cottonwood Camp.** Forest Service Road 100 enters the Red Rock Valley just above the Red Rock Lake game refuge.

Chick's Motel, just off Highway 287 in Alder (406/842-5366, about $50) is the only conventional motel in the area. It has a restaurant attached. The **Virginia City KOA** (406/842-5677, tent $24–27, RV $31–45) is in fact just east of Alder and is open to campers all year. **Upper Canyon Outfitters** (406/842-5884, www. ucomontana.com) operates a guest ranch for anglers, hikers, and horseback riders, and offers fly-fishing lessons on the Ruby River and special programs for women. In the fall, the focus is on hunting. Basic rates (June–mid-Sept.) start at $160 for the first person, $100 for each additional person, with an extra fee for meals. A wide variety of packages are available.

Ruby Springs Lodge (2487 Hwy. 287, 406/ 842-5250 or 800/278-7829, www.rubyspringslodge.com, $4,500 per person per week, including guided fishing), one mile north of Alder off Highway 287, is an exclusive fishing lodge catering to 12 guests at a time. If you can't stay for a week, shorter stays are possible.

The **Alder Steakhouse and Bar** (406/842-5159, 4–10 P.M. daily, $16–25) is Alder's dinner restaurant. It's also just a short hop to Virginia City, where Bandito's has excellent dinners.

Laurin

Laurin preserves a hint of this tiny community's Gallic genesis in its pronunciation: With little apparent respect for the original French, you say "law-RAY." Jean Baptiste Laurin established a trading post and stage stop along the banks of the Ruby River in the late 1860s and eventually amassed large agricultural holdings in the area. Laurin built St. Mary's Church, a handsome and substantial Catholic church constructed of local stone, as a gift to the town he founded.

Robber's Roost

Between Alder and Sheridan, along the old stage route between Alder Gulch and Bannack, is the roadhouse and bar once known as Pete Daly's Place. This two-story log bar and dance hall was built in 1863 and became associated with Henry Plummer and his band of ne'er-do-wells. After two outlaws were lynched by vigilantes nearby, Pete's Place became known as Robber's Roost. Bullet holes in the walls attest to the character of the Alder Gulch bar scene.

A full-length porch with hitching rail opens onto the first-floor bar and gambling hall; upstairs was the dance floor. On the veranda, dancers could catch a breath of air or desperados could plot mayhem as the situation demanded.

Sheridan

Sheridan (pop. 699, elev. 5,079 feet) was established in 1866 as mining spread from Alder Gulch and northeast to the Tobacco Root Mountains. Sheridan grew into a prosperous trade center catering to miners and ranchers, a fact reflected in the handsome period storefronts.

The **Moriah Motel** (220 S. Main, 406/842-5491, www.moriahmotel.com, $62 and up) has downtown rooms equipped with fridges and microwaves, plus a laundry room for guests' use. If you'd rather stay in an old Victorian house, the **Ruby Valley Inn B&B** (3209 Hwy. 287, 406/842-7111, www.ruby-valleyinnllc.com, $85–90) is comfortable and welcomes anglers and others.

There are a few local restaurants, and Twin Bridges' Old Hotel is nearby with gourmet dinners. In town, the **Mill Creek Inn** (102 Mill St., 406/842-5442, 7 A.M.–2 A.M. daily, $5–15) serves Mexican food (try the wet burrito) in addition to the requisite steaks.

The Jefferson River Valley

At Twin Bridges the Jefferson River collects its mighty tributaries—the Big Hole, Beaverhead, and Ruby Rivers—and flows north to its appointment with the Missouri at Three Forks. For much of this 80-mile journey the Jefferson and its valley are open, wide, and relaxed, as if they too enjoy the spectacular mountain scenery rising above them. The ragged peaks of the Tobacco Root and Highland Mountains contain granite intrusions that are cousins to the mineral-rich formations near Butte.

The Jefferson's deep holes and brushy banks, which hampered Lewis and Clark's journey upriver, now excite sportspeople. Brown trout of storied size lurk in the shade of the overgrowth; river floaters, more captivated by the rugged mountain scenery than challenged by the current, enjoy the river's leisurely pace.

East of LaHood, the river drops into the Jefferson Canyon. Stop and watch for bighorn sheep along the high sheer cliffs. In a limestone formation high on the side of the canyon are the Lewis and Clark Caverns, one of the nation's largest developed cavern systems.

HISTORY

After Lewis and Clark ascended to Three Forks in 1805, their journey became a series of conjectures about which river fork, and which fork of forks, to follow to the Continental Divide. At Three Forks the Corps of Discovery chose the Jefferson. They could have saved themselves hundreds of miles of rambling in the upper Jefferson drainages if they had heeded Charbonneau's advice and traveled up Pipestone Creek near Whitehall. They would have surmounted the Continental Divide in 20

miles and found themselves in the Columbia River drainage.

Near Twin Bridges the captains chose to follow the Beaverhead River. A few miles upstream, Sacagawea recognized Beaverhead Rock, an immense limestone outcropping rising above the river, as a landmark for her people, the Shoshone.

The gold rush of the 1860s produced the inevitable smattering of gold camps in the Jefferson Valley, with towns such as Silver Star booming when the gold market allowed. Marble quarries and open-pit talc mines have proved to be more resilient and more profitable. The real economic vitality of the region, however, derives from the ranches that spread across this wide valley.

The little crossroads of **LaHood** is named for Shadan LaHood, a Lebanese immigrant who moved to Montana in 1902. After a few years of selling dry goods to settlers from his horse-drawn wagon, he established a general store along the Jefferson River. LaHood Park, at the site of the original store, became the nation's first Civilian Conservation Corps camp and is still in operation as a restaurant.

LEWIS AND CLARK CAVERNS

Leave I-90 at Three Forks or Whitehall and follow back roads through Jefferson River Canyon for a scenic loop-road alternative to the interstate. The quickening pace of the river as it cuts through walls of steeply tilted sedimentary rock makes this a popular expedition for floaters.

High on the north side of the canyon in a vein of exposed limestone is Lewis and Clark Caverns

State Park on Highway 10, west of Three Forks 19 miles, or 13 miles east of Whitehall (406/287-3541, tours 9 A.M.–4:30 P.M. May 1–June 14 and Aug. 20–Sept. 30, 9 A.M.–6:30 P.M. June 15–Aug.19, $10 adults, $5 children 6–11). When a ramrod of granite magma thrust up the Tobacco Root Mountains about 70 million years ago, sedimentary layers laid down hundreds of millions of years earlier rose to flank the new mountains in steeply pitched strata. In an exposed face of Madison Limestone, rainwater began to erode the porous rock. Many millions of years later, water has cut 3,000-foot-long chambers and passageways 300 feet below the surface, making this the third-largest cavern in the United States.

Water carrying minute traces of minerals has stained the many stalagmites and stalactites into wonderful colors. Fanciful minds have assigned the caverns' rich abundance of exotic formations theme chambers, with such names as Hell's Highway, the Lion's Den, and the Organ Room. Tours last about two hours; visitors should be sure on their feet and ready to negotiate stairs. Take a jacket—the caverns remain at 50°F.

The caverns stand three miles from the highway. Along the route are a campground, several picnic areas, and a vista point overlooking the Jefferson. Light snacks are available at the visitors center. There is also a self-guided nature trail near the upper picnic area; watch for snakes.

WHITEHALL AND VICINITY

The town of Whitehall sits along the Jefferson River in the shadow of the main spine of the Rocky Mountains. Originally a stage stop between Helena and Virginia City, Whitehall was named for the large white ranch house of an early settler. The town evolved once the Northern Pacific pushed through in 1889.

Many of downtown Whitehall's buildings have been adorned with **murals** depicting Lewis and Clark's travels through the Jefferson Valley. The series of 12 murals begins with a painting of Corps of Discovery members hauling a boat up the Jefferson River

and ends with the corps floating back down the river on their way back east. Downtown Whitehall is pretty small, so it's easy to take a short break from I-90 to stroll past these rather spectacular murals.

Silver Star

After an eventful early history, Silver Star has settled into a gentle doze. One of the oldest settlements in the state, the town was founded by Green Campbell, who was issued Montana land patent No. 1 in 1866. The town sits on the southernmost extreme of the rich Boulder Batholith, and miners extracted hefty amounts of gold, silver, and lead from the Highland Mountains. Silver Star was the only town between Virginia City and Helena during the high-flying 1870s, booming as it serviced the needs of local miners and settlers.

Legend contends that Edward, Prince of Wales, spent three days in Silver Star in 1878. It's been pretty much downhill ever since.

TWIN BRIDGES AND VICINITY

Twin Bridges slumbers near the confluence of the Ruby, Beaverhead, and Big Hole Rivers. Lewis and Clark rested here before continuing up the Beaverhead. At Three Forks the captains named the mightiest of the Missouri forks for President Jefferson. At the forks of the Jefferson, they decided to name each for the cardinal virtues of the president: Philanthropy, Philosophy, and Wisdom. Later settlers waxed less poetic, renaming the rivers the Ruby, the Beaverhead, and the Big Hole. History is silent as to whether the later generation considered these attributes of President Jefferson.

Twin Bridges is now a good base for anglers and a thoroughly pleasant place to stop for the night if you're touring this part of Montana.

For many, Twin Bridges is the object of a pilgrimage just to go to the **R. L. Winston Rod Company shop** (500 S. Main St., 406/684-5674). This company makes well-regarded fly-fishing rods.

King's Motel (307 S. Main, 406/684-5639 or 800/222-5510, www.kingsflatline.com, $55 and up) is a tidy, pleasant little motel with a wide variety of cabin-style rooms ranging from single rooms with kitchenettes to units that sleep up to seven people. Dogs are permitted for an extra $10. Cabin accommodations are available at **Stonefly Inn** (409 N. Main, 406/684-5648, www.thestoneflyinn.com, $59 and up, includes breakfast). At either of Twin Bridges' motels, the owners will gladly set you up with fishing guides. (It's best to call in advance if this is what you have in mind.)

The best food in town is at **⟨ The Old Hotel** (101 E. 5th Ave., 406/684-5959, Tues.–Sun. May–mid-Oct., Thurs.–Sun., mid-Oct.–Apr., call for hours, dinners $20–25, dinner reservations recommended), where the Scottish-born owner turns out wonderful meals, and where

there's always a good veggie option. The Old Hotel also has two B&B suites for $125.

East of town, **Healing Waters Fly Fishing Lodge** (270 Tuke Ln., 406/684-5960, www. hwlodge.com, Apr.–Nov., $595 per angler per day, $395 nonangler) is highly acclaimed for both its top-notch guides and its amenities.

Beaverhead Rock
Between Dillon and Twin Bridges is Beaverhead Rock, a landmark to settler and Indian alike. The excited Sacagawea recognized the huge outcropping and told the rest of the Corps of Discovery that they were in her homeland. Three hundred feet high, it is apparently the leading edge of land thrust eastward by mountain building to the west.

I-15: Butte to Helena

Between Helena and Butte, I-15 crosses over the Boulder Batholith, an intrusion of magma that shot up from the bowels of the earth like a piston about 70 million years ago. The formation is made largely of granite, but in places it also contains an almost incomprehensible wealth of valuable minerals. Near towns such as Clancy and Jefferson City, gold was panned, mined, and dredged. The orderly dikes of processed gravel tailings from streambeds lie like welts across the landscape.

The old town of Boulder lies at the center of this rich mining area. Its spent mines have been put to new use. Radon gas, in low concentrations, occurs naturally in the mineshafts. People who suffer from a variety of ailments, including cancer, asthma, and lupus, have found relief descending the mines and breathing the radon-rich air. Called "health mines," these strictly non-AMA-approved facilities have become so popular that peak seasons are reserved for weeks in advance.

HISTORY
About 120 years ago, this forlorn piece of nondescript mountain landscape was one of the

busiest and most populated in Montana. Rich but diffident deposits of gold first attracted placer miners in the 1860s. Gold camps sprang up in every gulch. After the surface deposits were exhausted, many camps developed into industrial mining towns as capitalists brought in more highly mechanized techniques to mine and smelt underground silver, lead, and gold. A final reprise of Montana's mining boom years came in the early decades of the 20th century, when gold dredges reworked the tailings from old mines for the trace amounts of gold missed by earlier mining methods. By redigesting mining refuse and stream bottoms in a rich muddy soup, dredges were able to isolate what mineral wealth remained, leaving acres of mine tailings.

Between Helena and Boulder, place names recall important early settlements and boomtowns: Jefferson City, Prickly Pear Gulch, Montana City, Wickes, Corbin—towns that once vied with Helena and Butte in importance during territorial days. Now little remains, save a citation in a history book and mounds of worked gravel, these towns long ago having slumped from narcolepsy into dilapidation.

MIRACLE CURES IN MONTANA RADON GAS MINES

In 1950 a California woman who suffered from arthritis accompanied her husband into a uranium mine near Boulder. She noted a marked relief from the constant pain to which she had grown accustomed. She related her experiences to a fellow arthritis sufferer. The friend also visited the Boulder mine, and her stay produced the same rapid recovery.

Word of the "miracle cure" soon spread, reaching an early peak when *Life* magazine sent a news team to cover the "stampede" of people arriving to seek this underground cure.

Just why the cure seems to work hasn't been adequately explained. Radon gas is a naturally occurring gas formed when radium, in the process of aging, oxidizes. This radioactive gas occurs in Basin-Boulder mines in levels deemed safe for miners but in concentrations considered therapeutic by the mines' many promoters. Sympathetic researchers contend that radon gas stimulates the pituitary gland to produce health-giving hormones and natural steroids, which can ease or eradicate the pain of conditions caused by hormonal dysfunction.

The recommended "cure" involves a careful regimen of contact with radon gas. Patrons are asked to spend no more than one hour at a time in the mines no more than three times per day. About 30 hours of contact with radon gas is considered to be the optimum treatment. Within the mines, there are sofas, tables, and chairs for the visitors' comfort; card games and reading are the usual pastimes.

Radon gas therapy is *not* medically accepted in the United States (the European medical establishment is less hostile to radon gas therapy), and the owners stress that the mines are open for people seeking *nonmedical* treatment. There is no guarantee of a cure.

There are, however, many moving testimonials from people who have found relief from aggravated and long-standing afflictions. The list of physical conditions for which radon gas may be efficacious grows as the number of afflicted visitors grows. Sufferers of arthritis, migraines, eczema, asthma, diabetes, and allergies have testified to the mines' healing virtues.

If you have questions about the "health mines," contact the **Boulder-Basin Chamber of Commerce** (www.bouldermtchamber.com) or contact the following mines directly at **Free Enterprise Health Mine** (406/255-3383, www.radonmine.com); **Earth Angel Health Mine** (406/225-3516); **Merry Widow Health Mine** (406/255-3220, www.merrywidowmine.com).

Radon therapy is very popular; if you are considering a visit, call ahead for reservations, and don't be surprised if the facilities are all booked up. Also, don't come expecting a four-star spa; accommodations can be quite rustic.

Boulder and Basin survived the decline of Montana's mining industry by establishing a somewhat more diversified economy. As early as the 1880s, Boulder Hot Springs attracted tourists and weekenders to its spa resort. Boulder was also the trade center for ranchers in the Boulder River Valley. Basin struggled on as a rail center for local gold and silver mines until the 1940s, when the presence of uranium met the demands of a changing world. After a brief flurry of activity, these radium-rich mines became the radon health mines that currently energize the local economy.

BOULDER AND VICINITY

Named for the large stones littering its valley, Boulder (pop. 1,352, elev. 5,158 feet) began as a stage stop between Fort Benton and Virginia City in the 1860s. Its prominence as a trading center was enhanced when the state built the Montana Home for the Feeble-Minded here in 1892. Now known as the Montana Developmental Center, the facility houses and trains developmentally disabled citizens.

Old Boulder

The town center of Boulder, with its sprawl of

red-brick storefronts, retains much of the flavor of a frontier commercial center. Its most prominent landmark is the **Jefferson County Courthouse,** built in 1889. Its grand scale and gargoyles betray the German education of designer John Paulsen, who also designed the administration building for the Home for the Feeble-Minded. Both are listed on the National Register of Historic Places.

Boulder Hot Springs

One of the earliest tourist facilities in the state, Boulder Hot Springs (406/225-4339, www.boulderhotsprings.com) began in 1883 as a spa for the rich and influential in Helena and Butte. Over the years the lodge has been redesigned and reinterpreted in fashionable, ever more grandiose architectural vernaculars. The earliest wooden-frame hotel was replaced by a Queen Anne clapboard lodge, only to be renovated in Spanish mission style. The imposing lodge at Boulder Hot Springs is undergoing another rejuvenation, this time as a New Age–style health and spiritual retreat. A corner of the huge lodge has been renovated (the rest seems to be perpetually under construction) and is open with both hotel and B&B options. Basic hotel rooms cost $65–85; B&B rooms range from $99–139. Swimming and soaking are free to all guests. Various types of massage and other healing arts are also available.

Nonguests can stop by for a swim in the 90–95°F outdoor pool, then plunge into indoor hot and cold pools or sit in the steam room for $6 adults, $5 seniors, $3 children. Boulder Hot Springs is three miles south of Boulder on Highway 69.

Elkhorn

The silver-mining town of Elkhorn began in the 1870s and flourished until the early 1890s, when the international silver market bottomed out. Although only the ghosts of the town remain, Elkhorn is reckoned to be one of the best-preserved mining camps in the state. Buildings of note include **Gillian Hall,** a two-story bar and dance hall, and **Fraternity Hall,** a meetinghouse built in the neoclassical style. Elkhorn is six miles south of Boulder on Highway 69, then 12 miles

north on gravel Elkhorn Road. During winter the trip is best made on cross-country skis.

Accommodations and Food

Many travelers elect to stay a few miles out of town at **Boulder Hot Springs** (see above), but there are a couple of options downtown.

The red brick **Castoria Inn** (211 S. Monroe, 406/225-3549) dates from 1889 and is listed on the National Register of Historic Places. It currently offers bed-and-breakfast and motel rooms for under $50. Similarly inexpensive, the **O-Z Motel** (114 N. Main, 406/225-3364) is an older motel in the center of historic Boulder.

For campers, the area offers pleasant RV parks with easy access to fishing in the Boulder River. Try the **Sunset Trailer Court** (4th and Adams, 406/225-3387) or the RV campground at the **Free Enterprise Health Mine** (149 Depot Hill Rd., 406/225-3383).

You'll find food at **Phil and Tim's Bar & Bowl** (406/225-3201). Otherwise, try heading to **Mountain Good Restaurant** (124 Main, 406/225-3382, 6:30 A.M.–2 P.M. Mon.–Sat.), a classic old downtown café.

BASIN

Located in narrow Boulder River Canyon, Basin is an old mining town that has avoided the ghost-town destiny of many other mining camps. By luck or connivance, Basin always successfully managed to market what it has. Gold prospectors such as Granville Stuart helped found the community, but silver mines put Basin on the map during the 1880s. The town fell into a long doze after a spurt of gold mining during the 1920s, then reactivated when the uranium market developed during World War II. The radon gas present in many of the old mines is now marketed for its reputed health-giving benefits.

Basin's main street exhibits structures from more prosperous times. The **Masonic Hall** dates from the early 20th century, as does the old boardinghouse in the Sockerson Block. Watch the hillsides near Basin for old flumes and mine adits.

Over the past few years, Basin has attracted artists and musicians, giving the tiny town a

SOUTHWESTERN MONTANA

lively alternative feel. Locals have formed the **Montana Artists Refuge** (406/225-3500, www.montanaartistsrefuge.org), a residential program for all types of artists. Refuge residents live and work in two historic downtown brick buildings, and they have plenty of chances to collaborate with each other and with the Basin community. The Refuge's big fund-raiser, a fairly wild jazz brunch, is usually held the first weekend of June; it's a great time to visit.

Support the local artists with a visit to **Basin Creek Pottery and Gallery** (82 Basin St., 406/225-3218); the resident potter gets his clay from local mining sites.

If you've been hurtling down I-15 and need to stretch your legs, turn off the interstate south of Basin at the Bernice exit (exit 151) and drive a couple of miles east to the **Bear Gulch trail.** While it's not exactly wilderness, the trail through open forest and meadows is a good break from the road.

Accommodations and Food

Most of the health mines provide accommodations and campgrounds for their guests. Be sure to reserve ahead. The RV campground at the **Merry Widow Health Mine** (two blocks off Basin Creek Rd., 406/225-3220, www.merrywidowmine.com) is open to the public, but spaces go quickly. The Merry Widow also offers quite basic motel accommodations for $40–55 (five-night minimum; $10 per night surcharge for shorter stays). The small **Basin Canyon Campground** run by the Forest Service (406/287-3223) is five miles north of Basin on I-15, then three miles east on Forest Road 172. It's free but has no piped water.

The Silver Saddle Bar and Cafe (109 Basin St., 406/225-9995, 7:30 A.M.–8 P.M. daily) serves good basic food in an authentic Western atmosphere. Right across the street, **Leaning Tower of Pizza** (110 Basin St., 406/225-9790) has pizzas for $12–15.

Helena

Montana's capital city straddles one of history's richest gold strikes: Last Chance Gulch. Unlike its contemporary boomtowns, Helena (pop. 26,353, elev. 4,124 feet) managed not only to survive but to prevail through good times and bad. Like a snake swallowing its tail, Helena transformed itself from seething gold camp to trade center, then to capital city, and finally into a cultural and tourist center.

In Montana, only Butte can approach Helena in sheer historicity, but history has left Helena a richer legacy of monuments and architecture. From the elegance of the State Capitol and the Cathedral of St. Helena to the stone shacks on Reeder's Alley, the highs, lows, and middlings of the state's history each have their testimony here. Excellent museums and galleries present and preserve the best of Montana's past and present.

People in Helena are both insiders and outsiders. The state is by far the city's largest employer, and Helena's bright friendly character derives in part from internalizing the lessons of political life. Citizens greet you as if they seek to be popularly elected.

But at the weekend, the insiders go outside. Helena is unbelievably well-situated for recreation. With fishing and boating on nearby lakes on the Missouri, hiking and skiing in Helena National Forest, and exploring old ghost towns and other reminders of the past always just nearby, the Helena area tempts the traveler with a rich brew of history and outdoor activity.

HISTORY

Helena began, as did so many other gold camps, as the cry went up, "Just one last chance before we leave." In this case, four former Confederate soldiers were panning for gold in 1864 in a narrow gulch called Prickly Pear, just below the crest of the Continental Divide. The "Four Georgians," as they were later known, found color in their pans in the draw they called Last Chance Gulch.

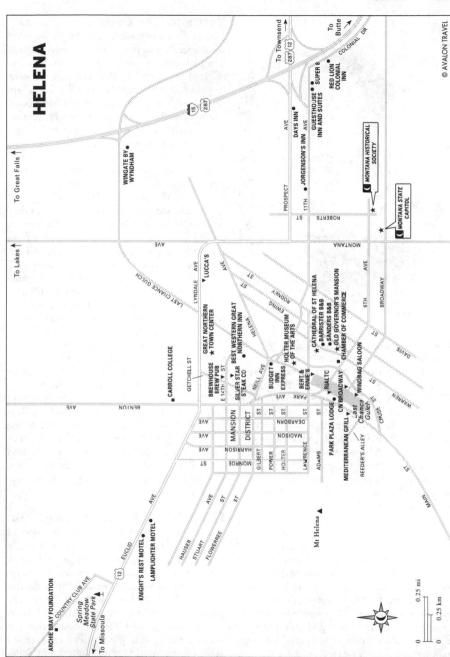

HELENA

To Great Falls →

To Lakes →

To Townsend →

To Butte →

WINGATE BY WYNDHAM

COLONIAL DR

DAYS INN

JORGENSON'S INN AND SUITES

GUESTHOUSE INN AND SUITES

SUPER 8

RED LION COLONIAL INN

PROSPECT

11TH

ROBERTS ST

MONTANA

AVE

MONTANA HISTORICAL SOCIETY

MONTANA STATE CAPITOL

LAST CHANCE GULCH

LUCCA'S

LYNDALE AVE

GREAT NORTHERN TOWN CENTER

BEST WESTERN GREAT NORTHERN INN

EWING ST

RODNEY ST

HELENA ST

NEILL AVE

CARROLL COLLEGE

GETCHELL ST

BREWHOUSE BREW PUB

E 14TH ST

SILVER STAR STEAK CO

BUDGET INN EXPRESS

BERT & ERNIE'S

HOLTER MUSEUM OF THE ARTS

CATHEDRAL OF ST HELENA

BARRISTER B&B

SANDERS B&B

OLD GOVERNOR'S MANSION

CHAMBER OF COMMERCE

WINDBAG SALOON

RIALTO

Last Chance Gulch

6TH AVE

BROADWAY

DAVIS ST

WARREN ST

MAIN ST

CROSS ST

BENTON AVE

PARK AVE

MANSION DISTRICT

DEARBORN ST

MADISON ST

HARRISON AVE

MONROE AVE

GILBERT ST

POWER ST

HOLTER ST

LAWRENCE ST

ADAMS ST

PARK PLAZA LODGE

MEDITERRANEAN GRILL

CN BROADWAY

REEDER'S ALLEY

Mt Helena ▲

HAUSER AVE

STUART ST

FLOWERREE ST

EUCLID AVE

KNIGHT'S REST MOTEL

LAMPLIGHTER MOTEL

COUNTRY CLUB AVE

ARCHIE BRAY FOUNDATION

Spring Meadow State Park

To Missoula →

0.25 mi

0.25 km

© AVALON TRAVEL

SOUTHWESTERN MONTANA

SOUTHWESTERN MONTANA

© BILL MCRAE

Helena has a rich architectural heritage.

Word spread, and the rush was on. By 1876 the town had grown to 4,000 inhabitants.

At the time, Montana was a territory lacking a cohesive center. Because of the boom-and-bust nature of its initial settlements, the focal point of Montana moved from strike to strike. The earliest territorial capital, Bannack, was almost deserted by the time the center of government moved to Virginia City. In turn, Helena attracted the territorial capital in 1875.

Helena had advantages that the other mining centers lacked. The gold, then the silver and lead, were richer in Helena than in other early settlements. Helena was midway on the stage routes between Fort Benton—the uppermost steamboat reach on the Missouri—and Virginia City and other mining areas in southwestern Montana. Newcomers quickly realized that wealth was in trade, not mining, and gravitated to Helena, the largest center of population in the territory. Trade quickly underpinned mining to support Helena's economy. Onetime miners, now important captains of industry, built huge mansions on the city's west side.

Battle for the Capital

Helena first overtook Virginia City in 1875, when voters chose it to be the territorial capital. The real battle began when Montana was recognized as a state in 1889. The feud between Copper Kings Marcus Daly and William Clark ricocheted across the state. What had been a grudge match of political influence became war as each backed a different city to be capital of the new state of Montana in a statewide election in 1894.

While each of the industrialists had solid power bases in Butte, the wrangle involved Anaconda, the city that Daly had built, and the established capital of Helena, where Clark had major mining investments. The attack politicians of our time could take lessons from the acrimonious battles of the Copper Kings. Each man controlled newspapers; each shamelessly bought and influenced votes. ("It came through the transom" is an expression still used in Montana to explain a windfall gift from a patron.) In the end, Helena only just won the statewide vote, retaining its hold as the capital.

Helena continued to hold sway over the rich and powerful during the late 1890s and early years of the 1900s, as is witnessed by its elaborate architecture of the period. Be they ranchers, miners, or tradesmen, the rich from across the state hadn't "arrived" until they had engaged in the mansion-building competition that thrived on the west side of Last Chance Gulch. The concentration of wealth in Helena is legendary. In the late 1880s there were more millionaires in Helena per capita than anywhere else in the nation.

◖ MONTANA STATE CAPITOL

The state capitol (1301 6th Ave.) was begun in 1899. This imposing structure, domed with a cupola of Butte copper, was enlarged in 1912 by the extensions containing the present legislative wings. The statue on the dome commemorates an odd episode in Montana history. After the bruising fight for state capital between Helena and Anaconda, the Capitol Commission ran off with the books. When this statue arrived at the railroad station from a foundry in Ohio,

© BILL MCRAE

the Montana state capitol

no one knew who had ordered it, who had paid for it, or what it was meant for. The foundry's records were shortly destroyed in a fire, leaving the mysterious statue no history and no future. The builders of the capitol needed statuary for the top of its dome, and the *Goddess of Liberty* found its way to the top.

Significant paintings and murals decorate the capitol. In the House Chamber hangs *Lewis and Clark Meeting the Flathead Indians at Ross's Hole* by Charlie Russell, one of his largest and most acclaimed works. In the lobby of the House of Representatives, six paintings by E. S. Paxson detail the state's history. Free guided tours of the capitol are given on the hour (9 A.M.–3 P.M. Mon.–Sat., noon–4 P.M. Sun. May–Sept., 10 A.M.–2 P.M. Sat. only Oct.–Apr.) The capitol is also open for self-guided tours (8 A.M.–5 P.M. Mon.–Sat.). For information, contact the Montana Historical Society (406/444-2694, www.montanacapitol.com).

THE CAPITOL AREA

Known in local parlance as the East Side, the area around the capitol is directly south of the downtown area and contains many buildings of historic interest.

Probably the first thing a summer visitor should do while in Helena is take the hour-long train tour offered by **Last Chance Tours** (406/442-1023, www.lctours.com, $7 adults, $6.50 seniors, $6 children 4–12). This open-air train tour does a quick drive-by of most of Helena's historic and scenic properties; the traveler can decide what to explore in further depth. On the route are buildings in the capitol area, Last Chance Gulch, Reeder's Alley, the mansion district, and Carroll College. Catch the "Last Chancer," as the tour train is nicknamed, just outside the Montana Historical Society at 6th Avenue and North Roberts Street, across the street from the capitol. In June tours are at 11 A.M., 1, and 3 P.M.; in July and August at 11 A.M., 1, 3, and 5:30 P.M.; in September at 11 A.M. and 3 P.M.

Montana Historical Society

The Montana Historical Society (225 N. Roberts St., 406/444-2694, www.montanahistoricalsociety.org, 9 A.M.–5 P.M. Mon.–Wed. and Sat.,

9 A.M.–8 P.M. Thurs., $5 adults, $1 children) is Montana's premier museum, mixing fine art, an exhibit charting the state's history, and changing exhibits. Of special interest is the **MacKay Gallery of Charles M. Russell Art,** one of the nation's largest public collections of Russell's art. If Western art seems like an oxymoron to you, come marvel at the brilliant use of color and composition by this unschooled cowboy artist.

The **Montana Homeland Exhibit** tells the story of Montana, beginning with Indian prehistory and moving on through the era of settlement. Three rooms contain more than 2,000 artifacts. Other galleries change exhibits but often contain fascinating displays of frontier photographs. Of interest to historians and researchers are the library and photo archives.

Old Governor's Mansion

From 1913 to 1959, Montana's governor lived at the Old Governor's Mansion (304 N. Ewing St., 406/444-4789). Built in 1883 by a local entrepreneur, the 20-room residence is now owned by the Montana Historical Society, which has restored the ornate building to its historic splendor. Tours operate on the hour (noon–3 P.M. Tues.–Sat. May–Sept., noon–3 P.M. Sat. Oct.–Apr., $4 adults, $1 children).

Cathedral of St. Helena

The Cathedral of St. Helena (530 N. Ewing St., 406/442-5825, 7:15 A.M.–6 P.M. except during services, free) was begun in 1908 but wasn't finished until 1924. Modeled after Cologne Cathedral, Helena's largest church dominates the skyline with its 230-foot twin spires. Its stained glass was fashioned in Germany, although the images of the Seven Sacraments seem out of a Burne-Jones pre-Raphaelite painting.

LAST CHANCE GULCH

In the 1860s, Prickly Pear Creek snaked down from the mountains through a thicket of mining claims called Last Chance Gulch. As mining gave way to commerce, the gulch remained the main street; its winding path, and especially the one-claim-sized business buildings, still reflect its mining past. The old business district

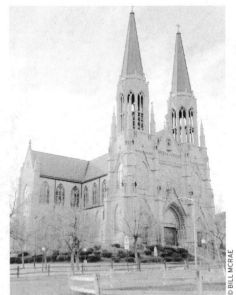

© BILL MCRAE

The Cathedral of St. Helena is modeled after Cologne Cathedral.

of Helena is still impressive, even after a 1933 earthquake destroyed some of its buildings.

Much of Last Chance Gulch is now a pedestrian mall, designed in the 1970s to make this historic main street more attractive to tourists and businesses. Have a look at the handsome empty storefronts and decide if it has worked.

The extensive infrastructure of historic business buildings in Helena proves that the capital's most significant occupation was commerce, not mining. Several walking-tour maps to the Last Chance Gulch area are available from the chamber of commerce and from **Downtown Helena** (225 Cruse Ave., 406/447-1530). Notable buildings not to miss include the following:

The Power Block (58–62 N. Last Chance Gulch) was built in 1889; note that on the southeast corner, each of the five floors has windows grouped in corresponding numbers of panes. The **Securities Building** (101 N. Last Chance Gulch), built in 1886, is a Romanesque former bank with curious carved thumbprints between the first-floor arches. The **Montana Club** (24 W. 6th Ave.) was Montana's most

© BILL MCRAE

Reeder's Alley is a reminder that not all Helena prospectors lived like millionaires.

prestigious private club: Membership was open only to millionaires. The club's present building was designed by Cass Gilbert, who designed the U.S. Supreme Court Building.

The **Atlas Building** (7–9 N. Last Chance Gulch) is one of Helena's most fanciful; on a cornice upheld by Atlas, a salamander and lizards do symbolic battle. **Reeder's Alley** (308 S. Park Ave.) is a winding series of one-room brick shanties built in the 1870s to house the mining camp's many bachelors. Today, it's a theme alley dedicated to shops and places to eat.

Visit the Wells Fargo Bank (350 N. Last Chance Gulch, 406/443-0136) to see the **Gold Collection,** displaying gold in many forms, from nuggets to leaves.

OTHER SIGHTS
West Side Mansions

Montana's grandest historic homes grace the hillside above Helena. In an area roughly bounded by Stuart, Monroe, Dearborn, and Power Streets stand dozens of imposing monuments to the economic clout of their merchant, mining, or ranching owners. The mansions display a bewildering assortment of styles; Mark Twain described these Helena homes as "Queen Anne in front and Mary Ann behind." In all their opulence, these are what money could buy in Helena during the boom years of 1880–1900.

None of the old homes are regularly open for viewing, but a walk through these beautiful old neighborhoods is a must for anyone with an interest in historic homes.

Downtown Environs

Given all the beautiful architecture in Helena, it is ironic that the city's most distinctive building is the **Civic Center** (corner of Neill and Fuller), built in 1921 as the Masonic Algeria Shrine Temple. This exercise in high camp is a Moorish revival edifice with a 175-foot minaret, onion dome, and intricately modeled exterior brickwork. It now houses Helena's municipal offices and a performance hall.

Just east of downtown is the new **Great Northern Town Center,** a new development on 11 acres of land that was until recently unused rail yards. The development has several

JEANNETTE RANKIN: A LIFE OF PRINCIPLE AND PEACE

It's almost a cliché that Montana breeds strong women, but Jeannette Rankin stands out as one of the most forthright of the bunch.

Born in 1880 into a Missoula ranch and timber family, Jeannette was a serious child who considered Chief Joseph a personal hero. After stints teaching at a country school outside Missoula and working in a San Francisco settlement house, she attended social-work school in New York. There she became involved in the women's suffrage movement, and she went on to work in Washington State and Montana to obtain the right to vote for women. She was a good public speaker, and after a taste of politics she became convinced that politics, not social work, was the most effective way to change the world.

In 1916, Rankin ran for Congress as a Republican and was elected to the House of Representatives. She was the first woman elected to national office in the United States. The first day she took her seat in the House, President Woodrow Wilson asked Congress to authorize official United States entry into World War I. Rankin voted against war, which upset many of her constituents and led to her defeat when she ran for the Senate in 1918.

Fresh out of Congress, and increasingly engaged in the nascent peace movement, she went to Europe and helped found the Women's International League for Peace and Freedom. On her return to the United States, Rankin worked as a peace activist in Washington, D.C. Sensing that the South was a good place for a peace movement to take root, she also bought a farm in Georgia. Montana remained her voting place, however, and in 1940 the state again elected her to Congress.

After Pearl Harbor, Rankin was the only member of Congress to vote against entry into World War II. She cast her vote saying, "As a woman I cannot go to war, and I refuse to send anybody else."

Rankin was not returned to Congress in 1942, but she remained active in women's, children's, and peace issues, all of which she had supported in Congress. In 1968 she led a group of women in a march protesting the Vietnam War. Rankin died in 1973.

significant public buildings, including a new federal courthouse, plus a hotel, several restaurants, shops, and a carousel. As a modern commercial district, the Great Northern Town Center harmonizes nicely with Helena's classic Western architecture.

Overlooking Helena from the northeast is **Carroll College,** a private Catholic college with a student body of 1,400. Carroll stands on 63 acres atop a bluff still known as Capitol Hill. The site was offered for the state capitol in 1895, but the landowner wanted $7,000 for the real estate, and the frugal Capitol Commission went elsewhere.

Fort Harrison

Established in 1895, Fort Harrison, just north of Helena on Highway 12, was one of the U.S. Army's last defensive garrisons against ructions in the West. Although the troops were never called out, the fort remained active through World War I. By 1922 the fort was given over to the Veterans Administration and turned into a large veterans' health facility. Fort Harrison still operates as a veterans hospital, but its most interesting buildings are its 1905 officers quarters. Built of brick, these imposing three-story duplexes boast wide verandas and gabled roofs. Early-20th-century army life in Montana was extremely genteel, judging by these lodgings. Buildings at Fort Harrison are closed to the public.

Marysville

Seven miles north of Helena off Highway 279, this almost ghost town has just enough life left to feed passersby. The **Marysville House,** in the midst of abandoned general stores, churches, and hotels, is housed in the old train depot and is known for its ample meals.

GALLERIES
Holter Museum of the Arts
This museum (12 E. Lawrence St., 406/442-6400, www.holtermuseum.org, 10 A.M.–5:30 P.M. Tues.–Fri., 10 A.M.–4:30 P.M. Sat., 11 A.M.–4:30 P.M. Sun., free) displays very good changing exhibits of contemporary art and offers workshops, readings, and a gallery store. Summer visitors should check out the auction exhibition; early in August the works are auctioned off at a big party.

Last Chance Gulch Galleries
Several private Western art galleries range along Last Chance Gulch, including **Ghost Art Gallery** (21 S. Last Chance Gulch, 406/443-4536) and the **Upper Missouri Artists Gallery** (7 N. Last Chance Gulch, 406/457-8240).

Archie Bray Foundation
The Archie Bray Foundation (2915 Country Club Ave., 406/443-3502, www.archiebray.org) is a studio workshop, classroom, and gallery for ceramic artists. The brickyard and kilns of the **Western Clay Manufacturing Company** have stood just outside Helena for more than 100 years. Archie Bray, whose father began the business, was approached by local artists to use the brickyard's huge beehive kilns to fire ceramics. Bray, who was already active in the Helena arts scene, decided to dedicate a portion of the factory to the ceramic arts. In 1951 he founded the Archie Bray Foundation, now a world-famous facility for training talented young potters and a space in which resident artists can experiment and exhibit.

Visitors can watch potters in workshops and view works for sale in the gallery. The old kilns and outbuildings still stand, while avant-garde ceramics, colorful and abstract, are strewn about with guileless abandon.

THE ARTS
The **Myrna Loy Center for the Performing Arts** (15 N. Ewing St., 406/442-0287, www.myrna-loycenter.org), named for the late film actress who hailed from the Helena area, is housed in the revamped 1880s jail. A performance space, gallery, and art-film theater combine to make this a jewel in Helena's cultural crown.

The **Grandstreet Theatre** (325 N. Park Ave., 406/447-1574) is Helena's community theater. Grandstreet works closely with drama students from Carroll College and conducts a theater school for young people.

RECREATION
Hiking is as close as **Mt. Helena,** the city's 620-acre park on the west side of Last Chance Gulch. Seven trails wind up and across the mountainside; some ascend to Mt. Helena's 5,468-foot peak, and others dawdle in meadows. To reach the park, follow the ravine behind Reeder's Alley on foot or drive to the top of Adams Street behind the mansion district.

A good diversion for hot kids is **Spring Meadow Lake State Park** (406/495-3270, $5 non–Montana residents), a small lake just west of Helena off Euclid Avenue. A trail rings the lake, but the real attractions are the beaches lined with swimmers and anglers in summer.

Great Divide Snowsports (406/449-3746, www.skigd.com), 22 miles northwest of Helena near Marysville, is a ski and snowboard hill with 1,503 feet of vertical drop, five double chairlifts, about 140 trails, and reasonable rates. Adults ski for $29 weekends, $19 weekdays; seniors pay $20, and children's rates run $14–24. The season runs from mid-December to early April. In summer the ski area offers horseback rides (Wed.–Sun. June–Aug.).

The municipal **swimming pool** (1203 N. Last Chance Gulch, 406/447-1559) is at Memorial Park. There are **tennis courts** at the park behind the Civic Center (Neill St. at Park Ave.) and at Barney Park (Cleveland St. and Hudson St.). Both parks also have picnic facilities and playgrounds.

Holter, Hauser, and Canyon Ferry Lakes in the vicinity of Helena provide excellent fishing, boating, and even windsurfing.

ACCOMMODATIONS
Under $50
Most of Helena's hotels and motels are located at the fringes of the city at busy intersections.

One notable exception is the modest but well-situated **Budget Inn Express** (524 Last Chance Gulch, 406/442-0600 or 800/862-1334, $44 and up). It's in the heart of downtown and right around the corner from a large natural-foods store.

Knight's Rest Motel (1831 Euclid Ave., 406/442-6384 or 888/442-6384) is a good value with double rooms at $44. Pets are allowed.

$50-75

The **Lamplighter Motel** (1006 Madison Ave., 406/442-9200, $62 and up) offers accommodations in homey cottage units. Some are family units with full kitchens, and several are two- or three-bedroom units. Pets are $5 extra.

The **Helena Super 8** (2201 11th Ave., 406/443-2450 or 800/800-8000, $75 and up) has an exercise room, guest laundry, and free high-speed Internet access.

Jorgenson's Inn (1714 11th Ave., 406/442-1770 or 800/272-1770, $71 and up), with an indoor pool, exercise equipment, guest laundry, and restaurant, is a large motel near the capitol.

$75-100

The **Guesthouse Inn & Suites** (2101 11th Ave., 406/443-2300 or 800/541-2743, www.helena-countryinn.com, $82), near I-15, has an indoor pool, hot tub, steam room, and sauna, and an on-site restaurant. Pets are welcome for a $6 fee.

Over $100

The **Best Western Great Northern Hotel** (835 Great Northern Blvd., 406/457-5500 or 800/829-4047, $150) is at the center of the new Great Northern Town Center district. Rooms are very large and nicely furnished, and the hotel offers a complimentary breakfast, 24-hour business center, high-speed Internet access, an indoor pool, and fitness center. Restaurants and shopping are right out the front door.

The **Red Lion Colonial Hotel** (2301 Colonial Dr., 406/443-2100 or 800/422-1002, $108) is one of Helena's finest, with indoor and outdoor pools, sauna, hot tub, free airport shuttle, restaurant, and lounge.

Those who simply can't get enough of

Helena's historic homes might consider spending a few nights at **The Sanders Helena's Bed and Breakfast Inn** (328 N. Ewing St., 406/442-3309, www.sandersbb.com, $130), an impressive mansion built in 1875 by Montana's first U.S. Senator. This National Registry property is amazingly well-preserved and filled with lovely furnishings, many original to the home. Even though a great deal of care is taken to preserve period authenticity, all of the seven bedrooms have private baths, telephones, and hair dryers, and the entire mansion is air-conditioned. All of the rooms have a TV tucked away for inveterate small-screen fanatics, although more in keeping with the spirit of the place are the radio alarms, each tuned to the local public radio station. Breakfasts are served in the formal dining room, a showpiece of carved oak moldings.

Just down the street is another historic inn, **The Barrister B&B** (416 N. Ewing St., 406/443-7330 or 800/823-1148, http://thebarristermt.tripod.com, from $114), an 1874 mansion located near St. Helena Cathedral. Its features include ornate fireplaces, antique stained-glass windows, and carved staircases. Modern niceties are also in evidence, including air-conditioning, TVs in rooms, all private baths, and a guest business center with a fax machine, copier, and wireless Internet access.

The nicest downtown hotel is the **Park Plaza Lodge** (22 N. Last Chance Gulch, 406/443-2200 or 877/774-3536, www.parkplazamt.com, $109 and up), a well-appointed, newly renovated hotel with an indoor pool.

The **Days Inn** (2001 Prospect Dr., 406/442-3280 or 800/325-2525, $109) is right near the Prospect exit off I-15.

Wingate by Wyndham—Helena (2007 N. Oakes at 1-15 exit 193, 406/449-3000 or 800/228-1000, $112 and up) is one of Helena's newest hotels, offering free continental breakfast, indoor pool, exercise center, and large, nicely furnished rooms.

Camping

The **Helena Campground and RV Park** (5820 N. Montana Ave., 406/458-4714), three miles north on Montana Avenue, has a pool and playground. **Moose Creek Campground** (406/449-5490, www.fs.fed.us/r1/helena) is a very pleasant spot in the Helena National Forest just east of the Continental Divide. It's 10 miles west of Helena on Highway 12, then 4 miles south on Rimini Road. The Bureau of Land Management maintains a couple of campgrounds on Canyon Ferry Lake, about 20 miles east of town.

FOOD
Breakfast and Lunch
It makes sense in a town fueled by the business of politics that there are as many or more good choices for lunch in Helena as for dinner. Clustered in the Last Chance Gulch area are several good restaurants that serve a busy and boisterous lunch clientele. **Bert and Ernie's** (361 N. Last Chance Gulch, 406/443-5680, 11 A.M.–10 P.M.) serves a sandwich-dominated menu with a wide selection of beers. Sandwiches run $6–9; dinner prices hover around $12.

The **Windbag Saloon** (19 S. Last Chance Gulch, 406/443-9669, 11 A.M.–10 P.M.) was a brothel named Big Dorothy's until 1973. With this colorful history and filled with namesake politicians, the Windbag is one of Helena's unique restaurants. The burgers (about $7) are the thing for lunch, with steaks on the dinner menu. The Windbag is one of the few restaurants open on Sunday night in Helena.

For lunch in a Helena institution, go to the **Rialto** (52 N. Last Chance Gulch, 406/442-1890, 11 A.M.–9 P.M.). Try the burger in this venerable old bar with a café up front. The **Brewhouse Brew Pub and Grill** (939 Getchell St., 406/457-9390, 11 A.M.–10 P.M. daily) serves Lewis and Clark Brewery beers and ales along with good pub food (the brewery is immediately downstairs from the brewpub, and offers free samples of their handcrafted beers and ales).

Helena's most famous sweets sanctuary is **Parrot Confectionery** (42 N. Last Chance Gulch, 406/442-1470, 9 A.M.–6 P.M. Mon.–Sat.), a soda fountain and candy factory that isn't just old-fashioned but actually *old*. Try the handmade chocolates or a malted milk; the Parrot's sole feint to solid food is its renowned chili.

Helena has several excellent bakeries. The **Park Avenue Bakery** (44 S. Park Ave., 406/449-8424) offers European-style pastries, real French bread, and specialty desserts. A great cheese Danish and a cup of their fine coffee induces a near out-of-Montana experience. Try the (**Sweetgrass Bakery** (322 Fuller Ave., 406/443-1103) for healthful breads, muffins, sweet rolls, and other baked goods. **Great Harvest Bakery** (1133 Helena Ave., 406/443-5623) makes hearty breads from Montana-grown wheat, plus delicious cookies, scones, and muffins.

Fine Dining
Tasty Northern Italian cuisine appears at (**On Broadway** (106 Broadway, 406/443-1929, 5:30–10 P.M. Mon.–Sat.) in a light, airy, red-brick atmosphere. Another bastion of fine Italian cookery is **Lucca's at the Carriage House** (234 ½ Lyndale, 406/457-8311, www.luccasitalian.com, Wed.–Sun. 5 P.M.–9:30 P.M.) is a very intimate (just eight tables) restaurant with excellent appetizers, pasta, and meats, and a carefully chosen wine list. The lamb chops with mint pesto and balsamic-roasted shallots are $26.

The **Mediterranean Grill** (42 South Park Ave., 406/495-1212, 11 A.M.–9:30 P.M. Mon.–Sat., 10 A.M.–2 P.M. Sun.) offers a pan-Mediterranean menu: Excellent pasta, pizza, and Italian dishes are paired with Moroccan and Turkish specialties (the owner is Turkish).

The (**Silver Star Steak Company** (833 Great Northern Blvd., 406/495-0677, 11 A.M.–9 P.M. Mon.–Sat.) is at the center of the new Great Northern district. As one of Helena's most popular restaurants, you'll need reservations most evenings, but the steaks and atmosphere are both notable. Expect to pay $22 and up for prime rib and steak.

For two of Helena's most unique dining experiences, you'll need to leave town. In the old near-ghost-town of Marysville near the Great Divide Ski Area, **Marysville House** (153 Main St., Marysville, 406/443-6677, from 5 P.M. Tues.–Sat. summer, from 5 P.M. Wed.–Sat. the rest of the year) doesn't have a huge menu, but the 24-ounce T-bone steaks, grilled half chickens, and oyster skillets at this rustic frontier-era restaurant keep locals coming back for more. Marysville is seven miles north of Helena on I-15, then nine miles west along Highway 279, and a final six miles south along the gravel road to Marysville.

East Helena is a separate town from Helena, five minutes south on I-15. It was home to the smelter for the ores carved out of the famed Last Chance Gulch mines. Today, this workers' town is a little worse for wear, but its historic red-brick downtown is a great spot for savvy restaurateurs looking for inexpensive rent. **Capella's** (24 W. Main, 406/439-2680) offers French- and Caribbean-influenced cuisine such as calamari served with jalapeno grits and herb-encrusted beef tenderloin with cognac sauce. The talents behind this new and notable restaurant have substantial résumés: The owner operates one of Helena's top catering companies, and the chef previously cooked at New York City's Waldorf Astoria Hotel.

INFORMATION AND SERVICES

The **Helena Chamber of Commerce** is at 225 Cruse Avenue (406/442-4120 or 800/743-5362).

The central **post office** is located at 2300 North Harris Street (406/443-3304). The **Lewis and Clark County Library** is at 120 South Last Chance Gulch (406/447-1690).

St. Peter's Hospital is at 2475 Broadway (406/442-2480).

The **Helena National Forest Ranger Station** is at 2001 Poplar Street (406/449-5490). The **Department of Fish, Wildlife, and Parks** office is at 1420 East 6th Avenue (406/444-2535).

The *Independent Record* is Helena's daily paper. Find **Montana Public Radio** at 91.7 FM and 107.1 FM.

The **Eleventh Ave. Clean and Coin Laundromat** is at 1411 11th Avenue (406/442-9395).

TRANSPORTATION

Helena is served by Horizon, Northwest, SkyWest, and United airlines. The **airport** is east on Washington Street, or you can take the airport exit from I-15. **Rimrock buses** link Helena with Missoula, Butte, and Great Falls. You'll find the **bus station** at 5 West 15th Street (406/442-5860).

Hertz rents cars at the airport (406/449-4162), and **Budget** is at 1930 North Main Street (406/442-7011). Call a **cab** at 406/449-5525.

Townsend and Upper Missouri

At Three Forks, the Jefferson, Madison, and Gallatin Rivers unite into the Missouri River. It's no wonder, with such an abundance of water around, that Townsend and aptly named Broadwater County boast of their recreational facilities. Perhaps not surprising in an area so close to the state capital, there is an embarrassment of riches in state parks along the Missouri, providing fishing, hunting, boating, and windsurfing opportunities. Visitors can even engage in a more traditional pastime: panning for gold. Several

old mines provide pay dirt and teach prospecting skills.

TOWNSEND

Townsend (pop. 1,867, elev. 3,833 feet) has always made the most of its location. Set up in advance of the arrival of the first Northern Pacific train in 1883, Townsend was laid out with a deliberate sensibility, as if it were intended for bigger things. Prosperous farmers and ranchers along the Missouri nourished the strapping town; with the completion of

Highway 12 linking central Montana to the west, Townsend became a transportation crossroads. When the Canyon Ferry Dam was built in the 1940s, Townsend planted its flag over the lakes' recreational opportunities.

Today, Townsend is a pleasant town filled with trees and parks, seemingly dedicated to recreation on the nearby lakes and along the Missouri River.

Sights

At the **Broadwater County Museum** (133 N. Walnut, 406/266-5252 1 A.M.–5 P.M. daily May 15–Sept. 15, donations), there are relics of the region's history, including early mining tools from Confederate Gulch.

Where the Missouri River enters Canyon Ferry Lake just north of Townsend is the **Canyon Ferry Wildlife Management Area.** A 5,000-acre delta wetland, this is an exceptional place for viewing migrating waterfowl and nesting birds, including ospreys and loons. Beavers and white-tailed deer are also present. From Townsend, follow Highway 12 east to Harrison Road and turn north one mile.

Recreation

The upper Missouri Valley is lined by the Elkhorn Mountains to the west and the Big Belt Mountains to the east, each a part of the immense Helena National Forest. While these ranges are not particularly developed for the hiker and camper, the combination of mountain shelter and verdant river meadows makes the area famous for its hunting. **Monte's Guiding and Mountain Outfitting** (16 N. Fork Rd., 406/266-3515, www.montes-guiding.com) offers both guided fishing trips and big-game hunting expeditions.

As elsewhere in Montana, cattle drives have become high recreation around Townsend. **Montana High Country Cattle Drive** (7837 Hwy. 287, 406/266-2498 or 800/654-2845) organizes three five-day drives each summer; prices run $1,750 per person, including tent lodging, chuckwagon meals, horses, and help from real ranchers and outfitters. During the drive, information programs focus on natural history and issues facing contemporary ranchers.

Accommodations and Food

Both of these motels are comfortable, convenient, and offer rooms with rates under $50 per night: The **Lake Townsend Motel** (413 N. Pine, 406/266-3461 or 800/856-3461) is in a quiet spot one block off the highway. Each room in this tidy personable place has its own theme, and there's an outdoor hot tub. Pets are permitted with a deposit. The **Mustang Motel** (412 N. Front St., 406/266-3491 or 800/349-3499) is right along Highway 12 and accepts pets for an extra $5. Some rooms have refrigerators and microwaves; one room is wheelchair accessible.

More upscale lodging is available north of town at the **Canyon Ferry Mansion B&B** (7408 Hwy. 287, 406/266-3599, www.canyonferrymansion.com), with rooms starting at $139. The 28-room mansion is a popular place for weddings and family reunions.

To find campgrounds, follow Highway 12 or 284 north along Canyon Ferry Lake; the Bureau of Reclamation and the Bureau of Land Management run 12 campgrounds along the lakeshore.

As much landmark as it is a restaurant, bar, and casino, the **Mint** (305 Broadway, 6 A.M.–midnight) also has lighter meals and sandwiches. The **Horseshoe** (500 N. Front St., 406/266-3800) is open for three meals a day with good quick food. Stop for pizza, soup, and sandwiches at **Full Belli Deli** (209 S. Front St., 406/266-5459), which also makes its own sausages and cured meats.

The name **Cowboy Coffee and Steakhouse** (316 N. Front St., 406/266-3348, 6 A.M.–8 P.M. Mon.–Thurs., 6 A.M.–9 P.M. Fri.–Sat., 8 A.M.–2 P.M. Sun.) seems expansive but indicates that this newly relocated restaurant's roots are as a coffee shop. Expect a friendly welcome and good home-style cooking; main courses are $8–20.

Information

The **Townsend Area Chamber of Commerce** is at 412 North Front Street (406/266-4104).

SOUTHWESTERN MONTANA

The **Helena National Forest Office** is at 415 South Front Street (406/226-3425).

THE UPPER MISSOURI LAKES

North of Townsend, three dams in rapid succession impound the Missouri. Because they are near major population centers and are served by good roads, these lakes are among the most popular and developed in Montana. Canyon Ferry, Hauser, and Holter Lakes are well trod by local anglers, boaters, and campers, but they bear up pretty well considering their heavy use.

The range of recreational options is boggling: There are 25 state, Bureau of Land Management, and Bureau of Reclamation parks on Canyon Ferry Lake alone, which makes a brief overview difficult. Contact the Department of Fish, Wildlife, and Parks (1420 6th Ave., Helena, 406/444-2535) for more complete information.

Canyon Ferry Lake

Canyon Ferry Dam was built in the 1950s by the Bureau of Reclamation, creating the largest of the three lakes on the upper Missouri. Canyon Ferry backs up 25 miles of reservoir with almost 80 miles of shoreline. At the south end nearest Townsend, the lake is widest and the surrounding countryside rolling, gentle, and treeless. To the north the reservoir narrows and begins to flow into a steep canyon.

On the east side of the lake, about 18 miles north of Townsend, is a sharp ravine in the Big Belt Mountains called **Confederate Gulch.** In 1864 a couple of Confederate soldiers discovered incredibly rich gravel beds here. While it lasted, individual pannings yielded up to $1,000 in gold. A boomtown surged up immediately; called Diamond City, it grew to 10,000 people and was as rowdy and tough as the economics and the era allowed. By the 1870s the gold played out, but one last blast with a huge water-cannon-like hydraulic sluice dislodged another million dollars in gold. Today, almost nothing remains of the fabulously rich workings of Confederate Gulch.

Today, however, there is popular fishing and boating at Canyon Ferry. The lake is heavily and regularly stocked with rainbow trout, and they are usually hungry and scrappy enough to make a lucky angler feel skilled. Most of the facilities, both public and private, cluster at the northern end of the lake.

Follow Canyon Ferry Road (or Montana Avenue) east nine miles out of Helena to reach the lake. If coming north on Highway 12, turn on Highway 284 eight miles north of Winston. Rent a boat or windsurfing equipment at **Yacht Basin Marina** (3555 W. Shore Rd., 406/475-3440).

On the southern end of the lake, the campgrounds thin out. The most convenient **campsites** are at Silo, seven miles north of Townsend on Highway 12, where there are both public and private campgrounds. At the privately owned **Silo's RV Park** there's **Silo's Inn** bar and restaurant (406/266-3100, 5–9 P.M.).

Hauser Lake

Built in 1908 by Montana Power, Hauser Dam is named for Samuel Hauser, an early Montanan who advocated damming the Missouri to harness electricity for regional mining enterprises. At this 3,720-acre lake, heavily used for boating and waterskiing, the fishing is OK for smallmouth bass and kokanee salmon.

There are two scenic, practically adjacent public campgrounds on Hauser Lake. If the beach at **White Sandy,** seven miles northeast off I-15 on Highway 453, is full, then continue a few yards farther to **Black Sandy.**

While at Hauser Lake, try your hand at sapphire mining. The **Spokane Bar Sapphire Mine** (5360 Castles Rd., 406/227-8989), 10.5 miles east of Helena via York Road, offers buckets of sapphire-laden gravel. Here the novice can wash gravel to discover highly colored sapphires as well as garnets, rubies, and gold. A gallon bucket of gravel from the sapphire mine costs $25, and it's best to come equipped with a screwdriver and tweezers, essential tools of the gravel mining trade.

【 Holter Lake and the Gates of the Mountains

Holter Lake is the most awe-inspiring of the

three upper Missouri Lakes. Behind the dam lies the Gates of the Mountains, so named by Meriwether Lewis:

July 19th, 1805: This evening we entered the most remarkable clifts that we have yet seen. These clifts rise from the waters edge on either side perpendicularly to the hight of 1,200 feet. Solid rock for the distance of 53/4 miles. I entered this place and was obliged to continue my rout until sometime after dark before I found a place sufficiently large to encamp my small party; from the singular appearance of this place I called it the gates of the mountains.

The Missouri cut a deep gorge through thick deposits of limestone; although the flooding of Holter Dam (built in 1913) has decreased the rush of the river through these gates, it is still a startlingly dramatic landscape of geologic and human history. Wildlife viewing, historical vignettes, geologic curiosities, and drop-dead beautiful riverscapes make this one of Montana's most compelling side trips.

Gates of the Mountains Inc. (406/458-5241, www.gatesofthemountains.com), two miles east from the Gates of the Mountains exit off I-15, offers guided open-air **riverboat tours** (Memorial Day–Sept., $11 adult, $10 senior, and $7 child) of the entire canyon. During the two-hour trip, travelers usually see bighorn sheep, mountain goats, eagles, ospreys, and deer. Guides point out Indian pictographs along the limestone cliffs. The departure schedule is complex; call or check the website for times.

Plan your day carefully, and disembark from the boat at Meriwether Picnic Area. The boat captains allow passengers to break the trip at this point. Here at the site of Lewis and Clark's 1805 camp are trails that lead up into the **Gates of the Mountains Wilderness Area,** a 28,560-acre wildlife reserve within the deep limestone canyons along the east side of the Missouri River. It was back in this remote and precipitous area that 16 young firefighters died in 1949, a tragedy that led to the writing of Norman Maclean's best-selling book *Young Men and Fire.*

If you lay over at the wilderness area, be certain to know when to expect a returning riverboat, and save your ticket stub.

Known simply as **The Bungalow** (406/235-4276 or 888/286-4250, $125–145), Charles Power's 1911 country lodge is now one of Montana's most historically significant bed-and-breakfasts, located near the small town of Wolf Creek in the Gates of the Mountains canyon country. Charles Power was one of the engines of early Montana capitalism. Beginning rather humbly as a trader at Fort Benton in the 1870s, by the time of his death Powers owned 95 different corporations, controlled four square blocks of downtown Helena (including Helena's most architecturally significant, the Power Block), and was one of the state's richest men. When it came time to build a country home, Power turned to Robert Reamer, the architect who designed the Old Faithful Lodge in Yellowstone Park. For furnishings, Power turned to young interior designer Marshall Fields. Many of the original furnishings remain in the stately log lodge, which offers four guest rooms (one with private bath).

There are three public **campgrounds** along Holter Lake, all on the east side. Turn south from I-15 at the Wolf Creek exit, cross Wolf Creek, then turn north (left) on Recreation Road and proceed a few miles to the bridge. Turn south on Bear Tooth Road after crossing the Missouri. Continue three miles to **Holter Lake State Park.** Four miles up the same road are **Log Gulch** and **Departure Point State Parks.**

SOUTHWESTERN MONTANA

THE MISSOURI HEADWATERS AND SOUTH-CENTRAL MONTANA

More than any other part of the state, this country of broad valleys, rugged mountains, lush ranches, and trout-laden rivers is what people expect to find in Montana—and it doesn't disappoint. From the Yellowstone River, the longest undammed river in the Lower 48, to the Beartooth Highway, declared by the late Charles Kuralt to be one of the most spectacular drives in the United States, to the serene history-laden Missouri headwaters, this is country that cuts deep into the soul.

The Missouri headwaters, where the Jefferson, Madison, and Gallatin Rivers merge and create the Missouri, anchor the northwestern corner of this region. In the northeastern corner, the Crazy Mountains rise wildly from the plains. The Beartooth and Yellowstone Plateaus are at the southern edge. Rivers roll off south-central Montana's mountain ranges—the Beartooths, the Absarokas, the Gallatins, the Madisons, the Gravellys, and the Tobacco Roots—and course north to the Missouri.

Anglers are lured to the Madison, Gallatin, and Yellowstone Rivers by trout. People do run rivers, hunt, and mountain bike here, but the fishing draws pilgrims from around the world. The hatches of salmon flies and caddis flies are as closely watched as the seasons, and most everyone knows brown from rainbow from cutthroat. See specific sections under *Recreation* for more information.

PLANNING YOUR TIME

Start in **Bozeman,** which has decent air service and is a good place to transition from the rest of the world to Montana. Use it as a place to

© JUDY JEWELL

HIGHLIGHTS

((Museum of the Rockies: Home to many varied collections, this museum is best known for its dinosaur bones, including the *Tyrannosaurus rex* skull excavated in eastern Montana in 1990 (page 206).

((Missouri Headwaters State Park: At the Missouri headwaters it's not immediately apparent which of the three braided streams is the true main stem of the river. Lewis and Clark followed the Jefferson upstream; it provided the best path west to the Continental Divide (page 216).

((Norris Hot Springs: Not only is this small hot springs pool a good place to soak, it's also one of the most fun places around to hear live acoustic music (page 219).

((Fishing the Madison River: The 50-mile stretch of the Madison River from Quake Lake (near Yellowstone Park) north to Ennis is an almost continuous riffle, and the abundant trout are eager to grab passing morsels (page 221).

((Big Sky: Skiers and snowboarders should try to arrange a winter trip to Big Sky – ride the tram all the way to the top of Lone Mountain, take a big gulp as you look at the drop, and point your skis downhill (page 228)!

((Beartooth Highway: This 68-mile-long road climbs to 10,947 feet and crosses alpine meadows and snowfields on its run from Red Lodge to Yellowstone National Park. It'll take at least half a day to drive (page 254).

((Norris Geyser Basin: This ever-changing thermal area may not be as well-known as Old Faithful, but it's far more atmospheric and a better place to hike past geysers and boiling pools (page 265).

((Lamar Valley: It may not have the spectacular geothermal features found in other areas of Yellowstone National Park, but this wide valley on the stretch of road between Cooke City and Gardiner is the best place in the park to spot the famous Yellowstone wolves. The best time to see them is around dawn (page 267).

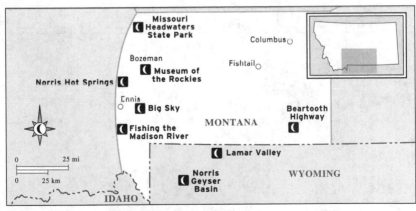

LOOK FOR ((TO FIND RECOMMENDED SIGHTS, ACTIVITIES, DINING, AND LODGING.

SOUTH-CENTRAL MONTANA

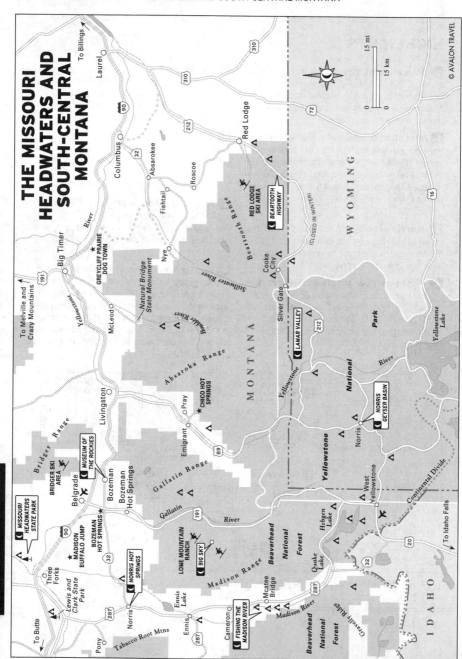

THE MISSOURI HEADWATERS AND SOUTH-CENTRAL MONTANA

SOUTH-CENTRAL MONTANA

© AVALON TRAVEL

decompress, but don't make it your sole destination in this spectacular region. While you're settling in, visit the **Museum of the Rockies** and spend an afternoon just wandering up and down Bozeman's bustling Main Street. If you have a week to spend in this region, devote the first day to Bozeman.

Those with even a peripheral interest in the Lewis and Clark Expedition should plan to head to **Three Forks** for day 2. Visit the Missouri Headwaters State Park, and make a side trip to the Madison Buffalo Jump, where Native Americans herded bison over the edge of a cliff. The Sacajawea Hotel is downtown Three Forks's biggest landmark and a fine place to spend the night.

On day 3, head south up the Madison River, around the corner at West Yellowstone (don't bother to stop here unless you're heading into the park), then down (north) the Gallatin River to the **Big Sky area.** Either the 320 Ranch or Buck's T-4 make a good resting place. Stop and fish or hike.

Continue down the Gallatin back to Bozeman on day 4, head east, and spend the night in **Livingston,** maybe right downtown at the Murray Hotel.

Ramble around downtown Livingston's galleries in the morning of day 5, then head south to **Chico Hot Springs** for the night.

Hike around Chico on day 6, then drive about 25 miles south to Gardiner or Mammoth. Explore the extrahot hot springs in that part of Yellowstone.

On day seven, get up just before dawn and drive to **Cooke City.** As the sun rises, keep your eyes open for wolves in Yellowstone's **Lamar Valley.** Continue on the Beartooth Highway to Red Lodge. If you're continuing your journey to the east, spend the night in Red Lodge or Billings. Otherwise, make it a long day by returning to Bozeman.

HISTORY

The hunting ranges surrounding the Missouri headwaters were coveted and often fought over by Native Americans. Bannock, Blackfeet, Crow, Flathead, and Shoshone all considered it sacred hunting ground. As the Blackfeet gained control of the northern plains, they drove other tribes out of the Missouri headwaters area. The Shoshone moved south and west, the Crow tended to stay off to the east, and the Flathead crossed over from the Bitterroot Valley less often.

Lewis and Clark arrived at present-day Three Forks in July 1805 and declared it the headwaters of the Missouri. Clark and his party returned to the forks on their way back east; from the headwaters they traveled up the Gallatin, crossed Bozeman Pass at Sacagawea's suggestion, and reached the Yellowstone River near the site of present-day Livingston. They floated the Yellowstone to its confluence with the Missouri, where they were joined by Lewis and his men.

Fur-bearing animals quickly caught the eyes of white trappers and mountain men. Miners made some forays into the mountains, but homesteaders and ranchers were ultimately more successful. Tourism, spurred on by dude ranches and fly-fishers, is now evident in most towns.

Bozeman and Vicinity

Bozeman (pop. 29,459, elev. 4,754 feet), home of Montana State University, lies at the foot of the Gallatin Valley, with the Gallatin and Madison Ranges to the south, the Bridger Range to the northeast, the Tobacco Roots farther west, and the Big Belts way off north and west.

It's a lovely setting, and Bozeman makes the most of its physical attributes, with hiking and skiing practically out the back door. However, what makes Bozeman such a great destination for a traveler is the town. More than any other Montana city, Bozeman has maintained its handsome old downtown as a business center, which makes the city seem centralized and community-focused. Add some excellent restaurants, art galleries, inexpensive lodging options, and an outgoing youthful population, and you've got Montana's most beguiling urban experience—though it's not to be mistaken for the real Montana.

HISTORIC BOZEMAN

One fortune seeker who passed through Bozeman in 1882 claimed it was the nicest place he'd been since St. Paul. In a letter to his sister, he told of "two churches, court house, fine large brick school, and the nicest lot of small dwelling houses all painted white with green lawns and level as a floor. There are lots of brick store buildings here. That is something you don't see the whole length of the Yellowstone River." Many of these attractive buildings remain: To embark on a historical downtown walking tour, with a foray into residential areas, start at the large brick building at Main and Rouse; it once housed city hall, but was first the opera house, with the original sign remaining over the front door for years afterward. Historic business buildings along Main Street include the **Baxter Hotel** (eat in one of the restaurants it now houses, or simply step in and admire the lobby), the **Hotel Bozeman,** the **Ellen Theatre,** and **Holy Rosary Church.** Historic homes cluster in the

neighborhood between Main Street and the university, especially along Willson Avenue. The Sigma Alpha Epsilon fraternity house at Willson and College is known locally as the **Storey Mansion.** It was the home of the son of Nelson Storey, the first cattleman to drive cattle up from Texas to the Gallatin Valley.

Sunset Hills Cemetery, immediately south of Lindley Park, is now home to John Bozeman, Chet Huntley, and most of the people for whom Bozeman's buildings and streets are named. The old part of the cemetery is off to the west; if you're really interested in exploring the graves, stop at a bookstore and pick up a copy of the cemetery guide produced by MSU art students.

Find downloadable walking-tour brochures of Bozeman's historic neighborhoods at www.bozemancvb.com.

MONTANA STATE UNIVERSITY

Founded in 1893, MSU (406/994-0211, www.montana.edu) is the state's oldest university. Originally the "ag school" in the state system, it is now a haven for some 12,000 outdoorsy students with a technical bent. The university, located south and west of the city center (take 7th Avenue south from Main Street to find the campus), is dominated by unremarkable modern buildings and, except for the Museum of the Rockies at the edge of campus, isn't really much of a destination.

MUSEUMS
◖ Museum of the Rockies

At the southeast corner of the MSU campus is the Museum of the Rockies (600 W. Kagy Blvd., 406/994-3466, www.museumoftherockies.org, 8 A.M.–8 P.M. daily Memorial Day–Labor Day, 9 A.M.–5 P.M. Mon.–Sat., 12:30–5 P.M. Sun. Labor Day–Memorial Day, $8–10 adults, $4–7 students 5–18, free for kids under 5; planetarium admission only, $3). The collection is eclectic, but most people know the museum

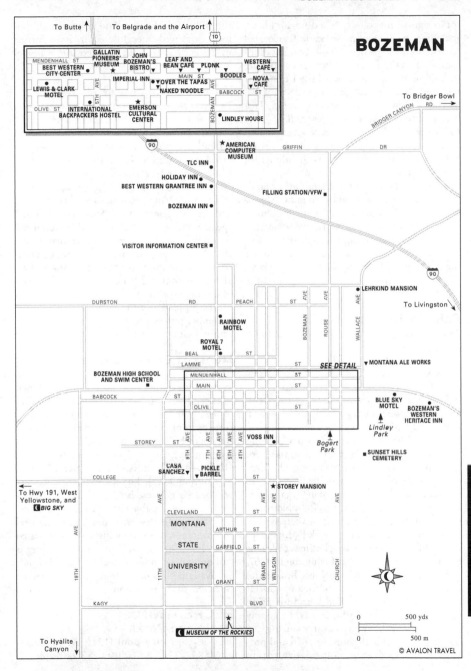

BOZEMAN

To Butte

To Belgrade and the Airport

10

MENDENHALL ST

GALLATIN PIONEERS' MUSEUM

JOHN BOZEMAN'S BISTRO

BEST WESTERN CITY CENTER

IMPERIAL INN

LEAF AND BEAN CAFÉ

PLONK

MAIN ST

OVER THE TAPAS

NAKED NOODLE

BOODLES

WESTERN CAFÉ

NOVA CAFÉ

BABCOCK ST

LEWIS & CLARK MOTEL

5TH AVE

INTERNATIONAL BACKPACKERS HOSTEL

EMERSON CULTURAL CENTER

OLIVE ST

BOZEMAN

LINDLEY HOUSE

To Bridger Bowl

BRIDGER CANYON RD

90

AMERICAN COMPUTER MUSEUM

GRIFFIN

DR

TLC INN

HOLIDAY INN

BEST WESTERN GRANTREE INN

BOZEMAN INN

FILLING STATION/VFW

VISITOR INFORMATION CENTER

LEHRKIND MANSION

To Livingston

90

DURSTON

RD

PEACH

ST

AVE

AVE

WALLACE AVE

RAINBOW MOTEL

BOZEMAN

ROUSE

ROYAL 7 MOTEL

BEAL

ST

LAMME

ST

SEE DETAIL

MONTANA ALE WORKS

BOZEMAN HIGH SCHOOL AND SWIM CENTER

MENDENHALL

ST

MAIN

ST

BABCOCK

ST

OLIVE

ST

BLUE SKY MOTEL

BOZEMAN'S WESTERN HERITAGE INN

STOREY

ST

9TH AVE

7TH AVE

6TH AVE

5TH AVE

4TH AVE

VOSS INN

Lindley Park

Bogert Park

SUNSET HILLS CEMETERY

CASA SANCHEZ

PICKLE BARREL

COLLEGE

ST

STOREY MANSION

To Hwy 191, West Yellowstone, and BIG SKY

19TH AVE

CLEVELAND

ST

AVE

AVE

AVE

MONTANA

ARTHUR

ST

STATE

GARFIELD

ST

11TH

UNIVERSITY

GRAND

WILLSON

CHURCH

GRANT

KAGY

BLVD

MUSEUM OF THE ROCKIES

To Hyalite Canyon

0   500 yds

0   500 m

© AVALON TRAVEL

for its significant collection of dinosaur bones, including the *Tyrannosaurus rex* skull excavated in eastern Montana in 1990—the largest dinosaur skull ever found. The dinosaur exhibits are housed in the spacious new Siebel Dinosaur Complex. It's a good place to take the kids, and adults may want to prepare by reading Jack Horner's book *Dinosaurs Under the Big Sky* before their visit. Horner, the renowned paleontologist in charge of the museum's impressive paleontology department, was the model for the paleontologist in *Jurassic Park*.

The museum also offers a sampling of modern art, pioneer history, and astronomy. Almost as popular as the dinosaurs is the museum's planetarium, where the impressive projection system simulates flying through space. The museum's extensive photo archive includes many images of and by Native Americans. Many of these photos can be browsed on the museum's website.

Gallatin Pioneer Museum

This museum (317 W. Main St., 406/522-8122, www.pioneermuseum.org, 10 A.M.–5 P.M. Mon.–Sat. Memorial Day–Labor Day, 11 A.M.–4 P.M. Tues.–Sat. Labor Day–Memorial Day, $3) took over the old county jail in 1982; there are still jail cells and a gallows among the Indian artifacts, old household items, and barbed wire collections.

Other exhibits feature the story of John Bozeman, a mountain man and immigrant guide of the 1860s; his namesake trail, essentially a spur of the Oregon Trail leading to Montana's gold country, ran along what is now a section of I-90. Frequent attacks by Sioux and Cheyenne bands plagued sojourners on the Bozeman Trail. Bozeman was killed, perhaps by Blackfeet (or perhaps by a business colleague or a jealous husband), near Livingston in 1867.

Largely as a reaction to John Bozeman's murder, Fort Ellis was established in 1867 at the site where William Clark and his party camped on July 14, 1806. It was the supply post for the U.S. Army cavalry during the Battle of the Little Bighorn in 1876 and provided military escort for railroad surveyors in the 1880s. The fort itself no longer stands, but local guys with metal detectors have turned up relics that are incorporated into a model at the museum.

American Computer Museum

Lest you think that all historical museums in Montana focus on early settlers, take note of the American Computer Museum, located in a small shopping center just north of I-90 on 7th Avenue (2304 N. 7th Ave., Bridger Park Mall, 406/582-1288, www.compustory.com, 10 A.M.–4 P.M. Fri.–Wed., 10 A.M.–8 P.M. Thurs. June–Aug., 10 A.M.–4 P.M. Tues.–Wed. and Fri.–Sat., noon–4 P.M. Sun. Sept.–May, $5 ages 13 and up, $3 children 6–12). You'll not see one old kitchen utensil in this surprisingly absorbing museum. Instead, ponder computers that seem immense and confusing and realize that they are little more than 20 years old. There's also an exhibit that focuses on printing presses and includes a replica of the Gutenberg press and an actual page from the original Gutenberg Bible.

Montana Grizzly Encounters

Although the Grizzly Discovery Center in West Yellowstone is a more fully developed facility, if you can't get there and really want to see a grizzly bear on your trip to Montana, stop by **Montana Grizzly Encounters** (80 Bozeman Hill Rd., 406/586-8893, www.grizzlyencounter.com, 9 A.M.–7 P.M. daily summer, 10 A.M.–4 P.M. Thurs.–Sun. winter, $7 adult, $5 children 3–12). The center has rescued several bears that were bred in captivity but living pretty miserable lives. Their new home near Bozeman Pass provides a more natural environment while allowing visitors to watch them play, forage, and snooze. The center is still quite new and will likely expand as funds are available. It's off I-90 at exit 319 between Bozeman and Livingston.

RECREATION
Pools and Parks

The 50-yard **city pool** (1211 W. Main St., 406/587-4724, $4 adults, $2 children) is adjacent to the high school. Regular morning, noon, and evening lap swims are scheduled. **Bogert Park** (303 S. Church Ave.) has an outdoor swimming pool, an ice rink, and a summertime Saturday morning farmers' market. Just south of Bogert Park, pick up the **Gallagator Linear,** a walking, running, skiing, and biking trail that runs from South Church Avenue and Storey Street to 3rd Avenue and Kagy Boulevard.

Lindley Park is just on the eastern edge of downtown, on the south side of East Main Street. The Sweet Pea Festival takes over the park early each August, and it's a good spot for a picnic at other times. During the winter, it's a good place for an easy cross-country ski.

Bozeman Hot Springs

Once a dilapidated extension of the neighboring KOA campground, Bozeman Hot Springs (81123 Gallatin Rd., 406/586-6492, 7 A.M.–10 P.M. Mon.–Thurs., 7 A.M.–sundown Fri., sundown–11 P.M. Sat., 8 A.M.–10 P.M. Sun., $7.50 adult, $6.50 age 5–12, $3.50 age 4 and under) has been refurbished with the addition of a small outdoor pool, several new soaking pools, a sauna, a steam room, a fitness center, and a spa. The main pool is indoors, in a large room with just a whiff of sulfur in the steamy air, and the atmosphere is homey and family-oriented rather than overly plush.

Hiking

Hyalite Canyon is about a half hour south of town via South 19th Avenue and Hyalite Canyon Road. Drive to the end of the road to launch a five-mile hike past nearly a dozen waterfalls to Hyalite Lake, then go another two miles to reach Hyalite Peak. One drainage over from the Hyalite Lake hike, another five-mile hike leads to pretty Emerald Lake in a high cirque. Turn left off the road shortly after the youth camp at Hyalite Reservoir to reach this trailhead.

The trails in this area are well-maintained and well-signed. Many of the trails, campgrounds, and fishing-access points in Hyalite Canyon are designed to allow people of differing physical abilities to use them. The trails are rated from easiest to most difficult; one of the easy trails is a 0.5-mile paved loop from Langhor Campground with nature trail signs in both type and braille.

North of town, the **Bridger Foothills National Recreation Trail** starts at the **M Picnic Area** on Bridger Drive (head north on Rouse; it becomes Bridger Drive) and continues for 21 miles to the Fairy Lake Campground. From there it's a two-mile hike to **Sacagawea Peak.** To drive to the **Fairy Lake Campground,** take Bridger Drive for 24 miles to Forest Road and go another seven miles to the campground. If you're just up for a short hike, start at the same place and hike up to the "M" for a great panorama of Bozeman and Bridger Canyon.

Another good view of the city and surrounding mountains comes from **Peet's Hill,** right in town at the corner of South Church and Storey, across the road from the entrance to the Gallagator Linear trail. It's a short and rewarding climb up the hill.

Skiing

Big Sky and neighboring **Moonlight Basin,** one hour to the south, form the state's largest downhill ski resort; on the same mountain, find good cross-country skiing at **Lone Mountain Ranch** (406/995-4644).

Bridger Bowl (15795 Bridger Canyon Rd., 406/587-2111 or 800/223-9609, www.bridgerbowl.com, mid-Dec.–mid-Apr., $43 adults, $15 children 6–12, $35 seniors, half-day and multiday passes available), 16 miles northeast of town up Bridger Canyon Road, is Bozeman's local nonprofit ski mountain. It's just as snowy as Big Sky, though smaller, less glitzy, and less expensive. During the ski season a free shuttle bus runs several times daily between Bridger and the Gallatin County Fairground (901 N. Black Ave.). Call 406/586-2389 for a ski report.

Cross-country skiers can head up Bridger Canyon to the groomed trails at **Bohart Ranch Cross Country Ski Center** (16621 Bridger Canyon Rd., 406/586-9070, www

SOUTH-CENTRAL MONTANA

.bohartranchxcski.com, Dec.–Mar., $15 adults, $8 children 7–12). Lessons and rentals are also available. During the summer the trails are used for mountain biking, hiking, and horseback riding (bring your own horse). There are also cross-country ski trails at Hyalite Reservoir, 18 miles south of town; Bozeman Creek, five miles south of town; and Stone Creek, 10 miles northeast of Bozeman. Call the Forest Service (406/522-2528) for details on these trails.

In downtown Bozeman, **Chalet Sports** (108 W. Main St., 406/587-4595) rents skis and bikes.

Fishing

Although there aren't any major trout streams flowing through Bozeman, the town is close enough to the Gallatin, Yellowstone, and Madison Rivers to support several good fly shops and outfitters. Right downtown is **The Bozeman Angler** (23 E. Main St., 406/587-9111 or 800/886-9111, www.bozemanangler.com). **River's Edge** (2012 N. 7th Ave., 406/586-5373, www.theriversedge.com) and **Montana Troutfitters** (1716 W. Main St., 406/587-4707 or 800/646-7847, www.troutfitters.com) are also convenient. Any of these shops can set you up with a guide, and each shop has good information on current fishing conditions on its website.

Other Activities

Rent rafts, kayaks, and other recreational equipment from **Northern Lights** (1716 W. Babcock St., 406/586-2225). The staff here can also supply recreational information, especially concerning climbing routes in Hyalite Canyon, Gallatin Canyon, and at Bozeman Pass.

Pick up a copy of the **Bozeman Big Sky Outdoor Recreation Map** at any bike or outdoor store; it shows routes for the area's hiking and mountain biking trails.

Golf **Bridger Creek** (2710 McIlhattan Rd., 406/586-2333) or **Cottonwood Hills** (8955 River Rd., 406/587-1118), both public courses.

YogaMotion (in the Emerson Annex, 111 S. Grand Ave., 406/585-9600, www.yogamotion.com) welcomes drop-in students.

EVENTS

The **Gallatin County Fair** is held the third week of July.

One of Bozeman's pleasant surprises is the **Intermountain Opera** (406/587-2889, www.operabozeman.org), which stages one production a year (with three performances).

Early August is a festive time in Bozeman. During the first week of the month, booths from local restaurants line up along Main Street for the **Bite of Bozeman,** a big picnic-cum-dinner party that is part of the **Sweet Pea Festival** (406/586-4003, www.sweetpea-festival.org, first full weekend of August), a big arts festival. As the music, dance, and theater bustles in Lindley Park, people gear up for the costumed Sweet Pea Ball, held at the Gallatin Gateway Inn. A parade and plenty of musical and arts events are scheduled for the festival weekend. It's a good idea to book your hotel room well in advance of this festival.

September marks the start of the season for the **Bozeman Symphony Orchestra and Symphonic Choir** (406/585-9774). Performances occur approximately once a month through April.

SHOPPING

There's plenty of shopping to be done on and around Main Street, with many shops focusing on Western-style interior decorating and others offering designer cowboy clothes.

Northern Lights (1716 W. Babcock St., 406/586-2225) has equipment and clothing for hikers, climbers, campers, and cross-country skiers. For a large selection of kayaks, rafts, and canoes as well as discounted outdoor gear and clothing, head a couple of miles west of town on Highway 191 to Northern Lights' outlet-style store, **The Barn** (83 Rowland Rd., 406/585-2090).

Montanaphiles, baseball lovers, and jazz buffs alike will thrill to the collection at **Vargo's Jazz City & Books** (6 W. Main St., 406/587-5383). The shelves are packed with new and used books on topics both mainstream and obscure, and Fran Vargo is a great person to talk with about books, music, and beyond. **Country Bookshelf** (28 W. Main St., 406/587-0166) is an exceptionally good general bookstore with many books autographed by their Montana authors.

If you need special camera supplies, stop by **F-11** (16 E. Main St., 406/586-3281, www.f11photo.com). It's one of the best photo supply shops in the state, serving both film and digital photographers; many camera repairs are done in-house.

GALLERIES

A number of art galleries dot downtown Bozeman; most stay open until 8 P.M. on the second Friday of the month, June–September, for an **Art Gallery Walk.**

Emerson Center for the Arts and Culture

The Emerson (111 S. Grand, 406/587-9797, www.theemerson.org) houses artists, craftspeople, performers, and a café. Visitors can browse the studios and galleries, stop for lunch at the Café Internationale, and attend evening performances.

Montana Trails (219 E. Main St., 406/586-2166, www.montanatrails.com) specializes in Western art both traditional (occasional works from artists such as 19th-century Swiss painter Karl Bodmer and Montana cowboy artist Ace Powell pop up here) and contemporary. It's a pretty approachable place for browsers. A little more serious, with a scholarly bent, is the **Thomas Nygard Gallery** (135 E. Main St., 406/586-3636), focusing on 19th- and 20th-century American art.

Indian Uprising Gallery (25 S. Tracy Ave., 406/586-5831) shows contemporary Native American art, largely from Plains Indian tribes.

Another good contemporary gallery is **Visions West** (34 W. Main St., 406/522-9946), which also has a branch down the road in Livingston.

Rather off the beaten track, but worth a visit for the bronzes of Tom Thornton (based on traditional Western stories passed through a dream-world filter), the gestural twisted-wire horse sculptures of Tina DeWeese, and the

lovely scenery, is **Cottonwood Gallery** (14190 Cottonwood Canyon, 406/763-4221, www.deweeseart.com, www.tomthorntonbronze.com). Hours are irregular here, so call first.

ACCOMMODATIONS
Under $50

Travelers who prefer not to stay in standard motel accommodations have a choice in Bozeman. The **International Backpackers Hostel** (405 W. Olive St., 406/586-4659, www.bozemanbackpackershostel.com, $20 bunk in co-ed dorm room, $42 private room) could pass for a big MSU group house, with no curfew. It's a big, old, somewhat shabby (but not creepy) Victorian just off Main Street.

The **Bozeman Ranger District** (406/522-2520, www.fs.fed.us/r1/gallatin, $30) rents out a number of rustic cabins in the Gallatin National Forest. They're generally equipped with woodstoves but have no running water, and they may require a substantial hike from road's end. For a list of cabins, call the ranger station or visit the website.

$50-100

Most convenient to shopping and dining downtown are the following motels. On the east side of Bozeman, the pet-friendly **Blue Sky Motel** (1010 E. Main St., 406/587-2311, www.bluesky-motel.com, $55–95) is an easy stroll or drive to downtown. The rooms are small and certainly not luxurious, but there's a big front lawn where guests often hang out and a city park next door. The handy park and the management's pet-friendly attitude make this a good place to stay with a dog. From I-90, exit 309 is closest to this end of town.

The other good budget choice, on the 7th Avenue strip, is the extraclean and well-run **Royal 7 Motel** (310 N. 7th Ave., 406/587-3103 or 800/587-3103, www.royal7inn.com, $51–87). The rooms at the Royal 7 are considerably nicer than what you'll find in other budget motels in town. In the same area, the **Rainbow Motel** (510 N. 7th Ave., 406/587-4201, $65–75) has a small outdoor pool. **Bozeman's Western Heritage Inn** (1200

E. Main St., 406/586-8534 or 800/877-1094, www.westernheritageinn.com, $88 and up) is a very comfortable motel with spacious rooms, including some with kitchenettes, plus a fitness room, hot tub, steam room, suites with whirlpools, and free light breakfast. Pets are permitted.

Right at the I-90 exit is a bundle of motels. One locally owned place, **Bozeman Inn** (1235 N. 7th Ave., 406/587-3176 or 800/648-7515, www.bozemaninn.com, $55 and up), has a pool and a large hot tub; pets are allowed. The adjoining restaurant, Santa Fe Red's, is popular, although better food is available downtown. The relatively new **TLC Inn** (805 Wheat Dr., 406/587-2100 or 877/466-7852, www.tlc-inn.com, $59–75) has a sauna, hot tub, continental breakfast, and some pet-friendly rooms.

Over $100

A fairly average but conveniently located motel that's significantly cheaper in the off-season is the **Best Western City Center** (507 W. Main St., 406/587-3158, www.bestwestern.com, $100 and up), on the edge of downtown not far from the university. There's a pool plus a restaurant and lounge.

Also convenient is the **Lewis & Clark Motel** (824 W. Main St., 406/586-3341 or 800/332-7666, www.lewisandclarkmotel.net, $100 and up), a large complex that includes a 20-yard indoor pool, fitness center, sauna, hot tub, plus a restaurant and lounge.

The **Voss Inn** (319 S. Willson Ave., 406/587-0982, www.bozeman-vossinn.com, $100–120 s, $120–140 d), in a 120-year-old mansion on a lovely and well-situated neighborhood street, is Bozeman's premier bed-and-breakfast. The six guest rooms are furnished with antiques, and each has a private bathroom. Breakfast is served in the guest parlor or in guests' rooms, and afternoon tea is served in the parlor.

◖ **Lehrkind Mansion** (719 N. Wallace Ave., 406/585-6932 or 800/992-6932, www.bozemanbedandbreakfast.com, $139–189) is owned by former Yellowstone National Park rangers, who are full of good travel hints. The house,

a fanciful antique-filled Victorian with a huge hot tub on the back deck, is joined by an old farmhouse with several more guest rooms.

East of town off I-90, **Howler's Inn** (3815 Jackson Creek Rd., 406/586-0304 or 888/469-5377, www.howlersinn.com, $115–195) is a little different from your average B&B—it's also a wolf sanctuary. Income from the B&B supports wolves who can't be released into the wild; they live in a three-acre fenced enclosure. The rooms are comfortable, with views of mountains and wolves, and guests may use the hot tub and sauna.

Silver Forest Inn (15325 Bridger Canyon Rd., 406/586-1882 or 877/394-9357, www.silverforestinn.com, $80–140) is a good base for Bridger Bowl skiers. The 1932 log home has been renovated as a six-room B&B; the turret room has incredible views of the Bridger Mountains. Some rooms share baths.

One of Bozeman's nicest conventional motels is the **Best Western GranTree Inn** (1325 N. 7th Ave., 406/587-5261 or 800/624-5865, $108 and up). It's a ways from downtown, but an indoor pool, hot tub, laundry room, restaurant and lounge, and an airport shuttle are all available.

One other chain motel out near the I-90 interchange that's surprisingly pleasant is the **Holiday Inn** (5 Baxter Ln., 406/587-4561 or 800/366-5101, www.hibozeman.com, $115 and up). Services and amenities are quite good and include an indoor pool, hot tub, exercise and game rooms, restaurant and lounge, room service, laundry room, massage therapist, and free airport shuttle; kids stay—and eat—free, and pets are welcome too.

Even though it's 15 miles from town in the Highway 191 hamlet of Gallatin Gateway, travelers to Bozeman shouldn't overlook the historic ◖ **Gallatin Gateway Inn** (406/763-4672 or 800/676-3522, www.gallatingatewayinn.com, $149 and up). The old railroad hotel has been extensively renovated but not substantially altered from the original. Huge arched windows and ocher walls give the lobby an airy Mediterranean feel, and the rooms, which range from smallish in the hotel proper to spacious suites in buildings behind the main lodge, are graceful and comfortable. There's an outdoor pool and hot tub, a casting pond, tennis courts, and places to hike or mountain bike just out the back door. About 10 miles west of town, the **Gallatin River Lodge** (9105 Thorpe Rd., 406/388-0148 or 888/387-0148, www.grlodge.com, $270) is located on a large ranch in the Gallatin Valley. All six suites have elegant oak Mission-style furniture. Each has a private bath containing a large whirlpool tub and shower. Packages are available with or without guide service; a three-night stay with guide service runs $1,575 per person, double occupancy. Without the guide, it's $1,175 per person.

Consider renting a cottage or lodge from **Bozeman Cottage Vacation Rentals** (406/585-4402 or 888/415-9837, www.bozemancottage.com, $740 per week and up). A variety of well-maintained houses, many located in Bozeman's close-in residential neighborhoods, are available. Nightly rentals can sometimes be arranged.

A property management company with a number of high-quality houses and apartments for short-term rentals or more extended stays is **Intermountain Property Management** (406/586-1503 or 888/871-7856, www.montanavacation.com). They have listings all over south-central Montana.

Camping

Tent campers can head for one of the three **Gallatin National Forest campgrounds** (406/522-2520, www.fs.fed.us/r1/gallatin, mid-May–mid-Sept., $11) in Hyalite Canyon: **Langhor** is 11 miles south of town on Hyalite Canyon Road, and **Hood Creek** and **Chisholm** are another six and seven miles down the same road, respectively. Reach Hyalite Canyon Road by heading south on 19th Avenue.

Convenient though rather expensive camping is available at the **Bozeman KOA** (81123 Gallatin Rd., 406/587-3030 or 800/562-3036, tent $29, RV $44 and up, cabins $55), eight miles south of town on Highway 191, next door to Bozeman Hot Springs.

FOOD

Bozeman's prosperous trendiness is reflected in its restaurants—not a bad thing for the hungry traveler. In fact, Bozeman has a higher concentration of great restaurants than any other city in the state. That doesn't mean that all the best meals are served in posh new cafés, but the emphasis on fresh ingredients and vivid flavors resonates even in more modest venues.

Casual Meals

At the **Western Cafe** (443 E. Main St., 406/587-0436, 5 A.M.–3:30 P.M. Mon.–Fri., 5 A.M.–1 P.M. Sat., $5–10), you can experience old-time Bozeman; cinnamon rolls come out of the oven at 8 A.M., tabs must be paid before the first of the month, the grill cook is quick, and there's a jackalope head mounted above the milk dispenser. In short, it's an old-fashioned Western diner.

For those who would rather drink coffee than eat, the **Leaf and Bean** (35 W. Main St., 406/587-1580, 6 A.M.–10 P.M. Mon.–Thurs., 6 A.M.–11 P.M. Sat., 7 A.M.–10 P.M. Sun.) is a good place to hunker down with the morning paper, a pastry, and an espresso drink.

 Cateye Café (23 N. Tracey St., 406/587-8844, 7 A.M.–2:30 P.M. Wed.–Mon. and 5–9:30 P.M. Thurs.–Sat., breakfast and lunch about $7, dinner $15–20) is a good-natured and hip spot with a strong streak of retro. All diners, kids and adults alike, are provided with toys to play with while waiting (sometimes for quite a while) for meals to come. At dinner, the homemade meatloaf is tasty.

Another stylish and rightly popular breakfast or lunch spot is **Nova Cafe** (312 E. Main St., 406/587-3973, $7–12); the menu items are good takes on standards such as breakfast burritos or Belgian waffles, and the specials (lemon blackberry ricotta pancakes) are often inspired. Gluten-free baked goods are available.

Over the Tapas (19 S. Willson Ave., 406/556-8282, 11 A.M.–3 P.M. Mon.–Fri. and 5–10 P.M. Mon.–Sat., small plates $4–14) is a good place to while away an evening running up your tapas bill. But it's also easy to get out of here pretty cheaply; a large helping of delicious patatas bravas and a tortilla con chorizo are each only $4.

Two doors down is the **Naked Noodle** (27 S. Willson Ave., 409/585-4801, 11 A.M.–9 P.M. Mon.–Sat., noon–9 P.M. Sun., $7–12), a casual spot for a pasta or Asian noodle meal. Pick your favorite style of noodle and then add a sauce and various toppings such as meat, seafood, veggies, or cheese. (This makes it an excellent place to bring a picky eater!) There are also set menu items if you're feeling uninventive.

For downtown's best pizza and good local ales, go to **MacKenzie River Pizza** (232 E. Main St., 406/587-0055, 11 A.M.–10 P.M. daily, closes at 9 P.M. winter weekdays, $7–10). The food is pretty good, and it's a great value, making it immensely popular with Bozeman's student population.

The **Soup Shack Garage** (451 E. Main St., 406/585-8558, 11 A.M.–9 P.M. daily, $6–11) has a large outside patio where you can spend your summer evenings sipping homemade soup and eating mesquite-grilled burgers.

Montana Ale Works (611 E. Main St., 406/587-7700, 4 P.M.–late daily, $13) has a huge room full of pool tables and serves microbrews from all over the region. The menu ranges from burgers and huge delicious salads to steak and seafood, and both the food and the wine list are way better than is common at a brewpub.

Serious wine drinkers should head to **(** **Plonk** (29 E. Main St., 406/587-2170, 11:30 A.M.–2 A.M. daily, $12–18), a wine bar with a small but good lunch and dinner menu and the most studiously hip atmosphere in town. They offer a wide selection of wines by the bottle or by the glass, as well as more than 60 beers, and a surprising selection of cheeses.

Near the university, some casual places cater to students and locals. The **Pickle Barrel** (809 W. College St., 406/587-2411, 11 A.M.–10:30 P.M. daily, $6–7) is not much bigger than the genuine item. All they've got are sandwiches, but they're giant, satisfying things, with any of the steak-and-cheese sandwiches getting a special recommendation. There are picnic benches out front so you can hang around and eat, then finish the gorge with an ice-cream cone from the equally tiny place next door. (It's actually part of the Pickle Barrel, but

the buildings are too small to fit main course and dessert in the same place.) Pickle Barrel also has a downtown location at 219 E. Main Street, inside the Rockin' R.

The deli at the **Community Food Co-op** (908 W. Main St., 406/587-4039, 7 A.M.–8 P.M. daily, store open until 10 P.M.) serves a wide variety of vegetarian soups, salads, and casseroles.

If you're staying on the 7th Avenue motel strip and lack the energy to leave your street, there are alternatives to McDonald's and Taco Bell. At the Bozeman Inn, **Santa Fe Red's** (1235 N. 7th Ave., 406/587-5838, 9:30 A.M.–2 A.M. daily, $8–13) serves decent Southwestern-style food.

Fine Dining

The cosmopolitan (for Montana) atmosphere at **Boodles** (215 E. Main St., 406/587-2901, lunch Mon.–Sat., lunch and dinner daily, dinner $18–33) is just right for contemplating a selection of New American dishes featuring duck breast, lamb, porterhouse steak, and game. It also has a good bar with a wide selection of fine wines.

From its basement location, **Looie's Down Under** (101 E. Main St., 406/522-8814, lunch Tues.–Fri., Sunday brunch, dinner nightly, $14–32) features high-quality Italian and continental cuisine as well as sushi (from the restaurant upstairs). The tasty grilled sea bass is served with a corn and lobster hash and vanilla rum butter.

John Bozeman's Bistro (125 W. Main St., 406/587-4100, 11:30 A.M.–2 P.M. and 5–9:30 P.M. Tues.–Sat., $12–34) has risen from its American bistro ex-hippie roots to become one of Bozeman's fine dining restaurants. The menu is global in its scope; order seafood in a Thai red curry sauce over soba noodles while your companion has a Cajun-spiced steak with prawns.

If you're hankering for a venison chop served with butternut squash–pear hash, pick up and drive out to the **Gallatin Gateway Inn** (Hwy. 191 at Gallatin Gateway, 406/763-4672, 5:30–9:30 P.M. nightly, entrées $16–32). The food is very good, and the atmosphere sublime.

Also worth a little drive is the classy yet thoroughly Western **(** **Mint Bar & Café** in Belgrade (27 E. Main St., 406/388-1100, 4 P.M.–2 A.M. daily, $19–46), which features hand-cut steaks, seafood, and martinis. **Gallatin River Grill,** in the Gallatin River Lodge south of Belgrade (9105 Thorpe Rd., 406/388-0148 or 888/387-0148, 5–9 P.M. nightly, entrées $28–32) serves dinner nightly in a dining room with fir floors, oak furnishings, and an early-1900s oak back bar where diners sometimes spot white-tailed deer grazing by the trout pond.

NIGHTLIFE

The 1939 Works Progress Administration *Montana, a State Guide Book* characterized Bozeman as "an old and decorous town. Local ordinances prohibit dancing anywhere after midnight and in beer halls at any time. It is illegal to drink beer while standing, so all Bozeman bars are equipped with stools."

Well, things have loosened up a little bit since the 1930s. College students have a nasty habit of standing up to drink, and the electronic gaming machines now endemic in bars threaten to make barstools obsolete.

At the **Crystal Bar** (123 E. Main St., 406/587-2888), both the decor and decorum sometimes seem a bit tenuous. This Main Street fixture was once dominated by cowboys, but now students and tourists join the mix. Crystal's rooftop terrace is surrounded by chicken wire to keep patrons from tossing beer bottles onto the sidewalk below.

At the classy but relaxed **Rockin' R** (211 E. Main St., 406/587-9355), the mixed crowd is usually sprinkled with poets and lefties. Head down to the corner of Main and Rouse, to the old Bozeman Hotel building, to find the **Zebra Club** (15 N. Rouse Ave., 406/585-8851) with cocktails and indie bands.

Head north to the **Filling Station VFW** (2005 N. Rouse Ave., 406/587-5009) for music from local bands, many playing alternative Western music. It's also at least a quasi-official stop for scores of Harley riders on their way to the annual Harley-Davidson Festival in Sturgis, South Dakota. The **Cat's Paw** (721 N. 7th Ave., 406/586-3542) is a band bar with

enough space to sponsor big shows; it's also a casino with a popular card room.

Nightlife doesn't necessarily include alcohol at the **Leaf and Bean** or the **Emerson Cultural Center,** both of which often have music in the evenings.

SERVICES AND INFORMATION

The **Bozeman Area Chamber of Commerce** is at 2000 Commerce Way, near the 19th Avenue exit from I-90 (406/586-5421 or 800/228-4224, www.bozemancvb.com). More convenient is the **Downtown Bozeman Visitor Center** (224 E. Main St., 406/586-4008).

Bozeman Deaconess Hospital is at 915 Highland Boulevard (406/585-5000).

Find the **public library** at 220 East Lamme Street (406/582-2400). Pick up **Yellowstone Public Radio** at 102.1 FM in and around Bozeman. Good alternative tunes come out of KGLT at 91.9 FM.

TRANSPORTATION

Gallatin Field is eight miles west of town, near Belgrade. Served by Delta, Horizon, Northwest, Frontier, and United Airlines, flights come in daily from Seattle, Salt Lake City, and Denver.

Automobile rentals are available at the airport through **Budget Rent-A-Car** (406/388-4091 or 800/527-0700), **Alamo/National** (406/388-6694 or 800/227-7368), **Hertz** (406/388-6939 or 800/654-3131), and **Enterprise** (800/261-7331). Shuttle service between Gallatin Field and downtown Bozeman is provided by **Karst Stage** (406/556-3540 or 800/287-4759, www.karststage.com) and **All Valley Cab** (406/388-9999).

If you're over 21 and have a motorcycle license, you can rent a Harley from **Yellowstone Harley Davidson** (540 Alaska Frontage Rd., Belgrade, 877/388-7684, www.yellowstoneharley.com, rentals May–Sept.).

Greyhound stops in Bozeman on its way across I-90/94 (1205 E. Main St., 406/587-3110 or 800/231-2222). **Rimrock Trailways** (800/255-7655) provides bus service to Billings and Missoula from the same bus terminal.

SOUTH-CENTRAL MONTANA

Three Forks and the Madison River Valley

Even if the notion of the Missouri headwaters doesn't automatically stir your blood, a visit there probably will. There's something *big* about the place where three lively trout streams join up to make their way across the plains that gives the spirit an almost geological uplift.

All three of the Missouri's forks come straight from the mountains. The Madison Range flanks the Madison Valley to the east; to the west are the northerly glacier-cut Tobacco Root Mountains and the southerly low Gravelly Range.

The Madison River, which forms the middle fork of the Missouri, starts in Yellowstone National Park and joins with the Jefferson and the Gallatin at Three Forks. Mention of the Madison quickens the pulse of anglers across the United States; people come from all over to fish here, and the valley sports several guest ranches to accommodate them.

The Madison Range has obvious current geologic activity. The eastern front is moving along a fault. A lurching move in August 1959 jacked the mountains up and dropped the valley floor. The southern end of Hebgen Lake (just west of Yellowstone National Park) rose, the northern end dropped, and a rock slide buried campers and blocked the Madison River, forming Quake Lake.

FISHING STRATEGIES

Fish the lower Madison (below Ennis Lake) for brown trout or the upper river for the now-scarce rainbow trout, and be prepared to catch a generous number of whitefish as well. The state once stocked the Madison with hatchery trout, but this practice was discontinued and wild populations were doing well on their own until whirling disease came along (see sidebar).

Along with the beautiful riffled water and trout come crowds. To avoid them, look for spots far from Highway 287 and fish early or late in the season. Although the high waters make most stretches of the Madison too turbulent for fly-fishing until late June, some

stretches (especially inside Yellowstone Park) are OK for flies by early June, and turbulent waters don't seem to deter anglers when the salmon flies hatch around the end of June.

July and August are when the caddis hatch, and anglers flock to the upper Madison. North (downstream) of Ennis Lake, the river warms up too much for good summer fishing; try this area in the spring or fall. Fly-fishing is usually good through mid-October on most of the Madison.

Some areas of the Madison River are closed to fishing from a boat; bait fishing is prohibited along some stretches, and for a 30-mile stretch of the upper river, catch-and-release fishing is mandated. Special regulations will usually be posted at fishing-access areas, but check ahead with the Department of Fish, Wildlife, and Parks or your fishing guide.

THREE FORKS AND VICINITY

Three Forks (pop. 1,845) gets its name from the confluence of the Gallatin, Madison, and Jefferson Rivers, which occurs on a wetland plain surrounded by mountains just north of town. A large factory on the edge of town produces talc. (In mountains to the south of town, deeply buried marble deposits have further metamorphosed into talc, making this a major talc-mining area.)

Just west of Three Forks, Highway 287 follows the Jefferson River through fossil-ridden limestone that's been jostled into a tilted position. For a few miles the land is open and dry; past Lewis and Clark Caverns, the Madison River flows through a gorge of high buff-colored hills. This road, which eventually leads to Cardwell, is a pleasant alternative to the interstate.

◖ Missouri Headwaters
State Park

Well before Lewis and Clark camped at the site of Missouri Headwaters State Park (four miles northeast of Three Forks on Road 286,

WHIRLING DISEASE

In the 1990s it looked like the Madison River fishery was doomed. Trout populations were down by as much as 90 percent due to whirling disease. Although over 150 rivers in the state have been infected, the Madison has now recovered significantly from this parasitic disease, thought to have originated in Europe, where brown trout have largely developed immunity to it.

The disease is caused by a parasite that infects the head and spine of fingerling trout, causing them to swim erratically. In addition to their whirling swimming, infected fish may have a darkened tail, twisted spine, and deformed head with a shortened and twisted jaw. Although rainbow and cutthroat trout are most susceptible, the condition can affect any salmonid species.

Researchers have worked on ways to ameliorate the damage of whirling disease, including identifying resistant fish, and preventive measures have significantly helped prevent the spread of *Myxobolus cerebralis*, the protozoan spore that causes the illness. Because there is no known cure for the disease, it is important that anglers follow these precautions:

- Remove all mud and aquatic plants from your vehicle, boat, anchor, trailer and axles, waders, boots, and fishing gear *before* departing the fishing access site or boat dock. If you've been fishing in infected streams, it may be a good idea to wash boots, waders, and fishing equipment in a bleach solution. Be sure to rinse the bleach off thoroughly so it doesn't damage the waders.

- Drain all water from your boat and equipment – including coolers, buckets, and live wells – *before* departing the fishing access site or boat dock.

- Dry your boat and equipment between river trips.

- Don't transport fish – dead or alive – from one body of water to another.

- Don't dispose of fish entrails, skeletal parts, or other by-products in any body of water or in a garbage disposal. Put them in the garbage for disposal in a landfill.

- Don't use salmon, trout, or whitefish parts as bait.

Find more information on whirling disease online at www.whirling-disease.org.

406/994-4042, www.fwp.state.mt.us/parks, daylight hours, year-round, camping from May 1–Sept. 30, free for Montana residents, $5 day-use fee for nonresidents), this area where the Madison, Jefferson, and Gallatin Rivers join up to form the Missouri was well traveled. It was a disputed hunting area and the site of frequent battles between the Crow and the Blackfeet. The mountain and river bands of the Crow had regular rendezvous at the headwaters, where they'd hunt, fish, and later, trade with whites.

When the Corps of Discovery reached the Missouri headwaters on July 27, 1805, Lewis and Clark concluded that none of the three rivers was sufficiently larger than any other to warrant calling it the Missouri and calling the other two feeder streams. They solved this dilemma by declaring them "three noble streams" and took the opportunity to name them after the President (Jefferson), the Secretary of State (Madison), and the Secretary of the Treasury (Gallatin). Actually, river-naming was not foremost in Lewis's and Clark's minds—they were far more preoccupied with meeting the Shoshone, from whom they hoped to obtain horses.

Try to visit the headwaters early or late in the day, when the light comes in low and opens you up to some special magic held by the rivers and bluffs. Good information stations discuss local flora and fauna as well as Corps of Discovery history. The headwaters site includes an old hotel and log cabin from Gallatin City, built in 1864 with the somewhat deluded thought that steamboats would be able to navigate to this point. (The city did not thrive.) A small cave is painted with several faded and damaged Native

© PAUL LEVY

Plan to spend a few hours exploring the Missouri Headwaters.

American **pictographs;** follow the trail south from the main interpretive center to see it.

If bird-watching appeals to you more than steeping yourself in Lewis and Clark lore, there are herons, ospreys, Canada geese, and songbirds along the headwaters trail. Climb Lewis Rock or Fort Rock to scan the cliffs for golden eagles. Vegetation here is characteristic of the plains: prickly pear and pincushion cacti, bluebunch wheatgrass, big sagebrush, saltbush, and buckwheat brush. The headwaters area is also a popular fishing spot.

Madison Buffalo Jump State Monument

The semicircular limestone cliff at Madison Buffalo Jump State Monument (seven miles south of Logan, 406/994-4042, www.fwp.mt.gov/parks, daylight hours, year-round, free for Montana residents, $5 for nonresidents) has changed little since Native Americans regularly drove bison over its edge. In fact, bone shards are still scattered in the dirt at the foot of the cliff, and tepee rings are clustered around the top. Buffalo jumps were commonly used

before the introduction of horses; fleet-footed men dressed in skins would lure the bison to the edge of the cliff, then somehow manage to get out of the way as the herd plunged over.

Headwaters Heritage Museum

Downtown Three Forks's historical museum (202 S. Main St., 406/285-4778, Mon.–Sat. 9 A.M.–5 P.M. daily June–Sept.; free) has a good collection of photographs and an archaeological display among the exhibits. But perhaps most memorable is the mount of a 29.5-pound brown trout—the largest ever caught in the state.

Pony

Nestled just below the Tobacco Root Mountains about 30 miles southwest of Three Forks and six miles up a paved road from Harrison, Pony comes off as something of a ghost town, but it actually has about 180 residents. There are a few fancy new houses on the hills above the abandoned Victorians and the brick bank building. Pony took its name from Tecumseh "Pony" Smith, who mined gold here in 1868. Gold, silver, and some tungsten were mined in Pony through the early part of the 20th century, and an early 1990s attempt at cyanide-process gold mining netted virtually no gold and left cyanide in the groundwater.

The Pony Bar, which is still doing business, used to be a boardinghouse for men. When the second-floor residents got tired of running downstairs and out back to the outhouse, they constructed a "pee trough" running down the hallways and into a drainpipe.

Fishing

There's fishing access to the Missouri River and its tributaries at **Headwaters Park.** The **Drouillard Fishing-Access Site** offers entry to the Jefferson River on Highway 10 two miles west of Three Forks. The **Sappington Bridge** crosses the Jefferson on Highway 287 at Highway 10, and the **Williams Bridge** is just to the east. The Jefferson is deeper and slower than the riffly Madison, but fishing very early or late in the day will often yield brown trout as well as a host of less prestigious whitefish, carp, chubs, and suckers.

Cobblestone, Grey Cliff, and **Black's Ford** fishing-access sites are on the lower Madison River between Highway 84 and the Missouri headwaters. To reach this stretch of the Madison, head south on Highway 286 (off I-90 east of Three Forks) or east from Norris on Highway 84, then north on Highway 286. Camping is permitted at these undeveloped riverside spots, but care should be taken not to stray onto the surrounding private land without permission. The relatively warm lower Madison, while popular, does not share the incredible reputation of the river's cooler upper reaches.

There are several pullouts on Highway 84 near the bridge nine miles east of Norris, and the more ambitious angler can head up the trail into Beartrap Canyon (see below under *Other Recreation*).

C Norris Hot Springs

At Norris Hot Springs (406/685-3303, www .norrishotsprings.com, 4–10 P.M. Wed.–Sun. May–Sept., 4–9 P.M. Wed.–Thurs., 2–10 P.M. Sat.–Sun. Oct.–Apr., $5, no credit cards),

just east of Norris on Highway 84, the natural springs fill a small pool lined with wooden boards. Hot water shoots into the air and showers down onto a corner of the pool, lowering the temperature of the water from the source temperature of 120°F to about 104°F. From one side of the pool bathers can look out onto the nearby wetland, which is frequently visited by wildlife. The hot springs has also become a great place to hear acoustic roots music (7 P.M. Thurs.–Sun., $7 admission when there's music).

Other Recreation

Beartrap Canyon, a Bureau of Land Management wilderness area east of Norris, is a steep gorge cut by the Madison River. A hiking trail starts three miles down a dirt road from the Red Mountain Campground (about nine miles east of Norris on Highway 84) and runs seven miles up the canyon. A dam at the southern end holds back Ennis Lake; hiking is prohibited around the dam, forcing hikers to retrace their steps to leave the canyon. The trail is popular with both hikers and anglers and can get crowded on summer weekends.

Events

The lively and popular **Three Forks Rodeo** is held the third weekend of July. A mid-April high school rodeo also draws big crowds.

The second weekend of August brings **Rockin' the Rivers** (406/285-0099, www.rockintherivers.com) to town. This huge outdoor music festival draws up to 15,000 to hear performers such as Journey, Nazareth, and a Styx cover band (Bonnaroo it ain't).

Each September, Headwaters State Park is the site of the **John Colter Run** (406/587-4415), a seven-mile dash through the prickly pears commemorating Corps of Discovery member Colter's 1808 feat of survival when he was stripped naked and hunted by Blackfeet Indians and still managed to escape. Clothing and shoes are permitted on this run.

Accommodations

Three Forks's grand **C Sacajawea Hotel** (Main St. and Ash St., 406/285-6515 or

888/722-2529, www.sacajaweahotel.com, $95–115, lower rates off-season) has been a local landmark since 1910, and in recent years has been through a succession of owners, with several extended closures. When we visited in the spring of 2008, it was open and offering the nicest digs in town, but it was once again on the market. From the rocking chairs on the wide front porch to the big claw-foot bathtubs in some of the rooms, the Sac has an easygoing yet refined comfort.

In downtown Three Forks, the **Broken Spur Motel** (124 W. Elm, 406/285-3237 or 888/354-3048, www.brokenspurmotel.com, $63) is a comfortable and well-run place with free continental breakfast. Just off the I-90 exit west of downtown, **Fort Three Forks Motel** (Highway 287 near I-90 exit 274, 406/285-3233 or 800/477-5690, http://fort3forks.com, $77 and up) has nice motel rooms and a small RV campground. Pets are accepted at both places for a small fee.

Bud Lilly's Anglers Retreat (16 W. Birch, 406/285-6690 or 406/284-9943, $65 and up) offers sleeping rooms (shared bath) and furnished apartments in a restored railroad workers hotel. As the name suggests, Lilly (a well-known fishing guide and conservationist) rents most of his lodgings to anglers who are spending a bit of time in the area.

Camping

The **Missouri Headwaters State Park campground** (four miles northeast of Three Forks on Road 286, 406/994-4042, http://fwp.mt.gov/parks/, May 1–Sept. 30, $12 camping fee includes day use) has brushy riverside sites perfect for those on a Lewis and Clark pilgrimage. Read their journals first if you doubt the importance of bringing mosquito repellent.

There's also a large state park campground (with showers) at **Lewis and Clark Caverns** (19 miles west of Three Forks on Hwy. 2, 406/287-3541, http://fwp.mt.gov/parks/, $15 camping May–Sept., $13 Oct.–Apr., $40 cabin May–Sept., $25 Oct.–Apr.).

From Norris, about 30 miles south of Three Forks, head east on Highway 84 for nine

miles to find **Red Mountain** (406/683-2337, www.blm.gov/mt/, May–Dec., $8), a Bureau of Land Management campground near the bridge over the Madison River. For a secluded spot, try **Potosi** (about eight miles south of Pony, 406/682-4253, www.fs.fed.us/r1/bdnf/, June–Sept., free).

Food

The dining room at the **Sacajawea Hotel** (Main St. and Ash St., 406/285-6515 or 888/722-2529, www.sacajaweahotel.com, 11 A.M.–9 P.M. daily, lunch $6–9, dinner entrées $17–25, bar menu 5:30–8:30 Wed.–Sat., $5–12) is a classy but laid-back place, with reliable if not particularly inspired meals. It's a pleasant place for I-90 travelers to take a break for lunch. The bar scene is comfortable, with a wide range of generally friendly locals and travelers. The bar is a reclaimed bridge trestle that was originally part of a bridge that spanned the Great Salt Lake.

At the **◖ Willow Creek Café & Saloon** (six miles southwest of Three Forks in Willow Creek, 406/285-3698, 11 A.M.–9 P.M. Tues.–Sun., 8 A.M.–9 P.M. Sun., dinner $6–21), the food is a cut above what you'd expect to find out here, and both the restaurant and the bar are easy spots in which to while away a couple of hours. Locals think nothing of driving for miles to eat barbecued ribs at Willow Creek. Next door to the restaurant, the **Willow Creek Gallery** is worth a visit.

Just off I-90 at the Three Forks exit, stop at **Wheat Montana** (406/285-3614, 6 A.M.–8 P.M. daily, sandwiches $6–7) for anything from a muffin to a deli sandwich to a giant bucket of flour or a loaf of bread. This is one of several retail outlets for a large local wheat farm, which sells their chemical- and pesticide-free wheat nationwide.

Thanks to the fact that Montanans will go out of their way for a good charbroiled steak, Logan's **Land of Magic Dinner Club** (11060 Front St., 406/284-3794, 5–9 P.M. nightly, reservations recommended, $14–29), housed in a great old log building six miles east of Three Forks, has been pulling in customers for more

©PAUL LEVY

The road from Virginia City drops dramatically into the Madison River Valley near Ennis.

than 25 years. Aside from the steaks, the Land of Magic is known for its shrimp, its duck à l'orange, and its wine list. Come prepared to work your way through relish tray, soup, salad or shrimp cocktail, potato, bread, and ice cream in addition to your entrée.

Information

The **Three Forks Chamber of Commerce** (406/285-4753, www.threeforksmontana.com) is a good resource for information about local businesses and sights. The **visitors center** is housed in a railroad caboose just around the corner from the huge landmark Sacajawea Hotel.

ENNIS AND VICINITY

Ennis (pop. about 1,000, elev. 4,927 feet) is known for its superb fishing, for all the cowboys that come to town on the weekends, and for its lively Fourth of July rodeo and popular October Wild Game Cook-off.

Originally founded as a supply station for the gold towns of Virginia City and Nevada City shortly after gold was discovered in Alder Gulch, ranching has become Ennis's economic

mainstay. Many of the area's ranches are now owned by wealthy investors who hire real ranchers to manage and run the cattle (or buffalo, as in the case of Ted Turner's nearby ranch). Anglers flock to Ennis in the summer, when they outnumber the cowboys on Main Street.

Ennis's Main Street, not long ago a small strip with a couple of rancher bars, a café, and a fly-fishing shop, is now lined with gift and antique shops and real estate offices.

Fishing the Madison River

The 50-mile stretch of the Madison River from Quake Lake (near Yellowstone Park) north to Ennis is an almost continuous riffle, and trout are eager to grab passing morsels. The Madison is also the state's most trout-dense river. This makes for good fishing for beginning fly anglers, but it also means the river can get crowded. The first 30 miles of the Madison (from Quake Lake to Varney Bridge) is a catch-and-release area, with no live bait permitted.

The state maintains several fishing-access sites on the Madison River near Ennis. **Ennis FAS** is on Highway 287 just south of Ennis;

SOUTH-CENTRAL MONTANA

© JUDY JEWELL

Fishing access sites are numerous along the Madison River, and are good spots for anyone to stop and enjoy the scenery.

Burnt Tree Hole is one mile west of Ennis on Highway 287, then two miles south on the county road; **Eight Mile Fork** is four miles down the same county road; **Varney Bridge** is another six miles down the road. All of these spots except Ennis have informal no-fee camping sites; there's a small fee to camp at Ennis. To reach **Valley Garden FAS,** turn north from Highway 287 onto the county road 0.25 mile south of town and travel two miles. **McAtee Bridge,** 18 miles south of Ennis, also provides access to the Madison.

Ennis Lake (Ennis Reservoir or Meadow Lake) is a silty shallow reservoir backed up by a rather small Montana Power dam on the Madison just below the lake. Because it's so shallow, Ennis Lake gets very warm during the summer. The warm water makes for pleasant swimming but causes rampant algae growth and is generally rough on fish downstream. Because of the warm water, it's best to fish the lower Madison (downstream of Ennis Lake) during the cooler weather of the spring and fall.

Floating the Madison River
Float the Madison, but take care where you go. Beartrap Canyon is for white-water experts, and the multichanneled stretch between Cameron and Ennis is tough for a novice to navigate. A popular and easy trip runs 30 miles from Quake Lake (put in at the Highway 87 bridge four miles from the lake) to the Varney Bridge in Cameron. This stretch of the river passes several campgrounds. Fishing from a boat is restricted on certain stretches of the Madison. Check the current regulations before casting a line.

Bozeman-based **Montana Whitewater** (800/799-4465, www.montanawhitewater .com, $129) runs daylong trips on the Madison through Beartrap Canyon's big rapids. Rafters are given the option of walking around the Class IV Kitchen Sink rapids.

Other Recreation
Madison Meadows (406/682-7468) is a public nine-hole golf course just west of town.

Many old logging roads in the hills south of

Ennis are closed to motorized traffic and make good mountain-bike routes. Get the current road-closure information at the Ennis Ranger Station. The Gravellys are popular with elk hunters, but the recent road building and logging have threatened elk habitat, partly because the logging roads have brought more hunters to previously remote areas.

September brings upland game-bird hunters to the area for Hungarian partridge and sharptail, blue, and ruffled grouse.

Accommodations

$50-100: Riverside Motel (346 E. Main St., 406/682-4240 or 800/535-4139, www.riversidemotel-outfitters.com, $70–145) is a good choice—it's just on the edge of downtown Ennis, next to a little riverside park. A large grassy area is used for fly casting, and a pond is stocked for kids' fishing. The units are detached, like little cabins, and the more expensive ones have kitchenettes and two or three bedrooms. One of the Riverside's owners is a fishing guide; let him know if you're interested in fishing the Madison, Big Hole, Jefferson, or Yellowstone Rivers.

At the **Sportsman's Lodge** (north of town on Hwy. 287, 406/682-4242 or 800/220-1690, www.ennissportsmanslodge.com, $55 and up), you have a choice of regular motel units or rustic cabins, all set in a nicely landscaped property. Pets are allowed in some rooms, and the motel has its own private airstrip. The **Fan Mountain Inn** is on the north edge of town (204 N. Main St., 406/682-5200 or 877/682-5200, www.fanmountaininn.com, $55 and up).

Lake Shore Lodge (406/682-4424, open mid-May–Sept., $50 and up) rents fully equipped cabins on Ennis Lake. Camping space for RVs and tents, outfitter services, and boat rentals are all available here.

A couple of Ennis's nicest motels are just south of town. The **El Western Resort** (4787 Hwy. 287 N., 406/682-4217 or 800/831-2773, www.elwestern.com, cabins $85–95, kitchenette cabins $135–250, lodges $275–425) sits on 17 wooded acres near the river. Accommodations are in duplex log cabins, which range from simple sleeping cabins to more luxurious lodges complete with kitchens, fireplaces, and up to four bedrooms. Right next door on Highway 287, the **Rainbow Valley Lodge** (406/682-4264 or 800/452-8254, www.rainbowvalley.com, $70 and up) is the only motel in town with a pool. The rooms are large and nicely furnished in a Western style. You have a choice of one- or two-bedroom units, kitchen units, and rooms with patios overlooking the river. The Rainbow Valley is the only motel in town that does not accept pets in the rooms, although they can arrange for very reasonably priced horse boarding.

About 34 miles south of Ennis, **West Fork Cabin Camp** (1475 Hwy. 287 N., 406/682-4802 or 866/343-8267, www.wfork.com, $70–100) has housekeeping cabins and an RV campground (there are also some tent sites). It's a great location, right on the Madison, about halfway between Ennis and West Yellowstone.

Over $100: Tucked in back of the bank on Main Street, the **Ennis Homestead** (206 2nd St., 406/682-4086, www.ennishomestead.com, $1,500 per week and up) offers the most upscale lodgings in town on the grounds of the estate of Ennis's founders. It's a little gated adults-only community with just-so two-bedroom log cabins with kitchens and laundry facilities.

The area south of Ennis, near the town of Cameron, has several fishing-oriented lodges. **The Old Kirby Place** (34 miles south of Ennis, west of MP 15 on Hwy. 287, 406/682-4194 or 888/875-8027, www.oldkirbyplace.com, $195 per person includes meals, three-night minimum) is noted for its log lodge and bunkhouse dating from the 1880s, its great location, and its fabulous fishing. Food is good, and local fishing guides often drop in for dinner to chat and share fish stories.

The eight-cabin **Diamond J Ranch** (14 miles east of Ennis, 406/682-4867 or 877/929-4867, www.diamondjranch.com, late June–early Aug., $1,350 per person per week) has operated as a guest ranch since the 1930s. In addition to fishing, horseback riding, and early autumn bird hunting, the Diamond J has indoor tennis courts and a swimming pool.

The Lodge at Sun Ranch (1520 Hwy. 287 N., Cameron, 406/682-3031, www.papoosecreek.com, from $900 per person double occupancy for three nights, includes meals) is a luxurious retreat with an eco-friendly ethic; the owners have actively worked to improve the local habitat and invite local ecologists in to talk with the guests. Stay in a room in the large lodge or in a renovated homesteader cabin. The cost of a stay here includes many amenities, although guided fishing and horseback trips are extra.

Just north of Ennis, between the Madison River and Jack Creek, the **Madison Valley Ranch** (307 Jeffers Rd., 406/682-3214 or 800/755-3474, www.madisonvalleyranch.com, $1,525 per person for three nights lodging and two days of guided fishing) is an all-inclusive fishing lodge.

Camping
Ennis Fishing-Access Site (http://fwp.mt .gov, May–Nov., $12) just out of town on the south side of the bridge, is a more developed campground than most of the state's fishing-access sites.

Once you get south of Cameron, there are plenty of public campgrounds. **Ruby Creek** and **Palisades** are Bureau of Land Management campgrounds (406/683-2337, www.blm.gov/ mt, $8) just off Highway 287 about 25 miles south of Ennis.

About 34 miles south of Ennis, near the West Fork rest area, find both the **West Fork Madison** (406/682-4253, www.fs.fed.us/r1/ b-d, late May–mid-Sept., $7) and the **Madison River** (late May–mid-Oct., $8) Forest Service campgrounds.

Food
Ennis's restaurant of note is the **(Continental Divide** (47 Geyser St., 406/682-7600, 5:30–10 P.M. daily May–Oct., $26–36, reservations recommended), where creative, sophisticated bistro-style meals are served in a setting that's not too intimidating to be a real treat. It's in a seemingly unlikely location north of town near Ennis RV Village; however, views are great from the outside dining area.

Local ranchers hang out at the **Silver Dollar Saloon** (131 E. Main St., 406/682-7320) and the **Longbranch Saloon** (125 E. Main St., 406/682-7370, 10 A.M.–2 A.M. daily). Both places also have steak restaurants; the one at the Longbranch is better.

At **Cowboy Heaven** (319 E. Main St., 406/ 682-7773) you can swill espresso, smoothies, or milkshakes and eat tasty baked goods.

Down the road in Cameron, spend a spirited Saturday night at the **Blue Moon Saloon** (406/682-4612). Still farther south, in the West Fork area, the **Grizzly Bar & Grill** (406/682-7118, 11 A.M.–9 P.M. daily, $12–27) cooks its excellent steaks in an open-pit grill.

Events
Mid-June brings **Pioneer Days** to Ennis. The Fourth of July weekend **rodeo** is taken seriously here. Mid-October, shortly after the start of hunting season, Ennis holds its **Wild Game Cook-off.** Visitors can taste the dishes and vote for their favorites. Both the rodeo and the cook-off are known statewide as happenin' events. Call the chamber of commerce at 406/682-4388 (www.ennischamber.com) for details.

Shopping
Many of the anglers who flock to Ennis come with nonfishing spouses. Main Street shopkeepers have taken note, and Ennis is now a fun place to while away an afternoon browsing antique and home decor shops. There are also several fly-fishing shops in town, including **Madison River Fishing Co.** (109 Main St., 406/682-4293 or 800/227-7127) and **The Tackle Shop** (127 Main St., 406/682-4263). These shops can also recommend guides.

If the fishing is off, would-be anglers can head west on Highway 287 to Twin Bridges for a shopping spree at the **R. L. Winston Rod Company,** where the extremely well-regarded rods are handcrafted.

Information and Services
The **Madison Valley Public Library** (210 E. Main St., 406/682-7244) may be the

only library that lends fishing rods as well as books! The **Ennis Chamber of Commerce** (406/682-4388, www.ennischamber.com) is a good source of general information about Ennis and member businesses. The area around Ennis is part of the Beaverhead Deer Lodge National Forest. The local **ranger station** (just west of town at 5 Forest Service Rd., 406/682-4253, www.fs.fed.us/r1/b-d) has maps and information on recreation and camping.

Call the **Madison Valley Hospital** at 406/682-4222.

CLIFF LAKE AND WADE LAKE

If you aren't able to make the drive in to Red Rock Lakes Wildlife Refuge but would like to see some wildlife, try Cliff Lake and Wade Lake. These turquoise lakes are about six miles west of Highway 287 via Forest Service Road 8381 (find this road just north of where Highway 87 joins Highway 287).

The road in to the lakes passes the ghost town of Cliff Lake, crosses the "Missouri Flats," a high sagebrush prairie with abundant bird life, and climbs to the forested lakeshores. Trumpeter swans sometimes appear here in the winter, and raptors live and nest around the lakes. Moose are also common. Wade Lake has good trout fishing.

The southern road to Cliff and Wade Lakes snakes in through humpy sagebrush and pine-covered hills from Highway 87, north of where Raynolds Pass crosses the Continental Divide into Idaho at a remarkably level 6,834 feet. It takes its name from Captain Raynolds, who headed a scientific expedition in 1860. Jim Bridger was the scientists' guide. There's now a fishing-access site just south of Highway 287 near Raynolds Pass.

Accommodations and Food

There are three very pleasant Forest Service **campgrounds** in the area: **Wade Lake, Hilltop,** and **Cliff Point,** all near Wade Lake Resort.

The utterly charming ◖ **Wade Lake Cabins** (406/682-7560, www.wadelake.com, $75–125) are simple housekeeping cabins (each with its own outdoor gas grill in addition to the more

The road to Cliff Lake is off the beaten path and quite lovely.

traditional kitchen setup) for rent year-round. Bathrooms are in a separate shared bathhouse. At Wade Lake, the focus is on low-impact recreation. During the summer, anglers come to fish the lakes, known for their huge rainbow and brown trout. A wood-fired hot tub is especially welcome in the winter, when the resort caters to cross-country skiers, grooming 35 miles of trails. Winter visitors are especially likely to see wildlife; lots of animals winter in the area. A three-night minimum stay is required, no credit cards are accepted, and pets cannot be accommodated. Rates rise a bit in the winter, when the resort hosts will shuttle your food and gear from the road while you ski in to your cabin. Canoes and motorboats are available for rent at the lodge.

Over on the far side of Cliff Lake, about one mile from the lakeshore, **Wilderness Edge Retreat** (406/682-4611 or 866/226-7668, www.wedgeretreat.com, mid-May–mid-Oct., $65–515) has a handful of very nice new log lodges (the largest has five bedrooms) as well as the resort's original rustic cabins with

SOUTH-CENTRAL MONTANA

© JUDY JEWELL

refrigerators, outdoor grills, and a shared bath-house. Dogs are permitted in the rustic cabins but must stay out of the larger houses. The resort can arrange fishing trips and horseback rides, and guests may rent small motor boats, canoes, kayaks, and mountain bikes.

QUAKE LAKE AND HEBGEN LAKE

South on Highway 287 toward Hebgen Lake, the mountains rise off the plain of the Madison Valley. Hebgen Lake is the reservoir formed by the damming of the Madison River in 1915. The lake's north side has a smattering of resorts and private campgrounds; several public campgrounds are on the lake's less-trafficked south side.

Late on the night of August 17, 1959, the Madison River Canyon shuddered as an earthquake with a magnitude of 7.5 started a giant landslide. A 7,600-foot-high mountain collapsed into the river, burying campsites at the Rock Creek Campground and damming the Madison to form Quake Lake. Twenty-eight people were killed. A couple of large fault blocks dropped and tilted north. A huge tidal wave swept across Hebgen Lake, over Hebgen Dam (six miles away), and into the Madison River Canyon. Amazingly, Hebgen Dam held.

Dead trees now stand in Quake Lake, the Madison River is still choked with rubble, and a "ghost village" near the east end of Quake Lake is a jumble of buildings swept up and dropped by floodwaters. Reach the ghost village via the road across from Cabin Creek campground.

A visitors center now overlooks the site of the landslide. It's open Memorial Day to Labor Day (406/646-7369), with an admission fee of $3 per vehicle.

Recreation

The **Lee Metcalf Wilderness Area,** just north of Hebgen Lake, and the adjacent **Cabin Creek Wildlife Management Area** are crisscrossed with trails. Several trails start at the end of Beaver Creek Road, and a trail heads out from Cabin Creek Campground to the wilderness area and other trails. Consult a Gallatin National Forest map, available from the ranger stations in West Yellowstone or Ennis, before setting out.

Even when the lake is iced over, fishing continues on Hebgen Lake. Brown and rainbow trout predominate and can be large. Smaller populations of cutthroat, whitefish, and arctic grayling also live here. Fishing is not quite as good on Quake Lake, which was one of the Madison River's prime fishing areas before the 1959 earthquake.

Hebgen Lake is a popular boating and water-skiing spot, and although people do windsurf on the lake, it's probably not worth planning an entire vacation around it.

There's backcountry cross-country skiing on Hebgen Mountain and less challenging trail skiing at Refuge Point on Hebgen Lake. Stop by the ranger station in West Yellowstone for more information.

Accommodations

Most Hebgen Lake establishments shut down from late September until early May because of snowfall. When West Yellowstone is booked up or seems too hectic, these resorts can be a good place from which to stage trips into Yellowstone National Park. See the camping section for ski-in cabin information.

Campfire Lodge Resort (155 Campfire Ln., 406/646-1448, late May–mid-Sept. $50 and up) is on the Madison River between Hebgen and Quake Lakes. It's a laid-back place, with rustic kitchenette cabins.

Kirkwood Resort & Marina (11505 Hebgen Lake Rd., 406/646-7200 or 877/302-7200, www.kirkwoodresort.com, cabins $79–119) is on Hebgen Lake and rents cabins, tepees ($25), RV sites, and boats. This resort does stay open year-round. On Highway 191, just south of where Highway 287 comes in, the **Madison Arm Resort** (406/646-9328, www.madisonarmresort.com, $130–150) has log cabins, larger prefab cottages, an RV park, lakefront tent sites, and a marina.

Yellowstone Holiday (16990 Hebgen Lake Rd., 877/646-4242, www.yellowstoneholiday .com, cabins $67–115) is on a flat grassy patch

SOUTH-CENTRAL MONTANA

© PAUL LEVY

Dead trees in Quake Lake are the result of a 1959 earthquake.

of land between the road and Hebgen Lake about 13 miles northwest of West Yellowstone. Although it's mainly an RV park, there are also some cute cabins (bring your own linens, towels, and cooking utensils).

⟨ Parade Rest Guest Ranch (7979 Grayling Creek Rd., West Yellowstone, 406/646-7217 or 800/753-5934, www.paraderestranch.com, $190 per person per day, all-inclusive, lower rates for children) caters to anglers and their families. Although fishing is a major focus, this is a traditional guest ranch with daily guided horseback rides. Parade Rest, which is located near Hebgen Lake, is a well-established guest ranch with close ties to many local fishing guides. (It's best to arrange for guide service well in advance.)

Firehole Ranch (11500 Hebgen Lake Rd., 406/646-7294, www.fireholeranch.com, $365 per person per day and up, includes meals and all activities except guided fishing) is a luxurious Orvis-endorsed fishing-oriented vacation ranch, with in-house fishing guides and a full complement of other recreational activities.

Hebgen Lake Mountain Inn (15475 Hebgen Lake Rd., 406/646-5100 or 866/400-4564, $125) has newer motel rooms with full kitchens on a bluff across the road from the lake and the USS Happy Hour Bar.

Camping

Cabin Creek and **Beaver Creek** Forest Service campgrounds are on the Highway 287 side of Hebgen Lake. To the east, **Rainbow Point** (on the Grayling Arm of Hebgen Lake) and **Bakers Hole** (on the Madison River above Hebgen Lake) are public campgrounds close to West Yellowstone, and are often full of RVs. **Spring Creek, Rumbaugh Ridge,** and **Lonesomehurst** are Forest Service campgrounds on the less-traveled south shore of Hebgen Lake. Contact the Hebgen Lake Ranger Station (331 Hwy. 191 N., West Yellowstone, 406/823-6961, www.fs.fed.us/r1/gallatin) for details. A lot of snow falls here in the winter, and virtually all of these places shut down between late September and early May.

Not far removed from camping are the Forest Service cabins (406/823-6961, www.fs.fed.us/r1/gallatin, $30) in the Hebgen Lake area.

SOUTH-CENTRAL MONTANA

These cabins are rustic, with outhouses and (in our experience) resident mice.

Food

The resorts along the north shore of Hebgen Lake offer what there is to be found in the way of food and drink. The **USS Happy Hour Bar** (15400 Hebgen Lake Rd., 406/646-7281) is a particularly appealing bar with a view of Hebgen Lake. If it's choice you want, head down the road to West Yellowstone, where restaurants proliferate.

Information

The deluxe **Earthquake Lake Visitor Center** (Hwy. 287, 406/682-7620, 8:30 A.M.–6 P.M. daily, June–Sept., $3 per car) sits above Quake Lake. The **Hebgen Lake Ranger Station** (406/823-6961) is actually on the northern edge of West Yellowstone.

Big Sky and the Gallatin Valley

Highway 191 follows the swift Gallatin River north from Yellowstone National Park through a narrow valley speckled with dude ranches and resorts. The Madison Range is west of the Gallatin Valley; the Gallatin Range rises to the east. In the rugged northern part of the Madison Range, the Spanish Peaks rise as high as 11,000 feet.

Tourism is not new to the Gallatin Valley. The Milwaukee Pacific Railroad built the Gallatin Gateway Inn in 1927 at the terminus of its tourist spur line down from Three Forks. Tourists generally dined at the hotel but slept in their train cars before boarding buses to Yellowstone National Park. Once tourists began traveling more by car than by train, the railroad was forced to sell off the elegant hotel, which passed through a series of owners and foundered for many years; fortunately, it was never the victim of remodeling and is now an elegant historic landmark.

SIGHTS

Big Sky, Montana's largest ski resort, is on Lone Mountain about one hour north of West Yellowstone. The slopes of Lone Mountain have been grazed since the 1890s, and dude ranches began to spring up a few years later. When native son Chet Huntley retired from the newscasting business, he started up Big Sky Resort in what he figured was the ideal spot to blend development with the natural environment; though at the base of the lifts, the Huntley Lodge and its swarming parking lot now teeter on the edge of overwhelming nature.

Development here has not led to wide use of street addresses. Instead, businesses are located by the "village" they occupy: The Huntley Lodge and ski lifts are in the development known as Mountain Village; Meadow Village is toward the base of the mountain; the West Fork–Town Center area is in between, about 2.5 miles from Highway 191 and six miles from Mountain Village.

While in Big Sky, you may hear about the **Yellowstone Club,** but unless you're one of the elite, you won't see it. Billing itself as the world's only private ski and golf community, it's so exclusive that outsiders can't even browse its website, much less its grounds.

Soldiers Chapel commemorates Montana's native sons who died in the infantry in World War II. The log chapel is on Highway 191 near Big Sky. Sunday services are held here.

SKIING AND SNOWBOARDING

Skiing at Big Sky is not cheap, but there is an enormous amount of terrain here. For those who just can't get enough, a Big Sky–Moonlight Basin combination pass is available. It's $93 for adults, $83 for seniors and college students with ID, and $73 for youth ages 11–17.

◖ Big Sky

Big Sky (406/995-5900 snow phone, 800/548-4486 reservations, www.bigskyresort.com,

$78 adults, $58 students with ID and youth ages 11–17, children 10 and under ski free) is the state's biggest and best downhill ski resort. Eighty-five trails lace two mountains (Lone Peak is the big one; Andesite Mountain is right next to it and has mostly beginner trails), covering over 3,800 skiable acres. An average of 400 inches of snow falls each year, and there are enough lifts, including a tram to the top of 11,166-foot Lone Peak, to keep lines fairly short. The tram, with its two 15-passenger cars, stops just 16 feet short of the summit and opens up lots of steep terrain. (For those who deem it too steep, it's perfectly fine to get back on the tram and ride down to some nice intermediate-level slopes.) The vertical drop is an amazing 4,350 feet, and the longest runs go on for six miles (from Liberty Bowl to Mountain Mall). Just off the Ram Charger high-speed quad, a terrain park offers several rails and a half-pipe, with terrain for all levels of snowboarders. Half-day and multiday rates are also offered, as is night skiing from December 26 to March 31. Big Sky's winter season runs from mid-November through mid-April.

Moonlight Basin

Montana's newest ski resort (406/993-6000, www.moonlightbasin.com, $51 adults, $41 college students, seniors, and youth ages 11–17, free for kids 10 and under) is right around the corner from Big Sky, on the northern face of Lone Mountain. To reach the ski area, continue about two miles past Big Sky's Mountain Village. The views from Moonlight's slopes are spectacular, and it helps to know that the resort has made an effort to protect the environment.

Although it's not as expansive as Big Sky, Moonlight Basin does have trails to suit every level of skier or boarder, and cheaper lift tickets than what you'll find at most high-mountain resorts. It's an especially good place for beginners because there's plenty of gentle terrain. The five lifts include three quads, a triple, and a high-speed detachable six-passenger chairlift. One lift and some terrain are actually shared with Big Sky Resort.

Cross-Country Skiing at Lone Mountain Ranch

Cross-country skiers can buy daily passes for the trail network at Lone Mountain Ranch (406/995-4644 or 800/514-4644, www.lm-ranch.com, $20 adults, $15 seniors, children 12 and under free). The nearly 50 miles (80 km) of trails are groomed for both traditional and skate skiing and cross a variety of terrain with some good views of the Gallatin Valley. The grooming here is exceptionally good, and the snow quality is usually very good, making for smooth, relatively fast skiing. Unless you're visiting on a holiday or on a beautiful weekend day, it's not supercrowded and, even though you're usually not far from the lodge, it feels like a true wilderness. Lessons and naturalist-guided tours into Yellowstone National Park are also offered. Cross-country skiing is usually possible from early December through mid-April.

Other Cross-Country Skiing and Snowshoeing Areas

Cross-country skiers can also head to the **Spanish Creek Cabin** on the edge of the Lee Metcalf Wilderness Area, about 10 miles north of Big Sky. It's rented out December 1–April 30 for $30 per night. Call the Bozeman Ranger Station (406/522-2520) for reservations.

Rent snowshoes from the Lone Mountain Ranch or **Grizzly Outfitters** (Meadow Village, 406/995-2939) and head for **Moose Tracks,** a dedicated snowshoe trail starting at the base of Andesite and Lone Mountains. Find the snowshoe trail behind the Mountain Village near the base of the Swift Current Express lift.

GALLATIN RIVER RECREATION
Floating

The Gallatin is popular with white-water enthusiasts; it's a challenging river to float, with some huge rapids in the lower canyon, the 20-mile stretch between Big Sky and the mouth of Gallatin Canyon, which is the focus of outfitters' half-day raft trips. Two rafting outfitters have their headquarters on Highway 191 near Big Sky. **Montana Whitewater Raft Company** (Hwy. 191, mile marker 64, seven miles north of the Big Sky turnoff, 406/995-4613 or 800/799-4465, www.montanawhitewater.com, $49 half day, $81 full day) and **Geyser Whitewater Expeditions** (Hwy. 191 next to Buck's T-4 Lodge, 406/995-4989 or 800/914-9031, www.raftmontana.com, $51 half day, $88 full day) both run daily whitewater trips.

Fishing

Fishing access to the Gallatin River is easy: The road runs alongside it much of the way from Yellowstone to Bozeman, and there are many pullouts—de facto fishing-access sites. There's an official site at the Axtell Bridge, between Gallatin Gateway and Bozeman Hot Springs. Fish don't grow large in the cold waters of the upper Gallatin, but most anglers pull something from the riffling waters of this stretch. The West Fork comes in near Big Sky, and the combined waters flow through a canyon with exceptionally good fishing. Fishing from a boat is prohibited on the Gallatin.

The salmon flies hatch from late June through early July on the Gallatin, but there's good fishing for brown and rainbow trout April through October. **Gallatin Riverguides** (Hwy. 191, 0.5 mile south of the Big Sky turnoff, 406/995-2290, www.montanaflyfishing.com) leads fishing trips year-round. **Lone Mountain Ranch** and **320 Ranch** (see below under Guest Ranches) also provide fishing guides, as does **Wild Trout Outfitters** (406/995-4895 or 800/423-4742, www.wildtroutoutfitters.com). Guide rates vary widely depending on the sort of trip that's arranged and how many anglers participate, but count on spending $325–425 for a day of private guided fishing. Costs per person go down dramatically when two or three people share a guide.

OTHER RECREATION

Hikers flock to the **Lee Metcalf Spanish Peaks Wilderness Area** during the summer. Trails, most more suitable to overnight backpacking than to day hiking, cross the peaks. Trailheads sprout on Highway 191 between Big Sky and Bozeman; the Cascade Creek hike is especially popular, and the trail can be crowded on the weekends. The Swan Creek trail heads out of the Swan Creek campground and follows the creek 11 miles to the Gallatin Divide.

From Big Sky proper, hike along the North Fork trail, one mile off the main road, just above Lone Mountain Ranch. This ridgeline path heads deep into the Spanish Peaks, where it connects with other Forest Service trails.

Backpackers can hike up almost any creekside trail and catch the **Gallatin Divide Trail,** which runs north-south along the divide between the Gallatin and Yellowstone Rivers from the Yellowstone National Park boundary to Hyalite Peak, just outside Bozeman. The trail passes lakes, petrified forests (don't carry out petrified wood unless you have a permit from the ranger station), and badlands; lucky hikers will see moose and possibly bears.

Big Sky's gondola runs all summer long, transporting **mountain bikers** up Lone Mountain. It's $19 for a single ride, $30 for a full day of downhill biking. Bike rentals are available near the base of the gondola (406/995-5840, $63 for 2 hours includes lift) or from **Grizzly Outfitters** (Town Center, 406/995-2939), where full-suspension mountain bikes rent for $45 per day.

The **Big Sky Golf Course** (Meadow Village, 406/995-5780, early June–mid-Sept., $69), a challenging course along the banks of the West Fork of the Gallatin River, was designed by Arnold Palmer and is open to the public.

A free nine-hole **disc golf course** starts behind Huntley Lodge. If you can fathom the idea of renting a disc, they're available at Big Sky Sports.

Jake's Horses (406/995-4630 or 800/352-5956, www.jakeshorses.com, $37 one-hour ride, $83 dinner ride) offers a wide variety of guided trail rides around Big Sky. Find the stables three miles south of Big Sky on Highway 191.

Long multipitched climbs right near the highway make the Gallatin Canyon popular with **climbers,** even though the rock is crumbly and rather unstable.

Events

The **Music in the Mountains** concert series (406/995-2742, www.bigskyarts.org) brings classical, jazz, country, and blues music to the slopes on weekends in late July and early August.

ACCOMMODATIONS

There are several lodging options at Big Sky. Motel rooms, cabins, and condominiums are all available at different elevations on Lone Mountain. During the winter, a shuttle bus runs between all of the lodging spots and the ski lifts. Room prices are somewhat fluid and can vary greatly by season and by day of the week. Additionally, each place will have different room types available. It's best to call and see what's available to fit your needs.

$50-100

Big Sky's lowest rates are at **The Corral Motel** (five miles south of Big Sky on Hwy. 191, 406/995-4249 or 888/995-4249, www.corralbar.com, $70–100), a small motel attached to a popular restaurant and bar.

Over $100

On Highway 191, **(Best Western Buck's T-4 Lodge** (406/995-4111 or 800/822-4484, www.buckst4.com, $139–159) is a very nice lodging with two large outdoor hot tubs. During the winter, room rates jump about $10–20. Small pets are permitted with a $5 fee. The restaurant here is also notable. **Whitewater Inn** (47214 Gallatin Rd., 406/995-2333 or 800/548-4486, www.bigskyresort.com, $119–163) is on Highway 191 near Buck's. The big attraction here is the motel's indoor pool, which has a slightly cramped water slide emptying into it.

Somewhat apart from the Big Sky bustle is the **(Rainbow Ranch Lodge** (Hwy. 191, five miles south of the Big Sky turnoff, 406/995-4132 or 800/937-4132, www.rainbowranch.com, $245–270 suites, $600 cabin) on the Gallatin River. Although the main lodge at this resort was destroyed by fire in the spring of 2008, a four-bedroom, four-bath riverside cabin about a mile away was spared, as was the giant hot tub.

On the road up Lone Peak, between Meadow and Mountain, the **River Rock Lodge** (3080 Pine Dr., 406/995-4455 or 800/995-4455, www.riverrocklodging.com, $160–260) has Big Sky's most comfortably elegant lodgings. The tasteful Western-craftsman decor has a practical note, like the handsome wool blankets and down comforters on each bed.

Many of the accommodations at the Mountain Village are owned by Big Sky Resort. Surprisingly, there's not a huge variation between winter and summer rates here. Rooms at the **Huntley Lodge** (Mountain Village, 406/995-5000 or 800/548-4486, www.bigskyresort.com, $168–412) and the adjacent **Shoshone Condominium Hotel** ($285–843) offer easy ski-in, ski-out access to the main base area. There are two swimming pools, a steam room, hot tubs, and great access to the slopes. Under the same management and also part of the Mountain Village is the rather swank **Summit at Big Sky** ($221–508), a high-rise hotel-condominium complex with a wide variety of room configurations. Big Sky Resort operates several other condo developments in the Mountain Village; the resort's website has a good schematic, and telephone reservations clerks are generally quite helpful.

Resort Property Management (406/995-4800 or 800/548-4488, www.rpmbigsky.com, $200 and up at Meadow level, $400 and up Mountain level) rents a staggering array of lodging choices, ranging from reasonably priced suites that can accommodate up to eight people to many condos and homes for nightly rental. Many of these properties have hot tubs.

North of Big Sky, in the town of Gallatin Gateway, the historic **(Gallatin Gateway Inn** (406/763-4672 or 800/676-3522, www.gallatingatewayinn.com, $149–189) has been beautifully restored to landmark status. Rooms are either in the historic main lodge or cottages tucked behind the lodge. There's a very nice outdoor pool and hot tub, as well as a casting pond and tennis courts.

Guest Ranches

(Lone Mountain Ranch (406/995-4644, www.lmranch.com), halfway between the highway and the ski lifts, is a little different from the other Big Sky lodgings. Originally a working cattle ranch, it has become a great cross-country ski resort (some say the nation's best), and during the summer it's a dude ranch with special programs for anglers and for children learning to ride. Different packages are offered, but a standard summertime seven-day stay in a small cabin, including all meals, costs $2,860 for the first person, plus $2,200 for each additional adult, $1,445 for a child ages 4–5, or $535 for a child ages 2–3. Winter rates for a weeklong stay are $2,355 for the first person, plus $1,475 for each additional adult, $1,020 for each child 4–12, $525 for ages 2–3.

Another noteworthy guest ranch, the **Nine Quarter-Circle Ranch** (5000 Taylor Fork Rd., 406/995-4276 or 995-4876, www.ninequartercircle.com) specializes in families and has plenty of children's activities. The Nine Quarter-Circle, which is near the northwest corner of Yellowstone National Park, has been in operation since 1912 and accommodates its guests in log cabins, all with private baths and woodstoves. Meals are served in the handsome central lodge. Activities include horseback riding, fishing, overnight pack trips, and square-dancing. Weekly rates start at $1,743 per person double occupancy, with discounts for children.

The **320 Ranch** (205 Buffalo Horn Creek, 406/995-4283 or 800/243-0320, www.320ranch.com, $133–353), another guest ranch that has been around since the beginning of the 20th century, is 12 miles south of Big Sky and six miles north of Yellowstone National Park. Lodging is in cabins (some with kitchenettes) or larger log houses; the most interesting is the McGill cabin, the home of Dr. Caroline McGill, Montana's first woman physician and former owner of the 320. Even if you're not sleeping at the 320, it's a good place to stop for a meal.

Camping

Spire Rock is a small Forest Service campground about 15 miles southeast of Gallatin

Gateway. Other good bets are **Moose Creek Flat,** five miles north of Big Sky on Highway 191; **Swan Creek,** just north of Moose Creek Flat; and **Greek Creek,** just north of Swan Creek. On Highway 191 about eight miles south of Big Sky, **Red Cliff** is a riverside Forest Service campground about 50 yards off the highway. These campgrounds are part of the Bozeman Ranger District of the Gallatin National Forest (3710 Fallon St., Bozeman, 406/522-2520, www.fs.fed.us/r1/gallatin, mid-May–mid-Sept., $11) and can be reserved online (www.recreation.gov).

FOOD

There's no dearth of good food around Big Sky. Down on Highway 191, **Buck's T-4 Best Western** (just south of the Big Sky turnoff, 406/995-4111, 6–9:30 P.M. nightly, reservations recommended, $23–49) serves some of the best dinners around. Buck's specializes in wild-game dinners; try the wild boar stew. A cheaper way to go is eating off the bar menu ($10–20); an open-faced steak sandwich goes for $12.

Also at the highway, **Rainbow Ranch** (406/995-4132), although devastated by fire when we visited in spring 2008, plans to rebuild and continue serving meals. If they are open, it's well worth a visit.

Another good dinner spot is halfway up the hill at **Lone Mountain Ranch** (406/995-2782, 7–9 A.M., noon–2 P.M., and 5:30–8:30 P.M. daily, dinner reservations required, $20–30). The views from the comfortable Lone Mountain bar are especially seductive after a few times around the cross-country ski trails. Also offered here is a sleigh ride to a family-style dinner, cooked on a wood stove in a remote cabin ($85, reservations required).

For lunch or a takeout dinner, try the deli in the **Country Market** (Meadow Village, 406/995-2314). They make delicious soups, sandwiches, and salads. Also in the Meadow Village, **La Luna** (406/995-3280, 11 A.M.–3 P.M. Mon.–Fri. and 5–9 P.M. Mon.–Sat., $10–12) is a very popular place for Mexican- and Thai-inspired food in a casual setting. The (brand-new in 2008) brewpub, **Lone Peak Brewery**

(406/995-3939, 11 A.M.–8 P.M. daily) serves lunches and an oatmeal stout named "Hippie Highway."

Between Meadow and Mountain, in the Westfork area, the **Blue Moon Bakery** (Westfork Plaza Mall, 406/995-2305, 7 A.M.–10 P.M., $5–12) serves soups, pizzas, and large tasty sandwiches in addition to bread, bagels, and breakfast pastries.

Out on Highway 191 at the Big Sky turnoff, the **Bugaboo Café** (47995 Gallatin Rd., 406/995-3350, 7–10:30 A.M., 11:30 A.M.–2:30 P.M., and 5:30–9 P.M. Tues.–Fri., 7 A.M.–2 P.M. and 5:30–9 P.M. Sat., 7 A.M.–2 P.M. Sun., $9–23) has good food and a relaxed environment. For lunch, try a flank steak sandwich ($8.25); dinner options run the gamut from gourmet mac and cheese to grilled halibut.

Up on the ski hill, **Huntley Lodge** has a fancy dining room, but happy hour at **Chet's Bar** (also in the lodge) is more fun. Sandwich shops, pizza joints, Chinese food, and cafeterias are all well represented and easy to find in Mountain Village.

About five miles south of Big Sky on Highway 191, Western atmosphere abounds at the **Corral Bar Steakhouse Cafe** (42895 Gallatin Rd., 406/995-4249, 4–10 P.M. nightly, $11–37); stop by the bar if you're not up for dinner. Just across the highway from the Corral Bar, dinners at the **320 Ranch** (205 Buffalo Horn Creek, 406/995-4283, dinner nightly, $12–28) is worth a stop for good Montana-style steak, trout, and wild-game dinners with a few little gourmet twists, such as a honey-Dijon sauce on the Rocky Mountain oysters.

The **Half Moon Saloon,** three miles south of Big Sky on Highway 191 (45130 Gallatin Rd., 406/995-2928), is a comfortable place to stop for a beer. The smoked and barbecued baby back ribs are the house specialty, and Montana's best bar bands are booked on the weekends.

In the northern valley, almost to Bozeman, the **Gallatin Gateway Inn** (406/763-4672, $16–32) serves elegant yet robust dinners ranging from pasta to a venison chop.

PRACTICALITIES
Information and Services
For information specifically on the downhill ski area and its lodgings, contact **Big Sky Resort Association** (406/995-5000 or 800/548-4486, www.bigskyresort.com). General area information is available from the **Big Sky Chamber of Commerce** (406/995-3000 or 800/943-4111, www.bigskychamber.com).

Big Sky's **medical clinic** is at the base of the Mountain Village (406/995-2797).

Transportation
Bozeman's Gallatin Field is the closest airport.

During the ski season **Karst Stage** (406/388-2293 or 800/287-4759, www.karststage.com) runs a shuttle from the airport to Big Sky. Reservations are required; fare is $45–50 one-way. During the spring, summer, and fall, Karst discontinues their regular shuttle service between the airport and Big Sky but does provide transportation in a custom van.

Another good option, and the best bet during the spring, summer, and fall, is **Mountain Taxi** (406/995-4895 or 800/423-4742, www.bigskytaxi.com). They charge $140 for a single person in a van and $5 more for each additional person up to a total of four. Groups of five or more people pay $40 per person.

Shuttle buses (www.skylinebus.com) run frequently between Big Sky's Meadow and Mountain villages. For information on car rentals, see the *Bozeman* section.

Livingston and the Paradise Valley

Back when passenger trains still crossed southern Montana, Livingston was the gateway to Yellowstone National Park. Parkgoers would change trains at the Livingston depot and take the rail spur to Yellowstone.

Nowadays, travelers with a little time to pass can stock up on some of the world's most coveted flies in Livingston, cast them into the Yellowstone River, soak in the hot springs at Chico, or wander out of the broad sun-filled Paradise Valley into the Absaroka-Beartooth Wilderness Area. There's really no sense in a pell-mell dash to often hectic Yellowstone when there are so many places to linger around just to the north.

LIVINGSTON

Livingston is a weird place. Stand by the jukebox at a downtown bar and a lovely woman in evening dress may invite you to party with author Tom McGuane and actor Peter Fonda. Or maybe you'll be the lucky person to meet the guy dressed in full buckskins, up visiting from Los Angeles. At the very least you'll hear a good fishing story.

While Bozeman quickly gained a reputation as a straitlaced town, Livingston, 26 miles east, never had any such opprobrium to live down. It's a town with a history of such Wild West legends as Calamity Jane and Kitty O'Leary, also know as Madame Bulldog.

Few towns have seen the gentrification boom as much as Livingston. What was, a few years back, a sleepy and rough-edged town with a local artist and a writer or two is now a mandatory way station on the glam tour of Montana. For lively Livingston-based fiction, read Jamie Harrison's *The Edge of the Crazies* or any of Thomas McGuane's books set in Montana.

Livingston (pop. 7,279, elev. 4,490 feet), the Park County seat, is situated at the wind-tossed northern end of the Paradise Valley on the banks of the Yellowstone River. The Absaroka Range, rising up in the south, dominates the town, and the Crazy Mountains show up to

the northeast. After its northerly run up from Yellowstone National Park, the Yellowstone River turns east at Livingston, where I-90/94 meets the river and ushers it from the state.

History

Mt. Baldy (or Mt. Livingston), southeast of Livingston in the Absaroka Range, was the site of winter vision quests by Crow braves. William Clark camped on the Yellowstone River south of Livingston on July 15, 1806. Several days later, Crows stole his party's horses, forcing the explorers to build dugouts and bullboats.

Livingston's comparatively mild climate led Nelson Storey to select it for the terminus of his cattle drive from Texas in 1866, à la Larry McMurtry's *Lonesome Dove*—a trip prescient of Montana's development as cattle country.

Livingston became a major railroad division point and locomotive-repair site in the 1880s, and a boom set in. Ever since then, Livingston's history has been a cycle of booms and busts. When tourists flocked to Yellowstone National Park via train, rail passengers debarked from the main Northern Pacific line to catch the Park Branch Line to Gardiner, and Livingston flourished.

With the good times came legendary rambunctiousness described in the Works Progress Administration's *Montana, A State Guide Book:*

The old Bucket of Blood, 113 Park St., one of the many old-time Montana saloons so named, was probably a little rougher than most. It...was the center of a group of resorts of the same kind, including a gambling dive run by Tex Rickard, Kid Brown, and Soapy Smith until the Klondike rush took them off to the Yukon. Madame Bulldog, once Kitty O'Leary, ran what was euphemistically known as a dance hall. Her joint, she said, was a decent one. Announcing that she would stand for no damfoolishness, she saved the wages of a bouncer by polishing

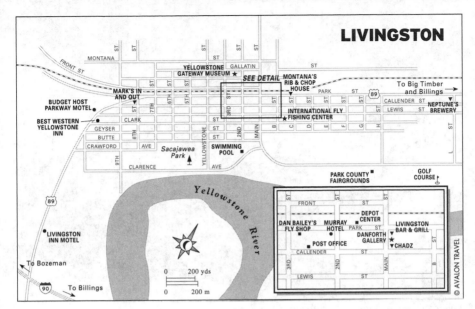

off roughnecks herself. Her dimensions, like her sensibilities, were pachydermal; she tipped the scales at 190, stripped. And stripped she was most of the time. Calamity Jane was one of her associates for a time, but legend has it that they fell out, whereupon Madame Bulldog tossed Calamity into the street, "as easy as licking three men." When asked whether Calamity Jane really tried to fight back, one who knew both women replied succinctly, "Calamity was tougher'n hell, but she wasn't crazy!"

Sights

The **Depot Center** (200 W. Park St., 406/222-2300, www.livingstonmuseums.org, 9 A.M.–5 P.M. Mon.–Sat., 1–5 P.M. Sun., late May–late Sept., $3 adults, $2 children and seniors) is a well-curated historical, cultural, and art museum housed in the historic Northern Pacific Railway Depot. The depot was built in 1902 and resembles an Italian villa. The park next to the depot is the site of many summer festivals.

The other historical museum in town, the

Yellowstone Gateway Museum (118 W. Chinook St., 406/222-4184, www.livingstonmuseums.org, 10 A.M.–5 P.M. daily June–Aug., 11 A.M.–4 P.M. Tues.–Sat. Sept., $4 adults, $3.50 seniors, $3 children 6–12) is tucked into an old schoolhouse and a hundred-year-old Northern Pacific car across the tracks from downtown. (Cross the tracks at B Street or 5th Street; the museum is two blocks from the tracks.) Among the displays are a room devoted to railroading, many items from Yellowstone National Park's early days, a display dedicated to Calamity Jane, and a bicycle collection. This is Park County's historical museum, and it houses the county archives.

At the **Fly Fishing Discovery Center** (215 E. Lewis, 406/222-9369, www.livingstonmuseums.org, 10 A.M.–6 P.M. Mon.–Sat., noon–5 P.M. Sun. June–Sept., 10 A.M.–5 P.M. Mon.–Fri. Oct.–May, $3 adults, $2 seniors, $1 children 7–14), exhibits focus on the history of fly-fishing (check out the beautiful vintage rods and reels) and fish ecology. One exhibit room is devoted to an incredible collection of flies tied by master fly-tiers from around the world. The Fly Fishing Center's best perk is a series of free

© PAUL LEVY

Livingston has a thriving downtown.

summertime fly-casting lessons held on the center's front lawn each Tuesday and Thursday evening, 5–7 P.M. Equipment is provided for people who don't have their own.

Livingstonians ran amok in the late 1970s, listing every eligible site on the National Register of Historic Places. There's great pride taken in the restoration of downtown buildings to their original Western look, and it does look splendid. Look for elaborate brickwork and faded signs painted on the sides of the downtown buildings. Don't neglect the residential streets. Yellowstone Street, three blocks west of Main, was a tony address around the end of the 19th century. The east side of town, near G Street and Callender, was the figurative "other side of the tracks," where the blue-collar railroad workers lived. To round out the tour, visit the 300 block of South B Street. The four matching houses on the east side of the street were once Livingston's brothels.

Recreation

Fishing is Livingston's recreation of choice, and many locals make their living from guiding. **Dan**

Bailey's Fly Shop (209 W. Park St., 406/222-1673 or 800/356-4052, www.dan-bailey.com) is a good first stop for any angler; the staff can also set you up with a guide. Guide services and a huge selection of flies are also available from **Anderson's Yellowstone Angler** (406/222-7130, www.yellowstoneangler.com), which has a shop just south of town on Highway 89.

The Absaroka Range rises up just south of Livingston. One convenient trailhead into the Absarokas is **Suce Creek,** about 10 miles south of Livingston off the East River Road. Trails beginning here provide access to Livingston Peak, the north fork of Deep Creek, Blacktail Lake, and Elephant Head Mountain. About three miles farther south on the East River Road, the **Deep Creek** trail heads to the Davis Creek Divide.

Timber Trails (309 W. Park, 406/222-9550) rents and repairs bicycles.

The nine-hole **Livingston Golf and Country Club** (406/222-1100) is a public course on View Vista Drive at the foot of Main Street.

The city **swimming pool** is near the foot of Main Street just east of Sacagawea Park.

CALAMITY JANE

It's a little hard to pin down many facts on Martha Jane Cannary (better known as Calamity Jane), largely because she was one of the West's most notorious liars.

Martha's father moved his wife and children west from Missouri in the early 1860s. He was ostensibly a Mormon lay preacher bound for Salt Lake City, but the Cannarys seem to have landed in Virginia City, Nevada, during the 1865 gold rush. As a teenager, Martha Jane set to wandering around the West, picking up what work she could.

Like many other women of the West, she became a prostitute, but she also demonstrated both an aptitude for and interest in such male-dominated pursuits as army scouting and prospecting, and she often showed her more tomboyish side. Says the Works Progress Administration's *Montana, A State Guide Book*, "She was given to shooting up saloons, and to raising hell with tongue and quirt."

She may have been a lover of Wild Bill Hickok's, but it's unlikely. Stories of her secret marriage to Wild Bill and of a daughter, Janey, resulting from the union are unsubstantiated. But her theatrical bent did lead to a stint with Buffalo Bill's Wild West Show. Her theatrical career, however, as well as many other projects, was cut short by her alcoholism.

Castle, Harlowton, Big Timber, and Livingston were all her haunts. She lived in Livingston off and on; she had a cabin at 213 Main Street for several impoverished and unhappy years. She was 51 when she died outside Deadwood, South Dakota, in 1903. According to her wishes, she was buried next to Wild Bill in the Deadwood cemetery.

For a fact-based eloquent novel, try Larry McMurtry's *Buffalo Girls*, which chronicles the lives of Calamity Jane and her comrades.

Events

The **Livingston Roundup Rodeo** is on the Fourth of July weekend. It kicks off with a parade and segues into a lively Professional Rodeo Cowboys Association (PRCA) rodeo (406/222-7277). An arts festival takes over Depot Square during this weekend.

The **Yellowstone Boat Float** (406/224-4414), a three-day mid-July event, runs 110 miles from Livingston to Columbus, following the route of Captain Clark and his party on their return from the Pacific. The float is open to all, any sort of boat is permitted, and like the river, it's "wet, wild, and dam free."

During the first week of August, Livingston hosts the **Park County Fair.**

Arts

It may be a little surprising that a scrappy railroad town like Livingston has become something of an artists' colony. But the beautiful light and stunning scenery (not to mention the trout fishing) of the Paradise Valley work in counterpoint to Livingston's raucous edge

to make this one of the state's most prestigious addresses.

Russell Chatham is Livingston's most renowned artist. His oils and lithographs evoke the places where the plains come up against the mountains. You'll see mostly lithographs at **Chatham Fine Art** (120 N. Main St., 406/222-1566). **Tierra Montana** (116 N. Main St., 406/222-3000) exhibits paintings, sculpture, and high-quality crafts, including the weavings of owner Ben Maestas. Other galleries along the same stretch of Main Street are the **Danforth Gallery** (106 N. Main St., 406/222-6510), which focuses on contemporary Montana artists, and **Livingston Center for Art and Culture** (119 S. Main St., 406/222-5222), featuring regional artists and offering classes, workshops, and an open ceramic studio. Within the Center for Art and Culture is the **Parks Reece Gallery** (406/222-5724), featuring Reece's whimsical paintings and prints.

South of town in the Sleeping Giant Trade Center (5237 Hwy. 89 S.), find the **Burl Jones**

Roche Jaune Galerie (406/222-8719), with Western art, including Jones's bronzes.

Accommodations

The **((Murray Hotel** (201 W. Park St., 406/222-1350, www.murrayhotel.com, $89–220), across the street from the Depot Center, has enough character to hold its own in a lively, quirky town like Livingston. Like much of the rest of downtown, the Murray is listed in the National Register of Historic Places, and its interior architecture recalls the grander side of the Old West. The Murray has been restored with panache, retaining the eccentricities that have traditionally made it a haven for "writers, artists, and film people." (Film director Sam Peckinpah lived in a Murray Hotel suite in the 1970s and reputedly shot up the ceiling.) The hotel is very dog-friendly. Be sure to visit the rooftop hot tub.

On the east end of town, the **Rainbow Motel** (5574 Hwy. 89 S., 406/222-3780 or 800/788-2301, www.rainbowmotelmt.com, $45–80) is an older motel that allows most pets. There's a nice grassy area with some picnic tables outside this friendly motel, which is a block from the Yellowstone River. An adjacent campground and RV park is run by the same folks.

Most of Livingston's motels are west of downtown, near the intersection of I-90 and Highway 89, the road to Yellowstone. The **Livingston Inn Motel** (5 Rogers Ln., 406/222-3600, www.livingstoninnmotel.com, $90 and up) is a well-run place that's been recently renovated. **Budget Host Parkway Motel** (1124 W. Park St., 406/222-3840 or 800/727-7217, $56–85) has a heated outdoor pool and much lower winter rates (kitchenettes are available for an extra charge, and an outdoor barbecue area is open to all guests). Pets are permitted for an extra $5.

Facilities at the **Best Western Yellowstone Inn** (1515 W. Park St., 406/222-6110 or 800/826-1214, www.theyellowstoneinn.com, $110 and up) include a restaurant, lounge, heated indoor pool, and convention meeting rooms. Near the I-90 exit on the west end of town, the **Quality Inn** (111 Rogers Ln.,

406/222-0555 or 800/424-6423, $130) has an indoor pool and is one of the nicer places in this area.

South of town right on the river, the **River Inn Yellowstone Cabins** (4950 Hwy. 89 S., 406/222-2429 or 888/669-6993, www.yellowstoneriverinn.com, $125–145) has a couple of cabins and a tiny sheepherder's wagon ($40) that can serve as an extra bedroom.

Three miles south of town, the **Blue-Winged Olive** (5157 Hwy. 89, 406/222-8646 or 800/995-1366, www.bluewingedolive.net, $100 s, $150 d) is a B&B catering mostly to anglers, who appreciate its proximity to the Yellowstone and to several spring creeks. (The big early-morning breakfasts are also a plus.)

Camping

Unless you're looking for RV camping, it's better to drive a ways up the Paradise Valley to find a site, but in a pinch there are private campgrounds in Livingston. About 18 miles south of town, **Yellowstone's Edge** (3502 Hwy. 89 S., 406/333-4036, www.mtrv.com, May–Oct., $40 RV) is a particularly well-equipped and well-situated RV park.

The **Forest Service** (406/222-1892, www.fs.fed.us/r1/gallatin, $30–35) rents several cabins in the Livingston district. Not all cabins have electricity or drinking water; most have wood heat.

Food

The back bar at the **((Livingston Bar and Grill** (130 N. Main St., 406/222-7909, 5–9 P.M. nightly, entrées $23–32) dates to the early 1900s and comes from the original Livingston Bar, which was supposedly Calamity Jane's favorite spot in Livingston. Calamity probably wouldn't recognize much on the menu today, which includes a chipotle-barbecued pork chop. And she probably wouldn't know her way around the extensive wine list either. The dining room is beautiful but relatively casual.

The specialties at **Montana's Rib & Chop House** (307 E. Park, 406/222-9200, 11:30 A.M.–2 P.M. Mon.–Fri., dinner from 5 P.M. nightly, $5–29) are ribs, hand-cut steaks, and Louisiana-style seafood. The atmosphere is casual and friendly, and its dining room is spacious and stylish.

At the Murray Hotel, the **2nd Street Bistro** (201 W. Park St., 406/222-1350, dinner from 5 P.M. nightly, $16–24), the simple wood tables and chairs and big windows allow diners to keep an eye on downtown Livingston. That is, if they lift their faces from their crab cakes and Mediterranean fish stew; the food here is quite good.

Chadz (104 N. Main St., 406/222-2247, 7 A.M.–2:30 P.M. daily, $2–7) is a good place to spend the morning hanging out with the locals, who gather at the tables or sip coffee and read on the comfy couches. Stop in for coffee and a scone or lunch on a rice bowl.

Stop for a burger and a shake at a local institution: **Mark's In and Out** (Park St. and 8th St., 406/222-7744, 11 A.M.–10 P.M. daily, Mar.–Oct., about $5) has been around since the 1950s and is a good place to sample the locally made Wilcoxson's ice cream (which is also available in most grocery stores throughout the state).

The **Sport** (114 S. Main St., 11 A.M.–9 P.M. daily, burgers $8, dinners $17–28), is another local institution where the old-time Montana atmosphere comes with the burgers and beer.

Don't be surprised to find yourself propped up against a bar in Livingston. The town's wild reputation is supported by a wealth of bars. The bar at the **Murray Hotel** may host tea-drinking hotel guests early in the evening, but it eases into rowdiness later at night. Spot Livingston's literati at the Murray or the **Owl** (110 N. 2nd St., 406/222-1322).

Just east of downtown, the microbrews at **Neptune's Brewery** (110 N. L St., 406/222-7837) are quite tasty, and because it's a full bar rather than a brewpub, the taps don't shut down at 8 P.M.

Information and Services

The Livingston **Chamber of Commerce** (303 E. Park St., 406/222-0850, www.livingston-chamber.com) is housed in a former railroad crew headquarters a couple of blocks east of the Depot Center.

For information on hiking, camping, Forest Service cabin rentals, and fishing, stop by the ranger station on Highway 89 about one mile south of Livingston (406/222-1892). **Livingston Memorial Hospital** is at 504 South 13th Street (406/222-3541).

Transportation

Three eastbound and three westbound **Greyhound** buses (1404 E. Park, 406/222-2231) stop in Livingston daily. **Rimrock Stage** uses the same terminal and provides daily service to Billings and Missoula. Bozeman and Billings have more car rental agencies, but **Yellowstone Country Motors** (207 S. 2nd St., 800/497-1001) has vehicles for rent.

PARADISE VALLEY

The never-dammed Yellowstone River flows through the Paradise Valley and separates the eastern Absaroka Range and the western Gallatin Range. The valley starts narrow, squeezing through Yankee Jim Canyon near Yellowstone National Park, then broadens enough for ranches to spread out on the valley floor.

Yellowstone's volcanoes spat out the Absaroka Range—a high lava field with relief etched by erosion from water and glacial ice. The Absarokas are lush wet mountains, more characteristic of western Montana than the dry peaks east of the Continental Divide. The same Yellowstone lava flows covered folded sedimentary rocks of the Gallatin Range.

Sights

Come to the Paradise Valley for the Yellowstone River, its valley, and the surrounding mountains. A few miles south of Livingston, the paved but potholed East River Road leaves Highway 89. Both roads along the Yellowstone are lovely, but East River Road gives a better view of the way people live in the valley.

The upper Yellowstone River cuts through the gneiss of narrow **Yankee Jim Canyon,** 15 miles north of Gardiner. Jim George, also known as Yankee Jim, built the first road into Yellowstone National Park. He charged a toll to

© JUDY JEWELL

The Yellowstone is one of the few undammed rivers in the West.

travel the road, and when the Northern Pacific claimed its right to the roadbed, the railroad was forced to build Yankee Jim another road farther up the hill.

Jardine, an old mining ghost town five miles up Bear Gulch from Gardiner, has seen several spurts of mining activity. Both gold and arsenic were mined here, with arsenic production continuing until the end of World War II. The late 1980s saw another attempt to mine gold from Jardine, but the town is notable chiefly as home to some well-preserved mining relics. Hiking trails starting in Jardine lead into the Absaroka-Beartooth Wilderness.

Down between Corwin Springs and Gardiner, you may spot some pretty normal-looking blue-painted houses off the road to the west. These are one remaining sign of a spiritual group whose presence rocked the Paradise Valley for a time. During the 1980s and 1990s, the **Church Universal and Triumphant** (known locally as CUT) bought more than 25,000 acres of land north and west of Gardiner. This spiritual community believes in developing harmony between the land and its inhabitants, but drew much criticism for its land use and environmental track record, not to mention its accumulation of weapons, and the local community was very wary of them. The church's leader, Elizabeth Clare Prophet, developed Alzheimer's disease in the late 1990s and since then things have quieted down a bit. The church has worked with the federal government on land and wildlife issues (including allowing a limited number of Yellowstone bison to cross church land in order to access nearby Forest Service land), and many members have become more integrated into the local community, easing some of the tensions.

Fishing

The Yellowstone River is a blue-ribbon trout stream. Summer and fall are the most popular seasons to fish the Yellowstone. In early summer the salmon flies and caddis flies hatch. Around August, trout feed on grasshoppers near the river's edge. Numerous fishing-access sites dot both Highway 89 and East River Road.

Besides the Yellowstone, a couple of "spring creeks" challenge the skillful angler.

The two most notable of these, Nelson's and Armstrong's, are on private land and a fee is charged for fishing them. For details, ask at Dan Bailey's Fly Shop in Livingston or at any other local angler's shop. Another good source for advice, gear, or access to private fishing spots is **Angler's West** (406/333-4401, www.montanaflyfishers.com), just off Highway 89 at Emigrant.

Hiking

Start at the Pine Creek campground, about one mile south of the town of Pine Creek on the East River Road, to hike the popular and lovely trail up Pine Creek. Pine Creek Falls is just a short hike from the campground; Pine Creek Lake is another three or four steep miles up the mountain.

Mill Creek reaches into the Absaroka-Beartooth Wilderness Area. The lower stretches of Mill Creek Road, heading east from the town of Pray to the wilderness boundary, are good for mountain biking, and the foot trail continues into the wilderness area. Thompson Lake, Elbow Lake, Mt. Cowan, and Passage Creek Falls are some of the destinations for hikers. Snow Bank campground is a handy jumping-off point.

In the Gallatin Range, hike or cross-country ski just about any drainage: **Trail Creek** (there's cross-country skiing near the Forest Service cabin); **Big Creek** (28 miles south of Livingston, then west up Big Creek Road, trailhead is across from Mountain Sky Ranch); or **Rock Creek** (with access to a trail network).

The hike up **Tom Miner Basin** starts at the Tom Miner campground and includes an interpretive trail in the Gallatin Petrified Forest. To reach the trailhead, turn west off Highway 89 between mile markers 16 and 17 onto Tom Miner Creek Road. Follow signs to the campground, approximately 12 miles from the highway. The petrified forest trail is about two miles round-trip.

Chico Hot Springs

Even if you're not staying at the lodge, stop by Chico Hot Springs (406/333-4933,

relaxing in the pool at Chico Hot Springs

© JUDY JEWELL

8 A.M.–11 P.M., day pass $6.50 adults, $2 seniors, $4 children 6–12, under 6 free) for a swim. The pool is huge, and it's always a great place to people-watch. (See *Accommodations* below for more information.)

Other Recreation

The East River Road is a pleasant road ride for cyclists who don't mind a few potholes. Mountain bikers will want to turn off the main road and head up into the hills.

The upper stretches of the Yellowstone River, particularly through Yankee Jim Canyon, have some challenging white water. After the river leaves the canyon and enters the Paradise Valley, it calms down enough for novice floaters to navigate it without much difficulty. Gardiner's **Yellowstone Raft Company** (406/848-7777 or 800/858-7781, www.yellowstoneraft.com) runs raft trips on the Yellowstone. Half-day trips are $31 for adults, $21 for children; full-day trips are $72 for adults, $52 for children.

During the winter, sign on with **Absaroka Dogsled Trek** (406/222-4645, $125 for 2 hours) based at Chico Hot Springs. Trips range from a two-hour introduction to a full-day trek ($340).

Horseback rides start from Chico Hot Springs's **horse barn** (406/333-4933, $30 for 1 hour) throughout the day and are suited to riders of all abilities. Another local outfitter, **Rockin' HK** (406/333-4505, www.rockinhk.com, day-long ride $200) leads day-long trips into Yellowstone's backcountry; they also combine horse packing trips with fishing.

Accommodations

◖ **Chico Hot Springs** (406/333-4933 or 800/468-9232, www.chicohotsprings.com, $49–355), halfway between Livingston and Gardiner in Pray, is the sort of spot you want all your friends to know about and everybody else to ignore. The lodge here is built around a large hot springs–fed swimming pool. The original rooms in the circa-1900 lodge are cramped and Spartan, but the rooms aren't where most guests spend their time (and rooms in the lodge addition and the newer cabins and cottages are spacious and nicely furnished). Yellowstone National Park is right down the road, and there's plenty of hiking and fishing in the Paradise Valley, soaking and swimming in the pool, elegant dinners in the hotel dining room, and rowdy good times in the lively bar. There's an outfitter on the premises with horses, fishing gear, and bicycles for rent. Rooms in the main lodge start at $49 for a very small room with shared bath and run to $89 (private bath); newer lodge buildings have rooms ranging $125–225; there are cabins (no kitchens) for $79–89, and log houses for $169–355. Dogs are permitted in the rooms at Chico ($20 per stay).

Although Chico is the most renowned place to stay in the Paradise Valley, there are several other good places to stay between Livingston and Gardiner. **Pine Creek Store & Lodge** (2496 East River Rd., 406/222-3628, www.pinecreeklodgemontana.com, June–Sept., $60–80), 12 miles south of Livingston, rents quintessential Montana resort cabins in a friendly community with easy fishing access to the Yellowstone. The

fairly rustic cabins, all with electric heat, sleep 2–6 people, and pets are allowed. The excellent **Pine Creek Café,** open Wednesday–Sunday, is also part of the complex.

Just up the road from the hot springs, find the **Homestead Cabin at Old Chico** (406/333-4772, www.homesteadcabin.com, $135–195, $750–1,000 per week). The tiny community of Old Chico consists of a scattering of old cabins; this one has been fixed up in a way that retains a sense of rusticity but adds a touch of elegance. The cabin sleeps four and has a full kitchen; pets are permitted ($20).

Guest Ranches

At the **Yellowstone Valley Ranch** (38401 Hwy. 89 S., 406/333-4787 or 800/626-3526, www.yellowstonevalleyranch.com, $3,195 per person, double occupancy for six nights, all inclusive), 14 miles south of Livingston, anglers stay in tastefully decorated cabins perched just above the Yellowstone, affording wonderful river views and good fishing. This is emphatically a fly-fishing lodge, where anglers spend their days with some of the Paradise Valley's best guides. Beginning fly-fishers are welcome, and benefit from the two-to-one guest/guide ratio. Shorter stays are also possible, and nonfishing companions get a much-reduced rate.

Mountain Sky Guest Ranch (406/587-1244 or 800/548-3392, www.mtnsky.com, June–late Aug., $3,185–3,955 per adult for one week all inclusive, $2,065–3,185 per child) is a family-oriented guest ranch set up in Big Creek with great views of Emigrant Peak, across the Paradise Valley in the Absaroka Range. Riding is one of the core activities here, but fishing, tennis courts, a pool, hot tub, and sauna are also available, and there's a well-developed program for kids, from infants to teens. Each guest is matched with a horse to ride for the week's stay, and either breakfast rides or 9 A.M. rides are scheduled daily. Ranch staff run van trips into Yellowstone National Park for hikes and wildlife viewing and can assist anglers on ranch streams and ponds. The food at Mountain Sky is first rate, and the "rustic" cabins are a far cry from the typical Montana rustic cabin (there are also modern cabins available). It's best to book far in advance. During the late spring and early fall, it's possible to stay for less than a week, at $285–325 per person per night.

Camping

Pine Creek campground (406/222-1892, www.fs.fed.us/r1/gallatin, Memorial Day–Labor Day, $11) is 10 miles south of Livingston, then six miles east of Highway 89 up Pine Creek Road (reservations at 877/444-6777, www.recreation.gov). Pine Creek Falls is a short hike from the campground, and Jewell and Pine Creek Lakes are three miles up the trail.

Sites may also be reserved at **Snowbank** (406/222-1892, www.fs.fed.us/r1/gallatin, Memorial Day–Labor Day, $11), 20 miles south of Livingston on Highway 89, then another 15 miles east on Mill Creek Road.

Closer to Gardiner and Yellowstone National Park, **Tom Miner/Petrified Forest** Forest Service campground (406/848-7375, www.fs.fed.us/r1/gallatin, June–Oct., $7) is eight miles west of Highway 89 on Tom Miner Road (36 miles south of Livingston). The Gallatin Petrified Forest is a two-mile hike from the campground. The many fishing-access sites on the Yellowstone are also de facto campgrounds.

The Forest Service has **cabins** for rent up Trail Creek, 20 miles southwest of Livingston, and Big Creek, 28 miles south of town, then eight miles west on Big Creek Road. These cabins are rented year-round for $30 per night; winter visitors may need skis or a snowmobile to reach them. Contact the Livingston ranger station (406/222-1892) for reservations.

Food

The restaurant at **Chico Hot Springs** is known statewide for its gourmet fare (406/333-4933 or 800/468-9232, dinner nightly and Sunday brunch, dinner $23–36; reservations strongly recommended). Penny-pinchers can eat at the resort's **Poolside Grille** (lunch and dinner daily, $3–14).

The other place to find really good food in the Paradise Valley is the casual **Pine Creek Café** (2496 East River Rd., 406/222-3628, 9 A.M.–2 P.M. and 5:30–9 P.M. Mon.–Fri., 8 A.M.–2 P.M. and 5:30–9 P.M. Sat.–Sun. summer, closed Mon.–Tues. winter, $6–22). It's worth the trip for the rainbow trout tacos or a buffalo sloppy joe; in good weather there's deck seating.

Local color is enhanced by the horse-barn decor at the **Livery Stable** (406/333-4688, 5:30–9 P.M. nightly, $9–20) on the west side of the highway in Emigrant. The trout dinner is good; the steaks are variable.

GARDINER

A year-round route into Yellowstone National Park, Gardiner (pop. 851, elev. 5,314 feet) has become known for its Church Universal and Triumphant neighbors (who are not your run-of-the-mill Western neighbors, even in the "New West") and has gained additional notoriety as the site of the slaughter of Yellowstone National Park buffalo.

Buffalo frequently carry brucellosis, a bacterial infection that causes newly infected cattle to miscarry their pregnancies, causing a great deal of concern among ranchers. In the winter of 2007–2008, about 1,600 Yellowstone buffalo were rounded up and shipped to slaughterhouses when they migrated north from the park seeking lower elevations with winter forage. Other buffalo have been driven back into the park. In 2008 an agreement among the State of Montana, the National Park Service, and the Church Universal and Triumphant provided a corridor for a limited number brucellosis-negative bison to cross the church's ranch north of the park to winter grazing grounds south of Yankee Jim Canyon. Although this is a step forward, this issue will probably persist for some time.

The Gardiner entrance to Yellowstone is marked by the Roosevelt Arch, dedicated in 1903 by Theodore Roosevelt. It's the only park entrance open to cars year-round. The road between Gardiner and Cooke City is plowed during the winter.

Events and Recreation

The rodeo comes to Gardiner in mid-June, usually on Father's Day weekend. Contact the **chamber of commerce** (406/848-7971, www.gardinerchamber.com) for details.

Boats aren't allowed on Yellowstone National Park's rivers, but **Yellowstone Raft Company** (406/848-7777,www.yellowstoneraft.com, half-day $35 adult) and **Flying Pig Raft Company** (406/848-7510 or 866/807-0744, www.flyingpigrafting.com, half-day $39 adult), both headquartered in Gardiner, run trips on the Yellowstone River outside the park.

Local outfitters guide visitors on a wide variety of trail rides and fishing trips. **Hell's A Roarin' Outfitters** (406/848-7578, www.hellsaroarinoutfitters.com) is based in Jardine and offers a wide range of activities, including horseback rides and fishing trips; **Parks' Fly Shop** (406/848-7314, www.parksflyshop.com) is on Highway 89 in downtown Gardiner and can set you up with a guide. Richard Parks is author of a comprehensive fishing guide to Yellowstone National Park and is the local go-to guy on many conservation issues.

The Gallatin National Forest has a **ranger station** (406/848-7375) in Gardiner near the park entrance.

Accommodations

Not surprisingly, during the summer, many of the accommodations in Gardiner are on the expensive side. Parkgoers may prefer to reserve well in advance and stay in the lodge or cabins at Mammoth Hot Springs, which cost about the same. From mid-September through May, lodging prices drop significantly.

The **Absaroka Lodge** (406/848-7414 or 800/755-7414, www.yellowstonemotel.com, $112) is well-situated on the banks of the Yellowstone River. Kitchenettes are available for $5–10 extra. The **Best Western by Mammoth Hot Springs** (406/848-7311 or 800/828-9080, www.bestwesternmontana.com, $144 and up) has an indoor pool and is set back off the highway just north of Gardiner on Highway 89 with views of the river.

At the **Yellowstone Village Inn** (406/484-7417 or 800/228-8158, www.yellowstonev-inn.com, $109–149), a nicely decorated place set up on a hill above the highway, there's an indoor pool and sauna, and a few suites with kitchens.

The **Super 8** (Hwy. 89, 406/848-7401, www.yellowstonesuper8.com, $89–145) is about what you'd expect; nothing fancy, but a clean room with a bed.

On Highway 89, the **Westernaire Motel** (406/848-7397 or 888/273-0358, www.yellowstonemotel.com, $75 and up) is a good budget choice. In the same price range are the **Yellowstone River Motel,** just east of Highway 89 near the park entrance (406/848-7303 or 800/797-4837, www.yellowstonerivermotel.com, $70–95); **Hillcrest Cottages** (406/848-7353 or 800/970-7353, www.hillcrestcottages.com, $60–100); and the **Jim Bridger Court** (406/848-7371 or 888/858-7508, www.jimbridgercourt.com, $75), with rustic cabins.

If you stay at the child- and pet-friendly **Gardiner Guest House** (112 Main St., 406/848-9414, $90–135), run by guide Richard Parks and his wife, Nancy, you'll come away knowing just a bit more about the area, its critters, and its issues. There are four rooms in the Victorian house and a cabin out back.

Just north of town, the **Yellowstone Basin Inn** (406/848-7080 or 800/624-3364, www.montanaguide.com/maiden, $75–350) has attractive standard rooms and suites on a hillside overlooking the highway and the river.

Camping

Yellowstone RV Park (406/848-7496) and **Rocky Mountain** (406/848-7251) are RV campgrounds right in Gardiner. **Eagle Creek** is the nearest Forest Service campground; it's four miles northeast of town on the road to Jardine.

Food

For lunch, join park employees for sandwiches on the deck at the **Sawtooth Deli** (406/848-7600, 8 A.M.–9:30 P.M. Tues.–Sat., $7–8) or relax for a while with a tasty panini sandwich and a new book at **Tumbleweed Bookstore and Cafe** (Hwy. 89, 406/848-2225, $7–8).

Gardiner's fancy restaurant is the **Yellowstone**

Mine in the Best Western (406/848-7336, 6–11 A.M. and 5–9:30 P.M. daily, $8–22), and a good casual rib joint is **Antler's** inside the Comfort Inn. For something a little bit Western, head to **Red's Blue Goose Saloon** (406/848-7037) on Park Street.

About eight miles up the road in Corwin Springs, **The Lighthouse** (752 Hwy. 89 S., 5:30–9 P.M. daily, $13) has pan-Asian food, including spicy curries.

Transportation

One of Yellowstone National Park's concessionaires, **Xanterra** (307/344-7901, www.travelyellowstone.com), runs bus tours of the park. From late May through mid-September, buses leave Gardiner every morning at 7:45 A.M., tour the Grand Loop of Yellowstone's roads, and return to Gardiner at 6:15 P.M. The fee is $65 adults, $32.50 kids 8–15, free for children under age 8.

Big Timber to Laurel

The Boulder River flows between the Absarokas and the Beartooths to Big Timber, passing ghost towns, church camps, and dude ranches on the way. Near Big Timber, the Boulder pours into the Yellowstone River, which around here changes from a cold-water trout stream to the broad warm home of paddlefish.

This whole area was Crow territory before white settlers moved in during the 1870s. When the railroad came through, a small settlement sprang up near the mouth of the Boulder River. This town, called Dornix (meaning "Rock Pile"), never made it as a railway station. In 1883 the town of Big Timber was founded just to the west. Ranching (especially sheep ranching), tourism, and recreation now support the local economy.

BIG TIMBER AND VICINITY

A mostly quiet and well-kept-up ranch town, Big Timber (pop. 1,768, elev. 4,072 feet) is not a forested spot. William Clark, who passed this way on the return from the Pacific, named Big Timber Creek for the stand of cottonwoods shading its confluence with the Yellowstone. Today it might be called "Big Wind" or "Crazy View" for the frequent gusts, and the nearby mountain range are far more noticeable than the trees.

Crazy Mountain Museum

A garden at the entrance to the Crazy Mountain Museum (I-90 exit 367, Cemetery Rd., 406/932-4878, 10 A.M.–4:30 P.M. Tues.–Sat., 1–4 P.M. Sun., Memorial Day–Labor Day, free) spotlights native plants collected by Lewis and Clark on their journey across Montana. Also outside, a Norwegian *stabbur*, a supposedly rodent-proof pantry building, has been built to acknowledge the area's Norwegian heritage. Indoors, historical photos are mixed with several striking modern photos, and one small room is filled with a collection of chaps.

Fish Hatchery

Yellowstone cutthroat trout of all ages live in the pools of the fish hatchery north of town on McLeod Street (406/932-4434). Trout are taken from the hatchery to stock lakes across the state.

Greycliff Prairie Dog Town

Pull off the interstate to visit the communal burrows of Greycliff Prairie Dog Town (Greycliff exit from I-90, 406/247-2940, $2 non–Montana residents). It may not sound like much, but prairie dog behavior is kind of a kick to watch, and even the most jaded wildlife observer is likely to leave with half a roll of film exposed with shots of chortling prairie dogs. They're very social animals, and it's easy for humans to make up little stories about their inner lives as the prairie dogs nuzzle, groom, and play with each other. They're also very vocal, giving sharp yelps or "barks" when

LEWIS AND CLARK MEET THE PRAIRIE DOG

The Corps of Discovery first encountered prairie dogs in what is now Nebraska. Foreshadowing their future relationship with dogs in general, the captains had one of the animals cooked for dinner. Lewis gave roasted prairie dog a favorable review, declaring it "well flavored and tender." The corps soon decided, however, that the burrowing rodents were too difficult to shoot, and the enlisted men spent the better part of September 7, 1804, pouring barrels of water into prairie dog burrows in an effort to flush out a specimen to send to President Jefferson. Finally, one popped out alive, and the study commenced.

Lewis recorded:

Ther mouth resemble the rabit, head longer, legs short, & toe nails long ther tail like a ground Squirel which they shake and make chattering noise ther eyes like a dog, their colour is Gray and Skin contains Soft fur...the Village of those animals Covs. about 4 acrs of Ground on a Gradual decent of a hill and Contains great numbers of holes on the top of which those little animals Set erect make a Whistleing noise and whin allarmed Slip into their hole – we por'd into one of the holes 5 barrels of water without filling it. . . .

Lewis called the critter a "dog" because of its bark; Clark pressed for "ground rat" or "burrowing squirrel." It was soon commonly known as a "barking squirrel," except by the French, who stuck with *petit chien*, "little dog."

A live prairie dog was shipped from Fort Mandan to the White House, and although it arrived on the East Coast in sickly condition, it soon regained its health. One can only imagine Thomas Jefferson's delight at finding a barking squirrel at his door.

© JUDY JEWELL

Call it a prairie dog, ground rat, or barking squirrel . . . you'll find plenty of these social animals just off I-90 at Greycliff.

---

alerted to possible danger. When this danger cry goes out, all the surrounding prairie dogs scuttle into their burrows.

Crazy Mountains

The Crazy Mountains, north of Big Timber, are a spectacular isolated range. To reach them from Big Timber, drive north on Highway 191 (the road to Harlowton) and follow signs for Big Timber Canyon. **Halfmoon Campground** and a trailhead into the mountains are about 15 miles from the pavement.

Recreation and Events

Sunbaked I-90 travelers may enjoy a stop at the **Big Timber Waterslide** (nine miles east of Big Timber at exit 377, 406/932-6570, 10 A.M.–7 P.M. daily June–Labor Day, $15.95 adults, $11.95 ages 4–12). A caveat: This waterslide has a few years on it, and if your kids are used to huge fancy water parks, they may not be overly impressed with this one.

Boulder River **fishing-access sites** include **Big Rock,** four miles south of Big Timber, and **Boulder Forks,** at the confluence of the Main

Boulder and West Boulder Rivers in McLeod. Fish the Yellowstone from **Grey Bear,** six miles west of Big Timber on the frontage road, or **Pelican,** just east of the Greycliff exit on the frontage road.

In the Crazy Mountains, hiking trails start from the **Halfmoon Campground.**

The **rodeo** is held the last weekend in June.

Accommodations

The 🟢 **Grand Hotel** (139 McLeod St., 406/932-4459, www.thegrand-hotel.com, $59–155), built in 1890, has been restored as a bed-and-breakfast hotel. This is a great place to stay: The rooms are cozy, the full breakfasts are staggeringly good, there's a sauna in the upstairs hallway, and the adjoining restaurant and bar are good places to while away an evening.

The **River Valley Inn** (600 W. 2nd St., 406/932-4943 or 877/899-1397, $75) is a newer motel and a good option if you can't stay at the Grand and want to be in town.

The **Buckin' Horse Bunkhouse,** southeast of Big Timber on Bridger Creek (exit 384 from I-90, then 3.6 miles south on Bridger Creek Rd., 406/932-6537, www.bunkhouse.biz, $125), rents a B&B cabin that's rustic on the outside but nice on the inside. Horseback rides (even cattle drives) can be arranged. Another pleasantly rustic B&B ranch, the **Burnt Out Lodge** (248 Upper Deer Creek Rd., 406/932-6601 or 888/873-7943, www.burntoutlodge. com, $97–107, breakfast included) has rooms (each with a private entrance and bath) in a log lodge on a working ranch. Guests are welcome to get involved in ranch activities.

Camping

Spring Creek Camp and Trout Ranch (406/932-4387) has cabins ($30–65) and some tent sites but is essentially an RV park ($27–36) in a quiet spot two miles south of Big Timber on Boulder River Road. Ponds here are stocked with rainbow trout. The **Big Timber KOA** is just off the interstate next to the waterslide (406/932-6569, $29–38). Besides tent and RV sites, there are cabins for rent ($46), a swimming pool, and hot tubs.

Nineteen miles north of Big Timber, up Big Timber Canyon, **Halfmoon Campground** (406/932-5155, www.fs.fed.us/r1/gallatin, Memorial Day–Labor Day, $5) features hiking trails into the Crazy Mountains.

Food

You can breakfast at the 🟢 **Grand Hotel** (5–9 P.M. nightly, $18–27) only if you're a guest there, but tasty dinners are served up to the public, and there's a friendly bar off to the side of the lobby. Don't miss the Montana twist on the menu items, such as the hearty appetizer of elk rellenos with lime cilantro avocado sauce ($10).

Information

The **Sweetgrass County Chamber of Commerce** (406/932-5131, www.bigtimber. com) runs the local visitor center, located at exit 367 on I-90. Find the **Forest Service** at 225 Big Timber Loop Road (406/932-5155).

BOULDER VALLEY

It's hard to pick Montana's most beautiful river valley, but this one's a strong contender. Small wonder then that celebrities and novelists have become the modern-day homesteaders here.

Sights

Drive up the Boulder River Valley 25 miles south of Big Timber to the **Natural Bridge State Monument.** The limestone cliffs have been warped, lifted, dropped, and eaten away by weak river-water acids, leaving a spectacular gorge with a 100-foot waterfall. The eponymous natural bridge across the falls collapsed in 1988. Trails course the park, but there are no campsites.

Just down the road from the natural bridge, the **Main Boulder Ranger Station** dates from 1905. There are pictographs in the caves west of the ranger station.

Forty miles up the Boulder River from Big Timber, the ghost town of **Independence** recalls a past of gold mining and stock-promotion schemes. The final four miles to Independence are best driven in a high-clearance four-wheel-drive vehicle.

SOUTH-CENTRAL MONTANA

Recreation

When the Yellowstone River is brimful of muddy water, the rocky Boulder River usually runs clear. Upriver from Natural Bridge, the Boulder is populated with rainbow and cutthroat trout; below the tall falls at the bridge, browns and rainbows predominate.

Follow Boulder River Road to its end to pick up a trail into the **Absaroka-Beartooth Wilderness Area,** a remote high country studded with alpine lakes and covered with wildflowers late in the summer. It's a good spot for a week of backpacking.

In the winter, the Boulder River Road is maintained for snowmobiling starting about 30 miles south of Big Timber and continuing to the wilderness boundary. Snowmobilers often spot the many elk and moose that winter in the Boulder Valley. For more information on snowmobiling, call the Forest Service in Big Timber (406/932-5155).

Accommodations

The Boulder Valley didn't support miners or farmers for long, but dude ranchers have done well by it. The **Hawley Mountain Guest Ranch** (45 miles south of Big Timber, 406/932-5791, www.hawleymountain.com) offers reasonably priced weeklong (Sunday to Sunday) packages including cabin, meals, horseback riding, flyfishing, and river floating. Accommodations are either in the lodge or in one of three cabins. Weekly all-inclusive rates are $1,555 s, $2,430 d; cabins are about $2,895 or $3,270 per week for two people.

For less-expensive lodgings, the tidy **McLeod Resort** (16 miles south of Big Timber, 406/932-6167, www.mcleodmt.com) has a campground ($15 tents, $20 RVs), cabins ($30 and up), and a guest house ($1,000 a week for up to eight people) set alongside the West Boulder River. The cabins and the houses have cooking facilities, but cooking utensils are not provided in the cabins.

Camping

The Gallatin National Forest is studded with campsites south of Big Timber (406/932-5155,

www.fs.fed.us/rl/gallatin, $5), but you have to drive a ways to reach them. **Falls Creek Campground** is 30 miles south of town on Boulder River Road, with **Aspen Grove, Chippy Park,** and **Hell's Canyon** Campgrounds all within the next 10 miles. **Hicks Park Campground** is 50 miles south of Big Timber on the same road. Turn right (west) at McLeod to reach the **West Boulder Campground,** 30 miles southwest of Big Timber, with a trail into the Absaroka-Beartooth Wilderness. The **McLeod Resort** (see *Accommodations* above) also offers tent and RV camping.

Food

If the name of the (**Road Kill Bar and Cafe** (15 miles south of Big Timber, 406/932-6174, 11 A.M.–close Wed.–Sun.) makes you grin, and if their motto, "From your grille to ours," doesn't put you off, you'll find heaven in McLeod. This Boulder Valley landmark is a convivial place to stop for a drink or a meal. During the summer, there's often a band—don't be shy about dancing, and don't forget to look up and admire the arched plank ceiling in the bar (behind the false front, the place is a Quonset hut).

REED POINT

Tiny Reed Point has barely changed from the early 20th century, when this was a booming trade center for local farmers and ranchers. In the 1920s, Reed Point was a major center for sheep ranchers; an estimated 48,000 sheep grazed in the mountains above the town.

Historic old buildings still grace the four blocks of the downtown area, linked by authentic plank sidewalks. It's fun to saunter along the streets, admiring the old shops and storefronts.

However, Reed Point has one other unique characteristic: the **Running of the Sheep.** Started in 1989 as a fund-raiser for the tiny community's library, school, and other public facilities, the sheep drive has become an institution. Held on the Sunday of Labor Day weekend, the event consists of watching several thousand sheep scampering down Reed Point's main street, eating grilled lamb and sausages, and attending the parade and street dance that follow the drive. The Associated Press reports one local wag as stating: "It's like the running of the bulls in Spain, only a whole lot safer."

RAPELJE

In the late 1990s, Rapelje, 25 miles north of Columbus and surrounded by wide-open flatlands, was on the brink of becoming a ghost town when residents decided to stage a mountain bike race in order to raise funds to keep the local café in business. Area ranchers allowed the construction of trails on their private property and found a promoter to put on a small race. That race has grown to a 24-hour marathon, held on the June weekend closest to the summer solstice. The course follows county roads that wind through coulees and hills with spectacular mountain views. Shorter recreational rides are also offered. Mountain bike central in town is the **Rapelje Stockman Cafe** (406/663-2231, http://stockmancafe.googlepages.com/), collectively owned by a group of townspeople.

COLUMBUS AND THE STILLWATER RIVER

Thirty-seven miles east of Big Timber at the mouth of the Stillwater River, Columbus (pop. 1,931) is renowned for the **New Atlas Bar** (see *Food and Nightlife* below). But back before the New Atlas was the main thing people thought of when they thought of Columbus, the town was known for its frequent name changes. Previously it has been called Eagle's Nest, Sheep Dip, and Stillwater.

The jagged peaks of the Beartooth Range form the jawline of the horizon to the south. On the road down from Columbus, through Absarokee to Red Lodge, take in the fine views of former Crow country.

A lovely little town with one of the state's great names, Fishtail is worth a stop, if only for a soda at the mercantile. Of course, a brief stop will only make you wish you'd stayed longer, so plan on hanging out for a while.

If merely hanging around this lovely country sounds too unstructured, sign on with **Paintbrush Adventures** (86 N. Stillwater Rd., Absarokee, 406/328-4158, www.paintbrushadventures.com) for a trail ride ($45 for two hours) or day hike ($75). They also offer extended pack trips and guided fishing trips. Another outfitter, **Absaroka River Adventures** (113 Grove St., Absarokee, 406/328-7440 or 800/334-7238, www.absarokariver.com, half-day $37 adults, $20 children), offers white-water trips on the Stillwater River (not a contradiction!).

Accommodations

Although there are several chain motels, including a Super 8, up on I-90 at the Columbus exit, the most comfy place to spend the night in the Stillwater country is Absarokee, where the ☾ **Stillwater Lodge** (28 Woodard Ave., 406/328-4899, http://stillwaterlodge.net, $68–84) is a small motel with comfortable, thoughtfully decorated rooms. Another pretty place in this little town is **The Big Yellow House** (Main St., Absarokee, 406/328-7220, http://thebigyellowhouse.biz, $30–75), which dates from about 1904; guests have use of the kitchen to make their own dinners and breakfasts. Guests can either stay in one of the house's three bedrooms (shared bath) or in a cottage next door.

If you'd like to experience life as a Fishtail local, stay at the **Fiddler Creek Cabins** (406/328-4949, www.montana-cabin-rentals.com, $750 per week and up), eight miles southwest of Fishtail.

Camp at **Pine Grove** or **Emerald Lake** campgrounds (406/446-2103, www.fs.fed.us/r1/custer, May–Sept., $9) out of Fishtail, or at **Jimmy Joe** or **East Rosebud Lake** out of Roscoe.

Food and Nightlife

In Dean, longtime area favorite **Montana Hanna's Trout Hole Restaurant** (406/328-7400, dinner from 5 P.M. Thurs.–Sun., $20–26) is a family restaurant serving a variety of steaks in addition to the namesake rainbow trout. The view from the huge windows onto fields giving way to mountains is half the attraction here. The Stillwater Saloon next door is also a big draw.

In nearby Roscoe, the **Grizzly Bar and Restaurant** (406/328-6789, 11 A.M.–midnight daily, $8–25), housed in a lovely log building along the East Rose Bud River, offers a reason to linger in this attractive hamlet. Although the menu emphasizes steak and prime rib, it also includes pasta, seafood, scallops, Alaskan king crab, and line-caught Alaskan halibut.

It's hard to find a bar that's as simultaneously stately and seedy as Columbus's **New Atlas Bar** (522 E. Pike St., 406/322-4033)—it has a great back bar and more animal heads than most non-Montanans have seen in a lifetime. Don't expect anything here to be prettied up for refined sensibilities, and don't suppose that because there are no ashtrays on the bar that it's a nonsmoking joint: Spittoons are provided for ash and spew.

LAUREL

Located at a transportation crossroads, Laurel (pop. 6,421) is a town that has often been passed through by history. The town grew up as the railhead for the Red Lodge–area coal mines that fueled the Northern Pacific's Montana steam engines, and became the railroad hub of the entire Yellowstone Valley. Access to rail lines made Laurel a candidate for other industry. Currently, a Cenex oil refinery dominates the skyline.

With railroading and refining, Laurel maintains an industrial ambience at odds with the fruitful valley it sprawls in. Boosters of Billings repeat a mantra about the day when Billings stretches clear to Laurel. It's not clear that there's much to gain or lose for either city; it would be hard times for the farms in between, however.

Sights

As the Nez Percé Indians fled from the Battle of the Big Hole in 1877, they struck eastward toward Yellowstone National Park. Here they hoped to encounter their allies the Crow and seek asylum in southeastern Montana. By this time, however, the Crow were working closely with the U.S. Army. They repudiated the Nez Percé, whose leadership realized they had but one choice remaining: escape to Canada.

They pressed up the valley of the Clark Fork of the Yellowstone and crossed the Yellowstone at Laurel. Colonel S. D. Sturgis and the new Seventh Cavalry caught up with the Nez Percé on September 13, about nine miles north of Laurel, in Canyon Creek. Indian sharpshooters took positions in the sandstone bluffs above the valley and held off the infantry until the Indian caravan was safe in the Musselshell Valley. At the Battle of Canyon Creek, the army lost three men, and the Nez Percé claimed three wounded.

Follow Highway 532 north of Laurel nine miles to visit the scene of the Canyon Creek battle. The **Chief Joseph-Sturgis Battlefield Monument** commemorates the event.

Closer to town, in **Fireman's Park,** a statue of Chief Joseph serves as a memorial to the combatants at the battle.

Accommodations and Food

The classiest place in town is the **Howard Johnson Inn** (310 S. 1st Ave., 406/628-8281 or 877/210-5626, www.thehojo.com, about $100), with a pool on the premises and a nice restaurant and health club next door. Rooms at the **Welcome Travelers Motel** (620 W. Main St., 406/628-6821) are a few dollars less expensive; kitchenettes are available, and they can arrange scenic airplane rides.

Information

Contact the **Laurel Chamber of Commerce** (406/628-8105, www.laurelmontana.org) for more information.

Absaroka-Beartooth Wilderness

This is Montana's high country: Granite Peak, towering 12,799 feet in the Beartooth Range, is the state's highest point and a formidable climb. Geologically and ecologically different from one another, the Absaroka and the Beartooth Ranges share a plateau and a wilderness area. The accommodating Beartooth Plateau tilts from a low northwestern Absaroka corner to the soaring Beartooths in the southeast.

The Beartooths were uplifted, eroded, partially blanketed with lava from Yellowstone's volcanoes, and covered with glaciers. The limestone cliffs of the Beartooth Range rise from high tundra cut through by steep canyons.

The weather in the Beartooths can change quickly and with arctic severity. Come prepared for a snowstorm, even in midsummer.

The Beartooths are largely above the timberline, and alpine meadows are the characteristic vegetation. The growing season here is about 45 days, and the plants and the soil are sensitive to trampling. During the late summer, snowbanks sometimes turn pink as microorganisms on the snow's surface die and turn red.

RED LODGE

Red Lodge (pop. 2,455, elev. 5,555 feet) is supposedly named for red clay–decorated Crow lodges. Once part of the Crow Reservation, this area was taken from the Indians in 1882; coal mining commenced a few years later. The mines became the basis for the town, and many immigrants came to work in Red Lodge; Finns were particularly well-represented. Mining dropped off in the 1930s, and an explosion at the nearby Smith Creek Mine in 1943 halted large-scale coal mining in the area. Red Lodge is now a resort and jumping-off point for travelers on the Beartooth Highway and is also visited by many Montanans for its good spring skiing.

Sights

Red Lodge's downtown remains vital and is a showcase of historic preservation. Pick up a walking-tour map from the visitors center (or download it from www.redlodge.com) and ramble through the sandstone and brick edifices of the late 1800s. Red Lodge's Old Town, near the high school, was the town's business center from 1886 to 1893.

The **Carbon County Historical Museum** (224 N. Broadway, 406/446-3667, 10 A.M.–5 P.M. Mon.–Sat. summer, 10 A.M.–5 P.M. Tues.–Fri., 11 A.M.–3 P.M. Sat. winter, $3 adults, $2 students) has exhibits on rodeos, Native Americans, and mining. Another historical artifact, Liver Eatin' Johnson's cabin, is on the north end of town next to the visitors center. It's probably apocryphal, but Mr. Johnson was said to have avenged his Flathead wife's death by eating the livers he'd ripped from Crow Indians.

Red Lodge's biggest attraction, besides its recreation and its many restaurants and shops, is the **Beartooth Nature Center** (615 2nd St. E., 406/446-1133, www.beartoothnaturecenter.org, 10 A.M.–5 P.M. daily May–Oct., 10 A.M.–2 P.M. daily Nov.–Apr., $6 adults, $5 seniors, $2.50 children), which provides a home for native animals that can't be returned to the wild.

Skiing

Red Lodge Mountain (406/446-2610 or 800/444-8977, www.redlodgemountain.com, $46 adults, $39 teens, $16 children under 13) is a ski resort six miles west of town with a vertical drop of 2,400 feet and seven chairlifts, including two high-speed quads, to ferry skiers to the 70 trails. Ski season runs from early December through mid-April, sometimes later. Spring skiing is especially popular at Red Lodge.

Red Lodge Nordic Ski Area (406/425-0698, www.beartoothtrails.org, $5 adults, $3 children 13 and under) has nine miles of groomed trails west of town on Hwy. 78, with lessons and rentals available. Find notes about other trails in the area from the Nordic association's website.

Hiking and Other Recreation

Head up the West Fork of Rock Creek for hiking and fishing. The often-crowded **Wild**

Bill Lake, six miles from Red Lodge on West Fork Road, is wheelchair-accessible for fishing. Toward the end of the road, trailheads sprout up. Just out of Basin Campground, the **Basin Lakes National Recreation Trail** is an easy day hike leading to two lakes (with some brook trout) and a few tumbledown prospectors' cabins. At the road's end, the **West Fork Trail** puts you at the Absaroka-Beartooth Wilderness boundary, a one-mile hike from a waterfall, five miles from a mountain lake, and 10 miles from Sundance Pass.

Many of the area's Forest Service campgrounds are near hiking trails. The **Corral Creek Trail** starts near Sheridan Campground, and Parkside Campground is on the high winding road to the trailhead for the **Hellroaring Lakes Trail,** which leads to a lovely chain of mountain lakes.

Golf at beautiful and challenging **Red Lodge Resort and Golf Club** (406/446-1812), southwest of town on Red Lodge Mountain Road. Swim at the 25-yard-long mile-high **city pool** (14th and Hauser, daily June–Aug.).

Events

The **Red Lodge Music Festival** (www.redlodgemusicfestival.org) brings top high-school musicians to train with professionals. Both students and faculty perform over a nine-day span in mid-June.

The **Red Lodge Rodeo** is on Fourth of July weekend.

Mid-July brings the **Beartooth Rally** and a huge swarm of Harleys to town, making Red Lodge into the Sturgis of the Rockies.

The last weekend in July is devoted to the **Montana Old-Time Fiddle Contest** (www.montanafiddlers.org).

Mountain men (406/446-3043, www.redlodge.com/rendezvous) descend on Red Lodge in late July and early August. The encampment on the south end of town features music, dance, black-powder shoots, and trade goods, including buckskin garments, black-powder rifles, Indian beadwork, and pewter ware.

Red Lodge's ethnic diversity is celebrated each August during the **Festival of Nations** (www.

festivalofnations.us). Lots of music, lots of food, and lots of people fill downtown. The town fills up for this celebration, so be sure to book rooms in advance if you want to stay in Red Lodge during the second week of August.

It may take an early March trip to Red Lodge to really believe that there is such a sport as ski-joring. Visit the rodeo grounds for the **National Ski-Joring Finals,** and watch horses pull skiers around a circular course loaded with jumps and gates. The town's **Winter Carnival** happens around the same time of year.

A personalized event can be yours at the **Canyon Wedding Chapel,** four miles south of Red Lodge (406/446-2681 or 800/823-2681). Both religious and civil wedding ceremonies are accommodated here.

Accommodations

During the busy summer season or on peak ski weekends, perhaps the easiest way to book a room in Red Lodge is to call the **central reservations service** (406/446-3942 or 877/733-5634, www.redlodgereservations.com). Book a vacation home through **Red Lodging** (406/446-4700 or 877/733-5634, www.redlodging.com).

Lodging can be pricey in Red Lodge in the summer. Expect prices to drop dramatically in the spring and fall, and to be somewhat lower in the winter.

If you're a fan of old downtown hotels, your best bet in Red Lodge is, without question, the (**Pollard Hotel** (2 N. Broadway, 406/446-0001 or 800/765-5273, www.pollardhotel.com, $90–300). Back when it was known as the Spofford, it hosted Calamity Jane and Buffalo Bill. Now after extensive renovation, there are even racquetball courts, a health club, and a sauna. Rooms are comfortable (though the least expensive ones are quite small), and many include in-room steam baths and whirlpool tubs.

For a full-scale, full-service resort, the (**Rock Creek Resort** is four miles south of town on Highway 212 (406/446-1111 or 800/667-1119, www.rockcreekresort.com, $130 and up). Accommodations range from single rooms to three-bedroom townhouses ($355). During ski season, Rock Creek offers packages including bed, breakfast, and skiing. A pool, tennis courts, health club, volleyball, croquet, horseback riding, and mountain-bike rentals keep Rock Creek's guests occupied. The resort also features two restaurants.

Quite a bit less fancy but still comfortable is the alpine-looking and dog-friendly **Yodeler Motel** (601 S. Broadway, 406/446-1435, www.yodelermotel.com, $108–118), which has half-basement rooms (which are not unpleasant) and, for a few dollars more, rooms that are fully above ground. Amenities here include an outdoor hot tub and in-shower steam baths, which work quite well, even though they initially seem improbable, and are something to look forward to after a day of mountain biking or skiing.

The chalet-like **Chateau Rouge** (1501 S. Broadway, 406/446-1601 or 800/926-1601, www.chateaurouge.com, $119–139) is a good value, with rooms in studios or two-bedroom condos ($89 and up). These rooms can be made up to sleep a crowd if necessary. There's an indoor pool and hot tub.

LuPine Inn (702 S. Hauser, 406/446-1321 or 888/567-1321, www.lupineinn.com, $119–143) is off the main drag on a stream and has a large indoor pool, fitness center, hot tub, sauna, indoor playground and game room, and guest laundry; pets are permitted. Another attractive and convenient chain motel is the **Comfort Inn** (612 N. Broadway, 406/446-4469 or 888/733-4661, $155).

A newly built log lodge houses the creekside **Rocky Fork Inn B&B** (718 S. Broadway, 406/446-2967, www.rockyforkinn.com), which is just about the most luxurious place to stay in town.

Camping

The **Red Lodge KOA** (406/446-2364 or 800/562-7540, May–Sept., $28 tent, $35 RV), four miles north of town on Highway 212, has a swimming pool and sites for both RVs and tents. **Perry's RV Park and Campground** (406/446-2722, late May–Sept., $20 tent, $30 RV) is on Rock Creek 1.5 miles south of town.

To find Forest Service campgrounds (406/446-2103, www.fs.fed.us/r1/custer/, May–Sept., $11), head south on Highway 212. Reach **Cascade** and **Basin** campgrounds via Red Lodge Mountain Road, which starts right near the ranger station. These are good spots for hikers heading into the Absaroka-Beartooth Wilderness. Farther south on Highway 212, find turnoffs for **Sheridan** and **Ratine. Parkside, Limber Pine, Greenough Lake,** and **M-K** are all part of the Rock Creek Recreation Area 11 miles south of Red Lodge and virtually at the foot of the Beartooth Highway. All of these spots except for Cascade have running water and charge $11 to camp.

Food

It's not hard to find a meal in Red Lodge—the town boasts of having more restaurants per capita than any other place in Montana. One particularly pleasant spot is [**Bridge Creek Backcountry Wine Bar** (116 S. Broadway, 406/446-9900, 8 A.M.–10 P.M. daily, dinner $12–35), a lovely little place with sidewalk seating, a coffee bar, and a small gourmet market as well as a regular sit-down restaurant section. At lunch, a variety of wraps and sandwiches are offered ($6–9); dinners range from soba noodles with veggies to duck pot pie. Wine pairings are suggested on the menu.

The **Red Lodge Pizza Company** (115 S. Broadway, 406/446-3933, 11 A.M.–10 P.M. Sun.–Thurs., 11 A.M.–11 P.M. Fri.–Sat. summer, 11 A.M.–9 P.M.daily winter, $3–4 per slice) serves passably good pizza, and it's available by the slice, making for a quick inexpensive lunch. It's also a good place to bring kids.

For a casual lunch or dinner, **Bogart's** (11 S. Broadway, 406/446-1784, 11 A.M.–9 P.M. daily) is a longtime Red Lodge favorite serving pizza and large portions of fairly standard Mexican food in a comfortable cabin-like setting.

A bright spot for the bleary-eyed, **Coffee Factory Roasters** (6 S. Broadway, 406/446-3200) roasts beans and serves espresso and desserts. Find the other kind of brewing at **Sam's Taproom** (417 N. Broadway,

406/446-4607, 2–8 P.M. daily), adjacent to the Red Lodge Ales Brewing Company. Another good place to get a beer is **Natali's** (117 N. Broadway, 406/446-3333), though if you really want to kick up your heels, that's best done across the street at the **Snow Creek Saloon** (124 S. Broadway, 406/446-2542).

Red Lodge's fanciest dining is offered by **The Dining Room** (406/446-0001, 7–11 A.M. and 5–9 P.M. daily, dinner $18–28) at the Pollard Hotel. Steaks are from natural Angus beef from Montana; chops, fresh seafood, pasta, and game dishes also appear on the menu, and the wine list is extensive.

Cafe Regis (16th and Word, 406/446-1941, 6 A.M.–2 P.M. Tues.–Sun., $6–8), located in a nicely renovated old grocery store two blocks west of the main drag, has a less touristy feeling than most Red Lodge restaurants. The back doors open onto a patio that bumps up against town's community gardens. It's safe to say that the Regis has the best barbecued tofu in town (it really is good).

Head seven miles east of town to the **Bear Creek Saloon** (Hwy. 308, 406/446-3481, 5–10 P.M. Thurs.–Sun., May–Sept. and Dec.–Mar., $8–27), known as much for its pig races as its food (though the charbroiled steaks are tasty). Every 15 minutes, another group of porkers toes the line. Thanks to special state legislation, it is legal to bet on the pigs.

Information and Services

The chamber of commerce **visitors center** (601 N. Broadway, 406/446-1718, www.red-lodge.com) has the expected brochures, plus an RV dump station. The **ranger station** (406/446-2103) is on Highway 212.

Beartooth Hospital is at 600 West 21st Street (406/446-2345).

If you're setting out to drive the Beartooth Highway, be sure to gas up in Red Lodge.

Transportation

Fly into Billings; it's about 60 miles from Red Lodge. Also 60 miles away is the Cody, Wyoming, airport. Car rentals are available at the either airport.

◖ BEARTOOTH HIGHWAY

Make sure there's gas in the tank, fresh batteries in the camera, an extra sweater in the back seat, and at least three hours to spare before setting out on the 68-mile-long Beartooth Highway. Built in 1936 and now a National Scenic Byway, the road climbs to 10,947 feet and crosses alpine meadows and snowfields. The Beartooth Highway is closed by snow most of the year—most years it's open from the end of May to mid-October.

The road climbs Rock Creek Canyon out of Red Lodge and switches back four times, crossing as many vegetation zones, starting in a valley of Douglas fir and lodgepole pine and topping out in alpine meadows strewn with boulders and wildflowers. Near Beartooth Pass, pink snow betrays the presence of high-elevation algae.

Watch for the Bear's Tooth, a tall spire left after a glacier devoured the rest of the peak. North of the summit of Beartooth Plateau, Granite Peak juts above the landscape.

Hiking

The high country around the Beartooth Highway is crossed by hiking trails and speckled with lakes. Hiking trails across fragile alpine terrain are rarely forged paths; rather, they're less precise routes marked by rock cairns. For a short hike through an alpine meadow, drive up to the fire lookout on **Clay Butte** and hike a little over a mile along the ridge.

For a longer trek, take **Trail 614** at the switchback in the road up to the lookout and hike about four miles (generally downhill) around Beartooth Butte to Beartooth Lake. There's a lovely campground at Beartooth Lake, and a loop hike around the butte passes several other lakes in its seven-mile course.

Skiing

Early in the season, it may seem more appropriate to ski. The Red Lodge International Summer Ski and Snowboard Camp uses the area, and the public is welcome to use the **ski lifts** (406/446-3446, 8 A.M.–1:30 P.M., $35) near Beartooth Pass from about Memorial

Day through July 4, or however long the snow lasts. Because the slopes are nearly vertical, skiers and boarders must be able to demonstrate expert abilities before getting on the lift.

Fishing

Many of the alpine lakes on the Beartooth Plateau have been stocked with trout. The hikes in are lovely, the fishing's generally good, and Pat Marcuson details every fish-bearing Beartooth lake and stream in *Fishing the Beartooths,* published by Falcon Press. Remember that the road dips down into Wyoming here—buy a Wyoming fishing license in Cooke City or at the Top of the World store before going after the rainbow, cutthroat, and brook trout in Beartooth Lake.

Camping

The only motel along the road from Red Lodge to Cooke City is a tiny and extremely basic place connected to the **Top of the World Store** (307/587-5368, $55–79), but there are plenty of places to pitch a tent along the Wyoming stretch of the Beartooth Highway (406/446-2103, www.fs.fed.us/r1/custer/, July–Sept., $8–11). High on the Beartooth Plateau, **Island Lake,** about 40 miles west of Red Lodge, and **Beartooth Lake,** three miles farther west, have trails leading to the many alpine lakes to the north. **Fox Creek,** seven miles east of Cooke City, and **Crazy Creek,** about three miles farther east, don't have the alpine quality of the higher campgrounds, but they are convenient and attractive wooded riverside spots.

COOKE CITY AND SILVER GATE

John Colter was the first white person in the area, leading the 19th-century parade of mountain men, traders, prospectors, and speculators. Until 1882 this was still recognized as Crow land, and relatively few whites intruded. By 1883, however, Cooke City, named after the son of a Northern Pacific financier, was a booming mine town. Gold, silver, and lead were extracted from the mountains, but because of the remoteness, the boom didn't last.

Unmined lodes remain around Cooke City, but it's still hard to get to them, and until recently the mining costs were reckoned to be too high to maintain much of an operation.

Other than occasional mining speculation and attendant high-level wheeling and dealing, Cooke City (elev. 7,651 feet) is a tourist town. There's just one street to reckon with here, and it's easy to walk from one end of it to the other. Even in the summer, when drivers spill off the Beartooth Highway, there's an easygoing rustic flavor. During the winter, when the Beartooth Highway shuts down, Cooke City is open via the road through Yellowstone Park to Gardiner. Silver Gate, three miles west of Cooke City, was established as a resort town shortly after construction of the Beartooth Highway. Together the two towns have about 140 year-round residents.

Recreation

There is some gold in the hills around Cooke City, and fortune seekers may enjoy panning in the local streams.

Beartooth Plateau Outfitters (406/838-2328 or 800/253-8545, www.beartoothoutfitters.com) runs hunting, fishing, and horse-packing trips. **Skyline Guide Service** (877/238-8885, www.flyfishyellowstone.com) also leads trips into Yellowstone Park and the Absaroka-Beartooth Wilderness Area.

For a short forest hike to a waterfall, start at the Range Riders Lodge in Silver Gate.

Northeast of Cooke City, on the edge of the Absaroka-Beartooth Wilderness, there's a **"grasshopper glacier,"** a glacier with dark bands of grasshoppers frozen into it. To reach the glacier, drive a high-clearance four-wheel drive up the LuLu Pass-Goose Lake Road (near Colter Campground). The road stops at the Absaroka-Beartooth Wilderness border. Continue on foot (or horseback) along the old road to Goose Lake, then take the trail northeast to the saddle between Sawtooth Mountain and Iceberg Peak. Turn right at the saddle and climb the first rock ridge, from which the glacier is visible on the north side of Iceberg Peak. The hike from the road's end to this point is four miles. Topographical maps of the area are available at the Cooke City Store. Hikers should prepare for harsh weather any time of year.

Snowmobile rentals are readily available in town during the long winters.

Accommodations

Most accommodations in Cooke City are older serviceable motels and cabins; they're neither fancy nor expensive. For a budget place, the **High Country Motel** (406/838-2272, www.cookecityhighcountry.com, year-round, $55–85) is very nice, with both motel rooms and cabins, including a few with kitchens. The **Alpine Motel** (406/838-2262, www.cookecityalpine.com, year-round, $75), also has well-kept rooms and a few suites. Extended families and other groups should inquire about renting cabins at **Antler's Lodge** (406/838-2432 or 866/738-2432, www.cookecityantlerslodge.com, $75–135). **(€ Elk Horn Lodge** (406/838-2332), right along the main drag of Highway 212, also has both cute kitchenette cabins ($99) and motel rooms ($84). Just east of town, **Big Moose Resort** (406/838-2393, www.bigmooseresort.com, $75–90) is the tiniest touch fancier and well off the main drag.

Down the road in Silver Gate, **Grizzly Lodge** (406/838-2219, www.yellowstonelodges.com, $50–75) has basic, but OK, cabin-style rooms right near Soda Butte Creek. The other lodgings in Silver Gate are all owned by a group of people who are working to give this tiny town some vitality without destroying its woodsy laid-back beauty. **Pine Edge Cabins** (406/838-2371, www.pineedgecabins.com,

$89–140) are open all year. The charming 1930s-era **Silver Gate Cabins** (406/838-2371, www.silver-gate-cabins.com, $72–150) all have kitchens; there are also some motel rooms here.

The only real deviation from the small motel and cabin format in the area is the **Super 8** (406/838-2070, $85) in Cooke City. If you want to stay someplace a little more modern, this is it.

Camping

Chief Joseph, Soda Butte, and **Colter** are Forest Service campgrounds (406/446-2103, www.fs.fed.us/r1/custer, July–mid-Sept., $8–9) just east of Cooke City on the Beartooth Highway.

Food

If you're dizzy from the elevation, sit on the porch of the **Beartooth Cafe** (406/838-2475, 11 A.M.–10 P.M. daily Memorial Day weekend–Sept., dinner $13–25) and gobble a burger or a sandwich ($7), stroke the town dogs, then order a beer from the impressive list of imports and microbrews. Breakfast at **The Bistro** (406/838-2160, 7 A.M.–10 P.M. daily summer, 8 A.M.–5 P.M. daily winter, dinner $12–23) is a good bet, and the French-influenced dinners are surprisingly good. Stop at the **Miner's Saloon** (406/838-2214, lunch and dinner, open year-round, $8–25) for either a beer or a full meal (try the fish tacos). The saloon is loaded with historical touches, and the food is as fresh as you'll find in remote Cooke City, where it's nearly impossible to grow a vegetable.

Yellowstone National Park

There are many reasons why Yellowstone National Park (307/344-7381, www.nps.gov/yell, $25 carload for seven-day pass, $12 per person on bicycle or foot, $20 motorcycle, $80 Interagency Annual Pass good for most federal recreation sites) is such a popular destination. First, its incredibly violent geological history left not only a giant caldera but also geysers, hot springs, and other geothermal oddities. Second, largely because it became protected as the country's first national park in 1872, the wildlife is abundant and diverse. Third, the county is just plain beautiful.

Most of the park is in Wyoming, but three of its entrances—West Yellowstone, Gardiner, and Cooke City—are in Montana. For an excellent in-depth guides to the entire park, see *Moon Yellowstone & Grand Teton* by Don Pitcher (Avalon Travel Publishing).

The park is set up for motorists—spin through a couple of loops, watch Old Faithful spew, cruise by Yellowstone Lake, peer down into Yellowstone Canyon. If you're lucky, maybe you'll see some wildlife. This is all reasonably satisfying, but perhaps not worth the veritable pilgrimages people make to Yellowstone.

There are plenty of ways to make a park visit more enriching. Classes at the **Yellowstone Association Institute** can provide focus (see below under *Information*). Read up on natural history and geology. If you're anything of an angler, bring fishing gear and pick up a fishing permit at a visitors center or ranger station. Find out from a ranger where wildlife is likely to be spotted and spend some time there with binoculars and perhaps a camera or sketchpad. Follow the trail of the Nez Percé through the park, or become obsessed with the exploits of mountain men such as John Colter.

Yellowstone Park closes for a couple of weeks early in December and from mid-March until May, but for those willing to make the effort to get in there during the winter, there's a wilder park to explore than most summertime visitors glimpse. Winter snows drive the animals down to lower elevations, where they find easier winter grazing. Snowmobiling has traditionally been a big part of winter at Yellowstone, but plans to phase it out are underway; this has precipitated lots of legal and political wrangling.

A 20-year road construction project designed to improve Yellowstone's notoriously potholed roads commenced in 2001. Much (though not all) of the work is done at night, causing regular nighttime road closures. Check with the park if you plan to drive through at night.

THE LAND

Six hundred thousand years ago, a volcano erupted from the deep magma pocket underlying Yellowstone and left an immense hole, or caldera, gaping in the central part of what is now the park. Subsequent lava flows filled the caldera, and glaciers refined the landscape, carving out Yellowstone Lake.

The Madison and Gallatin Ranges are to the west and north of Yellowstone Park's high plateau; the Absaroka Range is off to the east. South of Yellowstone, in Wyoming, the Tetons shoot to 12,000 feet.

Flora and Fauna

The wide range of habitats in Yellowstone can be broken down into ecological zones: The aquatic zone is home to trout, beavers, moose, eagles, ospreys, and otters. Low grasslands include rabbits, badgers, pronghorn, and in the winter, elk and bison. Forests contain elk, mule deer, mountain lions, and coyotes. The huge fires of 1988 have played a crucial part in the lodgepole pine's life cycle (their resinous cones require fire to release the seeds), and burned areas are now carpeted by midsummer wildflowers and a lush growth of young trees. A climax forest of Engelmann spruce and subalpine fir and areas of alpine tundra top off the park's ecological zones. Elks, deer, and bears are attracted to the edges between high meadows and forests.

SOUTH-CENTRAL MONTANA

Yellowstone National Park cannot be thought of as a distinct entity. Surrounding areas are also part of the ecosystem, and the tendency of animals to naturally walk across unnatural park boundaries can be a source of conflict. The reintroduction of wolves into Yellowstone made area ranchers famously uneasy. Wolves were exterminated in the early 1900s because of their predatory nature. Without their predation, the population of other animals in the park, notably elk, burgeoned. The reintroduction of breeding wolf packs in the park met with everything from enthusiasm to fear that wolves would make the park unsafe for children. However, the reintroduction has been a great success, and there has never been a serious wolf attack on humans in North America. The best wolf viewing is in the Lamar Valley, during the early morning hours.

HISTORY

The history of the Sheepeaters, thought to be descendants of outcast Bannock and Shoshone Indians, tells of being in the area around the Yellowstone geysers "from the beginning."

John Colter was the first white person to describe the fantastic land of fire pots and blowholes, which was soon called "Colter's Hell." The U.S. Geological Survey explored Yellowstone in 1870, which led to its establishment as the first national park in 1872. For 14 years, park superintendents and their small crews worked as virtual volunteers marking park boundaries and routing poachers and other troublemakers. In 1886 the U.S. Army took over and spent the next 30 years bringing law and order to Yellowstone. Since 1916 the rangers of the National Park Service have patrolled the park.

Over the past century, notions as to how a national park should be managed have changed considerably. Bears were once tourist attractions as they begged for food at campsites and foraged in the open garbage dumps; they are now managed to maximize their "wildness." Fire-control procedures have also changed; for the park's first 100 years, fires were suppressed. This policy was discontinued in 1972, leaving

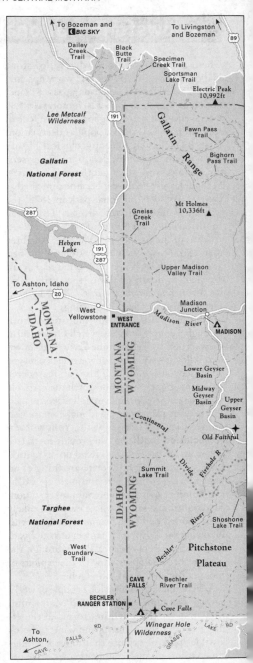

YELLOWSTONE NATIONAL PARK

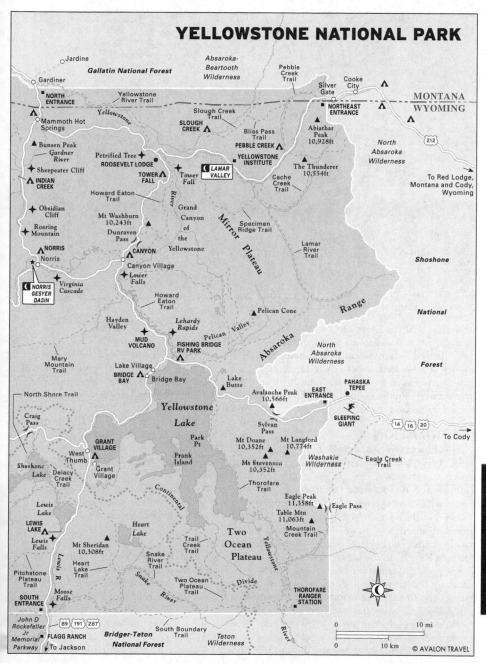

Jardine

Absaroka-
Beartooth
Wilderness

Gallatin National Forest

Pebble
Creek
Trail

Silver
Gate

Cooke
City

Gardiner

MONTANA
WYOMING

NORTH
ENTRANCE

Yellowstone
River Trail

NORTHEAST
ENTRANCE

Yellowstone

Slough Creek
Trail

212

Mammoth Hot
Springs

SLOUGH
CREEK

Bliss Pass
Trail

Abiathar
Peak
10,928ft

North
Absaroka
Wilderness

Bunsen Peak
Gardner
River

Petrified Tree
ROOSEVELT LODGE

PEBBLE CREEK

YELLOWSTONE
INSTITUTE

Sheepeater Cliff

LAMAR
VALLEY

The Thunderer
10,554ft

To Red Lodge,
Montana and Cody,
Wyoming

INDIAN
CREEK

TOWER
FALL

Tower
Fall

Cache
Creek
Trail

Obsidian
Cliff

Howard Eaton
Trail

River

Grand
Canyon

Roaring
Mountain

Mt Washburn
10,243ft

of

Specimen
Ridge Trail

Lamar
River
Trail

Shoshone

NORRIS

Dunraven
Pass

the

Mirror

Norris

CANYON

Yellowstone

National

NORRIS
GESYER
BASIN

Virginia
Cascade

Canyon Village

Plateau

Lower
Falls

Pelican Cone

Range

Howard
Eaton
Trail

Forest

Hayden
Valley

Lehardy
Rapids

Pelican Valley

North
Absaroka
Wilderness

MUD
VOLCANO

FISHING BRIDGE
RV PARK

Absaroka

Mary
Mountain
Trail

Lake Village

Lake
Butte

PAHASKA
TEPEE

North Shore Trail

BRIDGE
BAY

Bridge Bay

Avalanche Peak
10,566ft

EAST
ENTRANCE

Craig
Pass

Yellowstone

Park
Pt

Sylvan
Pass

SLEEPING
GIANT

14 16 20

Lake

GRANT
VILLAGE

Mt Doane
10,352ft

Mt Langford
10,774ft

To Cody

West
Thumb

Frank
Island

Mt Stevenson
10,352ft

Washakie
Wilderness

Eagle Creek
Trail

*Shoshone
Lake*

Delacy
Creek
Trail

Grant
Village

Thorofare
Trail

Eagle Peak
11,358ft

Eagle Pass

Lewis
Lake

Continental

Heart
Lake

Table Mtn
11,063ft

Mountain
Creek Trail

LEWIS
LAKE

Mt Sheridan
10,308ft

Trail
Creek
Trail

Two
Ocean
Plateau

Lewis
Falls

Snake
River
Trail

Yellowstone

Pitchstone
Plateau
Trail

Lewis R

Heart
Lake
Trail

Snake

Two Ocean
Plateau
Trail

Divide

THOROFARE
RANGER
STATION

SOUTH
ENTRANCE

Moose
Falls

River

River

John D
Rockefeller
Jr
Memorial
Parkway

89 191 287

FLAGG RANCH

To Jackson

**Bridger-Teton
National Forest**

South Boundary
Trail

Teton
Wilderness

0   10 mi

0   10 km

© AVALON TRAVEL

SOUTH-CENTRAL MONTANA

© JUDY JEWELL

Bison graze along the Madison River.

large stands of trees ready to fuel a wildfire. In 1988, when fires broke out, they were initially allowed to burn uncontrolled, but when hot dry weather looked unlikely to break, fire crews were sent in to the park. Ironically, the first snowfall finally quelled the fires, which burned 36 percent of the park.

INFORMATION

The **Yellowstone Association** (307/344-2293, www.yellowstoneassociation.org) sells books in park visitors centers, and it runs the **Yellowstone Association Institute,** a field school with classes ranging from Yellowstone history to wildlife photography to fly-fishing, including many day hikes and longer back-packing trips. The institute is based in the old "Buffalo Ranch" in the Lamar Valley.

For good information concerning issues affecting the entire Yellowstone ecosystem, contact the **Greater Yellowstone Coalition** (406/586-1593, www.greateryellowstone.org).

Within the park, **Xanterra** (307/344-7311, www.travelyellowstone.com) is the sole concessionaire, providing all lodging and dining.

WEST YELLOWSTONE AND VICINITY

The site of a stiff competition between nature and motel space, West Yellowstone (pop. 1,232, elev. 6,666 feet) is the west entrance to the park. Here you'll find all the tourist schlock you'd ever want to see, and experience the out-of-doors purveyed as recreation, a commodity that'll bring people here and make them spend money. But never mind. It's great country, and if mass tourism gets you down, come in the off-season (spring) and share the place with buffalo grazing on south-facing hills, huge crows, relaxed locals, and false-fronted buildings shut down until the crowds return.

Sights

Trains once brought most visitors to Yellowstone National Park, and the **Yellowstone Historic Center** (104 Yellowstone Ave., 406/646-1100, www.yellowstonehistoriccenter.org, 9 A.M.–9 P.M. daily Memorial Day–mid-Sept., 9 A.M.–6 P.M. daily mid-Sept.–mid-Oct. and mid-May–Memorial Day; $6 adults, $5 seniors, $4 children, $15 family) is housed in

© JUDY JEWELL

The Grizzly and Wolf Discovery Center in West Yellowstone is home to former "problem" bears.

the old Union Pacific Railroad Depot and has exhibits on the park's history, from those railroad days up to the regeneration following the fires of 1988. The bookstore here is worth a browse; it has a strong regional section and a good selection of field guides.

Just outside the national park entrance, a huge statue of a bear heralds the entrance to the nonprofit **Grizzly and Wolf Discovery Center** (201 S. Canyon, 406/646-7001 or 800/257-2570, www.grizzlydiscoveryctr.org, open 8 A.M.–dusk year-round, $9.75 adults, $9 seniors, $5 children 5–12). The center has gathered orphaned or "problem" bears from all over the world and confined them with fences and moats to provide a walk-through wildlife-viewing experience. The center also houses a small gray wolf pack (all of the wolves were born in captivity) in a one-acre compound. The center really does put a strong focus on education, and the animals are fascinating to watch; although it's essentially an upscale zoo, it's worth a visit if you're not in a rush to get into the park.

The **Yellowstone IMAX** theater (101 S. Canyon St., 406/646-4100, www.yellowstoneimax.com, 9 A.M.–9 P.M. daily, $9 adults, $6.50 children) features an eye-popping presentation on Yellowstone's natural history on a six-story screen. Movies start on the hour. But remember not to let the just-like-being-there quality of IMAX keep you from actually *being* in the park.

Fishing

West Yellowstone is a good hub for fishing the area's trout streams. The Madison, both in and out of the park, is the most celebrated river, but there are smaller streams worth fishing: Grayling, Duck, and Cougar Creeks, and the South Fork of the Madison. Inside the park, the Firehole River is a favorite of many anglers. Venture into nearby Idaho and try Henry's Fork of the Snake River. Fishing season gets going on Memorial Day weekend (except on Yellowstone Lake and its tributary streams, where the season opens June 15) and runs through the first Sunday of November. State fishing licenses aren't needed inside the park, but a Yellowstone fishing permit, available from any park visitors center or ranger station ($15 for three days) is required.

If you need someone to initiate you into the mysteries of fly-fishing, find a guide to be your guru. Even experienced anglers can benefit from a guide's knowledge of local conditions. They don't come cheap, however; expect to pay about $400 a day for a guided float or wading trip. **Bud Lilly's Trout Shop** (39 Madison Ave., 406/646-7801, www.budlillys.com) employs some of West Yellowstone's best guides. **Madison River Outfitters** (117 Canyon St., 406/646-9644, www.madisonriveroutfitters. com) is another good source of fishing expertise in West Yellowstone, as are **Jacklin's** (105 Yellowstone Ave., 406/646-7336, www.jacklinsflyshop.com) and **Arrick's** (37 Canyon St., 406/646-7290, www.arricks.com).

Recreation

Rent bikes from **Free Heel and Wheel** (40 Yellowstone Ave., 406/646-7744). The Rendezvous Cross-Country Ski Trails (see below in *Recreation*) are well suited to summer mountain biking. A bicycling and walking route runs along the old Union Pacific rail bed from West Yellowstone to Island Park, Idaho. When park traffic dies down in early October, the West Yellowstone Chamber of Commerce (406/646-7701, www.wyellowstone.com/bicycle) organizes a day ride to Old Faithful.

To find a horse for hire, head west on Highway 20 (the Targhee Pass Highway) toward the Idaho border. There you'll find guided rides at **Diamond P Ranch** (2865 Targhee Pass Hwy., 406/646-7246).

Winter Recreation

During the winter, the only ways into the park from this direction are via cross-country skis, snowmobile, or snowcoach. Snowcoaches, customized 10-passenger vans with treads, ferry passengers to Old Faithful and other thermal basins. **Yellowstone Alpen Guides** (555 Yellowstone Ave., 406/646-9591, www.yellowstoneguides.com, $99 adults, $89 seniors, $79 children) runs several snowcoach tours, including one with a bit of cross-country

skiing worked in. **Yellowstone Expeditions** (406/646-9333 or 800/728-9333, www.yellowstoneexpeditions.biz) runs cross-country ski, snowshoe, and snowcoach trips in the park, including multiday ski and snowshoe trips using comfy yurts as a base camp.

The **Rendezvous Cross-Country Ski Trails** (www.rendezvousskitrails.com) comprise 15 miles of trails groomed for both traditional cross-country and freestyle (skating) skiing. The trailhead is just off Yellowstone Avenue, about three blocks west of Canyon Street. Loops can be selected according to skill and stamina, and for that special Montana touch, there's a biathlon loop for gun-slinging skiers. During the summer, the mountain bikers use the Rendezvous's trails.

The **Riverside trails** start where Madison Avenue ends (at Boundary). These trails aren't as meticulously groomed as those at Rendezvous, but they offer a little more scenic punch. The trail network goes right into the park, where it runs along the Madison River. It's easy skiing, with a basic trip of about 2.5 miles. There's a good chance of seeing wildlife from these trails.

Although some restrictions have been placed on snowmobiles in Yellowstone National Park, they are still permitted. Note that reservations (307/344-7311, $10 per day per snowmobile for the first day and $3 per day for each day thereafter, does not include the $15 park entrance fee) and a valid driver's license are required, and that snowmobiles must travel in groups of at least two and no more than eleven. The West Yellowstone entrance to the park can accommodate 550 snowmobiles a day. Most of these 550 snowmobiles come in with commercial snowmobile guides, who make the necessary reservations.

Snowmobiling has long been a major wintertime activity in West Yellowstone. After years of hand-wringing about how to limit snowmobile use of Yellowstone, the park has imposed limits on the number of snowmobiles allowed in the park, and requires snowmobilers to be part of guided trips. Find a guide at **All Yellowstone Sports** (301 Madison Ave., 406/646-7656 or 800/548-9551), **Two Top Snowmobile**

Rentals (645 Gibbon Ave., 406/646-7802 or 800/522-7802, www.twotopsnowmobile.com), or **Yellowstone Adventures** (131 Dunraven St., 406/646-7735 or 800/231-5991, www.yellowstoneadventures.com). Also, many hotels and motels rent snowmobiles; ask when you make reservations. Expect snowmobile rentals to run $115–150 per day, with an additional $40 or so guide fee.

Events

The **Rendezvous Marathon Ski Race** is held early in March. A winter festival has sprung up around this event, which is shortly followed by the **World Snowmobile Expo.** The spring months, when the park is closed for road plowing, are relatively quiet in West Yellowstone. During the first two weeks of April, Yellowstone's roads are open to bicycle and pedestrian traffic but not to cars. Everything is usually up and going again by mid-April.

Entertainment

The **Playmill Theater** (29 Madison Ave., 406/646-7757, $15, reservations recommended) runs family-oriented shows on summer evenings.

Accommodations

West Yellowstone Central Reservations (406/646-7077 or 888/646-7077, www.yellowstonereservation.com) can book you into anything ranging from an RV park to a fancy hotel. Most of West's "downtown" motels are family-run places that have been around for years. Some of the smaller places shut down in the winter; others have lower winter rates.

Under $50: The most distinctive budget rooms in town are the hostel rooms at the **Madison Hotel** (139 Yellowstone, 406/646-7745 or 800/838-7745, www. madisonhotelmotel.com, Memorial Day–Oct. 5), a log-hewn cross between an old downtown hotel and a youth hostel built in 1912 and relatively little changed since then. Hostel rooms provide bunks at $28, while private rooms are $49 d. The rooms at the adjacent Madison Motel are less charming but equipped with TVs and

bathrooms, and run $85 and up. (Check-in for both locations is in the gift shop.)

The **Gallatin National Forest** (406/823-6961) rents rustic (no electricity or bathrooms) cabins for $30 per night at Beaver Creek, Cabin Creek, and Basin Station.

$50-100: Moving up the scale a bit, the small and centrally located **Alpine Motel** (120 Madison Ave., 406/646-7544, www.alpinemotelwestyellowstone.com, May–Oct., $74 and up) offers basic rooms (no phones) near the park entrance. In the same area is **City Center Motel** (214 Madison Ave., 800/742-0665, www. yellowstonevacations.com, $79 and up). The same folks run the **Pony Express Motel** (at Firehole St. and Boundary St., 800/323-9708, www.yellowstonevacations.com, $59 and up), a simple budget motel on a side street close to the park; pets are accepted here.

The **Lazy G** (123 Hayden St., 406/646-7586, www.lazygmotel.com, $56 and up), located on a quiet street a few blocks off the main drag, has in-room refrigerators and an outdoor eating area with a gas grill and picnic tables.

Set just off a busy street, the **Yellowstone Inn** (601 Hwy. 20, 406/646-7633 or 800/858-9224, www.yellowstoneinn.net, $80–136) is a small inn with nicely decorated cabin-style units. Pets are allowed here.

Moose Creek Cabins (220 Firehole Ave., 406/646-9546, www.moosecreekcabin.com, $89–151) has cute older log cabins with kitchenettes, cable TV, hookups for X-Box or Playstation and DVD players, dining area, and sitting area; larger units are available to house families.

Three Bear Lodge (217 Yellowstone Ave., 406/646-7353 or 800/646-7353, www.threebearlodge.com, $95 and up) is a popular motel with a pool.

Over $100: At the **Hibernation Station** (212 Gray Wolf Ave., 406/646-4200 or 800/580-3557, www.hibernationstation.com, $109 and up), modern log cabins with faux-rustic log furniture are clustered tightly together. Cabins range from small sleeping cabins to multiroom cabins with kitchens.

For comfortable rooms in a newer motel, the **Yellowstone Lodge** (251 S. Electric St., 406/646-0200 or 877/239-9298, www.yellowstonelodge.com, $99 and up) is a good bet. It's a few blocks from downtown, near the Rendezvous ski trails, and has an indoor pool. The **Stage Coach Inn** (209 Madison Ave., 406/646-7381 or 800/842-2882, www.yellowstoneinn.com, $116) is a West Yellowstone classic with a historic lodge atmosphere and a great lobby. There's a hot tub and sauna here, and during the winter it's a hub for snowcoach tours.

One of West Yellowstone's most upscale lodgings is **((West Yellowstone Conference Hotel & Holiday Inn Sunspree Resort** (315 Yellowstone Ave., 406/646-7365 or 800/646-7365, www.yellowstoneholidayinn.com, $181). Facilities include an indoor pool, sauna, hot tub, and exercise room; there are several two-bedroom units, plus a restaurant and lounge. All rooms have coffeemakers, microwaves, and refrigerators.

Camping

The campgrounds in the town of West Yellowstone are mostly for RVs, although **Rustic Wagon RV Park** (637 Hwy. 20 W., 406/646-7387, $36–40 RV, $29 tent), **Wagon Wheel RV Park** (408 Gibbon Ave., 406/646-7872, $36–40 RV, $29 tent), and **Hideaway RV Park** (320 Electric St., 406/646-9049, $28–32 RV, $18.50 tent) reserve some space for tent campers. The Rustic Wagon and the Wagon Wheel also has cabins for rent (about $60).

Bakers Hole (Hebgen Lake Ranger Station, 406/823-6961, www.fs.fed.us/r1/gallatin, mid-May–mid-Sept., $14) is the closest public campground to West Yellowstone. It's just three miles north of town on Highway 191. Blue herons nest on the Madison River just across from the campground.

Food

Start your day with the friendly folks at **Mocha Mamma's** (40 Yellowstone, 406/646-7744, 9 A.M.–6 P.M.), a coffee bar located in the Freeheel and Wheel bike shop. If you want a full breakfast, the **Running Bear Pancake House** (538 Madison Ave., 406/646-7703, 7 A.M.–2 P.M. daily, $5–8) is a longtime local favorite, with great filling breakfasts.

Head toward the back of the **Book Peddler** (106 Canyon St., 406/646-9358, 7:30 A.M.–10 P.M., $2–8), where soup and sandwiches, pastries, and espresso are served in a friendly relaxing atmosphere. For a good to-go deli sandwich, swing by **Ernie's Deli** (406 Hwy. 20, 406/646-9467, $6). Another good breakfast or lunch spot is **((Uncle Laurie's Riverside Café** (237 Hwy. 20, 406/646-7040, 7 A.M.–4 P.M. Mon.–Sat., box lunches $8.50) a laid-back place at the corner of Electric Avenue and Highway 20.

West's best dinners—indeed the only ones that don't have a mass-preparation feel to them—are at **((Sydney's Mountain Bistro** (38 Canyon St., 406/646-7660, 11 A.M.–9 P.M. daily, $3–32), a small place with good pasta, excellent steaks, and a good selection of wine.

Find the local brewpub, **Wolf Pack Brewing Co.**, in the Best Western Desert Inn (139 Canyon Ave., 406/646-7725, noon–8 P.M. daily, sandwiches $8). Their specialty is German-style lagers, which go well with the pub's bratwursts.

Step out onto the main drag for the slowly cooked meats from **Beartooth Barbeque** (111 Canyon Ave., 406/646-4252, 11 A.M.–9 P.M., $10–20).

Even when everything else is closed in town, you'll probably be able to get dinner at **Bullwinkle's** (119 Madison Ave., 406/646-7974, 10 A.M.–2 A.M., $6–28), a saloon and restaurant with a wide-ranging menu, a surprising number of good wines by the glass, and several Montana beers on tap.

The best pizza in town is at **((Wild West Pizzeria** (14 Madison Ave., 406/646-4400, 11 A.M.–9 P.M., most meals about $10); they also serve pasta and sandwiches.

Information and Services

The **chamber of commerce** (30 Yellowstone Ave., 406/646-7701, www.westyellowstone-chamber.com) has the expected array of brochures and a friendly staff. During the summer, rangers from **Yellowstone National Park** have an outpost in the chamber of commerce information center. The **Hegben Lake Ranger Station,** just north of West Yellowstone on Highway 191 (406/646-7369, www.fs.fed.us/r1/gallatin) can provide information on the nearby Gallatin National Forest. **Gallatin National Forest Avalanche Center** (406/587-6981, www.mtavalanche.com) posts daily avalanche reports outside the post office during the winter.

Find a **medical clinic** (406/646-7668) at 236 Yellowstone Avenue.

Transportation

West Yellowstone Airport is open during the summer, but it's often easier (and cheaper) to fly in to Bozeman and rent a car there. **Karst Stage** (406/388-6404 or 800/517-8243, $94 and up one-way, reservations required) runs a shuttle between the Bozeman airport and West Yellowstone.

To rent a car in West, contact **Big Sky Car Rental** (415 Yellowstone Ave., 406/646-9564 or 800/426-7669). **Budget** (406/646-7882 or 800/231-5991) has an office at the airport.

Buffalo Bus Lines (406/646-9564 or 800/426-7669, from $58 adult, $45 child) runs tours through the park.

MADISON JUNCTION

From West Yellowstone, follow the Madison River into the park. This is one of Yellowstone's premier fishing areas—the warm water of the Firehole River joins the cooler Gibbon River at Madison Junction, providing an ideal trout habitat.

Between Madison Junction and Norris Geyser Basin, the road follows the Gibbon River. Stop at 84-foot **Gibbon Falls.** Like Madison Junction, the falls perch on the edge of the main Yellowstone caldera.

◖ NORRIS GEYSER BASIN

Yellowstone's most spectacular and changeable thermal area, Norris Geyser Basin may not be as well known as Old Faithful, but it's far more atmospheric and a better place

to actually hike past numerous geysers and boiling pools.

Norris is situated over the junction of two major faults (one that runs down from Mammoth Hot Springs and another coming over from Hebgen Lake). These crustal cracks provide conduits for heat to rise to the earth's surface. Steam vents, hot springs, and geysers are all manifestations of this surface heat.

Sights

Between 1886 and 1916, when the army ran Yellowstone, some troops were based at the remote Norris outpost. The old Soldier Station has been renovated and now houses the **Museum of the National Park Ranger.** History buffs and fans of rustic architecture will enjoy this stop, but for most people, time is better spent hiking around the geyser basin.

Pick up a map of Norris's trail system and strike out through steam clouds, whiffs of sulfur, spurts of water, and brilliantly colored mineral deposits. Because the landscape here is relatively malleable, the map and signposts may not include all of the current thermal activity, but this unpredictability is part of Norris's charm. Be careful, stay on the trail, but do explore at least one of the two loops.

The path around **Porcelain Basin** is less than one mile long but has expansive pale (porcelain-hued) views of terraced hot springs and geysers. The more forested **Back Basin** loop is about 1.5 miles long and passes a near-boiling pure green spring that takes its color from the combination of the blue spring water and the yellow sulfur of the basin wall. **Steamboat Geyser,** which has rare 300-foot-high eruptions (and more frequent minor spurts), is also on the Back Basin loop.

Camping

There is a park campground across the road from **Norris Geyser Basin** (mid-May–Sept., $14) and another one between Norris and West Yellowstone at **Madison Junction** (reservations available at 866/439-7375, May–Oct., $18.50) Between Norris and Mammoth, there's camping at **Indian Creek** (mid-June–mid-Sept., $12).

MAMMOTH HOT SPRINGS AND VICINITY

The grand arch leading into Yellowstone from Gardiner, dedicated by Theodore Roosevelt in 1903, was the original entrance to the park and is still the only entrance open to cars year-round.

Elks winter around Mammoth, spending much of their time, it seems, in the hotel parking lot.

Sights

Stop by the **visitors center** for an overview, a movie, and, if necessary, fishing or backcountry permits. Schedules for ranger-led hikes and discussions are also available.

A boardwalk climbs the terraced hot pools. The pools are not static; as the flow of hot groundwater through limestone changes, so do the formations. Groundwater combines with burps of carbon dioxide from underground magma to form carbonic acid, which dissolves limestone. Limey carbonated water emerges from the ground at Mammoth Hot Springs, and the lime is deposited as travertine. Thermophilic bacteria and algae live in the hot water, tinting the white travertine with their brilliant colors. Pick up a brochure at the foot of the trail to take the self-guided tour of the springs. Take care to stay on the boardwalk; the hot pools are frequently boiling hot, and they may have very thin crusts around them. People and animals have died in thermal pools.

The U.S. Army was the park's original overseer, and its headquarters, Fort Yellowstone, is behind the visitors center. It has been used as the **National Park Service Headquarters** for the park since 1918.

During the summer, the Mammoth campground amphitheater is the site of nightly **talks by park rangers**.

For a roadside glimpse of the park, try Xanterra's **bus tour of the Grand Loop** (307/344-7311, www.travelyellowstone.com, $63 adults, $31.50 ages 8–15). Call ahead or sign up at the activities desk in the Mammoth Hotel; buses leave at 8:30 A.M. daily. Xanterra also offers tours in historic yellow buses (no, not school buses); from Mammoth they go across the Beartooth Highway ($87 adults, $43.50 age 15 and under), across the park's northern edge to the Roosevelt corrals for a stagecoach ride ($44 adults, $22 age 15 and under), and on several other wildlife-spotting tours.

Midway between Mammoth and Tower Junction, the **Blacktail Plateau** offers both a scenic drive and hiking trails. Follow the dirt road through grasslands and along a stretch of the old Bannock Trail, used by the Bannock Indians to cross from present-day Idaho to the eastern plains.

Mammoth's steaming pools and ghostly white terraces are particularly appealing in the winter, when it's not unusual to see elk lying in the hot pools. **Snowcoach tours** (307/344-7311, www.travelyellowstone.com, around $100) leave Mammoth and head to Old Faithful.

Recreation

Hot springs empty into the Gardiner River at the 45th parallel, and this is one place where hot springs bathing is sanctioned. The parking lot is just over the state line in Montana. It's about a five-minute walk down the path to the springs, which are officially open 8 A.M.–6 P.M. Remember to bring a bathing suit.

Register for **trail rides** at the Mammoth Hotel activities desk. A one-hour ride costs $35.

During the winter, the Mammoth Hotel rents **ice skates** and **cross-country skis.** Guided ski tours are available, as is a snowcoach shuttle service to other areas of the park.

Accommodations

Mammoth Hot Springs Hotel (307/344-7311, www.travelyellowstone.com, mid-May–mid-Oct. and mid-Dec.–early Mar.) has both hotel rooms (starting at $115 with bath, $85 without) and cabins ($107 with bath, $75 without). As in all national park lodges, the rooms are fairly simple, with no TVs, telephones, air conditioning, or WiFi.

Camping

The campground at Mammoth is small by

local standards—only 85 sites. It's open year-round and costs $14 per night, but no reservations are taken. Showers are available for a couple of bucks at the Mammoth hotel.

Food

Mammoth Hot Springs Hotel Dining Room (6:30–10 A.M., 11:30 A.M.–2 P.M., 5–10 P.M. daily, $13–29) is a *relatively* fancy restaurant open during the hotel's summer and winter seasons (during winter, dinner service ends at 8 P.M.). Dinners are pretty good, but not exactly memorable. Although many visitors chow down on the breakfast buffet ($10), the menu items are tastier. The **Terrace Grill** (6:30–10 A.M., 11:30 A.M.–2 P.M., 5–10 P.M. daily May–mid-Oct.) is in the same complex, and the atmosphere is decidedly casual. The **Mammoth General Store** offers basic foodstuffs year-round. Remember, you didn't come to Yellowstone for a culinary experience.

Information and Services

General park information is dispensed at the **visitors center** in Mammoth (307/344-2263).

The **Mammoth Hot Springs Clinic** (307/344-7965) is near the visitors center.

The main Yellowstone **post office** is to the side of the Park Service administration building in Mammoth. Foreign currency can be exchanged at the front desk of any Yellowstone hotel.

TOWER JUNCTION AND VICINITY

Tower Junction is where the Mammoth–Cooke City road is joined by the road to Yellowstone Canyon. There's a small settlement here: a ranger station, a lodge with cabins, and a campground three miles south at Tower Falls.

Tower Falls

The falls, nestled into a rocky gorge, are a popular sight. A more meditative viewing is often afforded by taking the short but steep hike to the bottom. Bannock Indians found a safe place to cross the Yellowstone River just above the falls; it's now referred to as Bannock Ford.

Lamar Valley

Elks and bison winter in the Lamar Valley, east of Tower Junction. Coyotes are also commonly spotted jogging across the valley floor, and this is usually the best place in the park to see wolves. The wolves, which were reintroduced into Yellowstone in 1995, now number about 270, and several packs frequent Lamar Valley. Get up *early* if you really want to see a wolf (dawn is the best viewing time) and be aware that the local wolves are way larger than the more common coyotes and range in color from almost blond to jet-black. Bring along a spotting scope or a good pair of binoculars and considering enrolling in a field seminar with the Yellowstone Association Institute (307/344-2293, http://yellowstoneassociation.org/institute), which bases its classes on Yellowstone's wolves in the Lamar Valley; lodging is available for course participants in simple guest cabins.

Recreation

The **Buffalo Plateau Trail** swings north of the park into Montana on its 21-mile run from the trailhead three miles west of Tower Junction to Slough Creek Campground. It's best to wait until late July for this hike because the varied terrain includes Slough Creek, which can be difficult to cross when it's carrying lots of water. **Slough Creek Campground** is also the trailhead for an 11-mile hike (or wintertime cross-country ski trip) up Slough Creek to the northern edge of the park. Hikers should also check with park rangers to learn about current trail conditions.

In the winter, the road to Tower Falls becomes a **cross-country ski trail.** A private viewing of the falls is worth the three-mile, generally uphill slog.

Specimen Ridge, southeast of Tower Junction, is home to a petrified forest—in fact, petrified forests are stacked deep in this area. The mud and ash coughed up by volcanoes provided soil on which new trees could grow, only to be covered when the next volcano erupted. Erosion has uncovered some of the top layers; it's conjectured that 44 layers of forest exist. Naturalists lead day-long hikes on Specimen Ridge during July and August; details are available at any park visitors center.

Accommodations

Prices at **Roosevelt Lodge** (307/344-7331, www.travelyellowstone.com) start at $67 for a rustic cabin without a bath; a cabin with a bath is $112. Roosevelt's season is short—early June through August. There's an emphasis on things Western here: Stagecoach rides leave several times a day for a half-hour tour ($9.50 adults, $7.65 children), and cookouts at nearby Yancey's Hole involve a horseback or church-wagon journey (see below under *Food*).

Camping

Nearby campgrounds include **Tower Falls,** open late May to mid-September; **Slough Creek,** open late May through October; and **Pebble Creek,** open mid-June to early September, $12, no reservations accepted.

Food

If you want a meal that's longer on experience than on cuisine, try the **Old West Dinner Cookout** (307/344-7311 or 866/439-7375). Jump on a horse or climb into a church wagon at Roosevelt Lodge and ride to Yancey's Hole for a slab of steak and other picnic fare. Dinner and an hour-long horseback ride cost $66 ($56 children 8–11). Wagon riders pay $55 ($45 for children).

The **Roosevelt Lodge** (7–10:30 A.M., 11:30 A.M.–3 P.M., 5–9 P.M., early June–Aug., dinner $15–25) prides itself on the ribs and baked beans served at its family-style restaurant.

BILLINGS AND SOUTHEASTERN MONTANA

Southeastern Montana is the most "Western" of Montana's regions. Historically, it is the West of the early trapper and hunter and of the clash between Indian and infantry. It was the Montana of the cattle drover and the great cattle barons. Today, it is still home to thousands of American Indians, and it is still unashamedly cowboy country.

However, in times gone by, all this land was once beachfront property. It's hard to believe, looking at the dry and dusty buttes and rolling prairies of southeastern Montana, that amphibious dinosaurs and palm trees were once native to this area. For millions of years this was the shoreline of vast inland seas. Southeastern Montana's most distinctive geologic formations—badlands, prairies, and sandstone bluffs, as well as the coal

and oil they mask—all date from a primeval maritime past.

The Yellowstone River is the locus of the entire region. As the river moves eastward through the prairies, it picks up the waters of three major southerly tributaries: the Bighorn, the Tongue, and the Powder. As it discharges into the Missouri, the Yellowstone is the largest free-flowing river in the United States.

As the principal avenue of entry and exit in Montana during the pioneer days, the Yellowstone took out the region's wealth of furs, brought in soldiers, and transported cattle and sheep to eastern markets. Towns like Miles City, Glendive, and Billings grew up on its banks as railroads extended up the valley. Within memory, ranchers on the "North Side," up to Jordan country, and on the "South Side,"

HIGHLIGHTS

◖ Billings Historic District: Once the center of Billings, the old hotels and storefronts on Montana Avenue were largely derelict until reborn as art galleries and upscale night clubs (page 276).

◖ Yellowstone Art Museum: This regional art museum features part of the fabulous Bair art collection, plus a shop for local crafts (page 277).

◖ Pictograph Cave State Monument: Prehistoric Native Americans etched figures onto cave walls at this archaeological site overlooking Billings (page 279).

◖ Pompey's Pillar National Monument: In 1806 the Corps of Discovery climbed this bluff, and William Clark carved his name in the rock (page 285).

◖ Range Riders Museum: This museum tells the story of Miles City from Custer-era fort to cow capital of the West (page 289).

◖ Makoshika State Park: This badlands park preserves a stark wilderness of gumbo buttes, eroded rock, and prehistoric fossils (page 293).

◖ Carter County Museum: This museum has a significant collection of dinosaur fossils, collected locally by Ekalaka's longtime high school science teacher (page 301).

◖ Medicine Rocks State Park: The eerie sandstone promontories at this park were sacred to the native Indians of the prairies (page 303).

◖ Little Bighorn Battlefield National Monument: One of the country's epochal battles, the Battle of the Little Bighorn is recounted here in chilling detail (page 311).

◖ Horseshoe Bend: The Bighorn River trenches a 1,000-foot-deep canyon through underlying limestone (page 321).

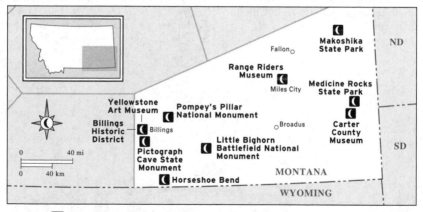

LOOK FOR ◖ TO FIND RECOMMENDED SIGHTS, ACTIVITIES, DINING, AND LODGING.

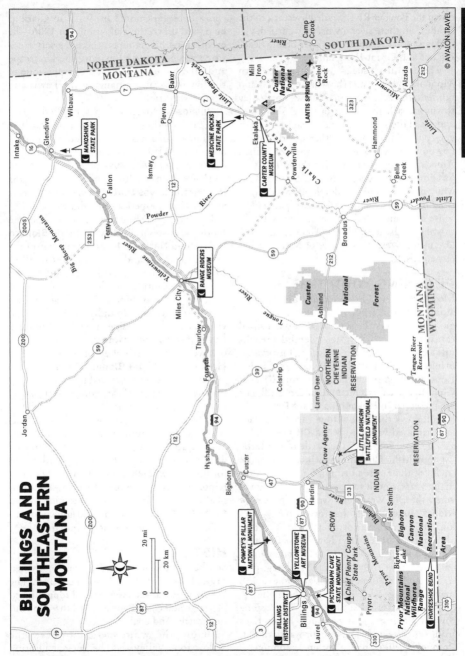

SOUTHEASTERN MONTANA

© AVALON TRAVEL

BILLINGS AND
SOUTHEASTERN
MONTANA

down the Powder River, trailed livestock to the "Valley." In these river towns, they partied, visited, and stocked up on groceries before heading out to their far-flung ranches.

The dominant social unit in southeastern Montana today is still the working ranch and family farm, and the same Yellowstone Valley towns are still the center of trade, shopping, and social life. This is about as real as the West gets, but it's not a Western theme park. Today, cowboys are stockmen, Indians are Native Americans, and the spirit of the Wild West has grown up into agribusiness. Southeastern Montana is not a highly developed tourist destination, but for the traveler with patience, a sense of humor, and an interest in wildlife, pristine landscapes, Native America, and the lore of the West, this corner of Montana has few equals.

PLANNING YOUR TIME

Most travelers will explore southeast Montana along I-90 and I-94, which traverse the region. I-94 enters the state at **Wibaux,** a small ranch town with a rather splendid French-influenced stone church and a long history that brings together French noblemen and Teddy Roosevelt. I-94 meets the Yellowstone River at Glendive, where scenic and austere badlands are preserved in **Makoshika State Park.** I-94 then follows the Yellowstone through a badland-rimmed valley to **Miles City.** Founded as a military fort after the Battle of the Little Bighorn, Miles City was the center of the cattle trade for the entire northern Great Plains for many years, and it's still unabashedly a town where the Old West spirit lives on. The **Range Riders Museum** tells the story of the region's long and eventful history. The Wild West isn't all history in Miles City: Late May's **Bucking Horse Sale** is a cross between a rodeo and a bacchanal that truly brings the cowboy spirit to life. A clutch of new hotels at I-94 exit 138 makes this a good spot to spend the night.

As I-94 passes west along the Yellowstone toward Billings, a flat-topped butte rises from the irrigated fields of corn and alfalfa. **Pompey's Pillar,** now a national monument,

was a landmark noted by William Clark as he passed down the Yellowstone in 1806—he even carved his name on the hill's soft sandstone walls. Stop and explore the landscape and hike to view Clark's autograph—one of the few physical remnants of the Lewis and Clark Expedition.

Billings is Montana's largest city and a good base for exploring southeastern Montana. The downtown area has several good restaurants, busy watering holes, and cultural institutions like the **Yellowstone Art Museum** and the **Western Heritage Center.** Just outside of Billings is **Pictograph Caves State Park,** which preserve ancient Native American cave drawings.

I-90 enters southeastern Montana from the south and passes just below the **Little Bighorn Battlefield National Monument.** One of the most disturbing and resonant sites in all of Montana, the battlefield has a good visitors center and historic drives that interpret the calamitous events of June 1876. The actual battle site still feels profoundly haunted. If you visit in late June, consider attending **Custer's Last Stand Reenactment,** the centerpiece of a weekend's worth of events in and around Hardin called **Little Bighorn Days.**

Between the routes carved by I-94 and I-90 lies the extreme southeast corner of the state, a land of vast ranches and Indian reservations. Worthy of a road trip, this is a landscape of far-flung rural communities, pine-fringed buttes, and wildlife—large populations of grouse, deer, and antelope make this a popular spot for hunters. **Ekalaka,** one of the state's most remote towns, is also one of the most authentically Western. It's also near **Medicine Rocks State Park,** a landscape of sandstone promontories that were sacred to local Indians.

HISTORY

Southeastern Montana's history is closely tied to the history of the Yellowstone River. The Yellowstone was the avenue that brought in explorers, soldiers, and settlers, and that took out furs, cattle, and coal.

Before the white man, however, the Yellowstone Valley was the ancient hunting

WHEN THE BUFFALO ROAMED

The buffalo, or the American bison (*Bison bison*), as it is properly known, once ranged over most of the North American continent. Between Pennsylvania and the Continental Divide, and from the lower Mississippi and the Arkansas River north to the northern Alberta border, these shaggy members of the cattle family roamed over 40 percent of the continent in herds of up to a million animals. They were migratory creatures, following the seasons north and south.

Eastern Montana was ideal buffalo country, no matter what season. Huge herds that summered on the Canadian plains moved south to winter on the Montana prairies, while equally numerous herds from the grasslands of Colorado and Wyoming migrated north to summer on the plains of Montana. Perhaps as many as 60 million of these animals once roamed the continent, and as many as four million lived in Montana alone.

As previously agricultural Indians entered Montana from the east, the vast herds of buffalo soon changed the lifestyle of the Native Americans. Bison had always been an element of the Indian culture, but when the Indians were forced onto the plains, the buffalo's importance altered.

In ways that are difficult to imagine today, the buffalo provided the means of life for the early Plains Indians. The hide provided tepee coverings and leather for moccasins; the flesh was eaten fresh in season and also preserved for later consumption (steaks from the hump were delicacies). The bones were used to create tools, from bone-splinter awls (with buffalo sinew for thread) to shoulder-blade hoes. Dried manure was used in campfires. Even the dried tail was used – as a flyswatter.

Before the introduction of horses and firearms, the Indians hunted buffalo with bow and arrow, often using buffalo "jumps" or *pishkuns*. The unsuspecting animals were stampeded off cliffs in large herds, after which the tribe harvested the dead and wounded. When the rifle and the horse met on the plains of Montana, the destruction of the vast herds began in earnest.

The development of new tanning techniques in the East allowed tanners to turn dried buffalo hides into soft marketable leather, changing forever the lives of the prairie Indians. In the 1840s most of the fur-bearing mammals of the West had been trapped out; by the 1860s and 1870s the great buffalo hunt was on. Waves of new white settlers (many displaced by the Civil War) moved west and joined the slaughter. Entire herds were completely wiped out in the course of a summer, as sharpshooters picked off the animals while they grazed. The animals were skinned, the hides shipped east by steamboat or rail, and the carcasses left to rot. Areas of the northern plains were white with bleached bones where the large herds had been slaughtered, and as the buffalo became scarce, a trade developed in dried buffalo bones, used for fertilizers.

By 1884 the buffalo was effectively extinct in the United States. In 1908, when the government created the National Bison Range near Moiese in northwestern Montana, it was stocked mostly with animals from Canada.

As the buffalo passed, so did the life of the Plains Indian founded on the buffalo. The basis for a nomadic warrior society was gone, leaving the Indians with no source of food, shelter, or support – except the U.S. government.

grounds for Native Americans, especially the Crow Nation. The valleys of the Yellowstone and the rivers that feed it were rich with game and furs, and the prairies that adjoined the rivers teemed with buffalo. As the Sioux and Cheyenne were forced into this corner of Montana, fierce intertribal rivalries flared.

The Yellowstone was not explored by whites until 1806, during Lewis and Clark's return voyage. Clark and his party floated most of the way down the river in dugout canoes. Upon reaching the confluence with the Missouri, he noted that because of the enormous abundance of game along the Yellowstone, the valley would be advantageous for a trading fort.

Within a year, at the mouth of the Bighorn, near present-day Custer, traders erected the territory's first structures. Beginning with Fort Ramon, established by Manuel Lisa in 1807 and named after his infant son, and soon followed by other forts, this location drew adventurers and frontiersmen who came to trade, trap, and explore the wilderness.

The list of those who passed through these forts reads like a who's who of the early West: Jim Bridger, Father De Smet, John Bozeman. The mouth of the Bighorn River was traditionally the head of navigation for steamboats on the Yellowstone River.

Soon after, white settlers moved in to exploit the rich Yellowstone country, and others, with gold prospecting in western Montana on their minds, followed the Bozeman Trail north to the Yellowstone Valley across Sioux and Cheyenne tribal land. The resulting conflicts with these tribes generated some of the most famous battles of the western Indian Wars, including the Battle of the Little Bighorn.

The eradication of the buffalo and the incarceration of the Indians left the prairies empty, but by 1880 huge herds of Texas cattle filled the "open range." The Northern Pacific Railway pressed up the Yellowstone Valley at the same time, bringing in settlers and establishing trade centers like Billings and Miles City. Homesteaders replaced cattle barons, but they made only a tentative impact on this vast and arid, almost hostile and ungiving, land.

The coal and oil development at the end of the 20th century has done as much to change the landscape and character of southeastern Montana as a century of agriculture.

RECREATION

Southeastern Montana lacks the mountainous terrain of western Montana but many outdoor enthusiasts return year after year to enjoy its wide-open spaces. In fact, in many smaller communities, the fall hunting season is the busiest tourist season.

Hunting and Fishing

Southeastern Montana is a hunter's dream. Trophy-size mule deer haunt brushy coulees, and game birds such as pheasant and wild turkeys are abundant. Obtaining hunting access is relatively easy. The Department of Fish, Wildlife, and Parks's Region 7, which encompasses most of southeastern Montana, has the state's highest number of landowners signed up in the Block Management Program. The program opens and maintains access to 3.2 million acres of private land for recreational purposes. (A list of participating farmers and ranchers is available from the Department of Fish, Wildlife, and Parks office in Miles City.) An increasing number of ranchers run outfitting and guide services.

As the Yellowstone River winds through its wooded valley, it attracts anglers with its wealth of walleye, northern pike, smallmouth bass, ling, channel catfish, the occasional trout, and sauger. The river's lower reaches, especially near Glendive and Sidney, are home to the paddlefish. Public fishing sites on the Yellowstone are plentiful because the Department of Fish, Wildlife, and Parks is in the process of locating access areas every 12 miles along the river.

For trout fishers, the Bighorn River is the real news in southeastern Montana; below Yellowtail Dam, the Bighorn becomes one of the state's best trout-fishing areas, and Yellowtail Dam in the Bighorn Canyon has got to be one of the most awe-inspiring brown trout and walleye holes in the West. Because much of the Bighorn flows through the Crow

Reservation, access is limited. The upper reaches of the Tongue River also provide good trout fishing.

Agate Hunting

The moss agates of the Yellowstone Valley are known around the world for their quality. Starting at the mouth of the Bighorn and continuing to its confluence with the Missouri, the Yellowstone passes through gravel beds rich with the semiprecious stones. It takes a trained eye to spot the yellowish matte exterior of an agate in the rough, but often the jostling of the river will have chipped the surface, and its translucent interior will be visible. Stop at a fishing-access area or along a bridge to search for agates. The **Glendive Chamber of Commerce** also offers guided boat tours on the Yellowstone specifically tailored for agate hunters.

INFORMATION

For general information on southeastern Montana, request the **Custer Country**

Regional Tour Guide (800/346-1876, www. custer.visitmt.com).

Reach the **Custer National Forest offices** at P.O. Box 2556, Billings, MT 59103 (406/657-6361). The regional **Department of Fish, Wildlife, and Parks** office is at 2300 Lake Elmo Drive in Billings (406/247-2940).

Getting There and Around

Billings has the largest airport in Montana, with service from Delta (SkyWest), United, Alaska/Horizon, and Northwest. With the 2008 closing of Big Sky Airlines, air service to other Southeast Montana communities has been curtailed; check to determine if **Great Lakes Airlines** (www.greatlakesav.com) has picked up the routes, as rumored at press time. You'll need an automobile to travel off the interstate in southeastern Montana. **Rimrock Stages** (800/255-7655, www.rimrocktrailways.com) offers once-daily east-west service to the major towns along I-94 and south toward Denver on I-90.

Billings

Billings (elev. 3,117 feet) is Montana's largest city, with a population of more than 130,000 in the greater urban area. Billings's physical setting is striking: The Rimrocks—sandstone cliffs several hundred feet high—ring the city; from them, five mountain ranges are visible. The Yellowstone Valley here is wide and green. Billings is primarily a sales and trade center, with some oil refining and energy generation enlivening its economy.

Billings makes much of being the largest city in the vector north of Denver and between Spokane and Minneapolis, and boasts of being the capital of the "Midland Empire," a vague principality consisting of eastern Montana, northern Wyoming, the western Dakotas, and on an expansive day maybe even some of Canada's prairie provinces. Certainly, to judge by the license plates at the stockyards or at one of the shopping malls, Billings is the service

center for much of the northern plains. It's a city that is proud of its comparative wealth and growth, and as the center of a vast agricultural area, it has a strong sense of purpose and vitality.

Billings is also home to two institutions of higher learning. The state's oldest, Rocky Mountain College, was founded in 1878. Rocky Mountain, affiliated with the United Methodist and Presbyterian Churches and the United Church of Christ, has 800 students. Montana State University at Billings, formerly Eastern Montana College, offers two- and four-year degrees to some 4,500 students.

TOURS OF BILLINGS

Get an entertaining overview of Billings's sights taking the two-hour **Fun Express Bus** (406/254-7180 or 888/618-4386, www.montanafunadventures.com, 10:30, 11:30 A.M.,

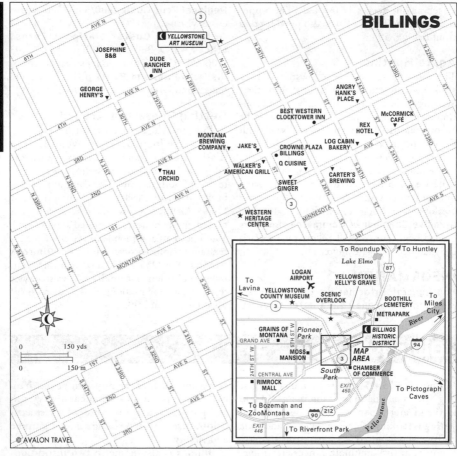

12:30 P.M. Mon.–Sat., June–Sept., call for winter hours, $20 adult, $15 students and military, $10 ages 6–12, under 6 free). Stops include historic downtown Billings, Black Otter Trail on the Rimrocks, Boot Hill, and several museums. Arrange pickup from your hotel or meet at the Moss Mansion (914 Division St.). In addition to the standard introduction tour, daily van tours include options such as tours of local brewpubs, hat makers, and chocolatiers. In summer, guided tours are also offered to Little Bighorn Battlefield, Lewis and Clark sites, and other destinations in southeast Montana.

DOWNTOWN BILLINGS
◖ Billings Historic District

The Billings Historic District stretches along Montana Avenue from 23rd to 26th Streets. Here, paralleling the old Northern Pacific tracks, is the heart of old Billings. Late-19th-century hotels and commercial buildings crowd in around themselves, and although the area is still filled with local color, so to speak, it's also filled with galleries, music clubs, and interesting restaurants. The bar and restaurant at the **Rex Hotel,** once frequented by Buffalo Bill Cody, is a major island of gentrification, as are the newly refurbished Northern Pacific

© BILL MCRAE

Historic Montana Avenue is once again a hotspot for bars and restaurants.

Railway depot buildings. Other old hotels have been converted to art galleries, and others to jazz clubs and martini bars. This is one of the most diverse areas in Billings, which is otherwise a pretty conformist city.

Western Heritage Center

The Western Heritage Center (2822 Montana Ave., 406/256-6809, www.ywhc.org, 10 A.M.–5 P.M. Tues.–Sat., 1–5 P.M. Sun., adults $3, students and seniors $2, children under 12 free) is housed in the old Parmly Library, built in 1901 by Frederick Billings in honor of his brother Parmly. The center is a museum of the history and culture of the Yellowstone Valley. Historical photos, period clothing, art, Western crafts, historic artifacts, and interpretive exhibits are featured.

◖ Yellowstone Art Museum

The Yellowstone Art Museum (401 N. 27th Ave., 406/256-6804, www.artmuseum.org, 10 A.M.–5 P.M. Tues.–Wed. and Fri.–Sat., 10 A.M.–8 P.M. Thurs., noon–5 P.M. Sun., also open Mon. Memorial Day–Labor Day, $7

adults, $5 seniors, $3 children 6–18, under 6 free), located in the old county jail, mounts up to 20 exhibits a year in its five galleries. Known by its acronym, YAM, the center is devoted to securing and displaying contemporary regional and Western art, although it houses international and historic pieces as well. Recent acquisitions focus on drawings and paintings by Will James and Charley Russell; the collection of contemporary Western art is significant. There's also a museum shop with local gifts and books.

Moss Mansion

Just west of the downtown area is a district of beautiful old Victorian homes. Only one of these is open to the public, but for anyone interested in late-19th-century architecture, a walk along these streets (between Division and 3rd Streets, and Lewis and Yellowstone Streets) is a pleasant diversion.

The Moss Mansion (914 Division St., 406/256-5100, www.mossmansion.com, guided tours on the hour, 10 A.M.–3 P.M. summer, call for hours off-season, $7 adults, $5

© BILL MCRAE

Moss Mansion is one of Billings's grandest historic homes.

seniors and students, $4 children 6–12) was built by an early Billings bank president who engaged Henry Hardenberg, the architect of the Waldorf-Astoria Hotel in New York City, to design his Billings home. Completed in 1903, the three-story sandstone mansion has pronounced European touches. In fact, each room seems to be designed to reflect a different European country, from the Moorish entry hall to the Tudor dining room. Most of the original furniture and fixtures remain.

THE RIMROCKS

The Rimrocks are worth a visit, if only for the views from the top. From **Black Otter Trail** off Airport Road, five mountain ranges are visible. To the southeast are the Bighorns, farther west are the Pryors, to the southwest are the Beartooths, and northwest are the Crazies and Snowies.

Yellowstone Kelly's Grave

On the Rimrocks along Black Otter Trail is Yellowstone Kelly's Grave, placed here at his request at a site overlooking the Yellowstone River.

Luther Kelly was an adventurer of an old-fashioned sort, better suited to fiction than reality. He came west after the Civil War and found the rough-and-ready life here to his liking, despite his cultivated Eastern background. He learned both the Crow and Sioux languages and campaigned with General Miles when the Army forced the Indians onto reservations following the battle at Little Bighorn. Kelly later ventured to Alaska and later still became a provincial governor in the Philippines. Back on this continent, he became an Indian agent in Nevada, where he also mined for gold. He died in California, and his body was returned to this site in 1928.

Boothill Cemetery

Follow Black Otter Trail to the eastern base of the Rimrocks to find Boothill Cemetery, one of the only reminders of the old town of Coulson. At rest here are 52 early residents, many after meeting violent ends. Coulson's sheriff, "Muggins" Taylor, is buried here, as is Henry Lump, the man who killed him. Taylor was the Army scout who brought news of the Custer massacre to the world via Fort Ellis in 1876.

THE LEGEND OF SACRIFICE CLIFFS

Dominating the skyline south and east of Billings across the Yellowstone are the Sacrifice Cliffs. These 200-foot escarpments figure in a Crow legend. As recounted by Mark Brown in *The Plainsmen of the Yellowstone*, Crow storyteller Old Coyote told of two brothers, both warriors, who returned to their village to find it ravaged with smallpox.

They saw the dead on scaffolds. These brothers were courting two sisters. They saw many scaffolds on a cliff and climbed up there. One said to the other, "Take a look at these dead. What if they were the girls we were courting?" They recognized the sisters.

Their oldest brother was one of the chiefs. He was dead. There was no one to care for the people. They dug into their parfleches. They took out their best clothes and put them on. One had a grey horse. This was his best horse. They got on this horse, rode double. They rode through the camp and sang songs just like when there was no sickness, some lodge songs, and lastly their brothers' songs. After this ride, they went up to the cliff and rode along the rimrock singing their own songs. Then they blindfolded the horse and turned toward the edge of the cliff singing the Crazy Dog Lodge song. They were still singing when the horse went over the cliff.

Yellowstone County Museum

Also on the Rimrocks, near the airport, is the Yellowstone County Museum (1950 Terminal Cir., 406/256-6811, 10:30 A.M.–5 P.M. Mon.–Fri., 10:30 A.M.–3 P.M. Sat., free). This community museum features an old steam engine from the Northern Pacific, a pioneer cabin, a sheepherder's wagon, a roundup wagon, and homesteader and Indian artifacts. Diorama fans will be uplifted by its display of life in the early years of Yellowstone settlement, and outdoors near the picnic tables is a telescope for viewing Billings and vicinity.

◖ Pictograph Cave State Monument

The most unusual of Billings's Rimrock attractions is the Pictograph Cave State Monument (406/247-2940, 8 A.M.–8 P.M. daily May–Sept., $5 per vehicle for non–Montana residents). Located southeast of Billings on the south side of the Yellowstone, the caves were inhabited for about 10,000 years. A succession of cultures has lived here, beginning with a tribe of prehistoric hunters. Excavations have yielded almost 30,000 cultural artifacts of early Paleo-Indians, making this one of the richest archaeological sites in Montana.

The road into the monument passes by spectacular cliffs and ponderosa pine forests. At the site, three caves have been cut into the sandstone

© BILL MCRAE

Billings from the Rimrocks

© BILL MCRAE

Boothill Cemetery contains the graves of many colorful characters from Billings's early years.

by water erosion. The best-preserved cave paintings are in Pictograph Cave. Here, buffalo, elk, prehistoric animals, and figurative and abstract designs are just visible on the sandstone walls of the cave. That the paintings have survived at all is amazing, especially after repeated assaults by vandals with spray paint. However, nature eventually washed off the spray paint, and the colors of the painting, made from plant resins, cherry juice, animal fat, charcoal, and soil, once again show through. The other two caves, Ghost Cave and Middle Cave, were also inhabited by prehistoric Indians.

A hard-surface 1,000-foot trail links all of the caves from a central parking lot. A very nice picnic area (but no camping sites), water, and toilets make this a great place to stop and explore. The abundance of birdlife along the rims and the presence of typical prairie flora make the monument grounds a mini nature hike. To find Pictograph Cave State Monument, take exit 452 from I-90 and follow the signs south along Coburn Road for five miles.

ZOOMONTANA

Billings's small zoo (2100 Shiloh Rd., 406/652-8100, 10 A.M.–5 P.M. daily May–Sept. 24, 10 A.M.–4 P.M. winter, $6 adults, $4 seniors, $3 children 3–15) is devoted to northern hemisphere temperate species. It features native animals including river otters, owls, and ferrets, as well as more exotic species such as a Siberian tiger and Seca deer. In addition, there are a number of gardens and nature exhibits on the 70-acre property. The Discovery Center features hands-on exhibits and educational displays. To reach ZooMontana, take I-90 exit 446 and follow the signs west.

RECREATION

The **Billings Mustangs,** a farm team for the Cincinnati Reds, train in Billings and constitute just about the only organized spectator sport besides rodeo. The Mustangs play at Dehler Park (2611 9th Ave.); call 406/252-1241 for a schedule. City parks cater to the casual athlete. **Pioneer Park,** between 3rd and 5th Streets on Grand Avenue, is a beautiful old park near the downtown area featuring tennis courts, jogging paths, and plenty of picnic space. The swimming pool is at **Athletic Park** (N. 27th at 9th Ave. N.). **Riverfront Park,** located along the Yellowstone River just off I-90, has picnic tables, jogging paths, fishing access, boat access for nonmotorized boats, and lots of room to romp. No overnight camping is allowed. Take exit 446 north to King Avenue, follow it to South Billings Avenue, and follow South Billings Avenue to the park.

Lake Elmo State Recreation Area (2400 Lake Elmo Rd., Billings Heights, 406/254-1310) offers swimming, fishing, nonmotorized boating, and picnic areas. Boat rentals are available. Non–Montana residents pay $5 per vehicle entrance fee. No overnight camping is allowed.

There are several public golf courses in Billings. **Briarwood Country Club** (3429 Briarwood Blvd., 406/248-2702) has 18 holes and is south of Billings along Blue Creek. The **Par Three Golf Course** (Central Ave. at 19th St. W., 406/652-2553) has 18 holes. The **Lake**

YELLOWSTONE MOSS AGATES

Agates and sapphires are Montana's two official gemstones. Although agates occur worldwide, dendritic agates from the Yellowstone Valley are highly valued for their unusual figurations. Often called moss agates, the interiors of these stones reveal startlingly realistic mini-landscapes when correctly cut and polished.

Agates are made when gases form bubbles within cooling igneous strata. These cavities are slowly filled with water carrying a silica solution tinted with mineral traces, usually iron. As the silica hardens, it forms regular bands of color of varying intensity. Successive layers of colored silica are laid down within the cavity. As the overlying rock is eroded, the nodes of agate are freed from their setting.

Moss agates are different from banded, or riband, agates because of the presence of plumelike formations within the stone. Small fractures allow the penetration of minute amounts of waterborne minerals into the silica node, which forms treelike or featherlike apparitions in the translucent stone as it hardens. Combined with bands of color within the agate, these formations make landscape images of trees and sunsets, or trees along a lakeside. The verisimilitude of moss agates can be uncanny.

These agates, often called picture agates, occur almost exclusively in the Yellowstone Valley between the mouth of the Bighorn River and the Missouri. Why this should be so is a matter of speculation. As the Bighorn, Tongue, and Powder Rivers drain a common area of Wyoming, some theories propose that the agates formed in volcanic ash and lava beds near the watersheds of these rivers and later washed downstream to the Yellowstone. This explanation seems rational, but no appropriate igneous formations have been found in Wyoming.

If you know what you are looking for, agates are not hard to find, but it takes a trained eye to spot them in the rough. Only if they are scuffed or broken do they reveal their translucent interior; otherwise they are a dirty yellow-white.

Agate hunting is a favorite pastime for many locals, and many shops carry baskets of cut agates or agate jewelry for those who are not willing to hunt for their own. The same locals and shopkeepers are usually willing to lend advice to novice agate hunters. The best agate-hunting seasons are early spring and midsummer, when snowpack runoff scours out the gravel beds. Inquire at the local chamber of commerce to find out if there are guided agate-hunting tours. Just be sure not to cross private property without permission.

Hills Golf Course (406/252-9244) is near Lake Elmo State Park in Billings Heights. Follow Lake Elmo Road past Lake Elmo and turn at Wickes Lane. A new golf course is the **Peter Yegen Golf Course** (3400 Grand Ave., 406/656-8099).

ACCOMMODATIONS

Generally speaking, Billings features two major centers for accommodations: downtown and the I-90 exits, where you'll find a great many chain hotels.

$50-75

The **Cherry Tree Inn** (823 N. Broadway, 406/252-5603 or 800/237-5882, $50 and up)

is just north of downtown. It features a complimentary continental breakfast, exercise room and sauna, and allows small pets. Just down the hill from the airport, the **Rimview Inn** (1025 N. 27th St., 406/248-2622 or 800/551-1418, $58 and up) features large well-equipped rooms. Included is a complimentary continental breakfast; all rooms have refrigerators, and some have full kitchens. Two- and three-bedroom units are also available.

Across from Billings Clinic and an easy walk to downtown, the **Riverstone Billings Inn** (880 N. 29th St., 406/252-6800 or 800/231-7782, $68 and up) offers continental breakfast, a guest laundry, and nicely furnished rooms. Also close to downtown, the **Dude Rancher Inn** (415 N. 29th St., 406/259-5561 or 800/221-3302, $71 and up) is a small and venerable motel with a pronounced Western atmosphere. The coffee shop here is a popular place for breakfast. Pets are allowed.

Along I-90, just off exit 446, you'll find at least a dozen large newly built motels; barring a major event, you should have no trouble finding rooms without reservations. If you want to call ahead, try any of these (with rooms between $65–$75): **Billings Super 8 Lodge** (5400 Southgate Dr., 406/248-8842 or 800/800-8000) has a free continental breakfast. **Ramada Limited** (1345 Mullowney Ln., 406/252-2584) has a pool and hot tub, and pets are permitted. The **Days Inn** (843 Parkway Lane, 406/252-4007 or 800/325-2525) offers free breakfast.

$75-100

The ⟨ **Josephine Bed and Breakfast** (514 N. 29th St., 406/248-5898 or 800/552-5898, www.thejosephine.com, from $95) is in a historic home close to downtown. All five rooms, including one two-bedroom suite, have private baths.

Also comfortable is the **Best Western ClockTower Inn** (2511 1st Ave. N., 406/259-5511 or 800/628-9081, from $87). Right downtown, this motel offers a pool, sauna, restaurant, exercise room, and a guest laundry; it's an easy walk to bars and restaurants on the trendy Montana Avenue strip.

Over $100

At I-90 exit 447, Hampton Inn Billings (5110 Southgate Dr., 406/248-4949, from $129), offers large comfortably furnished rooms convenient to the interstate. Facilities include a pool, fitness room, and complimentary breakfast.

At the center of downtown is the **Crowne Plaza Billings** (N. 27th St., 406/252-7400 or 800/588-7666, from $170). The Crowne Plaza offers the service and amenities you'd expect in an executive hotel (such as an indoor pool, health club, and hot tub), but with the added privilege of doing so in Montana's tallest

building (23 stories). The hotel underwent a complete renovation in 2008.

Camping

The **Billings Metro KOA** (3087 Garden Ave., 406/252-3104 or 800/562-8546) has 115 RV sites, 60 tent-camping sites, and a pool, playground, and minigolf course, all right next to the Yellowstone. The KOA is off exit 450. The Billings KOA has the honor of being the first KOA in North America.

FOOD

The Billings restaurant scene is diverse, featuring several ethnic cuisines. But don't fool yourself; this is really red meat country.

Breakfast and Light Meals

A popular spot for a hearty old-fashioned breakfast or lunch is the **McCormick Café** (2419 Montana Ave., 406/255-9555, 7 A.M.–4 P.M. Mon.–Fri., 8 A.M.–3 P.M. Sat., 9 A.M.–1 P.M. Sun.), located in a historic hotel in the city's oldest district. Just down the block is the **Log Cabin Bakery** (2519 Montana Ave., 406/294-5555, 6 A.M.–3 P.M. Mon.–Sat.), with excellent breads, cookies, desserts, coffee, and lunchtime panini.

Support local farmers at **Grains of Montana** (926 Grand Ave., 406/259-7142, 7 A.M.–9 P.M.), a bakery, sandwich, and pizza restaurant that features bread products created with spring wheat flour from the owner's farm.

Another good, locally-owned option for light meals is a brewpub. Billings has several notable small breweries which also offer burgers and snacks; see *Bars and Nightlife* below.

Steaks and Fine Dining

Steaks share top billing with gourmet fare at several downtown restaurants. There's a good view of the city from the 20th-floor **Montana Sky** in the Crowne Plaza Billings (27 N. 27th St., 406/252-7400, 6:30 A.M.–2 P.M. and 5–10 P.M. Mon.–Fri., 6:30–11 A.M. and 5–10 P.M. Sat.–Sun.). Steaks and seafood entrées average $24. **Jake's** (2701 1st Ave. N., 406/259-9375, 11 A.M.–2 A.M. Mon.–Fri.,

4:30 P.M.–2 A.M. Sat., $18–25) combines a lively bar scene with steaks, chops, and a selection of more internationally eclectic dishes.

Billings's dining hot spot is **Walker's American Grill** (2700 1st Ave. N., 406/245-9291). The stylish bar and dining room feature a large selection of tapas plus up-to-date New West cuisine ranging from steaks and pasta to duck and seafood ($19–$28). Grilled pork loin is served with broccoli white-cheddar risotto and sun-dried tomato pesto.

The old Billings Historic District on Montana Avenue is filling with excellent restaurants and beckoning bars and clubs. The **Rex Hotel** (2401 Montana Ave., 406/245-7477, 11 A.M.–2 A.M. Mon.–Fri., 4 P.M.–2 A.M. Sat.–Sun., $18–30) combines excellent aged beef with Italian dishes, game, and fresh fish in a refurbished and elegant old hotel. **Q Cuisine** (2503 Montana Ave., 406/245-2503, 4:30–11 P.M. Mon.–Sat.) in the refurbished Carlin Hotel, is another hip new restaurant—the bar is the city's top martinis-and-jazz destination while the coolly retro dining room serves sophisticated cuisine, with entrées $16–24. Seared scallops with red pepper cream sauce is $20.

The city's top choice for Mediterranean-style cooking is **Enzo Bistro** (1502 Rehberg, 406/651-0999, 5–9 P.M. daily). Main courses range from wood-fired pizza to rib-eye steak stuffed with shallots and blue cheese; fresh fish is a specialty, with about have the menu dedicated to fish and seafood flown in to ensure freshness. Grilled halibut with wild mushroom balsamic gastrique is $26.

Another historic building turned into a good restaurant is **George Henry's** (404 N. 30th St., 406/245-4570, 11 A.M.–9 P.M. Mon.–Fri., 5:30–9 P.M. Sat., $16–24). The 1882 home, not far from downtown, is now in the business of serving tasty steaks, seafood, salads, and light meals. Also not far from downtown is the **Granary** (1500 Poly Dr., 406/259-3488, 5–10 P.M. nightly, $18–33), a light and airy restaurant in an old mill with good beef, a selection of chicken dishes, and seafood. The outdoor deck here is a delightful spot in good weather.

Ethnic and Other Options

Billings is blessed with good Asian food; main courses at the following restaurants range $8–16. Along the Montana Avenue strip is **Sweet Ginger** (2515 Montana Ave., 406/245-9888, 11 A.M.–10 P.M. Mon.–Sat.), serving pan-Asian dishes, including sushi, Thai, and Korean food. **Thai Orchid** (2926 2nd Ave. N., 406/256-2206) has a good selection of vegetarian dishes. Near the hotels off I-90 exit 446 is **Jade Palace** (2021 Overland, 406/656-8888, 11 A.M.–9:30 P.M. daily), which mixes Cantonese and Szechuan cuisine in an attractive setting. If you're itching for sushi, you'll find it at **NaRa Oriental Restaurant** (3 Custer Ave., 406/245-8866), near the corner of Division and Montana Avenues. NaRa also serves Korean dishes in addition to Japanese specialties.

A longtime favorite for southern Mexican cooking, **Mamacita's** (1404 6th Ave. N., 406/252-9950) features house-made tortillas and salsas.

Less formal dining is available, of course: Grand Avenue is the strip where all of the fast-food places huddle.

Bars and Nightlife

Like other Montana communities, Billings has a nightlife centered on bars and restaurants. The **Rex Hotel** (2401 Montana Ave., 406/245-7477) began as an experiment in urban renewal through drink. By putting a trendy bar in an old hotel in the dilapidated historic district along the tracks, the developers began the rejuvenation process of Billings's most historic district. Several other clubs and bars now line the streets down by the tracks, including the **Carlin Club** (2501 Montana Ave., 406/245-2500), which features Billings's best live jazz scene.

Jake's (2701 1st Ave. N., 406/259-9375) is one of the liveliest bar scenes downtown. Jake's is the kind of bar where, after a couple of drinks, everyone seems single. In a city this would seem threatening, but in Billings it seems endearing.

Other nightspots of note include the **Monte Carlo** (2828 1st Ave. N., 406/259-3393), a horseshoe bar and casino with piano entertainment, and **The Western**, a rowdy watering hole on the "wrong" side of the tracks (2712 Minnesota Ave., 406/252-7383) that starts early and goes late.

Billings has a number of brewpubs, where you can sample local brews and dine on pub grub. **Montana Brewing Company** keeps things lively with good homemade beer and lots of local student activity (113 N. Broadway, 406/252-9200). **Yellowstone Valley Brewing Company** (2123 1st Ave. N., 406/245-0918) hosts Saturday evening live music in its "garage pub." **Angry Hank's Place** (2405 1st Ave. N., 406/252-3370) offers microbrew ales in a converted filling station. **Carter's Brewing** (2526 Montana Ave., 406/252-0663) has a brewpub located in an old railroad building right beside the tracks at the heart of Montana Avenue's nightclub district. Their Derailed IPA is a thing of beauty. **Pug Mahons** (3011 1st Ave. N., 406/259-4190) is an Irish pub just west of downtown. They don't brew beer but offer lots of draft beer options and a choice of Irish food specialties.

EVENTS

MetraPark (near the corner of 6th Ave. N. and Exhibition Dr., 406/256-2400, www.metrapark.com) is the major venue in Billings for concerts, rodeos, fairs, and just about any other event that requires extensive seating and exhibition space. Seasonal events include the **MontanaFair**, a large agricultural affair with a rodeo, carnival, and horse racing held during the middle of August. The **Northern International Livestock Exposition** is a large and prestigious livestock show held in October and featuring five nights of rodeo. Check the website for concert dates or sports engagements.

Live theater is presented in several venues. The **Alberta Bair Theatre** (2801 3rd Ave. N., 406/256-6052) hosts performance events, including theater by the Fox Committee for the Performing Arts, the Billings Symphony, and events featuring visiting artists. Venture Theater (2317 Montana Ave, 406/591-9535) is an ambitious acting troupe with a large theater space at the heart of Montana Avenue's nightlife scene. The group mounts musicals, dramas,

and comedies and also offers improv evenings several times each month. **Billings Studio Theatre** (1500 Rimrock Rd., 406/248-1141) is a local community theater featuring old and new favorites of the popular stage.

SHOPPING

The downtown area of Billings hasn't fared so well as shoppers have deserted older businesses in favor of newer shopping centers with chain stores on the city's fringes. A few older businesses persist in their original locations.

Billings is a good place to get outfitted with Western goods. **Lou Taubert Ranch Outfitters** (114 N. Broadway, 406/245-2248) is an established Western store with a wide selection of boots, hats, and gear. **Al's Bootery** (1820 1st Ave. N., 406/245-4827) offers a wide selection of boots as well as silver jewelry.

Several art galleries in Billings emphasize Western and Montana art. **Flatiron Gallery** (2 Custer Ave., 406/256-7791) features contemporary Montana artists. **Thomas Minckler Gallery** (2511 Montana Ave., 406/245-2969) offers historic Western art and artifacts plus rare books. **Toucan Gallery** (2505 Montana Ave., 406/252-0122, 10 A.M.–5 P.M. Mon.–Sat.) is located in the historic district and features contemporary local arts and crafts.

INFORMATION

The chamber of commerce **visitor center** is at 815 South 27th Street (406/245-4111 or 800/735-2635, http://billingscvb.visitmt.com). The main **post office** is directly behind the chamber of commerce at South 26th Street and 9th Avenue South. The downtown branch is at 2602 1st Avenue North.

Speedy Wash is downtown (2505 6th Ave. N., 406/248-4177, 6 A.M.–11 P.M. daily). **The Laundry Room** is near I-90 exit 446 (3189 King Ave. W., 406/652-2993, 7 A.M.–9 P.M. daily).

For a **local weather forecast** call 406/652-2000. For **road conditions** information call 406/252-2806.

The **Fish, Wildlife, and Parks** office is at 2300 Lake Elmo Drive (406/247-2940). The **Custer National Forest headquarters** is at

2602 1st Avenue North (406/248-9885). The **Bureau of Land Management** office can be reached at 406/255-2888.

Billings Clinic is at 9th Avenue North and Broadway (406/657-4000). **St. Vincent's Hospital** is at 1233 North 30th Street (406/657-7000).

Listen to Montana Public Radio at 91.7 FM.

TRANSPORTATION

Billings is the largest air link in Montana. Horizon, United, Delta, Frontier, Allegiant, and Northwest each fly into Logan Field several times daily. Logan Field sits atop the Rimrocks at the junction of Airport Road and North 27th Street. **Hertz, Budget, Avis,** and **National** all operate car rental agencies at the airport.

Rimrock Stages buses (2501 1st Ave. N., 800/255-7655, www.rimrocktrailways.com) provides service to communities along I-94 and to Denver along I-90. **MET** is the city's public transport system; call 406/657-8218 for information.

East Toward Miles City

Between Billings and Miles City lies an area of rich farmland and pastureland fed by the waters of the Yellowstone and shaded by cottonwoods. Irrigated farming is the mainstay of the local economy, with corn, sugar beets, and soybeans the most prevalent crops. Feedlots, where cattle are wintered or fattened, are also common.

Past the steep sandstone bluffs that rise out of the valley floor, beyond the reach of the center-pivot sprinklers, the badlands and prairies begin. Out here it's suddenly sagebrush and cactus, dusty roads, and cattle country. Small towns like **Forsyth** serve the needs of farmers, ranchers, and travelers alike.

When traveling the Yellowstone Valley, one is always following in someone's footsteps. The wide fertile valley cut by the river has been used for centuries as a thoroughfare, first on foot and horseback, then later by steamboat, railroad, and most recently by automobile along I-94.

Initially the wildlife brought people to the valley. Archaeological remains indicate that prehistoric Indians have lived here for thousands of years. Following Lewis and Clark (who left a signature at **Pompey's Pillar National Monument**), trappers exploited the region's abundance of fur-bearing animals and established trading forts at favorable points. By the end of the 19th century the range was being settled by big cattle and sheep outfits. Then the valley began to fall to the plow.

Coal-fired electricity-generating plants built at **Colstrip** by the Montana Power Company in the 1970s sparked a huge debate in the state, as ranches sitting atop coal reserves were tempted and coerced to sell their mineral rights. Ecologists found allies in Indians and cowboys alike as the effects of the coal-fired plants on the environment became known. In the end the plants went in, but not before families and neighbors were divided over the issues surrounding economic growth, environmental damage, and rapid change in traditional communities.

◖ POMPEY'S PILLAR NATIONAL MONUMENT

Pompey's Pillar has always been a landmark. Indians used it as a lookout and for sending smoke signals, but the Corps of Discovery put Pompey's Pillar on the map. In July 1806, William Clark and his party were paddling down the Yellowstone when they sighted this 200-foot-high sandstone outcropping in the middle of the wide valley. Clark named the formation after Jean Baptiste, the son of Sacagawea and Charbonneau, the French trapper and adventurer who accompanied the corps. Clark had nicknamed Jean Baptiste "Little Pomp," meaning Little Chief. Clark wrote:

July 25th, 1806, at 4 P.M.: Arrived at a remarkable rock situated in an extensive bottom. This rock I ascended and from its top had a most extensive view in every direction. This rock, which I shall call Pompy's Tower, is 200 feet high and 400 paces in secumpherance and only axcessable on one side. The nativs have ingraved on the face of this rock the figures of animals &c near which I marked my name and the day of the month and year. From the top of this Tower I could discover two low Mountains and the Rocky Mts covered with snow one of them appeared to be extencive.

Some of the pillar's petroglyphs still remain and are reckoned to be the work of the Shoshone Indians who lived in this area before the current Plains tribes moved west. But the real curiosity here is Clark's signature, carved in the rock and still legible after 200 years. Clark was not the last to sign Pompey's Pillar. A pair of crossed hatchets, insignia medallions worn by members of the corps, were probably carved by an enterprising corpsman while Clark finished his signature. Capt. Grant Marsh, pilot of the steamship *Josephine*, added his graffiti in 1875.

Climb the boardwalk staircase to see Clark's signature; continue on to a good vista of the Yellowstone Valley and surrounding rimrock hills. There are picnic tables near the river, but no overnight camping is allowed.

The Bureau of Land Management operates a visitors center at Pompey's Pillar and charges a $7 fee for each vehicle. The site is open 8 A.M.–8 P.M. daily April 30–Labor Day, and 9 A.M.–4 P.M. daily Labor Day–October 28. The rest of the year, vehicle access and the visitors center are closed, but visitors are free to park at the gates and walk in to the monument, about 0.75 mile.

FORSYTH

Forsyth (pop. 1,944, elev. 2,515 feet), nestled beneath a rim of rough gumbo badlands along the banks of the Yellowstone, is a pretty little town with lots of trees and Western character. The presence of Colstrip to the south has elevated Forsyth above the general economic malaise assailing other small Montana towns without developing it into an affluent parody of its historic self. For the traveler, Forsyth offers recreational opportunities and a friendly place to spend the night.

Forsyth is named for Gen. James Forsyth, a U.S. Army officer who first landed here in 1875, before the town existed. Steamers stopped here to refuel their engines from the abundant stands of cottonwood.

The town was established in 1880 and earned its own post office when the Northern Pacific arrived in 1882. The elaborate buildings along Main Street, including the imposing Rosebud County Courthouse, indicate the wealth of the young community during the early years of the 20th century.

Sights

The **Rosebud County Pioneer Museum** (1300 Main St., 406/356-7547, 9 A.M.–7 P.M. Mon.–Sat., 1–7 P.M. Sun., May–Sept., free) houses artifacts from the area's early years of settlement and photographs of pioneer days.

Recreation

Forsyth is well-placed to serve as a center for hunters, as it is the hub of many country roads that quickly take the outdoors person into prime big-game territory. Pronghorn, mule deer, and white-tailed deer are the usual quarry. Also, with the fields that line the river and the river itself both serving as habitat, bird hunters are rewarded with ample prey.

With fishing-access sites practically within city limits, Forsyth also welcomes anglers. The **Rosebud State Recreation Areas,** directly east and west of the city, offer fishing and boating access and camping. If you stop for a picnic, don't forget to look for agates.

The **Forsyth Golf and Country Club** (three miles west of Forsyth, exit 93 at Frontage Rd., 406/356-7710) has nine holes, rentals, and a clubhouse. The course winds up a steep gumbo canyon in the badlands just outside of town.

Accommodations

$50-75: You'll find nicely furnished rooms at

COLSTRIP, A TOWN BUILT ON COAL

South of the bluffs of Yellowstone Valley proper, the underlying sandstone changes from Eagle Formation to Fort Union Formation sandstone. While there are no visual differences between the two, there is a vast difference in mineral wealth. In the 15 million years between the two sandstone-making periods, tropical forests laid down vast deposits of peat alongside the ancient seas and riverbanks. When the climate changed, these deposits in turn were covered by others, and the peat slowly turned to coal.

The coal in this part of Montana is highly prized. It is covered by a modest layer of overburden (rock and soil) and makes for easy strip-mining. Strip-mining removes the overburden by levels, revealing the coal seam, which is then gouged out by enormous power shovels. The coal is low-sulfur bituminous, which burns cleaner and at a higher temperature than soft coal from other parts of the country.

These considerations have made Colstrip, a town of 2,500 residents astride huge coal deposits, appealing to mining and energy interests. When Montana Power began to build coal-fired generators at Colstrip in the 1970s, Montanans were galvanized around the issues of progress, ecology, and heritage.

The amount of coal to be mined here was enormous. Entire ranches would be devoured by the strip mines. The generators would pollute the air, which is pristine in almost the entire eastern part of Montana. However, the plants would bring economic growth to some of the state's most marginally successful agricultural communities.

Instantly, battle lines were drawn. Environmentalists concerned with air quality joined with ranchers worried about wells and the lowering of the water table. (Coal seams function as aquifers, because coal is porous, and the water table in this part of Montana is often the shallow layer of coal underlying almost everything in the eastern third of the state.) Other farmers and ranchers, who had struggled for decades against the weather, insects, and bad

markets, were understandably excited by the prospect of finally earning a living from the land, albeit by a troubling method.

Even the Indian tribes were divided: the Cheyenne fought to cancel coal leases on the reservation and filed to have the reservation reclassified as an area with Class 1 air standards, usually granted only to wilderness areas. The Crow, on the other hand, sold mineral rights and watched strip mines operate on the reservation.

Grassroots opposition to the coal-fired power plants found its focus in the Northern Plains Resource Council and its leaders in articulate farmers and ranchers who feared the changes in environment and community that the growth of large-scale mining would entail. Development at Colstrip was a deeply divisive issue to rural Montanans. As traditional "leave me alone" libertarians who resented environmentalists as cowardly predator-lovers, these farmers and ranchers found the same mistrusted environmentalists to be allies against the juggernauts of big business and big development.

In the end, Colstrip electric generators 1 through 4 went in after many delays and courtroom battles. However, the state instituted tough reclamation laws and levied a severance tax on coal sold out of state. The generators have left as many scars on rural Montana culture as they have on the plains near Colstrip.

In the late 1990s, the future of the generators seemed sealed. Several of the utilities that funded the original development of Colstrip were threatening to pull out. A scant 20 years after they were built, the enormous coal-fired generators seemed destined to be mothballed. However, with the new Bush administration in Washington stressing coal-fired energy generation, Colstrip has roared back to life in the 21st century. Current debate centers on the development of methane gas reserves, and familiar industry-environmentalist battle lines are drawn with local ranchers caught in the middle.

The **RestWel** (810 Front St., 406/356-2771, $55). Convenient to interstate travelers, rates at the RestWel include continental breakfast; some rooms have kitchenettes.

The **Westwind Motor Inn** (W. Main at Hwy. 12, 406/356-2038 or 800/356-2038, $60) has a pretty location near fishing access along the Yellowstone. The inn provides a continental breakfast; pets are permitted in the rooms. The **Rails Inn** (3rd and Front Streets, 406/356-2242 or 800/621-3754, $60) has a hot tub and lounge. Rooms come with a complimentary hot breakfast at the motel's café.

$75-100: The **Best Western Sundowner Inn** (1018 Front St., 406/356-2115 or 800/332-0921, $80) has senior discounts available, and all rooms are equipped with refrigerators and coffeemakers; pets are allowed.

Camping

There are campsites at both of the **Rosebud State Recreation Areas** on the east and west ends of town. **Wagon Wheel Campsites** (exit 95, 406/356-7982) welcomes both tent and RV campers.

Food

For home-style food 24 hours a day, go to the **Speedway Diner** (811 Main St., 406/356-7987) in downtown's vintage Howdy Hotel. The specialty is chicken fried steak ($8). **Fitzgerald's Restaurant** (109 S. 10th, 406/346-4444) offers casino action in addition to quality steaks.

Miles City

Miles City (elev. 2,371 feet) is an attractive town located at the confluence of the Tongue River and the Yellowstone. Gumbo buttes vaguely fringed with juniper ring the town. Miles City is the second-largest city in southeastern Montana, with almost 8,500 inhabitants. It's a major trade center for farmers and ranchers who, in their pickup trucks, converge on the city for livestock sale days, during harvest for parts, or as often as an excuse can be found to "go to Miles."

HISTORY

Miles City was born in the aftermath of the Battle of the Little Bighorn. After the defeat of Custer's Seventh Cavalry, the Army decided to establish a permanent military presence in eastern Montana to protect settlers and to drive the Sioux back onto reservations. In the fall of 1876, six companies of the Fifth Cavalry under the command of Gen. Nelson Miles established a military cantonment at the mouth of the Tongue River and arranged for the building of Fort Keogh. The civilian settlement that grew up downriver was initially known as Milestown. Fort Keogh, the largest military fort built in Montana, was finished in 1878, and Miles City reestablished itself on the Tongue River's opposite shore.

Miles City quickly became important as a trade center. The military payroll made for a relatively affluent citizenry, encouraging a stable base for the trades and mercantile. Steamboats were the vehicle for almost all transportation in the early days, and Miles City was an important port. The steamboats brought up goods for Fort Keogh and the young community of Miles City and took out a wealth of buffalo bones and hides.

After the Army had subdued the Sioux in 1877, and after the buffalo hunters had completed their own devastation, the vast prairies along the lower Yellowstone drainage were opened up for grazing. The first of the huge trail drives north from Texas was in 1879, and for the next 10 years Miles City was the center of a grazing region that summered tens of thousands of southern cattle. The Northern Pacific Railway arrived in 1881, providing a railhead to eastern slaughterhouses and markets. These boom years in the 1880s justified Miles City's swaggering boast of being the "Cow Capital

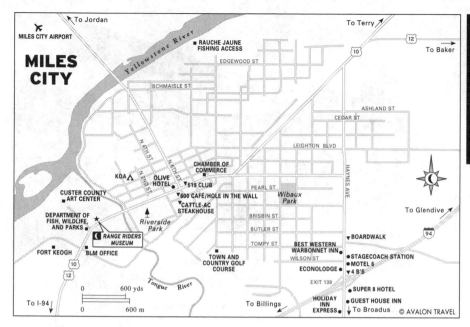

MILES CITY

To Jordan
To Terry
MILES CITY AIRPORT
To Baker
RAUCHE JAUNE FISHING ACCESS
EDGEWOOD ST
SCHMAISLE ST
ASHLAND ST
CEDAR ST
LEIGHTON BLVD
CHAMBER OF COMMERCE
KOA
OLIVE HOTEL
519 CLUB
PEARL ST
Wibaux Park
CUSTER COUNTY ART CENTER
600 CAFÉ/HOLE IN THE WALL
CATTLE-AC STEAKHOUSE
To Glendive
DEPARTMENT OF FISH, WILDLIFE, AND PARKS
Riverside Park
BRISBIN ST
BUTLER ST
RANGE RIDERS MUSEUM
TOMPY ST
BEST WESTERN WARBONNET INN
BOARDWALK
FORT KEOGH
BLM OFFICE
WILSON ST
STAGECOACH STATION
TOWN AND COUNTRY GOLF COURSE
MOTEL 6
ECONOLODGE
4 B'S
Tongue River
EXIT 138
0   600 yds
0   600 m
To I-94
To Billings
SUPER 8 HOTEL
HOLIDAY INN EXPRESS
GUEST HOUSE INN
To Broadus
© AVALON TRAVEL

of the West," for as its population and wealth grew, so did its reputation as a hard-drinking rough-and-tumble cow town.

Miles City Today

The old downtown, or what is left of it (the city was victim to a suspicious number of arson fires in the 1980s), contains remnants of Western boomtown architecture. Elements of the town, especially the bars and Main Street, have changed little since they were built.

Fort Keogh still exists, at least in name. Indian hostilities on the northern plains ended in 1877, after General Miles defeated both the Sioux in southeastern Montana and Chief Joseph in the north-central part of the state. Fort Keogh remained an Army post until 1900, at which time it became a remount station where horses were trained for the U.S. Army. In 1924 the fort was transferred to the control of the Department of Agriculture, and an agricultural test station was established. The Livestock and Range Research Station at Fort Keogh is known primarily for its role

in developing the purebred "Line One" of the Hereford cattle breed. But it is not known for its sensitivity to historic monuments. The original buildings of Fort Keogh fell into decrepitude, and many were simply burned. The only remaining building open for viewing, an officers' duplex, is at the Range Riders Museum.

SIGHTS
Range Riders Museum

Every community in eastern Montana has a local museum. If you see only one, make it the Range Riders Museum in Miles City (406/232-6146, 8 A.M.–8 P.M. daily, Apr. 1–Oct. 31, or by appointment, $5 adults, $1 students, $0.50 children under 6). Located at the western edge of the city, near the confluence of the Tongue and Yellowstone Rivers on West Main Street, it contains enough items to impress even the most jaded of museum-goers.

A one-room school, a frontier cabin, tepees, and a sheep wagon have been moved onto the grounds and maintained in period condition with authentic furnishings. A building from

© BILL MCRAE

The Range Riders Museum commemorates the days of the open range.

Fort Keogh, officers' quarters, is open to visitors and is a vivid reminder of just how civilized life was on the Yellowstone in 1878.

Inside the museum is an excellent gun and weapon collection, artifacts and memorabilia from the settling of the West, Indian art and artifacts, old photos, a southeastern Montana settlers "hall of fame," fossils, and more. There's also a reproduction of an 1890s Miles City street.

The best display also harkens back to Fort Keogh. In 1990, curator Bob Barthelmess presented his labor of love: a complete reconstruction of Fort Keogh at 1:80 scale. Housed in a room with an artfully painted trompe l'oeil landscape of the valley, the fort is re-created with painstaking detail and accuracy. It's really amazing—both the model and what the original must have been.

Custer County Art Center

The Custer County Art Center (Water Plant Rd., 406/232-0635, 9 A.M.–5 P.M. Tues.–Sat. May–Sept., 1–5 P.M. Tues.–Sat. Oct.–Apr., free) is in the historic Miles City Water Works building. The center is housed in a 1924 structure designed to filter and hold the city's water, and the galleries are in the water-holding tanks. The center emphasizes Western art, not surprisingly, along with frequent talks, readings, and a "quick draw" contest. There's also a nice picnic ground around the museum, under some ancient cottonwoods. Turn north at the Fish and Wildlife office off Highway 10 one block west of the Range Riders Museum.

Downtown

Downtown Miles City is still intact enough, despite the efforts of arsonists, to look like the cattle-trading capital it was in times past. There's an undeniably Western flavor to the city, with its old bars, saddleries, cafés, and the clientele to appreciate them. Most of the downtown area is now listed on the National Register of Historic Places.

PRACTICALITIES
Recreation
Riverside Park, on West Main at the Tongue River Bridge, has tennis courts and swimming

in a natural lake. **Wibaux Park** has a good playground for kids and is easy to find from I-94 by following South Haynes Avenue from the Broadus exit toward town and turning south two blocks at South Strevell. The **Town and Country Golf Course** (Montana Ave. and S. 4th St., 406/232-1600) is a private nine-hole club open to the public.

Twelve miles southwest of Miles City on Highway 12, **Woodruff Park** has picnic sites in grassy swales and pine trees. Although there are no formal trails, a nice wander along the ridges is enjoyable. Overnight camping is also allowed, although no water is provided, and garbage has to be carried out. Cross-country skiers use the park in winter.

White-tailed and mule deer are abundant in the countryside around Miles City, making it a good headquarters for hunters. Consider using an outfitter if you are new to the area. **Ray Perkins Outfitters Service** (1906 Main St., 406/232-4283) offers game-bird and big-game outfitting.

Accommodations

$50-75: The always affordable **Motel 6** (1314 S. Haynes Ave., 406/232-7040, $54 d) is one of many hotels at I-94 exit 138. The **Econolodge** (1209 S. Haynes, 406/232-8880 or 800/456-5026, $75 d) has an indoor pool and complimentary continental breakfast.

Downtown is the **Olive Hotel** (502 Main St., 406/232-2450 or 800/228-2000, $55 d), the only historic and original Miles City hotel in operation. The Olive is so well-established that even fictional characters (such as Gus McCrae of *Lonesome Dove*) stay there. The Olive is a Montana institution, and its 1899 lobby is listed in the National Register of Historic Places. Rooms are perfectly comfortable but not exactly luxurious. It's a good choice if you plan to spend your evening in the downtown bars, however.

A **Super 8** (406/232-5261 or 800/800-8000, $67 d) is south of the exit 138 interchange on Highway 59.

$75-100: The **Best Western War Bonnet Inn** (1015 S. Haynes Ave., 406/232-4560 or 800/528-1234, from $99) is one of the city's best, with an indoor pool, hot tub, and a business center.

The **Holiday Inn Express** (1720 S. Haynes, 406/232-1000 or 888/700-0402, $98) has complimentary breakfast, an indoor pool, and guest laundry.

Over $100: The newest hotel on the strip is the **Guesthouse Inn and Suites** (3111 Steel St., 406/232-3661 or 800/214-8378, from $110), with an indoor pool and hot tub, complimentary hot buffet breakfast, and a variety of large suites, including family suites with a separate bunk room for kids.

Camping

The **Miles City KOA** (1 Palmer St., 406/232-3991) is near the Tongue–Yellowstone River juncture. It features a pool, tent sites, laundry, and hot showers from May to November. The **Big Sky Campground** (406/232-1511) is just off the Baker interchange (exit 141) and is open to both RVs and tents from May to November. Not much shade is available, though.

Food and Nightlife

There's a large concentration of fast-food restaurants, a 24-hour truck stop, and a dependable 24-hour **4-Bs** (406/232-5772) restaurant at the I-90 exit 138. Locally owned options also exist. For tasty food at extremely reasonable prices, go to the buffet at the **Boardwalk** (906 S. Haynes Ave., 406/232-0195). **Stagecoach Station** (3020 Stower, 406/234-2288, 11 A.M.–9 P.M. daily) is a full-service family restaurant with a pronounced Western theme.

There's more character if not better food downtown. Here, among the easily recognized fast-food and sandwich joints, are authentic Miles City eating experiences. A landmark is the old diner-like **600 Cafe** (600 Main St., 406/232-3860, 6 A.M.–2A.M. daily), full of character and characters, both local. It's a great place to catch the pulse of this old cow town. The dining room at the historic Olive Hotel is now called **Mexico Linda** (501 Main, 406/234-2450, 11 A.M.–9 P.M. daily) and offers high quality Mexican food; main courses are $7–$14.

Club 519 (519 Main St., 406/232-5133,

5–9 P.M. nightly) features steaks in the historic First National Bank building (built in 1910). **The Cattle-Ac Steakhouse** (501 Pacific, 406/234-6987, 11 A.M.–10 P.M. Mon.–Sat.) offers good beef in a casino and dance-hall atmosphere. Full dinner at these establishments will range $12–22.

A night out in Miles City is a great way to experience one of the legacies of the Old West. Miles City started as a watering hole for thirsty soldiers, and it is still a major meeting place for stockmen and ranch hands. Miles City is exceptionally blessed with great old bars, and some of them have not changed appreciably (except for the addition of the ubiquitous gambling machines).

The ◖ **Montana Bar** (612 Main St.) is probably one of the greatest bars in the state, remarkably unchanged since it opened in 1902. You can imagine the many tall tales told and livestock trading that went on here. Other good bars are the **Range Riders** (605 Main St.), the **Bison** (618 Main St.), the **Log Cabin** (710 Main St.), and the bar at the **Olive Hotel** (501 Main St.). Also check out the **Golden Spur,** near the hotel strip at I-94 exit 138 (1014 S. Haynes, 406/232-3544), where you can taste Miles City's own microbrew, Milestown Draught.

Events

The **Miles City Bucking Horse Sale** is the one event that Miles City is known for throughout the West. On the third weekend in May, rodeo stock contractors and bacchants from just about everywhere gather in Miles City to watch young untamed horses buck. The most promising of these mounts are then sold at auction as rodeo broncs.

The Bucking Horse Sale is one of the biggest parties in the state, although the actual rodeo is now the central event in a weekend's worth of events that includes horse racing, a street dance, a barbecue, cowboy poetry readings, and the like. Don't let these more civilized pursuits fool you: This is a flat-out celebration of the Dionysian element of the Old West. Admission to the rodeo is $17 per person for reserved seats; general admission seats are $12;

children under 12 get in $2 cheaper in either section. For information, including tickets, contact the chamber of commerce or go to www.buckinghorsesale.com.

Shopping

Where better to buy your Western togs than in the Cow Capital of the West? The **Miles City Saddlery** (808 Main St., 406/232-2512, 9 A.M.–5 P.M. Mon.–Sat.) will outfit you (and the horse you rode in on) with quality Western gear. Boots, cowboy hats, spurs, pearl-snap shirts, and handmade saddles: It's all here. In a happier era, Main Street was lined with shops, each peddling its own handmade boots and saddles.

Check out the local arts-and-crafts scene at the **Wool House Gallery** (419 N. 7th St., 406/232-0769, 1–5 P.M. Tues.–Sat. Apr.–Dec.), located in a former railroad wool warehouse and now featuring woodworking, steel sculpture, paintings and drawings, and a small railroad museum of Miles City.

Services

The **post office** is at 106 North 7th Street. The **Holy Rosary Hospital** is at 2102 Clark Street (406/232-2540).

If the sky is threatening stormy weather, call the **weather service** for an update at 406/232-2099, and check the **road conditions** by dialing 406/232-2099.

Montana Public Radio is heard locally on KEEC 90.7 FM.

Information

The Miles City **Chamber of Commerce** is located at 901 Main Street (406/232-2890, www.mcchamber.com).

The **Bureau of Land Management** office (406/233-4333) is across from the Miles City Sales Yards, about one mile west of the Tongue River Bridge. The **Department of Fish, Wildlife, and Parks** (406/232-0900) is just south of the BLM office.

Getting There

The **Rimrock Stages** bus station (406/232-3900) is at 2210 Valley Drive East.

The Lower Yellowstone

Between Miles City and its confluence with the Missouri, the Yellowstone becomes a languid prairie river flowing through increasingly arid badlands. The trees and the small towns thin out, and a kind of sullen barrenness grips the landscape.

This is ranch country, rugged and desolate. Since the days of the big cattle drives in the 1880s, the plains along the lower Yellowstone have been home to large holdings of livestock. Towns such as **Terry, Glendive,** and **Wibaux** had their beginnings as trade and rail centers in the early days of the West. Their economies are still largely tied to agriculture, although oil and gas production have bolstered them somewhat in the recent years of poor cattle, sheep, and grain markets.

This area is also home to curious opportunities for the traveler. **Makoshika State Park** near Glendive offers startlingly rugged badlands filled with fossils, hiking trails, and wildlife. It also offers the chance to pull into old towns like Terry and Wibaux and experience the life of modern stockmen on their own turf.

Until the end of the Indian Wars of 1876–1877, this was Indian country, with the Sioux harassing travelers on the Yellowstone as they passed through. When the Northern Pacific was surveyed, hundreds of soldiers were needed to protect the engineers from the Indians. At this time, the only whites living in this part of Montana were rough-hewn loners who cut cottonwood for steamer fuel in summer and shot buffalo in winter.

By 1877 the Indians were mostly incarcerated on reservations, and the land opened to settlement and exploitation. One of the last great herds of buffalo on the open range was slaughtered in the Terry area in the early 1880s, just in time for the hides to be shipped east on the first trains running on the Northern Pacific.

The prairie was soon overrun with herds of Texas longhorns. Glendive and Wibaux were major railheads for the shipment of the cattle to Eastern markets and were rough-and-ready cow towns in their day. After the hard winter of 1886, when vast herds of free-range cattle died, the cattle industry was reborn in areas like Wibaux, where the cattle barons of the open range then founded ranches.

GLENDIVE

Like other towns on the Yellowstone, Glendive (pop. 4,729, elev. 2,069 feet) seems like an oasis of green and trees after crossing the sere plains that surround it. Although agates are common all along the Yellowstone, Glendive probably has the best agate hunting in the state. One of the best collections of this beautiful stone can be found here, and organized float trips on the river are available to the would-be collector. Although the paddlefish lives in much of the lower Yellowstone, the Glendive area is the paddlefish capital of Montana. Makoshika State Park, a preserve of colorful and austere badlands at the southeastern edge of town, offers camping, hiking, wildlife viewing, and fossil hunting.

Glendive began as Fort Canby, a military camp built to protect railroad workers as they laid the track for the Northern Pacific up the Yellowstone Valley in the late 1870s. The train actually arrived in the settlement on July 4, 1881. The name Glendive is apparently a corruption of "Glendale," the name given to a nearby creek by Sir George Gore on his hunting trip in 1856. (A more colorful story maintains that the name is a reference to a particularly earthy bar on the site named Glen's.)

◖ Makoshika State Park

The rugged beauty of 8,800 acres of heavily eroded badlands, as well as good facilities, makes Makoshika the area's premier attraction. The same geologic buckling that formed the oil-rich Cedar Creek Anticline (which sponsored an oil boom here in the 1970s) raised these badlands hundreds of feet above the prairie. As water eroded the exposed land,

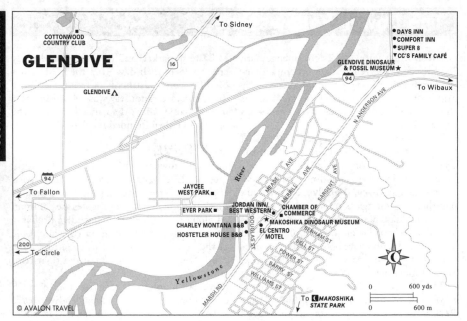

it cut through the layers of the Fort Union Formation and revealed a lower, earlier stratum, the Hell Creek Formation. Embedded in the Fort Union Formation is a rich record of fossil life, including the enormous remains of such beasts as triceratops and tyrannosaurus. In 1990 a volunteer paleontologist sat down for a lunch break on what turned out to be a huge triceratops skull. The excavated skull is now on display at the park visitors center.

Today in Makoshika Park, deep ravines have been cut from ridgetops into box canyons whose walls contain fossils. Although fossil hunting is not encouraged in park lands, the park offers stunning overlooks onto the badlands and many opportunities for recreation. Park admission is $5 per vehicle for non-Montanans, plus $12 to camp.

As the road leaves Glendive it quickly climbs up a series of steep switchbacks onto a plateau. From here the road continues 12 miles along steep ridges and barren canyons with frequent viewpoints and picnic areas. Two maintained trails allow hikers access to the steep canyon walls and valley floors and to the fantastically sculpted formations carved by erosion.

The **Cap Rock Nature Trail** is an interpretive trail that drops 160 feet onto the canyon walls. It passes a short natural bridge, pedestal rocks, fossil beds, and a gumbo sinkhole. A brochure available at the trailhead relates geological history and explains how the formations occurred. About 0.5 mile farther in, the **Kinney Coulee Hiking Trail** winds down a canyon through juniper trees and eroded formations that take on fanciful shapes. This steep trail is about one mile long and puts you onto the valley floor. The brochure also identifies common plants and animals along the path.

Makoshika Park is also a good wildlife-viewing area. Most noteworthy is a summer population of turkey vultures. Golden eagles are common, as are hawks. Coyotes can be heard howling at night. Mule deer hide out here by day and descend to the valley floor by night.

At most overlooks there are picnic tables, and there is a visitors center at the park entrance. Overnight camping is allowed at the

PADDLEFISH AND MONTANA CAVIAR

Paddlefish occur in only two places on earth: in the upper Missouri drainage and in the Yangtze River in China. No paddlefish had been seen in the United States since 1912, and the species was feared extinct. Then in 1962 a fisherman near Intake landed a grotesque-looking specimen weighing 28 pounds, with no scales and a prominent snout. Since then, the sport of paddlefishing has become a popular early summer recreational pursuit in eastern Montana.

The paddlefish is a member of a primitive family that includes the sturgeon. Among its peculiarities are a three-chambered heart, a skeleton of cartilage instead of bone, a long life span (up to 30 years), and its snout, which can be up to two feet long on an adult. It eats only plankton, which it strains out of river water flowing through its gills. This means that the paddlefish won't rise to bait. Instead, it can only be snagged from the river depths where it lurks.

And thus, the *sport*, not art, of paddlefishing. Anglers use heavy rods and line as well as heavy weights (or even spark plugs) to drop the line to the bottom of the river. The line is jerked along the bottom, with the hopes of snagging a paddlefish from its muddy lair. Once on the hook, a tremendous battle ensues, because paddlefish frequently weigh upward of 80 pounds (the record paddlefish, apprehended in the Missouri, weighed 142.5 pounds).

The popularity of paddlefish snagging has begun to worry wildlife experts. In recent years, a disproportionate number of fish taken were huge and old. While exciting for the angler, the ages of the fish being taken has convinced the Fish and Wildlife Department that there aren't sufficient numbers of young fish surviving in the Yellowstone and Missouri. As a result, fewer paddlefish permits are available.

While not all paddlefish flesh is edible (much of it is ominously dark and strong-tasting), a large paddlefish yields an abundance of delicate white meat, which tastes like and shares texture with monkfish.

Since 1989 the Glendive Chamber of Commerce has been authorized to collect paddlefish roe to make into commercially processed caviar. (Actually, paddlefish anglers donate the roe to the chamber, in return for having their fish cleaned.) Although the caviar is not available in Glendive, or anywhere else in Montana (the Fish and Wildlife Department expressly forbids sale of the caviar in Montana to reduce the risks of a caviar black market), it fetches high prices on the international caviar market. However, anyone can order Glendive paddlefish caviar as long as it is shipped to an out-of-state address. If you'd like to order some, call the Glendive Chamber of Commerce at 406/365-5601. The chamber has so far collected over $1 million from the sale of paddlefish roe. Part of the money has been used for county parks and paddlefish research; a full 60 percent of the proceeds is returned to the community through grants.

---

campsite one mile inside the park. Drinking water is available. Trailers are not allowed past the campground because the road becomes quite steep. A road guide to the park is available at the chamber of commerce or park entrance for $1.

To reach Makoshika State Park, follow Merrill Avenue south from downtown and turn under the railroad tracks on Barry Street. Follow the signs right on Taylor Avenue to the park access road. For more information, contact the Park Manager at P.O. Box 1242,

Glendive, MT 59330, or phone the visitors center at 406/365-6256. The park is open all year, but heavy rain or snow may make the roads impassable.

Other Sights

The **Frontier Gateway Museum** (Belle Prairie Rd., 406/377-8168, 9 A.M.–noon and 1–5 P.M. Mon.–Sat., 1–5 P.M. Sun. and holidays, June–Aug.; 1–5 P.M. daily May and Sept.) has several interesting exhibits. In addition to artifacts of local history, seven historic buildings have been

SOUTHEASTERN MONTANA

© BILL MCRAE

The badlands of Makoshika State Park are rich in dinosaur fossils.

moved to the site, as well as a collection of old fire engines. The museum basement houses a replica of old downtown Glendive. A unique exhibit here is a display of evidence from the area's past murder trials.

Makoshika Dinosaur Museum (11 W. Bell St., 406/377-1637, $3 adults, $2 students and seniors, children 5 and under free) offers a glimpse of Glendive's ancient life with full-size dinosaur replicas, fossil bed recreations, and dioramas. The museum also offers daylong fossil digs for both adults and kids.

Glendive's community art center, called **The Gallery** (109 N. Merrill, 406/365-6508, noon–4 P.M. Mon.–Fri.), is in the West Plaza mall. The Gallery features works by local artists, including sculpture.

Downtown Glendive has several interesting old buildings. A brochure with a walking tour of Glendive is available from the chamber of commerce.

Glendive also has attractive parks. **Lloyd Square Park,** 1.5 blocks west of Merrill Avenue on Gresham Street, has an outdoor

pool and tennis courts. On the west end of the Bell Street Bridge is **Eyer Park,** with a playground and picnic grounds. On the other side of the road is **Jaycee West Park** with more tennis courts.

Due to open in 2008 is the 20,000-square-foot **Glendive Dinosaur and Fossil Museum** (I-94 exit 215, 406/377-1141, www.creationtruth.org). This facility presents a Christian view of the fossil record, linking dinosaur extinction with Noah's flood. Murals of local dinosaur life, 23 full-size models of dinosaurs, and exhibits corrective of evolution are featured.

Recreation

Intake, an irrigation diversion 16 miles northeast of Glendive, is the center for **paddlefishing,** although paddlefish are found south to Miles City and in the Missouri as well. The State Department of Fish, Wildlife, and Parks closely supervises paddlefishing areas to limit abuses and overfishing. The season begins in May and ends on July 15, and a special permit beyond the usual fishing license is necessary.

Another reason to take to the river is to hunt for agates. From March to October **guided agate float trips** can be arranged by the Glendive Chamber of Commerce (P.O. Box 930, Glendive, MT 59330, 406/365-5601).

The **Cottonwood Country Club**(406/365-8797), north after the Highway 16 exit to Highland Park Road, is a challenging nine-hole course.

Accommodations

Under $50: If you're looking for inexpensive, the **El Centro** (112 S. Kendrick Ave., 406/377-5211, $47) is downtown on a quiet street, and rooms have refrigerators and microwaves.

$50-75: At I-94 exit 215 are the **Days Inn** (406/365-6011, $59) and the **Super 8** (406/365-5671 or 800/800-8000, $67). Pets are permitted at both places.

A historic 1912 prairie-style home is now the **Hostetler House B&B** (113 N. Douglas St., 406/377-4505 or 800/965-8456, $55 and up). The two guest rooms share a bath and use of

THE SIGHTS OF TERRY

The little ranch town of Terry sits along the Yellowstone midway between Miles City and Glendive, with prairies to the south and rugged badlands to the north. If you are traveling east, it's time to realize that you're well and truly on the plains of Montana. At Miles City, the Yellowstone is a wide green valley with irrigated pastures and fields. At Terry, 40 miles downstream, only a fringe of green isolates the river from the encroaching prairies.

Although the town doesn't offer many facilities for the traveler, it does have the **Prairie County Museum** (105 Logan, 406/637-4040, 9 A.M.-3 P.M. weekdays, 1-4 P.M. weekends, Memorial Day</#208>Labor Day), housed in an elegant late-19th-century bank building. Its exhibits include horse-drawn carriages, rebuilt offices and businesses, and historical photographs. The museum staff can direct travelers to several Indian tepee rings and buffalo jumps in the hills around Terry.

Evelyn Cameron, a pioneer photographer, took spectacular pictures of Terry and the surrounding area during the late 19th and early 20th centuries. Some of her photos hang in the **Cameron Gallery**, next door to the county museum, with the same hours and shared admission charges. A book, *Photographing Montana* by Donna Lucey, and a PBS special have each celebrated this remarkable pioneer photographer. Check out the website www.evelyncameron.com for more information on Cameron, with many examples of her stirring photos.

---

a hot tub. Many of the furnishings are handmade, and others are heirlooms. The B&B is just one block from the Yellowstone and close to swimming pools, tennis courts, and downtown. You are guaranteed a friendly welcome from hosts who grew up in the Glendive area.

$75-100: Another landmark mansion turned B&B is **Charley Montana B&B** (103 N. Douglas, 406/365-3207 or 888/395-3207, $85 and up). This 25-room 8,000-square-foot home of a local rancher, built in 1904, features original family furnishings. Of the five guest rooms, four share a bath.

The **Jordan Inn** (223 N. Merrill Ave., 406/377-5655 or 800/824-5067, $76) is Glendive's landmark downtown hotel, with a restaurant and bar. The newer motel portion of the original Jordan Inn is now the **Best Western Glendive Inn** (222 North Kendrick Ave., 406/377-5555 or 888/453-6348), with an indoor pool and sauna. Dining facilities are shared with the Jordan Inn, which is adjacent.

The **Comfort Inn** (1918 North Merrill, 406/365-6000 or 800/228-5150, $92) is convenient to I-94, has an indoor pool, and offers free continental breakfast.

Camping

The **Glendive RV Park and Campground** (206 1st St., Highland Park, 406/365-6721) has both RV and tent facilities, plus a swimming pool and camping cabins with air-conditioning and TVs! The **Green Valley Campground**, 0.5 mile north on Highway 16 (406/365-4156), has its own fishing pond. There's also a campground at **Makoshika State Park.**

Food

The best dining in downtown Glendive is the dining room at the **Jordan Inn** (223 N. Merrill Ave., 11:30 A.M.-10 P.M.). At I-94 exit 215 is **CC's Family Cafe** (1902 N. Merrill Ave., 406/377-8926, 6 A.M.-9 P.M. Sun.-Thurs., 6 A.M.-10 P.M. Fri.-Sat.).

Services

The **Glendive Medical Center** is located at 202 Prospect Drive at Ames Street (406/345-3306). **Econo Wash** (1212 W. Towne) is open daily 6 A.M.-10 P.M.

The **chamber of commerce** is at 313 South Merrill Avenue (406/365-5601). You'll receive a free moss agate just for stopping by.

Getting There

Glendive is 35 miles west of the North Dakota border on I-94. Glendive is served by the **Rimrock Stages** bus line.

WIBAUX

Wibaux (WEE-bo) is a quintessential cattle town (pop. 567, elev. 2,634). This small eastern Montana community has seen some of the West's most colorful characters, and it has been an actor in some of the West's most colorful periods. Today, it is a comfortable corner of Montana whose past feels relatively recent.

History

The Northern Pacific first passed through this area in 1881, spawning a tiny community called Mingusville. It became the railhead for the huge cattle ranches that grew up along the North Dakota–Montana border. (It was also the local party town; neighboring Dakota counties were "dry.") This area was coveted grazing land in the days of the open range, but the disastrous winter of 1886 spelled the end of the trail-drive days.

Among the investors who made a successful change to rancher was a Frenchman, Pierre Wibaux, who arrived in Montana in 1883. He is rumored to have made it through 1886 by feeding his cattle cottonwood branches, and with an influx of French capital, he was able to buy up livestock at low prices from desperate fellow cattlemen. By the mid-1890s there were 65,000 head of cattle bearing his brand, the W Bar.

So it was no mere act of hubris when Wibaux presented the Northern Pacific authorities a petition in 1894 asking that Mingusville, the principal railhead for Wibaux's ranch, be changed to Wibaux. The authorities sensibly complied.

In this corner of the United States, these were days of interesting characters. Just over the border in North Dakota, the Marquis de Mores established the town of Medora. This French nobleman founded a huge cattle ranch and meatpacking plant in the middle of nowhere, built a manor house for his wife, and waited for fortune to come and visit. Instead, he welcomed

such visitors as Teddy Roosevelt, who had established a cattle ranch nearby after the deaths of both his mother and his wife. Pierre Wibaux was another fixture in this stylish set.

Wibaux spent his final years in Miles City. His original ranch, with its elaborate home and outbuildings, burned some years ago.

St. Peter's Catholic Church

Pierre Wibaux left a legacy in Wibaux that seems very rich for such a small town. In 1884 Wibaux's father sent him money to build a church. St. Peter's Catholic Church was built the next summer out of native stone and lava rock. St. Peter's reveals its French background: Its quiet rootedness recalls a Normandy churchyard more than a pioneer parish eight miles from North Dakota. It is an imposing structure on the prairies, in summer covered with green ivy, rising above the town that Wibaux built. Consider when this handsome church was built; places like Glendive and Billings were little more than rail sidings. Beyond the church is a statue of Pierre Wibaux looking north toward the location of his old ranch.

Wibaux County Museum

Wibaux's W Bar Ranch was 14 miles north of the present town. To conduct business in town, he built an office and bunkhouse. This small clapboard "town house" now houses the Wibaux County Museum (112 Orgain St. at Wibaux St., 406/796-2381, 9 A.M.–5 P.M. Mon.–Sat., 1–5 P.M. Sun., May 15–Sept. 30, free). Tours are conducted daily at 1, 2, and 3 P.M. Memorial Day–Labor Day. The town house has been returned to its original 1892 condition, including the grounds, which French gardeners had designed with a pond, flower beds, and a grotto. The museum houses personal belongings and furniture as well as items typical of the open range days.

Centennial Car Museum

In 1964, during the New York City World's Fair, Montana sent a railcar containing promotional exhibits about the state, as it was celebrating its centennial as a territory in the same

© BILL MCRAE

Wibaux's fieldstone Catholic church was built by Norman French immigrants.

year. Today, the railcar contains the Centennial Car Museum (E. Orgain, 406/795-2289, 9:30 A.M.–5:30 P.M., Memorial Day–Labor Day, free). Inside are Indian and pioneer relics, including the museum's pride, a human vertebrae with an arrowhead imbedded in it, which has been unofficially dated to a period at least 2,000 years ago.

Accommodations and Food

The **Beaver Creek Inn** (400 W. 2nd Ave., 406/796-2666) has a picnic area, some handicap-accessible rooms, and an adjacent restaurant **Genie's Kitchen** (300 W. 2nd Ave., 406/796-2228, 7 A.M.–8 P.M.), with home-style cooking.

For local color, go to the bar-restaurant in the **Palace Hotel** (Main St., 406/796-2426) or the **Shamrock Bar** (Main St., 406/796-8250) both of which offer up light meals and good times.

Information

The Wibaux **chamber of commerce** can be reached at P.O. Box 159, Wibaux, MT 59353 (406/795-2412).

The Southeastern Corner

SOUTHEASTERN MONTANA

In the far southeastern corner of Montana, between the Yellowstone River and Montana's border with Wyoming and the Dakotas, is a vast wedge of prairie and forested uplands that contains some of the state's best rangeland. In the 1880s, during the heyday of open-range cattle ranching, this land was highly prized. Longstanding agricultural trade towns like **Baker, Ekalaka,** and **Broadus** serve as outposts of society in this little-visited corner of Montana outback.

For lovers of the backcountry, there are a number of reasons to make the journey, however. **Medicine Rocks State Park** is a strangely evocative collection of sandstone monoliths that was considered sacred by Native Americans. Ekalaka's **Carter County Museum** contains a significant collection of dinosaur fossils collected by a local amateur paleontologist.

BAKER

Located 81 miles from Miles City and only 12 miles from North Dakota, Baker (pop. 1,695, elev. 2,929 feet) is a bustling commercial center with good recreational facilities. Baker first boomed during the early years of its founding, when the railroad came across Montana in the 1900s. Most of the downtown was built during this time. In the 1960s and 1970s, nearby oil and gas exploration brought a new spate of civic building. Even though the oil boom has gone a bit bust, Baker has experienced enough prosperity to distance it from its roots as an agricultural trade center.

The most notable aspect of Baker is Baker Lake, a reservoir in the center of town that's the focus of summer water sports. At Triangle Park and the lake's south end, there's a swimming and picnicking area.

Nearby Ismay decided to celebrate its centennial as a community in 1993 by renaming itself something that would garner some attention—like Joe. The town's namesake—former

San Francisco 49ers and Kansas City Chiefs quarterback Joe Montana—was flattered but didn't bother to attend the festivities.

Sights

The **O'Fallon Historical Museum** (2nd St. at Fallon, 406/778-3265, 9 A.M.–noon and 1–5 P.M. daily June–Sept., closed Sat. Oct.–May, free) contains artifacts from the area's Indian past and early settlement years, plus six historic buildings. The real highlight here is an enormous stuffed steer—at almost 4,000 pounds it's one of the world's largest.

Accommodations

The **Montana Motel** (716 E. Montana Ave., 406/778-3315 or 800/779-8353, $70 and up) has both brand new rooms plus newly remodeled rooms, all with fridges, microwaves, and free wireless Internet.

Camping

Baker makes tourists welcome with free camping. Tent campers are encouraged to throw up a tent in **McClain Memorial Park** (Hwy. 12 at 3rd St. W.). In the same complex is **Walt's RV Memorial Park,** which offers free RV camping with hookups.

Food

Good home-style food is available at **Sakelaris's Kitchen** (121 Lake City Shopping Ctr., 406/778-2202, 6 A.M.–7 P.M., $8–14) in the Lake City Shopping Center. **Jane's Home Cookin'** (23 S. 1st St. W., 406/778-3647, 7 A.M.–4 P.M.) serves homemade soups and pies. If you want a drink with your steak, go to the **Corner Bar & Casino** (1 S. Main, 406/778-3278, 11 A.M.–10 P.M., $9–16).

Services

The **Fallon County Hospital** (406/778-3331) is at 320 Hospital Drive. Call the **sheriff's office** (406/778-2879) in case of emergency. The **chamber of commerce** (406/778-

SOUTHEASTERN MONTANA

© BILL MCRAE

The buttes and prairies of southeastern Montana were the northern terminus of 1880s cattle drives.

2266) can be reached at P.O. Box 849, Baker, MT 58313.

EKALAKA

Ekalaka (pop. 410, elev. 3,457 feet) is known affectionately as "the town at the end of the road," for there is only one paved road to it. It is reached by first going to Baker (not exactly the center of the world itself) and turning south for an additional 35 miles. No one just turns up in Ekalaka by mistake, but there are ample reasons to make the trip.

The Medicine Rocks, an Indian holy site, are 11 miles north of town. Three units of the Sioux Division of the Custer National Forest are within one hour of the town limits. The Carter County Museum is known nationally for its collection of local dinosaur skeletons. The town buildings don't bother to hide their age or history.

But the real pleasures of Ekalaka are highly subjective and understated. Ekalaka is for the traveler who will smile to see a main street on which original stone buildings still house bars

and stores, and street benches on which locals sit and chat; for a traveler who finds pleasure in a forest of scattered pines atop limestone cliffs; for a traveler who is content to watch the sunset at the site of ancient Indian rites; and for the traveler who enjoys a quiet drink listening to the conversations of ranchers in old bars. Anybody beguiled by the languor of the West will find Ekalaka fascinating. Time, if not prosperity, has been kind to Ekalaka; the town is much as the 1930s left it, for better or worse.

◖ Carter County Museum

The Carter County Museum (Main St., 406/775-6886, 9 A.M.–5 P.M. Tues.–Fri., 1–5 P.M. Sat.–Sun., free) is worth a detour. For any fan of dinosaur remains, this is one of Montana's best small museums, as its collection is nationally known. Ekalaka country is particularly rich in fossil remains, and Marshall Lambert, a science teacher at the local high school, was a keen amateur paleontologist. His discoveries of entire dinosaur

THE LIFE AND TIMES OF THE LIVESTOCK BRAND

It is impossible to know who first used brands in Montana; however, Meriwether Lewis marked his bags with his own brand, and the 1850 inventory of goods at Fort Union lists a branding iron valued at $2.50. By the time the first territorial legislature met in 1864, livestock numbers were great enough for the government to enact a law regarding the recording of brands. Registering brands was meant to limit livestock loss resulting from straying (a problem in the days of the open range) and to help prosecute rustlers.

A state commission was formed to regulate brands throughout the state, thus eliminating brand duplication. But the problem of rustling remained. Certain brands are easily altered: a "running iron" can change E-Y to B-K within minutes. Also, because a brand is proof of ownership, any animal stolen while young and unbranded and then branded with someone else's brand becomes that person's property.

But early laws lacked teeth. Rustlers were an especially virulent problem in central Montana, and exasperated ranchers took enforcement into their own hands. Vigilantes under the direction of Granville Stuart are reported to have summarily executed up to 60 alleged rustlers during the summer of 1884. Alarmed, the legislature quickly passed laws controlling the movement of livestock. Those laws form the basis of Montana's present-day system of brands records.

To halt the movement of stolen animals, livestock inspectors examine all animals moved across county lines and when a change of ownership takes place. Livestock presented for sale at an auction yard must be accompanied by a permit of transport and must pass a brand inspection at the sales yards. Montana law also provides for range detectives, who investigate suspected rustlers.

BRAND LORE

Contrary to popular belief, brands are not a cowman's vanity plate. Most early brands were not the owner's initials. One problem is that all characters and symbols are not equally effective as brands, and some brand more cleanly than others. For instance, Bs and 8s are notoriously hard to apply; the hot iron will simply singe an indistinguishable blotch on the animal's flesh. Letters such as Y and N are preferred because their clean lines are easily read. Other letters present the problem of being too easy to alter.

Generally speaking, two-figure brands are preferred over three-figure brands: to a cattleman, it's one fewer irons to apply. The same brand can be registered to different people if it is applied to different parts of the animal. Cattle have six typical brand areas: the hips, ribs, and shoulders – on both the left and right side. HS on a right shoulder is a different brand from HS on a left hip. The same rules apply to horses, except that horses are never branded on the ribs but rather on the jaw.

Montana law allows brands to be registered for animals besides cattle and horses: sheep brands, for example, as well as brands for buffalo, elk, deer, hogs, and mules.

Brands must be reregistered every 10 years for a $50 fee. Brands that are not reregistered become available to newcomers. When applying for a brand, one specifies what letters are preferred, and the registrar sends a selection of brands not already taken that use those characters. (Most obvious combinations are already taken.) Two-figure brands have cachet, because they are more authentic, but the Brand Commission no longer issues any new two-figure brands. The only two-figure brands available are those established brands that have been allowed to lapse. In the back of Montana livestock newspapers you will see ads for two-figure brands. A good brand with some history can bring $1,500.

Recently, ranchers have experimented with freeze branding. Instead of hot irons searing the flesh, extremely cold irons, dipped in liquid nitrogen, freeze the animal's hair follicles, causing the hair to grow in white. The brand then shows up in contrast. Obviously, this method works best on dark animals.

OLD TIMES IN EKALAKA

While other cities have founding fathers, Ekalaka has a founding bartender. Claude Carter, a Nebraska buffalo hunter who knew the weaknesses of his fellow settlers, was intending to establish a bar along Russell Creek when his wagon of logs bogged down several miles short of his destination. "Hell," Carter was reported as saying, "any place in Montana is a good place to build a saloon." His bar, the Old Stand, was the founding business of Ekalaka, and tradition places the date in the 1860s. In those days, Ekalaka was known as "Pup Town" for a nearby prairie dog colony.

David Russell, the first white homesteader in the area, moved to the Old Stand settlement in 1881. His wife was a Sioux woman named Ijkalaka ("Swift One" in Siouan), a niece of Sitting Bull. When the post office came in 1885, it was named for her.

skeletons, including the only remains of the Pachycephalosaurus found in the world, allow the Carter County Museum to boast a collection of bones to rival the best museums in the country. There's also a good selection of Indian artifacts, minerals, and exhibits on the early pioneer settlement of the area. A planned expansion of the paleontology exhibits is scheduled to open in 2010.

Medicine Rocks State Park

The Medicine Rocks State Park, 11 miles north of Ekalaka on Highway 7, contains a series of sandstone outcroppings carved by the wind into weird and mysterious shapes. Some of the buttes tower 80 feet above the pine-clad countryside, and others wind along the hilltops like trains. The Sioux called the area *Inyan-oka-la-ka,* or "Rock with a hole in it," for the strange holes and tunnels in the stone. Legend maintains that the Indians used the area for vision quests and other rituals, and they considered the rocks to be sacred and full of "medicine," or spirit power. Sitting Bull and his Sioux and Cheyenne warriors reportedly camped here before the Battle of the Little Bighorn, waiting for guidance from their medicine men. The mile-square park welcomes picnickers, campers, and sightseers; it is open daily with free admittance. At the entrance to the park is a hand pump with good water, and tables, fire pits, and latrines are also provided. Beware of snakes.

Other Sights

"One road in" is Ekalaka's motto. However, for the explorer who has no fear of gravel roads, this corner of Montana offers little gems of beauty and adventure, and other ways out.

Three sections of the **Sioux Division of the Custer National Forest** lie within easy striking range of Ekalaka. South of town along a well-traveled gravel road are the **Chalk Buttes.** These stark white cliffs sit atop rocky forested buttes and can be seen for miles. The Chalk Buttes have long served as landmarks for travelers and stockmen. Fighting Butte, or Starvation Rock, is the most northerly of the Chalk Buttes. Its flat top is inaccessible but for a treacherous single-track path. According to Indian legend, members of one tribe, seeking to escape pursuers of another tribe, fled up the precipitous path leading to the summit. Once there, the pursuing Indians simply guarded the single-file access to the butte and waited for their foes to die of thirst and starvation.

According to a Bureau of Land Management official, species of grass grow on the top of Fighting Butte that occur nowhere else in the Ekalaka area. One local sheep rancher grazed sheep on these unusual grasses, to his eventual chagrin: A windy storm blew up, and the entire herd of 600 drifted with the wind to fall off the sheer sides to their deaths.

Recreational opportunities are more numerous in the other sections of the Sioux Division of the Custer National Forest. In the **Ekalaka Hills,** southeast of Ekalaka, there are two camping areas. **Macnab Pond** is located in piney hills seven miles southeast of town on Highway 323 and one mile east on a gravel

© BILL MCRAE

The area near Ekalaka now known as Medicine Rocks State Park was sacred to the Sioux.

road. Watch for signs. Trout have been planted in the pond.

Ekalaka Park is more remote. Follow signs for **Camp Needmore,** three miles southeast on Highway 323, and after arriving at Camp Needmore follow Forest Service Road 104 (Rimrock Carter Road) five miles. Although there are no official trails, hiking among the ponderosa pines and sandstone outcroppings is easy and interesting. Wildlife is abundant, and during the spring there is a good display of wildflowers.

If you like this kind of lonely open country sprinkled with buttes and pines, and if you feel adventurous, a day trip to **Long Pines,** the third section of the Sioux Division of the Custer National Forest, is well worth it. Follow Prairie Dale Road to Mill Iron off Highway 323 (three miles south of Ekalaka) for about 10 miles, and turn south on Forest Service Road 107 (Snow Creek Road). This gravel road follows the main spine of the Long Pines. Wildlife viewing is especially good here.

Raptors love the sandstone bluffs (this is the nation's primary breeding range for merlin falcons), as do deer, coyotes, and wild turkeys. Just short of the North Dakota border lies **Capitol Rock,** a huge deposit of volcanic ash eroded into the shape of the nation's capitol. Again, hiking is informal, as there are no maintained trails. Camp at Lantis Spring Campground, about 15 miles into the national forest, where water is available. If you camp informally, make sure you heed fire restrictions and carry garbage out.

If you follow Snow Creek Road out, you end up in Camp Crook, South Dakota, on the Little Missouri. Camp Crook was a station on the Deadwood Stagecoach route.

Accommodations

The **Midway Motel** (406/775-6619, Apr.–Nov., $55), on Highway 7 as it enters Ekalaka, offers basic rooms. The **Guest House** (406/775-6337, $45) is an updated hotel on Main Street. Pets are allowed, and it's open all year.

Camping

Cline Camper Court, west of town (406/775-6231), is open April–December but has no tent sites. **Ekalaka Park** is a Forest Service campground. Go three miles south on Highway 323, then follow signs on the improved road for another six miles; it's open May–November. **Macnab Pond,** another Forest Service facility, is seven miles south on Highway 323, one mile east on the improved road; both sites have toilets and water, and Macnab has fishing.

Food
The revered **Old Stand Bar** (406/775-6661, 11 A.M.–9 P.M.) is on Main Street and still offers steaks ($12–$17) and cocktails. The **Wagon Wheel Cafe** (406/775-6639, 7 A.M.–7 P.M.), just up the street, is a friendly place for a lighter meal; chicken fried steak is $9.

BROADUS
There's something about the Powder River that excites the phrasemaker. "A mile wide, an inch deep," "Too thin to plow, too thick to drink," the sayings go. There is some truth to these statements: When the Yellowstone discharges into the Missouri, the Powder River has contributed only 5 percent of the flow but 50 percent of the silt. The broad grassy valleys of the Powder River and the Little Powder River have been home first to vast herds of wildlife and later to equally vast herds of cattle.

Nestled in the cottonwoods along the river, Broadus (pop. 451, elev. 3,030 feet) is an attractive ranching town. Oil revenue allows the town extras like a good school system and new county offices.

History
The early Indians spent summers hunting here, where buffalo, prairie elk, deer, pronghorn, and game birds were abundant. Later, after westward Indian migration began, these hunting grounds were at the heart of bitter disputes between the Crows, who claimed it as a homeland, and the Sioux alliance.

A sad presaging of the great buffalo annihilation came in 1854 through 1856, when Sir George Gore, an Irish sportsman, came to hunt the Powder River country. Gore was no rugged survivalist; his entourage included

several guides, 20 servants, 112 horses, 12 yoke oxen, six wagons, and 21 carts for ammunition. After spending the winter at the mouth of the Tongue River, Gore killed local game in such numbers that finally the Crow protested.

After the Sioux were interned and the buffalo eliminated from their range, the rich Powder River country became the avenue into Montana for Texas cattle drives. The cattle boom lasted barely 10 years, but it survived long enough to form much of the iconography of the Old West.

Market forces, a disastrous winter, and the influx of homesteaders all contributed to the decline of the cattle drover and the establishment of the cattle rancher. By the 1890s, ranches and settlements were springing up along the Powder and its tributaries. Broadus, and euphonious crossroads like Sonette, Olive, Epsie, Liscom, Quietus, Mizpah, and other "South Side" outposts, began as trading centers and post offices.

Located near the confluence of the Powder and the Little Powder Rivers, Broadus became the dominant trading center for the southeastern corner of Montana. Oil was discovered in Belle Creek, south of Broadus, in 1967. Within six years the field had produced more than $1 billion in oil alone; Belle Creek also produces significant amounts of natural gas.

Sights
The **Powder River Historical Museum** (102 W. Wilson, 406/436-2862, 9 A.M.–5 P.M. Mon.–Sat., Memorial Day–Sept. 30, free) has a collection of artifacts illustrating local history, along with old cars, an old buggy, and the old Powder River County Jail. The **Mac's Museum,** a collection of Indian artifacts and seashells, is also here now, as is the local visitors center.

Cattle Drives
The Powder River country is seeing another surge of cattle droving these days, although this time they're put on for fun. Expect to trail cattle with suitably gentle horses, do chores, eat chuckwagon food, sleep out, and (the one

SOUTHEASTERN MONTANA

inauthentic amenity) shower. Contact **Powder River Wagon Trains & Cattle Drives** (P.O. Box 676, Broadus, MT 59317, 406/436-2350 or 800/492-8835, www.powderrivercattledrive.com) if a recreational cattle drive sounds like fun. Expect to pay about $2,100 to join a six-day drive, including all meals, sleeping accommodations, horse, and tack; cattle drives usually take place in mid to late July.

Accommodations

Three of Broadus's motels are now operated by one office, called the **Broadus Motels** (the office is at the Quarter Horse Motor Inn, 101 N. Park, 406/436-2626). You'll be given a choice of an older or a newer unit, with prices ranging from $62–$70. Rooms in each of the motels are equally well-furnished, comfortable, and conveniently located; kitchen rooms are also available. Broadus Motels also offers more adventurous accommodations in summer, including tepees, cowboy cabins, and a sheep wagon.

Another lodging alternative is to stay at a guest ranch. **Doonan Gulch Outfitters** (406/427-5474), 25 miles west of Broadus off Highway 212, also operates the 【 **Oakwood Lodge B&B** in a spacious new log lodge on their ranch. Each of the three guest rooms ($70) has a private bathroom.

Camping

Town and Country Trailer Village, located one block west of Highway 212 East (406/436-2595, Apr.–Nov.), and **Wayside Park,** located just south of the junction of Highways 212 and 59 (406/436-2510), both offer tent and RV camping.

Food

The attractive 【 **Judge's Chambers** restaurant (101 S. Wilbur, 406/436-2002) serves "prairie food" made from local products, including vegetables and herbs from the chef's garden in summer. This is the most refined food for miles, so do plan to stop. The restaurant incorporates local specialties prepared by European-trained chefs. It's definitely worth calling ahead to make sure the restaurant is open before making the drive to Broadus, though; at present it's open 11 A.M.–9 P.M. Thursday–Saturday from early June through October only. The **Montana Bar and Cafe** (111 E. Wilson, 406/436-2454, 7 A.M.–9P.M.) serves three meals a day, with homemade pies a favorite.

Outfitters

The Powder River country is home to an abundance of outfitters. The local twist on hunting is to go after prairie dogs rather than, say, elk. **Powder River Outfitters** (406/427-5497, www.powder-river-outfitters.com) offers archery, deer, pronghorn, and game-bird hunting; ask for Ken. **Doonan Gulch Outfitters** (Russell Greenwood, S. Pumpkin Creek Rd., 406/427-5474) offers hunting for big game and "varmints," rockhounding, hiking, and a B&B.

Services

Powder River Medical Service (406/436-2651) is at 507 N. Lincoln. Contact the **sheriff** at 406/436-2333. The **chamber of commerce** (406/436-2611) is at P.O. Box 484, Broadus, MT 59317.

Crow and Northern Cheyenne Reservations

The Crow and Northern Cheyenne Reservations are basically the upper drainages of Montana's Tongue and Bighorn Rivers. The landscape combines the lyricism of rough sandstone bluffs and uplands covered with ponderosa pine forest with the austerity of the high, barren prairies. And underlying everything here are the vast coal deposits of the Fort Union Formation.

Except for the river valleys and small reservation towns like **Hardin**, there is scarcely any development. Like the Custer National Forest to the east, the reservation lands seem to be maintained in a kind of ad hoc trust. While this has preserved the beauty and integrity of the area, it has hindered the economic development of the tribes.

This region has always been Indian land, first by tradition, later by decree. The Crow settled here 300 years ago. Later, other tribes vied for room on these rich hunting grounds south of the Yellowstone. When traders first came to barter with the Indians for furs, they came here; when the Army came to subdue the Indians, they came here as well. One of the most stirring events in Western history took place on these plains: the clash between the 7th Calvary under General George A. Custer and the assembled warriors of the Sioux and Northern Cheyenne, commemorated at **Little Bighorn National Monument.** And there is something more than history, as well; the mixed prairies and forests of these reservations have a cultural weight, their openness and limitlessness a statement of animistic potency.

HARDIN

Even though Hardin (pop. 3,384, elev. 2,966 feet) is not on the Crow Reservation, it serves as the primary trading center for residents of the reservation and the ranches to the north and west. It's a pleasant town, with a local museum that's worth a visit, and it is a good base for trips to the Little Bighorn Battlefield, Bighorn Canyon, and the Crow and Northern Cheyenne Reservations.

The confluence of the Little Bighorn and Bighorn Rivers was a strategic outpost during the Indian Wars. The steamboat *Far West* maneuvered up the Bighorn to the mouth of the Little Bighorn in June 1876 to pick up wounded soldiers after the Reno-Benteen battle. In 1877, the year after the Custer battle, Bighorn Post was built on the cliffs above the confluence. Renamed Fort Custer, it was apparently rather a grand fort, in the manner of Fort Keogh; it was abandoned in 1898.

By 1906 the Dawes Act opened the reservation to white settlement. The next year, only nine years after Fort Custer ceased its patrol of the Crows, the Chicago, Burlington, and Quincy Railroad built a spur line down to the present site of Hardin, both to bring in new settlers and to serve their needs.

During World War II, many Japanese-American internees were brought into Montana to work sugar-beet fields because farmers were experiencing a labor shortage. A large number worked in the Hardin area; some settled here after the war.

Bighorn County Historical Museum

The Bighorn County Historical Museum (exit 497, 406/665-1671, www.museumonthebighorn.org, 8 A.M.–6 P.M. daily May–Sept., 9 A.M.–5 P.M. Mon.–Sat. Oct.–Apr.) has 20 historic restored buildings open for viewing in summer, including a handsome 1917 German Lutheran church, an old post office and store, and old farm buildings, including a 1916 farmhouse that's never been renovated and particularly evokes early-20th-century rural life. The museum contains rotating exhibits and a good selection of books on local history and lore. The museum also has a visitors center, picnic tables, and bathrooms.

Other Sights and Recreation

Stop by the **Jailhouse Gallery** (218 N. Center, 406/665-3239) to see exhibits on

Native American culture and art, and works by local artists.

Custer Park has a playground and picnic tables. Take exit 495 south on Crawford Street, but resist the urge to veer off to Yellowtail Dam, and instead follow Crawford until 3rd Avenue.

Hardin's community **pool** (621 W. 8th St., 406/665-2346) is Olympic-sized and indoors.

Accommodations

The **Lariat Motel** (709 N. Center, 406/665-2683, $52 and up) is clean and basic, and allows pets.

The **American Inn** (1324 Crawford, 406/665-1870 or 800/582-8094, $79 and up) has two guest laundries, a hot tub, pool, and 140-foot waterslide. Also part of the complex is a lounge, restaurant, and casino, as well as a playground and barbecue area.

A historic brick hotel in downtown Hardin has been converted into the **(Hotel Becker B&B** (200 N. Center, 406/665-2707, June–Sept., $75 d and up). There are seven guest rooms, each with its own bathroom (though some baths are across the hall). The owner-hostess is a good cook and travel adviser.

Another local B&B is the **(Kendrick House Inn** (206 N. Custer, 406/665-3035, www.kendrickhouseinn.com, $90 d and up), a historic boardinghouse updated to offer five charming guest rooms; an all-you-can-eat breakfast is included. Families and small pets can sometimes be accommodated with advance notice. Just across the street in another historic building, where the owners of Kendrick House have opened a teahouse with light lunch and dessert service.

Camping

The **KOA** (406/665-1635) is one mile north of Hardin on Highway 47. **Grandview Campground** (406/665-2489) is south of Hardin on Highway 313.

Food

Hardin is not a place for cuisine. The fast food outlets at exit 495 present one option. **The Purple Cow** (406/665-3601, 7 A.M.–9 P.M.),

just north of I-90 on Highway 47, is a vintage roadside diner with meals $7–12.

Events

The Hardin Chamber of Commerce sponsors the annual **Little Bighorn Days,** whose main feature is the **Reenactment of Custer's Last Stand** (406/665-1672 or 888/450-3577, www.custerslaststand.org). The event is held on the Friday, Saturday, and Sunday closest to the anniversary of the battle on June 26. In addition to the battle, the actors stage the events that led up to the conflict. It's a huge swirl of horses, tepees, and warriors, with more than 200 participants, and the drama is matched by the dust. The reenactment is held six miles west of Hardin, not at the battle site. Other events during Little Bighorn Days include a rodeo, an 1876 grand ball, Indian dancing, and special tours of the Little Bighorn Battlefield.

Tickets to the reenactment are $20 for adults and $8 for children. There are two shows on Saturday, and one each on Friday and Sunday. Tickets and information are available through the chamber of commerce or the website.

Information

The **chamber of commerce** (406/665-1672) can be found at 21 East 4th Street. The **post office** is at 406 North Cheyenne. The **Bighorn County Memorial Hospital** (406/665-2310) is at 17 North Miles.

THE CROW INDIAN RESERVATION
Before the White Man

The present-day Crow Indians derive from Hidatsa tribes who originally lived along the Mississippi headwaters. Of Siouan linguistic stock, they were an agrarian people who lived in earth lodges and made pottery. Sometime during the 1600s the Crow left the larger Hidatsa tribe and began to move westward, first settling in the Black Hills area. Increasingly, lands as far west as the Powder, Tongue, and Bighorn River drainages were added to their hunting grounds, and by the 1770s the tribe had settled onto its historic homelands south of the Yellowstone.

When William Clark first traveled through Crow territory in 1806, the Crow were a wandering tribe of hunters living in tepees along the Bighorn. The horse had been introduced to the Crow only about 50 years before, and even though only 3,500 members belonged to the tribe, they already owned about 10,000 horses. The Crow had almost totally given up agriculture (though they continued to raise tobacco) and were nomadic within their hunting grounds. Crow women were famous for their bead and quill work, and Crow men were great horsemen and hunters. They were also proud of their long hair and may have been *les beaux homes* ("the handsome men") recorded by the French explorers, the Verendryes. The tribe was organized first by family, then by matrilineal clan. Known as the Absaroka in Hidatsan, or "children of the large-beaked bird," they were considered to be as crafty and enterprising as the raven, hence the English name Crow.

Friendly Relations

From their first contact with white explorers and traders, the Crow have maintained mostly friendly relations with European settlers. Montana's first trading post, Fort Ramon, was built in 1807 at the juncture of the Bighorn and Yellowstone to serve the beaver-pelt trade with the Crow. Although the Indians initially were not exactly willing partners in the beaver trade (they chafed at trapping and trading pelts for more goods than they had need for), the presence of white traders in Crow territory led to a long-standing and important alliance between the Europeans and the Crow.

In 1833, Fort Cass was built on the same grounds as the abandoned Fort Ramon. By this time the main article of trade was buffalo hide, and this time the Crow were interested. A complex relationship between the Indians and whites emerged: The traders provided tobacco, food, guns, manufactured goods, clothing, and liquor, while the Crow provided pelts and hides and protection from the hostile Blackfeet to the north. The whites and the Indians hunted together, sharing knowledge and cultures.

But the Crow became economically dependent on trade with the whites, a dependency served by plundering the riches of their homeland. While Indians like the Crow were instrumental in exterminating the vast herds of buffalo in the West, the buffalo remained their source of food and shelter. By the 1880s the buffalo had disappeared from its range on the Yellowstone.

The alliance with the agents of the United States was also strategic for the Crow in their ongoing warfare with rival Indian tribes. The warlike Blackfeet to the north endangered their lucrative trade with the whites, while the Sioux and Cheyenne to the east threatened traditional Crow hunting grounds. The treaties of Fort Laramie in 1851 and 1868 guaranteed the Crow homelands against incursions by whites and by other Indian tribes, especially the hostile Sioux confederacy.

It wasn't just political concerns that provided the bond between the Crow and the white settlers. Their friendship lasted several generations and weathered many altercations. And while the U.S. government was not especially solicitous to the Crow (though they were treated somewhat less abjectly by the United States than some other tribes), the Crow remained faithful allies. Crow scouts accompanied Custer and his troops during his fateful Montana tour of June 1876.

The Reservation Today

In 1965 the Bighorn River was dammed near the site of Fort Smith. This beautiful rugged landscape became the Bighorn National Recreation Area in 1968. By trapping sediment, cooling the water, and maintaining a steady flow, the dam changed the Bighorn from a slow-moving catfish river to a crystal-clear blue-ribbon trout stream, one of the best fisheries for trophy-size trout in the country.

This once-remote corner of the Crow Reservation suddenly became popular with hunters, anglers, and tourists, but the Crow considered the Bighorn Canyon and the adjacent Pryor and Bighorn Mountains to be sacred lands. In 1973 the tribe voted to close all hunting and fishing to non-Indians on the reservation, citing its rights to the Bighorn under the Fort Laramie treaties. The state of Montana took the tribe to court in order to open public access to the river. The case, known as the Battle of the Bighorn, went all the way to the U.S. Supreme Court, which in 1981 found for the state. There are now four fishing-access sites along the river within the reservation.

The present Crow Reservation, much reduced from the 1868 land grant, contains 37,000 square miles of rolling prairie and rugged foothills drained by the Bighorn River, making it Montana's largest reservation. There are about 7,000 tribal members, with a majority living on the reservation. The Crow language, a cousin to Siouan and Assiniboin, is spoken by more than 80 percent of the tribe. The retention of their native language is a combination of tradition (no Crow addresses another Crow in English) and the fact that the federal government never mandated English-only boarding schools on the Crow Reservation.

Chief Plenty Coups State Park

Chief Plenty Coups, the last of the great Crow war chiefs, is credited for advocating peaceful relations with the whites and for being the first Crow leader to recognize the need to adapt to the new life of the reservation. When the U.S. government opened the Crow Reservation to individual allotments in 1887, the young chief applied for his 320 acres, just west of Pryor off Highway 416, along a pretty stretch of Pryor Creek. It had been revealed to Chief Plenty Coups in a vision quest almost 30 years before that he would live out his life there, "where the plums grow."

Chief Plenty Coups attempted to set an example of how the Crow might coexist with the white settlers. He stressed education and mediated conflicts between his tribesmen and the whites. He cultivated his holding and built a two-story log home and a store, symbolically forsaking the tepee and the hunting lifestyle of the prairie nomad. He and his wife lived there until his death in 1932.

A stirring orator, Plenty Coups became a sort of celebrity, traveling to Washington,

D.C., frequently to represent his people. While he was staying in Washington he visited Mt. Vernon, home of the first president. He then conceived of dedicating his land on the reservation as a memorial to the Crow Nation. The Chief Plenty Coups Monument was dedicated in 1928 as a "token of my friendship for all people, both red and white." It is now a Montana state park.

The 40-acre park (406/252-1289, www.fwp. state.mt.us/parks, free for Montana residents, $2 day-use fee for nonresidents, children under 6 free) houses a museum of Crow culture, Plenty Coups's home and store, his grave, and a gift shop featuring Crow crafts. The spacious grounds allow plenty of room to stretch your legs, and there is a well-developed picnic area (but no overnight camping). The park is open 8 A.M.–8 P.M. daily, and the museum is open 10 A.M.–5 P.M. May 1–September 30.

Recreation

The Bighorn River below Yellowtail Dam has become one of the country's most famous trout fisheries. The newfound popularity of the Bighorn has concerned the Crow, who object to the influx of people onto reservation land along the river. The state now maintains four fishing-access sites within the reservation. Do not attempt to fish on private land without getting permission. Anglers should stay within high-water marks, in or on the river, to avoid trespassing on Crow land. More than a dozen outfitters in the Fort Smith area rent boats and offer guide services. The following also offer guest lodging in addition to guided fly fishing: **Bighorn Country Outfitters** (P.O. Box 7828, Fort Smith, MT 59035, 406/666-2326 or 800/835-2529, www.bighornkingfisher.com) and **Fort Smith Fly Shop and Cabins** (P.O. Box 7872, Fort Smith, MT 59035, 406/666-2550, www.flyfishingthebighorn.com).

Events

The **Crow Fair** is the biggest event of the year and is perhaps the largest Native American gathering in North America. During the third weekend of August, the tribal campgrounds near Crow Agency become a sea of tepees, pickup trucks, and RVs as thousands of tribe members and visitors rendezvous to celebrate Crow heritage. Traditional games are played, including innocent-seeming "hand games," where money is gambled in a variation of the shell game. Some of the Crow dress in traditional garb, which shows off their complex and colorful beadwork. The costumes largely come off during the dance contests. There is also a parade, an all-Indian rodeo, and horse racing. Visitors are welcome, and bead goods and Indian food are for sale. Bring sunscreen and a hat, and be prepared to get dusty. For more information, contact the Crow Tribal Council (below) or visit the website http://crowfair.crowtribe.com.

Information
The **Crow Tribal Council** (406/638-3700, www.crowtribe.com) can be contacted at P.O. Box 159, Crow Agency, MT 59022.

Contact the **Bighorn National Recreation Area** (406/666-2412, www.nps.gov/bica) at P.O. Box 458, Fort Smith, MT 59035.

◖ LITTLE BIGHORN BATTLEFIELD NATIONAL MONUMENT
The Battle of the Little Bighorn was one of those epochal historical moments when individual strands of fate, personality, and history wove a whole that is larger and more meaningful than any sum of its parts. Upon hearing the story of Custer and Sitting Bull, an elemental part of the psyche either rejoices at the victory of the American Natives or condemns the triumph of savagery. To stand on the sere slopes of the Wolf Mountains and ponder the events of 1876 is to sense that something much more than a battle between armies and cultures took place. The issues at stake continue to resonate as the historical march of culture confronting culture goes on.

The centerpiece of the monument is the battlefield, although the museum and interpretive center are also fascinating. However, change is coming to this remote historic corner of

Montana: The Crow tribe has recently built a casino and deli just outside the park boundaries.

George Armstrong Custer
However hackneyed the observation, George Armstrong Custer was, and remains, an enigma. He graduated last in his class at West Point. He served the Union in the Civil War. He became the youngest general in the history of the Army after General Lee surrendered to him; he was later court-martialed for ordering the shooting of Army deserters in Kansas.

Once reinstated, Custer—demoted to a lieutenant colonel—became commander of the Seventh Cavalry. His exploits made him and his wife colorful and frequent guests at New York society functions. He fell afoul of the Grant administration for allegations made in congressional hearings about corruption involving the president's brother and Indian trading licenses. Custer was arrested again.

A New York newspaper publisher who championed Custer as a future presidential candidate used his presses to mold opinion in Custer's favor. Released again, the 36-year-old Custer led 265 men to death on the Little Bighorn when he went on the offensive against a united war party with upward of 3,000 Sioux and Cheyenne warriors.

The Sioux and Cheyenne
This butterfly of a man confronted representatives of an ancient culture. The Sioux and Cheyenne were settled into one reservation in eastern Wyoming and the western Dakotas by the conditions of the Fort Laramie Treaty of 1868. However, the discovery of gold in 1874 in South Dakota's Black Hills immediately caused the treaty to be broken by gold hunters. Sioux and Cheyenne warriors, responding to these incursions onto their reservation and to the age-old need to migrate to hunt buffalo, began to leave their reservation. Under the leadership of such warriors as Sitting Bull and Crazy Horse, they camped in the drainages of the Powder, Tongue, and Rosebud Rivers, their numbers growing as more and more natives became disenchanted with their treatment. Here,

for one last reprise, they practiced the centuries-old culture of the Plains Indian.

From here they also raided settlements and harassed travelers. The Commissioner of Indian Affairs ordered the Indians back onto the reservation, threatening military action if they did not comply by January 31, 1875.

The Sioux and Cheyenne did not respond, and the Army was sent to force them to move.

The Battle of the Little Bighorn

Three separate expeditions were sent out to campaign against the hostiles. These troops were to move from three different directions into the southeastern corner of Montana, where the Indian forces were known to be encamped. Custer's Seventh Cavalry followed the Rosebud River up to its divide with the Little Bighorn, where he was to wait for the two other columns. Instead, he divided his own command into thirds, and on June 25, 1876, took the offensive against one of the largest Indian forces ever gathered.

The details of the engagement at the Little Bighorn are best left for the traveler to discover at the battle site. What actually happened is complex, far from certain, and compelling.

Perhaps we learn of Custer and the Sioux too early in life, when complex issues seem too simple. The battlefield is not merely a place for boys of all ages to gloat in the memory of battle. The site is as chilling as Civil War battlefields, where you sense the past and somehow recognize the end of a culture and an epoch with a tightened and hollow gut. This is Montana's most haunted ground.

Battlefield Sights

The battle site is 15 miles east of Hardin, one mile east of Highway 90. The **visitors center** (406/638-2621, www.nps.gov/bica, 8 A.M.–9 P.M. daily Memorial Day–July 31, 8 A.M.–8 P.M. Aug. 1–Labor Day, 8 A.M.–6 P.M. spring and fall, 8 A.M.–4:30 P.M. winter, $10 per vehicle, $5 per pedestrian) is situated below the crest of the hill where the last stand took place. It contains some interesting exhibits and should be visited before going on to the

battlefields. Exhibits explain the Indian background to the conflict, the military strategies, the contemporary lifestyles of both cultures, and also display artifacts of the battle. Probably the most arresting of the exhibits is a raised-relief map of the entire battle area, which uses colored lights (indicating soldiers and Indians) to show the ebb and flow of the battle. There is also a good bookshop where you'll want to pick up further reading or a tape to play in your car as you tour the battlefield. Downhill from the visitors center is Custer National Cemetery, where some war dead from this and other conflicts are buried.

In 2003 the National Park Service unveiled the **Little Bighorn Battlefield Indian Memorial,** dedicated to Indian lives and perspectives on the conflict. The memorial consists of bronze spirit statues representing fallen Indian warriors and a spirit gate for the dead Army soldiers, plus story panels, petroglyphs, and plaques with writings of Indian leaders.

One quarter mile up the hill is Last Stand Hill Monument, where the last of the Seventh Cavalry died. Grave markers stand where the bodies of soldiers were found. They are interred in a common grave under the monument, which bears the names of the dead. Custer is buried at West Point.

To look down the grassy hillside at the markers, some standing alone, others huddled together, many clumped together around the swale where Custer's own body was found, is to vividly experience the full horror of the battle.

The paved road winds past the monument on a seven-mile loop road to the **Reno-Benteen Battlefield.** Maj. Marcus Reno and three of the Seventh Cavalry's companies were ordered by Custer to lead the first offensive against the Sioux and Cheyenne village on the Little Bighorn River. They retreated up to this ridge, where they took up defensible positions. During the melee, the main Indian attack was directed north to Custer's command. Reno was joined by Capt. Frederick Benteen and the cavalry's pack train, the last third of Custer's original unit. On this hill, behind the bodies of slaughtered pack horses, these soldiers withstood 48 hours of attack by the victorious Sioux and Cheyenne before the Indians, almost inexplicably, retreated. A self-guided walking tour of the battlefield begins at the parking lot. Park rangers and Native Americans give free tours and programs relating to the battle.

Down the road in Garryowen is the site of the Reno battle and the **Custer Battlefield Museum** (406/638-1876, www.custermuseum. org, 8 A.M.–8 P.M. daily summer, 9 A.M.–5 P.M. daily winter; $5 adults, $3 seniors, children under 12 free). The privately owned museum has some superb Indian crafts, a collection of historic photos, a recreation of Sitting Bull's campsite, and the tomb of an unknown soldier. There's also a gift shop and gallery.

Accommodations

The Custer Battlefield is about as lonely and forlorn a place as you can imagine. However, some amenities have grown up nearby, and Hardin is only 15 miles away.

The closest lodging is **Little Big Horn Camp** (406/638-2232), at the Custer Battlefield exit off I-90. This is mostly a campground but there is a small motel with basic rooms ($45).

Food

At the I-94 interchange at the battleground there's a good restaurant and gift shop, the **Custer Battlefield Trading Post and Cafe** (406/638-2270, 8 A.M.–9 P.M. summer, 9 A.M.–5 P.M. winter). Indian tacos, actually a variety of fried bread, are featured ($8). The gift shop has a nice selection of Indian crafts and books. There's also a deli in the **Little Bighorn Casino** (406/638-4000, 8 A.M.–9:30 P.M. Mon.–Fri., 8 A.M.–11 P.M. Sat.–Sun.), the Crow tribe's casino.

THE NORTHERN CHEYENNE RESERVATION

Located between the Crow Reservation and the Tongue River, the Northern Cheyenne Reservation was granted to the Cheyenne Indians after a period of wandering and incarceration following the Battle of the Little Bighorn. The Northern Cheyenne Reservation contains 444,500 acres, almost 90 percent of which is controlled by tribal members. About 3,500 Cheyenne live on the reservation. Characterized by patches of dry prairie ringed by sandstone uplands covered with ponderosa pines, the area is rich in prairie wildlife and game birds, and the Tongue River affords the angler opportunities for walleye, smallmouth bass, and, south near the Tongue River Reservoir, trout.

Highway 212 cuts across the reservation on its way between the Little Bighorn Battlefield and the Black Hills of South Dakota, and it's an absolutely beautiful drive.

Onto the Plains

French traders first encountered the Cheyenne Indians in 1680, when they were living in present-day Minnesota. At that time they were an agricultural people who lived in earth-and-log cabins. The pressure of settlements to the east forced all Indian tribes to migrate west. The Cheyenne, however, were not pushed west by white settlers but by the hostile Sioux, who had been previously displaced. Driven onto the plains, the Cheyenne lost their agricultural arts and divided into two federations: the Northern Cheyenne in Montana and the Dakotas, and the Southern Cheyenne in Colorado. By the time Lewis and Clark toured the West, the Northern Cheyenne tribe was living near the Black Hills. They lived in tepees and existed almost totally off the largesse of the buffalo. Their agricultural past had faded into tribal myth.

The Northern Cheyenne soon were expeditiously allied with the Sioux because of the presence of two common enemies: the settlers and soldiers, and their traditional rivals, the Crow, on whose hunting grounds the two tribes were increasingly intruding.

The Conflicts

When gold was discovered in the Black Hills in the 1870s, treaties barring non-Indians from the area were promptly ignored, and the resulting gold rush and cavalry action forced the Cheyenne (and other Plains tribes) into greater confrontation with the whites. In

1875, when all Western tribes were ordered onto reservations, the Northern Cheyenne refused, choosing to live their traditional life on the prairies.

The victory of the Indians over Custer's forces in 1876 earned the Cheyenne brief freedom. Within a year of the Battle of the Little Bighorn, all tribe members were forced onto reservations, with the majority in Oklahoma with the Southern Cheyenne. During the winter of 1878–1879, about 300 of the Northern Cheyenne fled the Indian Territory and attempted to make their way back to rejoin their brethren then sequestered on the Tongue River. After many battles and skirmishes with the cavalry, only 60 of the fleeing Northern Cheyenne lived to be reunited with the tribe remaining in Montana. In 1884 the government granted the tribe its own reservation.

Development

Like other Indian tribes who were settled on what were once considered marginal lands, the Northern Cheyenne have had to fight to resist the development of their lands by outside interests. The reservation sits on the vast coalfields of the Fort Union Formation. In the 1970s, coal companies sought to open up the area for strip mining. The tribe faced a painful decision: whether to allow the mining and reap the economic benefits, which would bring jobs to the area and allow the building of needed public facilities, or to maintain the integrity of the land in its natural state.

By 1972, energy companies were poised to exploit 70 percent of the reservation, but the following year the tribe voted to cancel the leases. After protracted legal maneuvering, the U.S. government upheld the Cheyenne's wishes. During the same period the Northern Cheyenne sought and finally obtained the first redesignation of air quality (to "pristine") ever granted to a reservation, thereby inhibiting development of coal-fired generators near the reservation (the enormous generators at Colstrip are 20 miles north). The tribe did decide to allow oil exploration in the 1980s, but no viable reserves were found.

Sights

The tiny town of Busby was the site of a historic and culturally significant **reburial** in 1993, when remains of Northern Cheyenne killed during the Indian Wars were retrieved from the Smithsonian and other East Coast museums and reburied in their homeland. The remains got to the museums as a result of an 1880s ballistics study commissioned by the Army—they wanted to see how effectively their new carbines were killing Indians. In 1990 a federal law permitted the remains to be returned to the reservation, where they're now buried in a circle near the Two Moon Monument on Highway 212.

The **St. Labre Indian School** was established in Ashland in 1884, after a Catholic soldier stationed at Fort Keogh contacted his bishop to tell him of the woeful state of the Cheyenne, who were wandering, starving, and homeless on the Tongue River. The bishop bought land on the river, and in 1884 four nuns from Toledo, Ohio, established the school and mission.

The mission remains a center of Cheyenne cultural and educational life, currently schooling 700 students. The mission also operates alcohol treatment, employment counseling, and other social services. Its modern chapel, built from local stone in the shape of an enormous tepee, dominates the campus. Tours are available. On the mission grounds, the **Cheyenne Indian Museum and Ten Bears Gallery** (406/784-2200, 8:30 A.M.–4:30 P.M. daily Memorial Day–Labor Day) displays and sells examples of the tribe's fabulous beadwork.

Accommodations

Although the tribal headquarters for the Northern Cheyenne is located at Lame Deer, Ashland is the reservation's primary trading town and has the reservation's only motel, the **Western 8** (406/784-2400, $45).

Food

Dining opportunities are rather perfunctory. In Ashland there's the **Justus Inn** (406/784-2701, 11 A.M.–10 P.M.), which features a full menu. The **Charging Horse Casino** (406/477-6677, 7 A.M.–10 P.M.), 0.5 mile east of Lame

© BILL MCRAE

The St. Labre Mission church was designed to resemble a traditional tepee.

Deer, has a full-service restaurant with main courses from $8–13.

Events

There are two powwows, a large one in Lame Deer on the Fourth of July and another in Ashland over Labor Day. Cheyenne powwows feature dancing contests, Indian singing, and lots of food.

Information

Contact the **Northern Cheyenne Nation** 406/477-6284, www.cheyennenation.com) at P.O. Box 128, Lame Deer, MT 59043.

CUSTER NATIONAL FOREST, ASHLAND DIVISION

Across the Tongue River from the Cheyenne Reservation is eastern Montana's largest block of national forest. Like other isolated islands of woodland within the vast archipelago of the Custer National Forest, the Ashland Division (406/784-2344, www.fs.fed.us/r1/custer) is largely overlooked by travelers, save the hunters who come to stalk trophy mule deer and wild turkeys.

As in the other forests of southeastern Montana, here ponderosa pine savannas are interspersed with short-grass prairie, and isolated sandstone bluffs rise up spookily from the plains. The entire area is rich in wildlife, especially birds.

Like the other Custer forests, this is largely an undeveloped destination for visitors. But before dismissing these remote areas, adventurous travelers should consider stopping to enjoy the vast and lonely expanses of these high-prairie grasslands and woodlands.

Three areas of the Ashland Division have been designated as riding and hiking areas. They are off-limits to motorized vehicles, making them ideal for nature study and wildlife viewing.

© BILL MCRAE

the Tongue River near Ashland

While the Forest Service had horses in mind when they called it a riding area, the rough but open landscape is also ideal for mountain-bike exploration. There are no maintained hiking trails, but the nature of the landscape allows for considerable ambling and scrambling.

Red Shale Campground is six miles east of Ashland and has 16 units. Other campsites are more remote. The **Holiday Springs** campsite is of interest not only because it serves as a campground but also because the Forest Service maintains a rental cabin there. Whitetail Cabin sleeps four and has electrical power (though no water): It costs $30 per day. The cabin and campsite are about 18 miles east of Ashland, up the East Fork of Otter Creek.

While cross-country skiing is possible almost everywhere in the area when there's enough snow, the Forest Service has developed two loop trails near Camp's Pass, 20 miles east of Ashland. This area, near the defile where the highway enters the national forest from the east, contains some of the roughest land in this section of the Custer National Forest.

Bighorn Canyon and the Pryor Mountains

Nothing in the prairies and valleys of the Crow Reservation prepares the traveler for the magnitude and sheer drama of Bighorn Canyon and the Pryor Mountains. The Bighorn River follows a wide wooded valley from St. Xavier upstream to **Fort Smith** along Highway 313, where suddenly the land ends in upheaval, with bright red clinker stone topping gravel bluffs. The road climbs four miles up a series of steep switchbacks onto a plateau. At the base of the eroded face of the Pryors, an enormous canyon opens up, with the waters of **Yellowtail Reservoir** a ribbon of blue below thousand-foot cliffs.

Bighorn Canyon isn't particularly on the way to anywhere; you must really want to be there to get there at all. Much of the land around the canyon is Crow Reservation land and off-limits to most visitors. Despite the

information on many road maps, you cannot get from the dam at Fort Smith on the northern end of the canyon to the recreational access areas to the south (a distance of only 25 miles)—unless you have a boat or want to drive a couple hundred miles around and about and down and through Wyoming and back up into Montana, because the Crow do not allow non–tribe members to cross tribal land. This isn't a problem for the locals, who tend to use the reservoir for boating, but a traveler on a schedule will need to make plans to see the entire canyon.

The Land

Bighorn Canyon cuts through walls of limestone between the Pryor Mountains and the rugged Bighorn Mountains in Wyoming, revealing 500 million years of geologic history. Both the Pryors and the Bighorns were formed when Paleozoic-era sedimentary rock was shoved eastward by the rising Rocky Mountains and upward by a bulwark of rising igneous magma. Limestone that had been laid down 300 million years ago was forced to the surface, forming first the Bighorn Mountains in Wyoming and, trailing behind in Montana, the Pryors.

The Bighorn River rises in Wyoming and flows north uneventfully until it comes to the limestone plateau just east of the Pryors. Here the river has cut into the fault line between the two mountain ranges and has carved out one of the deepest and most dramatic canyons in the northern United States.

HISTORY
Early Inhabitants
Bighorn Canyon and the Pryor Mountains were home to many early Indians. Although the Crow were to adopt this land as their own many centuries later, prehistoric nomadic Indians lived here, where the prairies meet the mountains and where limestone caves provided easy shelter. Crow tradition describes the indigenous people of Bighorn as "dwarfish," strong, and without fire. Bad Pass Trail, which skirts the rim of the Bighorn Canyon, led these early Indians from the grassy plains of Montana to the Great Basin country of Wyoming.

The tortured landscape seems to have induced a sense of wonder in these early residents, for several sites appear to have been places of worship (such as the Medicine Wheel in the Bighorn Mountains of Wyoming). The stone remains of vision-quest structures are found along rocky cliffs in the Pryors.

The area became the homeland of the Crow when they arrived here in the 17th century. The land around the canyon and the Pryors was considered especially sacred. Because Bad Pass Trail led through their territory, incursions by other tribes often led to skirmishes and feuds.

White Settlement
Early adventurers operating out of the various trading forts at the confluence of the Yellowstone and Bighorn Rivers trapped in the Bighorn country. John Colter, who "discovered" Yellowstone National Park, was the first white to explore the Pryors, and Jim Bridger, tale spinner and backwoodsman, claimed to have been the first to float the Bighorn River. Frontier missionary Father De Smet said the first Catholic mass in the state, under a large cottonwood tree near Fort Smith in 1840.

The first white settlement resulted from the Bozeman Trail. Established by John Bozeman in 1864, it cut off from the Oregon Trail and veered north up to the Yellowstone Valley and thence to the goldfields of western Montana.

The Bozeman Trail crossed into Montana near Decker and crossed the Bighorn River at the northern end of the canyon. In Wyoming the trail crossed Sioux land, which the tribe greatly resented. (The Crow tolerated the whites as long as they moved across their land without settling.) A series of forts was built by the military to protect settlers and miners from the Sioux as they passed through the prairies. The most northerly of these, Fort C. F. Smith, was located at the crossing of the Bighorn in 1866.

The hostility of the Sioux, however, was to prove greater than the military's endurance, as the forts were perpetually under siege. After the Hayfield Fight in 1868 near Fort Smith, and the second Fort Laramie Treaty, the Bozeman Trail was closed and the fort left deserted.

A second, more peculiar adjunct to the local history came at the end of the 19th century, when the area was given over to guest or dude ranches and celebrity homesteaders. Writers Will James and Carolyn Lockhart both ran ranches in the Bighorn and Pryor country. The buildings at Hillsboro Dude Ranch along Bighorn Canyon are now open to visitors.

BIGHORN CANYON NATIONAL RECREATION AREA– NORTH DISTRICT
The Bighorn Canyon National Recreation Area was designated in 1968 after the completion of Yellowtail Dam. The resulting 71-mile-long Bighorn Lake extends the full length of dramatic Bighorn Canyon.

The recreation area also divides the Crow

SOUTHEASTERN MONTANA

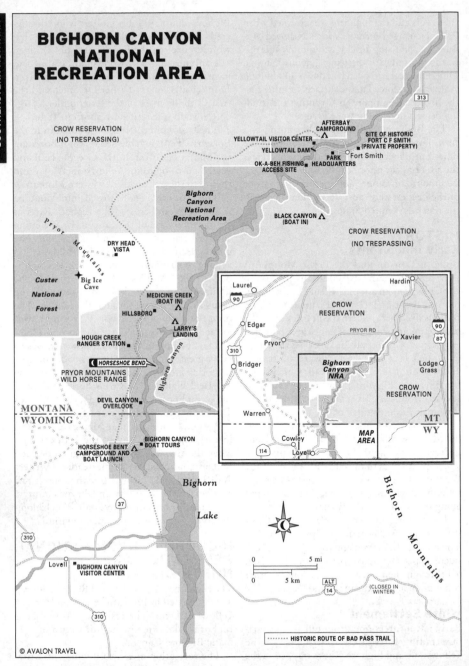

BIGHORN CANYON NATIONAL RECREATION AREA

CROW RESERVATION
(NO TRESPASSING)

313

AFTERBAY
CAMPGROUND

YELLOWTAIL VISITOR CENTER
YELLOWTAIL DAM
OK-A-BEH FISHING
ACCESS SITE

SITE OF HISTORIC
FORT C F SMITH
(PRIVATE PROPERTY)

PARK
HEADQUARTERS

Fort Smith

*Bighorn
Canyon
National
Recreation Area*

BLACK CANYON
(BOAT IN)

CROW RESERVATION

(NO TRESPASSING)

DRY HEAD
VISTA

Pryor Mountains

Custer

National

Forest

Big Ice
Cave

MEDICINE CREEK
(BOAT IN)

HILLSBORO

LARRY'S
LANDING

HOUGH CREEK
RANGER STATION

HORSESHOE BEND

Bighorn Canyon

PRYOR MOUNTAINS
WILD HORSE RANGE

DEVIL CANYON
OVERLOOK

MONTANA
WYOMING

HORSESHOE BENT
CAMPGROUND AND
BOAT LAUNCH

BIGHORN CANYON
BOAT TOURS

Bighorn

37

Lake

310

Lovell   BIGHORN CANYON
VISITOR CENTER

310

Laurel

90

Hardin

CROW
RESERVATION

Edgar

PRYOR RD

90
87

Pryor

Xavier

310

Bridger

*Bighorn
Canyon
NRA*

Lodge
Grass

CROW
RESERVATION

Warren

MT
WY

Cowley

**MAP
AREA**

114   Lovell

Bighorn

Mountains

ALT
14   (CLOSED IN
WINTER)

········· HISTORIC ROUTE OF BAD PASS TRAIL

0   5 mi

0   5 km

© AVALON TRAVEL

© BILL MCRAE

Yellowtail Reservoir backs up through Bighorn Canyon.

Reservation. The Crow consider the land around the canyon to be sacred; they guard it as a de facto wilderness and do not allow access to non–tribe members. This means that the recreation area has a North District at Fort Smith, Montana, and a South District at Lovell, Wyoming. No direct land route connects the two districts. Lacking a boat, the visitor who wishes to see both halves of the recreation area will have to skirt the Crow Reservation by public highway, a journey of at least three hours by car.

While tourists may enjoy the scenery and the history of the Bighorn Canyon, the recreational opportunities make the canyon a favorite with locals. Fishing and boating are very popular, and for good reason. Boats are without any doubt the conveyance of choice, because exploration of the canyon by any other method is either impossible or illegal. Hiking opportunities also exist on unmaintained trails or old roads. More experienced travelers might be tempted to explore the area's many caves. There is a $5 per-vehicle fee for access to the recreation area.

Yellowtail Visitor Center

Although the Yellowtail Visitor Center (406/666-3234, 9 A.M.–5 P.M. daily Memorial Day–Labor Day) remains open, tours of Yellowtail Dam, the tallest dam in the Missouri River drainage, are no longer offered because of security concerns. The visitor center offers a good museum exhibit of traditional Crow life in Bighorn Canyon.

Sights

Fort C. F. Smith is located on private land; it can only be visited during a ranger-led tour. Prior arrangements are suggested; contact the Fort Smith Visitor Center. The tour involves a 0.25-mile hike. Ask about the **De Smet Tree,** under which Father De Smet said the first Catholic mass in Montana in 1840.

Recreation

To reach **Ok-A-Beh Boat Landing,** turn south at Fort Smith and ascend the steep face of the Bighorn Plateau, here burned to bright red clinker by the intense heat of ancient smoldering underground coal seams. The road will deposit you at just about the same elevation you started at, but on the other side of Yellowtail Reservoir in Bighorn Canyon. Think twice about making this 11-mile trip if your brakes are poor or your vehicle pulls hard on hills. Otherwise, the road to Ok-A-Beh is a great vantage point from which to overlook the canyon, the Crow Reservation, and the Pryor and Bighorn Mountains.

Boat facilities at Ok-A-Beh include a landing, a fish-cleaning area, and gas, oil, and boating supplies. Shore fishing is almost impossible at public-access sites in the North District of Yellowtail Reservoir, but fishing by boat is good for brown trout and walleye. Boat rentals are available at the **Ok-A-Beh Marina** (406/666-2349). Remember to have the appropriate state fishing licenses, because the reservoir spans both Montana and Wyoming and there is no license reciprocity. If you happen to have your scuba gear along, you'll find the area's best diving off the northern end of the reservoir, around Ok-A-Beh Landing.

Fishing below the reservoir, however, is a different story. The Bighorn River downstream (north) of the dam is a world-class fishery for trophy-size brown and rainbow trout. Much of the access to the river falls under the jurisdiction of the Crow, who do not allow access by non–tribe members. In the immediate area of Fort Smith, however, there are two public-access sites. Afterbay Dam, just below Yellowtail Reservoir, provides a boat launch and fishing access.

No motorized vehicles are allowed on the Bighorn River below Afterbay Dam. Boat rentals are available from the outfitters and fishing gear stores at Fort Smith.

Because the Bighorn is both heavily fished and carefully monitored for access, anyone uncertain of the area and its conditions should consider using the services of a professional outfitter to guarantee fishing success and compliance with trespassing laws.

The same laws that limit fishing access also limit the number of maintained hiking trails in the area. One very short jaunt, the **Beaver Pond Nature Trail,** leaves from the parking lot of the Yellowtail Visitor Center to overlooks of beaver ponds in Lime Kiln Creek. For the more ambitious, **Om-Ne-A Trail** leads from Yellowtail Dam to the Ok-A-Beh boat launch. This three-mile hike skirts the canyon rim and offers great views.

Accommodations

The little community of Fort Smith offers some motel space, although lodgings are geared to anglers on package fishing trips. Both found along Highway 313, the **Bighorn Angler Motel** (577 Parksdale Ct., 406/666-2233, $83 d) and the **Bighorn Trout Shop Motel** (406/666-2375, $125 d) offer gear and bait in addition to very comfortable rooms.

A larger selection of lodgings is available in Hardin, 42 miles north on Highway 313. See *Hardin* in the *Crow and Northern Cheyenne Reservations* section.

Camping

Camping is a more economical means of staying over in Fort Smith. At **Afterbay,** the National Park Service maintains a free 30-site campground. **Cottonwood Camp** (406/666-2391) offers all of the usual niceties plus boat rentals and shuttle service to fishing-access sites. On Yellowtail Reservoir, the Park Service maintains a boat-in-only campsite with minimal facilities at the head of **Black Canyon,** five miles south of Ok-A-Beh by boat.

Food

While making motel reservations, check with your guide or outfitter because many of the outfitters will offer room and board to their angling guests. **Polly's Place** (866/676-5597, 7 A.M.–9 P.M. daily Apr.–Nov., $10–20) offers tasty pasta, steaks, and fish. Polly's is just north of the highway in the center of tiny Fort Smith.

Outfitters

The Bighorn River below Yellowtail Dam has blue-ribbon trout fishing. Many outfitters offer fishing, floating, and hunting packages. If the trout are luring you to the Bighorn, these outfitters are serious about fishing and promise results.

Bighorn Fly and Tackle Shoppe (P.O. Box 7597, Fort Smith, MT 59035, 406/666-2253 or 888/665-1321, www.bighornfly.com) offers rentals and sage advice with its guide service. **Bighorn Angler** (P.O. Box 7578, Fort Smith, MT 59035, 406/666-2233, www.bighornangler.com) offers boat rentals, accommodations, a tackle shop, and full guide service. Check www.visitmt.com for a full list of outfitters in Fort Smith.

BIGHORN CANYON NATIONAL RECREATION AREA— SOUTH DISTRICT
Bighorn Canyon Visitor Center
The South District has its headquarters at the **Bighorn Canyon Visitor Center** (307/548-2251, 8 A.M.–6 P.M. daily Memorial Day–Labor Day, 8 A.M.–5 P.M. the rest of the year; $5 per vehicle) at the junction of Highway 14A and Highway 310 in Lovell, Wyoming. In this solar-heated building, visitors will find information on the canyon's wildlife, geology, and history. There is also a raised-relief map of the recreation area that reduces a monumental landscape to a comprehensible scale. Self-guided cassette tours of the history and geology of the area are available. The rangers lead special activities, including campfire programs at Horseshoe Bend Campground. Check the information board at the visitors center for details.

◖ Horseshoe Bend
The South District contains the best access to dramatic views onto the canyon. As Highway 37 leaves the Lovell area, it climbs onto a plateau with strangely desertlike features such as thorn bushes and barren rocky slopes. This almost lunar landscape is broken as the road drops onto Horseshoe Bend, where a wide expanse of the lake passes into Bighorn Canyon to the north.

Other Sights Along Highway 37
Highway 37 (misleadingly known as the Trans-Park Highway; no road connects both halves of

the park) then passes into the **Pryor Mountains Wild Horse Range,** where one of the country's last herds of wild mustangs runs free.

Within the boundaries of the Wild Horse Range is the most spectacular view onto Bighorn Canyon. Where Devil Canyon meets Bighorn Canyon, sheer 1,000-foot-high cliffs tower above the waters of the lake. From **Devil Canyon Overlook** atop one of these cliffs, the views are literally breathtaking as well as vertigo-inducing. Informational signs explain the precipitous landscape.

A short hike off the highway near the campsite at Barry's Landing leads to the remains of **Hillsboro,** a ghost town originally built by an early white settler, G. W. Barry. After several financially unsuccessful attempts at mining and horse ranching in the first decade of the 20th century, Barry converted his settlement into Cedarville Dude Ranch, a guest ranch for tourists. Most of the original buildings are still standing. Highway 37 ends at **Barry's Landing,** a boat launch established by Barry, who offered boat tours of the canyon. Barry's Landing is now maintained as a boat launch and campsite by the Park Service.

After crossing the Montana state line, Highway 37 parallels the ancient **Bad Pass Trail,** the path used for centuries by Indians as they passed from the plains and valleys of Montana to the Great Basin land of Wyoming. Travois trails and stone cairns are still visible along the trail. You can get a feel for the Bad Pass Trail if you hike or drive up Dryhead Road (an unimproved road that begins where the paved portion of Highway 37 dead-ends at the turnoff for Barry's Landing) into **Lockhart Ranch.**

Carolyn Lockhart was a successful journalist who left the *Boston Post* for the life of a Bighorn Canyon homesteader and Western novelist. Lockhart and her companion weathered the Depression years only to fight the government when it claimed that the two women had not improved on the homestead. Lockhart was awarded the title to her land in 1936. The original structures still stand abandoned at her ranch. Dryhead Road continues to parallel Bad

Pass Trail for another 12 miles beyond the Lockhart Ranch but is passable only to high-clearance vehicles or hardy hikers.

Recreation

While fishing is certainly a popular pastime on Yellowtail Reservoir, waterskiing, swimming, nautical sightseeing, and even scuba diving are the order of the day. **Horseshoe Bend Campground and Boat Launch** is located on the northern end of Bighorn Lake (a wide section of Yellowtail Reservoir), just before it disappears northward into the defiles of the canyon. Besides its role as a boat-in area, Horseshoe Bend serves as a hub of other recreational activities, including supervised swimming. Free canoe trips into the canyon are offered by rangers, as are evening campfire programs. Check the information boards at the visitors center in Lovell for details.

Boat rentals are available from the Horseshoe Bend Marina. A second boat launch is located 17 miles farther north at Barry's Landing.

From Horseshoe Bend Campground, **Crooked Creek Nature Trail** wends 0.25 mile through the arid landscape. Self-guiding brochures identify plant and animal life. **Medicine Creek Trail** follows the rim of Bighorn Canyon for almost two miles from Barry's Landing to Medicine Creek Campground. In addition to these maintained trails, options for hiking in the Bighorn Canyon area are dictated only by the energy and forethought necessary to strike out on your own. The area is full of old mining, logging, and ranching roads. With the help of a ranger and a Forest Service map, much of the area is open for exploration.

Spelunking is another activity offered to the adventurous in the Bighorn region. The entire area is a huge uplift of limestone, which has eroded for millions of years. The result is networks of caves, filled not simply with mineral formations but also with the archaeological remains of early Indians. The Park Service and the Bureau of Land Management limit access to many of the caves, but most (such as the Bighorn Caverns) are open to experienced spelunkers on request. Ask at the visitors center in Lovell,

or at the Cody, Wyoming, Bureau of Land Management office for permission, keys, and information on specific dangers. Most caves will require a four-wheel-drive vehicle for access.

Accommodations

Lovell, Wyoming, is 12 miles south of the recreation area and is the closest community to the South District. The **Econo Inn** (595 E. Main, 307/548-2725, $60), at the east end of Main Street, is near a restaurant. The **Western Motel** (180 West Main Street, 307/548- 2781, $96) is comfortable and quiet, with newly remodeled rooms.

Camping

Campgrounds are available in the recreation area. At **Horseshoe Bend Campground** there are 126 sites; it has the most modern facilities. Seventeen miles downriver is **Barry's Landing Campground** with 14 sites, but bring your own water. **Medicine Creek Campsite** is a hike-in or boat-in-only area two miles north of Barry's Landing with primitive facilities.

THE PRYOR MOUNTAINS

Rising to the west of Bighorn Canyon are the low, greatly eroded plateaus of the Pryor Mountains. Although these mountains are not very high on the Montana scale, they form a curious destination for the traveler. The Pryors are so extraordinarily rich in Indian tradition and sites that the parts of the range that fall in the Crow Reservation are considered sacred and treated as wilderness. The area is also rich in limestone caves, noted both for their mineral formations and archaeological interest.

The Pryors are surrounded by the Crow Reservation and the Bighorn National Recreational Area. They are therefore not easily accessible, but the difficulty of getting in is more than made up for by the reward of being there. This is really remote country, with tepee rings and ice caves, bighorn sheep and mustangs, views over holy lands, all amply served by Forest Service roads. Although a high-clearance vehicle is a good idea, the Pryors cry out for exploration by mountain bike.

Sights

In the mid-1960s, public concern became focused on about 200 wild horses living in the Pryors, remnants of larger herds that roamed the remote areas of the West. In 1968 the Bureau of Land Management established the **Pryor Mountains Wild Horse Range** on 44,000 acres on the Montana-Wyoming border. The ancestry of these animals is mixed. Some horses are merely escapees from ranch herds; others derive from Indian pony stock, which in turn was generated from imported Spanish horse lines. "Tiger stripes" on the legs or back are characteristics derived from Spanish breeds. A dominant stud, his harem of mares, and their foals form common mustang social units.

Wild-horse viewing is easiest along Highway 37 coming north from Wyoming into the Bighorn Recreation Area. For the more adventurous, the meadows and box canyons of the Pryors are a more memorable place to see the herds.

Bighorn sheep, for which this entire area was named, have been restocked in the Pryors. Deer and elk are common, and the area is popular in the fall for hunting.

The remoteness of the Pryors makes them tempting destinations for a certain kind of adventurer. Mountain bikers will find this a compelling challenge because of the flora and fauna (where else can one pedal among wild horses?) and also because of the area's archaeological wealth. Most important, there are many deserted roads from the days when these mountains were mined and logged.

The Forest Service map of the Custer National Forest indicates a great number of caves, many open to public access. **Big Ice Cave** was once a popular picnic spot for day trips in the early years of the 20th century. It was closed for many years except to guided tours by the Forest Service but is now open for informal exploration. There are picnic grounds and wilderness camping opportunities nearby. Big Ice Cave is found at the top of the Pryors, along Forest Service Road 3093. Spelunkers are advised to check with the Bureau of Land Management or the Forest Service for details of access to other caves, because some are locked in order to prevent vandalism and to protect the unsuspecting from specific dangers.

Almost the best reason to venture into the Pryors is the last one reached, at least by civilized routes. Past Big Ice Cave on Forest Service Road 849 is **Dry Head Vista,** a panoramic viewpoint with Bighorn Canyon dropping away 4,000 feet below.

New Age Experience

It can't be called a guest ranch, they're not exactly outfitters, and it's only kind of like going camping—**Sacred Ground's Happy Heart Ranch** (406/245-6070, www.sacredgroundintl. org) offers something else altogether. Guests spend a week sleeping in tepees and experiencing traditional Native American ways of life, which may mean riding and hiking, observing plants and wildlife, attending ceremonies, meeting tribal elders and teachers, or spending time alone. It's all flexible, with a focus on a personal interaction with nature. The cost for a week is about $1,200, with some special guest-worker rates available.

Camping

Within the bounds of the **Custer National Forest** are a couple of camping areas. **Sage Creek Campground** is the most northerly; bringing water is a good idea for the squeamish, even though there are several natural springs with potable water. **Crooked Creek Campground** is farther in (near Big Ice Cave) and more rudimentary, and it requires a more energetic motor vehicle.

Getting There

This isn't as simple as it looks. Maps show a road south from the little town of Pryor. Called Pryor Gap Road, it is in fact the old roadbed of an abandoned rail spur line. It's not in very good shape, but it is the shortest way into the Pryors from southeastern Montana. It also crosses Crow land, and sometimes access has been denied. It's best to check on road conditions and access before starting up the gap.

The standard but somewhat indirect way into the area is from the west, via Highway 310, onto Pryor Mountain Road two miles south of Bridger, or north and east from Warren, Montana, along Sage Creek. About 20 miles of gravel road later, you will arrive in the canyons of the Pryors.

From the Wyoming side, if you have a four-wheel-drive vehicle, there are several rough and scenic routes into the Pryors. Cowley Airport Road turns into a four-wheel-drive road called Crooked Creek Road. In its rough-and-ready fashion it leads past tepee rings and the two highest peaks in the Pryors before reaching Crooked Creek Campground. For the very hardy, a road leads up to (or more prudently, down from) Dry Head Vista, along Sykes Ridge Road. Before attempting either route, ask locals for directions and cautionary tales.

INFORMATION

For details on the Wild Horse Range and other destinations, the **Bighorn Canyon Visitor Center** (307/548-2551, www.nps.gov/bica) is at the junction of Highways 310 and 14A at the east end of Lovell.

Yellowtail Visitor Center (406/666-2358) is located at the end of Highway 313 at Fort Smith.

The **Beartooth Division of the Custer National Forest** (406/446-2103, www.fs.fed.us/r1/custer) has jurisdiction over the national forest in the Pryor Mountains.

The **Bureau of Land Management office** (307/587-2216) in Cody, Wyoming, has the keys to many of the caves in the Bighorn Canyon area.

The Lovell, Wyoming, **Chamber of Commerce** (307/548-7552) can be reached at P.O. Box 322, Lovell, WY 82431.

THE JUDITH BASIN AND CENTRAL MONTANA

Central Montana is the state's hybrid province: here, hundreds of miles from the Rocky Mountains' front range, isolated mountain peaks rise up like islands from the surrounding prairie. Called outliers, these ranges are literally habitat "islands" to plants and wildlife otherwise found only in the fastness of the Rockies and represent some of Montana's most curious geologic history.

About 50 million years ago, vast amounts of magma began to rise randomly along faults and fractures in overlying rock. In some cases, as in the Highwood Mountains, volcanic eruptions occurred. Sometimes the magma pooled under existing sedimentary levels, bulging these strata up to mountain height (the Big Snowy Range). In other cases, magma flowed along fractures until lakes of lava formed at their ends. Erosion has eaten away the softer sedimentary casts, leaving spiny lava outcrops (like Square Butte).

The molten rock that hardened into mountains in central Montana is unusual. Not only has it proved to be rich in gold, silver, and lead, it also contains minerals that are rare elsewhere. Some of the world's bluest and most valued sapphires are mined on Yogo Creek in the Little Belt Mountains.

Between the mountains are prairie-like plateaus—the Judith Basin is the largest and most central of these—that were an ample home first to buffalo, and then, in the same pattern as the rest of eastern Montana, to livestock and farmers. But the mountains inevitably intrude, and nowhere on the central Montana prairies are they out of sight.

© BILL MCRAE

CENTRAL MONTANA

HIGHLIGHTS

◖ Historic Lewistown: Lewistown has one of the loveliest locations in the state, in a verdant valley below round-peaked mountains. The old town center is remarkably intact, showing the handiwork of immigrant stonemasons who quarried local sandstone to create a handsome downtown business district (page 330).

◖ Lewistown Art Center: You may be miles from the centers of Montana art, but the Lewistown Art Center is an island of sophistication – and the gift shop is an excellent spot to pick up souvenirs (page 331).

◖ Big Springs: A fish hatchery may not seem like a compelling destination on the surface, but the hatcheries are here due to Big Springs, the world's third largest freshwater spring. More a park than a hatchery, it's a lovely spot for a stroll and a picnic (page 331).

◖ Ghost Towns: In the mountains above Lewistown, gold rush-era ghost towns molder in the valleys where miners thronged in the 1880s, seeking their fortunes. Back-road routes link these towns, making for an interesting afternoon drive through high mountain meadows (page 332).

◖ White Sulphur Springs: Its hot mineral waters popular with Native Americans for centuries, this old ranch town is still a fascinating destination for hot springs enthusiasts. Successful cattle and sheep men displayed their wealth by building prestigious homes here. Aptly named, **The Castle** is a fabulous 1890s home that now houses the Meagher County Historical Museum (page 342).

◖ Harlowton: This is the archetypal Montana town, located on rolling prairies with mountains rising in every direction. The entire downtown area is on the National Register of Historic Places, a fascinating relict of Montana's 1910s homesteading era. The **Graves Hotel** is the grandest of all the historic buildings built when the railroad pushed through (page 349).

◖ Charles M. Bair Family Museum: A rambling ranch house containing a fascinating collection of European furniture, impressionist and cowboy paintings, silver, and Indian artifacts, the Bair family's home on the range is absolutely unique (page 351).

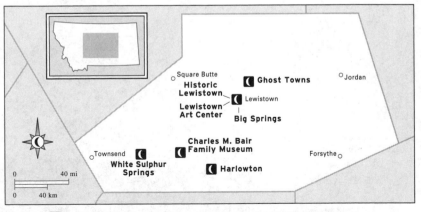

LOOK FOR ◖ TO FIND RECOMMENDED SIGHTS, ACTIVITIES, DINING, AND LODGING.

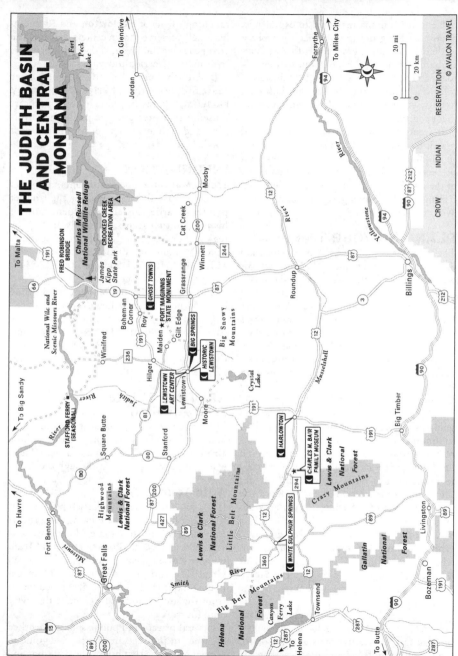

THE JUDITH BASIN AND CENTRAL MONTANA

© AVALON TRAVEL

Central Montana managed to experience, almost headlong and after the fact, every phase of the state's history. Prospectors followed cattle barons, who were hurried out by the railroads and homesteaders. Fossil-fuel exploration followed giddily, and the region's hub city, Lewistown, is now quickly becoming a retirement community.

It seems odd that such a rich, central, and practical region should be one of the last settled in Montana. But the area's potent amalgam presents the traveler with a telescoped menu of the state's best offerings in hiking, hunting, fishing, wildlife viewing, scenery, and flat-out Western culture.

PLANNING YOUR TIME

The Judith Basin and central Montana is a place of quiet, uneventful beauty. While not a major destination, it's worth spending a night or two here to explore this agricultural heartland. If you're crossing the state, consider taking either Highway 12 or 200, both of which transect this region. Each leads to plenty of worthy diversions for amateurs of history and recreation.

Spend a morning exploring **Lewistown**'s handsome downtown, with stops at **Lewistown Art Center** and perhaps a picnic at the **Big Springs,** a lovely park and fish hatchery at the world's third largest freshwater spring. Several gold-rush **ghost towns** in the surrounding mountains make a good excuse for an afternoon drive past grain fields and through lovely mountain meadows. If you plan to be in Lewistown in mid-August, consider taking in one of the many events at the **Montana Cowboy Poetry Gathering,** one of the West's largest Western poetry festivals.

Wind through the Little Belt Mountains to **White Sulphur Springs,** where you can unwind in the hot mineral pools at the **Spa Hot Springs.** Anglers should explore the **Smith River,** a blue-ribbon trout stream in a remote mountain canyon.

East on Highway 12, the road follows the old tracks of the Milwaukee Road, which once brought farmers and ranchers to this isolated landscape of foothills and prairies. The old

ranching towns of **Harlowton** and **Roundup** have well-preserved town centers that are little changed since the 1930s. A sleepy historicity is their main attraction today.

There's history of a different sort near Martinsdale at the **Charles Bair Family Museum,** a sprawling ranch house cum art museum that preserves the paintings, furniture, and artifacts of one of Montana's most notable ranch families.

INFORMATION

Travel Montana's central Montana district is called Russell Country, after the frontier painter Charlie Russell, who spent most of his life painting scenes and landscapes of the region. For free travel information, contact Travel Montana at P.O. Box 3166, Great Falls, MT 59403, 406/761-5036 or 800/527-5348, www.russell.visitmt.com.

The **Bureau of Land Management office** is on Airport Road in Lewistown (406/538-7461). Most of the mountains in the area are part of the **Lewis and Clark National Forest,** Jefferson Division. The Forest Supervisor's Office can be reached at P.O. Box 871, Great Falls, MT 59403, 406/791-7700.

GETTING THERE AND AROUND

Much of central Montana is within a couple of hours of Great Falls or Billings, both of whose airports are served by major air carriers. There is no public transportation through the area.

Auto Tours

If you're a fan of Charlie Russell paintings or Montana history, or just looking for a theme for your central Montana explorations, consider taking the **C. M. Russell Memorial Trail.** Charlie Russell spent most of his life between Great Falls and the Judith Basin, and images of the unique landscape, as well as noted events from the area's early history, made their way onto his canvases.

Several private and public sponsors worked together to produce an interpretive guide to central Montana that brings the paintings and landscapes back together. The free guide, available from most tourism offices or directly from the Russell Country office listed above, keys 25 of Russell's most famous paintings to the landscapes and stories that were part of their genesis. The interpretive points, marked by signs, stand mostly along Highway 200 between Great Falls and Lewistown, with a profusion around Russell's old stomping grounds at Utica. It's a great day trip through beautiful country—one that makes Russell's achievement even more meaningful.

Lewistown

Nestled along Big Spring Creek at the foot of the Judith, Big Snowy, and Moccasin Mountains, is Lewistown (pop. 5,813, elev. 3,960 feet), the hub of central Montana (actually, the exact center of the state is located at 1105 W. Main St.). Lewistown is a lively trading center for farmers and ranchers in the fertile Judith Basin country and provides ample facilities and temptations for the traveler. Besides the city's many buildings of historic and architectural interest, within 30 miles are hiking trails, mountain lakes, trout streams, wildlife viewing, and ghost towns.

HISTORY

Big Spring Creek Valley was strategically located as settlement and trade entered central Montana. Fort Sherman trading post, founded in 1873, served hunters, trappers, and Crow Indians. The Carroll Trail, a stage route connecting Missouri River steamboats with the gold camps at Helena, was established one year later and passed near the trading post. Camp Lewis, a temporary military post, was built to protect commerce along the trail in the same year.

The Métis

The first permanent settlement came in 1879, when Métis families settled along Big Spring Creek. The half-French, half-Chippewa Métis had lived on the prairies of the northern United States and southern Canada until the Riel Rebellion of 1870. Dislocated by the English, the Métis fragmented and drifted westward in search of a homeland. Louis Riel joined the Big Spring Creek Métis in the early 1880s, but in 1884 he returned to Canada with most of his people to organize and resist English Canadian incursions against the Canadian Métis.

After the second Riel Rebellion failed in 1885, the Métis drifted back into Montana as "landless Indians," most of whom were eventually settled on the Rocky Boys Reservation. Some Métis remained on Big Spring Creek and established homesteads. Francis Janeaux opened a store and laid out part of his land for the town that eventually became Lewistown.

Taming the Territory

Meanwhile, the Judith Basin was opening up. Granville Stuart established the DHS, a huge open-range cattle ranch, east of Lewistown in 1880. Other ranchers moved in to graze the rich prairies. Prospectors discovered gold at Maiden in the Judith Mountains the same year. The central Montana gold rush was on, and mining camps like Gilt Edge, Maiden, and Kendall boomed.

Even though the Indian Wars of 1876–1877 had effectively crushed the fighting force of the Native Americans of Montana, in 1880 the U.S. Army established Fort Maginnis to protect fledgling settlements from Indian attack. None occurred, and the indolent soldiers became more of a problem to local residents than the hostiles they purported to deter. The fort was closed in 1890.

Lewistown remained a rough-and-ready frontier town longer than comparable Montana communities. Rustlers preyed on local ranches, finding ample shelter in the rugged Missouri Breaks north of town. A shoot-out on Main Street in 1884 ended the careers of two suspected ringleaders, known to

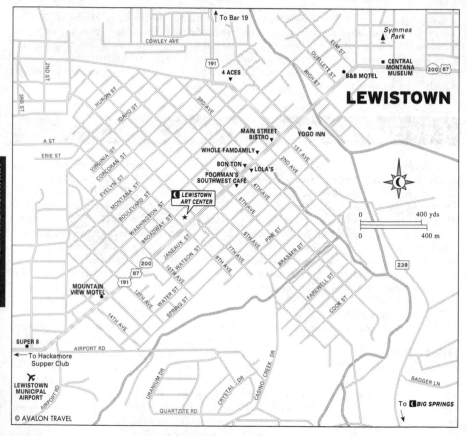

their contemporaries as Rattlesnake Jake and Longhair Owen.

Lewistown was incorporated in 1899, and in 1903 the Central Montana Railroad (bought in 1908 by the Milwaukee Road) reached this center of mining and ranch trade. What was taken out in cattle or gold was dwarfed by the numbers of homesteaders who came in. The Judith Gap and Lewistown area was quickly and heavily settled by hopeful farmers: Nearly 6.5 million acres of land were opened for settlement. The hegemony of the open-range ranches was broken, and by 1920, mining had declined in importance. The fertile countryside of central Montana sheltered homesteaders from some of the vicissitudes encountered by settlers elsewhere, and the gracious homes and buildings of Lewistown bear testimony to the community's long-standing stability.

SIGHTS
Historic Lewistown

Lewistown has one of the prettiest physical settings in the state and almost matches its natural attributes with its graceful early-20th-century architecture. Three neighborhoods are listed as historic districts in the National Register of Historic Places. The chamber of commerce (408 N.E. Main St.) provides brochures with walking tours of Lewistown. Not to miss: the **Fergus County Courthouse,** at 8th Avenue and Main, built in 1907 in

© BILL MCRAE

downtown Lewistown

mission style; behind it, on Broadway and 7th, is a wooden frame building that originally served as officers' quarters at Fort Maginnis; immediately next door is a wonderful example of a sandstone "four-square" home. The **Silk Stocking District,** an area bounded by Boulevard and Washington Streets at 2nd and 3rd Avenues, contains a mix of arts-and-crafts style and neo-Georgian homes built by early haberdashers (hence the name). Dominant throughout, and especially downtown along Main Street, are buildings made of sandstone bricks carved by immigrant Croatian stone carvers.

Central Montana Museum
Located in the same complex as the chamber of commerce (403 N.E. Main St., 406/538-5436, 9 A.M.–5 P.M. daily, Memorial Day–Labor Day, free), this local museum features Indian relics, homesteader memorabilia, and reminders of life on the open range.

Lewistown Art Center
Specializing in Montana art, this small gem of a gallery (801 W. Broadway, 406/535-8278, www.lewistownartcenter.org, 11:30 A.M.–5:30 P.M. Mon.–Sat., free) mixes traveling shows of regional art with a good selection of local arts and crafts in its gallery shop. The center features 12 exhibits per year and also offers art classes, workshops, and a variety of performing arts.

Big Springs
A scenic place for a picnic is the Big Springs, the source of Upper Big Spring Creek. Big Springs is the world's third-largest freshwater spring, discharging 62,700 gallons of water a minute—more than three million gallons per hour. Water from the spring is bottled and sold as drinking water throughout Montana. Some of the water is diverted into Big Springs Fish Hatchery, Montana's largest. Near the hatchery, along the stream and among trees, there's a lovely picnic area; tours of the hatchery are available. Follow 1st Avenue south to Country Club Road and follow signs for the hatchery; Big Springs is six miles south of Lewistown.

CENTRAL MONTANA

GRANVILLE STUART, AMBITIOUS PRAIRIE PIONEER

Granville Stuart – statesman, rancher, vigilante, writer, ambassador, and librarian – was among those early Montana settlers who thrived on challenge. Born to Scottish parents in West Virginia in 1834, Stuart accompanied his family to California during that state's gold rush. While returning east, he and his brother James detoured north through Montana. On Gold Creek, near Drummond, they discovered gold in 1858 and essentially started the Montana gold rush. But Granville was canny enough to realize that the real way to make money in a gold camp was to supply goods to miners, and he opened a store in Bannack in 1862. He also operated a small farm and soon ran a lumber company as well. He saved his money and began to dabble in ranching in the Deer Lodge Valley.

Stuart was elected to the Territorial Council in 1871 and to the lower house twice, in 1876 and 1879. By 1879 he moved cattle out of western Montana and onto the plains of the east. He helped found the DHS Ranch east of Lewistown, the first large ranch in this part of the state.

Entire towns of rustlers sprang up in the inaccessible Missouri Breaks to prey on these early ranches. At a meeting in Helena in 1884, the Montana Stockgrowers Association named Stuart – a founding member of the association – as president. Stuart presented the cattlemen's concerns about rustling to the legislature and to the administrators of Fort Maginnis, which the U.S. Army had built in the hay yard of the DHS Ranch. When the branches of the government failed to adopt appropriate measures, Stuart and other fed-up ranchers founded "Stuart's Stranglers," a vigilante gang that broke the back of organized rustling. Estimates of the number of suspected rustlers killed in 1884 vary, but at least 25 died, and perhaps as many as 100.

The winter of 1886-1887 dealt with Stuart as sternly as others on the Montana prairies. He swore that he would never again winter an animal he couldn't shelter. In 1891 he became the state land agent, and he selected 600,000 acres of government land for lease, whose proceeds still support the state school system. In 1894 he was named envoy to Paraguay and Uruguay by President Cleveland. Stuart retired to Montana in 1899 and became the Butte public librarian until his death in 1918.

Although not formally educated, Stuart was an avid reader with a taste for Byron, Shakespeare, and the Bible. His memoir, *Forty Years on the Prairie*, is fascinating reading.

◖ Ghost Towns

Note that most of the following ghost towns are located on private land. Landowners have reportedly been restricting access for several reasons, including liability and to keep people from packing everything off. If you're keen on actually investigating one of the following gold camps first-hand, call the chamber of commerce to find out what the current state of access is. Otherwise, just driving the public roads to the ghost towns makes for a nice afternoon drive.

Gold was discovered in 1880 in the Judith Mountains; by 1881 **Maiden** claimed a population of 6,000, making it larger than Lewistown, with which it vied for county seat when Fergus County was formed in 1882. To reach Maiden, take Highway 191 north from Lewistown for 10 miles, then turn east on a good secondary road, the Maiden Road, for nine miles. This gold camp burned in 1905, making the inevitable ghost town a bit more spectral.

The road up Warm Springs Creek in the Judith Mountains to Maiden is scenic, and it continues five miles over a steep pass (this is not a road for trailers) to **Gilt Edge,** another gold camp gone bust. Gilt Edge boomed when gold was discovered in the early 1890s. Calamity Jane Cannary claimed that Gilt Edge was her favorite town; she also claimed that she was

© BILL MCRAE

Judith Mountains vista

the local law enforcement. A few intact brick buildings and more disintegrating plank buildings remain. Gilt Edge can also be reached by traveling Highway 200 east from Lewistown for 14 miles, then turn north another mile.

Farther west in the Moccasin Mountains is **Kendall,** a gold camp that reached its zenith in the first years of the 20th century. The foundations of the union hall and a bandstand are among the remains. Take Highway 191 north to Hilger, then turn west for about six miles.

Charlie Russell Chew-Choo

It's a real groaner of a pun, but this dinner train through farm and ranch land north of Lewistown has proved to be a popular summer weekend activity. The train, made up of historic dining cars, leaves from Spring Creek Junction and travels to Denton, a 3.5-hour ride through some lovely country filled with wildlife, and over the vertigo-inducing Hanover Trestle.

A prime-rib dinner is included in the ticket price ($90 adult, $50 children 12 and under), along with Western entertainment. During Lewistown's Cowboy Poetry Gathering, the trip is accompanied by cowboy rhymes. The train has a somewhat erratic schedule, but generally runs most Saturdays from June through September, with several "polar express" runs in December. Contact 800/216-5436 or www. montanacharlierussellchewchoo.com for departure times and reservations.

RECREATION
Fishing

The Lewistown area offers great trout fishing. Big Spring Creek issues forth from a spring seven miles south of town, and locals consider it one of the best fishing streams in the state. Turn south on 1st Avenue and follow signs to Heath or the State Fish Hatchery. Warm Springs Creek is also good trout fishing in a more rural setting. Take Highway 191 north 10 miles to the intersection of Warm Springs Creek Road.

Lake anglers are also in luck. **Crystal Lake,** high in the Big Snowy Mountains, affords excellent recreational opportunities, including good fishing for rainbows. No motorized boats are allowed. Good hiking trails, overnight camping, and picnicking make Crystal Lake a popular destination for locals. Crystal Lake is 35 miles south of Lewistown; follow Highway 200 west seven miles, then follow well-signed gravel roads 28 miles south (or turn off at Moore; it's 21 miles to the lake from here).

Hiking

The gentle domed peaks of the Big Snowy Mountains provide surprisingly challenging and rewarding hikes. From the south end of Crystal Lake, **Uhlhorn Trail** leads up an initially steep grade to the Big Snowy Crest. High, moderately flat alpine meadows open out across the saddle of the mountains, with great views across the plains of eastern Montana. At the crest the trail divides. To the west a two-mile-long trail leads to Ice Cave, a cool and exciting place to explore with a flashlight. A longer hike involves following the crest trail to the east. The trail continues through meadows until, about six miles in, the ridge narrows to Knife Blade Ridge. The trail skirts abrupt drops on both sides before reaching Greathouse Peak, about 10 miles from the crest trailhead.

Other Parks

Closer to town, **Symmes Park** has a picnic area, tennis courts, and a playground, and is located right behind the chamber of commerce and museum at Highway 200 and Prospect Avenue. The city swimming pool and water-slide is in **Frank Day Park** (6th Ave. and Cook St., 12 blocks south of Main). Also at Day Park is Open Market, a farmers' and crafters' market held on summer Saturday mornings.

Golf

The **Pine Meadows Golf Course** (south of Lewistown on Spring Creek Rd., 406/538-7075) is a nine-hole course situated above a pastoral mountain stream. The **Judith Shadows Golf Course** (off Marcella Rd., 406/538-6062) is the town's new 18-hole course.

ACCOMMODATIONS
$50-75

The **Mountain View Motel** (1422 W. Main St., 406/535-3457 or 800/862-5786, $50 and

up) is located near restaurants and convenience stores and also has two two-bedroom houses and one two-bedroom suite, all fully furnished, for daily or weekly rent; pets are allowed.

The **Super 8** (102 Wendell, 406/538-2581, $68 and up) stands on the hill west of town. On the east edge of town is the well-maintained **B & B Motel** (520 E. Main St., 406/535-5496 or 877/538-3563, $65). Pets are allowed with a $3 charge.

$75-100

The **Yogo Inn** (211 E. Main St., 406/538-8721 or 800/860-9646, www.yogoinn.com, $95 and up) is Lewistown's most comfortable lodging. The Yogo was developed out of the old train station by a consortium of local citizens, and it caters to the small convention trade. The Yogo has the kinds of amenities (indoor and outdoor pools, a spa, good restaurant, lounge, meeting rooms) that dignify this class of motel.

Camping

Mountain Acres (406/538-7591) is principally an RV park, located just north of Lewistown on Highway 191. Tent campers will prefer **Crystal Lake,** 35 miles south of town.

FOOD

The **Garden Restaurant** at the Yogo Inn (211 E. Main St., 406/535-8721, 6 A.M.–9 P.M. daily) has Lewistown's most varied menu, featuring local trout along with beef, pasta, and seafood; main-course dishes range $12–28.

The **♦ Main Street Bistro** (122 W. Main St., 406/538-3666, 11 A.M.–8 P.M., Mon.–Thurs., 11 A.M.–9 P.M. Fri.–Sat.), adds continental flavors to the Lewistown dining scene, with pasta dishes, salads, and fresh vegetables. Although the decor is plain, someone in the kitchen clearly knows a thing or two about good cooking. Grilled pork chops are served with apple and red bell pepper compote; dinners range $10–18. Combining Southwestern cooking and a used bookstore, **Poor Man's Book and Southwest Cafe** (413 W. Main St., 406/535-4277, 7 A.M.–3 P.M. Mon.–Sat.) is an unusual mix for Lewistown. The food is very good as well as inexpensive, and you can browse the bookshelves while you wait. A pleasant addition to Main Street's dining scene is **Lola's** (319 W. Main St., 406/535-5720, 11 A.M.–9 P.M. Mon.–Thurs., 11 A.M.–10 P.M. Fri. and Sat.), with espresso drinks, light meals, ice cream, desserts, and crepes.

Elsewhere, steaks are the order of the day. The **(Hackamore Supper Club and Casino** (two miles west of Lewistown on Hwy. 200, 406/538-5685, 5 A.M.–10 P.M. Fri. and Sat., 4 A.M.–9 P.M. Sun.) is only open on the weekend, but its mix of steaks and Italian cooking is the best in the area. Grilled pork chops with porcini mushroom sauce is $19. During the rest of the week, good steaks and seafood are available from **Bar 19** (one mile north of downtown on Hwy. 191, 406/538-4949, 5 A.M.– 10 P.M. Tues.–Sat., $12–24).

Go to the **Whole Famdamily** (206 W. Main St., 406/538-5161, 11 A.M.–9 P.M. daily) for home-style cooking; this is the kind of place that has great pies and huge sandwiches.

For a treat, take the kids to the **Bon Ton** (312 W. Main St., 406/538-9650, 10 A.M.–8 P.M. Mon.–Thurs., 10 A.M.–10 P.M. Fri.–Sat.), an old-fashioned soda fountain that celebrated its 100th year in 2008. In addition to ice cream treats, the Bon Ton serves sandwiches and soup.

EVENTS

Lewistown's biggest summer festival is the **Montana Cowboy Poetry Gathering.** Every year the number and quality of the poets increase, with homespun artists coming from all over the western United States and Canada. Headquartered at the Yogo Inn, but with functions held in a variety of locations around Lewistown, the gathering happens in mid-August. It's a great time to visit Lewistown, as the festival is really taking off in popularity and reputation, with new functions and activities added every year. Be sure to make reservations well in advance. For more information, contact the Lewistown Art Center (406/535-8278, www.lewistownartcenter.org).

SERVICES

The **Lewistown Area Chamber of Commerce** stands at 408 Northeast Main Street (406/535-5436 or 800/216-5436, www.lewistownchamber.com).

The **Carnegie Public Library** is at 701 West Main Street (406/538-5212). The **Central Montana Medical Center** is at 408 Wendall Avenue (406/538-7711). The **post office** is at 204 3rd Avenue North (406/538-3439).

Winter storms can be intense in the local mountains. To check **local road conditions,** call 406/538-7445.

East of Lewistown

Once the traveler descends from the pass of the Judith Mountains 10 miles east of Lewistown, unadulterated eastern Montana lies ahead. The ponderosa pines quickly thin and give way to short-grass prairie; mountain valleys flatten into wide coulees surmounted by sandstone bluffs. Ranches displace farms, and gray rain clouds from the west veer upward, cauterized by heat rising off the prairies. Somewhere hereabouts, the Great Plains begin in earnest.

This part of Montana is more often traversed than visited: Even by Montana standards, this is pretty forlorn country. Nonetheless, it bears the

memories of a violent history, sporadic development, and early settlement. Today, in the tradition of the glory days of the West, this outpost of central Montana supports large ranches, access to the vast **Charles M. Russell National Wildlife Refuge,** and tiny communities like **Winnett** known mostly for their watering holes.

CHARLES M. RUSSELL NATIONAL WILDLIFE REFUGE, WESTERN UNIT

The Western Unit of the Charles M. Russell National Wildlife Refuge forms the northern border of much of this area. Created in 1936, the 1.2-million-acre CMR, as it is known locally, is the second-largest wildlife refuge outside of Alaska. Highway 191 is one of two paved roads into the refuge; the other is 125 miles east. Anyone who wishes to visit the refuge must be willing to drive, sometimes for great distances, on gravel and dirt roads. The rustlers and outlaws who holed up here did so for a reason: It's hard country to navigate. However, isolation conducive to thieving is also conducive to wildlife.

Travelers without high-clearance vehicles are advised to cross the Fred Robinson Bridge on Highway 191 and take the **Self-Guided Nature Trail,** a 20-mile loop north of the Missouri. Those with more versatile vehicles can explore the back roads of these rugged, isolated, and uninhabited badlands on the south side.

Sand Creek Road leaves the pavement four miles south of the Fred Robinson Bridge, at the refuge headquarters, and winds through badlands, with several side roads giving onto the river bottoms. A much longer road (and in bad weather one more dubiously passable) leaves Highway 191 near the crossroads at Bohemian Corners (and runs north from Highway 200 at Winnett) and leads into some of the roughest and most historic wildlands in the refuge. **Crooked Creek Recreation Area** is located at the mouth of the Musselshell River, where the waters of Fort Peck Lake meet steep gumbo canyons.

Many travelers will find this rugged but eerily beautiful country reason enough to visit the refuge, but don't forget the wildlife. Deer, pronghorn, and elk range through the refuge in profusion. Bighorn sheep, coyotes, and prairie dogs can be seen by the sharp-eyed, and more than 200 bird species have been sighted.

Backcountry Byways

The BLM has designated some scenic off-road routes under its protection as "Backcountry Byways." The **Missouri Breaks Back Country Byway** makes a loop west of Highway 191 and travels through rough badlands, with views onto the Missouri River and its canyon. The byway begins within the Charles M. Russell National Refuge and continues along the boundary of the Upper Missouri Wild and Scenic River area. Turn west on Knox Ridge Road one mile south of the Fred Robinson Bridge. The most questionable part of the entire route immediately looms as the dirt road climbs up a very steep grade to the top of the breaks. After this point, the road becomes much less stressful; however, do not attempt this route if it's at all wet.

The Bureau of Land Management's designated route splits off Knox Ridge Road and turns north toward the river along Lower Two Calf Road. From it, several side roads drop onto the river bottom. Sweeping views of the Missouri and wildlife sightings make this byway both instructional and awe-inspiring. The route rejoins Knox Ridge Road and returns to Highway 191 across high prairies.

The entire loop road is 73 miles long; at the western junction of Knox Ridge and Lower Two Calf Roads, the traveler can also continue 12 miles to Winifred and paved Highway 236.

Camping

Informal camping is allowed in most areas of the CMR, with established campgrounds at **James Kipp State Park,** at the Fred Robinson Bridge on Highway 191. The campgrounds at **Crooked Creek** have a boat launch, but no fresh water.

Information

Contact the Charles M. Russell National Wildlife Refuge at P.O. Box 110, Lewistown, MT 59547 (406/538-8706).

WINNETT AND VICINITY
History

Walter Winnett's ranch along McDonald Creek evolved in 1909 from an open-range camp to a small town as homesteaders who settled the valley needed a center for commerce. The Milwaukee Road extended to Winnett (present pop. 185, elev. 2,960 feet) in 1917, just as drought hit. The community began to fray, then in 1919 oil was discovered at Devils Basin, the first oil strike in central Montana. Despite the bad years for farmers, Winnett's population boomed with the hope of more oil strikes. At Cat Creek, on the

THE OPEN RANGE

As with the Big Open region just to the east, the prairies of central Montana saw the requisite historical phases of boom and development come late and peremptorily. There was little settlement – of a law-abiding sort – until the 20th century, making this one of the last areas of Montana to be settled.

To the north of Winnett, trappers, wolf hunters, and woodchoppers (for the steamboats) were the only permanent residents along the Missouri River, and they lived in rough camps that passed for towns. As steamboat trade dwindled, the settlements increasingly became hideouts for rustlers and outlaws; Kid Curry and his gang had a pied-à-terre in a knocked-together river town called Rocky Point. The Breaks, as this rough country was known, became synonymous with rustlers and ne'er-do-wells. An 1870 census found 170 people living along the Missouri from Fort Benton to North Dakota; the count included only one white woman.

On the prairies that spread out eastward from the Judith Mountains, cattlemen like Granville Stuart soon established huge open-range ranches. By the 1880s, lawlessness was so rife that Fort Maginnis, raised on the flats next to Stuart's DHS Ranch, spent more time pursuing rustlers than intimidating Indians.

The confluence of the Missouri and Musselshell Rivers hosted numerous rustler gangs: In this wild country of brushy badlands, box canyons, and primitive settlements, wayward cowboys could trail stolen cattle and horses into secret ravines, alter their brands, and sell them to traders or trail them to Canada. Once in Canada, they would steal other livestock and trail them south into the States.

As the situation worsened, Stuart and a posse of like-minded vigilantes met at a bar in Gilt Edge and decided to take matters into their own hands. During the summer of 1884, "Stuart's Stranglers," as the vigilantes called themselves, took the offensive against the rustling rings along the Missouri. In a series of shoot-outs and hangings, at least 17 men were killed by the vigilantes in Rocky Point, at the mouth of the Musselshell, and other hideouts along the Missouri. Spurred on by their success, Stuart's Stranglers took their show on the road, and in secret raids across eastern Montana killed an estimated 100 more suspected thieves.

So the ranchers rid themselves of the threat of rustlers, but because these stockmen did not own the land they grazed, soon homesteaders carved the open range into half-section parcels.

CENTRAL MONTANA

Musselshell River, drillers discovered significant reserves of oil in 1920. A pipeline was laid to Winnett, a refinery was established, and the railroad shipped out the first tanker of oil in 1921. By 1923, Winnett had a population of 2,000 people.

But the boom was short-lived; within 10 years, Winnett had lost three-quarters of its population, even though Cat Creek continued to produce oil. Ranching and farming, much of it on arid and marginal land, again took over as the area's primary economy.

Accommodations

In this vast unpopulated area, there are few lodging options. In reality, only bad luck,

car trouble, or the spirit of adventure should catch you spending the night out here. In the tiny community of Grassrange, the motels vie for the trucking trade. The grimly efficient **Grassrange Motel** (406/428-2242, $48) is the third wheel of a bar-café complex. Also in Grassrange, the **Little Montana Truckstop** (406/428-2270) has an RV park and showers.

Food

In Winnett, the **Kozy Korner** (406/429-2621) is open daily 6 A.M.–9 P.M. At the crossroads of Highways 87 and 191 there's the **Bohemian Corner Cafe** (406/464-2321), open 7 A.M.–9 P.M. The **Grassrange Bar** (406/428-2242) also serves food, as do the town's truck stops.

LANDSCAPES CARVED BY ANCIENT RIVERS

Geologically speaking, relatively recent events created the distinctive landscapes of Central Montana. About 20 million years after the Rockies formed, a vast surge of volcanic activity forced molten rock to the surface in many parts of the Judith Basin. Not all lava erupted; some molten rock squeezed up through fissures and faults or fed into underground reservoirs, called laccoliths. Erosion has exposed these formations – steep vertical ridges of volcanic stone, called dikes, running in straight lines across the landscape. One of the most prominent laccoliths in Montana, Square Butte, rises spectacularly from the plains near Geraldine.

Edging down from the north, ice age glaciers reached the Great Falls area, where they trapped river flow and glacial meltwater that would have normally flowed north and east along the ancestral Missouri drainage, forming Glacial Lake Great Falls. About 15,000 years ago, the present site of Great Falls was flooded by 600 feet of melted ice. Water stretched from the Highwood Mountains to the Rocky Mountain foothills. As the lake grew and the glaciers receded, this vast body of water cut a new spillway. About 10,000 years ago, the overflow of Glacial Lake Great Falls roared through this channel, until the melting glaciers revealed a lower watercourse. The glacial lake spillway, called the Shonkin Sag by geologists and the Big Sag by locals, remains a deep U-shaped valley, 500 feet deep and one mile wide, along the base of the Highwood Mountains and Square Butte. All that's left of the huge river that once flowed here are the awesome canyon that it cut and a few shallow lakes.

The Judith Basin

Bounded by the mountain ranges of central Montana, the broad basin of the Judith River contains some of the state's richest agricultural land. Streams course through fields and meadows; abundant crops and well-nourished livestock share this fecund domain.

For centuries, this open prairie supported hundreds of thousands of buffalo. After their decimation, the first open-range ranches of Montana prospered here. The Milwaukee Road and the Great Northern vied for supremacy in the Judith Basin, each luring settlers (and hence passengers and freight) by extensive advertising campaigns. The dryland farms were so successful that the Judith Basin became the poster child of the Montana homestead movement. Unfortunately, even here farmers could not survive on homestead allotments during cycles of bad years. Today, small communities like **Stanford, Hobson, Utica** and **Judith Gap** only just hang on as trade centers for local farmers and ranchers.

Information

For information about the Judith Basin area, contact the **Judith Ranger District, Lewis and Clark National Forest** (P.O. Box 434, Stanford, MT, 406/566-2292).

STANFORD AND VICINITY

Stanford (pop. 454, elev. 4,200 feet) was the Judith Basin's most important trade center for grain and livestock in the early 1900s. It has managed to survive the vicissitudes of drought and bad markets better than its neighbors, and the town's wide streets and well-kept homes make it a handsome anomaly in central Montana.

Stanford's **Judith Basin Museum** (203 1st Ave. S., 406/566-2281, 9 A.M.–noon and 1–5 P.M. Mon.–Fri., Memorial Day–Labor

YOGO SAPPHIRES

Montana's most famous gemstones are Yogo sapphires, found in a small area of the Little Belt Mountains just south of Utica called Yogo Gulch. The primary rock in this mountain chain is Precambrian limestone laid down more than 575 million years ago; however, the narrow vein of rock that holds precious Yogo sapphires is much younger.

About 50 million years ago, molten magma rose into the overlying limestone, where it slowly cooled to form a dike an average of eight feet in width but over five miles long. As the magma in the dike crystallized, atoms of oxygen combined with atoms of aluminum to form corundum, the mineral form of aluminum oxide. The corundum formed tiny, perfectly shaped transparent crystals rather than the usual blue-gray prisms. Moreover, virtually every crystal in this dike contained traces of iron and titanium that gave each crystal a beautiful cornflower-blue color, the signature hue that makes Yogo sapphires the most precious gemstone mined in the United States.

Although it is not known that Native Americans gathered sapphires in Yogo Gulch, in fact the word *yogo* means "blue sky" in the Piegan Blackfoot tongue. The discovery of sky-blue sapphires in the Little Belts awaited the Montana gold rush, when seemingly every drainage in Montana was explored by prospectors. Low-level gold deposits in Yogo Gulch were sufficient for a town site of nearly 1,000 miners to spring up in the early 1880s, but the lack of sustainable deposits caused the boomtown to go bust by the 1890s.

One hardened prospector named Jake Hoover persevered here despite the disappointing volume of gold nuggets. Over the years he had collected the small, brilliantly blue stones that appeared along the creek and in his gold pan. He sent a small cigar tin of these stones to Tiffany's in New York City for valuation in 1895 – and in return received a check for $3,750, with the price set at a paltry $6 per carat for top-quality stones!

Hoover and his business partners quickly staked claims along the dike and began sapphire mining in earnest. The mine later changed hands: By the time the British firm of Johnson, Walker, and Tolhurst ceased mining in 1929, more than 16 million carats worth of sapphires had been extracted from Yogo Gulch.

The Yogo mines lay dormant until 1956, when production began again. New technology and mining techniques have meant that miners can now follow the Yogo dike deeper and farther than before. Yogo sapphires are unusual in that they are mined using hard-rock mining techniques, involving underground tunnels and blasting or sluicing to extract the alluvial deposits that contain the rough stones.

Because of their intense blue color, Yogo sapphires have gained a loyal following among the world's royal and wealthy. Queen Elizabeth II's engagement ring featured a Montana Yogo sapphire; however, it seems that Princess Diana's sapphire engagement ring from Prince Charles was composed with a Sri Lankan sapphire, not a Yogo sapphire, as was widely reported at the time. The largest cut Yogo sapphire is a 10.2-carat gem in the Smithsonian Institution in Washington, D.C.

Day) features a collection of more than 2,000 salt and pepper shakers and frontier-era household items. Stop at the **Basin Trading Post** along Highway 200 to see an exhibit on a dastardly white wolf from homesteader days.

The **Sundown Motel** (west along Hwy. 200, 406/566-2316) stands next to Stanford's best steakhouse, the **Sundown Inn** (406/566-9911). Rooms go for $48 for a double.

The **By Way Cafe** (south of Stanford on Hwy. 200, 406/566-2631) is that uniquely Montanan institution, the combination truck stop, restaurant, and liquor store. In the center of town is the **Wolves Den** (81 Central Ave., 406/566-2451, 8 A.M.–10 P.M.), which specializes in pizza.

HOBSON AND UTICA

The **Judith Basin Cattle Pool** was one of the earliest open-range outfits in the state. During the boom years of the 1880s, investors bought

THE JUDITH GAP

Named for the wide and desolate divide between the Big Snowy and the Little Belt Mountains, the Judith Gap has been a transportation corridor for centuries. Crow Indians crossed the gap to hunt buffalo in the Judith Basin; Blackfeet warriors later pushed south across the area to menace the Crow along the Musselshell River. Traders used this notoriously windy pass to reach erstwhile settlements and gold camps in central Montana. Both the Great Northern and the Milwaukee lines laid track over the Judith Gap to reach homestead towns.

The first settlement in the area was the old crossroads of U-bet, which thrived as a stop on the old Carroll Trail stage line during the 1870s. U-bet was a well-loved watering hole for early cowboys. When Richard Harlow's Montana Railroad pushed through the Judith Gap in 1903, it too named its station U-bet.

During the homestead rush, a telling division of sentiment regarding alcohol led to the establishment of two communities. North Garneill was "dry," while nearby South Garneill (incorporating U-bet) had a guesthouse, saloon, and the accoutrements of an Old West town. In some kind of victory, today only North Garneill survives, if only diffidently and under the abridged name of Garneill.

The **U-bet and Central Montana Pioneers Monument** at Garneill is a huge block of granite on a concrete base. Embedded in the base is an array of local rocks. There are two large, nearly identical pear-shaped stones here, found by early settlers near Winnett. Apparently carved by Indians, their meaning has been lost.

cattle and then pooled them together to be run by hired cowboys. Calves were branded with the same brand as their mothers; in the fall they were sold, trailed to railheads, and shipped to feedlots for fattening.

Utica was the hub for open-range cowboys in the Judith Basin during the 1880s; here they gathered the immense herds of cattle to divide them according to brand. It was a raucous time: After a summer of sometimes lonely cattle herding, the cowboys had a chance to kick up their heels and celebrate being back in town. Painter Charley Russell worked the ranges here, and many of his paintings feature the unique skyline of the Judith Basin.

Not much is left in Utica except a bar and a museum, both appropriate memorials to the ghosts of cowboys past. When the Great Northern line went through, Utica was bypassed for Hobson (pop. 244, elev. 3,940 feet), 10 miles down the Judith River.

Art of another sort has its heyday around here in late summer. Hobson-area businesses sponsor hay-bale decorating in a contest called "What the Hay?" as a fun and humorous diversion (there's also a sizable pot of prize money awarded). Watch for large round hay bales wearing clothing, paint, old tires, hats, and whatever makes a good visual joke.

The **Utica Museum** (406/423-5208, 10 A.M.–5 P.M. Sat.–Sun., Memorial Day–Labor Day) preserves Utica's cowboy heritage with tools, saddles, and wagons.

Light meals are served at Utica's old bar, the **Oxen Yoke Inn** (406/423-5560, 11 A.M.–9 P.M. daily). In Hobson, the (**Black Bull Bar and Steakhouse** (Central Ave., 406/423-5391, Mon.–Thurs. 11:30 A.M.–1:30 P.M. and 5–9 P.M., Fri.–Sat. 11:30 A.M.–1:30 P.M. and 5–10 P.M., Sun. noon–8 P.M.) is the local steakhouse. At the junction of Highways 200 and 191 is **Eddie's Corner** (406/374-2471), a popular truck stop with a café open 24 hours a day.

HARNESSING JUDITH GAP WINDS

About ten miles north of Harlowtown on Highway 191, at the edge of Judith Gap, the always-gusty pass between the Judith and the Musselshell River drainages, is Montana's largest wind farm. In 2005, Chicago-based Invenergy Services erected 90 massive wind towers on the prairie (the highway cuts right through the midst of the wind farm). Each of the towers is 262 feet tall and is powered by a wind turbine with three 126-foot-long blades. Each of the turbines is capable of producing 1,500 kilowatts of power at maximum generating strength (one kilowatt of power provides enough electricity for 240 to 300 homes). The entire wind farm generates upwards of 135 megawatts of electrical power, which is consumed by a local utility, NorthWestern Energy, with 320,000 electrical customers in Montana. Invenergy has announced plans to add another 35 turbines, which would boost electrical production at this central Montana wind farm by another 52.5 megawatts. Even if you're not planning to travel on Highway 191, it's worth the detour to view the wind farm. The towers are very impressive, and their slowly spinning arms provide a surrealistic addition to the expansive landscape.

CENTRAL MONTANA

© BILL MCRAE

wind turbines near Judith Gap

White Sulphur Springs and the Belt Mountains

CENTRAL MONTANA

The wide basin of the Shields and Smith Rivers stretches between the Missouri and Yellowstone drainages. Although hemmed in by five mountain ranges, the valleys are vast and flat. White Sulphur Springs lies at the center of this valley network. The hot springs for which the town is named were first enjoyed by Indians; by the early 20th century, developers advertised them as America's answer to Europe's famous spas in Baden-Baden.

As elsewhere in central Montana, the mountains drew early settlers to mining camps. Diamond City in Confederate Gulch in the Big Belt Mountains, just west of White Sulphur Springs, was the site of one of the state's earliest and richest gold strikes. Three veterans of the Civil War found the deposits in 1864; by 1867 the town's population had swollen to 5,000, and it had a reputation for wildness and wealth.

The gravels were extraordinarily rich. Legends tell of single pans containing a thousand dollars' worth of gold; in one day miners claimed 700 pounds of gold from one strike. But the diggings were shallow; by 1870 the boom was over and the gold camp deserted, but not before prospectors extracted an estimated $16 million from the gulch. There's little left at Diamond City except ghosts; tiny former mining towns like **Monarch** and **Neihart** struggle on.

The basin offers unparalleled recreational opportunities. The Shields and Smith Rivers, and also Belt Creek, hold pedigrees as great trout streams. The Smith River passes through a deep limestone canyon, making it inaccessible to land vehicles for 61 miles; this section has become a favorite for river floaters.

◖ WHITE SULPHUR SPRINGS

White Sulphur Springs (pop. 984, elev. 5,200 feet) was named for the white deposits left by the hot water that burbles up in the city's public park just off Highway 12. The 115°F waters only faintly smell of sulfur, but weary travelers have soaked in them for centuries. Today, the flow is tapped for use in the Spa Hot Springs Motel; it also heats the town bank.

White Sulphur Springs had long been a popular hot springs for local Indians; Crow Chief Plenty Coups recalled pilgrimages by warriors to the medicinal mud baths. James Brewer chanced onto the area in 1866, as stagecoaches rumbled through along the Carroll Trail. Brewer developed the hot springs as a stage stop for travelers; the waters here are said to resemble the famous springs at Baden-Baden in Germany, and references to Baden-Baden dot his early promotional literature. However, the grand hotel and spa envisioned by early boosters never materialized.

Notoriety of another sort has clung to White Sulphur Springs. Two noted Montana writers, Walt Coburn and Ivan Doig, hail from local ranches. The latter's *This House of Sky* is autobiographical and is set hereabouts.

The Castle

The gracious homes built in White Sulphur Springs during the 1890s are testimony to the wealth of open-range ranchers who found the wide valleys hospitable for raising cattle and sheep.

The Castle, a mansion built in 1892 out of locally carved granite, now functions as the **Meagher County Historical Museum** (310 2nd Ave. N.E., 406/547-2324, 10 A.M.–6 P.M. daily, May 15–Sept. 15, $3 adults). It contains a selection of artifacts from the region's early history and some beautiful period furniture. The mansion is well restored, and the carved wood and moldings are to die for.

Floating and Fishing the Smith River

The Smith River gets off to an easygoing start in the wide basin around White Sulphur Springs but soon passes into a narrow canyon cut through extensive limestone formations. On the 61-mile stretch between old Camp Baker and Eden Bridge, the river can only be

© BILL MCRAE

Now a museum, The Castle was built by a prominent local rancher.

reached by boat. The extreme remoteness of this portion of the Smith, along with excellent wildlife viewing and old-fashioned excitement, make this float very popular.

The Smith also offers excellent fishing for brown and rainbow trout. The state maintains two fishing-access sites and campgrounds in otherwise inaccessible portions of the river north of White Sulphur Springs. Take Highway 360 west and follow signs to Smith River (18 miles) or Fort Baker (26 miles).

Because of increased traffic on the river, the Department of Fish, Wildlife, and Parks (406/454-3441) has begun to limit the number of **float trips** down the Smith. Only 73 commercial launches are allowed during the summer, and permits for public float trips not run by outfitters are now distributed in a lottery. Even the campsites are available by reservation only. For up-to-date information on Smith River float trip regulations, including a list of sanctioned outfitters, check out http://fwp.mt.gov/parks/recreation/smithriver.

Most outfitters will offer four-, five-, and

six-day trips down the Smith; the difference in the length of trips is the pace. Four days is breakneck and exhausting, whereas six days is leisurely and suited to anglers. A full Smith River trip costs around $3,000.

The following outfitters are among the best and most environmentally sensitive. Try **Paul Roos Outfitters** (P.O. Box 621, Helena, MT 59601, 406/442-5489 or 800/858-3497, www.paulroosoutfitters.com), or contact **Smith River Flyfishing Expeditions** (532 Jack Creek Rd., Ennis, 406/682-7288).

One of the best local fishing and hunting outfitters is **Avalanche Basin Outfitters** (P.O. Box 17, White Sulphur Springs, MT 59645, 406/547-3962, www.avalancheoutfitters.com), which offers guided fishing trips on the Smith and other local rivers.

Accommodations

The new **All Seasons Inn and Suites** (808 3rd Ave. S.W., 406/547-8888 or 877/314-0241, $70) has a pool and a complimentary continental breakfast.

The **◖ Spa Hot Springs Motel** (202 W. Main St., 406/547-3366 or 800/898-3303, www.spahotsprings.com, $63) has White Sulphur Springs's trademark hot water piped into indoor and outdoor pools. Nonguests can drop by for a swim and soak for $5. Under new ownership (a retired chiropractor), the motel and springs are going through a renaissance. All beds have been fitted with Sealy Posturepedic mattresses, and the entire facility, including the guest rooms, has been extensively remodeled. The mineral pools are drained and cleaned nightly, making this a very clean spa.

Camping

The **Springs Campground** (Hwy. 89, 406/547-3921) is convenient for RV campers. Consider camping lakeside at **Newlan Creek Reservoir,** 10 miles north of White Sulphur Springs, or along **Sutherlin Reservoir,** 12 miles east on Highway 12.

Food

The **Stockman's Bar and Steakhouse** (117

JOHN RINGLING, SHOWMAN AND RANCHER

John Ringling was born in 1866 to a Wisconsin family seemingly predestined for big times in the big top. One of seven siblings who formed the Ringling Brothers Circus in 1884, John was perhaps the most entrepreneurial of the brothers. After years of touring the Midwest with its signature big tent (the tent could seat 4,000 and still had room for three rings of activities), Ringling led his brothers toward consolidation with the Barnum and Bailey Circus in 1907 to form "The Greatest Show on Earth."

With the world's largest circus in his back pocket, Ringling decided he needed another hobby. He purchased 100,000 acres of prime ranch land on the Shields River, not far from the town now called Ringling. He had major dreams for his Montana holdings: Not only would the ranch serve as a training camp for circus performers, but Ringling would also lead the tourist development of this part of Montana, basing his plans on the hot mineral springs at White Sulphur Springs.

Ringling was the chief financier and driving force behind the grandly named White Sulphur Springs and Yellowstone Park Railroad, an 18-mile-long line that linked the town of White Sulphur Springs with the mainline Milwaukee Road rail service at Ringling. This transportation link would bring travelers to White Sulphur Springs. Here, Ringling and other developers planned to build a grand spa hotel and resort based on the European style, where wealthy customers could come to "take the waters" in scenic splendor.

The rail line was built in 1910, but before the rest of Ringling's dreams of the spa lifestyle came into being, World War I broke out in Europe, causing worldwide recession and displacement. Managing the circus throughout this period of intense labor shortage and financial crisis preempted Ringling's Montana vision, and plans for the spa were soon abandoned. However, the Ringling family continued to own and operate their ranch until 1949.

Main St., 406/547-9985, 11:30 A.M.–9 P.M. daily) offers burgers and steaks; for the restaurant, go in the green door on the side street. **Montana K&L Roadhouse** (406/547-3638), just south of town, serves barbecued chicken and beef and more steaks.

Information

The **Meagher County Chamber of Commerce** can be reached at P.O. Box 365, White Sulphur Springs, MT 59645 (406/547-3366, www. meagherchamber.com). The **Lewis and Clark National Forest** office's address is P.O. Box A, White Sulphur Springs, MT 59645 (406/547-3361).

NORTH OF WHITE SULPHUR SPRINGS ON HIGHWAY 89

Actually anything but little, the Little Belt Mountains ramble across 1,500 square miles of central Montana. Formed by underlying folds in the bedrock, these broad arches expose rocks from a hodgepodge of sources,

including Precambrian sedimentary rock, limestone, and igneous intrusions. Silver has been mined in the Little Belts since the 1880s, but now more famous are the sapphire mines on Yogo Creek. Originally considered to be detritus from gold placer mining, the blue stones were analyzed and discovered to be sapphires of unusually high quality and a startlingly dark blue color. Like diamonds in South Africa, they occur in a "pipe" only eight feet across and three miles long. Sapphires have been mined commercially since 1896; the mines are not open to the public, but Yogo sapphires are available from local jewelers.

Recreation rather than mining seems to be the future of the Little Belts, however. Skiing, hiking trails, snowmobile tracks, and great fishing now characterize these pretty but undramatic mountains. The **Showdown Ski Area** (406/236-5522 or 800/433-0022; 24-hour snow line 406/771-1300), high in the Little Belts, holds the state's record for snowfall—33 feet in one winter. For your $35 lift

© BILL MCRAE

The Little Belt Mountains are famed for silver and sapphires.

ticket, you get access to 34 runs with a vertical drop of 1,400 feet, plus a terrain park. Facilities include a cafeteria, a bar, ski rentals, and a pro shop. Showdown is eight miles south of Neihart.

Neihart

There's not much life left in the old mining town of Neihart. It began in 1881 when silver was discovered; the rail line to Great Falls would have ensured growth if the silver market had remained stable, but Neihart was marginalized after the silver crash of 1893. Victorian-era homes and a log school testify to its more affluent days.

One oasis in Neihart is **Bob's Bar and Grill** (406/236-5955, 7 A.M.–8 P.M. daily), which also sells hunting and fishing licenses and offers motel rooms ($45 and up). Forest Service campgrounds abound along Highway 89 in the Little Belts: **King's Hill,** nine miles south of Neihart, and **Aspen,** six miles north of Neihart, are convenient to the highway.

The Lewis and Clark National Forest's **Belt Creek Information Station** (406/236-5511) is on Highway 89 in Neihart.

Monarch

Born a mining camp, Monarch has developed into a tourist center. Its sylvan character, access to fishing in Belt Creek, and bars and restaurants make this a favorite stop for hikers and skiers from Great Falls.

As Highway 89 drops out of the Little Belts and toward Belt Creek 10 miles north of Monarch, a roadside stop overlooks Belt Creek as it issues out of a canyon of white limestone cliffs. At the **Sluice Box State Monument,** trails lead up the creek beneath these cliffs. It's a good spot for a picnic or to try for a trout.

Rooms are around $65 for a double at the **Cub's Den** (406/236-5922), an all-purpose enterprise with a grocery store, gas station, and restaurant. The restaurant boasts a full lunch and dinner menu, from peanut butter sandwiches to steak and lobster. Next door is a casino and bar. The motel has a pool and hot tub, and a poolside continental breakfast is served; pets are permitted. The **Lazy Doe** (406/236-5439) serves lunch and dinner, and overlooks Belt Creek.

Recreation

The Little Belts along Highway 89 have been mined and logged. To explore the range on foot, travelers should hike into the headwaters of the Judith River—the South Fork, Lost Fork, and Middle Fork of the Judith are each served by good trails. The drainages cut through limestone canyons and are de facto wilderness areas.

For access to the hiking trails, follow the Judith River southwest from Utica along a good gravel road toward **Fred Ellis Memorial Recreation Area.** Follow signs to the trailhead.

SOUTH OF WHITE SULPHUR SPRINGS ON HIGHWAY 89
The Shields River
From the western slopes of the Crazy Mountains flows the Shields River. Highway 89 follows the river as it drains southward through lush farm and ranch land. In the 1860s frontiersman Jim Bridger led settlers up the Shields River, over Battle Ridge Pass, and into the Gallatin Valley

CENTRAL MONTANA

to western Montana gold camps. Settlement spread up the valley after the Northern Pacific reached Livingston in 1882; a stage coach line soon linked Clyde Park to the Yellowstone Valley, and a spur line of the Northern Pacific extended to Wilsall in the 1900s.

In the saddle between the Shields and Smith Rivers is Ringling, named for John Ringling of circus fame, who settled and ranched near here. A division point on the Milwaukee Road railroad, it now contains a grain-alcohol plant that converts local wheat and barley to gasohol. St. John's Catholic Church sits on a bluff above the town, dominating the skyline.

There's good fishing in the Shields River and its Crazy Mountain tributaries. Hiking trails to high mountain lakes in the Crazies depart from trailheads on Cottonwood Creek.

Highway 12 and the Musselshell Valley

The Musselshell River rises in the peaks of the Crazy, Castle, and Little Belt Mountains and flows east through a wide, wooded valley lined with farms and ranches. Here is some of the gentlest beauty in Montana; shaded by majestic cottonwoods, cattle graze along a rushing river flanked by steep sandstone cliffs. As everywhere in central Montana, mountains loom in the distance like ramparts.

Rarely in Montana does the integrity of the natural landscape seem so little in conflict with the pursuits of agriculture. The compromise that nature has made with the rancher seems only to have made the landscape more gracious.

Almost nowhere else in Montana have a region and a railroad been so closely linked as the Musselshell River Valley and the Milwaukee Road; the solid towns built alongside the railroad reflect the confident dreams of the settlers that it brought west. **Roundup** and **Harlowton** have endured as trade centers; however, the scope and solid stylishness of their old town centers contrast oddly with their present chastened realities. They wear their pasts awkwardly, like ill-fitting clothes—modest communities occupying towns built for larger purposes.

Other settlements—Shawmut, Twodot, Ryegate—didn't fare as well. Today all but ghost towns, these old communities are stone and brick monuments to the poignant and mostly unrealized dreams of an entire generation of Montanans. One exception to the rule of hard-luck agriculture was Charles Bair, an early and very successful sheep rancher. The rambling ranch house occupied by him and his daughters, now preserved as the **Charles M. Bair Family Museum,** is jammed with fine art and furniture from around the world, and is one of the true must-sees in central Montana.

Highway 12 parallels the old Milwaukee Road tracks and serves the farming, ranching, and mining communities that sprawl across this piece of Montana. This is one of the most beautiful drives in the state; east to west, it's more direct than the freeway.

HISTORY

The Musselshell Valley provided a rich hunting ground for early Indians, but it didn't historically belong to any single tribe; it was either shared or battled for. In the 1830s, part of the Crow tribe moved north from the Bighorn River Valley, settled along the Musselshell, and became known as the River Crow. Subsequent treaties established the Crow Reservation south of the Yellowstone, and the River Crow were removed from the Musselshell.

By the 1870s, open-range cattle companies grazed the valleys of central Montana. The U.S. Army established a trail linking Fort Custer on the Bighorn and Fort Maginnis near Lewistown; it crossed the river near the present town of Musselshell. Texas drovers considered this ford to be the last stop in the long trail from the south; thereafter, cattle fanned out to graze the rich prairies to the north. The Musselshell Valley and Judith Basin remained the province of open-range ranchers for almost 30 years.

© BILL MCRAE

CENTRAL MONTANA

The Milwaukee Road was the first railway to use electric engines, like this one displayed in Harlowtown.

Two of these ranches—the Twodot and the Seventynine—have passed into Western lore. Uncharacteristically, the big cattle outfits here shared the range with enormous sheep ranches, especially near Martinsdale and Sumatra.

Mining began in the 1880s at Castle, where a rich vein of silver was intermittently exploited. However, central Montana was far from any railroad—ox teams hauled the ore to Helena for smelting—which made further development of minerals unprofitable. Local residents began to call for a central Montana railroad. During the 1890s, Richard Harlow built the Montana Railroad in fits and starts and as financing allowed, eventually linking Lombard on the Missouri River to Harlowtown and Lewistown in 1903.

The Chicago, Milwaukee, St. Paul, and Pacific Railroad, on its way to Seattle, laid tracks up the Musselshell in 1908. The firm bought the Montana Railroad from Harlow, thereby extending into the Judith Basin. Coal deposits at Roundup were developed to fuel the Milwaukee's engines.

In 1915 the Milwaukee announced that it would electrify its engines between Harlowton and Avery, Idaho, which made it the longest stretch of electric railroad in North America at the time. The engines that pushed the trains uphill ran backward downhill, working both as brakes and as generators to recharge up to 60 percent of the electricity expended on the inclines.

Ad campaigns from the railroad convinced prospective settlers of the richness of central Montana. Towns sprang up along sidings, and farmers claimed the bottomland, half section by half section, signaling the end of the open range. The media trumpeted the bumper crops raised by these first-time farmers, and many immigrants responded, choosing new and seemingly secure lives and opportunities on the Montana prairies.

The decline of central Montana began with the droughts of the late 1910s and continued as later droughts combined with the Great Depression of the 1930s. Nature in Montana proved to be cruel; of the tens of thousands who moved to central Montana during the homestead era, only the frugal, driven, and lucky endured until the 1940s. The rural population decamped; coal mining at Roundup ended in the 1950s, and the Milwaukee Road, struggling since the 1940s, ended its central Montana rail service in 1980.

Today, agriculture nevertheless remains the backbone of local economies. Although large farms and ranches have replaced homesteads, rural life for many in central Montana is as unsure nowadays as it was for earlier, perhaps more naive, settlers.

FORSYTH TO ROUNDUP

Highway 12 climbs out of the Yellowstone Valley and across an arid plain before it drops into the Musselshell River Valley. Forsaken little towns like Vananda follow the old Milwaukee Road. They indicate both the hope and the disillusion of early homesteaders. This is historically sheep and cattle country, and the early prosperity of now-flagging communities like Ingomar and Sumatra was linked to vast nearby stretches of open prairie that needed a railhead for shipping livestock to outside markets.

Within the Musselshell Valley, irrigated farmland replaces the arid plains. Little towns like Melstone (pop. 166, elev. 2,897 feet) and Musselshell, once centers for homesteaders, are today crossroads and gas stations for travelers and local farmers. West of Melstone, the sandstone cliffs and bluffs of the Fort Union Formation shelter the valley; their rich coal veins enriched the local economy when the steam engines of the Milwaukee Road crossed the West.

Practicalities

One of the most famous bars in Montana is the **(Jersey Lily** (406/358-2278, 7 A.M.–midnight) in the little community of Ingomar. The bean soup here is the pièce de résistance and enjoys statewide fame. The Jersey Lily is the only business left in town, and only local ranchers and the occasional traveler keep the bar from going the way of the rest of the town. Plank sidewalks, hitching posts, and tumbleweeds in the street aren't added for effect: They're real. Enthusiasts of Western lore can test their mettle at the authentic outdoor privies.

ROUNDUP
History

Roundup (pop. 1,931, elev. 3,184 feet), by dint of etymology, was the beginning of the Great Montana Roundup—the centennial cattle drive in 1989, in which it mimicked its frontier role as a center of livestock roundups in the 1880s.

The Milwaukee Road railroad put Roundup on the map. In 1908 its steam engines arrived to create a demand for cheap coal in central Montana. The Bull Mountains, an uplift of sedimentary sandstone containing significant amounts of coal, are south of Roundup. Mines here became the Milwaukee's fuel source.

Highway 87 intersects Roundup north to south. Klein, a largely defunct community just across the Musselshell from Roundup, was once a vibrant mining community. Early immigrants solved the housing problem by building lodgings into the cliff side. Some of these cave homes are now used for livestock; some still house people. Watch for electric lines and TV antennas protruding from stone cliff-side dwellings.

Sights

The **Musselshell Valley Historical Museum** (524 1st St. W., 406/323-1403, 9 A.M.–6 P.M. daily, Memorial Day–Labor Day, donations) contains reminders of Roundup's dual heritage as pioneer cow town and mining camp.

Recreation

The **Pine Ridge Country Club** (one mile west on 13th Ave. W., 406/323-2880) is a nine-hole golf course with a log clubhouse dating from 1908. The municipal **swimming pool** is at 700 3rd Avenue West (406/323-1384).

Accommodations

The **Best Value Inn** (740 Main St., 406/323-1000 or 888/422-1224, $40) offers air-conditioned rooms with cable TV. Nonsmoking rooms are available, and dogs are allowed. On the north end of town is the **Ideal Motel** (926 Main St., 406/323-3371 or 888/323-3371, $42); some rooms have kitchenettes. The Ideal also offers RV hookups.

At **Cowbell Park,** off Highway 12 south of town, there is free overnight camping along the Musselshell River.

Guest Ranch

Runamuk Guest Ranch (733 Goulding Creek, 406/323-3614, www.runamukguestranch.com) is an 18,000-acre fifth-generation ranch that offers guests the opportunity to join in ranch activities either as overnight guests or for 5- to 7-day "ranch experience" vacations. Multiday packages include all meals, horseback riding, and accommodation in comfortable lodgings, which include a four-bedroom guest house, a cabin, and a one-bedroom apartment. Rates begin at $75 double for a basic overnight stay, $125 double for bed and breakfast, and $1,250 per person for a five-day ranch experience package.

Food

Good for a quick bite in Roundup is the **Busy Bee** (south on Hwy. 87, 406/323-2204). It's principally a diner that's open 24 hours a day; the large parking lot explains its popularity with truckers. Along the town's handsome old Main Street, try the **Pioneer Café** (229 Main St., 406/323-2622, 7 A.M.–7 P.M. Mon.–Sat., 7 A.M.–3 P.M. Sun.) for Western home-cooking, or the **Vault** (201 Main St., 406/323-1229) for pizza.

Information

Contact the **Roundup Chamber of Commerce** (P.O. Box 751, Roundup, MT 59072, 406/323-

1966, www.roundupchamber.com) for more information.

ROUNDUP TO HARLOWTON
History

The traveler is rarely out of sight of ponderosa pines on sandstone buttes or the cottonwood-lined Musselshell on this length of Highway 12. As elsewhere on the early Milwaukee Road, community hopes ran high: The huge now-defunct hotel at bypassed Lavina testifies to the ambitions of homestead-era settlers. At Barber, among the deserted storefronts, is Grace Lutheran Church. Built in 1917 by German homesteaders, it could be the prototype for the Little White Church in the Vale; it is also the smallest active Lutheran congregation in the nation.

Just east of Ryegate, Chief Joseph and the Nez Percé crossed the Musselshell in 1877 as they fled northward to Canada.

Practicalities

Near Lavina, the **Lavina Crossing Cafe** (south on Hwy. 3, 406/636-2112) is open 6 A.M.–8 P.M. If you want a break in Ryegate, try the **Ryegate Cafe** (107 1st St., 406/568-2279, 7 A.M.–8 P.M.).

At **Deadman's Reservoir,** north of Highway 12 between Barber and Shawmut, there are free undeveloped campsites, along with good fishing and views of the Big Snowy Mountains.

◖ HARLOWTON

The original settlement at this valley crossroads was called Merino, indicating the importance of sheep and wool production in the area. When Richard Harlow's Montana Railroad reached the village in 1900, the jubilant citizens renamed their town in his honor.

Harlowton (pop. 1,062, elev. 4,167 feet) was a division station for the old Milwaukee line; this and a flour mill provided a suitable basis for substantial early growth.

At Harlowton, Highway 191 cuts through north to south. Access to the Judith Basin and the Yellowstone Valley make Harlowton a hub of local travel.

CENTRAL MONTANA

© BILL MCRAE

The Graves Hotel reflects the grandeur of a past era.

Historic Harlowton

Harlo (as it is known to locals) has one of the best-preserved early-20th-century town centers in Montana, a perhaps unwelcome benefit of limited recent growth. Immigrant stonemasons cut sandstone from nearby quarries to build storefronts. Three blocks of the downtown area, now a historic district, are built of this handsome native stone. Especially notable is the grand **Graves Hotel** (106 S. Central Ave.), a lovely old stone building with wraparound porches and a third-story turret. Built in 1908, for many years the Graves was a beacon of hospitality in this remote part of Montana. It is currently closed.

Other Sights

The **Upper Musselshell Historical Society Museum** (11 S. Central Ave., 406/632-5519, 10 A.M.–5 P.M. Tues.–Sat., 1–5 P.M. Sun., May 1–Nov. 1, donations) offers two different locations in downtown, both containing local memorabilia, such as the requisite pioneer schoolroom re-creation, old conveyances, and an interesting display of serving vessels carved from 200 different kinds of wood.

On the corner of Central Avenue and Highway 12 is a circa-1915 Milwaukee Road Electric Locomotive. Trains pushed by engines like this were the first to climb the Rockies under electric, not steam, power.

Recreation

The **Jawbone Creek Golf Course** (406/632-9960), 0.5 mile north on Central Avenue, is a nine-hole course that incorporates an old cemetery as a hazard.

Accommodations

The **Country Side Inn** (309 3rd Ave. N.E., 406/632-4119 or 800/632-4120, $60 and up) is a handsome log motel with a new hot tub, sauna, and exercise room. In addition to non-smoking rooms and king-bed rooms, there's also one room that's wheelchair accessible; pets are allowed.

The **Corral Motel** (406/632-4331 or 800/392-4723, $59) is located 0.25 mile east of town at the junction of Highways 12 and 191.

There are three kitchenette rooms, plus three units with suite-style separate bedrooms.

Camping

There's camping at **Chief Joseph Park** near the eastern junction of Highways 191 and 12. This three-acre city park also offers a playground, picnic sites, and a fishing pond.

Food

At the crossroads of Highways 191 and 12 is **Wade's Cafe** (406/632-4533, 6 A.M.–10 P.M. daily), a truck stop open for three meals a day; during the summer there's a drive-in. For a steak, head to the **Sportsman's Bar & Steakhouse** (406/632-4848, 11 A.M.–9 P.M. daily), just east of Harlowton.

Information

Contact the **Harlowton Chamber of Commerce** at P.O. Box 694, Harlowton, MT 59036 (406/632-4694). The **Musselshell Ranger District Office** is just west of town off Highway 12, and can be contacted at P.O. Box F, Harlowton, MT 59306 (406/632-4391).

HARLOWTON TO THE CRAZY MOUNTAINS

West of Harlowton, the horizon is punctuated by the rugged peaks of the Crazy Mountains, the most dramatic of central Montana's ranges. Highway 191 cuts south along the eastern face of the Crazies to Big Timber and the Yellowstone Valley.

The Musselshell River skirts the northern edge of the Crazies; its headwaters are in the more modest peaks of the Castle and Little Belt Mountains. Highway 12 follows the Musselshell until it divides; it then follows the North Fork through a canyon and past Checkerboard, a pretty community sadly turned into a trailer court. Highway 294 follows the South Fork of the Musselshell and the old Milwaukee tracks, between the Castle and Crazy Mountains.

This is rich agricultural land: The wide green valleys provide open winter pasture, while nearby mountain slopes afford rich summer grazing, especially for sheep. In 1910 Charles Bair, the local sheep baron, shipped 44 railcar loads of wool out of Martinsdale, the largest single shipment of wool in the state's history. A famous local ranch was the Twodot, named for its cattle brand. Today, the little settlement of Twodot, little more than a school and a bar, serves Montana townsfolk as a shorthand epithet for any rural eastern Montana community.

At the tiny community of **Lennep,** one of the Milwaukee's electric powerhouses sits idly beside the road, a remnant of that railroad's early electrified service. Along a gravel road seven miles north of Lennep is the ghost of Castle, a silver-mining town that ran its boom-to-bust cycle in the last decades of the 1800s. Lennep was the site of the first Lutheran church service held in Montana, in 1891; the present church, built in 1910, commands a broad view over the valley.

【 Charles M. Bair Family Museum

The Bairs were one of Montana's wealthiest and most unusual ranch families, and their home was opened in 1996 as a museum. This is easily one of Montana's most intriguing sites. The museum reopened in 2006 after being shuttered for three years.

To say that the museum is in the family ranch house is to become involved in the kind of understatement that makes describing this collection so difficult. Certainly this house started out as a ranch house, but by the time the Bairs were through with it, the house had been added to sporadically until it was several hundred feet long and contained 26 rooms, many built just to house the family's art and furniture collections. In 2004, Sotheby's estimated the value of the Bair collections at $55 million.

Charles Bair's clout with the rich and powerful at the beginning of the 20th century in Montana made it easy for him to amass his astonishingly wide collection of Native American artifacts, including headdresses, beaded clothing, and parfleches from the last of the Montana tribes' great chiefs. He also accumulated an impressive collection of Western

CENTRAL MONTANA

MONTANA'S LATE GREAT BAIR FAMILY

Charles Bair came to Montana in 1883 as a conductor on the Northern Pacific Railway and went into ranching in 1891. At the time the land in central and southern Montana was just opening up to agriculture. Bair was able to acquire a sizable holding in the Musselshell River Valley – and grazing rights to acreage on the Crow Reservation. On these properties he amassed one of the largest herds of sheep in the world. At one point in the 1910s, he owned 300,000 head.

A large part of the Bair fortune was made in the Yukon. In 1898 Bair sold 25,000 head of sheep and invested in a company that developed a machine to heat and pressurize water. This hot water was then pumped into the gold-bearing permafrost along the Klondike River, freeing the gold from the frozen earth. Bair came back from the Yukon a much richer man. As befitted a man of power and influence, Bair was friends with many of the celebrities and politicians of his era, including many of the U.S. presidents of his time. He also cultivated friendships with artists, including Charlie Russell and J. K. Ralston (whose works he began to collect), Will James, and several early film stars. While operating on the Crow Reservation, Bair became acquainted with Chief Plenty Coups, the great chieftain who led the Crow toward a more agrarian life. Bair began to collect Crow artifacts, many of which were gifts from the chief.

Bair had two daughters, Marguerite and Alberta, who were educated at Bryn Mawr College. On their grand tours of Europe, the women began collecting the fine furniture and art that distinguish the Bair collection today. In time the art and furniture collection outgrew the family's original ranch house, so the daughters simply added more rooms. Eighteenth-century French furniture was a particular passion of the Bairs, as was Paul Storr silver.

Charles Bair died in 1943. Marguerite married the ranch foreman, Scotsman Dave Lamb, in 1938, and they continued to live at the ranch until their deaths in the 1970s. Alberta, who never married, also continued to live in the family mansion. She was a well-known and colorful character, equally at home sealing a lamb sale in a Miles City bar as dining with royalty in an English country manor. Alberta was known for her proclivity for red hats, fine automobiles, vodka, and outspoken views on nearly everything. She was 98 when she died in 1993.

By the end of her life, Alberta had become a fixture on the Montana cultural scene. The Bairs were one of the most philanthropic families in the state, funding museums, hospitals, libraries, colleges, and charitable organizations. The Alberta Bair Theater in Billings, the city's performing arts center, was one of their gifts. Each year, four students from each of four rural Montana counties are given full-ride four-year academic scholarships, also courtesy of the Bair family.

Alberta's will stipulated that the Bair family home be left as a museum for the people of Montana.

paintings by Charlie Russell, J. K. Ralston, and J. H. Sharp, as well as a gallery of inscribed photos of presidents and celebrities.

Charles Bair's penchant for collecting paled beside his daughters' enthusiasm for it. In their 20 trips to Europe, Marguerite and Alberta indulged in a passion for Louis XV furniture, Scottish china, Sevres pottery, antique textiles, and English silver—and that's just for starters. The Bair daughters were also smart enough to buy up a collection of late French impressionist

paintings by Edouard Cortes. When they couldn't find upholstery fabric opulent enough (or one could opine, sufficiently gaudy), they hired French mills to custom-weave designs to their specifications.

This is not your average Montana ranch house, and no matter what your preconceptions, you will be bowled over by the collection. It's not just the sheer abundance of priceless antiques and fine art from all over the world; it's also that in the Bair's democratizing artistic vision, a Charlie Russell oil painting of cowboys hangs over an 18th-century marble commode that once graced Versailles, or that a Crow vest embroidered with porcupine quills, feathers, and beads belongs next to an impressionist masterpiece. And when you think you've seen it all, there's always the White Bathroom.

The Bair Family Museum (406/572-3314, www.bairfamilymuseum.org, 10 A.M.–5 P.M. daily Memorial Day–Labor Day, 10 A.M.–5 P.M. Wed.–Sun. May 1–Memorial Day and Labor Day–Sept. 30, $5 adults, $3 seniors, $2 children 6–16, children five and under free) is located one mile south of Highway 12 at Martinsdale.

Recreation

The Crazy Mountains' heavily glaciated peaks loom mirage-like above the surrounding plains; isolated and spectacular, they are among Montana's undiscovered gems for hiking and high-mountain lake fishing. Legends abound as to how they got their name, but they all have to do with women gone crazy with grief.

Hiking trails into the east side of the Crazies depart from the U.S. Forest Service's **Halfmoon Campground,** 15 miles west of Highway 191 on a good gravel road. There are several steep ascents, and the snow lasts well into June at higher elevations, so plan your hikes carefully. A short day hike of five miles round-trip from the campground takes in views of jagged peaks rising impertinently from deep-blue lakes; there's even good trout fishing in the lakes, although not all are easily accessible. Mountain goats were transplanted here in the 1940s and have flourished.

To reach Halfmoon Campground, travel eight miles south of Melville on Highway 191. The road passes through bucolic ranch lands before entering Big Timber Canyon on its way to the trailhead.

Accommodations and Food

Harlowton and White Sulphur Springs provide the closest lodging and dining.

Guest Ranches

With the Crazy Mountains as a backdrop, it's no wonder that some of Montana's best guest ranches have developed such devoted audiences.

The **Sweet Grass Ranch** (Box 161, Melville Rte., Big Timber, MT 59011, 406/537-4477 summer, 406/537-4497 winter, www.sweet-grassranch.com) welcomes guests to live the good life at the base of the Crazy Mountains; it has been in the same family for five generations and still operates as a cattle ranch. Horseback riding is the principal activity, with daily trail rides on the ranch's mountain trails or out onto the high plains. This is a working ranch, so when the Angus need to be moved or checked on, guests are invited to go along to help. The ranch provides a variety of other real-life activities as well, including milking the cows and riding the fence line. Guests are welcome to fish local streams and lakes or hike in the Crazies; cookouts and rodeos are featured, and outfitted trips into the Crazy Mountain backcountry can also be arranged. The original lodge, where meals are served, is listed on the National Register of Historic Places. Lodging is either in the lodge (bathrooms down the hall), in secluded cabins with wood-burning stoves and private baths, or in small cabins à la frontier. There is a seven-day minimum stay, with rates beginning at $1,250 to $1,525 per week; children's rates are available.

Bonanza Creek Guest Ranch (Lennep Rte., Martinsdale, MT 59053, 800/476-6045, fax 406/572-3366, www.bonanzacreekcountry. com) is a large longtime working cattle ranch with a new focus on guest ranching. If your idea of a guest ranch stay is horseback riding by day and lounging in a private log cabin by night, Bonanza Creek is a good bet. Unlimited horseback riding is the main activity here, and as the ranch maintains a herd of 1,500 cattle, you'll probably have the chance to use a horse as God intended—to push cows around. Guests are also free to explore the ranch on mountain bikes, to head out fishing, or simply to kick back and relax. Lodging is in four new family-sized log cabins, each with a full bath, or you can opt for the tepee and the kids can camp out in the sheep wagon. Meals are served in the cathedral-ceilinged main lodge. Six-night stays are preferred ($1,600 adult, $1,000 ages 4–12), although shorter three-day stays are considered if the schedule allows. In May and October, single-night stays are $125 (meals not included).

The **Lazy K Bar Ranch** (Box 550, Melville Rte., Big Timber, MT 59011, 406/537-4404, www.lazykbar.net) is the state's oldest dude ranch. Writer Spike Van Cleve wrote about his humorous misadventures here with errant guests and horses in *A Day Late and a Dollar Short,* and in fact the Van Cleve family still owns the ranch. Rates at this venerable, au-thentically rough-around-the-edges institution start at $1,600 per week.

Camping

Free lakeside camping is available at **Martinsdale Reservoir,** two miles east of town on a local access road, and at **Bair Reservoir,** 11 miles west on Highway 12.

Information

For information on the Crazy Mountain area, contact the **Gallatin National Forest, Big Timber Ranger District** (P.O. Box A, Big Timber, MT 59011, 406/932-5155).

THE BIG OPEN AND NORTHEASTERN MONTANA

One of the state's least-visited areas, northeastern Montana is usually dismissed as an unwieldy piece of real estate that must be crossed to reach more verdant or populated destinations. But this vast region contains enormous reserves of wildlife, the homelands of three Indian tribes, and some of the state's best hunting and fishing. Some of the wildest rodeos in the state are permitted out here. At Fort Union, would-be frontiersmen in buckskins gather to shoot muskets. Local Indians look for new reasons to throw powwows. Memories of the Old West—of the open range, cattle rustlers, and the homestead movement—drift in and out of conversations.

Even though you probably won't plan your vacation around it, what you're likely to remember about this part of the state is the people. In some kind of contrast to the rugged terrain and remorseless weather, the inhabitants of this lonesome corner of Montana are genuinely friendly, if haughtily independent, and they are probably some of the most inveterate socializers you'll ever meet.

PLANNING YOUR TIME

Although the long straight asphalt ribbons of Highways 200 and 2 tempt the traveler to shoot across this isolated corner of Montana, in fact the region offers several unusual destinations that reward the road tripper who is willing to take a day or two and get off the main highway.

Off Highway 2 at the North Dakota border, **Fort Union** is a re-creation of the trading fort founded in the 1820s at the confluence of the Yellowstone and Missouri Rivers. More

© BILL McRAE

HIGHLIGHTS

◖ Fort Peck Interpretive Center and Museum: One of the world's largest dams, **Fort Peck Dam** spans the Missouri River, creating a vast body of water 134 miles long. Opened in 2004, the Fort Peck Interpretive Center and Museum displays the fossils discovered during the building of the dam and retells the area's native and Lewis and Clark history (page 367).

◖ Fort Peck Public Works Buildings: Fort Peck Dam was built at the height of the 1930s New Deal, and the town center features many massive old Public Works Administration buildings that exemplify the monumental lodge-style architecture of the period (page 367).

◖ Pioneer Town: This walk-through museum in Scobey brings together an entire frontier town's worth of old buildings and artifacts, recreating a 1910-era farming town on the edge of rolling wheat fields (page372).

◖ Medicine Lake National Wildlife Refuge: Long lake beds in abandoned channels of the ancient Missouri River form this refuge, an unlikely migratory bird stopover in the midst of the prairies (page 375).

◖ Fort Union Trading Post National Historic Site: Located at the junction of the Yellowstone and Missouri Rivers, Fort Union recreates an 1840s fur-trading fort in fascinating detail (page 376).

◖ Charles M. Russell National Wildlife Refuge: This refuge is hard to get to, but it preserves the wildlife ecosystem that Lewis and Clark experienced as they journeyed across the prairies in the 1800s. Its most popular site is the water-sport destination **Hell Creek State Park** on Fort Peck Dam, famous for fossil excavations (page 384).

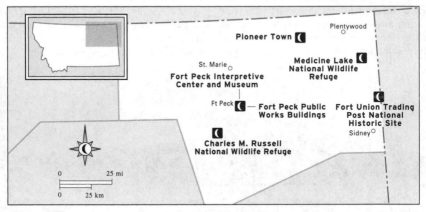

LOOK FOR ◖ TO FIND RECOMMENDED SIGHTS, ACTIVITIES, DINING, AND LODGING.

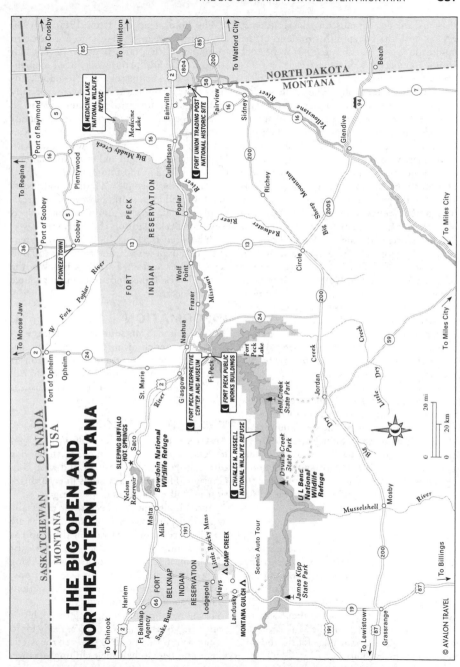

THE BIG OPEN AND NORTHEASTERN MONTANA

NORTHEASTERN MONTANA

To Crosby
To Williston
To Watford City
NORTH DAKOTA
MONTANA
Beach
Port of Raymond
MEDICINE LAKE NATIONAL WILDLIFE REFUGE
Medicine Lake
Bainville
FORT UNION TRADING POST NATIONAL HISTORIC SITE
Fairview
Sidney
Glendive
To Regina
Port of Scobey
Plentywood
Big Muddy Creek
Culbertson
Richey
Big Sheep Mountains
To Miles City
Port of Scobey
PIONEER TOWN
Scobey
Poplar
FORT   PECK
Redwater River
To Moose Jaw
W. Fork   Poplar River
Wolf Point
INDIAN   RESERVATION
Frazer
Missouri
Circle
To Miles City
Port of Opheim
Opheim
Nashua
Glasgow
FORT PECK INTERPRETIVE CENTER AND MUSEUM
FORT PECK PUBLIC WORKS BUILDINGS
Ft. Peck
Fort Peck Lake
Creek
Jordan
Little Dry
Dry
Big Dry
CANADA
USA
SASKATCHEWAN
MONTANA
St. Marie
River
SLEEPING BUFFALO HOT SPRINGS
Saco
Bowdoin National Wildlife Refuge
Hell Creek State Park
CHARLES M. RUSSELL NATIONAL WILDLIFE REFUGE
Devil's Creek State Park
Nelson Reservoir
U L Bend National Wildlife Refuge
Musselshell
Mosby
River
To Chinook
To Billings
Harlem
Ft Belknap Agency
Snake Butte
Malta
Milk
FORT   BELKNAP   INDIAN   RESERVATION
Little Rocky Mtns
CAMP CREEK
Scenic Auto Tour
James Kipp State Park
Lodgepole
Hays
Landusky
MONTANA GULCH
Grassrange
To Lewistown

20 mi
20 km

© AVALON TRAVEL

than just an open-air museum, the rebuilt fort evokes both the sweep of history and of the landscape. Come here in late June for the **Fort Union Rendezvous,** a reenactment of a fur-trader's rendezvous.

Fort Peck Reservoir is one of the world's largest, and even if dams aren't usually your favorite destination, there's plenty of reason to make the detour to Fort Peck. The town boomed during the New Deal 1930s and has some massive buildings, including a 1,100-seat theater still in operation as an excellent **summer stock theater** with a five-play season. Near the power-generation towers is a new **interpretive center** offering Native American and frontier history plus a rich collection of fossils discovered during the dam-building.

On the edge of the Fort Peck Indian Reservation, Wolf Point isn't really a tourist town, but in late July the **Wolf Point Stampede** brings lots of top-notch cowboys and cowgirls to town for one of Montana's top rodeos.

Farther west, the **Little Rockies** are an isolated mountain range that saw a lot of activity at the turn of the 20th century, when gold was discovered here. Gold-rush ghost towns like **Zortman** and **Landusky** are worth exploring for lovers of Western history.

Along Highway 200, the remoteness of the countryside is the main reason to make the trip. Isolated ranches fill the vast landscape of the **Big Open** between Sidney and Mosby. At the center of this uncrowded region is **Jordan,** gateway to the **Charles Russell National Wildlife Refuge** and to recreation on the southern shores of Fort Peck Reservoir at **Hell Creek State Park.**

HISTORY

The Sioux, Assiniboin, and Blackfeet Indians shared these buffalo-rich plains in shifting, suspicious alliances. The development of transportation corridors reaching across Montana's northern tier—first with steamboats on the Missouri River in the 1830s, then with the Great Northern Railway up the Milk River valley in the 1880s—set the stage for the Indians' removal to reservations.

The homestead era from 1900 to 1930 brought the greatest changes to northeastern Montana. With a farm family on every half section, these arid plains were forced momentarily to yield a bounty of grain. Scandinavians and other Northern Europeans were especially attracted to this unsettled area, and many small villages dominated by a Lutheran or Methodist church spire were settled with vague utopian aspirations. The varying climate, leagued with Depression-era drought and insect infestations, brought an end to most homesteads.

Many of the unemployed farmers and tradesmen did find local work, however. The greatest of all Public Works Administration projects was Fort Peck Dam on the Missouri River, built between 1933 and 1940. Employing tens of thousands of workers and flooding 250,000 acres of river bottom, Fort Peck is one of the world's largest dams and an important source of hydroelectricity.

INFORMATION

Travel Montana's **Missouri River Country** region covers much of northeastern Montana. Write for their free travel information at P.O. Box 387, Wolf Point, MT 59201, or call 406/653-1319 or 800/653-1319. The website is at www.missouririver.visitmt.com.

TRANSPORTATION

Amtrak's Empire Builder (800/872-7245) traverses northern Montana, with service east from Portland and Seattle and west from Chicago. There are daily stops in each direction at Wolf Point, Malta, and Glasgow.

Automobile travelers need to be especially aware that parts of northeastern Montana are very isolated: Not every dot on the map has a gas station, nor in fact does every dot exist in a form that's helpful to travelers. Along Highways 2 and 200, gas up whenever possible. Don't count on 24-hour service stations to help you cross the area at night.

If you are thinking of driving through this region in winter, make sure you're ready for it. Winter winds find nothing between the Arctic Circle and here to halt their chilling advance.

While winters are not particularly snowy, cold temperatures—Glasgow's average reading in January is 10°F—combine with these winds to produce even more intense chill factors. Make sure your vehicle is winterized and travel with plenty of warm clothing and a sleeping bag.

The Little Rocky Mountains

The Little Rockies are the easternmost of central Montana's volcanic outlier mountains. The core of the range, blanketed by displaced tilted layers of limestone, contains significant deposits of gold. The usual mix of prospectors, ne'er-do-wells, and colorful characters rushed in during the 1890s, founding Zortman and Landusky. Outlaws from the Missouri badlands, a kind of resort community for rapscallions, made these mining camps their local watering holes. Such criminals as Kid Curry and Butch Cassidy were habitués of the remote and lawless Little Rockies.

THE FORT BELKNAP INDIAN RESERVATION

From the Little Rockies north to the Milk River lies the 645,000-acre Fort Belknap Reservation, home to the Gros Ventre and Assiniboin Indians. These two tribes were rivals in the complex intertribal politics characteristic of the 1800s. The Assiniboin are a Siouan people who drifted west as settlement to the east displaced them from their traditional home near Lake Winnipeg. After arriving on the plains, the Assiniboin became fierce rivals of the Blackfeet Indians. After smallpox decimated their numbers in the 1830s, the tribe settled along the Milk River to hunt the diminishing buffalo.

How the Gros Ventre (French for "Big Belly") came by their name is something of a mystery; not only the French but also the Blackfeet and Shoshone referred to the tribe as the "Belly" people. One theory holds that in sign language the tribe was indicated by gesturing to the ribs, where early Gros Ventre tattooed symbols.

The Gros Ventre were allied with the powerful Blackfeet Nation. This Native American cartel roamed freely across northern Montana,

terrorizing Indians and white settlers alike. But increasing trade with the whites, especially for whiskey, demoralized the tribes. Old alliances were scrapped, and the Blackfeet and Gros Ventre fell to fighting. The Gros Ventre soon found themselves siding with their old enemies, the Assiniboin and the U.S. Army, against the marauding Blackfeet. The Gros Ventre settled on the northern slopes of the Little Rockies. The U.S. government built Fort Belknap in 1871—in part to protect the tribes from each other—and in 1887 created the reservation.

Sights

At Hays, along the flanks of the Little Rockies, Jesuit F. H. Eberschweiler founded **St. Paul's Mission** in 1886 to instruct the Gros Ventre. The early church was built of logs and contained instructional paintings; it burned during the 1930s and was rebuilt in stone. Some original log outbuildings dating to the 1890s remain.

Behind Hays, leading up People's Creek into the Little Rockies, is **Mission Canyon.** A gravel road passes beneath steep limestone cliffs riddled with caves. After 0.5 mile, the road leads to a **natural bridge,** where water has carved through the limestone, leaving an arch 60 feet above the valley floor.

Events

Milk River Indian Days, held in Fort Belknap usually on the last weekend of July, features contest dancing, a marathon run, and a giveaway; in mid-June, the **Hays Mission Canyon Dance** is held in the canyon behind the town. The public is welcome to attend these celebrations.

Information

Contact the Tribal Offices, Fort Belknap Agency (Box 66, Rte. 1, Harlem, MT 59526,

NORTHEASTERN MONTANA

Mission Canyon cuts through the Little Rocky Mountains.

© BILL MCRAE

406/353-2205, www.fortbelknapnations-nsn .gov) for information on tribal activities.

THE LITTLE ROCKIES

On the map, the southern border of the Fort Belknap Reservation looks as if someone took a bite out of it. In fact, that's about what happened. Prospectors found gold in the Little Rockies in 1884; by the 1890s, in contravention of treaties, miners overran the narrow gulches of these low mountains. The federal Indian agent for the reservation was unable to stop the influx, and he urged the Assiniboin and Gros Ventre tribes to sell a strip of land four miles wide and seven miles long to the Bureau of Land Management. The tribes received $350,000 for the land in 1895; in the early 1990s, the mines were producing $25 million a year in gold and silver.

History

Although rumors of gold in the Little Rockies were spreading abroad as early as the 1860s, the Blackfeet discouraged exploration. Development awaited Pike Landusky, a grizzled veteran of past gold rushes, Indian fights, and whiskey trading. He and a companion found gold in 1894 near the town that now bears his name; within months, hundreds of miners streamed in. The next year the government bought the land from the reservation, and within a decade, placer mining was replaced by more efficient but environmentally damaging cyanide stamp mills.

Even for mining camps, the towns of Landusky and Zortman drew more than their quota of rough characters. Pike Landusky was no milquetoast: In 1868 he went to the mouth of the Musselshell to trap and trade with the Indians; instead he was ambushed by a party of Sioux. The irascible Landusky seized his frying pan and started beating one of the warriors with it. Startled, the Sioux braves ceased their advance, and Landusky jerked the breechcloth off another and commenced lashing him in the face with the frying pan. Sensing a demonic presence, the Indians withdrew, leaving this dervish two ponies as an offering.

In an altercation with the Blackfeet, Landusky was shot in the jaw. The bullet

THE LEGEND OF SNAKE BUTTE

Snake Butte, southwest of Harlem, figures in a Gros Ventre Indian legend. In ancient times the nomadic Gros Ventre had no single place to bury their dead as they followed game across the prairies. According to legend, when hunting buffalo near Snake Butte, a child died, and the bereaved parents prepared the body and left it high on a lonely cliff on the butte.

When the parents returned to visit the body, as was customary, it had disappeared. The child's father found a wide trail leading from the burial area to a deep ravine in the side of the butte. The eerie trail bore the sign of scales, as if from a huge snake. The frightened parents returned to camp and related their story to a medicine woman. She vowed to visit the butte and spend the night on its peak.

The next morning she returned. Spirits had told her that deep beneath the butte lived a huge and evil snake; it had taken the child's body to warn the Gros Ventre that anyone who visits the butte will likewise disappear.

The exemplum obviously had little effect on the U.S. Army Corps of Engineers when they built Fort Peck Dam. They needed a source for riprap on the dam's face, and the igneous rock of Snake Butte (a diatreme radiating from the Little Rockies) was perfect. Workers quarried one million cubic yards of rock from the front of the butte and transported it 130 miles to the dam site.

The bad news is that the face of Snake Butte has been devastated; the good news is that the snake of Gros Ventre legend eluded capture.

---

shattered the bone and teeth, but Landusky simply fished the fragments out of his mouth, discarded them, and went on fighting.

Landusky was representative of other rough-and-tough characters in this neighborhood: This was not a delicate society. Jew Jake was the local barkeeper. His leg had been shot off by a lawman in Great Falls, and he used a Winchester rifle for a crutch. The Curry Gang, three brothers who side-stepped civility and the law, owned a ranch just south of town. Pike Landusky fell afoul of the Curry Gang when he objected to the wooing of his daughter by the youngest of the Curry boys, Lonnie. Sensing a slight, the eldest Curry, Kid, rode to town and shot Landusky dead at Jew Jake's bar. As a final humiliation, the third Curry brother, Johnny, moved in with Mrs. Landusky. The Currys gained national prominence after they formed the Wild Bunch with Butch Cassidy and the Sundance Kid and went on a spree of bank and train robberies.

Mining in Landusky and Zortman peaked in the 1910s. The second-largest cyanide mill in the world was erected in Zortman to leach gold out of quartz ore. By 1940 almost all activity had ceased, but in the 1980s the price of gold was high enough to justify reopening the mines at Zortman. In 1998 the Pegasus Mine closed again.

Zortman and Landusky

Both Zortman and Landusky have preserved the flavor of old gold camps and are protected as national historic sites. Although nominally considered ghost towns, neither has developed its old buildings as a tourist attraction. In Zortman the original jail still stands, and the Buckhorn Store and Bar still minister to the hungry and thirsty. The trailers and campers of today's miners contrast oddly with the rough log cabins of yesteryear. Landusky shows even fewer signs of life: A mining town is probably in extremis when its bar has closed.

Missouri River Breaks

Ten miles south of the Little Rockies lie the Missouri River Breaks. This province of rough badlands and river frontage has been included in the Charles M. Russell National Wildlife Refuge. Just about the only easily accessible part of the refuge is reached by a **self-guided auto tour** 0.5 mile north of the Robinson Missouri River Bridge off Highway 191. This

NORTHEASTERN MONTANA

20-mile drive along good gravel roads passes great wildlife viewing and scenic landmarks.

Accommodations
In Zortman, the **Buckhorn Store** (406/673-3162 or 888/654-3162) offers cabins with kitchenettes, campsites, and groceries. The **Zortman Garage** (406/673-3160 or 800/517-0372) also offers RV hookups and cabins.

Accommodations at either cost under $50 for a double.

Camping
One mile north of Zortman, the Bureau of Land Management maintains **Camp Creek,** a streamside campground. Another BLM campsite, **Montana Gulch,** is 0.5 mile west of Landusky.

The Milk River Valley

Between Malta and Glasgow, Highway 2 unrolls between cottonwoods and willows and the green thread of the Milk River. The prairies of northern Montana continue their expansive monotonous rhythm. Occasionally a ridge of uplands infringes—outriders from the wild Missouri Breaks just south—causing the horizon to hike up its skirts.

Ice age glaciers covered this part of Montana, homogenizing the prairie surface and obstructing the old Missouri River course. When the ice sheets retreated about 10,000 years ago, the Missouri found a more southerly valley to its liking. The sluggish Milk River, so named by Lewis and Clark, who thought its waters resembled "a cup of tea with the admixture of a tablespoonful of milk," has borrowed the old channel.

Eastern Montana's only hot-springs resort, a wildlife refuge dense with birdlife, and some of the state's best big-game hunting make a virtue out of these implacable prairies.

MALTA AND VICINITY
Yes, Malta (pop. 2,120, elev. 2,254 feet) was named for the Mediterranean island. No, Malta was not named for or by Maltese immigrants. As the Great Northern built across unpopulated northern Montana in 1887, enterprising employees spun the globe and then stopped it with a jab of the finger. Thus were deserted sidings along the Great Northern saddled with exotic names (Glasgow, Inverness, Kremlin, Havre). The siding at Malta jump-started the town.

Ranchers whose herds of cattle ranged the unfenced prairies needed a railhead, and thirsty cowboys needed a town to carouse in. Irrigated farms along the Milk River notwithstanding, this is still cattle country: Malta is a rancher's, not a farmer's, town.

Sights
Housed in the old Carnegie Library is the **Phillips County Museum** (133 S. 1st St. W., 406/654-1037, 10 A.M.–5 P.M. daily, mid-May to Sept. 30, $3 adult, $1 children). With displays of cowboy gear, Indian beadwork, and homesteader-era artifacts, it commemorates the area's history and also its prehistory. The museum features local dinosaur finds, including a 33-foot-long skeleton of "Elvis" the brachylophosaurus, a complete *T. rex* skull, and a 28-foot Albertosaurus skeleton.

To see more dinos and watch paleontologists in action, go to the **Dinosaur Field Station** (corner of Hwy. 2 and Hwy. 191, 406/654-5300, $5 adults, $3 youth 12 and under, 10 A.M.–5 P.M. Mon.–Sat., noon–5 P.M. Sun., Memorial Day–Sept.) for an intimate look into a working fossil laboratory. Visitors can see a number of fossil skeletons still under preparation as well as tour the high-tech lab. The Dinosaur Field Station is associated with the Judith River Dinosaur Institute; in fact, it is the huge success of the institute that led to the 2003-built field station. The fossil diggers recovered so many fossils locally that the Phillips County Museum ran out of room to display them.

THIS HERE'S THE WILD WEST

First the Plains Indians and the buffalo claimed the rich rangeland of the Milk River; then it was open-range cowboys and cattle. Just as the Indians entered remote areas of Montana after being displaced by homesteaders elsewhere, so settlement in the Judith Basin during the 1890s pushed untamed cowboys, desperadoes, and loners north into the Milk River valley.

From rugged hideouts in the Missouri Breaks and the Little Rockies, rustlers trailed stolen cattle to Canada and back, across the law-free expanses of Milk River country. The Hole-in-the-Wall Gang, led by Kid Curry, found cattle and horse theft too facile. In 1901 they held up the westbound Great Northern train five miles west of Malta. After stopping the train and blowing up the safe, the gang fled with a pile of worthless unfranked banknotes.

Painter Charlie Russell rode with other cowboys along the Milk River. One of his most famous paintings, *Loops and Swift Horses Are Surer than Lead*, re-created a 1904 episode that occurred just south of Saco. Early-rising cowpunchers found that 40 horses were missing from the remuda. A quick search revealed that a grizzly bear had entered camp, charged the horse covey, and was chasing the frightened horses across the prairie. The cowboys gave chase, and within seconds lassoed the furious bear.

Just two miles east of Malta is the **Bowdoin National Wildlife Refuge** (406/654-2863). Founded in 1936, this marshy lake is a major stopover for both migrating and nesting waterfowl. White pelicans are commonly seen (there are more than 800 nesting pairs), as are rarer white-faced ibises and night herons. In the spring, watch male sharp-tailed grouse as they drum their chests to impress the females. Access is by canoe or along a six-mile auto tour.

Fossil Digs

The **Judith River Dinosaur Institute** (P.O. Box 51177, Billings, MT 59105, 406/696-5842, www.montanadinosaurdigs.com) is an independent paleontological research organization that, among other projects, sponsors fossil excavations involving serious and qualified lay participants. There are three five-day summer sessions, each of which take on only up to 16 individuals.

Digs by the Judith Basin Dinosaur Institute are noteworthy for their level of participation. Rather than being a grunt for researchers who have all the fun, as is commonly the case when the public pays to be part of an excavation, here participants get involved in all parts of the process, including learning field and extraction skills and helping with lab work. Note that from year to year the location of the digs will change, and your excavation may not be in the Malta area.

Spaces go very quickly, so if you're serious about paleontology, inquire as soon as you start planning your Montana trip. Costs can change from year to year, depending on how remote the dig is. If the excavation is near a town, you have the option to camp or to rent a motel room, the costs of which are not included in the rates. If the dig is remote and camping is mandatory, three meals and non-alcoholic drinks are provided. Depending on the dig, costs can range from $900 to $1,600 per person per week. Participants must be 14 years of age or older.

Accommodations

Under $50: The **Sportsman Motel** (231 N. 1st St. E., 406/654-2300, $45) has comfortable older units, some with kitchenettes. The Sportsman also rents RV spaces, and restaurants are within easy walking distance.

$50-75: The nicest place to stay in Malta is the **Great Northern Motor Hotel** (2 S. 1st Ave. E., 406/654-2100 or 888/234-0935, $69), with updated rooms, a bar, restaurant, casino, and steakhouse. The hotel also offers inside parking—just the thing if you're visiting in winter. The pleasant **Maltana Motel**

NORTHEASTERN MONTANA

(138 S. 1st Ave. W., 406/654-2610, $60) is a very well-maintained older motel just one block from downtown on a quiet street.

Out on Highway 2, the **Edgewater Motel** (101 West US Highway 2 406/654-1302 or 800/821-7475, $72) offers an indoor pool, sauna, exercise facilities, and campsites. A restaurant is adjacent.

Food

For steaks, try the **Great Northern Motor Hotel** (2 S. 1st Ave. E., 406/654-2100, $12–16). For a lighter meal, go to the **Westside Restaurant** (west of Malta on Hwy. 2, 406/654-1555, 7 A.M.–8 P.M., $8–12) or the **Hitchin' Post** (east of Malta, 406/654-1882, 6 A.M.–9 P.M.).

Information and Services

Contact the **Malta Chamber of Commerce** at P.O. Box GG, Malta, MT 59538 (406/654-1776 or 800/704-1776, www.maltachamber.com). The **Phillips County Hospital** is at 417 South 4th Street East (406/654-1100). For emergencies, call the **sheriff** at 406/654-1211.

For a local **road report,** phone 406/265-1416.

SACO AND VICINITY

Saco (pop. 224, elev. 2,184 feet) is a little agricultural trading center named, like Malta, by the globe spinners at the Great Northern for Saco, Maine. Chet Huntley, the late TV newscaster, was born and educated near Saco, and the country grade school he attended now stands in a city park and serves as the local museum.

Camping and Fishing

Two miles off Highway 2 and adjacent to the Sleeping Buffalo Resort is **Nelson Reservoir State Park,** a 4,500-acre lake with camping along its banks. Locals use the reservoir for waterskiing and fishing for northern pike and walleye.

Accommodations and Food

There's one motel in town, the **Saco Motel** (207 Taylor, 406/527-3261, $45).

The **Circle V Cafe** is at 507 Taylor (406/527-3537, 6 A.M.–10 P.M.).

Sleeping Buffalo Resort

Unique along the northern tier, this rustic—some might say funky—hot-springs spa combines inexpensive accommodations, waterskiing, and aquatherapy. Named for large glacial rocks half buried in the prairies, the hot springs were tapped in 1924 when oil drillers struck a pool of hot, highly mineralized water at a depth of 3,200 feet. When the water reached the surface, the mineral gases ignited. The spring burned for six years.

Initially developed as an old-fashioned health spa, the hot springs at Sleeping Buffalo have been somewhat modernized and developed into a family recreational facility. Presently, the resort includes both indoor and outdoor hot pools (106°F), a waterslide, two bars, a restaurant, a nine-hole golf course, and rooms in venerable cabins or motel units starting at $45. It's a good idea to have a look at the rooms before you rent them: Upkeep hasn't been a priority.

Sleeping Buffalo Resort (Box 13, Star Rte. 3, Saco, MT 59621, 406/527-3370) lies 10 miles west of Saco on Highway 2, then one mile north along a good gravel road. The resort is open year-round.

Glasgow and Fort Peck

The largest Public Works Administration project of the 1930s New Deal era, Fort Peck Dam—holding one of the world's largest reservoirs—is an enormous tribute to the spirit that overcame the Great Depression. The old rail town of Glasgow, now the largest city in northeastern Montana, was the stepping-off point for the dam project and is now the livestock trading center of the region. Vivid history and unparalleled recreational opportunities, as well as tours of the enormous hydroelectric facilities and a new paleontology museum, make this northeastern Montana's most enticing stopover.

GLASGOW

The Great Northern established a wide spot along the rails called Siding 45 in 1887. The town, originally just a series of tents, became Glasgow in 1889. Glasgow (pop. 3,253, elev. 2,216 feet) grew fitfully as homesteaders and ranchers used the rail connections.

During the 1930s, Glasgow boomed as it became the primary trade and transport center for the shifting population of workers at Fort Peck Lake. Little shanty towns sprang up to serve the needs of the 10,000-strong labor force. This period of growth lasted less than a decade, and although few dam workers permanently settled in the area, Glasgow remains the focus for anglers and holiday makers at the reservoir.

More problematic for the city was the Glasgow Air Force Base. During the mid-1960s the population of Valley County nearly doubled with Air Force personnel and their families. Glasgow built new schools, redesigned the old downtown for more traffic, and prepared for sustained growth. When the Air Force pulled out in 1969, the city planners were left with a facility that, unlike Fort Peck, had no apparent afterlife. Currently, Boeing rents the base for flight training and equipment testing. The 1,200 living units on the base are being marketed as St. Marie's, a retirement community for military personnel.

Sights

The **Valley County Museum** (Hwy. 2 at 8th Ave. N., 406/228-8692) is one of eastern Montana's best museums. It presents a Lewis and Clark exhibit focusing on the natural history they documented while traveling up the Missouri River. Local history is presented in a series of dioramas. An authentic tepee and other artifacts are the focus of the Assiniboin exhibit, while a sheep wagon and chuck wagon commemorate the life of the early stockman; there's also a re-creation of a frontier town.

Accommodations

Under $50: On the west end of the Highway 2 strip, just across from the Pioneer Museum, is the **Star Lodge Motel** (406/228-2494, 903 6th Avenue N., $45), with in-room coffeemakers.

$50-75: La Casa Motel (238 1st Ave. N., 406/228-9311 or 877/228-9311, $50) is convenient to several chain and local restaurants, and allows pets. All rooms have microwaves and refrigerators.

The **Campbell Lodge** (534 3rd Ave. S., 406/228-9328, $50) is in easy walking distance of downtown shopping and offers discounts for AAA, AARP, and commercial travelers. The Campbell Lodge is two blocks from the city pool and recreation center.

$75-100: Glasgow's largest and newest motel complex is the **Cottonwood Inn** (406/228-8213 or 800/321-8213, $81 and up), east on Highway 2, on the edge of town. There's a good restaurant, pool, sauna, hot tub, guest laundry, meeting and small convention facilities, and over 100 rooms. A new wing offers a number of parlor suites. Adjacent, the hotel also operates an RV park.

Camping

For a campsite, consider driving the 17 miles to Fort Peck, or head to the **Cottonwood Inn** (406/228-2769), above.

Food

If you like a good steak and a Western bar atmosphere, then you'll treasure **(Sam's Supper Club** (307 1st Ave. N., 406/228-4614, 4:30–10 P.M. Tues., 11 A.M.–2 P.M. and 4:30–10 P.M. Wed.–Fri., 4:30–10 P.M. Sat.). The clientele, a mix of cowboys, anglers, and businessmen, converge here for the outstanding charbroiled beef (steaks $14–18) and good salad bar. **(Durum** (309 2nd Ave. S. 406/228-2236, 5 A.M.–9 P.M. daily) is quite a find in northeast Montana. A culinary-institute-trained chef has taken over the dining room of the Elks Club and prepares food of a quality and selection not often experienced in this corner of the state. House-made pasta, hand-cut aged beef from local ranches, and homemade soups make this a mandatory stop for food lovers.

Another Glasgow institution is **Johnnie Cafe** (433 1st Ave. S., 406/228-4222, 5 A.M.–10 P.M. daily), an old downtown diner that time forgot where locals gather to drink coffee and lunch on chicken-fried steak. The 24-hour dining room at the Cottonwood Inn's **Willows Restaurant** (east on Hwy. 2, 406/228-8213, main courses $8–18) offers chicken and pork dishes in addition to the compulsory steaks. **Eugene's Pizza** (193 Klein, 406/228-8552, 4 P.M.–midnight daily) serves Glasgow's best pizza.

Information

Contact the **Glasgow Chamber of Commerce** at 110 5th Street South (406/228-2222, www.glasgowmt.net). The **Department of Fish, Wildlife, and Parks** is on Highway 2 West (406/228-3700). The **Bureau of Land Management** office is west on Highway 2 (406/228-4316).

Transportation

Amtrak passes through Glasgow daily each way. Call 800/872-7245 for information; the depot (424 1st Ave. S.) is operated by Burlington Northern and endures Amtrak traffic without promoting it.

Budget Rent-A-Car (626 2nd Ave. S., 406/228-9325) is part of Newton Motors.

FORT PECK

Early traders built the original Fort Peck as an Indian trading post in 1867. Located right on the banks of the Missouri River for ease in loading and unloading steamboats, the trading post did a bang-up business with the Sioux and Assiniboin. The Great Northern Railway in 1887 chose to build through the gentle Milk River valley rather than traverse the intemperate badlands of the Missouri River, thereby bypassing the old fort.

Fort Peck Dam

In the fall of 1933, workers began to clear brush in preparation for the building of Fort Peck Dam. The largest and most ambitious of Franklin Roosevelt's Public Works Administration projects, construction of the dam created jobs for tens of thousands of people during the Great Depression and altered the face of Montana. At the time of its completion, Fort Peck was the world's largest reservoir. At 150 miles long, with a shoreline longer than California's, it is still the planet's second-largest earth-fill reservoir.

The Army Corps of Engineers justified the expense of Fort Peck ($150 million) by promising better river navigation, flood control, hydroelectric generation, and irrigation possibilities. But Fort Peck's biggest impact on Montana was the amount of jobs it provided. During the seven years of construction, at one time or another 50,000 people worked at the dam.

The Corps of Engineers built a showpiece town to house its personnel and serve as the dam headquarters. Named after the old trading post, Fort Peck also contained an enormous theater and a grand hotel, each built in the arts-and-crafts style characteristic of New Deal architecture.

But handsome, well-planned Fort Peck was not where the workers lived or played. The towns that grew up to serve this largely young, energetic, and migratory workforce quickly accrued reputations for wild times that would have made Dodge City jealous. Shanty boomtowns like Wheeler, New Deal,

FORT PECK FACTS

- Construction crews at Fort Peck Dam moved 130 million cubic yards of dirt and replaced it with four million cubic yards of gravel and 1.6 million cubic yards of riprap.

- The reservoir has the capacity to store 19 million acre-feet of water (the runoff from one third of Montana).

- The maximum depth of the lake is 220 feet.

- The dam stretches from bluff to bluff across the Missouri, a distance of 3.5 miles.

- The construction technique that built Fort Peck Dam is called "hydraulic fill." The sediment from the Missouri River bottom was pumped to the dam face as slurry, where it was drained into rock structures that trapped the mud and let the water drain away. More rock was then layered on top of this earth embankment.

and Park Grove shot up, invigorated with government cash and hard-won 1930s jouissance. For its first issue (November 23, 1936), *Life* magazine sent Margaret Bourke-White to Fort Peck to chronicle life on this new frontier. Little remains of this short and incandescent moment of Montana's development except derelict buildings and memories of landmarks like the Buckhorn Bar, destroyed by fire in 1983.

Fort Peck Power Plants

The Fort Peck Power Plants (near the junction of Hwy. 24 and Hwy. 117, 406/526-3411) offer tours of the turbines and electrical-generation facilities. Hour-long tours are free (9 A.M., 11 A.M., 1 P.M., 3 P.M. weekdays, on the hour from 9 A.M.–5 P.M. weekends and holidays, Memorial Day–Labor Day) and start in the Interpretive Center.

(Fort Peck Interpretive Center and Museum

Adjacent to the power plants is the Fort Peck Interpretive Center and Museum (406/526-3421, 9 A.M.–5 P.M. daily, May 1–Sept 30, free), opened in 2004, which presents the region's rich paleontological, natural, and human history. When the dam was built in the 1930s, workers found a wealth of fossils in the Missouri River badlands, and these specimens form the backbone of the center's impressive collection of ancient species. More recently, the Fort Peck area has become known as prime hunting ground for *Tyrannosaurus rex* specimens—three full skeletons have been unearthed in just the last decade and a cast of one of these is also on display here. In addition, the interpretive center contains exhibits on the native Sioux and Assiniboin and also details Lewis and Clark's journey along this stretch of the Missouri, an adventure-filled episode often neglected in popular histories. Kids will love the exhibits on local wildlife, including tanks filled with mammoth fish—including paddlefish and sturgeon—found in the deep waters behind Fort Peck Dam.

(Fort Peck Public Works Buildings

While the town of Fort Peck will not overwhelm the visitor with its sheer size, some of the old Public Works Administration buildings are astonishing relics. The **Fort Peck Theater** on Main Street was built in 1934 as a cinema in an imposing and somewhat squatty chalet style, all the better to accommodate its 1,100-patron capacity. It's hard to imagine a grander example of rustic New Deal architecture. For more than 30 years the theater has been home to one of the state's best summer theater companies (406/526-9943, www.fortpecktheatre.org). The theater stages five shows each summer, from late May through August. Tickets are $15 for adults and seniors, $10 for students kindergarten through high school, and $5 for preschool children.

The **Fort Peck Hotel** on Missouri Avenue and the dam's **administration building** on Kansas Avenue were built at the same time, and share the grandiose architectural vision of the 1930s.

Other Sights

There's excellent wildlife viewing just downstream from the dam. Starting at the Downstream Campground, the **Beaver Creek Nature Trail** winds along brushy streams and ponds; interpretive signs point out habitat and help identify species. Larger mammals, like deer, pronghorn, and buffalo, can be seen along an auto trail at the **Leo B. Coleman Wildlife Exhibit,** which begins on Big Horn Street, just across from the Fort Peck Theater.

If there's any question in your mind about the meaning of the term "badlands," then continue south of Fort Peck on Highway 24 toward Highway 200. Like a boat cresting waves, the road peaks and troughs through sandstone uplands and spectacular badland ridges and valleys. This land is adjacent to the C. M. Russell National Wildlife Refuge and offers opportunities for viewing pronghorn, mule deer, coyote, and other prairie residents.

Recreation

The Fort Peck area offers the best recreational opportunities in eastern Montana. The 245,000-acre reservoir contains sturgeon, northern pike, walleye, paddlefish, sauger, channel catfish, and lake trout. Locals also use the lake for waterskiing, sailing, parasailing, and windsurfing. There are six recreation areas within four miles of the dam and a dozen others farther afield. The best and most accessible fishing areas are south along Highway 24, along the Big Dry Arm.

If you're a compulsive walleye fisher, consider entering the **Montana Governor's Cup,** a very popular walleye fishing tournament held the second weekend of July at Fort Peck Lake. Hundreds of people from all over the West converge on Fort Peck to compete for nearly $40,000 in prizes. Contact the Glasgow Chamber of Commerce for information.

If you'd like to hire a guide for fishing on Fort Peck Lake or hunting on the Montana prairies, contact **Billingsley Ranch Outfitters**

(P.O. Box 768, Glasgow, MT 59230, 406/367-5577, www.montanahuntingfishing.com). For boat rentals, contact the **Fort Peck Marina** (406/526-3442). Boaters need to pay attention to storm and wind warnings: Intense thunderstorms build quickly along the prairies, and strong winds can create waves high enough to endanger small boats.

Fossil Hunting

From the mouth of the Musselshell River on, the Missouri River cuts down through the Hell Creek Formation, a geologic layer containing one of the richest records of prehistoric life in the world. Few anglers or boaters go to Fort Peck Lake without keeping an eye open for fossils, and others, taken by the area's Cretaceous-era outcroppings, come to the lake expressly to hunt fossils. Although vertebrate fossil excavation isn't allowed on the C. M. Russell Wildlife Refuge without a permit, nonvertebrate plant or shell fossils can be removed from public land. Banks of sandstone and shale often offer up fossils for viewing, particularly petrified fish, mollusks, and leaf imprints.

A word of warning: If you are exploring Fort Peck environs on back roads, head back to pavement at *the first sign* of rain; the gumbo hills quickly become impassably slick.

Accommodations

$50-75: The ◖ **Fort Peck Hotel** (on Missouri Ave., 406/526-3266 or 800/560-4931, $68), built to house visitors during Fort Peck dam's heyday, is one of Montana's most unusual lodgings. This venerable three-story hotel is on the National Register of Historic Places and contains 47 rooms, a bar, and a dining room. The spirit of the hotel hasn't changed much since the 1930s, but that is all the more draw for anyone who hankers for a taste of bygone days; however, the guest rooms are more modern after a thorough refurbishing in the 1990s. The hotel closes in winter; it's dependably open May through October, but it's worth calling to confirm spring and fall opening and closing dates.

Camping

Numerous campgrounds are scattered around Fort Peck Dam, all with access to fishing. Just under the bluff from the Fort Peck town site on Highway 117 is the **Downstream Campground;** it's in a great location, but bring the insect repellent. Likewise, the **Rainbow Campground** is three miles north of Fort Peck on Highway 117, where there's good fishing for walleye and northern pike. On the lake is **West End Campground,** three miles west of Fort Peck off Highway 24.

Food

The **Fort Peck Hotel** (406/526-3266, 6:30 A.M.–9 P.M. daily May–Oct.) offers tasty and imaginative food in a great dining room that's reminiscent of summer camp. For a short-order meal with cocktails, try the **Gateway Inn** (406/526-9988), "the best dam bar by a dam site," west of Fort Peck on Highway 24.

Information

For more information on Fort Peck Dam, contact the **Corps of Engineers** (E. Kansas St., 406/526-3411).

The Fort Peck office for the **C. M. Russell National Wildlife Refuge** is north along Highway 117 (406/526-3464). For information on the history of Fort Peck, visit www.fortpeckdam.com, with a great collection of vintage photos.

Fort Peck Indian Reservation and Vicinity

East of Fort Peck Dam, the Missouri River flows down a wide fertile valley lined by cottonwood trees. Extending north and south of the river are the relentless and austere plains. Also north of the river is the Fort Peck Indian Reservation, the state's second largest, home to the Yanktonai Sioux and Assiniboin tribes. Highway 2 follows the Missouri, linking old river-freighting centers and ranch towns like Wolf Point and Poplar.

HISTORY

In the late 1700s the Assiniboin Indians moved south out of Canada into Montana, where they lived along the Missouri River. They became willing partners with the early white traders. In 1837 smallpox raged through the Assiniboin Nation, killing an estimated two thirds of the tribe.

Greatly weakened as a society, the Assiniboin quickly agreed to the constraints and protections of early reservation treaties and settled along the Missouri. When smallpox again broke out among the Indians upriver at Fort Belknap, these Assiniboin quickly moved farther down the Missouri to live with the Yanktonai Sioux near Fort Peck, thereby avoiding the epidemic.

The Sioux Nation was one of the greatest of the Indian tribal confederations. The branch that came to inhabit the northern prairies of Montana is called the Yanktonai Sioux. They originally roamed the prairie provinces of Canada until forced into Montana. Here, rolling waves of displaced Indians came to a congested chaotic halt.

The Yanktonai were part of the alliance that fought Custer in 1876; this triumph didn't forestall their enclosure in the huge Indian territory north of the Missouri the following year. When the Great Northern sought to put a railway across northern Montana in the late 1880s, the U.S. government renegotiated the reservations to allow the railway right-of-way. The Sioux and Assiniboin were assigned to their present reservation in 1888.

Fort Peck Reservation was one of the worst-affected reservations under the Dawes Act. Seeking to turn these nomadic tribesmen into agrarian landowners, this federal program allocated homestead-sized pieces of land to individual Indians. The surplus land then became available to non-Indians. Because of the size of the Fort Peck Reservation (2.1 million acres) and the paucity of Indians (about 2,000 at the

NORTHEASTERN MONTANA

time), only 46 percent of the reservation is now owned by Native Americans.

WOLF POINT
History

Wolf Point (pop. 2,663, elev. 2,004 feet) began as a trading post on the Missouri. The thick groves of shady cottonwoods were home to early "wood hawks," who made a rugged living felling trees to feed the engines of steamboats that trundled the river between St. Louis and Fort Benton.

Along this stretch of the Missouri, the local Indians quickly learned that there was money to be made in selling wood. Cedarwood fetched a higher price than cottonwood; the canny natives would paint the ends of cottonwood logs red and then demand cedar prices for them. When the river was too low for the boats to approach the bank where the Indians were trying to sell wood, they would squat in the shallow water with only their heads above water to give the impression that the river was shoulder deep.

The name Wolf Point apparently derives from an event in the fur-trading days. During an especially harsh winter, trappers had good luck trapping and poisoning wolves. However, the wolves froze solid before they could be skinned, so the trappers piled the carcasses along the river's edge, to be skinned in the spring. But when the trappers returned, Indians had taken control of the landing, and the trappers were forced to abandon their booty. The putrefying wolves became a landmark for steamboat crews.

Wolf Point is now a trade town for local farmers and ranchers and a center for the Sioux and Assiniboin. Grain-storage facilities here can warehouse 1.5 million bushels of grain, making Wolf Point one of the state's most important terminals. The Wolf Point Wild Horse Stampede is the state's oldest organized rodeo and one of the best.

Sights

The **Wolf Point Area Historical Society Museum** (220 2nd Ave. S., 406/653-1912,

10 A.M.–5 P.M. Mon.–Fri., Memorial Day–Labor Day, free) contains artifacts from its early frontier and homesteading days, plus a reliquary devoted to native-son trick roper Montie Montana and his horse Rex.

If old tractors and farming implements are of interest to you, one of the nation's most complete collections of John Deere tractors is located north of Wolf Point. With more than 500 tractors, the **John Deere Tractor Collection & Museum** contains an example of every John Deere manufactured from 1923 to 1953. Although the collection is private, the owner is happy to show the tractors to interested visitors. Call 406/392-5294 and ask for Louis Toavs to set up a time to visit.

Accommodations

The **Homestead Inn** (101 Hwy. 2 E., 406/653-1300 or 800/231-0986, $63) has clean and comfortable rooms, complimentary coffee and donuts in the morning, microwaves, fridges, queen-size beds, guest laundry, cable TV, and free wireless Internet access; pets are permitted. Other motels string along Highway 2.

In downtown Wolf Point, the **Sherman Motor Inn** (200 E. Main St., 406/653-1100 or 800/952-1100, 6 A.M.–2 P.M. and 5–9 P.M., $55–70) offers a good restaurant, a lounge and casino, a fitness center, and meeting facilities on site.

Camping

Rancho Campground (406/653-1940) is one mile west on Highway 2. At the junction of Highways 2 and 13 (seven miles east of Wolf Point) is **R.B.W. Campground** (406/525-3740).

Food

Several drive-ins and fast-food parlors are strung along Highway 2, but it's worth driving downtown to find better atmosphere. The restaurant at the **Sherman Motor Inn** (200 E. Main St., 406/653-1100, 6 A.M.–2 P.M., 5 A.M.–9 P.M., main courses $9–17) is the nicest in town, with a menu that offers alternatives to the beef pervasive in most eastern Montana eateries. For Wolf Point's best steak ($14–18), go to the **Elk's Club Dining Room** (302 Main St., 406/653-1920, 5 A.M.–9 P.M.).

Events

The **Wolf Point Wild Horse Stampede** began as a Native American celebration of horse racing and horsemanship. Early cowboys found the event to their liking and joined in. The Stampede became a full-blown rodeo in 1915, after it was sanctioned by the Rodeo Cowboy Association. Today, it is the oldest and one of the most prestigious rodeos in Montana, where rodeo events alternate with Indian dancers in a mutual celebration of shared culture. The Wolf Point Stampede is held the second weekend in July, with three separate rodeos and parades. Contact the chamber of commerce for further details.

The Assiniboin celebrate **Red Bottom Day** west of Wolf Point at Frazer the third weekend of June. The powwow involves singing, traditional dancing, a giveaway, and a display of handmade wares.

Information

Contact the **Wolf Point Chamber of Commerce** at 201 4th Avenue South (406/653-2012, www.wolfpoint.com).

Getting There and Around

Amtrak's Western District ends (or begins) in Wolf Point, and one train daily passes through in each direction. The depot is on Front Street (406/653-2350).

POPLAR

Poplar (pop. 911, elev. 1,963 feet) is the agency town for the Fort Peck Indian Reservation. Like many a Missouri River town, Poplar had its fitful beginnings as an Indian trading post and freighting center for furs and buffalo robes. Its pulse quickened when the Great Northern went through in 1887, and the Fort Peck Reservation was carved out and centered here the following year.

Poplar is also home to **NAES College,** a tribal community college, and **A & S Industries.** A

tribally owned business, A & S employs more than 400 people to make camouflage netting and medical chests for the U.S. government. A large and heavy-producing oil field lies just north of town.

Sights

The **Poplar Museum** (406/768-5223, 11 A.M.– 5 P.M. daily, Memorial Day to Labor Day, free) is located in the old tribal jail east of Poplar on Highway 2. In addition to Indian artifacts, the museum relates the history of the Assiniboin and Sioux Reservation.

The **Fort Peck Assiniboin and Sioux Cultural Center and Museum** (Hwy. 2 east of town, 406/768-5155, ext. 2328, 9 A.M.–5 P.M. Mon.–Sat., May–Sept.) focuses on tribal history. Across Highway 2 is a new tribal arts center with variable hours.

Accommodations

Lee Ann's Motel (150 F St., Hwy. 2, 406/768-5442, $57) offers clean snug rooms, some with kitchenettes.

Food

Several drive-ins stretch along Highway 2, but if you want to drive into the center of Poplar, try the **Buckhorn Cafe** (217 2nd Ave. W. behind the bar) for light meals—the Indian tacos ($8) are a favorite. Steaks ($12–17), and good ones, are the specialty at the **American Legion Supper Club** (127 A St. E., 406/768-3923).

Events

The **Iron Ring Celebration,** held the third weekend of July in Poplar, commemorates a former Sioux chief with dancing and a powwow. The Assiniboin and Sioux collectively host **Oil Discovery Celebration,** a powwow held the last weekend of August to memorialize the 1950s discovery of oil on the reservation.

Information

Contact the **Fort Peck Tribal Council** at P.O. Box 1027, Poplar, MT 59255 (406/768-5155, hwww.fortpecktribes.org).

NORTHEASTERN MONTANA

The Northeast Corner

In Montana's northeast corner, the center does not hold. Up here the locals keep one eye on Canada, one on North Dakota, and their back to the rest of Montana.

Saskatchewan is at least as important to Plentywood and Scobey as is, say, western Montana. Canadians pour over the border by the thousands, both to shop and to carouse. Considering that goods are already significantly cheaper in the United States than in Canada, and that Montana doesn't even *have* a sales tax, for many Canadians shopping in northern Montana isn't a weekend's amusement but an economic necessity.

Montana has some of the nation's most relaxed liquor laws, while Saskatchewan has some of Canada's most restrictive. Montana allows gambling in many forms; Saskatchewan doesn't. Add up this equation and you have, in the middle of these arid unpopulated prairies, a couple of the most unlikely holiday towns in the country.

But this corner of Montana isn't just festivities and holiday making on the northern plains. Surrounding Plentywood and Scobey is rich farmland, pressed flat as table linen by ancient glaciers, with an occasional divot carved out for small farm ponds. Medicine Lake Wildlife Refuge is one of the state's foremost areas for viewing migratory waterfowl and other prairie species. Both Scobey and Plentywood offer fine museums that commemorate the homesteaders who helped tame the Wild West.

SCOBEY

With sufficient rain, Scobey (pop. 1,082, elev. 2,450 feet) is at the center of some of the state's most productive wheat-growing land. Like many other towns along the Great Northern Railroad, Scobey was settled principally by Scandinavians; it's now a trading town for local farmers and ranchers as well as for visiting Canadians. Only 17 miles from Saskatchewan, the Canadian influence is strong. Canadian radio is pervasive on the airwaves, the occasional "eh?" sneaks into conversations, and—most damning—Scobey is home to Montana's only curling rink.

☖ Pioneer Town

A project of the Daniels County Museum, Pioneer Town (406/487-5965, 12:30–4:30 P.M. daily Memorial Day–Labor Day, 1–4 P.M. Fri. or by appointment Labor Day– Memorial Day) is one of the state's best walk-through museums. Basically a re-creation of an early homesteader town, the 20-acre site contains 50 buildings, some with period furnishings. Included are a restored schoolhouse, barbershop, blacksmith shop, undertaker's office, a two-story hotel, two churches, vintage automobiles, and farm equipment. The county historical archives are also kept here. The last weekend in June brings Pioneer Days, with entertainment featuring the musical *Dirty Shame Show,* a parade, games, pancake fry, and barbecue. Pioneer Town lies just west of town off 2nd Avenue.

Accommodations

The **Cattle King Motor Inn** (406/487-5332 or 800/562-2775, $74), at the south edge of town on Highway 13, offers free continental breakfast, guest laundry, free WiFi, commercial and senior discounts, and one wheelchair-accessible suite; pets are $5 extra.

Food

The **Ponderosa** (102 Main, 406/487-5954, 11 A.M.–10 P.M.) is a bar and grill that also serves pizza. The **Slipper Lounge** (608 Main, 406/487-9973, 11 A.M.–10 P.M. Tues.–Sun.), next to the Cattle King Motel, is the local casino, supper club, and salad bar.

Information and Services

The **Daniels Memorial Hospital** is at 105 5th Avenue East (406/487-2296). Contact the **sheriff's office** at 406/487-2691. The **U.S. Border Patrol** can be reached at 406/487-2621

© BILL MCRAE

Scobey's Pioneer Town is an open-air museum of frontier Montana.

at the Port of Scobey. The border with Canada is open 8 A.M.–9 P.M. May 15–September 30, and 9 A.M.–6 P.M. the rest of the year.

For area information, contact the **Scobey Chamber of Commerce** at P.O. Box 91, Scobey, MT 59263 (406/487-5502, www.scobey.org).

PLENTYWOOD

Located just about as far as it could get from the centers of Montana trade and power, Plentywood (pop. 2,061, elev. 2,024 feet) is closer to Winnipeg than to state capital Helena; Minneapolis is closer than Dillon. But Plentywood isn't any the less Montana-like for it. In fact, Canadians love to visit Plentywood precisely because it is so much more wild and Western—that is, Montanan—than their prairie provinces.

By the way, only on a vast and treeless plain would a cowboy be reduced to calling a place Plentywood simply because (so the story goes) he found enough wood to build a fire.

History

For such a far-flung locality, Plentywood is in the mainstream of Montana history. The Sioux chief Sitting Bull and his followers passed through this area after the Battle of the Little Bighorn in 1876. After living safely for five years in southern Saskatchewan, they moved south and surrendered to U.S. Army officials at the present site of Plentywood.

After the military evacuated the Indians, the plains of northern Montana became rangeland. However, the presence of valuable cattle and horses, combined with the absence of any effective law enforcement, made the area popular with rustlers. The Outlaw Trail, so named by Butch Cassidy, crossed the Canadian line just north of Plentywood. Gangs of rustlers drove stolen Canadian cattle across the border here and followed Cassidy's trail across the most lawless and inaccessible parts of Montana on their way to markets in the Southwest.

During the early 1900s, some shady characters lived in the gulches north of Plentywood. Unembarrassed to smuggle whiskey, rob a train, or alter brands after ferrying livestock back and forth across the border, these denim-collared criminals earned the area a reputation,

Small towns alternate with wheat fields in northeast Montana.

according to an early brand inspector, as the "most lawless and crookedest" in the state.

After the Great Northern brought in homesteaders in the 1910s, Plentywood gained a different reputation. Shunning the two major political parties, early homesteaders formed the Farmer-Labor Party. During the 1920s, this socialist-leaning party controlled county politics. In the 1930 general election, 300 Sheridan County residents voted straight-ticket Communist Party.

Today, the county's progressive politics are expressed in the quality of its public institutions, parks, and recreational facilities.

Sights

The **Sheridan County Museum** (406/765-2219, 1–5 P.M. Tues.–Sun., Memorial Day–Labor Day, free), at the fairgrounds on the east side of Plentywood, contains memorabilia from frontier and homesteading days. On the museum grounds is the **Old Tractor Club,** a huge collection of vintage tractors and farm equipment.

Accommodations

The handsome **Sherwood Inn** (515 W. 1st Ave., 406/765-2810, $70) continues the illusion that there are forests here—a theme perpetuated by the presence of the lounge and casino **Robin Hood's,** restaurant **Fryer Tuck's,** and Maid Marian's Styling Salon, all part of the same complex. Rooms at the Sherwood range from standard rooms to suites with fridge, microwave, and separate bedroom, to fully equipped one-bedroom apartments. Wireless Internet is available.

Camping

Free campsites are available at the city park at the north end of Box Elder Street.

Food

For light meals, go to **Friar Tuck's** (515 W. 1st Ave., 406/765-2810, 11 A.M.–10 P.M. daily) at the Sherwood Inn, which offers a wide menu of Mexican dishes in addition to more standard American fare ($8–13). **Cousin's Family Restaurant** (564 W. 1st Ave., 406/765-1690, 7 A.M.–8 P.M. Mon.–Sat.) is also good for home-style cooking. For steaks ($10–18), drinks, and gaming, try the ◖ **Blue Moon**

Supper Club (406/765-2491, 11 A.M.–10 P.M. daily), an archetypal Montana steakhouse east of Plentywood on Highway 5.

Information and Services
Information is available through the **Plentywood Chamber of Commerce** (P.O. Box 4, Plentywood, MT 59254, 406/765-1607, www.plentywood.com).

The **sheriff's office** can be contacted at 406/765-1200. **Sheridan Memorial Hospital** is at 440 West Laurel Avenue (406/765-1420).

Reach the **U.S. Border Patrol** at the Port of Raymond (406/765-1852). The border is open 24 hours daily.

(MEDICINE LAKE NATIONAL WILDLIFE REFUGE
Medicine Lake lies in an old channel of the Missouri River. Before the ice ages, the Missouri flowed north from near Culbertson along this watercourse, eventually to empty into Hudson's Bay. Ice sheets blocked this channel about 15,000 years ago, and the Missouri sought more southerly outlets. Now the broad valley through which the river once flowed holds a series of shallow lakes.

Established in 1935, the Medicine Lake National Wildlife Refuge (406/789-2305) is a superior example of a prairie lake ecosystem. Containing 31,000 acres of lake, wetlands, and prairie, the refuge is home to enormous numbers of ducks (10 different species) and geese, as well as pelicans, herons, grebes, and cranes. Pronghorn and white-tailed deer are common along brushy coulees. In an area called the Sandhills are stands of chokecherry, buffalo berry, and native prairie grasses; hiking trails cross the rolling hills.

In 1976, a wilderness area was designated of 11,360 acres of the refuge. No motorized boats are allowed on the lake. On the 18-mile auto tour around the lake, one of the 10 stops is the **Tepee Hills Site.** Here, rings of stone indicate the sites of ancient Indian lodges perhaps 4,000 years old.

Fort Union and Vicinity

"A judicious position for the purpose of trade" is what Capt. William Clark recorded at the confluence of Montana's two mighty east-flowing rivers, the Missouri and the Yellowstone. Traders quickly agreed. The American Fur Company built the region's grandest fur-trading post here in 1828, overlooking the juncture of the two rivers. Fort Union prospered in the 1830s and 1840s as it became the undisputed focus of the Montana fur trade.

Today, the site is administered by the National Park Service, which is in the process of reconstructing the fort as it stood in 1851.

FORT UNION
History
Lewis and Clark camped at the confluence of the Missouri and Yellowstone Rivers on their way into Montana and again as they exited a year later. Upon arriving in late April 1805, they were glad to have made it to this famous landmark, where the forks of the Missouri divide. The captains allotted each member of the Corps of Discovery a dram of whiskey in celebration; the fiddle came out, and the evening was spent in song and dance. The expedition continued up the Missouri River.

Although overwhelmed with mosquitoes, Clark recognized the strategic nature of this site on his return trip. These two enormous, easily navigable rivers drained a vast region rich in wildlife. Whoever controlled the Missouri and Yellowstone confluence controlled the wealth of the two river basins.

During the early 1800s the Americans controlled trade on the Yellowstone and had made friends with the Crow Indians; however, the Missouri River all the way to Three Forks was controlled by the Blackfeet, who, through trade for firearms, were allied to the British in what is now Canada. The Americans repeatedly attempted to establish trade with the Blackfeet, with uniformly bloody results.

In 1828, John Jacob Astor of the American Fur Company ordered Kenneth McKenzie to build a trading fort at the confluence of the Yellowstone and Missouri, and to break the British hegemony over trade in the Missouri. McKenzie dispatched a trapper who spoke the Blackfeet language to induce warriors to accompany him back to Fort Union. Showered with gifts, the Blackfeet shortly entered into trade at Fort Union. With the Blackfeet suddenly compliant, and with steamboat service (starting in 1832) to Fort Union, all of Montana was open for exploitation. Until the 1850s, Fort Union reigned undisputed over Montana trade.

McKenzie—powerful, unscrupulous, and vain—built up Fort Union to be the most elegant habitation west of St. Louis. Liveried servants poured French wines into crystal goblets at his table; bagpipers piped as he entered his dining room; Native American chiefs were sometimes greeted by McKenzie in full chain mail. The list of guests at Fort Union reads like a who's who of the American West: painters Karl Bodmer, George Catlin, and J. J. Audubon, Germany's Prince Maximilian, Father De Smet, Jim Bridger, and Governor Isaac Stevens.

The enormous success of Fort Union was not based solely on geography. Although it was illegal to sell alcohol to the Indians, McKenzie established a still at Fort Union and used alcohol to cement native loyalty to his trading post and the United States. This was not a fine single malt that he traded to the Indians for furs: An early recipe for "Indian whiskey" cut McKenzie's homemade liquor with river water, cayenne pepper, tobacco, sagebrush, and a dash of strychnine.

The damage to the Plains Indians begun by alcohol at Fort Union was hastened by the arrival of the steamboat *Saint Peter* in 1837. The Assiniboin camped at Fort Union contracted smallpox from the crew; from here it spread quickly among the Indians in northern Montana.

An estimated 15,000 of them-two thirds of the tribe—died from the disease that year.

As fur-bearing animals in Montana approached extinction, Fort Union waned. By 1867 it had fallen into disrepair. Some buildings were dismantled to build Fort Buford two miles downstream, and the remainder was sold by wood hawkers as steamboat fuel.

🄲 Fort Union Trading Post National Historic Site

Behind 20-foot-high palisades situated on the high banks of the Missouri River, the reconstructed Fort Union Trading Post National Historic Site (Buford Rte., Williston, ND 58801, 701/572-9083, www.nps.gov/fous) is located only yards east of the Montana border in North Dakota and is again the focus of traffic at the Yellowstone and Missouri confluence. The **Bourgeois House** was the home of the fort's factor, or governor. The building was reconstructed as an exact replica of the surprisingly elegant 1851 house seen in paintings of the time; it now houses the visitors center and a good museum detailing the history of trade and early frontier life on the Missouri. The **Indian Trade House,** where natives swapped beaver, mink, and marten skins for rifles, trinkets, and whiskey, has also been reconstructed, as has a native village of tepees and earth lodges.

From the palisades, the Missouri and Yellowstone confluence can be seen, and it's easy to imagine steamboats pulling up to the embankment to load up with furs.

On the third week of June, the **Fort Union Rendezvous** takes place. At this reenactment of an 1800s trappers' gathering, hundreds of buckskin-clad, musket-bearing, tepee-dwelling people gather to celebrate frontier-era skills and fortitude. There are hatchet-throwing contests, food cooked à la frontier, and black-powder rifle shooting. On Labor Day weekend, the fort is the site of a living-history program, with actors and history buffs playing the parts of early traders, trappers, and natives, all in period garb.

It's important to note that Fort Union Trading Post National Historic Site is not a commercial reconstruction: This isn't a theme park, and it's not just for kids. The fort is one of the most informative and satisfying stops in this part of Montana, and is definitely worth a detour. The Fort Union Trading Post National Historic Site is open daily 8 A.M.–8 P.M. central time from Memorial Day through Labor Day. The rest of the year, it's open 9 A.M.–5:30 P.M. central time.

FORT BUFORD AND THE MISSOURI-YELLOWSTONE CONFLUENCE

Two miles farther into North Dakota are the remains of Fort Buford. Built in 1866 in the midst of hostile Sioux territory, the fort was conceived less as a military staging site than as a thorn in the side of the Sioux. It was at Fort Buford that Sioux leader Sitting Bull surrendered in 1881.

The old fort is now preserved as North Dakota's Fort Buford State Historic Site. Although about half of the buildings at old Fort Union were dismantled and brought here to be rebuilt, currently just three original buildings stand at Fort Buford State Historic Site: the stone powder magazine, a wood-frame officer of the guard building, and a wood-frame officers quarters, which contains a museum exhibit and interpretive center featuring artifacts and displays about the frontier military and Fort Buford's role in the history of the West. A reconstruction of the 1870s barracks is due to open in 2005. The fort's 1860s graveyard is definitely worth a visit: Reading the tombstones gives a fascinating glimpse of what life—and death—was like at this frontier outpost.

Just east of the ruins of Fort Buford along the same road is the confluence of the Yellowstone and Missouri Rivers. A nice picnic area on a broad embankment overlooks this historic crossroads. A respectful stillness seems to encroach: these two prodigious rivers, meeting beneath yellow bluffs in a tangle of cottonwoods, willows, and a crisp dialogue of waters, have embraced almost all of Montana. During the heyday of Fort Union, the confluence was farther upstream near the fort, but in accordance with some fluvial law, their junction has drifted eastward.

One half mile east of Fort Buford is the new **Missouri-Yellowstone Confluence Interpretive Center** (701/572-9034, 8 A.M.–6 P.M. daily May 15–Sept. 15, 9 A.M.–4 P.M. Wed.–Sun. Sept. 16–May 15, $5 adults, $2.50 children), which focuses on the natural and human history of the area, with an emphasis on the Lewis and Clark expedition.

CULBERTSON AND VICINITY

As the valleys of the Yellowstone and Missouri prepare to meet, a ridge of high gray badland buttes rises to the south. To the north the prairies begin their flat sweep to Canada.

The land here is rich, and grain production has dominated the local economy since the Great Northern Railway brought homesteaders here to plow. If good soil wasn't enough in itself, nature also found time to bury a wealth of oil here. A new crop for the region is wine: **Rolling Hills Winery** is eastern Montana's only winery, with a tasting room right along Highway 2 in Culbertson (406/787-5787, 2–7 P.M. Mon.–Fri., 10 A.M.–7 P.M. Sat.). Most of the wines produced are based on locally grown fruit, not grapes, and this may be your only chance to taste wines made from wild chokecherries, the sour but full-flavored fruit that local Indians and pioneers both used for sustenance.

Culbertson (pop. 716, elev. 1,921 feet) has come a long way since the day in 1892 when a young woman stepped from the train at Culbertson station and spent some time looking for the town. Where she came from, two buildings did not constitute a town. Early ranchers engaged in horse ranching. The many military forts along this length of the Missouri demanded a large number of mounts. Now a pleasant farming town, Culbertson sits at the crossroads between northern Montana and Saskatchewan.

Accommodations

The **King's Inn** (408 E. 6th, 406/787-6277 or 800/823-4407, $63) is a modern attractive motel with all queen beds along Highway 2. There's free camping in the city's **Bicentennial Park** (off 3rd Ave. E.), where you'll also find a playground and picnic area.

Food

The **Wild West Diner** (20 E. 6th, 406/787-5374, 7 A.M.–8 P.M. $8–12) is a classic roadside café with a pleasingly unassuming menu. **Stagecoach Casino** (602 2nd Ave. E., 406/787-6181, 11 A.M.–9 P.M.) has a full-service restaurant near the junction of Highways 2 and 16.

Information and Services

Contact the **Culbertson Chamber of Commerce** at P.O. Box 639, Culbertson, MT 59218 (406/787-5275). **Roosevelt Memorial Hospital** is at 818 2nd Avenue East (406/787-6281).

Highway 200: Fairview to Circle

The highway system in Montana almost exclusively follows river valleys or old rail lines, but there's one marked departure from the general rule. Highway 200 enters eastern Montana near the Yellowstone-Missouri confluence and, like a sensible highway, follows the Yellowstone Valley to Sidney. Then, perversely, it lights off west across the prairie toward nowhere in particular.

Between Sidney and Lewistown—a distance of almost 300 miles—Highway 200 passes through only three towns with gas pumps (Circle, Jordan, and Grassrange); their *combined* population approaches 1,500 people. As it connects these remote enclaves of humanity, Highway 200 intersects a part of Montana often called the Big Lonely. Unpopulated, marginally productive, and often starkly beautiful, this is one of the last vast frontiers left in the state.

FAIRVIEW

Squat on the Montana-Dakota state line and 11 miles east of Sidney is Fairview, a small farming town in the heart of sugar beet country. Fairview's principal claim to fame is that half the town is in North Dakota. There's camping in **Fairview City Park,** complete with RV hookups, a playground, a swimming pool, and picnic facilities.

SIDNEY AND VICINITY

Although stockmen had begun to establish ranches along this stretch of the Yellowstone

Valley in the 1880s, it took the Lower Yellowstone Project, a federally funded irrigation project begun in 1904, to put Sidney (pop. 4,774, elev. 1,928 feet) on the map. The wide fertile valley fell to the plow and hip waders. Sugar beets became the principal crop, inducing Holly Sugar to build a refinery here.

In the 1950s, Sidney found itself on the edge of the Williston Basin, a huge oil reserve. Sidney moved from sugar town to oil town seamlessly, accruing the economic benefits.

Mondak Heritage Center

One of the largest community museums in this part of the state, the Mondak Heritage Center (120 3rd Ave. S.E., 406/433-3500, noon–5 P.M. Mon.–Fri., 1–5 P.M. Sat.–Sun., $3 adults, $1 youth 11–18, 10 and under free with an adult) combines the function of a regional art center and local history museum. In addition to displays of area history, the basement houses a re-creation of an old-time Sidney street.

Accommodations

The oil boom of the 1990s has had an ameliorative effect on the quality of lodging in Sidney. The **Lone Tree Inn** (900 S. Central Ave., 406/433-4520, $78) and the **Richland Motor Inn** (1200 S. Central Ave., 406/433-6400, $100) are both modern attractive hotel-like lodging complexes.

NORTHEASTERN MONTANA

SHEEPHERDERS' MONUMENTS

You'll notice them on the tops of gumbo buttes in eastern and central Montana: steep piles of rock rising like parapets against the skyline. Known as sheepherders' monuments, they are the work of Scottish and Irish herders whose sheep-tending jobs gave them lots of free time on hilltops.

In many ways, the open range lasted longer for sheep ranchers than for cattlemen. Before the proliferation of stock reservoirs, sheepherders (Montanans never use the term *shepherd*) trailed sheep from pastures near "camp" to water every day. The range may have been fenced, but sheep needed the herder's extra inducement to behave sensibly. While at camp, herders typically kept watch over their flocks from nearby hills, mindful of predators and wayward sheep. Many ranches still employed herders – typically of Basque, Irish, or Scottish origin – through the 1950s.

Sheepherders always claim that they began to build cairns on the tops of high hills as windbreaks, but something more than utility went into it. Herders took pride in building the tallest, or the most tightly fitted, monument. Old-timers can still tell you which herder built every monument on the skyline.

Unfortunately, few ranches employ herders anymore, so remaining monuments have begun to slump a bit in their advanced age, and the monuments' survival is further threatened because vandals derive pleasure from toppling those convenient to highways. Please respect the age of these constructions – and the isolation, work, and pride that went into them.

Camping

Six miles east of Sidney on Highway 200 is **Richland Park.** This fishing-access area and campground is shaded by cottonwood and elm trees, and it provides latrines, potable water, picnic facilities, and a playground. If you plan to camp overnight, don't leave Sidney until you get permission and buy a $1 ticket from the Richland County Sheriff's Department (110 2nd Ave. N.W., 406/433-2919).

Food

For breakfast and light meals, try the **M & M** (south of Sidney on Hwy. 200, 406/433-1714, 5 A.M.–7 P.M. daily) or **Gulliver's** (120 E. Main, 406/433-5175, 7 A.M.–3 P.M.).

The Pizza House (710 S. Central Ave., 406/433-1971, 11 A.M.–1:30 P.M. and 5–10 P.M. Mon.–Fri., 11:30 A.M.–10 P.M. Sat.–Sun.) not only serves pizza but also has homemade soup and sandwich lunch specials. There's good Mexican cooking at **La Casita** (102 E. Main, 406/433-1839, 7 A.M.–9 P.M.).

For dining featuring steaks or seafood, go to the **South 40** (209 2nd Ave., 406/433-4999, 11 A.M.–10 P.M. Mon.–Thurs., 11 A.M.–11 P.M.

Fri.–Sat., 9 A.M.–10 P.M. Sun.) or the **Cattle-Ac Niteclub, Casino, and Steakhouse** (119 N. Central Ave., 406/433-7174, 11 A.M.–10 P.M. daily). Expect to pay $14–20 for a steak dinner at either of these restaurants.

Information and Services

You can contact the **Sidney Chamber of Commerce** at 909 South Central Avenue (406/433-1916, www.sidneymt.com). **Community Memorial Hospital** is located at 216 14th Avenue S.W. (406/433-7700).

RICHEY

Between Sidney and Circle, Highway 200 climbs over gravel hills and out of the Yellowstone drainage. The countryside opens into a wide basin garnished here and there with ranch buildings. In good years, deer and pronghorn are abundant, making this area popular with hunters.

The urban instinct is weak here—the little crossroads of Richey (pop. 189) represents one of this region's few experiments in city living. Richey is a pleasant little hamlet dominated by grain elevators; the **Richey**

NORTHEASTERN MONTANA

© BILL MCRAE

The Big Sheep Mountains mark the watershed between the Yellowstone and Missouri drainages.

Historical Museum (406/773-5656, 2–5 P.M. Mon., Wed., Fri., Memorial Day–Labor Day) commemorates the homesteading boom that followed the Great Northern line into town. The **Farmer's Kitchen Cafe** (406/773-5533, 6 A.M.–7 P.M.) serves tasty food designed to satisfy a ranch hand's appetite.

CIRCLE

Circle (pop. 644, elev. 2,450 feet) got its start as a cattle town during the open-range years. The biggest outfit hereabouts had a simple circle for its cattle brand, hence the name for the settlement that grew up beside it. Both the Northern Pacific and the Great Northern schemed about extending into Circle; this alone was sufficient to bring in grain-farming homesteaders who had plans for the flat grazing lands of the Redwater River Valley.

South of Circle are the Big Sheep Mountains, obviously named by people who hadn't seen a mountain recently. Actually little more than a series of high sandstone ridges, they mark the watershed between the Yellowstone and Missouri drainages. At one time, Audubon mountain sheep grazed along these chokecherry-laden bluffs. They live on in the name of the mountains only: Like the buffalo, early frontiersmen found them an easy, tasty prey and hunted them to extinction.

Sights

The **McCone County Museum** (west of town on Hwy. 200, 406/485-2414, 9 A.M.–5 P.M. Mon.–Fri. May–Sept., $2 adult, children 12 and under free) contains displays commemorating Circle's frontier history. On the museum grounds are a restored country schoolhouse, an old church, and a caboose from the Northern Pacific.

Accommodations

The **Traveler's Inn,** at the junction of Highways 13 and 200 (406/485-3323, $43), is Circle's sole lodging option.

Food

The best place to eat is **Kay's Family Dining** (east end of town on Hwy. 200, 406/485-3674, 7 A.M.–8 P.M.), for home cooking in a former Dairy Queen. The **Wooden Nickel** (Main St., 406/485-2575, 10 A.M.–10 P.M.) features local beef in burgers and steaks ($10–16).

Information and Services

Contact the **Circle Chamber of Commerce** at 406/485-2414. For emergencies, contact the **sheriff's office** at 406/485-3405.

There are two service stations, open until 9 P.M. For **road conditions,** call 406/365-2314.

The Big Open

West of Circle, the farms thin out, the fields coarsen into badlands, and signs of human habitation grow more scarce. From here to the banks of the Musselshell River 150 miles west, Highway 200 traverses a vaguely defined region of ranches, gumbo buttes, sagebrush, coyotes, and cowboys. It's known by many names: Big Dry Country, the North Side, Jordan Country, the Big Empty, the Big Lonesome, and the Big Open.

The last of these gained currency a few years ago when environmental activists proposed turning the area into an enormous wildlife park; it's hard to imagine how much more of a wilderness this forlorn and lonesome land could be. Garfield County, nearly the size of Connecticut, encompasses much of this area; it has the lowest population density in the Lower 48, with just 0.27 people per square mile.

But if you asked one of the locals, you'd be told there's not much room left. Out here, under a trademark big sky, where single farms and ranches engulf a whole township's worth of land, people get used to taking up space.

For better or worse, this is one of the last outposts of the frontier spirit: Cowboy hats are mandatory, the bar doubles as the community hall, and the rodeo club is the biggest extracurricular activity at the high school. Here more than anywhere else in the state, there is still some wild left in the West.

JORDAN AND VICINITY

No one comes to Jordan (pop. 364, elev. 2,800 feet) because of its interesting history or architecture. Like other late-germinating communities, many of the first settlers were outlaws. Homesteaders drifted through desultorily, recoiling when they discovered what a nasty piece of business the Big Dry Country was. Big ranches and big families have always ruled the rangelands. Now what makes Jordan exceptional is that it never bothered to change.

Jordan is remote. In 1931 only eight households had running water. Rural homes didn't have electrical service until 1952, and ranches didn't get telephones until 1956. Public transportation? Never had it, probably never will. The most isolated county seat in the continental U.S., Jordan is 175 miles from the nearest major airport, 85 miles from the nearest bus line, and 115 miles from the nearest train line. The local high school serves such a vast area that until the 1990s it maintained a public coed dormitory.

Once discovered, Jordan has always fascinated journalists. A New York radio station in 1930 identified Jordan as "the lonesomest town in the world." A local ranch woman contributed a column called "Timber Creek Riffles" to the *Wall Street Journal.* Jordan made it to the front page of the nation's papers in the 1970s when, in the aftermath of a break-in at the local drugstore, the sheriff deputized the men in the local bar as his posse. The sheriff got his man, but only after the gun-toting mob gave a visiting Associated Press journalist an eyeful of Western color.

A famous TV investigative reporter showed up in town a few years later to film a story about the farm and ranch crisis. Locals in the bar didn't much like his flashy ways; he conducted his on-screen interviews with his nose in plaster.

NORTHEASTERN MONTANA

© BILL MCRAE

Horses are still indispensable for ranch work in the Big Open.

The Montana Freemen

When the militia-like Freemen's movement found adherents in the area, Freemen moved here from other parts of the West in search of isolation. Jordan again made the national press in 1993 when the local Freeman militia issued "dead or alive" bounties for the duly elected county sheriff, attorney, and a federal judge. The conflict between the local adherents of Freeman philosophy and local authorities deepened when antigovernment zealots from across the West started streaming into a 920-acre ranch west of Jordan, to hole up and establish a Freeman world headquarters known as Justus Township. This self-declared free state administered under Freeman authority developed its own court and laws, elected officials, and bizarre banking practices. The Freemen in general refused to acknowledge the authority of any governing body except their own.

As the actions of the Freemen swerved from paranoid to nutty, the impact on the community intensified. Many of the people in the Freeman compound had family members who were anti-Freeman. Brother was pitted against brother, father against son, with the Freemen issuing bounties and arrest warrants for old friends and family alike. Many people around Jordan received death threats or were threatened with arrest and trial in a Freeman-style common-law court. With the Freemen increasingly wild-eyed and armed to the teeth, it was easy to believe that a bloodbath was imminent.

The FBI had been monitoring the Jordan Freemen for some time (in fact, operatives had infiltrated the compound posing as fellow antigovernment activists). Finally, in early 1996, the federal agents moved against the Freemen, capturing two of the ringleaders. The rest of the Freemen, numbering in the 20s, retreated to their heavily armed ranch compound, and the standoff began.

Within days, almost 600 federal law enforcement agents were in place in Jordan (the county fairgrounds was Operations Central), and as many as 200 journalists from around the world crushed into the little town, occupying every motel room, spare bedroom, and apartment for miles.

Obviously, life changed pretty quickly for tiny Jordan and its usually sanguine citizens. After enduring interview after interview with visiting film crews and a town suddenly overrun with strangers, many of the locals grew weary of the whole Freeman nonsense—you couldn't get a drink in the bar without a microphone being stuck in your face. After a couple of months without a resolution in sight, an area rancher drew up a petition that urged the FBI to use "reasonable force" to end the standoff. Within a couple of days, more than 200 Jordan-area citizens had signed the document. With the locals obviously growing restless, the FBI finally made a move. They turned off the Freemen's electricity and phone service. Within a matter of days, the Freemen began negotiations to give themselves up.

The standoff lasted 81 days. Remarkably, not a shot was fired during the entire confrontation, robbing the Freemen of guaranteed martyr status, seemingly a goal of hardened antigovernment extremists motivated by events at Ruby Ridge, Idaho, and Waco, Texas.

In 1998 the Freemen were tried in Billings. A

DINOSAUR COUNTRY

The dun-colored badlands that rise along the Missouri River, fantastically carved by erosion into sharp canyons and buttes, contain one of the world's richest chronicles of early life on earth. Paleontologists discovered some of the first and most important remains of dinosaurs in these desiccated hills. Today, the annual arrival of the summer "bone diggers" is almost an institution in Jordan.

In 1902, Dr. Barnum Brown of the American Museum of Natural History journeyed to the Jordan area to search for dinosaur remains. Brown cut quite a figure: He reported to the digs in a starched white collar and polished knee boots, popping his gold pince-nez on and off. The existence of large dinosaurs was still a matter of conjecture in scientific circles – the giant reptiles certainly didn't yet form part of the popular imagination.

What attracted Brown to this area was its Cretaceous-era badlands. Laid down by shallow marshy seas about 70 million years ago, these layers of mudstone, shale, and sandstone were normally covered by thick layers of more recent sediment. When the Missouri River cut its way through the badlands, it opened up a gorge through millions of years of geologic history. Here, in the arid bluffs of Garfield County, the earth had stored its memories of vanished life. In the stratified layers of sediment revealed by erosion, Brown reasoned, one should be able to find the band corresponding to the "Age of the Dinosaurs."

In a gumbo escarpment on Hell Creek, Brown found much more than he was looking for: two skeletons of *Tyrannosaurus rex*. The fossil-rich Cretaceous sediments, now called the Hell Creek Formation in honor of Garfield County's dinosaur haven, has continued to yield specimens. In 1988 a Jordan couple found the most complete tyrannosaurus skeleton to date (the 11th found in the area) along the shore of Fort Peck Lake. Triceratops has almost become Jordan's dinosaur mascot. Aquatic duck-billed dinosaurs and the mosasaur – a sea-serpent-like dinosaur – have also been found in the Hell Creek Formation. Smaller finds – dinosaur eggs, petrified mollusks, and fish – are common.

Later scientists have come to Jordan not to dig bones but to research theories. It was commonly known that dinosaurs (and, in fact, most early life-forms) were found only below a smudgy black band in the gumbo buttes, for instance. This thin layer of lignite coal in fact demarcates the Hell Creek and Fort Union sedimentary formations. Dr. Walter Alvarez, from the University of California at Berkeley, analyzed this layer closely, found that it contained traces of iridium embedded in similar sediments worldwide, and in 1979 proposed his asteroid-impact theory. According to Alvarez, a massive asteroid struck the earth, throwing dust into the atmosphere in such vast quantities that it caused a global winter, during which the dinosaurs became extinct.

Montana jury found eight of the Freemen guilty of 23 federal felonies. Notably, only one of the Freemen from Jordan was convicted of federal offenses. The Freeman issue is still a potent topic of discussion in Jordan, but don't be surprised if the locals don't want to talk about the situation with strangers. Family ties are still strained, and while not many local people agreed with the Freemen's sentiments (don't assume that everyone from Jordan is a sympathizer; in fact, the truth is the opposite), the sense of community fragmentation and hostility that the standoff produced will take a long time to dissipate.

Sights

Despite its reputation as the last stronghold of the Old West, Jordan is normally a friendly town with adequate facilities for the traveler. It is central to great hunting and to recreation and wildlife viewing on the C. M. Russell Wildlife Refuge and Fort Peck Lake.

The **Garfield County Museum** (406/557-2517, 1–5 P.M. daily, June 1–Sept. 1, free), just east of town, offers both historic and prehistoric overviews of the locality. A replica of a triceratops found north of town, an actual triceratops head, and other fossil remains are the highlights here.

A TALE OF DINOSAURS AND GLACIERS

In few places is the dinosaur fossil record so easily read as in northeastern Montana. Once a tropical seacoast, these prairies sprouted exotic vegetation, and dinosaurs of every size and description crowded in, hoping to eat and not be eaten. Some still-unknown event eradicated these exuberant life-forms about 70 million years ago; sediments continued to accumulate along the marshes, burying the remains of these ancient plants and animals.

After a prolonged altercation with ice age glaciers, the Missouri River cut a new channel across the prairies, revealing hundreds of feet of fossil-rich sediment in the deep gorge-like Missouri Breaks. The formation, named for Hell Creek near Jordan, where extensive fossil excavations have taken place, continues to yield its ancient secrets.

The ice sheets of the last ice age did more than divert the Missouri. They ground down the prairies north of the Missouri River's present channel to a uniform flatness.

Also on display are homesteader memorabilia, early photos, and a restored one-room school.

About eight miles west of Jordan is a curious landmark known as **Smokey Butte.** This promontory, which rises a thousand feet above surrounding prairie, is the easternmost of the many igneous intrusions that rose into mountains in central Montana. More curiously, the rock that makes up Smokey Butte, armolcolite, has never been found elsewhere except in rocks collected on the moon.

Accommodations

One of Jordan's original hotels, the **Garfield** (corner of Main St. and Hwy. 200, 406/557-6215, $45), is still in business and offers rooms in the hotel or in newer motel units. **Fellman's Motel** (Hwy. 200, 406/557-2209 or 800/337-1863, $48) is Jordan's other option.

Camping

Campers should go to **Kamp Katie** (406/557-2851), just west of the bridge, a pleasant enough campground on the banks of Big Dry Creek.

Food

The **Hilltop** (406/557-6287, 6 A.M.–9 P.M. daily), west of Jordan on Highway 200, is Jordan's only full-service restaurant.

Information and Services

Contact the **Jordan Commercial Club** for travel info at P.O. Box 370, Jordan, MT 59337 (406/557-2232). For emergencies, call the **sheriff's office** at 406/557-2882. The **C. M. Russell Wildlife Refuge** (406/557-6145) maintains a wildlife station in Jordan along Highway 200. Contact the **Bureau of Land Management** at 406/557-2376; the office is on Main Street.

For local **road conditions,** call 406/365-2314.

CHARLES M. RUSSELL NATIONAL WILDLIFE REFUGE

Known to locals, with widely varying degrees of affection, as the C.M.R., the 1.2-million-acre Charles M. Russell National Wildlife Refuge flanks the entire northern edge of Garfield County along the Missouri River. One of the largest refuges in the nation, the C.M.R. is home to an abundance of wildlife, including elk and bighorn sheep, which were once common on the prairies. Recently, ranchers have reported sightings of wolves and cougars, although it's not clear if these animals were passing through or if there are sustainable populations in the refuge.

Garfield County contains more of the C.M.R. than any other county; feelings run high here about having such a huge wilderness area (and its champion, the federal government) for a neighbor. Some local residents are still bitter about being displaced from their land along the Missouri when Fort Peck was built and about their grazing land in the Breaks

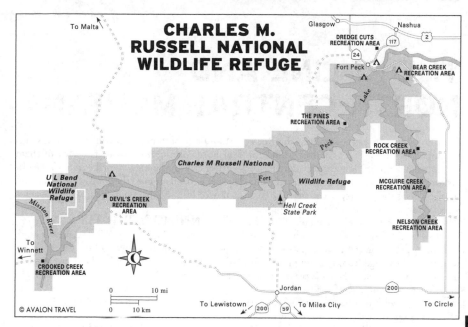

CHARLES M. RUSSELL NATIONAL WILDLIFE REFUGE

being turned into de facto wilderness, and are unhappy when what land they have left is overrun by errant herds of deer, pronghorn, elk, and worst of all, coyotes and wolves.

Unfortunately, heavy-handed interference on the part of the government and sheer old-fashioned cussedness on the part of the locals combine to make the C.M.R. much less accessible to visitors than it should be. Quite apart from the incredible wealth of wildlife—lacking only grizzly bears to replicate the Missouri River flora and fauna experienced by Lewis and Clark—the Missouri Breaks are dramatic and austere badlands that are still full of outlaw lore. At the center of the refuge is Fort Peck Lake, one of the largest manmade lakes in the world, important as a migratory waterfowl stopover, to say nothing about its stellar fishing and recreational possibilities.

There is public access to the refuge and Fort Peck Lake at two sites in Garfield County: Hell Creek State Park and Devil's Creek Recreation Area. Both sites offer good scouting for fossils.

Hell Creek State Park

The most popular site in the C.M.R. is Hell Creek State Park, 26 miles north of Jordan (406/232-0900). Developed as a recreation area for local anglers and boaters, Hell Creek offers a campground, marina (406/557-2345), store, and cabins. The road in, best attempted in dry weather, passes through rugged badlands. Elks, deer, waterfowl, eagles, foxes, and coyotes are pervasive. Entrance is $5 per vehicle for non–Montana residents, and camping is $15 per night.

Devil's Creek Recreation Area

Farther afield, along a dodgier road, is Devil's Creek Recreation Area, with undeveloped campsites, about 40 miles northwest of Jordan. Here the gumbo buttes fringed with ponderosa pines drop away in canyons to the lake's shore.

Information and Services

A regional office for the Charles M. Russell Wildlife Refuge (P.O. Box 110, Lewistown, MT 59597, 406/538-8706) is in Lewistown.

THE HI-LINE AND NORTH-CENTRAL MONTANA

From the dramatic eastern front of the Rocky Mountains to the long views of the Hi-Line, this agricultural heart of Montana has more for the visitor than a look at a topographic map would imply. This is the country where the Nez Perce were finally run down by U.S. Army troops, and where Chief Joseph gave his remarkable surrender speech. It's where dinosaur nests have revised scientific opinion on the ancient reptiles, transforming their image from flesh-ripping brutes into loving parents. It's where the Blackfeet have held fast to a small part of the land they used to race across with their horses, and where they now host a big annual powwow. And it's where cowboy artist Charlie Russell settled down to work in his log-cabin studio.

The Hi-Line was built by the Great Northern Railway—in fact, its name refers to its being the state's northernmost railroad line. Thousands of hardworking homesteaders, many of them European immigrants, took the train to the Hi-Line, stepped off onto the windswept plain, and plowed into the short-grass prairie.

PLANNING YOUR TIME

This is road-trip territory. While there's enough quiet history here to keep a buff occupied for days, for most travelers the Hi-Line and the Rocky Mountain Front will be experienced in transversal—on the way to elsewhere. Don't just blow through, however. **Great Falls** deserves a day, with the excellent **Lewis and Clark National Historic Trail Interpretive Center** and the **C. M. Russell Museum**. If you're here in late June, the **Lewis and Clark Festival** is a colorful event. Hundreds of living

HIGHLIGHTS

◖ Lewis and Clark National Historic Trail Interpretive Center: Montana's premier Lewis and Clark site, the center encapsulates the Corps journey across Montana in a fantastic structure overlooking the Missouri River at Great Falls (page 392).

◖ C. M. Russell Museum: The patron artist of Montana is Charlie Russell, and this museum offers the largest collection of his subtle and arresting Western art (page 392).

◖ First Peoples Buffalo Jump State Park: Ancient Native Americans stampeded bison off the cliffs here – today a new interpretive center relates the history and culture of the plains tribes that hunted here (page 393).

◖ Giant Springs Heritage Park: Underground aquifers burst from the cliffs above the Missouri River at this park, creating a unique ecosystem and a wonderful spot for picnicking (page 393).

◖ Square Butte Natural Area: Square Butte rises 2,400 feet above the prairies, an isolated volcanic plug capped with virgin prairie flowers and grasses. Bring a picnic and enjoy the views from one of Montana's most enchanted destinations (page 399).

◖ Fort Benton: Montana's oldest settlement, Fort Benton was the head of Missouri River boat traffic from the 1840s to the 1880s, making this a one-stop Montana history lesson (page 399).

◖ Upper Missouri River Breaks National Monument: From Virgelle to the backwaters of Fort Peck Lake, the monument preserves 150 miles of the Missouri River's prairie canyon as a near pristine wilderness (page 402).

◖ Havre Historical Underground Tours: Havre was once such a party town that some of its downtown businesses had to go underground – literally. Tours lead visitors to a circa-1900 business district that included brothels, barber shops, and bars (page 405).

◖ Old Trail Museum: Known nationally for its fossil collection, this Choteau museum is one of the state's top paleontology centers (page 414).

◖ Two Medicine Dinosaur Center: Visit the fossil gallery at this paleontology outpost to watch scientists prepare ancient dino bones, or schedule a hands-on encounter at a real fossil dig (page 415).

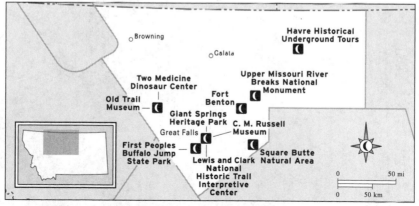

LOOK FOR ◖ TO FIND RECOMMENDED SIGHTS, ACTIVITIES, DINING, AND LODGING.

NORTH-CENTRAL MONTANA

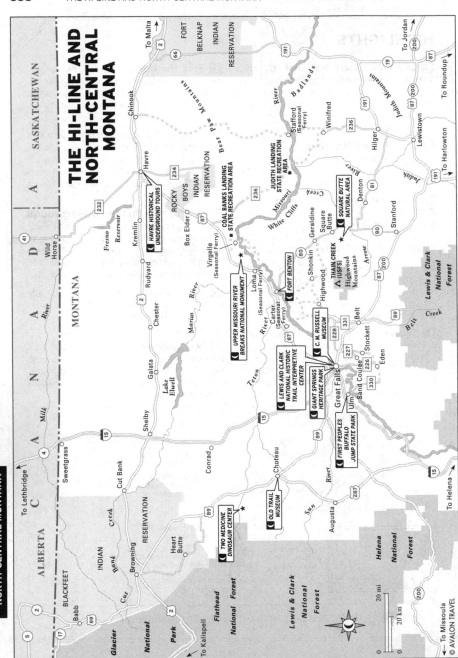

THE HI-LINE AND NORTH-CENTRAL MONTANA

history reenactors gather in buckskins and moccasins to relive frontier times.

Take back roads through **Shonkin Sag,** a weird landscape centered on an abandoned ice age channel of the Missouri, to reach **Fort Benton,** Montana's oldest town. Once the furthest upstream landing for Missouri riverboats, Fort Benton preserves many remnants of its trading post past—the trading fort is in the process of being reconstructed. The highlight of a Fort Benton visit will be a night at the **Union Hotel.** Built in 1882, this beauty is totally renovated and back in business.

East of Fort Benton, the Missouri River drops into a series of badlands canyons. Now preserved as part of the **Upper Missouri River Breaks National Monument,** the river and the landscapes remain much as Lewis and Clark saw them 200 years ago. Much of this territory can only be seen on multiday float trips, although travelers with high-clearance vehicles and a bit of time can explore the landscape on secondary roads.

Havre is now at the center of Montana's wheat-growing region, although a century ago the community found itself at a crossroads as both the United States and Canada began expansion onto the northern Great Plains. This rowdy, hell's-a-poppin' era is preserved in Havre's "underground" commercial district, which served the needs of thirsty cowboys, opium addicts, and love-starved plainsmen. **Havre Historical Underground Tours** offer a glimpse of this forgotten world.

The plains roll right up to the base of the **Rocky Mountain Front.** This strikingly dramatic landscape was once the grazing land for open-range cattle outfits, and the Western spirit lives on in the region's **guest ranches**—some of the state's most famous dude ranches are here. If you don't have time to spend a week in the saddle, at least plan a stop at one of the area's splendid **rural B&Bs.** Amateur paleontologists should plan an outing at one of Choteau's many dino sights. The new **Two Medicine Dinosaur Center** offers both day trips to fossil digs and multiday get-your-hands-dirty field excavation programs.

HISTORY

The Great Northern Railway defined the development of the Hi-Line. James J. Hill had rails laid across northern Montana after Montanans such as Marcus Daly and Paris Gibson convinced him that it was worth taking the trouble to compete with the Northern Pacific, whose line already ran across the southern part of the state. In order to keep the railcars filled, settlers were recruited for Gibson's town, Great Falls, and for the northern tier, which would be coaxed into producing grain.

Hill and Professor Thomas Shaw were proponents of dryland farming. Shaw developed a theory that called for deep plowing and unrelenting cultivation of the land, a method that was practiced widely and led to widespread erosion. Precious topsoil, catching a windy ride, blew completely out of the state.

Between 1910 and 1918, homesteaders, sometimes derogatorily called "honyockers," swarmed to Montana for free land. Typically, a family would get off the train, which had a boxcar full of their possessions, pay a "finder" $20 to lead them to their homestead, and start plowing. During the middle of the decade, the homesteader's life looked good. Wet weather helped crops flourish, and World War I inflated the price of grain. But when drought began in 1918 and didn't let up for years, homesteaders scattered almost as fast as the dry topsoil.

Wheat farming has remained a major part of the local economy, and one way of dealing with the dry windy climate is the strip agriculture you'll see wherever wheat's been planted, in which one strip of land is cultivated and the adjoining strip lies fallow.

PRACTICALITIES
Transportation

Amtrak's Empire Builder, taking its name from James J. Hill's sobriquet, crosses northern Montana daily in each direction traveling between Chicago and the West Coast, with stops in Havre, Shelby, Cut Bank, and Browning. Call 800/872-7245 for more information. Five major airlines serve Great Falls, but beyond that, there's little other public transport. Notably, there is no longer bus service between Great Falls and Havre, or along I-15 to Canada.

Information

Travel Montana provides excellent free travel information. Most of the Hi-Line falls within their Russell Country division (P.O. Box 3166, Great Falls, MT 59403, 800/527-5348, www.russell.visitmt.com). Ask for a free travel guide of the region.

Great Falls and Vicinity

Solid, wholesome, and prosperous, Great Falls (pop. 56,690, elev. 3,333 feet) suffers if compared to Montana's more dynamic and cosmopolitan cities. It's the kind of uneventful place that feels like a good place to raise a family. The casual explorer who doesn't venture off the long bleak 10th Avenue South commercial strip may well think that there's little reason to stop for more than a fill-up and a soda.

Look again, though: To start with, there's rich Lewis and Clark history here, albeit mostly obliterated by the hydroelectric dams that now rope in the once-awesome Great Falls of the Missouri. There's also the Charles M. Russell Museum, and the unexpected: contemporary art at the Paris Gibson Museum.

The Sun River flows into the Missouri at 10th Avenue South in Great Falls. The Highwood, Little Belt, and Big Belt Mountains crop up to the east, southeast, and south of town, while the main spine of the Rockies runs 50 miles west. But the Missouri River has always defined Great Falls—the falls themselves, remembered in the city's name; the Giant Springs, which now nourish hatchery trout; and the riverside parks beckoning bicyclists and anglers.

HISTORY

When sheets of glacial ice covered the northern Montana plains 15,000 years ago, present-day Great Falls was under 600 feet of water. Ice dams backed up glacial Lake Great Falls between Great Falls and Cut Bank, spilling out into the Shonkin Sag. Blackfeet controlled the area when Lewis and Clark spent June 15 through July 15, 1805, negotiating the Great Falls of the Missouri, actually portaging 18 miles in 13 days. A grizzly bear chased Lewis into the Missouri at one point; he was also impressed that there were "not less than 10,000 buffalo in a circle of two miles."

Paris Gibson first visited the river-bend site of present-day Great Falls in 1880 and quickly set to building a city there. He conferred with James J. Hill, of the Great Northern Railway, and in 1887 the Montana Central Railroad was built through Great Falls, connecting the Great Northern line to the mining centers farther south.

The Anaconda Company came into town in 1908 and built a copper-reduction plant, powered by a dam on Black Eagle Falls. The cheap electricity generated by the Black Eagle Dam and the others that followed on other falls spurred Great Falls to an industrial economy early on, with attendant labor union and political imbroglios.

SIGHTS

Be warned that street addresses are a little confusing in Great Falls. Avenues run east-west, streets run north-south, and both are named almost exclusively with numbers. Central Avenue divides north from south; most of the city lies east of the Missouri River; streets west of the river wear a W as part of their names.

For an introduction to Great Falls sights, take a tour on the **Great Falls Historic Trolley** (406/771-1100, www.greatfallshistorictrolley.com). Two tours are available: an hour-long "City Tour" ($13 adults, $5 children 5–12), and a two-hour "History Tour" ($22 adults, $5 children 2–12). Tours originate at the Visitor Information Center, (15 Upper River Rd., daily June–Sept. and year-round by

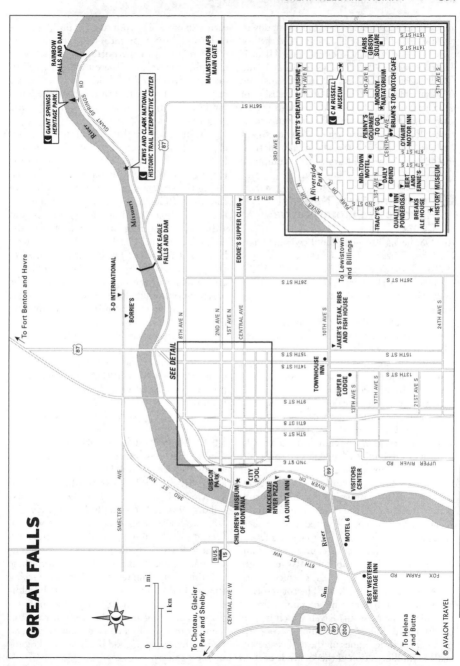

GREAT FALLS

To Choteau, Glacier Park, and Shelby

To Fort Benton and Havre

To Helena and Butte

To Lewistown and Billings

RAINBOW FALLS AND DAM

GIANT SPRINGS HERITAGE PARK

LEWIS AND CLARK NATIONAL HISTORIC TRAIL INTERPRETIVE CENTER

MALMSTROM AFB MAIN GATE

BLACK EAGLE FALLS AND DAM

3-D INTERNATIONAL

BORRIE'S

EDDIE'S SUPPER CLUB

SEE DETAIL

TOWNHOUSE INN

JAKER'S STEAK, RIBS AND FISH HOUSE

SUPER 8 LODGE

GIBSON PARK

CHILDREN'S MUSEUM OF MONTANA

CITY POOL

MACKENZIE RIVER PIZZA

LA QUINTA INN

VISITORS CENTER

MOTEL 6

BEST WESTERN HERITAGE INN

DANTE'S CREATIVE CUISINE

C M RUSSELL MUSEUM

PARIS GIBSON SQUARE

PENNY'S GOURMET TO GO

MORONY NATATORIUM

BRIAN'S TOP NOTCH CAFÉ

MID-TOWN MOTEL

O'HAIRE MOTOR INN

DAILY GRIND

TRACY'S

QUALITY INN PONDEROSA

BERT AND ERNIE'S

BREAKS ALE HOUSE

THE HISTORY MUSEUM

Riverside Park

Missouri River

Sun River

NORTH-CENTRAL MONTANA

0   1 mi
0   1 km

© AVALON TRAVEL

appointment). Both narrated tours visit downtown, the C. M. Russell Museum, and the historic homes district, while the longer Historic Tour adds on Giant Springs, the Lewis and Clark Interpretive Center, and Malmstrom Air Force Base. Call or check the website for departure times. The tour company also offers longer and more customized sightseeing tours through its sister organization **Tour de Great Falls** (same contact information); destinations include the Ulm Pishkum buffalo jump and specialized Lewis and Clark tours.

❰ Lewis and Clark National Historic Trail Interpretive Center

In 1998 the 5,500-square-foot Lewis and Clark National Historic Trail Interpretive Center (4201 Giant Springs Rd., 406/727-8733, www.fs.fed.us/r1/lewisclark/lcic, 9 A.M.–6 P.M. daily Memorial Day–Sept. 30, 9 A.M.–5 P.M. Tues.–Sat. and noon–5 P.M. Sun. Oct.–Memorial Day, $5 adult, children 15 and under free) opened on a cliff overlooking the Missouri's Great Falls. This $6 million facility instantly transformed Great Falls into a major Montana destination, giving the local tourist trade a badly needed focus.

The center doesn't break new ground for anyone who is already familiar with the Lewis and Clark Expedition, and the displays often seem a little cursory, given the complexity of the history involved, but it's a laudable enterprise just to *present* the complex issues represented by the Corps of Discovery: Enlightenment high ideals, American cultural imperialism (especially over Native Americans), the devastating extractive economic practices that followed, and the sheer catch-your-breath adventure, to name a few.

The exhibits follow the course of the journey, from St. Louis up the Missouri, into Montana, and to the Great Falls, which the explorers reached in June 1805. The corps spent a hellacious month portaging their boats around the falls of the Missouri River, which is lined by cliffs here. The two-story diorama of corps members pulling canoes up the cliff is an especially vivid illustration of the fortitude of these early explorers. Try your hand at pulling a specially weighted rope meant to reproduce the effort required in the portages, and let your thoughts marvel that these men—dressed in just moccasins and buckskins, and living on rations—had the strength to pull these boats for 18 miles, filled with a total of about a ton of gear.

The mazelike exhibits follow the expedition's journey across the Rockies, to the Pacific, and then back down the Missouri through Montana and back to St. Louis. Along the way, the center features a Mandan Indian earth lodge, a Shoshone Indian tepee, replicas of boats used by the expedition, and a display illustrating the difficulty of translating Lewis and Clark's English into local languages and back. The center does an especially good job of illustrating the contribution and cultures of the various Indian tribes the corps encountered along its route. A 158-seat theater shows a free 20-minute film covering the highlights of the expedition.

The interpretive center is located just off River Drive on Giant Springs Road, about three miles northeast of downtown Great Falls. From either Highway 87 or 10th Avenue South, just follow River Road west. If you're coming in from the east on Highway 200, turn north on the 57th Street bypass and follow the signs.

❰ C. M. Russell Museum

One of the finest museums in Montana, and a must-see for anyone interested in Western art, is the C. M. Russell Museum (400 13th St. N., 406/727-8787, www.cmrussell.org, 9 A.M.–5 P.M. daily May 1–Sept. 30, 10 A.M.–5 P.M. Tues.–Sat. and 1–5 P.M. Sun. Oct.–Apr., $9 adults, $7 seniors, $4 students). Charlie Russell's brilliant colors are astounding and complex—if you're familiar with these paintings only from reproductions, then seeing the original paintings is a real treat. In addition to Russell's own paintings, the museum displays painting and sculpture. The museum complex includes Russell's log-cabin studio and house; there's also a good bookshop and reproduction gallery.

The C.M. Russell Museum in Great Falls is a mandatory stop for anyone interested in Western art.

Paris Gibson Square Museum of Art

A few blocks from the Russell Museum, the Paris Gibson Square Museum of Art (1400 1st Ave. N., 406/727-8255, www.the-square.org, 10 A.M.–5 P.M. Mon.–Fri., 7–9 P.M. Tues., noon–5 P.M. Sat., free) mounts some surprisingly forward-thinking art exhibits housed in a handsome old school.

The History Museum

The Cascade County Historical Society administers the History Museum (422 2nd St. S., 406/452-3462, 10 A.M.–5 P.M. Tues.–Fri., $2 adults) is located in the High Plains Heritage Center. The museum, which has over 95,000 objects in its permanent collection, offers changing interpretive exhibits that tell the story of Central Montana with intriguing exhibits on Great Falls's early industrial history.

Children's Museum of Montana

The new Children's Museum of Montana

(22 Railroad Square, right behind the Civic Center, 406/452-6661, www.childrensmuseumofmt.org, 9:30 A.M.–5 P.M. Tues.–Sat. May–Sept., 9:30 A.M.–5 P.M. Wed.–Sat. and 9:30 A.M.–8 P.M. Thurs. Oct.–Apr., $3 for ages 2–60, $1 seniors, children 2 and under free) is just the thing if you're traveling with kids. Hands-on exhibits teach about Montana history and wildlife and feature science, math, and cultural activities, all while making sure kids are amused.

First Peoples Buffalo Jump State Park

Turn off I-15 at the Ulm exit, 15 miles south of Great Falls, and follow the state park signs six miles along good gravel roads to the buffalo jump, formerly called the Ulm Pishkun State Park. Tepee rings abound near the 30-foot-high buffalo jump, and there are supposed to be some pictographs there too. Poke around the base of the cliff for decaying buffalo bones, but wear boots to guard against the prickly pear and rattlesnakes, and don't carry off any souvenirs—the area is protected by the State Antiquities Act. The new visitors center (406/866-2217, 8 A.M.–6 P.M. daily Apr.–Sept., 10 A.M.–4 P.M. Wed.–Sat. and noon–4 P.M. Sun. Oct.–Mar.) is open year-round and does an excellent job of interpreting the past uses of the jump and how the Indians used the bison they slaughtered here. A prairie-dog town and picnic area share the *pishkun* site. Admission is $2 per person for non–Montana residents.

SPRINGS, RIVERS, AND DAMS

Everywhere you turn in Great Falls there's a park, and the pathway that links them all— the River's Edge Trail, a greenway along the Missouri and River Drive—is worth a special visit (see below under *Recreation*).

Giant Springs Heritage Park

The Giant Springs Heritage Park is three miles from downtown on River Road, and the Department of Fish, Wildlife, and Parks Visitor Center provides a vivid description of Lewis and Clark's portage of the falls, as

MISSILES ON THE PRAIRIE

Scattered among 23,000 acres of prairie surrounding Great Falls, tucked away in fields and meadows, are some 200 unremarkable enclosures of chain-link fencing and cement, more or less perfectly innocuous in appearance. But each of these facilities is home to a Minuteman intercontinental ballistic missile. Malmstrom Air Force Base in Great Falls is the headquarters for the Minuteman missiles.

The missiles were located in Montana for several reasons. Their fuel is sensitive to humidity, making the arid prairies a natural habitat. Also, the average elevation of 3,500 feet gives the missiles a head start, yielding a 6 percent fuel savings. And the fact that not many people live hereabouts probably didn't hurt either.

Each subterranean silo consists of an 80-foot-deep tube, launch equipment, and missile. The silo door *alone* weighs 108 tons. The launch facilities are controlled from a nearby underground chamber. Launch-control chambers have walls 4.5 feet thick and dangle in a 90-foot-deep pit, suspended by cables that allow the chamber to swing three feet in any direction.

Since the end of the Cold War, the Minutemen have been deactivated. Once staffed 24 hours a day in readiness for enemy attack, the sites now slumber, awaiting the arrival of another strategic threat. A flick of a switch would bring the system back to full readiness.

well as information and exhibits on fishing and hunting.

Giant Springs, a gushing natural spring that captured the attention of Lewis and Clark, is part of the Giant Springs Heritage Park. The genesis of this 134,000-gallon-per-minute fountain is in the Little Belt Mountains southeast of Great Falls. Exposed Madison limestone absorbs mountain snowmelt and rain, which then drains and flows underground through fissures to Great Falls, where it surges up and spews into the Missouri River. The mineral-rich water has proved to be a good fish-breeding medium, and there's a trout hatchery a stone's throw away from the springs. This is an enchanting place to picnic or just relax amid leafy lawns and the sounds of rushing water.

Black Eagle and Rainbow Dams

Downstream from the springs are overlooks onto the dams that harness Black Eagle and Rainbow Falls. Both of these dams have preserved the essential nature of the waterfalls. From the roadside overlook, look across the Missouri to the town of **Black Eagle,** a company town that was built up around the beginning of the 20th century to serve the copper-reduction works.

Ryan Dam

Head north on Highway 87 to visit the Ryan Dam, which marks the site of the Great Falls of the Missouri, described by Meriwether Lewis as "the grandest sight I ever beheld," with its roily cascades, foamy spray, and spiky rock projections.

Wildlife Viewing

Twelve miles north of town on Highway 87, the 12,300-acre **Benton Lake Wildlife Refuge** harbors nearly 200 bird species, including shorebirds, snow geese, tundra swans, burrowing and short-eared owls, and mammals such as rabbits, deer, and long-tailed weasels. Open to visitors April 1–October 31 during the daytime.

RECREATION

Bike or jog along the Missouri River on the **River's Edge Trail,** stretching from the 10th Avenue Bridge to Giant Springs Heritage State Park and past Crooked Falls. This rails-to-trails path has more than 13 miles of paved pathway and an additional 17 miles of single-track trail suitable for hiking or mountain biking. The River's Edge Trail is a great recreational asset to the city and a good place for travelers to take in both the urban and natural history of the area.

Swim outdoors (or take one of the waterslides) at **Electric City Water Park** (406/771-1265 1 A.M.–8 P.M. Mon.–Fri., 11 A.M.–6 P.M. Sat.–Sun., early June–Labor Day), just south of the 1st Avenue Bridge on River Drive. The city has also installed a Flow Rider, which lets hearty souls boogie-board the artificial waves. Kids will enjoy the state's largest children's water-play structure. Admission to the pool is $3 for adults, $2 for children ages 3–17, with addition charges for the waterslides and wave pool. Serious lap swimmers may prefer the beautifully named, carefully maintained **Morony Natatorium** (12th St. N. and 1st Ave. N.).

The Great Falls **Voyagers** are the Pioneer League farm team of the Chicago White Sox. Minor-league baseball fans can catch them throughout the summer at Centene Stadium. Call 406/452-5311 for schedule and ticket information.

The **Eagle Falls Golf Club** is a busy 18-hole public course on River Road next door to Legion Park. Across the river in Black Eagle, the **Anaconda Hills Golf Course** has recently expanded to 18 holes.

ACCOMMODATIONS

Great Falls lodgings are found basically in two areas. Several older, well-maintained hotels and motels are downtown and provide the best value for money, while along the 10th Avenue strip, amid the casinos, car lots, and malls, you'll find many inexpensive older motels, as well as several newer motel complexes. All of the usual chain hotels have properties along 10th Avenue South. On all but the busiest weekends, you'll have no trouble finding a room without reservations. Just remember that most of 10th Avenue South is a busy six-lane highway.

$50-75

Downtown, the pleasant **Mid-Town Motel** (526 2nd Ave. N., 406/453-2411 or 800/457-2411, $54 and up) has clean and simple rooms, a favorite locals' restaurant, and a bakery on-site, and accepts pets.

The **O'Haire Motor Inn** (17 7th St. S., 406/454-2141 or 800/332-9819, $72 and up) features an indoor pool, restaurant, and indoor parking. Some two-bedroom suites are available. The O'Haire's **Sip 'N' Dip** lounge was named by *Condé Nast Traveler* as one of the world's top watering holes—the authentic Tiki bar shares a glass wall with the hotel's swimming pool, affording drinkers a voyeuristic view onto the underwater frolics of the swimmers.

The **Quality Inn Ponderosa** (220 Central Ave., 406/761-3410 or 877/424-6423, $74), the new name for downtown's longtime Ponderosa Inn, has an outdoor pool, sauna, restaurant, lounge, and casino; microwaves and refrigerators are included in all rooms. Small dogs are permitted.

Out on 10th Ave. S., **Motel 6** (2 Treasure State Dr., near I-15 and 10th Ave. S., 406/453-1602 or 800/362-4842, $67 and up) is next door to restaurants and a casino.

$75-100

The **Super 8 Lodge** (1214 13th St. S., 406/727-7600, $78 and up) sits back off the 10th Avenue South strip and offers a continental breakfast. This is a good midprice choice.

The **Town House Inn** (1411 10th Ave. S., 406/761-4600 or 800/442-4667, $95 and up) has stylish rooms (including some that are in effect efficiency apartments), plus a casino, pool, sauna, hot tub, and restaurant. The Town House is near Holiday Village Mall, the area's largest shopping center.

$100 and Up

The **Best Western Heritage Inn** (1700 Fox Farm Rd., 406/761-1900 or 800/548-8256, from $119) is 0.25 mile off the highway and is the city's largest hotel. The recreational facilities are noteworthy, with two indoor pools, hot tubs, saunas, and a game room. Also on-site is a restaurant and a lounge/casino. Rooms are nicely furnished; executive suites with kitchenettes are available.

Great Falls's newest hotel occupies a lovely spot right on the Missouri River, a few blocks south of downtown. The **La Quinta Inn**

and Suites (600 River Dr. S., 406/761-2600 or 800/531-5900, from $129) is faced with stone and logs and offers great views west toward the distant Rockies. Rooms are large and nicely furnished; facilities include an indoor pool and sauna. Continental breakfast is included in room rates.

FOOD

Order breakfast 24 hours a day at **Tracy's** (127 Central Ave., 406/453-6108), a Great Falls institution. Another favorite spot for an old-fashioned and bountiful breakfast is **Brian's Top Notch Café** (718 Central Ave., 406/727-4255, 7 A.M.–3 P.M.).

   Penny's Gourmet to Go (815 Central Ave., 406/453-7070) is the storefront end of a catering business, offering soups, sandwiches, pasta, and salads at lunchtime. You can choose to eat in or take out.

   At night downtown, dining choices are limited. **Bert and Ernie's** (300 1st Ave. S., 406/453-0601, 11 A.M.–10 P.M. Mon.–Sat.) offers burgers, pastas, light entrées, and regional microbrews in an old brick storefront. **Ristorante Portofino** (220 Central Ave., 406/453-7186) has excellent Italian pasta and meats, with entrées ranging $8–15. **Dante's Creative Cuisine** (1325 8th Ave. N., 406/453-9599, 11 A.M.–10 P.M. Mon.–Sat., 2–10 P.M. Sun., $15–29) is Great Falls's current hot spot for stylish international cooking. In addition to steaks and seafood, Dante's specializes in creative Italian, Mexican, and Southwestern cooking. The **Breaks Ale House and Grill** (202 2nd St. S., 406/453-5980, 11:30 A.M.–9:30 P.M. Mon.–Thurs., 11:30 A.M.–10 P.M. Fri.–Sat., main courses $9–24) is a brewpub within a redbrick former warehouse that has been updated with plenty of industrial chic. The food here is very good, with buffalo short ribs, sandwiches, salmon crepes, and good homemade soups.

   A few blocks south of downtown, right along the Missouri River, is the **Mackenzie River Pizza Company** (500 River Dr. S., 406/761-0085, 11 A.M.–10 P.M. daily), with gourmet pizza, burgers, and sandwiches.

Traditional Great Falls Restaurants

Great Falls's unflappable sense of tradition extends to its favorite restaurants. For generations, two restaurants in Black Eagle, the old union town located on the north bank of the Missouri, have served up old-fashioned ethnic fare with high-minded zeal; full meals at both places range $15–28. At **Borrie's** (1800 Smelter Ave., 406/761-0300, 5–10 P.M. nightly), the menu leads with massive servings of Montana steaks and traditional Italian pastas laden with the hearty sauces of our immigrant forebears. At **3-D International** (1825 Smelter Ave., 406/453-6561, 11 A.M.–2 P.M. Mon.–Fri., 5–10 P.M. nightly), ethnic ecumenicism is practiced, with half the menu devoted to Asian food and half to traditional Italian. The menus at Borrie's and 3-D International say a lot about the early labor currents in industrial Great Falls, and besides that, the food is quite good. Because they are considered the best restaurants in the city by longtime residents, you'll need reservations to get in the door. There aren't many restaurants like these left, so do go.

   Otherwise, Great Falls has steaks, steaks, and steaks to offer the evening diner. **Jaker's Steak, Ribs, and Fish House** (1500 10th Ave., 406/727-1033, 11:30 A.M.–2:30 P.M. and 5–10 P.M. Mon.–Thurs., 11:30 A.M.–2:30 P.M. and 5–10:30 P.M. Fri., 5–10:30 P.M. Sat., 5–9 P.M. Sun., main courses $10–25) just about says it all, except that the place is also a casino. Not as fancy, **Eddie's Supper Club** (3725 2nd Ave. N., 406/453-1616, dinner only Mon.–Sat.) has been the steakhouse choice for meat lovers since 1944: More care is taken in the kitchen than on stylish redecoration. Expect cracked red vinyl booths, equestrian decor, and "cowboy-style steaks" ($15–28), which means fire-charred and enormous. If you're up to a short drive, head out to the **Bar-S Supper Club** (five miles east of Great Falls on Hwy. 200, 406/761-9550, 5–9 P.M. Wed.–Thurs., 5–10 P.M. Fri.–Sat., and 4–9 P.M. Sun., $15–25). Again, don't let appearances deceive. This venerable roadhouse has been serving magnificent steaks for years.

EVENTS

The **C. M. Russell Auction of Original Western Art** is an annual March event benefiting the C. M. Russell Museum, and bidders descend from all over the country to participate. Contact the museum at 406/727-8787 for details.

With tons of Lewis and Clark history in the area, it's natural for Great Falls to host the **Lewis and Clark Festival** (P.O. Box 2848, Great Falls, MT 59403, 406/452-5661, www.lewis-clarkia.com) in late June or early July. Frontier cooking, flintlock demonstrations, and fire-making are some of the things you'll see at the living-history encampment at Giant Springs State Park, where actors and docents in period dress recreate the daily life of the expedition's soldiers. Mini float trips and longer dinner float trips down the Missouri take in some of the river's historic sites, while other guided tours visit more out-of-the-way Lewis and Clark and naturalist destinations. Other festival events include dramatic readings, academic lectures on the Corps of Discovery, children's events, a buffalo barbecue, and a Western art show and sale. This is quickly becoming a major event in Great Falls. Many of the events are free.

Beginning the last Saturday of July and lasting eight days, the **Montana State Fair** (www.montanastatefair.com) takes over the town and the fairgrounds, located just west of downtown across the Missouri. Throughout the summer, the fairgrounds also host **horse races.**

INFORMATION AND SERVICES

The **Great Falls Chamber of Commerce** is at 710 1st Avenue North (406/761-4434, www.greatfallschamber.org). The **visitors center** is located just east of the 10th Avenue Bridge, beneath the "big flag" on Upper River Road.

The **public library** is at 301 2nd Avenue North (406/453-0349). Listen to **Montana Public Radio** at 89.9 FM.

Transportation

Southwest of town, **Great Falls International Airport,** the region's largest, is served by major airlines.

Rimrock Stage buses stop at 326 1st Avenue South.

Great Falls Transit System (406/727-0382) runs buses in and around town. Hail a **Diamond Cab** by calling 406/453-3241.

Fort Benton and Big Sag Country

East of Great Falls, the Rockies fade from view, the buttes and peaks of central Montana loom, and the Missouri leaves its wide valley to plunge into a badlands gorge. This transitional landscape between the prairies of eastern Montana and the foothills of the Rockies contains some of the most interesting history, geology, and scenery in the state. Here too are seldom-visited back roads leading to pleasant isolated towns like Highwood, Stockett, and Eden.

The region is also home to the oldest town in Montana—**Fort Benton.** Steamboats from St. Louis docked here in the 1840s (it was known as "the innermost port"), making it the stepping-off point for thousands of settlers and their chattel.

THE BIG SAG AREA

For travelers who like side roads and exploring the oddities of geology, there's no better detour than the byways of the Big Sag, or as it's more officially called, the Shonkin Sag. Part of this route is on unpaved roads, but except in extremely wet weather, these graded gravel roads present no challenges for cars and low-clearance vehicles.

The Shonkin Sag

Geologically speaking, relatively recent events created the distinctive landscapes of the Big Sag area. About 20 million years after the Rockies formed, a vast surge of volcanic activity forced molten rock to the surface in many parts of central Montana. Not all lava erupted;

some molten rock squeezed up through fissures and faults or fed into underground reservoirs, called laccoliths. Erosion has exposed these formations—steep vertical ridges of volcanic stone, called dikes, running in straight lines across the landscape. One of the most prominent laccoliths in Montana, Square Butte, rises spectacularly from the plains near Geraldine.

Edging down from the north, ice age glaciers reached the Great Falls area and then stopped. The leading edge of the glaciers trapped river flow from Missouri River tributaries that were south of the ice sheets and that would have normally flowed north and east along the ancestral Missouri drainage. Even though this was the ice age, the leading edge of the glacial advance saw seasonal thawing, which also created lots of fresh water. The result was the glacial Lake Great Falls, a reservoir created by the blockage of normal river drainage systems by ice-age glaciers. About 15,000 years ago, the present site of Great Falls was flooded by 600 feet of meltwater; water stretched from the Highwood Mountains to the Rocky Mountain foothills. As the lake grew and the glaciers receded, this vast body of water eventually cut a new spillway. About 10,000 years ago, the overflow of Lake Great Falls began to course through this channel, until the melting glaciers revealed a lower watercourse. The glacial lake spillway, called the Shonkin Sag by geologists and the Big Sag by locals, remains a deep U-shaped valley, 500 feet deep and one mile wide, along the base of the Highwood Mountains and Square Butte. All that's left of the huge river that once flowed here are the awesome canyon that it cut and a few shallow lakes.

Today, the Shonkin Sag is home to the small community of **Highwood** and scattered farms and ranches. To reach the Shonkin Sag, follow Highway 228 east from Great Falls or Highway 331 north from Belt. Highwood sits at the mouth of the sag. From here, gravel roads continue on to Geraldine or Fort Benton—both are well-signed and in good condition.

The more scenic choice is the Geraldine road. It continues up the Shonkin Sag to the little crossroads of Shonkin, then cuts south into a steep valley in the Highwood Mountains. The road leaves the mountains and again crosses the Shonkin Sag; Square Butte looms to the south across several marshy lakes, and a spiky palisade of igneous rock (a volcanic dike) marches across the valley. The county road ends at Geraldine and Highway 80. The landscape is curiously spare and beautiful. This is one of the most compelling side trips in the state.

Shonkin Sag continues southeast, following Highway 80 past Square Butte. Then it turns abruptly north, with tiny Arrow Creek borrowing the Missouri's ancient riverbed for a short and uneventful journey northward. Prominent white cliffs cap the ridges east of Square Butte. To the north, the Missouri is flowing through a canyon cut through the same formation. Lewis and Clark were much taken by the white cliffs along the Missouri, calling them "seens of visionary inchantment."

Travelers unable to make the full circuit around the Big Sag can get a taste of the landscape by taking a shorter side trip to Stockett, south of Great Falls. Before the last ice age began, the Missouri flowed in a channel slightly south of its present flow. The little towns of Sand Coulee and Stockett are nestled in the round-bottomed valley that was left when the Missouri abandoned this channel. To reach Stockett, follow Highway 227 south from the outskirts of Great Falls. Off-road enthusiasts can follow gravel roads through gently rolling landscapes, with great views onto the Rocky Mountain Front and the central Montana mountains, by continuing on to Eden, the Smith River valley, and Ulm.

Highwood Mountains

The Highwood Mountains are the deeply eroded remnants of isolated volcanoes that erupted about 50 million years ago. Although not tall (Highwood Baldy reaches 7,625 feet), these old craters host good trout streams. Like the other ranges of central Montana, the Highwoods don't overwhelm the traveler with size or severity. More meadow than peak, they are islands of green in a sea of grain fields. The Forest Service maintains a popular **campground** on Thain Creek.

Away from the main cluster of peaks, a series of isolated buttes marches to the east. While explosive volcanic events formed the Highwoods, unerupted pools of magma are responsible for these symmetrical but craggy peaks.

The most notable of these lava formations are **Round Butte** and **Square Butte,** east of the Highwoods. The unusual magma that formed these extrusions is a dark crystal-flecked rock called shonkinite, rare enough to be named after the central Montana area where it occurs in abundance. As the pools of shonkinite cooled underground millions of years ago, a lighter igneous rock floated to the top of the laccolith, like cream on milk. Called syenite, it's much lighter in color than shonkinite and forms the startlingly white cap on Square Butte.

(Square Butte Natural Area

The Square Butte Natural Area is a 2,000-acre preserve along the butte's high plateau and peaks, 2,400 feet above the prairies. Maintained by the Bureau of Land Management, this is one of the most unusual destinations in Montana. The steep sides of the butte have protected the native grasses and plants from overgrazing; Lewis and Clark saw such stands of grasses when they crossed the prairies 200 years ago. In a good year the plants reach waist level. Some varieties here are no longer found on rangeland. The wildflower display in May and June is astonishing, and deer, pronghorn, and birds are abundant.

The views are also spectacular. The core of the laccolith rises hundreds of feet above the plateau in cliffs and ridges of shonkinite and syenite. The Shonkin Sag runs along the north side of Square Butte (look for the escarpment of an ancient waterfall in the watercourse). Here, as at few other places, one can truly grasp the expanse of the plains. The mountains of central Montana perforate the otherwise limitless prairie horizon stretching outward for hundreds of miles.

Although ascending to the Square Butte Plateau is relatively easy (given a high-clearance vehicle and a little chutzpah), getting to the top of the volcanic plug requires a rigorous scramble up rough terrain. Square Butte is much more rugged than it looks from a distance. Don't attempt to climb it alone, and don't feel as if you have to. Heroism isn't required to enjoy the plant and animal life; a good picnic will do just as well.

Square Butte is accessible only through private land. The landowners ask that you check in with them before starting up the butte (usually this just means signing in at the parking area). The road is a four-wheel-drive track, and although adequately maintained, it is quite rocky. Cars with narrower axles than pickup trucks will need to straddle the tracks, as the trademark shonkinite can easily puncture the oil pan of a low-bellied car. Although a high-clearance vehicle is preferable for this road, at least one Honda Accord has made it up and back.

To reach Square Butte Natural Area, turn at the community of Square Butte and follow the signs. The road passes through a ranch yard. From here the top of the plateau is about three miles.

Accommodations and Food

The Big Sag area is within easy driving distance of Great Falls, Lewistown, Stanford, and Fort Benton, each of which offers a full range of lodgings and amenities. To reach **Thain Creek Campground,** follow road signs for Highwood from Highway 200, then turn up Highwood Creek for 18 miles on a good gravel road.

(FORT BENTON

Once the bustling head of Missouri River navigation, Fort Benton (pop. 1,654, elev. 2,600 feet) is now a quiet, even sleepy, town. When the fur trade boomed, steamboats struggled up the narrow sandbar-filled waters of the Missouri to discharge fortune-seeking trappers and prospectors and load up with furs. The Great Falls of the Missouri, 25 miles upstream, barred river travel farther upstream.

Fort Benton was built in 1846 and served primarily as a fur-trading post. By 1859 the

© BILL MCRAE

In Fort Benton, a statue commemorates Shep, a devoted sheepdog.

Mullan Road linked Fort Benton with Walla Walla, Washington, the easternmost outpost on the Columbia River system. The Whoop-up Trail led from Fort Benton to Alberta and was used to supply western Canada with illegal Indian whiskey. Incongruously, the fort was also a supply depot for Canadian Mounties charged with bringing order to the wild whiskey-sodden western territories.

Of the trading forts built in mid-19th-century Montana, only Fort Benton survives as a town today. History is well-displayed in Fort Benton's long green riverside park. And the Missouri River still flows by, as wide and muddy as ever, headed for an area that's still barely touched by roads.

Sights

The **Fort Benton Heritage Complex** (20th and Washington, 406/622-5316, 10 A.M.–5 P.M. Mon.–Sat., noon–5 P.M. Sun., mid-May–late Sept., $10 adults, $1 children under 12) is the overall name given to a multiblock complex that features the Museum of the Northern

Great Plains, the Museum of the Upper Missouri, a homestead village, the Upper Missouri River Breaks National Monument Interpretive Center, and historic archives with fantastic photos of Fort Benton in its heyday. One admission price gets you into all these sites plus tours of the restored old Fort Benton, which has largely been rebuilt by volunteers to resemble the original 30,000-square-foot trading post from the 1860s.

Walk down the river levee to find a statue of Lewis, Clark, and Sacagawea, sculpted by artist Bob Scriver from Browning, Montana; a keelboat replica built in the early 1950s for the movie *The Big Sky*; and the 15th Street Bridge, which has spanned the Missouri since 1888. Historical signs along the grassy riverside strip discuss riverboats, the fur trade, and wild times in the streets of 19th-century Fort Benton.

Facing the river at 1718 Front Street, the **Wild and Scenic Upper Missouri Visitor Center** has wildlife and archaeological exhibits and a Lewis and Clark slide show.

Among the town's historic buildings, the **Grand Union Hotel** (1302 Front St.) stands out. It was indeed grand when it was built in 1882—just as the railroad was poised to eclipse the steamboat as a means of transportation. The hotel has been magnificently refurbished and has reopened to overnight guests.

In front of the hotel is a bronze statue of **Shep,** Fort Benton's most famous canine denizen and an object of near-obsessive veneration for some (a Web search reveals some surprising websites). Shep was the faithful workmate of a local sheepherder. The herder died, and his body was ferried away by rail. Shep, however, kept vigil. The dog met every train into town for over five years. Shep's story became known across the country, and he became the darling of travelers and locals alike. However, Shep was eventually run over by a train and buried on a hill overlooking the depot. Read his story and weep.

Accommodations

$50-75: You may drive right by the **Pioneer Lodge** (1700 Front St., 406/622-5441, $55 and

SIGHTS ALONG THE MISSOURI

Downriver from Virgelle, the Wild and Scenic Missouri River passes beneath the White Cliffs, escarpments of white limestone looming above the river. Passing through the limestone are dikes of volcanic rock radiating from mountain ranges in central Montana.

Erosion has dealt harshly but creatively with these formations, incising them into landmarks for river travelers. The White Cliffs are often compared to the fortifications of ruined cities, with isolated towers and spires emerging in bas-relief from the canyon. Imaginative minds have accorded the formations fanciful names: Eye of the Needle, Citadel Rock, Steamboat Rock, Hole in the Wall.

Once past the PN Bridge, the river enters the Missouri Breaks. Here in a badlands gorge hemmed by outcrops of sandstone, erosion has segregated colorful but barren gumbo soil into buttes, bluffs, and canyons. Gangs of rustlers menaced early stockmen from these inaccessible ravines. Today, the fringe of pine and juniper shelters elk, deer, mountain sheep, and birds of prey.

In 1805, Lewis and Clark paddled upriver along this same expanse of the Missouri River. The beauty and monumentality of the canyon overwhelmed them. No self-respecting travel writer would dare attempt to match Meriwether Lewis's elegiac prose (or his spelling):

May 31st, 1805: The hills and river Clifts which we passed today exhibit a most romantic appearence. The water in the course of time has trickled down the soft sand clifts and woarn it into a thousand grotesque figures, which with the help of a little immagination and an oblique view are made to represent eligant ranges of lofty freestone buildings, having their parapets well stocked with statuary; columns of various sculpture both groved and plain, in other places with the help of less immagination we see the remains or ruins of eligant buildings; some collumns standing and almost entire with their pedestals and capitals; As we passed on it seemed as if those seens of visionary inchantment would never have an end; for here it is too that nature present to the view of the traveler vast ranges of walls of tolerable workmanship.

up) the first pass through, and maybe even the second time. The building used to be a general store. The rooms are comfortable and full of character, and they have TVs but no telephones.

Over $100: The ☾ **Grand Union Hotel** (704 14th Ave., 406/622-1882 or 888/838-1882, www.grandunionhotel.com) reopened as a lodging in late 1998. When it was built in 1882, the resplendent Grand Union was probably the finest hotel in the entire Montana territory. This beautiful Historic Register building adds a real touch of class to any stay in Fort Benton. Rooms are beautifully refurbished with tasteful period decor, and the restaurant serves perhaps the best meals in central Montana. In addition to standard guest rooms ($100–130), the hotel also offers suites with private sitting rooms ($130–180).

Camping

RV campers can pull up and spend the night for free in the city park, but there are no amenities. Tent campers are *not* encouraged to do the same.

Food

Bob's Riverfront Restaurant (1414 Front St., 406/622-3443, 6 A.M.–9 P.M., main courses $12–18) is the spot for a casual meal, with homemade pies, breads, and barbecue sauce, plus local Angus beef.

☾ **The Union Grille,** in the beautiful dining room at the Grand Union Hotel (406/622-1882, 5–9 P.M. Tues.–Sun. summer, 5–9 P.M. Wed.–Sun. winter, entrées $19–29), serves an eclectic regional menu with such dishes as roast chicken with huckleberry sauce, local trout crusted with pine nuts and citrus, and buffalo New York strip steak with truffled Lyonnaise potatoes. Outdoor riverside seating is available.

Information and Services

Contact the **Fort Benton Chamber of Commerce** (1500 Front St., 406/622-3864, www.fortbenton.com) for more information.

◖ UPPER MISSOURI RIVER BREAKS NATIONAL MONUMENT

East of Great Falls, the Missouri River leaves its valley and begins to cut through the prairie surface. In 1976 the sluggish river and the deep canyon it cuts were designated a Wild and Scenic River; 149 miles of river and 131,840 acres of adjacent land are preserved much as Lewis and Clark encountered them. Today, this makes for one of the great float trips in the nation, with tons of wildlife viewing enhancing the historic and scenic value of this last remnant of free-flowing Missouri River.

The Land

The austere gorge cut by the Missouri between Fort Benton and Fort Peck Dam is a relatively recent accomplishment. Until the most recent ice ages, the Missouri flowed north from this point until it debouched into Hudson's Bay. But when ice sheets blocked that outlet, huge ice-age dams, filled with the Missouri's flow and glacial melt, spilled over the plains. Almost surreptitiously the Missouri began to flow along the southernmost face of the glaciers, slowly cutting a new series of east-flowing channels all the way to the Mississippi. When the ice sheets began their last retreat 10,000 years ago, the Missouri remained in this new channel.

The precipitous and highly eroded walls of much of the Wild and Scenic Missouri's canyon are known locally as breaks or badlands. These strata, sedimentary remains of ancient seas, began to wash up in eastern Montana 80 million years ago. The 1,000-foot-deep gorge cuts through most of this geologic history. Erosion has isolated monoliths of sandstone, craggy outbursts of rock, and sheer cliffs of startlingly white limestone.

The soils are extremely infertile—rich in alkali and salt, they support little plant life except for occasional junipers and ponderosa pines. Along the river, however, there are beautiful groves of shade-giving cottonwoods. In its lower reaches, the Wild and Scenic Missouri merges with the C. M. Russell National Wildlife Refuge. Here elk, bighorn sheep, deer, beavers, mink, coyotes, and birds in abundance live along the riverbanks.

Exploring the Wild and Scenic Missouri by Boat

Only one road crosses the Missouri between Fort Benton and the Fred Robinson Bridge, north of Grassrange, 150 miles away. Only remote ranch-access dirt roads even come close to it. Without any doubt, the best way to see the Wild and Scenic Missouri is by boat. A float trip on the Missouri takes two forms: a trip with a guide and outfitter, or a well-planned float on your own. Each has its advantages.

While a traveler's independent streak might initially value a go-it-alone attitude, consider the following: There are no towns along the river, no shops, no restaurants, and no motels. You have to bring your own water—even boiled, the water of the Missouri, while potable, is far too muddy to be appealing for drinking. Portable toilets are now mandatory. There are no telephones or ambulances waiting if accidents occur (actually, heat stroke and sunburn are the greatest dangers). The Missouri is not a fast shoot-the-rapids river; it takes seven days to float all the way from Fort Benton to the Fred Robinson Bridge. When it's all over, you still have to get back to your vehicle, several hundred road miles back upstream.

If you do decide to float on your own, remember to sign in at the Bureau of Land Management visitors center in Fort Benton before putting in to the river. The stretch of the Missouri between Fort Benton and Loma is an easy one-day trip and is the most heavily used segment of the Wild and Scenic Missouri. For more information, contact the **Bureau of Land Management River**

Manager (Airport Rd., Lewistown, 406/538-7461, www.blm.gov/mt/st/en/fo/lewistown_field_office/UM.htm). During the summer, the BLM maintains an office at 1718 Front Street in Fort Benton (877/256-3252).

Outfitters

The following outfitters are among the best for guided trips on the Missouri. Each offers different packages involving trips of varying lengths (a minimum number of floaters is also usually required), and both rent canoes. Expect to pay $200–325 per person per day for completely guided and outfitted trips. Outfitted trips (they supply the canoe and food, but no guide) are roughly $175 per day. Canoe rentals are roughly $40 per day. The BLM provides a complete list of permit-holding outfitters on its website (see above).

Missouri River Outfitters (P.O. Box 762, Fort Benton, MT 59442, 866/282-3295, www.mroutfitters.com) was one of the first to offer trips down the Missouri; this company has been in business for more than 35 years. There are several choices of destinations, and depending on your schedule and interests, you'll choose either a three-, four-, or six-day trip. The outfitters provide all food, wall tents, cots, and camping gear, and you'll be expected to bring appropriate clothing. This outfitter also operates a canoe and kayak rental service for those who wish to plan their own trip.

Missouri River Canoe Company (Box 50, H.C. 67, Loma, MT 59460, 406/378-3110 or 800/426-2926, www.canoemontana.com) is a unique operation based out of the almost ghost town of Virgelle, once a railhead for Missouri River traffic. The old general store is now an antique store and the headquarters for this canoe outfitting and rental operation. The four boarding rooms above the store plus six homesteaders' shacks and a sheep wagon scattered around the old town site are offered to canoe clients on a B&B basis. As you might guess, any B&B operated by an antiques dealer is well-done and beautifully authentic; the as-was homesteaders' homes are especially evocative of bygone days.

Canoe trips are available in three forms.

Guided and outfitted trips range 1–12 days, including all transportation, food, and gear except a sleeping bag and personal effects. Outfitted but unguided trips are also available, including canoes, food, camp gear, and shuttle. Simple canoe rentals are also available. Bed-and-breakfast rates are $115; rustic cabins without breakfast begin at $45.

Exploring the Wild and Scenic Missouri by Car

While there's no substitute for a float trip down the Missouri, travelers who are on a tight schedule or fearful of water retain interesting options. On this section of the Missouri, only one gravel road bridges the river; other less-traveled roads cross the river on ferries.

The **Missouri River ferries** are among the last river ferries in the country. Licensed by the U.S. Coast Guard, these cable-drawn ferries connect obscure county roads for ranchers and farmers who live in this lonesome stretch of Montana.

The ferries are free during the day; simply pull up to the landing and drive onto the small plank barge. If the ferry is on the other side, the operator will cross to pick you up. If there is no sign of life, honk your horn. Out of consideration, plan to use the ferries within normal waking hours (also, there's sometimes a fee for late-night crossings). The ferries normally operate April to Thanksgiving; the rest of the year the river freezes over.

Ferries operate at Carter, Virgelle, and Stafford. The Carter Ferry links up with a network of country dirt roads in the Fort Benton–Highwood area, making a loop trip easy (if dusty).

Loma is where the Marias River flows into the Missouri. In 1805, when Lewis and Clark were traveling up the Missouri to its headwaters, they spent several puzzling days camped at the confluence. Their Mandan informants had not mentioned this particular river coming in from the north, and most of the men in the party believed that this large river was actually the main stream of the Missouri. (If you wonder how the Corps of Discovery could have been so flummoxed by so small a river as the Marias, remember that it was once much larger and is now impounded for irrigation by Tiber Dam.) Lewis, and eventually Clark, thought otherwise, and led the corps south, along what really was the Missouri. The mouth of the Marias became the site of **Fort Piegan,** established in 1831 for trade with the Blackfeet.

Downstream from Virgelle is the most scenic portion of the Missouri Breaks; **Coal Banks Landing State Recreation Area** is a popular departure point for float trips. From cars, the landscapes are dramatic, but there is no road access to the nearby White Cliffs area along the river.

The **Stafford (or McClelland) Ferry** is the most remote of the Missouri River ferries, linking dirt roads north of Winifred with a gravel road south of Chinook. It's a long road—about 80 miles—but it passes through breathtaking badlands, along the trail of Chief Joseph's last flight and battle, and through the lonesome and lovely Bear Paw Mountains. It's countryside not often seen by travelers. Note, however, that you should *not* attempt to drive on this road if rain threatens.

There's a bridge now at the site of the old Northern Pacific Ferry, at the juncture of the Judith River and the Missouri. The Judith adds its deep valley to the Missouri's gorge, making this a precipitous confluence. It's easily reached north of Winifred or south of Big Sandy by good all-weather gravel roads.

Practicalities

There aren't many lodging options in this remote stretch of badlands. You can call and ask for one of the charmingly authentic rooms at the 🄲 **Virgelle Mercantile,** now operated by **Missouri River Canoe Company** (406/378-3110), although their canoe clientele have first dibs. They offer a variety of lodgings—including homesteaders' homes, pioneer hotel rooms, and sheep wagons—that are some of the most unique accommodations in Montana. (See *Outfitters* above for more information.)

Otherwise, the closest lodgings are in Fort Benton and Big Sandy. Great Falls and Havre are close enough to serve as bases for day trips.

There are undeveloped campgrounds at the ranger stations at **Coal Banks Landing** near Virgelle and at Judith Landing north of Winifred.

The Hi-Line

More than any other part of Montana, this is the country the railroad built. James J. Hill, head of the Great Northern Railway, mounted an aggressive campaign to bring European immigrants to the Hi-Line—by train, of course. Towns named Zurich, Malta, Inverness, and Kremlin were supposed to welcome Europeans.

Today, this is the Montana known by Amtrak passengers, wheat farmers, and few others. Almost nobody comes here on vacation, unless it's to help their parents out with the harvest. Glacier National Park–bound Easterners zip past the grain elevators and filling stations, seldom turning from Highway 2 to explore the old downtowns.

However, the area does warrant a second glance. **Havre** offers tours of its "underground" city and its Native American buffalo jump are definitely worth taking in, and the Bear Paw Battleground has been elevated to National Monument status, with a visitors center and better facilities hopefully on the way. Other small grain-belt towns like **Chinook, Chester, Shelby,** and **Conrad** offer basic facilities for the traveler.

HAVRE

You wouldn't know it by the pronunciation, but Havre (HAV-er, pop. 9,621, elev. 4,167 feet) takes its name from the French city Le Havre. Originally it was called Bull Hook Siding, but James J. Hill pleaded for a name befitting the dignity of a Great Northern town. The locals complied, because Hill was ensuring the town's prosperity by making it a railway division point.

Raucous boom times came to town with the railroad and with cowboys in the 1890s. Gambling and prostitution both swelled to legendary proportions, some of which took place "underground" in Havre's below-street-level carousing and shopping district. By 1910 homesteaders were piling into the land office at Havre to claim their 160-acre plots. They were, as a whole, a much more serious bunch than the railroad workers, cowboys, bartenders, card sharks, and whores who had gathered around Hill's esteemed division point, but Havre did its best to resist the new morality imposed by farmers and prohibitionists.

Traces of this heritage linger in the drive-up bars and the gambling joints that are still thriving in downtown Havre. And why Havre's high school teams are called the Blue Ponies is anyone's guess.

🄲 Havre Historical Underground Tours

A century ago, some of Havre's pioneer businesses, including brothels, bars, and opium dens (as well as bakeries, butchers, laundries, and pharmacies) were located beneath the city streets. The tunnels that run through downtown Havre have been partially restored and opened as Havre Historical Underground Tours, or "Havre Beneath the Streets," one of the state's most interesting history lessons (120 3rd Ave., 406/265-8888, $10 adults, $9 seniors, $7 children). Many of the businesses are recreated with the exact fixtures and objects that were originally used in the underground district at the beginning of the 20th century, making this a fascinating snapshot of a bygone era. Access to the underground area is by tour only. Hour-long tours are offered throughout the year: on the half hour 9:30 A.M.–3:30 P.M. daily in summer, and 10:30 A.M.–3:30 P.M. Monday–Saturday in winter. Call ahead to confirm schedule times and for reservations. You'll need to be able to negotiate steep stairs

to access the tour, although wheelchairs are available once underground.

Other Sights

The **H. Earl Clack Museum** (306 3rd Ave., 406/265-4000, 10 A.M.–6 P.M. Mon.–Sat. and noon–5 P.M. Sun. Memorial Day–Labor Day, 1–5 P.M. Wed.–Sun. Labor Day–Memorial Day, free) presents the region's colorful history. The **Wahpka Chu'gn Buffalo Jump** provides the fodder for the museum's most interesting exhibits. At this archaeological site, which is directly behind the Holiday Village Shopping Center in Havre, Native Americans from three different prehistoric cultures, dating from 2,000 to 600 years ago, drove herds of bison off a cliff and then processed the slain animals for meat, hides, and tools. Excavations of the *pishkun* have uncovered Indian campsites, stone tools, and piles of buffalo bones. The site is open for tours only (Tues.–Sun. Memorial Day–Labor Day, $5 adults, $4 seniors, $3 students), which are operated by Clack Museum.

The remains of **Fort Assiniboine** are south of the intersection of Highways 2 and 87. The Clack Museum leads tours out to the old fort, built in 1879 to protect U.S. citizens from both the Blackfeet and the feared return of Sitting Bull from his exile in Canada. The fort was converted to an agricultural research station in 1913 and was used to house transients during the Depression.

Montana State University-Northern, formerly Northern Montana College, has a well-tended campus south of downtown and is a good place to sit in the shade. The Math-Science Building houses natural-history displays, including a stuffed specimen of the extinct Audubon mountain sheep once displayed above the bar of one of Havre's bygone high-class joints.

Ten miles south of Havre on Highway 234 is **Beaver Creek Park,** the nation's largest county park. With 10,000 acres of rolling hills and streams, the park is a popular place for picnics, camping, and for getting a sense of the lovely and remote Bear Paw Mountains.

These low mountains are 50-million-year-old volcanic humps that rise just enough above the surrounding prairies to provide welcome relief from the heat, and to sustain plants, wildlife, and streams otherwise absent from the plains.

From the park, follow back roads to the Chief Joseph Battleground, or to the Rocky Boys Reservation.

Rocky Boys Reservation

On the western edge of the Bear Paw Mountains south of Havre is the reservation named for Chippewa leader Stone Child, called Rocky Boy by the whites. Almost 2,000 Chippewa and Cree share this 108,015-acre reservation, which is entirely owned by tribal members.

Cree Indians came from the Upper Great Lakes area to the northern plains in the late 1700s and were allies of the Assiniboine and foes of the Sioux and Blackfeet. When bison began to disappear from the plains, the Cree became drifters in search of the last herds. They became known for their wandering on the northern plains and for their alignment with Louis Riel and his band of Métis.

U.S. authorities repeatedly tried to force the Cree to settle in Canada, and for many years the tribe was homeless. The Cree teamed up with another homeless group, Rocky Boy's band of Chippewa, who had been shorted out of reservation land in North Dakota. When Fort Assiniboine was abandoned in 1911, part of its acreage was set aside as a reservation for the Chippewa-Cree. Reservation life was not easy for these tribes, and employment on the reservation is still difficult to come by.

The tribes own and operate the Bear Paw Ski Bowl, a small downhill ski area (see below) and the Northern Winz Casino (406/395-5420, www.norhternwinz.com) in Box Elder. Contact the Rocky Boys Reservation at 406/395-4478 or www.rockyboy.org.

Recreation

When the sun beats down on the Hi-Line, consider a dunk in Havre's **city pool** (420 6th Ave., 406/265-8161).

Fish **Fresno Reservoir,** northwest of Havre,

for walleye, crappie, and northern pike. In **Beaver Creek Park** there's good fishing in two small lakes for pike and trout. Buy a fishing permit ($5) at the park headquarters located at the park entrance 10 miles south of Havre on Highway 234.

Tribal fishing and camping permits are issued by the Chippewa-Cree at their business office (406/395-4282) in Box Elder. The tribes also run the **Bear Paw Ski Bowl,** a small downhill ski area on the flanks of the Bear Paws, 26 miles south of Havre on the **Rocky Boys Reservation.** It's usually open mid-December through April 1.

Accommodations

$50-75: A couple blocks from downtown, but off the busy main highway, the **Budget Inn Motel** (115 9th Ave., 406/265-8625, $53) is a good deal, with well-maintained rooms and some kitchenettes. Commercial rates are available, and pets are allowed.

The attractive **El Toro Inn** (521 1st St., 406/265-5414 or 800/422-5414, $68) has a Spanish motif. A guest laundry is available, it's convenient for downtown shopping and dining options, continental breakfast is complimentary, and the city pool is just two blocks away; pets are permitted.

On the west end of town, near the fairgrounds and buffalo jump, is the **Havre Super 8 Motel** (166 19th Ave. W., 406/265-1411 or 800/800-8000, $66); pets are allowed with permission.

$75-100: The **Townhouse Inns of Havre** (601 1st St. W., 406/265-6711 or 800/442-4667, $85 and up) is a large motel complex with an adjoining casino and lounge. There's an indoor pool, sauna, and fitness room, and convention rooms are also available. The **Best Western Great Northern Inn** (1345 1st St., 406/265-4200 or 800/530-4100, $95 and up) is Havre's newest lodging, with nicely furnished rooms, an indoor pool and fitness room, and a complimentary breakfast bar.

Camping

The **Lions Campground** (west on Hwy. 2, 406/265-7121 or 888/265-7121) is fine for

RVs, but tent campers are better off heading toward the Bear Paw Mountains. It's only about 15 miles south on Highway 234 to the campgrounds at **Beaver Creek County Park** (406/395-4565), a huge park with 250 sites in several discrete campgrounds. Purchase a $5 camping permit at the park office, 10 miles south of Havre on Highway 234.

Food

Pizza Hut, McDonald's, and **Kentucky Fried Chicken** all rear their heads on the west end of town, but there are a few alternatives. **Nalivka's Original Pizza Kitchen** (1032 1st St., 406/265-4050, 11 A.M.–9 P.M. Tues.–Thurs. and Sun., 11 A.M.–10 P.M. Fri.–Sat., $7–14) is the locals' favorite for pizza, sandwiches, and pasta.

Andy's Supper Club (658 1st St. W, 406/265-9963, 4:30–10 P.M. daily, $15–25) is Havre's best steakhouse. You won't need to spend much time studying the menu, because it's basically just a list of steaks. Count on a massive meal, served in traditional Old Montana courses, complete with relish trays, salads, and pasta courses, all before the truly enormous steak arrives. Try the **Mediterranean Room** at the Duck Inn (1300 1st St., 406/265-6111, $15–29), for an exercise in amazing kitsch. Classical statues gaze at you as you ponder the admirably extensive (for northern Montana) menu of steaks and seafood.

For a less nutritious view of Havre, stop by the **Oxford Bar** (329 1st St.), where drinks are swallowed unnoticed when the gambling gets hot. Across the street at the **Palace Bar** (281 1st Ave.), there's a wonderful back bar and generous drinks.

Information and Services

You'll notice that the streets in Havre run parallel to the railroad tracks (Highway 2 is 1st St.); avenues are perpendicular to the tracks. Names for both rely principally on numbers, leading to maximum confusion.

For more information, contact the **chamber of commerce** (518 1st St., 406/265-4383, www.havremt.com). Find the **post office** at 306 3rd Avenue, just across from the lovely courthouse. The public **library** is just a couple of blocks away at the corner of 3rd Street and 4th Avenue.

Transportation

Amtrak's Empire Builder makes a brief layover in Havre, which is a restocking point. Trains arrive once daily in each direction; contact the station (235 Main St., 406/265-5381 or 800/872-7245) for schedule information.

Budget Rent-A-Car (Hwy. 2 W., 406/265-1156) is located at Tilleman Motor Company.

CHINOOK

Chinook (pop. 1,386, elev. 2,310 feet), the Hi-Line's remaining cattle town on the Milk River, is named after the warming wind that's saved many a cow from freezing or starving to death.

The **Blaine County Fair and Rodeo** and an accompanying art show and auction are held in mid-July. For more information, contact the **Chinook Chamber of Commerce** (P.O. Box 744, Chinook, MT 59523, 406/357-2100).

Bear Paw Battleground

The site of the Chief Joseph battlefield is 16 miles south of Chinook on paved Highway 240, in view of the Bear Paw Mountains.

This is where Gen. Nelson Miles overtook the Nez Perce, who were less than 40 miles from sanctuary in Canada. And it was here that Chief Joseph gave the speech for which he is most remembered:

It is cold and we have no blankets. The little children are freezing to death. My people, some of them, have run away to the hills, and have no blankets, no food; no one knows where they are—perhaps freezing to death. I want to have time to look for my children and see how many I can find. Maybe I shall find them among the dead.

Hear me, my chiefs. I am tired; my heart is sick and sad.

From where the sun now stands, I will fight no more forever.

THE NEZ PERCE AND THE BATTLE AT BEAR PAW

After the Nez Perce crossed the Missouri on their 1877 flight to Canada, they changed command and slowed down. They'd been on the run for four months and were tiring. Poker Joe, who'd proven himself to be a strong strategic leader, let Looking Glass, who pressed for a more relaxed pace, take over.

This pause gave General Nelson Miles and his battalion from eastern Montana the opportunity to attack the Nez Perce while they were still in U.S. territory. The Nez Perce were caught off guard, but they fought hard on the cold snowy prairie for six days before finally agreeing to lay down their arms.

Chief Joseph negotiated a ceasefire with Miles in which the Nez Perce would surrender their weapons but would see the return of their horses and their homeland in eastern Oregon. That night, White Bird – the only other Nez Perce chief still alive following the Bear Paw battle – led a band of Nez Perce toward Canada. More than 200 escapees made it to Canada, where they joined Sitting Bull and his Lakota followers.

Those who remained with Joseph were sent to Miles City, then to Kansas, and then to Oklahoma. Not until 1885 were they allowed to return to reservations in the Northwest.

The windswept patch of prairie has a few plaques and a trail through the grass that leads to small markers strewn over the battlefield, marking the sites of deaths and camps. The battlefield is now managed by the National Park Service as part of the Nez Perce National Historical Park. There's talk of building a visitors center if funding can be found.

In the meantime, there's a good local museum, the **Blaine County Museum** (501 Indiana, 406/357-2590, 8 A.M.–noon and 1–5 P.M. Mon.–Sat., noon–5 P.M. Sun., Memorial Day–Labor Day, donation), that's able to provide information about the battlefield. The museum also offers an audio-visual presentation called *40 Miles to Freedom,* which depicts the battle and siege at Bear Paw.

Accommodations

Bear Paw Court (114 Montana Ave., 406/357-2221 or 800/357-2224, $54) is a well-maintained court motel with cool neon two-bedroom units, and a free continental breakfast. At the attractive **Chinook Motor Inn** (100 Indiana Ave., 406/357-2248, $58), there's also a restaurant and lounge/casino.

Food

The **Pastime Lounge and Steakhouse** (406/357-2424) and the restaurant at the Chinook Motor Inn are the best bets for a meal in this small town.

WEST OF HAVRE

Every six miles or so, Highway 2 passes through yet another tiny town dominated by grain elevators and Lutheran church spires. Many are fancifully named (by the Great Northern), and most are just hanging on to existence. This is marvelous farmland for high-protein wheat, which fetches premium prices from bread and pasta makers.

Small towns like Joplin, Hingham, and Gilford don't have much in the way of facilities for travelers, but invariably there's a bar, a grocery store, and a coffee-klatch café in each town that would be glad to see a stranger.

Don't just whiz through **Kremlin.** Stop and look hard for the onion domes rising above the prairie—they're what give the town its name. (Actually, *nobody's* ever seen 'em, except a homesick Russian homesteader back in 1910 or so.)

The unenlightened may pass south of **Rudyard** on Highway 2 and dismiss it as a real hayseed town, but Rudyard natives have ended up doing such diverse things as running restaurant chains in France, creating art installations at the Whitney, and selling paintings in the Western art world that are valued in the six digits. Stop by and have a look at their new museum.

Inverness offers the **Inverness Supper Club** (101 Main St., 406/292-3801, 9 A.M.–11 P.M. daily), a favorite watering hole and steakhouse for local farmers and ranchers; it's also open for lunch.

Chester

A dam on the Marias River forms **Tiber Reservoir** (a.k.a. Lake Elwell) southwest of Chester (pop. 871, elev. 3,283 feet). It's the only recreational area for miles around and a haven for those seeking **campsites.** Boating is popular, fishing is mediocre for rainbows and perch, and there seems to be a largely untapped potential for windsurfing. A float trip along the Marias from below the dam to the Missouri River passes badlands and white cliffs not unlike those of the Wild and Scenic stretch of the Missouri.

If you're not a camper, perhaps you'd like to stay in a motel named after a local point of interest. The **MX Motel** (on Hwy. 2, 406/759-5564, $54) reminds passers-through that some missile silos slumber just off the highway around here.

Shelby

A boxcar was thrown from a Great Northern train here in 1891, and the site was named after Montana's general manager of the Great Northern, who swore the place would never amount to much. Shelby (pop. 3,216, elev. 3,283 feet) developed into a trade center, supplying cowboys and sheepherders with food and wild times. Oil was discovered north of town in 1921, and though the town's population swelled, it didn't quite live up to its own expectations. In 1923, Shelby hosted a prizefight between Jack Dempsey and Tommy Gibbons. A 45,000-seat arena was erected for this occasion; unfortunately, only 7,000 seats were filled for the fight.

The **Marias Museum of History and Art** (206 12th Ave., 406/434-2551) has memorabilia from the big fight and displays concerning the region's oil wealth.

The **Sweet Grass border crossing,** 24 miles north of Shelby on I-15, is open 24 hours and is the state's busiest Canadian port of entry.

Shelby is a stop on Amtrak's Empire Builder, which passes through once daily in each direction.

Like many hot Hi-Line towns, Shelby has a city **swimming pool** (105 12th Ave. N., 406/434-5311).

Accommodations

$50-75: Shelby has several motels and sees a lot of Canadian travelers. Downtown, **O'Haire Manor Motel** (204 2nd St. S., 406/434-5555 or 800/541-5809, $61 and up) has a fitness room and hot tub, free WiFi, guest laundry, and some two-bedroom units; pets are allowed. Also nice is the **Crossroads Inn** (1200 Hwy. 2, 406/434-5134 or 800/779-7666, $62 and up), with an indoor pool.

$75-100: The **Comfort Inn** (455 McKinley, 406/434-2212 or 800/442-4667, $99 and up), at the junction of I-15 and Highway 200, has a lounge and casino, exercise room and hot tub and allows pets.

Camping

Campers may want to swing seven miles south of town to **Williamson Park** on the Marias River.

Food

Country Skillet (406/434-2175, open 24 hours), is the spot for a hearty breakfast—it's in Shelby Travel Plaza truck stop just west of town. **Dixie's Inn & Dining Room** (406/434-5817, 11 A.M.–10 P.M. daily, $12–24), west of Shelby, is a good choice for a night out on the town, with steaks and seafood.

Conrad

Conrad (pop. 2,873, elev. 3,500 feet), although 24 miles south of the Hi-Line proper on I-15, shares an agricultural heritage and economy with the other towns along Highway 2. Dryland farming and big irrigation projects took off here and transformed it into a productive wheat-growing area. Conrad is within easy striking distance of Lake Elwell,

NORTH-CENTRAL MONTANA

a minor mecca for recreationists on the prairies. There's a **Super 8 Motel** (215 N. Main, 406/278-7676 or 800/442-4667, $69 and up)

handy to the freeway; the motel also features some kitchenettes and executive suites.

Blackfeet Indian Reservation

Just east of Glacier National Park and the Rocky Mountains, short-grass prairie rolls across the Blackfeet Reservation, a high plain cut through by creeks and dotted with lakes. Strong winds from the west, long and cold winters, and short hot summers make it difficult to ignore the weather here.

Among the reservation communities, **Heart Butte** is the most traditional; **East Glacier, St. Mary,** and **Babb** cater to tourists, with many businesses owned by non-Indians. **Cut Bank,** on the reservation's eastern border, has more in common with the Hi-Line towns to the east. **Browning** is home to the fascinating **Museum of the Plains Indian.**

Meriwether Lewis hoped to find the headwaters of the Marias River mingling with those of the Saskatchewan River up above the 50th parallel. On their return from the Pacific, Lewis and a small party of men traced Cut Bank Creek from its confluence with the Two Medicine River. (These two streams combine to form the Marias.) Unfortunately for Lewis, Cut Bank Creek comes out of the Rockies west of Browning, and, because of cloudy weather, he couldn't see the stars well enough to get an exact reading of how far north he was. All in all, it was enough to cause him to name their terminus Camp Disappointment. A highway marker and a wind-tossed hilltop picnic area now mark the site.

Lewis's side trip is also notable because it marks the only time anybody was killed during the expedition. Two Blackfeet were killed when, after sharing a campsite with Lewis's group, they tried to steal guns from the white explorers.

HISTORY

The Blackfeet, originally from north of the Great Lakes, moved west in the 1600s and established southern Alberta as their territory. What is now known as the Blackfeet Nation is composed of three distinct tribes: the Northern Piegan (Pikuni), the Southern Piegan or Blackfeet (Siksika), and the Blood (Kainai). By the 1700s, bands of Blackfeet had settled in what is now Montana. The Northern Piegan and the Blood mostly remained in Canada.

The Blackfeet formed tentative alliances with the neighboring Cree and Assiniboin, and considered the more distant Shoshone and Crow their enemies. When they first arrived on the northern plains, the Blackfeet had neither horses nor guns. They drove buffalo over *pishkuns,* steep cliffs, to kill them.

Horses, acquired from either the Shoshone or the Flathead, Nez Perce, and Kootenai tribes, made a tremendous difference in the everyday life of the Blackfeet. Buffalo were much easier to hunt from horseback, and once the tribe began trading for guns, were a snap to shoot down. The Blackfeet became skilled riders, and their fierce reputation was enhanced as they were able to stage wide-ranging raids.

When white explorers and mountain men arrived in the 1800s, the Blackfeet controlled the northern plains. White settlers feared the Blackfeet's raids as much as they vied for their business at trading posts. Early trading posts in Blackfeet country included Fort Piegan on the Missouri River near present-day Loma.

Contact with white traders and soldiers brought more of the valuable guns and ammunition, but also conflict and disease. The Blackfeet were decimated as much by smallpox and scarlet fever as by battle.

The U.S. government was eager to confine the Blackfeet, and in order to start the process along, marked the land north of the Yellowstone

WHY "BLACKFEET?"

Two legends tell of how the Blackfeet got their tribal name.

The first, and oldest, is a story about a man and his three sons. Obeying a vision, the man sent his sons west to hunt buffalo. The buffalo were where they were supposed to be, by the thousands, but they were difficult to approach. The sun appeared in a second vision and provided the father with black medicine with which to paint his oldest son's feet. It worked, and the son was able to run down the buffalo. His descendants are called Blackfeet. The man's other two sons weren't ignored. One became a warrior – his painted red lips earned his descendants the name "Bloods." And the third son returned home with clothes of distant tribes; his descendants became the Pikuni, or "Far-Off Clothing." Whites transformed this into "Piegan."

The less visionary explanation points to the fact that the tribe's long travels across scorched prairies to reach what is today Montana probably blackened their moccasins.

and south of Canada's Saskatchewan River, east of the Continental Divide and west of the confluence of the Missouri and Yellowstone Rivers, for a Blackfeet reservation. Pressure from whites wanting the land for their own uses resulted in an incredible shrinking reservation. The Blackfeet Reservation now comprises 1.5 million acres, with more than one third of that owned by non-Indians.

Oil drilling on tribal land has provided revenue for the Blackfeet since the early 1900s. Oil and gas now supply the tribe with most of their income and much controversy. Ranching, farming, and a pencil factory also contribute to the reservation economy.

Lakes dot the Blackfeet Reservation, and many of them are worth fishing. The tribe has a fishing information line (406/338-7413), and they'll provide advice on the necessary permits and current fishing conditions.

CUT BANK

This foothills oil and gas town of 3,105 souls was named by the Blackfeet for "the river that cuts into the white clay bank," or Cut Bank Creek. There was an initial burst of development when the Great Northern Railway came through in the 1890s and another big spurt in the 1930s when oil and gas were discovered nearby. Cut Bank is just east of the Blackfeet Reservation, and unlike Browning, it's not a thoroughly Indian town.

The city's heated outdoor **swimming pool** is at 320 2nd Avenue West (406/873-2452).

The last weekend of July brings Cut Bank's **Lewis and Clark Expedition Festival.** The **chamber of commerce** (P.O. Box 1243, Cut Bank, MT 59427, 406/873-4041) can supply details.

Accommodations

Newly built, the (**Glacier Gateway Plaza** (1130 E. Main, 406/873-2566 or 800/851-5541, $70 and up) has an indoor pool, hot tub, complimentary continental breakfast, and free high-speed Internet service. Owned by the same hoteliers, the **Glacier Gateway Inn** (1121 E. Railroad St., 406/873-5544 or 800/851-5541, $60 and up) is also new and comfortable with well-appointed rooms. You can't miss it—it's next to the 27-foot penguin. There are three themed rooms, one with a two-story tepee inside! The **Super 8** (609 W. Main, 406/873-5662, $72 and up) is adjacent to a shopping mall and restaurants and has an indoor pool and hot tub.

Food

The **Bon Appetit Cafe** (13 W. Main, 406/873-4010, 7 A.M.–7 P.M. Tues.– Sun.) serves breakfast all day. Get sandwiches at the **Smokehouse Deli** (5 N. Central Ave., 406/873-4747, 11 A.M.–3 P.M.). For dinner, look to the **Village Dining and Lounge** (601

W. Main, 406/873-5005, $8–$22), in the North Village Shopping Center, for sandwiches, steaks, pasta, and seafood.

BROWNING

Browning (pop. 1,065, elev. 4,462 feet) is the headquarters of the Blackfeet nation. It's 18 miles east of Glacier National Park, and many parkgoers zip through in a hurry to get to the mountains. Although Browning is not a fancy place—it can be hard to find a pay phone that works, and the café fare is no more compelling than the highway motel rooms—there is a certain spirit to the place, and there are reasons to stop here.

Sights

Browning's main attraction is the **Museum of the Plains Indian** (406/338-2230, 9 A.M.–4:30 P.M. daily June–Sept., 10 A.M.–4:30 P.M. Mon.–Fri. Oct.–May, $4 adults, $1 children 6–12), near the intersection of Highways 2 and 89. The exhibits of cultural artifacts are well-curated and professionally displayed, the slide show is vivid, and the gift shop is a good place to buy Indian art and jewelry without fear of getting inferior or inauthentic goods and with the assurance that the artist is being fairly compensated.

At the same highway intersection, the **Blackfeet Heritage Center and Art Gallery** (406/338-5425, 9 A.M.–5 P.M. daily May 1–Labor Day, 9 A.M.–5 P.M. Mon.–Fri. Labor Day–Apr.) exhibits and sells art, jewelry, and crafts from a number of Native American tribes.

The back roads of the reservation pass homes (with an occasional tepee pitched out back), lakes, oil and gas rigs, and a ceremonial sun lodge (a polygonal log-limbed structure). While common manners dictate that one shouldn't trespass, it is especially important not to enter tribal religious sites, such as a sun lodge.

Accommodations

The **War Bonnet Lodge** (406/338-7610, $76) is at the intersection of Highways 2 and 89; there's also a dining room and lounge. The **Western Motel** (121 Central Ave. E., 406/338-7572, $60) offers clean unfussy rooms with fridges and microwaves.

Food

Browning is no culinary mecca, but the **Jackpot Restaurant** at the Glacier Peaks Casino (Junction of Hwy. 2 and Hwy. 89 W., 406/338-2274, 10 A.M.–9 P.M.) is new and offers a broad menu.

Events

North American Indian Days are held the second week of July at the powwow grounds behind the Museum of the Plains Indian. Dancing and drumming are the highlights of the weekend activities. Teams of drummers come from all over the West to compete at this powwow, and their drumming is frequently rhapsodic. Stick games, jewelry peddlers, and the bustling encampment of tepees, tents, and pickups round out the scene. Spectators will quickly realize that this is *real,* not something trotted out for tourists, and while non-Indians are welcome, events aren't geared toward them.

Information

Information is available from the **Blackfeet Nation** (P.O. Box 850, Browning, MT 59417, 406/338-7276, www.blackfoot.org).

Rocky Mountain Front

The Rocky Mountains hoist themselves off the plains just west of Choteau and Augusta. It's as dramatic a transition as you'll find in any landscape: flat rangeland to the east, and wilderness mountains rising abruptly to the west. In winter, Chinook winds blow down off the mountains to warm the plains; the rest of the year, the wind just plain blows.

In this spectacular setting, near **Choteau** and **Augusta,** are found some of the state's best-loved and longstanding **guest ranches.** Many also operate as outfitters for fishing and hunting trips and lead pack trips into the Bob Marshall Wilderness.

Natural-gas pumps and missile sites dot the fields stretching out from the Rocky Mountain Front. Controversy has erupted between those who want to develop natural gas (and feel that it can be balanced with wilderness) and those who fear such gas exploration and mining will harm the Front's environment.

There's compelling ancient history here too: Near Choteau is **Egg Mountain,** where paleontologists discovered nests of egg-laying dinosaurs that may be the missing link between birds and reptiles. Although tours of the fossil beds are no longer offered, Choteau's **Old Trail Museum** has exhibits on these and other local dinosaurs, and the **Two Medicine Dinosaur Center** offers a gallery of dinosaur fossils and a variety of hands-on fossil dig programs for amateur paleontologists.

HIGHWAY 89: BROWNING TO CHOTEAU

Edging along the face of the Rocky Mountain Front, Highway 89 passes through bucolic ranching communities—the cattle and horses here have it very lucky, at least in summer. The scenery, with verdant pastures and wooded streams serving as foreground to the massive, near-vertical rise of the Rockies, is as dramatic as any in Montana.

While there aren't many developed tourist sites along this route—this remains first and last ranch country—there are two exceptional

bed-and-breakfasts in this rural area that warrant a stop.

Accommodations

If you're looking for historic character, then you'll love the (**Inn Dupuyer** (406/472-3241, www.3rivers.net/~inndupyr, year-round, from $85), located 34 miles north of Choteau in the little community of Dupuyer—the setting for several Ivan Doig novels. The original inn is a 100-year-old two-story log home that the owners carefully refurbished by constructing a modern home around the older building, largely encasing the log structure. While the dining room, kitchen, and a parlor area are new and commodious, the bedrooms and the common room are all in the historic log home. All four rooms have private baths and are carefully decorated with local period furnishings; the antique beds all have down comforters. The upstairs common room, with an old wood-burning stove, saddle tack, and rustic furniture, will make you feel as if you've just settled into a stylish 1890s ranch house. Off the back is a deck with great views onto the Front Range. Rates include a Western-style breakfast.

In Valier, the (**Stone School Inn B&B** (820 3rd St., 406/279-3796, http://stoneschoolinn.com, $85 and up) preserves a handsome three-story stone school building from 1911. The five large guest rooms, which take up the entire second floor, are beautifully furnished and each has a private bathroom. Guests share a library and game room; free WiFi is available throughout. This is quite an enterprise, and definitely worth the detour.

Food

A local favorite for excellent steaks and refined preparations of local meats and produce, the **Lighthouse Restaurant** (1162 Valier Hwy., 406/279-3798, 11 A.M.–10 P.M. daily May–Sept., 11 A.M.–10 P.M. Wed.–Sat. and 1–8 P.M. Sun. Oct.–Apr., $12–26) is right on the shores of Lake Frances in the center of Valier.

NORTH-CENTRAL MONTANA

© BILL MCRAE

The Rocky Mountain Front rises directly from the prairies.

CHOTEAU

Choteau (pop. 1,791, elev. 3,800 feet), at the feet of the Rocky Mountains, is not in Chouteau County; it's the county seat of Teton County. The town is built around the county courthouse, smack where Highway 287 crosses Highway 89.

The town has become known as a paleontological hot spot. Dinosaurs used this area as a breeding ground, and paleontologists (led by Jack Horner, now based in Bozeman at the Museum of the Rockies) have pieced together revolutionary dinosaur life theories based on bones and fossilized eggshells excavated at nearby Egg Mountain.

The Old North Trail, running from the Arctic to Mexico more than 8,000 years ago, was an important migratory trail for proto-Indians. Traces of it are still visible at the Pine Butte Preserve just west of present-day Choteau.

Catholic missionaries preceded the fur traders who started white settlement here. The town was named after Pierre Chouteau, who was associated with the American Fur Company.

(The first *u* in the name was dropped to distinguish the town from Chouteau County.) When fur trading died out, the economic mantle was picked up by cattle ranchers.

Choteau was home to novelist A. B. Guthrie until his death in 1991. Guthrie, best known for *The Big Sky,* was an environmentalist in this land of ranchers and natural-gas speculators.

◖ Old Trail Museum

When you're standing on Choteau's main street, Teton Trail Village, a cluster of old refurbished cabins loaded with period artifacts, is hard to miss, and you shouldn't. The biggest draw (besides the ice cream shop) is the Old Trail Museum (823 N. Main, 406/466-5332, otm@3rivers.net, 9 A.M.–6 P.M. daily Memorial Day–Labor Day).

The paleontology gallery features discoveries from the area's Two Medicine Formation, including a Maiasaura and an Einosaurus skull along with nestling, hatchling, and teenage Maiasaura skeletons and bones. New in 2008 is a full-bodied Maiasaura and a tribute to the 1978 Egg Mountain fossil bed discovery by Marion Branvold.

Other displays focus on more recent Choteau history, such as the Old North Trail and the story behind a contentious trial and hanging in the 1920s.

Egg Mountain

A nondescript hill west of Choteau, Egg Mountain is where paleontological history was made. The Egg Mountain site didn't yield just the bones of adult dinosaurs, but also hundreds of bones from juvenile dinosaurs. The most revolutionary find was nests of fossilized eggs, which strongly suggest that the dinosaurs here—dubbed Maiasaura (good mother lizards)—were nurturing animals. The finds at Egg Mountain suggest that female dinosaurs laid their nests in colonies (like modern social bird species), protected the nests from predators (pesky Albertosaurs), and cared for their juvenile young.

In the 1970s a local rancher discovered a cache of dinosaur remains in a shale-like

MAIASAURA, MONTANA'S STATE FOSSIL

As far as dinosaurs go, *Maiasaura* are practically heart-warming – enough so that Montana school children spearheaded a drive in 1985 to have this recently discovered reptile named as Montana's state fossil.

Maiasaura lived during the late Cretaceous period, about 80 to 65 million years ago, when this part of Montana was at the edge of vast saltwater swamps. *Maiasaura* grew to about 30 feet in length and were distinguished by duckbills, which enabled them to dredge coastal marshes for leaves, berries, and seeds. Although they walked on four feet, when they ran – and they were relatively fast for dinosaurs, sprinting at 12 to 18 miles per hour – they ran upright on their hind legs.

Maiasaura were the first dinosaurs to be found with their eggs, leading to new theories about saurian maternal instincts and a kinder, gentler reputation for ancient reptiles. At Egg Mountain, researchers found *Maiasaura* fossil skeletons alongside scooped-out holes in the ground about six or seven feet across. These holes were filled with up to 25 grapefruit-sized eggs. Nests were 25 to 30 feet across, roughly the size of a *Maiasaura*, which suggests that the dinosaurs lived and nested in colonies in order to protect and nurture their young.

Researchers estimate that Egg Mountain was home to roughly 10,000 *Maiasaura;* these individuals died when ancient volcanoes carpeted the area with volcanic ash. Because of this great population concentration, scientists also speculate that *Maiasaura* were migratory, returning to the rocky outcrop now known as Egg Mountain at nesting season.

Since their extinction, *Maiasaura* have traveled quite a distance from Egg Mountain. A *Maiasaura* bone fragment and a piece of egg shell flew on an eight-day Spacelab 2 mission with astronaut Loren Acton, making the "good mother lizard" the first dinosaur in space.

outcrop on Egg Mountain. In 1978, Marion Branvold, a rock-shop owner from nearby Bynum, found the first nests of fossilized eggs, which were later identified as Maiasaura, a new species of duck-billed dinosaur.

Tours of the excavation site are no longer available to the public. The Museum of the Rockies has purchased the Egg Mountain site and is currently using it for research purposes only.

If you just want to have a look at Egg Mountain from a distance (remember, you cannot just turn up and visit the site), there's a roadside marker for Egg Mountain just south of Choteau on Highway 287. For a closer look, turn off Highway 287 south of Choteau at the Pishkum Lake turn off. Continue down the road; when the road forks, don't take the road to Pishkun Lake—veer right. There are two big digging sites here: Egg Mountain, where evidence of many dinosaur nests has been unearthed, and the bone beds, final resting place of many Maiasaura.

(Two Medicine Dinosaur Center

Ten miles north of Choteau in the tiny community of Bynum is Two Medicine Dinosaur Center (406/469-2211 or 800/238-6873, www.tmdinosaur.org, $5 adults, $4 military and seniors 55 and up, $3 for children 4–12, free for kids 3 and under), a new addition to the area's dinosaur culture. The center is worth a stop to view the skeletal model of a Seismosaurus, the longest dinosaur every discovered; the first baby dinosaur remains found in North America; and Bob, or "block of bones" (hence the "bob" acronym). Bob is over 11 feet in length, weighs 5.5 tons, and contains over 100 dinosaur bones and fragments from at least three individuals and two separate species. Visitors can usually watch professional paleontologists extract and prepare fossils in the lab. The center also offers an array of hands-on programs that offer keen amateur paleontologists a chance to participate in a dig. A 3-hour program ($45) offers an introduction to basic fossil recognition, area history, and geology. One-,

NORTH-CENTRAL MONTANA

two-, and five-day programs offer a chance to help out in fossil excavations (see the website for details and dates). Prior reservations are required for all programs.

The Nature Conservancy's Pine Butte Swamp Preserve

Nestled between the Front Range and a former MX missile silo, this preserve stretches from the mountains to the plains across a rare (for this area) wetland. (More precisely, it's a fen, which means that the water actually flows.) Grizzly bears forage here and have historically used the brushy swamp as a corridor to the plains. This is now one of the easternmost outposts of the grizzly, which was native to the plains.

While access to the preserve is limited, there is one area open to visitors. Drive past the old Bellview schoolhouse (five miles west of Egg Mountain, along the same road) and turn right on a cut-across road. Drive northwest on this road for about two miles to an information kiosk. Park here, read the posted information, and take the trail starting at the kiosk. It's a short easy hike up a flower-strewn ridge to a view of glacier-carved Pine Butte, wetlands, glacial moraines, faint traces of the Old North Trail, and the Rocky Mountain Front.

Contact the Pine Butte Swamp Preserve (26 Meltwater Rd., Choteau, 406/466-5526) for more information regarding access and natural history programs offered through Pin Butte Guest Ranch (see below).

Another good wildlife area, southeast of Choteau, is **Freezout Lake,** a waterfowl area and wetlands that migrating birds use as a rest stop. Pelicans, blue-winged teal, and marsh hawks reside here, as do snow geese in the spring and tundra swans each fall. Nearby Priest Butte was the site of a Catholic mission for the Blackfeet.

Recreation

Take your pick of trails on the South Fork of the Teton River—many of them lead into the Bob Marshall Wilderness. **Our Lake** (called Hidden Lake on the trailhead sign)

is three miles up and in. Mountain goats are often visible above the lake. The hike to **Headquarters Pass** starts at the same trailhead (near the Mill Falls Campground) and passes a high waterfall on the Sun River on the way to expansive views. Grizzly bears are sometimes spotted in the area, so take precautions. It's not unusual to run into snowfields on the higher trails even in July.

Teton Pass Ski Area (406/466-2209, http://skitetonpass.com) has cross-country and downhill trails at Teton Pass. The relatively small downhill area has lift tickets for $27. Cross-country skiers headed for the Bob Marshall Wilderness Area often start from Choteau, because roads are plowed all the way to the mountains.

Fish **Pishkun Reservoir,** southwest of town, for kokanee salmon, northern pike, and rainbow trout.

Accommodations

The cheery **Bella Vista Motel** (614 Main Ave. N., 406/466-5711, $57) is located just across from the Old Trail Museum. At the **Big Sky Motel** (209 S. Main, 406/466-5318), rooms have microwaves and cable TV (some also include kitchens). The **Stage Stop Inn** (1005 Main Ave. N., 406/466-5900 or 888/466-5900, www.stagestopinn.com, $72 and up) has handsomely furnished rooms and a pool and hot tub. Complimentary continental breakfast is included.

Guest Ranches

Two of Montana's best guest ranches are tucked in behind the Rocky Mountain Front, west of Choteau.

For an old-fashioned horse-based guest ranch, it's hard to beat the (**Seven Lazy P** (P.O. Box 178, Choteau, MT 59422, 406/466-2044, www.sevenlazyp.com, closed in winter). In operation for more than 50 years, this beautifully located ranch offers lodging in comfortable log cabins large enough to sleep an entire family; each has a private bath and toilets. Meals are served in the gracious lodge headquarters, reached by a short bridge across a stream. The lodge common room, dominated by a stone fireplace and filled with comfortable rustic furniture, is an atmospheric place to hole up with a book or talk about the day's adventures. Activities include daily organized horseback riding, hiking, and fishing trips—or plain old relaxing. If you're considering a long-distance pack trip into the Bob Marshall Wilderness, the Seven Lazy P offers seven- to 10-day backcountry excursions. Rates run $205 per day double occupancy (four-day minimum), which includes all meals and horseback riding; the weekly rate is $1,390 per person. Pack trips run $270 per day, or $2,500 for 10 days.

Visitors are in for a slightly different experience at the (**Pine Butte Guest Ranch** (HC 58, Box 34C, Choteau, MT 59422, 406/466-2158). Stunningly located on the South Fork of the Teton River, with steep escarpments rising on all sides, Pine Butte has been a dude ranch since 1930. The original owners sold it to the Nature Conservancy, which is dedicated to preserving plants, animals, and natural communities by protecting the land and waters they need to survive. Consequently, in addition to traditional dude-ranch activities like trail rides, the ranch also sponsors daily naturalist hikes and programs along the Front Range, focusing on the area's unique natural history. During the spring and fall, the ranch sponsors a series of longer, hands-on workshops on topics such as grizzly bears, the local dinosaur digs, or nature photography. You'll leave the Pine Butte Ranch not only saddle sore but also wiser about the natural world of Montana.

Lodging is in very comfortable single or duplex cabins, each with private bathrooms and fireplaces; there's even a swimming pool. Meals are served in the lodge, which is filled with handmade furniture made by the ranch's original owner. Rates are $1,700 per week for adults, $1,300 for children (one-week minimum, Sunday-to-Sunday stays only). Room, board, naturalist tours, and horseback riding are included in the fee, as is Sunday transportation to and from the Great Falls Airport.

Camping

The free **Choteau city park campground** is right in town; turn off Highway 89 at the blinking light and follow the KOA signs. The city park is closer in than the **KOA** (406/446-2615), which is farther east. Choose the city park if flush toilets and running water are amenities enough; for hookups, showers, and campground fees, continue on to the KOA.

Mill Falls Campground is small, free, and well situated for hikers. Follow Highway 89 north out of Choteau and turn down the road to Teton Canyon.

Food

Summers heat up east of the Rockies, and Choteau is a good place to cool off with an ice cream cone. There's an ice cream parlor in the **Teton Trail Village** and another one right across the street at the **OutPost Deli** (819 7th Ave. N., 406/466-5330), which is also a good spot for a sandwich. The **Circle N** (925 N. Main Ave., 406/466-5531) is open daily for breakfast, lunch, and dinner, and serves steaks, burgers, and a Sunday buffet. Just passed the Old Trail Museum on the north edge of town, **Elk Country Grill** (925 North Main Ave., 406/466-3311, $8–18) offers good Western-style home-cooking, including authentic Dutch oven meals.

Events

The **Choteau rodeo** takes place on the Fourth of July.

Information

The Forest Service **ranger station** (406/466-5341) is on Highway 89 at the northern edge of town. An information kiosk is set up in Choteau during the summer, and the **Old Trail Museum** is another good source of information, especially for dinosaur details.

AUGUSTA

Even more so than Choteau, Augusta (pop. 284) is spectacularly located and is a good way to access the Bob Marshall Wilderness Area. As you head south on Highway 287 from Choteau, past mounded glacial moraines, the east face of the Rockies becomes closer and more dramatic. The road crosses the Sun River seven miles north of Augusta as it flows from the Rockies to the Missouri. The Blackfeet referred to the Sun as the Medicine River because they used mineral deposits from a side gulch medicinally. Gibson Reservoir, named after Paris Gibson, the founder of Great Falls and initiator of hydroelectric power on the Missouri, is on the Sun River right where the Rockies jut up from the plains. The dam was built in 1913 primarily to store and divert water for irrigation.

Augusta is home to the American Legion Rodeo, the state's oldest. It's also one of the best regarded, and people drive hundreds of miles to attend. The rodeo is held on the last Sunday of June.

Sights

Gibson Reservoir is 26 miles northwest of Augusta. Reach it via the road toward the south end of town with the sign to Willow Creek fishing-access area (Rd. 1081). On the way to the Rocky Mountain Front, the road crosses a moraine strewn with glacial erratics—boulders carried in glacial ice and then dropped where the ice melted. Once the road meets up with the Sun River, you come right up against the rocks, and the whole geologic idea of overthrust becomes startlingly clear.

The road ends just past the dam, and trails continue the length of the reservoir, past medicine springs and Native American pictographs, into the Bob Marshall Wilderness. Bighorn sheep, elk, and deer winter north of the reservoir.

The state bought land for **Sun River Wildlife Management Area** in the 1940s to provide wintering ground for the Sun River elk herd. Previous to that, the elk had competed with cattle on the plains and with bighorn sheep in the mountains. Thousands of elk now winter on the moraine between Gibson Reservoir and Augusta. Hunting is permitted here, although it's prohibited in the Sun River Game Preserve, which is part of the Bob Marshall Wilderness Area. The range is closed

in the winter (although elk are often visible from nearby roads) and open in the summer to bird-watchers, hikers, and mountain bikers.

Recreation

The trail from Mortimer Campground on Gibson Reservoir goes into the Bob Marshall Wilderness Area. Other trails into the Bob Marshall and Scapegoat Wilderness Areas start from Benchmark and South Fork Campgrounds, south of the reservoir. A trail starts at the South Fork Campground and passes through the Sun River Game Preserve on its way to the spectacular Chinese Wall, a 13-mile-long 1,000-foot-tall escarpment on the Continental Divide.

Accommodations

$50–75: The place to stay in Augusta is the **Bunkhouse Inn** (122 Main St., 406/562-3387 or 800/553-4016, $45), a 1912 hotel that started out in Gilman, which is now a ghost town. The old hotel was moved to Augusta, then renovated into a unique rustic inn. It has 10 rooms, all with shared baths (the owners point out that this is an improvement over the outhouses of the original hotel).

$75–100: The rural ◖ **Viewforth B&B** (4600 Hwy. 287, 406/467-3884, www.viewforth.com, $85), seven miles north of Augusta near the junction of Highway 287 and MT 408 (Fairfield Rd.), is a modern Craftsman-style home with incredible views toward the Rocky Mountain Front. The handsome, uncluttered home is surrounded by gardens and flocks of unusual Scottish sheep. There are two guest rooms, each with one queen bed and a private bathroom.

Camping

Settle in and contemplate geology at **Home Gulch Campground,** below Gibson Reservoir on the Sun River, 21 miles from Augusta. Five miles down the road, **Mortimer Campground** perches above the reservoir. A trail leads from Mortimer into the Bob Marshall Wilderness Area.

Three campgrounds south of Gibson Reservoir are on Road 234 (Benchmark Rd.)

west of Augusta. **Wood Lake** is 25 miles from Augusta, **Benchmark** is another five miles down the road, and **South Fork** is yet another mile on, at the end of the road. For information, call the ranger station at 406/562-3247.

Food

Restaurant choices are pretty much limited to the dining room at the **Buckhorn Bar** (120 Main St., 406/562-3344, 11 A.M.–9 P.M. daily), with burgers, chicken, and steaks, and **Mel's Diner** (121 Main St., 406/562-3408, 6 A.M.–7 P.M. daily May–Nov., 6 A.M.–5:30 P.M. Dec.–Apr.), a friendly café with good breakfasts and a famed buffalo burger.

Guest Ranches

The mountains behind Augusta harbor a clutch of excellent guest ranches. Since 1927 one of the state's most famous and beloved, **Klick's K Bar L** is currently for sale. If you're a fan of guest ranch experiences, keep an eye out for its reopening.

For a real outback Montana ranch experience, try the **Benchmark Wilderness Ranch** (422 County Line Rd., Fairfield, 406/467-3110, bmwranch@3rivers.net). The Benchmark Ranch is located deep in the Lewis and Clark National Forest, so far back that there are still no phones and no electricity (the otherwise modern comfortable cabins and lodge are powered with propane appliances and lights). You can drive to the ranch, or if you're traveling by plane, the ranch has its own airstrip. Cabins are located near a modern bathhouse. The advantage of this remote site is that you don't have to go far from your cabin to arrive in real wilderness. Benchmark specializes in backcountry horse pack trips ($240 per day per adult), which involve overnight camping trips to remote lakes and streams teaming with trout. Lodge-based programs are also available that include meals and horseback riding ($150 per day per adult). Cabins (with kitchens) are also sometimes available on a per-day basis ($70 for up to four guests). A la carte horseback riding is $70 per day. You'll get a friendly welcome at the Benchmark—the ranch has been in

operation since 1928, and you can rest assured that the stock and the hands here are some of the best in the state.

The **JJJ Wilderness Ranch** (P.O. Box 310, Augusta, MT 59410, 406/562-3653, www.triplejranch.com), located on Gibson Reservoir, operates a full-fledged dude ranch with horseback riding, nature photography, swimming in the heated pool, and fishing. Exploring the Front Range on horseback is the specialty of the Triple J, and you'll get plenty of hands-on instruction from the wranglers. Kids get a special welcome—there's even a special wrangler for kids who supervises rides and games. Lodging is in cabins, all with modern bathrooms and ample sitting room. Rates are $1,480 per person or $2,850 per couple per week, Sunday to Sunday only, and include all meals (including steak barbecues) and activities. The Triple J also runs five- to eight-day pack trips into the Bob Marshall Wilderness for $240 per person per day.

Information

The Forest Service operates a **ranger station** just down Willow Creek Road (406/562-3247).

BOB MARSHALL WILDERNESS AREA

This wilderness area was created in 1940, when three national forest primitive areas were combined and named for a New Yorker who was a strong advocate for wilderness and an inveterate hiker.

The Land

The eastern face of the Bob Marshall is characterized by overthrust—old rocks on young. The Sawtooth Range, which forms the Rocky Mountain Front, shows off faults, folds, and overthrusts in the layers of limestone jutting into the prairie. The rocks here are generally younger than those to their west. Oil and gas speculators have been petitioning the Forest Service since the 1940s for the right to drill in the Bob Marshall and Great Bear Wilderness Areas.

The eastern Sawtooth side of the Bob

The Sun River flows from the Bob Marshall Wilderness Area.

Marshall is, as expected, drier, windier, and more sparsely vegetated than the western Swan Range side. Bears, mountain goats (native, not transplants), elk, and bighorn sheep all thrive in this wilderness area.

Getting In

Despite its imposing appearance, the Rocky Mountain Front offers several entrances to the Bob Marshall Wilderness Area. Roads west from Choteau and Augusta end at trailheads, some near the wilderness boundary. There's a real visual punch gained by entering over the Front Range, where escarpments are pronounced, rather than from the west, across the trailing ends of the propped-up rocks.

The Benchmark trailhead west of Augusta is a particularly popular one, especially with horse

packers. Just to the north, trails from Gibson Reservoir lead right into the wilderness.

From the Headquarters Pass Trail, west of Choteau, continue on to Rocky Mountain Peak, the Bob's highest peak at 9,392 feet. This trail can also be followed to the Chinese Wall (see the following section).

Backpackers should plan to spend a minimum of five days to a week—distances are great. The Forest Service puts out a topographical map of the Bob Marshall, Great Bear, and Scapegoat Wilderness Complex. Use this map or U.S. Geological Survey (USGS) topos to select a route.

Destinations

Hikers and packers can start at virtually any trailhead and reach the **Chinese Wall.** This 1,000-foot-high escarpment near the Continental Divide is the hallmark of the Bob and can see a surprising amount of traffic during the summer. For solitude, it's worth studying the maps and consulting with rangers to pick a less-traveled area.

West of the Divide, the South Fork of the Flathead River cuts through the Bob and is a favorite with floaters and anglers, who usually come in from Holland Lake on the western border. East of the Bob Marshall's divide, anglers go after rainbow, brown, lake, golden, and cutthroat trout. Grayling are here too, but they must be released when caught.

The **Sun River Game Preserve** was established in 1912 to protect and develop big-game herds. It now covers much of the eastern half of the Bob Marshall Wilderness Area—the only part of the Bob where hunting is prohibited.

Information

Contact the Forest Service at the Choteau Ranger Station, Rocky Mountain National Forest, Choteau, MT 59422 (406/466-5341).

NORTH-CENTRAL MONTANA

BACKGROUND

The Land

Montana's borders rope in just over 147,000 square miles, making it the fourth-largest state behind Alaska, Texas, and California. The northern edge of the state spans the Canadian province of Alberta and catches two thirds of Saskatchewan and the eastern part of British Columbia to boot. North and South Dakota lie off to the east, Wyoming flanks much of the south, and the Idaho state line rims the Bitterroot Mountains at the western and southwestern borders.

Western Montana is where the state's name (from the Spanish word for mountainous) rings particularly true: Steep pitches and narrow north-south valleys line up from the Idaho border to I-15. The Continental Divide enters from Canada in Glacier National Park, twists through the western mountains, and exits on a high flat stretch of land just west of Yellowstone National Park. Central Montana is particularly varied, with high plateaus and isolated mountain ranges running in no set direction. The eastern part of the state, where the landscape gradually flattens out into the Great Plains, is coursed by the Missouri and the Yellowstone Rivers and a host of smaller valleys. Contorted badlands, eroded terraces, and steep rimrocks fringe river valleys and dot

© BILL MCRAE

the plains. Minerals, coal, and oil are concealed throughout the state, giving rise to the nickname "Treasure State."

GEOGRAPHY

More than 570 million years ago, Precambrian sand and mud deposits blanketed the land that would become western Montana, before the supercontinent of Pangaea broke up into Europe, Africa, and the Americas. Traces of blue-green algae are the only fossils found in Precambrian-era rocks, which can still be seen in western and central Montana, where later movements forced them to the surface. Glacier National Park is almost entirely Precambrian in origin.

Toward the end of the Mesozoic era, tectonic plates were scudding all over the earth. According to plate-tectonics theory, as the Atlantic Ocean widened, the North American Plate was shoved into the Pacific Ocean Plate, which slipped under the western edge of the continent. The crust of western Montana, then at the leading edge of the continental plate, crumpled, cracked, and faulted as it rammed into the Pacific plate. The crust of Montana eventually over-rode the Pacific plate and was then lifted high above sea level. About 70 million years ago, the Rocky Mountains were produced by this collision of tectonic plates.

Some sedimentary layers, laid down with older strata topped by younger, were scrambled during these crustal collisions, and in some places older rocks were forced up from the geologic basement and slipped on top of younger ones. This is especially apparent in Glacier National Park. As the Rockies lifted, older layers of rocks skidded eastward from what are now the Flathead and North Fork Valleys, ending up as the Lewis Overthrust on the eastern front of the Rockies. Volcanic intrusions further developed the Rockies and formed separate mountain ranges to the east of them.

As western Montana lifted, ancient seas rolled back off the eastern part of the state for the final time. Swamps and floodplains stretched across eastern Montana by the end of the Mesozoic era, about 65 million years ago. Many plants and animals lived on these sedimentary flats, and their remains, as oil, go into our gas tanks today. Peat swamps were prevalent; eventually they crumbled and rotted into thick veins of coal.

Volcanoes began erupting in present-day Yellowstone National Park about 50 million years ago. A monumental eruption 600,000 years ago shot magma over the West, leaving a large crater, or caldera. Recurrent outpourings of lava formed the high plateau that's there now.

Alternating wet and dry periods over the past 40 million years modified terrain all over the state. During dry spells, river valleys filled with sediments, nearly burying many mountain peaks. When the climate dampened, rivers washed away the fill to reexpose underlying structures. This deposit-erosion cycle has made eastern Montana a paleontologist's dream. The largest complete tyrannosaurus skeleton on record was unearthed in remote Garfield County.

Cenozoic glaciers advanced south about 15,000 years ago. Valley glaciers ran down from northwestern Montana mountaintops and scoured out broad U-shaped valleys along their route. East of the divide, glaciers plowed the land flat as far south as the Missouri. The Beartooth Plateau, just north of Yellowstone National Park, was glacier-covered at much the same time lava was flowing over it. An ice dam in Idaho backed up the Clark Fork River until most of the valleys in western Montana were covered by glacial Lake Missoula. When the ice dam gave way, which it did repeatedly, torrents of water barreled across the Northwest, scouring topsoil and carving river gorges all the way to the Pacific coast.

East of the Rockies, glacial Lake Great Falls formed at the southern edge of the glacial sheet and reached from Great Falls to Cut Bank. Glacial ice forced the Missouri River, which originally emptied into Hudson's Bay, to alter its course southward to the Mississippi; the Milk River now flows in a section of the Missouri's original bed.

The Plains

Erosion and uplifts formed the prairie landscape. Water, frost, and wind have cut gullies and gulches into the plains and sculpted benches or terraces along river valleys. Northeastern Montana prairie is broad, flat, and underlain by gravel beds. These high plains were formed 3–15 million years ago in a dry climate. The gravel layer allows efficient surface drainage, avoiding erosion and the channels and gullies of the badlands. Glacial debris has further enriched the soil, making this some of the state's best agricultural land.

Montana's badlands, desolate and vegetation-poor, tend to be found south of the Missouri, where glaciers did not deposit thick layers of good soil. Soft bedrock just beneath the surface of bare ground is easily eroded by rain; gullies form, with sediment outwashes spreading from their mouths. The bare, rain-pounded soil develops a hard crust, which exacerbates the runoff and makes it all the more difficult for any vegetation to take hold. The barrenness of the badlands perpetuates itself.

The Mountains

The ranges of the Rockies have different geologic histories and compositions. The Boulder Batholith, a mass of intrusive granite between Butte and Helena, is filled with mineral veins, especially copper and silver. The Absarokas and the Gallatin Range in south-central Montana are blanketed with volcanic rocks from eruptions in and around Yellowstone National Park.

In the far northwestern part of the state, glaciers shrouded the mountains, leaving them relatively rolling and softly shaped. Where glaciers ran down from high cirques into mountain valleys, there is a characteristic straightening of the valley's path and a U shape to its floor, unlike the V-shaped river valleys. Glaciers also pushed along gravel and soil; these moraines are still visible to the geologically savvy.

The isolated mountain ranges of central Montana are not part of the Rockies. Many of them were formed at the end of the Mesozoic era, about 20 million years after the Rockies rose, when molten granite shot up from the depths of the earth and bowed up the overlying sedimentary formations. Other areas of central Montana were lifted along faults to form high plateaus and buttes.

The Rivers

The Missouri and Yellowstone Rivers look on the map like a big crab's pincer, joined to the leg just over the North Dakota border and grasping a big chunk of eastern Montana. Western rivers such as the Clark Fork of the Columbia, the Flathead, and the Kootenai are tucked into mountain valleys. Rivers provided the way into Montana for the first white explorers, who were hoping to sail out on the Columbia. Trappers and traders also used the rivers as thoroughfares. Steamboats made the difficult trip up the Missouri from St. Louis through sandbars, rapids, and fallen trees to Fort Benton—until railroads took over the transportation business. Towns sprang up in the river valleys, and highways were built on their banks.

The dams that now harness water power and create reservoirs across the state have altered Montana's geography. Every large river but the Yellowstone has been dammed at some point, and millions of gallons of water are backed up in Fort Peck Reservoir on the Missouri and in Lake Koocanusa on the Kootenai River. The Great Falls of the Missouri, which took Lewis and Clark 22 backbreaking days to portage in 1805, are now a series of hydroelectric dams.

CLIMATE

There's as much variety in Montana's weather as there is in the state's topography. The Continental Divide splits Montana into two broad climatic regions. West of the divide, the climate is influenced strongly by mild marine air from the Pacific; to the east, harsher continental patterns prevail.

Stories of extreme weather abound in Montana. It can get *cold*; the lowest temperature in the lower 48 states was recorded at Rogers Pass, northwest of Helena, in 1954: −70°F. Hot summers are common, with temperatures of 117°F recorded in both Glendive and Medicine Lake.

During the spring, the winds shift, and moisture comes up from the Gulf of Mexico. These

MONTANA WEATHER LORE

Back before the Weather Channel, Native Americans and early settlers needed to know the weather forecast. As they spent the majority of the day outdoors, they came to recognize the signs that preceded or produced a change in the weather. Many of these signs of changing weather are still a part of the rural Montana folklore.

At sunset, watch for small rainbow-like reflections beside the sun. Called **sundogs,** these luminous spots indicate increasing moisture in the atmosphere. Old-timers predict rain or snow when sundogs appear. In the fall, a sundog to the north of the sun indicates impending snow; to the south, a warm rain.

When the moon is high in the sky, look for a wide reflective ring around it. A **ring around the moon** is also predictive of moisture; the number of stars within the ring equals the number of days before the rain or snow arrives.

Three days of east wind means a storm is imminent.

Expect rain 90 days after a heavy fog.

Animal activities are often thought to indicate weather changes. Skittish, rambunctious animal behavior precedes a storm. Horses standing stock still on a high hill during the heat of the day indicates an approaching thunderstorm.

Expect a rainstorm to continue as long as raindrops are still hanging from tree leaves; the rain is over as soon as birds begin to sing.

storms sweep through the Midwest and hit the east slopes of the Rockies. May and June are the wettest months over most of the state; the exception is in the northwest, which gets most of its moisture from winter Pacific storms.

July and August are usually the warmest months. It does rain during the summer, but brief thunderstorms are the norm. By September, the weather may start to change for the colder and wetter, but there is frequently a lovely Indian summer in October. Winter storms can begin anytime, but roads are often clear through early November.

Chinooks

Warm, dry winter winds coming off the east slopes of the Rockies and across the plains are called "Chinooks." As the Pacific air passes over the mountains, it unloads its moisture and is warmed on its eastern downslope run. Chinook winds carry an almost mythological force. They can bring incredibly rapid relief from frigid weather; in Great Falls, the temperature once rose from −32°F to 15°F in seven minutes, almost seven degrees a minute.

Droughts

Montana's dry spells can be as striking as its extremes in heat and cold. Average rainfall for the western part of the state is 18 inches per year, 13 inches for the east. Studies of almost 300 years' worth of tree rings have shown that, every 20-some years, the western United States experiences a drought. A five-year drought that started in 1917 in eastern Montana drove many homesteaders away from agriculture. This drought was coupled with particularly harsh winters. The 1930s saw not only economic depression, but (according to tree rings) the most severe drought since 1700. The 1980s proved to be another era of drought for much of the state. When it's too dry for prairie grasses to survive, ranchers are forced to buy expensive feed, or sell their herds and wait for rain.

Flora

Montana's geography dictates its habitats, and the flora and fauna can be considered in two broad categories: prairie and mountain. Precipitation and elevation are the major factors determining what grows where. The state's varied ecosystems provide a home to more than 2,400 types of vascular plants.

THE PRAIRIES

Nineteenth-century atlases called the plains the Great American Desert, an undeserved name that ignores the subtle variety of the grasses and plants found here. While the prairie is not known for its trees, the savannas of eastern Montana offer more than sagebrush and prickly pear landscapes. Willows take root in the river valleys, and Lewis and Clark noted a "scattering of pine and cedar" on the hills, and chokecherries and currants on lower ground. The cottonwoods that grow near river bottoms were prized for firewood and for dugout canoes.

Eastern Montana is mostly short-grass prairie—that is, a dry grassland supporting perennial grasses such as bluestem, bluejoint, bluegrama, June, wheat, and pine grass. Cheat grass grows in overgrazed areas; it starts strong but can't last through the summer. Other "nuisances" are feather grass and needle grass, which irritate the skin and eyes of sheep and cattle. Russian thistle, or tumbleweed, arrived with European immigrants and is almost universally reviled for its uselessness and prolific nature.

Prairie flowers include the buttercup, yellowbell, crocus, shooting star, bluebell, blanketflower, golden aster, and daisy. Blue camas and death camas grow in moist areas. Prickly pear and three other species of cactus still dog those who try to walk across the prairie. Milkweed, a common roadside plant, was variously used as eye medicine, gravy stock, and chewing gum by the Cheyenne. The deep thick roots of the Indian breadroot plant were an important food for eastern Montana Indians.

Chokecherry bushes are widespread on the northern plains and into the Rockies. Chokecherries were pounded, dried, and stored for the winter by Plains Indians. Indians also brewed a tea from the bark to relieve stomach ailments; unripe chokecherry purée was used by both Indians and white settlers to treat diarrhea.

Prairie sage is a traditional sacred and medicinal plant to many Montana Indians.

CONIFEROUS FORESTS

Most of western Montana supports lush growth, dominated by coniferous forests. Although there are some western Montana prairies (especially around the Mission Valley and Dillon), timbered hillsides are the rule. This category is usually broken down into at least two separate habitats: lower montane and higher subalpine. The highest peaks of Montana also support small areas of alpine tundra.

Ponderosa pine predominates low on the slopes. A little higher, Douglas fir takes over, and above that, lodgepole pine (a species that depends on fire for its propagation) may form dense stands. Western larch, western red cedar, western white pine, grand fir, aspen, and birch can also be found. Willows and alders sprout up along streambeds, and kinnikinnick, Oregon grape, and serviceberries are common elements of the understory.

Subalpine forests are rooted in subalpine fir and Engelmann spruce. Tasty huckleberries are the best-loved subalpine understory shrub. Alpine larch is another hardy high-elevation conifer. An autumn hillside of reddish-gold "evergreens" doesn't necessarily mean a lot of dead trees. Rather, it's probably a stand of larch, one of the few conifer species that drops its needles in the winter.

Wildflower meadows of glacier lilies, alpine poppies, columbine, Indian paintbrush, asters, arnica, globeflowers, white dryads, and bear grass color the midsummer hillsides. Dogtooth violets and mariposa lilies grow a little farther

GETTING ALONG WITH MONTANA'S BEARS

When a bear is spotted in western Montana, there's always the question: grizzly or black? Grizzly bears are huge; adults commonly weigh 600-800 pounds and stand four feet tall at their muscular shoulder humps. A grizzly's dish-shaped profile contrasts with the black bear's straight Roman nose. Black bears are also smaller (about 200 pounds and about three feet tall) and lack a shoulder hump.

Color is not a reliable distinguishing trait. No shade of brown is unusual for either bear; black bears can be honey-colored and are commonly cinnamon, while grizzlies are not always silver-tipped and grizzled looking.

But perhaps the ability to tell bears apart is not the most important thing to know when confronted by any ursine specimen.

SAFETY CONSIDERATIONS

Find out where bears, especially grizzlies, live, and take precautions. In Montana, grizzlies live in Glacier and Yellowstone National Parks and in wilderness areas throughout the Rockies. Rangers will usually know if bears have been spotted locally, and trails are sometimes closed because of bear activity.

Try not to surprise a bear. Stay alert and make some noise while hiking; many hikers wear bells. Keep strong odors down. Don't wear a fragrance, and don't cook strong-smelling foods (freeze-dried foods are almost odor-free). At night, keep food and smelly clothing inside a car or strung high in a tree. Sleep well away from the cooking area. Women are frequently cautioned to avoid bear country while menstruating.

If you do see a bear, give it plenty of room. Try to stay upwind of the bear so it can get your scent. If the bear becomes aggressive, drop something that may absorb its attention and climb the nearest tall tree. If this isn't possible, the next best bet is probably to curl up into a ball, clasp your hands behind your neck, and play dead, even if the bear begins to bat you around.

Bears can, and occasionally do, kill people, but most people who enter bear country have few problems. In fact, it is a special thing to see a grizzly. They are as impressive as they are rare. Precautions and respect for bears will ensure not only your continued survival, but theirs as well.

---

down the slopes. In the valleys and low on the hills, the state flower, the bitterroot, blossoms in early June. Serviceberry bushes turn white with flowers early in May and bear purplish berries late in July. This member of the rose family grows on the slopes and canyons of the Rocky Mountains.

ALPINE TUNDRA

Alpine conditions exist in a few places in Montana. Above the timberline (9,000–10,000 feet), the gray-green ground cover includes small low-lying vegetation: grasses, mosses, lichens, sedges, and krummholz (small, twisted trees pruned by the wind) of whitebark pine.

Fauna

Montana's wildlife is varied and abundant. Lewis and Clark's journals, the first written account of the region's flora and fauna, are filled with wonder at the vast numbers of animals they had never encountered in the eastern states.

Today, Montana hosts some 107 species of mammals, 382 kinds of birds, 86 sorts of fish, 17 varieties each of reptiles and amphibians, and 315 different mollusks and crustaceans.

THE PRAIRIES

Lewis and Clark found the plains fairly swarming with wildlife, and not just with "musquetoes," either. Just upstream from the confluence of the Missouri and Yellowstone Rivers, Lewis noted:

> The whole face of the country was covered with herds of Buffaloe, Elk & Antelopes; deer are also abundant, but keep themselves more concealed in the woodland. the buffaloe Elk and Antelope are so gentle that we pass near them while feeding, without appearing to excite any alarm among them; and when we attract their attention, they frequently approach us more nearly to discover what we are, and in some instances pursue us to a considerable distance apparently with that view.

They also reported encounters with rattlesnakes, wolves, black bears, grizzlies, beavers (one of which gave Lewis's dog a nasty bite), bighorn sheep (whose meat was reportedly a delicacy), a "polecat" (skunk), mule deer, and prairie dogs. On their trip up the Missouri, Lewis provided the first descriptions of the sage grouse, the western meadowlark, and the cutthroat trout.

The buffalo, bears, and wolves may be mostly gone from the prairies, but what Lewis called "our trio of pests"—mosquitoes, gnats, and prickly pear—remain.

Prairie life calls for adaptation, and many animals that live here dig burrows. Witness the **prairie dog.** It can metabolize its own waste water and survive for years without drinking. The black-tailed prairie dogs of Montana live in "towns" of burrows, which are occasionally sublet by burrowing owls.

Another burrowing animal is the **pocket gopher,** a long-clawed, small-eyed rodent that comes aboveground only for quick passes at mating. Pocket gophers get their nutrition—both food and water—from plants they suck, roots first, into their burrows.

While burrows may provide defense for many rodents and birds, the **pronghorn** relies on fleetness. Individuals have been clocked at 70 miles per hour. Their horn is part of a sheath composed of keratin (a fingernail-like protein) and fused hairs covering a core of bone. Pronghorns (which despite the common appellation are not antelopes) shed their horn sheaths annually and pass the winter and spring sporting the bare bony horn core. They are the only mammals that shed their horns (as opposed to antlers, which are, as a rule, dropped annually).

Deer, both white-tailed and the large-eared mule deer, roam the breaks of the big eastern Montana rivers. **Coyotes** still prey on both wild and stock animals. **Gray wolves,** edging in from Canada and Minnesota, have returned to the badlands of the Missouri River in recent years.

Rattlesnakes can turn up just about anywhere in eastern Montana, and it pays to watch where you put your hands and feet. Wear sturdy shoes for hiking. Although healthy adults rarely die from a rattlesnake's venom, a bite does warrant prompt medical attention.

There's abundant **insect** life on the prairie. Most everyone who's read a Western novel can conjure an image of grasshoppers scouring the grasslands and swarming around cattle, cowboys, and horses.

Although magpies seem to control Montana's airways, the sharp-tailed grouse, mourning dove, killdeer, bobolink, long-billed curlew, horned lark, western meadowlark, goldfinch, Brewer's blackbird, and sparrow hawk are all **birds** to be spotted above the eastern Montana plains.

Warm-water species of fish, such as paddlefish, walleye, northern pike, and channel catfish, inhabit the Yellowstone and the Missouri as they cross the plains.

CONIFEROUS FORESTS

Both **black bears** and **grizzlies** live in and around western Montana's forests. **Elks** live high in the summer, low in the winter. They're sometimes called wapiti, and they grow their antlers fresh every summer and shed them in the winter. **Moose** are common but private. **Mule deer** negotiate rough forest terrain; **white-tailed deer** run across more open areas. Transition areas between two types of habitat (such as the edges of a meadow or clear-cut) are usually good places to look for all sorts of wildlife. **Bighorn sheep, mountain goats,** and grizzly bears are all more likely to be seen high on the slopes of the Rockies.

Mountain lions have been showing up in some unlikely places, like the streets of Columbia Falls, the parks of Missoula, and the campgrounds of Glacier National Park. Big people can usually frighten them off with shouting and menacing gestures, but children and small adults have been attacked. Youngsters should hike within sight of adults.

Because of its predatory instincts, the **gray wolf** has been trapped, hunted, and poisoned to near extinction. Since receiving protection as an endangered species, wolf populations have made a comeback, mostly near Glacier National Park and in the far reaches of northwestern Montana. Even before wolves were introduced to Yellowstone National Park, some seemed to have slipped in unescorted. Montana's wolf population grew to over 420 before wolves were delisted as endangered species in 2008 by the Bush administration. Responsibility for wolf population management has passed to individual states, with Montana officials talking about instituting a hunting season for wolves.

The wolf's smaller relative, the **coyote,** has managed not only to survive the abuses given to predator species but to actually thrive in human-inhabited areas.

Birds such as dippers, Clark's nutcrackers, spruce grouse, owls, woodpeckers, jays, chickadees, wrens, sparrows, flycatchers, mountain bluebirds, western tanagers, warblers, rufous hummingbirds, waterfowl, bald eagles, ospreys, and hawks all find niches in the varied habitats provided by western Montana's forests.

Westslope cutthroat trout, the state fish, is native to Montana's streams and lakes. First described by Meriwether Lewis, its Latin name, *Salmo clarki,* remembers William Clark. The name cutthroat is just as revealing: These black-specked fish sport two red slashes under their jaws. Because of their tendency to hybridize with rainbow trout, cutthroat are becoming rarer.

Bull trout live mostly in northwestern Montana, especially in their native Clark Fork and Flathead drainages, although stream degradation from overlogging has severely damaged their habitat and reduced their numbers. They're olive green with orange or yellow spots on their sides and can run up to 30 pounds.

Brown trout were imported from Europe in the 1880s, and their numbers have now surpassed many native species. Browns have a reputation for being wily and tough to hook. Another introduced species, the **brook trout,** comes from the eastern United States. The backs of these fish have light-colored "worm tracks" on their otherwise dark olive backs.

Whitefish are silver-sided with olive-green backs and small mouths. They are usually five pounds or less and live in the western part of the state.

Arctic grayling are trout cousins; they're not common, but they can be caught in southwestern and south-central Montana. These small copper-colored or bluish fish are usually less than a foot long, with large dorsal fins.

Until recently, **kokanee salmon,** landlocked salmon with small dark spots on a blue-tinted body, thrived in Flathead Lake, where they'd been planted in the 1920s. Although changes in the lake's ecology have not favored the Flathead kokanee, they are still abundant in other parts of northwestern Montana.

ALPINE TUNDRA

Plants and animals pack as much as possible into the short cool summers of the high country.

Hoary marmots, ground squirrels, pikas, and **mountain goats** are commonly spotted around Logan Pass (6,680 feet), one of Glacier National Park's alpine communities. The **white-tailed ptarmigan** is the only bird living year-round on the tundra, although other species, such as **water pipits** and **finches,** summer here.

Environmental Issues

THE FUTURE OF MONTANA'S WOLVES

When Lewis and Clark crossed Montana in the early 1800s, gray wolves (*Canis lupus*) were commonly seen on the plains, and were, along with grizzly bears (also originally a prairie animal), the dominant predator of the plains wilderness ecosystem. But with the advent of the fur trade, and then agriculture based on livestock, the native wolf populations were gradually exterminated. By the 1930s, no gray wolves remained in Montana.

The rise of environmentalism and the passage of the Endangered Species Act (ESA) in 1973 created a new atmosphere of advocacy for reintroducing the wolf to the Western United States. Organizations including Defenders of Wildlife and the National Wildlife Federation spearheaded a successful effort to have wolves listed as "endangered" under the ESA's provisions. "Bounty" programs, which paid hunters to kill wolves, were discontinued, and it became illegal to kill wolves in the United States. In addition, provisions of the ESA called on the federal government to implement a plan for the recovery of the gray wolf population.

In the early 1980s, wolves from Canada began to move into northwest Montana, and by 1995 there were six wolf packs in that region. Advocates for wolves proposed boosting the recovery of wolf populations by actively restoring wolves to suitable areas in the Northern Rockies. Objections arose from livestock ranchers, hunters worried about the impact of wolves on game populations, and other concerned people, while environmentalists and wildlife advocates cheered on the reintroduction.

Eventually, the U.S. Congress held hearings and ultimately ordered the U.S. Fish and Wildlife Service (USFWS) to prepare an Environmental Impact Statement on the reintroduction of wolves to Yellowstone National Park and central Idaho. In 1995 and 1996, as part of its wolf recovery plan, the USFWS trapped 66 wolves in southwestern Canada and transplanted them to Yellowstone National Park and central Idaho.

The wolves quickly made themselves at home, reproducing and expanding their range faster than any of the experts had predicted.

One major objection to the reintroduction of wolves to the West was that wolves would devastate livestock herds. Even fans of reintroducing wolves acknowledged that wolves are highly efficient predators. To help address this concern, Defenders of Wildlife launched a program to compensate livestock producers when the reintroduced wolves preyed on their stock. By the end of 2002 the fund had paid out more than $270,000 to ranchers in the Northern Rockies.

In general, predation on livestock has been lower than predicted when the wolf reintroduction was first proposed, though it has still been significant. Fifty-two cattle, 99 sheep, nine dogs, and five llamas were confirmed lost to wolves in 2002 (these figures do not include livestock killed by predators but not conclusively confirmed as wolf kills). In those areas of Montana where Yellowstone wolves have dispersed, seven of 10 known wolf packs were involved in livestock depredation in 2002, and confirmed losses included 10 cattle and 71 sheep killed. Many wolves have been killed by the USFWS when it has been impossible to deter them from further predation.

By the mid-2000s, approximately 900 to 1,250 wolves were living in the northern Rockies in about 100 packs. While most of the population was in the Yellowstone Park area, some packs and individuals—the archetypal lone wolf—dispersed across other parts of Montana.

Beginning in 2005, ranchers in remote Garfield and McCone counties, which are adjacent to the vast C. M. Russell Wildlife Refuge (more than 300 miles north of Yellowstone, along the Missouri River), began to relate stories of abnormally high numbers of sheep and calves killed by predators, accompanied by sightings of canines that were described as wolves. The numbers of animals killed—by 2006 the tally included hundreds of sheep, dozens of young cattle, and even colts—convinced many ranchers that they were dealing with a wolf. According to USFWS regulations, individual ranchers are not allowed to kill a predatory wolf. Eliminating a predatory wolf falls to authorized USFWS agents.

In fall 2006 a large 105-pound male wolf was shot by USFWS hunters between Jordan and Circle—the first wolf seen in the area since the 1920s. The wolf was held responsible for the deaths of livestock worth tens of thousands of dollars. Under terms of the original reintroduction program, these ranchers were due reimbursement for the value of the livestock killed by the wolf—if the livestock-killing wolf was part of the reintroduced wolf population from Yellowstone.

The DNA of each of the reintroduced wolves from Yellowstone was on record, and after performing a DNA test on the wolf killed by the USFWS, researchers found that it was not part of the reintroduced population, but rather a wolf whose DNA matched wolves from northern Minnesota. Apparently the wolf had followed the Missouri River west from the woodlands of Minnesota before making its home in the Missouri badlands. Because the wolf was not part of the reintroduced population, affected ranchers were not able to apply for reimbursement for their dead livestock. The incidence of wolf sightings and heavy predation continues in eastern Montana; it is thought likely that wolves have set up a breeding population in the C. M. Russell Wildlife Refuge.

In 2008, citing the successful reintroduction of the gray wolf, the USFWS delisted the wolf as an endangered species. Responsibility for wolf population management now passes from the federal government to the individual states of Montana, Idaho, and Wyoming. Each of the states is required to come up with a wolf management plan that will allow for a population of at least 300 wolves, which is the minimum number required to maintain a stable population. In 2008, Montana had at least 422 wolves, including 39 breeding pairs, living in 73 packs. At the time of delisting, the state's wolf population was increasing about 25 percent annually. As part of its wolf management program, Montana officials are talking about instituting a hunting season for wolves.

POWER GENERATION ON THE GO

Coal-based power generation has been a political and environmental issue in Montana for more than 30 years, starting with Colstrip's enormous coal-fired plants in the 1970s. Now the development of coal bed methane gas is the principal topic of contention between energy developers and environmentalists.

Vast reserves of methane gas occur naturally in the coal beds that underlie much of southeastern Montana. Record high prices for natural gas has led energy companies to develop plans to tap into the coal seams and extract the gas, which would then be used for electric power generation.

However, extracting the coal bed methane may have serious consequences for ranchers and farmers who depend on groundwater for wells and springs. Underground coal is a natural aquifer for ground water—it's a porous layer of rock that allows the water to percolate below the landscape. Water is also what holds the methane gas in the coal beds. To extract the methane, wells are drilled into the coal seam and the water is pumped out. Methane gathers in the recesses formerly occupied by the water and is drawn to the surface and piped to power plants to be burned.

Pumping coal seams dry to extract methane also risks that wells drilled into the same coal aquifers will cease to provide water for rural residents of the region, meaning that longtime farms and ranches may suddenly have no access to water.

Methane gas development stalled until environmentalists and power-generation companies agreed on a plan to reinject the groundwater back into the coal seams after extracting the gas. Although this is costly for the power producers, it seems to address the concerns of ranchers and environmentalists.

Colstrip is no longer the only focus for power development in eastern Montana. The Great Northern Power Development Company is in the development phase of a huge power plant between Circle and Jordan along Nelson Creek. The planned development includes a 500-megawatt coal-fired power plant based on local lignite, plus a 60-megawatt wind-generation unit based on 50 wind towers.

THE GIFTS OF MINING PAST

One of Montana's founding industries was mining. The history of the huge mines at Butte—to say nothing of the 1860s Gold Rush, the sapphire mines, the silver and lead mines, and on and on—have all contributed mightily to the spunk and character of the state. However, recent years have revealed just what enormous environmental damage is now being exacted by the state's mining past.

Even though copper mining has ceased in Butte, the Berkeley Pit remains a mile-deep reservoir of toxic water. In the 1980s, investigations revealed that many homes in the Butte area, built on foundations made from mining tailings, were highly radioactive. The Butte-Anaconda area is the nation's single largest Superfund site. (The Environmental Protection

Agency's Superfund allows for cleanup of particularly toxic areas.)

Downstream from Butte, in the drainage of the Clark Fork River, recent restoration programs have been largely successful in reintroducing trout to this magnificent river. By the 1950s the river's chemical load was so high that it had become essentially sterile. However, the arsenic and heavy metals that flowed in the river for nearly a century haven't disappeared; many of these deposits are merely coated in mud.

Most of these toxic sediments lie behind the Mill Town Dam, just upriver from Missoula, which corrals the waters of the Clark Fork and Blackfoot Rivers at their confluence. The dam, an increasingly unstable log structure that was built in 1907 to generate electricity for an adjacent lumber mill, now serves primarily as a repository for sediment and mining wastes.

After years of debate about how to address the issues presented by the Mill Town Dam, NorthWestern Energy, the dam's owner, and Arco, which is liable for the contamination, agreed to an EPA recommendation to remove the structure and restore the rivers by extracting the toxic sediments from the river bottom—all without harming downstream fish populations.

The scope of the project was enormous: The price tag for removing the dam and the sediment was $120 million and involved removing the 500-foot-wide wooden dam and 2.6 million cubic yards of sediment. In 2008 the last of the dam and sediments were removed, and the rivers were rejoined as free-flowing streams of water.

However, by far the greatest human tragedy related to past Montana mining involves the small Northwest Montana community of Libby, site of a vermiculite (used in planting soil and kitty litter) mine. Libby residents discovered in the late 1990s that mixed in with the vermiculite, which many residents had spent their lives mining and that stood in piles around the town, was a mineral called tremolite, a rare and toxic form of asbestos. Tragically, the miners and many townspeople are now suffering from the effects of asbestos poisoning. Many have died from asbestos-related cancers, and even more are ill. Although the W. R. Grace Company (which owned the mine) *and* the government knew about the asbestos, nothing was done to stop the dust that contaminated the town. In 2000, after the *Seattle Post-Intelligencer* and other news sources began running stories on the asbestosis, W. R. Grace bought back the mine (which they'd sold years before), banned EPA officials from it, and backed off from promises to clean it up. In 2001 the W. R. Grace Company filed for bankruptcy, claiming it could not handle the deluge of personal-injury lawsuits. By the summer of 2001 about 5,500 Libby residents had been tested for asbestos. Nearly 20 percent of those tested had lung abnormalities. Many homes are contaminated, thanks to the free vermiculite insulation that was available for years in big piles outside the processing site. The EPA is managing an emergency cleanup of the town and has found contamination in places such as the high school athletic field.

As Montana enters the 21st century, its mining past is an increasingly heavy burden.

History

EARLY INHABITANTS AND EXPLORATION
The First Settlers

Proto-Indians first arrived in Montana from Asia about 10,000–15,000 years ago. After crossing the Bering Sea causeway, they traveled along the Great North Trail, the rift that opened up along the east face of the Rocky Mountains when the ice fields of the last ice age retreated into the mountains.

These people hunted big game and used tools made of chipped stone. Between 8000 and 6000 B.C., these early Indians lived principally on the plains and foothills. Around 5000 B.C., a desert climate developed, and game animals and the people who hunted them left.

Buffalo again spread across the region as a more moderate climate developed about A.D. 500. The hunters returned, probably from the south and west, bringing with them new techniques and cultural practices. These early dwellers were probably the ancestors of the Salish Indians. Before the introduction of horses, hunting techniques such as using a buffalo jump, or *pishkun,* were developed. Entire herds of buffalo would be stampeded off precipices and slaughtered for meat. The use of the tepee, or movable skin tent, was introduced. Pictographs and petroglyphs (rock paintings and carvings) were first made during this period.

Historic Indian Tribes

When white traders and settlers arrived in the region in the early 1800s, they did not find a land peopled with indigenous native tribes. Instead, the Indians of Montana were only recent immigrants, attempting to establish homelands and work out the cultural changes that their recent uprooting had caused. These tribes had been displaced as European settlement along the East Coast and in the Southwest increasingly forced Native American inhabitants from their traditional homelands, and they in turn displaced other tribes as all were forced north and west.

Some of the tribes that migrated to Montana during this period were not traditionally nomadic. Most came from woodlands in the Great Lakes–Mississippi Basin region, where they were sedentary, sometimes agricultural people who lived in permanent earthen dwellings. During the process of dislocation to the West, agriculture was lost and a hunting culture developed. The earth lodge was abandoned for the tepee. For these people, the buffalo became more than a food source: It was the central assumption on which their entire cultural life was predicated. Social organization was structured by warrior societies, and in some cases, by clan. Women were responsible for most of the daily work, save hunting and fighting. The Plains Indians shared an animistic religion.

The first tribe to enter Montana during the historic period was the Shoshone, who began to move into the southwestern corner of the state from the Great Basin area about 1600. They drove the resident Salish tribes (who had migrated from the Pacific Northwest several centuries earlier) farther north into the mountains. The Shoshone were fearsome warriors and the first Montana tribe to ride horses, which they had procured from the Spanish colonies.

The Crow Indians arrived in Montana shortly thereafter and settled along the Yellowstone River drainages, the first tribe to actually settle on the Montana prairies. The Blackfeet entered Montana from the north and east about a century later, around 1730, and brought the rifle. The Blackfeet, and their allies the Gros Ventre and the Assiniboin, soon established dominance over the northern Montana plains.

Further pressure from white settlement forced the Sioux and Northern Cheyenne into eastern Montana. The Cree and Chippewa tribes entered Montana in the 1870s as they were displaced from the Canadian prairies. As more and more tribes were squeezed into the area that would later become Montana, intertribal rivalries intensified. The Crow were hated enemies of the Blackfeet. The Blackfeet slaughtered the Salish or Kootenai Indians who dared to leave the safety of the mountains. As the Sioux entered Montana, they too became enemies of the Crow.

The Salish and Kootenai retained some traditions of the Northwest Indian tribes. Although these tribes once traveled over the Rockies to hunt buffalo, the presence of the fierce Blackfeet confederation on the prairies soon made these hunting expeditions too dangerous.

The Corps of Discovery

In 1803, President Thomas Jefferson purchased the Louisiana Territory from France for $11.25 million. The territory was understood to be the land west of the Mississippi to its Missouri headwaters, and north of the Arkansas River to the 49th parallel. Jefferson engaged his personal secretary, Meriwether

Lewis, to head an expedition to explore this new American territory and to search for a passage from the Missouri River to the headwaters of the Columbia River. Lewis in turn chose William Clark to be the cocommander of what Jefferson called the Corps of Discovery.

The two captains, three sergeants, 23 enlisted men, and Clark's black slave, York, left St. Louis in May 1804. In North Dakota they were joined by French trader Toussaint Charbonneau, who had traveled widely on the upper Missouri and spoke several Indian languages. One of Charbonneau's wives, a 15-year-old Shoshone girl named Sacagawea, gave birth during the spring. Lewis and Clark hired Charbonneau as interpreter and allowed the young mother and baby to accompany the Corps, as they later expected to travel through Shoshone territory.

The Corps entered Montana on April 26, 1805, passing the confluence of the Missouri and the Yellowstone Rivers. They wound their way up the Missouri, traveling in pirogues, huge French-Canadian dugout canoes. By July 25 they were at the Three Forks of the Missouri and were heartened by Sacagawea's claim that they were near her homeland. Nineteen days later, near Lemhi Pass, Lewis encountered the expedition's first Montana Indian (a Shoshone, who led them to Sacagawea's brother). They beached their pirogues, traded for horses, and proceeded down the Bitterroot Valley. On September 13 they crossed Lolo Pass out of Montana toward the Pacific Coast.

After a hungry and flea-ridden winter on the Oregon coast, the Corps started back up the Columbia. They backtracked to Lolo Pass and crossed into Montana on June 27, 1806. On July 1, at the point where Lolo Creek meets the Bitterroot River, the expedition divided. Clark took part of the Corps and retraced the previous journey to the Missouri headwaters, but this time followed the Gallatin River over the Bozeman Pass in order to explore the Yellowstone River Valley. Lewis took the rest of the men and followed old Indian trails up the Blackfoot River and then over the Rockies to the Great Falls in order to scout a more direct passage over the Continental Divide. While Clark had an uneventful journey down the Yellowstone, Lewis had a confrontation with a group of Blackfeet that left two Indian warriors dead.

The two parties met at the confluence of the Yellowstone and the Missouri on August 12. By September 23, 1806, they were in St. Louis. This amazing journey had an almost immediate impact on the history of Montana. Members of the Corps retold stories of vast amounts of wildlife, especially fur-bearing mammals. Within a year, the first fur trading fort was built in Montana.

Trading Posts

The first fur-trading post, Fort Ramon, was founded in 1807 by Manuel Lisa at the confluence of the Bighorn and Yellowstone Rivers, between present-day Billings and Miles City. Beaver, much sought for European fashions, was the major item of trade. Some Indian tribes, notably the Salish and Crow, maintained friendly relations with the white traders and trappers. The Blackfeet, who controlled the Missouri River area, were hostile to the Salish, Crow, and whites.

John Jacob Astor's American Fur Company built Fort Union at the confluence of the Yellowstone and Missouri in 1829 and finally induced the Blackfeet to trade peacefully by dispatching a Blackfeet-speaking trapper to bring them to the fort for a conference. The Blackfeet complied. Four thousand beaver pelts were taken from the heart of the heavily defended Blackfeet territory by Astor's trappers in 1838.

Fort Union and the American Fur Company soon ruled the Montana fur trade. As beavers were increasingly trapped out (and European fashion changed), trade continued in buffalo hides. By 1840 the era of the trapper and mountain man was over; almost three dozen trading forts had been built in Montana before the beaver was trapped to near extinction.

The Black Robes

Iroquois Indians accompanied French trappers to western Montana in the early 1800s. While the Iroquois were to teach the local Flathead and Nez Percé how to trap, they also passed on information about Christianity. The Montana Indians heard of "Black Robes" who possessed a Book of Heaven, whose "medicine" or power was great. The Flathead were greatly intrigued and sent four delegations to St. Louis to ask for a Black Robe to come and visit the tribe.

Finally, in 1840, Father Pierre Jean De Smet, a Belgian-born Jesuit, came west. Although the Indians' spiritual demands had more to do with the search for powerful medicine to protect them from the hostile Blackfeet than with traditional salvation, the Flathead and Nez Percé seemed genuinely friendly and anxious to learn the way of the Catholic fathers.

In 1841, St. Mary's Mission was established in the Bitterroot Valley near Stevensville. Here the Jesuits taught the Indians agriculture, music, milling, and, of course, religion. The original mission was abandoned in 1850 after De Smet made the mistake of starting missionary work with the Blackfeet. The Flathead were not eager to share their "medicine" with their enemies and lost interest in De Smet's projects. Another influential early church, St. Ignatius Mission, was established in 1854 in the Mission Valley among the Pend d'Oreille Indians.

Little attempt was made to bring Christianity to the Plains Indians until they were on reservations. Most of the early missionary work was done by the Catholic Church. Protestant missionaries entered the state only after white settlement had begun, when gold ore and high living induced the kind of bad doings best corrected by regular churchgoing.

WHITE SETTLEMENT AND INDIAN WARS
Gold

The trappers and traders of the early 19th century left little behind them except endangered species. There were no roads, no communications networks, and almost no settlements (from this era, only Fort Benton still exists as a community).

James and Granville Stuart discovered gold on Gold Creek near Deer Lodge in 1860. In

1862 gold was found on Grasshopper Creek near Bannack, and the next year saw prospecting along Alder Gulch near Virginia City. Last Chance Gulch, which was to become Helena, boomed in 1864.

These large strikes and many smaller mines attracted people of varied character to Montana. Fewer than 100 whites were in the state in 1860. By 1870 there were more than 20,000. Some men came to Montana to prospect for gold and get rich; others came to get rich by stealing and killing. Travel between the settlements of Virginia City, Bannack, and other mining camps became increasingly dangerous as "road agents" preyed on stagecoaches and miners.

For its protection, Virginia City elected Henry Plummer as sheriff. Plummer, however, doubled as leader of the principal gang of road agents, called the "Innocents." More than 100 people were killed by the Innocents during 1862–1863. In response, committees of vigilantes formed, which reached summary judgment and hanged the Innocents.

By 1870, approximately $100 million in gold had been extracted from Montana claims. The advent of great wealth and private property soon made firm government and community lawfulness imperative. In 1864, Montana became a territory, with Bannack its capital. Schools, churches, and other civic institutions were established in Virginia City. Miners began bringing their families out to the frontier to settle.

Treaties Made and Broken

While the Indians of the western mountains accommodated the arrival of white miners, trappers, and missionaries, the Plains Indians largely maintained their traditional ways during the first years of white ingress.

The first trail across the northern United States was the Oregon Trail. To protect travelers along its passage through Wyoming, the U.S. government produced the Fort Laramie Treaty in 1851, which was signed by the Crow, Gros Ventre, and Assiniboin. These tribes were assigned reservations in eastern Montana, as were the Blackfeet, who did not attend the meeting or sign the treaty, but were assigned a reservation in absentia.

The discovery of gold in the Rocky Mountains increased the demand for transportation routes across treaty Indian country. The Bozeman Trail, blazed during the 1860s, cut across Sioux tribal land to reach Montana's goldfields. Three military forts were built to protect the trail. Gold was also discovered in the Black Hills of South Dakota, country considered sacred by the Sioux, and prospectors flooded in.

These infractions by the whites infuriated the Indians. The U.S. government responded by unilaterally diminishing the size of the original reservations. The Sioux and Cheyenne, among the last of the tribes to be forced into Montana by white western expansion, were especially angry at the ongoing incursions. After the gold rush in the Black Hills, the Sioux quit the reservation completely and resumed their traditional plains lifestyle on the prairies of eastern Montana.

Army Versus Indian

The U.S. government in 1876 ordered the Sioux and the Cheyenne back onto the reservation. The Indians refused, and the Army was dispatched to compel them back. Three columns of infantry set out. The first column to arrive in Indian country divided, sending Gen. George Custer and the Seventh Cavalry on ahead to seek the hostiles. They found the combined Cheyenne and Sioux force (perhaps 3,000 warriors) on June 26, 1876. Custer rashly decided to do battle alone, and his entire command (265 men) was destroyed.

The next year, the Nez Percé under Chief Joseph fled from their Oregon homeland across Idaho and Montana, attempting to reach sanctuary in Canada. After a battle with the U.S. Army at the Big Hole in western Montana, the Nez Percé fled south to the Yellowstone Park area and then veered north, hoping to escape into Canada near Havre. Thirty miles from the border, Gen. Nelson Miles overtook the fleeing tribe. The Nez Percé, of Northwest origins, were sent to reservations in Oklahoma.

Custer's annihilation notwithstanding, by 1877 all of the Indians in Montana were incarcerated on reservations. In fact, many forces besides the Army had worked to weaken and inevitably subjugate the Indians. Diseases introduced from white settlements devastated Indian populations. An outbreak of smallpox among the Blackfeet in 1837 is reckoned to have killed three quarters of the tribe. Alcohol, illegally traded to the Indians, corrupted and debilitated the traditional warrior societies.

As trade evolved from peltry to buffalo robes, the Indians were unwittingly involved in exterminating the animal that provided the cornerstone of their entire traditional culture. Before white settlers reached the plains, 60 million buffalo lived in North America. By 1870, that number was down to 10–20 million. By 1883, after railroads crossed the West and settlers were streaming in after the Civil War, there were only 100–200 buffalo left in the United States.

With the buffalo largely exterminated, Native Americans were reduced to complete dependence on handouts from the government's Indian agents. By the mid-1880s the federal government spent $7 per year per Indian on a reservation, while it spent $1,000 per year on a soldier stationed in Montana's Indian land.

The Railroad Arrives

Riverboats were the only form of transportation linking Montana and the rest of the nation until the 1880s. Boats could reach as far inland as Fort Benton on the Missouri and to Pompey's Pillar on the Yellowstone, but real economic growth and settlement awaited the coming of the railroad.

The Union Pacific built a spur line north from Utah to Butte in 1881. The Northern Pacific crossed the length of Montana, linking Portland and Chicago in 1883. In return for opening the northern transcontinental line, the Northern Pacific was given a land grant: For every mile of track laid, the railroad received 40 sections (40 square miles) of land. In Montana alone, this amounted to 17 million acres.

The Great Northern stretched its service along the Montana-Canada border, joining Minneapolis and Seattle in 1893. The Milwaukee Road crossed central Montana on its way to Seattle in 1909. With access to coastal markets, Montana opened up to further development and immigration.

Cattle Country

Montana had a cattle trade in the western valleys and foothills since the 1860s as ranches grew up to feed the mining camps, and Texas longhorns had been trailed into Montana as early as 1866. But the era of the cattleman didn't really begin until the 1880s, when longhorn cattle were trailed north from Texas in great numbers.

Typically, the large "outfits" that brought cattle into Montana at this time were owned by a group of investors who bought shares in herds often numbering in the tens of thousands. Cowboys would herd these longhorns north from Texas, summer them free on the grassy unfenced prairies of Montana, and then round them up, sort them by brand, and sell them to eastern markets. This get-rich-quick scheme worked for many, because with a small investment in the startup animal, low labor costs with the cowboys, and no feed bills to pay, the profitability was great.

Initially, the fattened steers were trailed south into Wyoming to railheads on the Union Pacific. With the construction of the Northern Pacific along the course of the Yellowstone River in 1881–1882, railheads such as Wibaux, Miles City, and Billings became centers for the livestock trade and turned into full-blooded Old West cattle towns. In 1870 there were 48,000 head of cattle in Montana. By 1886, the height of the open-range period, there were 675,000 head.

Butte

In 1864, two miners staked a claim for gold on a lonely bluff near the Continental Divide at the headwaters of the Clark Fork River. The gold soon played out, but miners discovered something else: silver.

As a source of wealth, silver was as good as

gold, but the mining techniques were quite different. Gold can be panned from streams by individuals working alone and can be sold as powder or lumps. Silver, however, requires underground mining to extract the ore, which then must be refined by smelters. As mining at Butte developed in the 1870s, the era of the independent prospector passed and corporate mining began. Then, as silver ran out, copper became the lodestone of Butte mining.

The transcontinental railroads vied for lucrative contracts to take the refined metal to world markets. The railroads also brought in immigrants to work the deep veins. Railroads were built between Butte and Anaconda and between Butte and Great Falls to take the ore to smelters.

Butte, soon to be known as "the richest hill on earth," was dominated by smokestacks, peopled by immigrants, and undercut with 10,000 miles of mineshafts. It quickly became Montana's largest and wealthiest city. The city never slept: Miners worked the veins 24 hours a day, and bars, restaurants, and other businesses were always open to serve their customers. The huge influx of immigrants that poured into Butte during this period from Central Europe, Italy, Cornwall, Ireland, and China gave Butte its cosmopolitan flavor and its ethnic neighborhoods.

Other factors were not so positive. Butte was an environmental disaster. The pollution from the smelters soon killed all the vegetation within a 20-mile radius. The trees that weren't killed by smoke were cut for mine supports or to fuel the smelters. Smelting also used vast amounts of water, which was simply returned to streams laden with toxic chemicals and minerals. The mining process produced mountains of tailings, some of which were radioactive. Entire communities were built on these tailings.

EMPIRES GAINED AND LOST
The End of the Open Range
While Butte was booming during the 1880s and '90s, events conspired to end the Old West cattle days on the eastern prairies. The winter of 1886–1887 has been made most famous by

the grim drawing of the *Last of the 5,000* by artist Charlie Russell. A very dry summer led to a long, extremely cold winter. The warm-weather longhorn, summered on the drought-stricken plains, died in huge numbers as temperatures remained below zero for weeks. One half to three quarters of the cattle in Montana reportedly froze or starved to death. A single winter ended the era of the great cattle drives.

Sheep had played a part in Montana agriculture since the days of De Smet's St. Mary's Mission, but now the number of sheep on the plains increased considerably as ranchers realized that the hardy sheep were a good hedge against losses of the more temperate cattle. In 1870 there were just 2,000 head of sheep in the state, one for every 10 settlers; by 1900, with six million head, sheep outnumbered people 24 to one.

While the railroads opened up the growth of the cattle trade in Montana, they also brought in settlements. The open range was increasingly privately owned. The various homesteading acts of the late 1800s and early 1900s opened public land for settlement. With the hegemony of the big cattle outfits broken after 1886, homesteaders set up along the fertile valley bottoms, fencing off some of the best range and water access.

Homesteaders
Rail entrepreneurs like James Hill of the Great Northern quickly realized the benefits of establishing settlements all along his rail lines. Huge advertising campaigns were launched to tempt the homesteader to the plains of Montana. Rural European communities received advice from experts regarding the fertility of the Great Plains, and immigrants were given pamphlets as they disembarked onto U.S. soil.

Much of the promotional material presented by the railroads was fanciful, and some of it was flat wrong. It promised, for example, plenty of rain, fertile soil, and opportunities for all. Nonetheless, the advertising worked. The population of Montana grew 60 percent during the first decade of the 20th century, and the number of farms doubled.

While homesteading acts allotted 320 acres of "free land" per individual (a husband and

THE KINGS OF COPPER

During the boom years of copper and silver mining in Butte – in the 1870s and 1880s – the mines, the city, and the whole state were dominated by three men, called the Copper Kings.

William Clark made his first fortune mining and smelting silver, and extended his empire into banking and politics. Marcus Daly cannily bought up depleted silver mines in order to exploit the mines' rich veins of copper (electrical power created a market for copper wire, which turned copper from a junk metal to one of Montana's most precious commodities). Daly also had large business holdings in the lumber industry: His Butte-area mines used 40,000 board-feet of timber a day. Fritz Augustus Heinze cleverly manipulated the "Apex Law," which states that if a vein of ore surfaces on one person's claim, then that person has the right to the rest of the vein, no matter where it goes when underground. Because he owned the apex of mines owned by large mining interests, Heinze was able to thumb his nose at big business while becoming very wealthy.

Each of these men led an almost raucously public life. Heinze's wealth and reputation had less to do with his mining knowledge than with his control of the courtrooms. He courted public affection by publicly taking on the giant companies, such as Standard Oil, that were swallowing up Butte mining. Daly and Clark engaged in a fiercely contested rivalry involving wealth, political influence, and popular opinion. Each controlled newspapers, bought judges, and paid off legislators. A classic battle was fought in 1889 as Montana became a state. Daly favored Anaconda as state capital, while Clark lobbied for and triumphed with his choice of Helena. Daly got revenge by denying Clark a long-sought-after seat in the U.S. Senate. These and other battles were chronicled in the state press and were the stuff of public gossip and debate.

Butte was not the only area influenced by the era of the Copper Kings. Missoula and Hamilton were largely built by the Daly logging empire. Anaconda was essentially a Daly company town, built around his Washoe smelter, but with great pretensions. The growth of Great Falls was assured when smelters were built on the banks of the Missouri to refine Butte ore.

The political complexion of early Montana was largely established by events centered in Butte. Many of the early miners and prospectors who were attracted to the gold strikes of the 1860s and the boom of the 1870s were Southerners dislocated by the Civil War. They brought to Montana a strong hatred of Yankee Republicanism; most Irish immigrants were dependably Democratic. Both Daly and Clark fought their political battles from within the Democratic Party. Butte was the largest city in the state by far, and its population of workers, when unionized, voted unswervingly Democratic. To this day, Montana has a stronger Democratic Party than many Western states.

wife qualified for two allotments), even this quantity of land was insufficient to make a living in Montana. During good years with plenty of rain, the prairies provided adequate grazing, but most new settlers did not come to raise livestock (stockmen were seen as an anachronism). Farmers represented progress and the evolution of the West: They came to turn the soil over and raise grain.

Communities sprang up along the rail lines, particularly along the Great Northern's track through the Hi-Line and along the Milwaukee Road through central Montana. Towns were established near the rail sidings and usually consisted of a grain elevator, bank, hotel, and bar. Farms were "improved on" according to Homestead Act requirements, but were often little more than a tar paper or sod shack with ad hoc outbuildings for livestock. Eastern Montana has never been more populated than it was in 1918, with at least one homestead per square mile of arable land.

The Company

In the first years of the 20th century the Copper Kings Fritz Augustus Heinze, Marcus

Daly, and William Clark, largely to spite each other, each sold out to the buyer that was least likely to benefit the others. In each case it was Standard Oil. By 1906, Standard Oil, soon to reconfigure its holdings as the Anaconda Company, controlled almost everything in Butte. It became known simply as "The Company." Then, in the 1910s, when the Anaconda Company became yoked with the Montana Power Company, these two corporations controlled practically the whole state.

The Copper Kings had been largely beneficent to their workers and even suffered the unions gladly. Not so the Company. During the 1910s, Butte was a battlefield of labor-management disputes. Conditions in the mines worsened. The presence of "Wobblies" from International Workers of the World (IWW), a labor union that propounded revolutionary struggle during World War I, led to the Anaconda Company's targeting of "communist" influences that resulted in lynchings. The Great Depression further darkened conditions in Butte as the world price of copper fell 80 percent. Production of copper in 1933 was 10 percent of what it had been in 1929. The Company shifted much of its operations to Chile and Mexico, where copper was mined in open pits, involving lower labor costs. Butte, once one of the richest cities in the West, now faced massive unemployment problems.

The Dust Bowl Years

For a time the weather cooperated with the homesteaders in eastern Montana. Then, from the late 1910s to the mid-1920s, nature shifted gears. In 1916, Shelby, on the Hi-Line, received more than 15 inches of rain; in 1919, the third year of intense drought, the town received less than seven inches. Drought continued, coupled with high winds and grasshoppers. Range fires ruined crops and destroyed communities. Sixty thousand people had left Montana by 1925, representing 11,000 abandoned farms; 214 state banks failed, and Montana led the nation in bankruptcies. A few years later, disaster struck again. The stock market crash, combined with a second severe drought during the Dust Bowl years of the 1930s, eliminated many more farmers and ranchers.

The New Deal

As elsewhere in the United States, in Montana the Great Depression of the 1930s was followed by the spending programs of the New Deal. The works projects had a great impact on the state. Not only did programs like the Civilian Conservation Corps (CCC) and the Works Progress Administration (WPA) give employment and training to people who were out of jobs, but they produced monumental results. One of the largest public works projects in the country was Fort Peck Dam, completed in 1940 to dam the Missouri. Going-to-the-Sun Highway in Glacier Park was a CCC project. Dozens of roads, parks, fairgrounds, and other landmarks of public infrastructure were also built.

After the end of the New Deal era, government spending in Montana ceased to be a civilian affair and was given over to the military. Malmstrom Air Force Base was built in Great Falls in 1942 as a transit base for war materials shipped to the United States' then-ally the Soviet Union. By the 1950s it became a strategic air base that was assigned fighter jets to defend against the then-enemy Soviet Union. In the 1960s Malmstrom became the first center for the Minuteman missile system. Two hundred Minuteman missiles were buried in silos under 23,000 acres of central Montana prairie by 1970,, pointed at equivalent missiles in Russia. Glasgow Air Force Base brought population and business to that eastern Montana town until the base was closed in 1969.

Decline of the West

While the 19th century saw the buildup of wealth and influence in western Montana, the 20th century brought decline to the mining and logging industries that had fueled early growth.

Butte struggled on until 1955, when open-pit mining began, diminishing overhead and overburden at the same time. The old Butte communities were ripped apart as steam shovels tore into the soil. The huge Berkeley Pit swallowed up Meaderville, which was once a lively Italian neighborhood sitting on a vein of low-grade copper ore. Although Berkeley Pit revived industry in Butte for about 20 years, by the 1980s the Anaconda Company had sold all of its holdings in Butte. A mile high and a mile deep, Butte contained just a century's worth of riches.

Likewise, centralized ownership and over-production have crippled the timber-products industry. Huge companies control much of the timber production in Montana and have put local lumber mills and logging companies out of business. Much of the good timber on easily accessible private and state lands has already been harvested. With the old-growth trees gone, local loggers and mills have had to bear the expense of retooling machinery to accommodate smaller trees. Even though the loss of jobs and revenue in logging towns is a result of market forces, environmentalists usually receive the blame.

Coal and Oil

The 20th century saw other mineral development come to the eastern prairies. Coal had been mined in Montana since the early days of settlement, but large-scale exploitation of the incredible reserves of fossil fuels waited until the railroads arrived. The Northern Pacific developed Red Lodge, and later Colstrip, as sources of fuel for its steam trains, and the Milwaukee built up Roundup as its source. After trains were converted to electricity, coal mining ceased for several years. However, as machinery and technology refined the techniques of strip mining, the vast reserves of coal in the Fort Union Formation in southeastern Montana became more attractive.

In the 1970s, energy companies proposed building four electric generators in Colstrip, with the power to be sold to markets on the West Coast. Battles erupted in courtrooms and communities as the breadth of the mining and environmental damage became clear. The issues surrounding development sundered many communities as the benefits of conservation and economic opportunity were debated. Despite grassroots opposition from ranchers, Indians, and environmentalists, the generators went in.

Oil and gas exploration also brought wealth to some eastern Montana communities. Refineries helped Billings boom during the 1970s, and towns such as Sidney, Broadus, and Baker escaped the worst of recent agricultural downturns because of the presence of large nearby oil reserves. Plans are in place to build a new wind- and coal-fired generating plant between Jordan and Circle.

Farming and Ranching

Bad years still follow good in Montana agriculture. A series of good years in the 1960s and early 1970s brought prosperity and high land prices. The family ranch and farm began to modernize after borrowing against the inflated real estate values of the land. Then drought hit again, and land values fell. Farmers and ranchers found themselves with unsecured loans. The drought, bad markets, and financial breakdown of the 1970s and 1980s became known as the Farm-Ranch Crisis, an echo of earlier times and of an ongoing cycle.

Government programs in the 1970s and 1980s were designed to help the family farm and ranch but were too easily manipulated by unscrupulous investors. Huge tracts of cheap drought-stricken grazing land were bought up solely for the government payments available for plowing it. The broken land, plowed but not planted, simply drifted on the wind across the prairies while the investment "farmers" pocketed the payments.

Farms and ranches are large and far between in Montana. Those that remain have long histories and many experiences of lean times. Most are still operated as family businesses, with the work and pleasures shared by several generations living together on one farm or ranch site. While during much of the 20th century agriculture became more specialized and reliant on production of only one commodity (usually cattle or wheat), rural Montana is taking on the future with its eyes cast backward. A ranch that raises cattle, sheep, hay, and wheat and keeps chickens and a milk cow not only has diversified products to sell but also goes a long way toward being self-sufficient. The repeated cycle of boom and bust, rain and drought will continue, but after surviving four generations in eastern Montana, farmers and ranchers don't pretend to be in it for the money.

The New and Really Wild West

As people have become increasingly disillusioned with urban life, more and more look to the rural West as a place to relocate. Montana, with its spectacular scenery, great fishing, and comparatively low cost of living, has become a mecca for this second wave of homesteaders. Ranchettes and subdivisions are latter-day homesteads, and celebrity ranchers such as Ted Turner and Brooke Shields were late-20th-century versions of the Copper Kings.

Movie stars aren't the only ones who had an impact on rural Montana in the 1990s. Anyone who followed the news at the end of the 20th century knows that Montana is also a haven for wild-eyed antisocial misanthropes and antigovernment individuals and groups. In 1995 the nation learned that Montana was so law-hating that its citizens couldn't even endure a speed limit (never mind that the state quickly gained the highest per capita vehicle death rate in the nation). The Unabomber, the Freemen, and other gun lovers made Montana seem like a breeding ground for nutcases. When coverage of these fringe elements coincided with the outbreak of mad cow disease in Britain, enterprising (and characteristically wry) Montanans began boasting on bumper stickers, AT LEAST OUR COWS ARE SANE. Finally, in 1998, the state governor actually made an address to the press pleading for people to understand that not everyone in Montana is a scofflaw or lunatic.

Of course, he was right: A visitor to Montana in all likelihood will meet only gracious, law-abiding, and friendly people who are genuinely glad to see people of all makes and models visit their state. But it's undeniable that Montana has had a real public-relations nightmare in recent years and that there must be a reason for certifiably crazy and dangerous people to take refuge in the hills. Perhaps the state's long-standing "live and let live" philosophy fits too nicely with contemporary currents of violence and disenfranchisement.

Antigovernment factions in Montana form two basic groups. One is part of the more general influx of white separatists and neo-Nazis into the Pacific Northwest, where they hope to found an Aryan homeland. These people are generally in extreme western Montana, near the Idaho border. The second group is the equally disturbing Freemen movement. These latter-day "patriots" are Second Amendment zealots with massive weapons arsenals who are coincidentally often just clinging to economic survival on bankrupt farms and ranches. Freemen members are absolutely contemptuous of what they see as governmental interference in their sovereign individual rights and have gone as far as to issue dead-or-alive warrants for duly elected county officials that have dared to cross their paths (usually in order to collect on debt).

This fringe group became front-page news when Freemen (and women) from across the West came streaming into Jordan, Montana, where they set up a headquarters at the ranch of a notable and vocal sympathizer. The Freemen established their own government and currency, issuing death threats and bounties on people they considered their enemies. After the Freemen shattered the small-town harmony of Jordan, issued millions of dollars in bad checks, and threatened the lives of the sheriff, county attorney, and others who fell afoul of their self-made new laws, the FBI moved in. After federal agents snatched up the ringleaders in a helicopter raid, the remaining Freemen settled in for a long siege on their ranch. After 81 days, the Freemen gave themselves up only when the FBI turned off their electricity and phone service. The locals speculate whether it was the lack of hot water or Internet contact that drove the Freemen from their lair.

And then there was the Unabomber. Ted Kaczynski was apprehended in 1996 at his tiny homemade 10-by-12-foot cabin near Lincoln, Montana, and charged with the antitechnology bombing crimes of the Unabomber. In a federal trial in Sacramento, Kaczynski pleaded guilty to four bombings in 1985, 1993, and 1995 that killed two people and maimed two others. His plea bargain resolved all federal charges against him growing out of a 17-year string of 16 bombings that killed three people and injured 29. In return for a guarantee that he will not be executed, Kaczynski agreed to accept life in prison or a federal psychiatric facility without the possibility of parole.

Then, in 1998, a part-time Montana resident named Russell Weston Jr. entered the federal Capitol building in Washington, D.C., and fired on a number of people, killing two security guards.

If travelers need any kind of assurance that they'll be safe from antiestablishment zealots while visiting Montana, at least consider that most of the crazy folk from Montana prefer to play out their lives of crime outside of the state. Chances are very good that all the people you'll meet in Montana are going to be welcoming and sane—or sane enough.

Government and Economy

GOVERNMENT

Montana became a territory in 1864 and a state in 1889. The original state constitution of 1889 reflected the mining and timber interests that dominated the early days of the state. Partly because of that document's datedness and partly because of the climate of political reform in the late 1960s, Montanans voted to draft a new constitution. The results of the second Constitutional Convention in 1972 were a reformist, populist set of laws that affirms that the state government exists by consent of the people and for their benefit. The privileges of business and industry were diminished accordingly.

Montana granted women's suffrage in 1916, four years before the passage of the 19th Amendment. Jeannette Rankin, the first woman representative in the U.S. Congress, was elected from Montana in the same year.

The Montana Legislature is a bicameral, biennial body. There are 56 counties. Since the 1990 census there is only one federal House member (down from two). One particularity of the Montana primary system is its open ballot. Voters are not asked to identify party affiliation to receive a primary ballot; instead, they receive a voting form from both the Democratic and Republican parties. In the voting booth the voter marks only one form, and both are deposited in the ballot box. The system has been both hailed as the truest form of democratic voting and denounced as the most open to political hanky-panky.

Reservation Self-Government

Indian reservations make up nine percent of Montana and, even though a substantial amount of this land may be owned by non-Indians, tribal law prevails within reservation boundaries. Indian reservations are recognized by the federal government as independent political units. Legal jurisdiction is therefore something of a puzzle on reservations.

Tribes have certain inherent sovereign rights. Tribes can run their own schools, regulate transport and trade, and have their own constitutions, legislative councils, and tribal court and police systems. The state cannot tax reservation land or transactions that occur on reservations. While such legal considerations may not seem crucial to the traveler, Montana has in effect seven independent political entities within its borders. Visitors need to be aware that certain state laws do not apply on reservations.

Those cheap gas stations advertising cheap cigarettes aren't found just inside reservations by chance. State fuel and cigarette taxes aren't levied on those products sold by tribal members within reservations. Some local roads on reservation land are maintained by the tribes. Do not automatically assume that there is public access; sometimes use is reserved for tribal members. For instance, some of the Crow Reservation is off-limits to non-Indians.

Not all areas are open for recreation. The state does not have authority to regulate hunting, fishing, and recreation on reservations. Tribes can issue their own licenses for hunting and fishing, and may levy a user fee for hikers and campers. If you are not a tribe member, always check with tribal authorities before crossing reservation land.

ECONOMY

Montana is a rural state. Agriculture, mining, and the timber industry were among the founding trades of Montana and remain among its most important. Tourism is increasingly lucrative, and service industries like trucking and medical-treatment centers are major employers. Because it is so far from coastal markets or other significant population centers, it is unlikely that Montana will quickly become anything but a source of raw materials. Transport costs make industry unprofitable in so remote a state.

Agriculture

Montanans make strict differentiations between farms and ranches: Farms raise grain, and ranches raise livestock. To the purist, any amount of cultivation degrades a ranch to a farm. Even though most people think of Montana as primarily an agricultural state, less than 10 percent of the population makes a living from farming and ranching. Still, recent census figures indicate that the number of farms and ranches in Montana is increasing slightly (there are more than 15,000). Their average income has declined over the last decade, however. Beef cattle production is the most common form of ranching, with sheep production remaining a steady alternative. Spring and winter wheat are by far the most common crops, with barley a significant third. Along the

Yellowstone River, corn, soybeans, and sugar beets grow in irrigated fields. In the Flathead Lake region, sweet cherry orchards augment the local tourist economy.

Mining

The state of Montana was born of prospecting and mining camps. However, the copper, silver, and gold that established the Montana economy are largely depleted. Traditional centers of mining, such as Butte and Anaconda, have fallen on hard times as the world market has moved elsewhere to find cheaper, more easily mined minerals. But it's not that Montana has given up mining; copper, silver, and gold are still produced, but with modern techniques that don't demand an entire city's workforce.

Montana remains rich in other mineral wealth: from the unpronounceable molybdenum to the sublime Yogo sapphire to ordinary talcum powder. Thirty-foot-thick veins of bituminous coal lie under much of southeastern Montana and are unearthed by modern strip-mining techniques at places like Colstrip. The Stillwater Mine is the only U.S. source for valuable platinum. Oil and gas wells dot the eastern prairies.

Timber

About half of Montana's open land is forested. However, early overcutting and slow regrowth have limited the state's competitiveness in the world timber market. Many locally owned independent mills have been forced to close when they can't compete against large corporate "timber product" conglomerates, whose efficient automated factories have transformed logging from a lifestyle to a job, and which have largely practiced extractive "cut and run" logging with little concern for the forests' future. The forests still provide a living for enterprising Montanans, though: Christmas tree farms are found in northwestern Montana, and log-home manufacturers have moved Montana into the first ranks of home-kit producers in the nation. More log homes are shipped each year to Japan than remain in Montana.

MONTANA'S LIVESTOCK

Montana is one of the largest livestock producers in the nation, with 65 percent of its land in agricultural production (although only 8 percent of the population is engaged in ranching and farming). Different breeds of livestock have been developed for different needs and different environments, and ranchers put a lot of thought into the types of animals they raise. For Montanans, livestock breeds are another coded system of meanings that characterize individuals: Just as there are Ford or Chevy families, there are Black Angus or Charolais families, and each means something in the system.

CATTLE

Black Angus are probably the most prevalent cattle breed in the state. Ranchers prize these all-black beef cattle for their milking ability on the short-grass prairie and for their hardy disposition. These qualities make Angus cows the preferred mother stock in many herds, especially for ranchers who choose to crossbreed. Red Angus are just what they sound like: a deep red-haired version of the Angus breed, which is native to Scotland.

Hereford cattle come either horned or polled (that is, naturally unhorned) and are distinguished by their red bodies and white heads and legs. Herefords are as traditional a breed as Angus and share many of the same attributes, but they are somewhat less popular nowadays because of the horns on the larger and more vigorous variety, and because the udders of white-fleshed Herefords can easily sunburn, particularly when there's snow on the ground, causing the mothers to reject the hungry advances of newborn calves. Longhorn cattle established Montana cow towns like Miles City, but these cattle from Texas proved to be too delicate for Montana winters. Longhorn cattle are raised today mostly for rodeo stock.

So-called exotic breeds were brought to the United States in the 1960s from Europe to introduce larger bone structures into local Hereford and Angus cattle. Federal laws forbade the direct importation of live breeding stock but not the importation of semen. Exotic cattle made artificial insemination of cows an everyday occurrence on Montana ranches. Because exotic breeds (most are named for the European region where they originated, like Maine-Anjou or Charolais) are much larger than the Angus or Hereford, they produce larger calves. But larger cattle demand more food and range; the economic benefit of exotic cattle depends largely on the condition of the range.

The number of dairy cattle has fallen because transportation costs and centralization

The People

The first residents of Montana arrived from Asia via the Bering Strait land bridge more than 14,000 years ago, at the end of the last ice age. These prehistoric people were the ancestors of the North American Indians. However, the Indians who now live in Montana were not native to the area: They were forced westward after being displaced by other tribes and white settlers from the east (see the following sections).

Montana was one of the last states to be settled by whites. Only after gold was discovered in the 1860s did people start to build communities and settle in the state permanently. In addition to the gold diggers from other western states, like California, where gold had already played out, the first towns were peopled by Southerners who had been displaced by the Civil War. Railroads and the Homestead Act made Montana's free acreage tempting to the thousands of immigrants who poured into the United States in the early 20th century. Many communities still retain their strong European heritage.

of processing has made Montana dairy herds uncompetitive. It is cheaper to ship in milk from out of state than to ship in the feed to support a dairy cow.

SHEEP

The war between sheep raisers and cattlemen was never as fierce in Montana as in other western states because in harsh and unpredictable climates, sheep have proved to be a sensible livestock adjunct to cattle ranching. As a commodity, sheep have two basic values: wool and meat. Sheep that are best for wool production are not the best for meat production, however. In fact, the qualities exist in inverse proportion to each other. The larger and meatier the sheep, the coarser the wool. While all sheep produce wool, the staples that can be spun into fabrics for suits fetch the highest prices. In a bad year, the cost of shearing the sheep may be greater than the fleece price of poor-quality wool.

Black-face sheep produce the most desirable carcass (the most meat per pound of grain), but the wool is almost worthless for quality fabric-making. White-faced polled sheep like Columbias and Targhees are the sheep man's choice for midquality fleece and good-quality carcasses. If it's wool you're after, then the Rambouillet, with its large curving horns and fine fleece, and the Merino are Montana's best wool breed. If the wool market isn't good, however, you can't expect top price for these breeds' comparatively small-framed lambs.

HORSES

Most jobs on most Montana ranches could be done by various machines or vehicles, but many Montanans persist in using horses for everyday work. It's part of the heritage, and besides, grain is cheaper than gasoline. Most stock horses are quarter horses, known for their endurance and speed over short distances. Appaloosas are the horses with the spots on their hindquarters. Draft horses appear on farms and ranches occasionally, as fuel prices and whimsy dictate. Driving a team and wagon to feed stock is not common, but certainly not rare.

HOGS

Pigs are the single livestock commodity that has no Old West antecedent, but they are prevalent. Most farmers keep pigs simply because the ratio of feed to profit is lower than with other livestock: Put simply, pigs can utilize food disdained by sheep or cattle. Compare it to a diversified investment portfolio. Like sheep, hogs can serve as a hedge against bad grain or cattle markets.

NATIVE AMERICANS

There are approximately 56,000 Native Americans, representing 11 different tribes, living in Montana today (nearly 14 percent of the state's total population). The majority live on reservations, which make up nine percent of Montana's total land area.

Native Americans are often lumped together as "Indians," with the assumption that one culture, language, and history link these people. However, the tribes that now live in Montana come from very different traditions, speak different languages, and have not always been friendly toward each other.

Kootenai

The Kootenai tribe had settled in the Kootenai River area by 1500, and there is evidence that they are descended from the area's prehistoric inhabitants. Their original range included the northwestern corner of Montana and adjacent areas of Alberta and British Columbia. As a people, the Kootenai are closely related to Indians of the Columbia Basin, although they speak a language seemingly unrelated to other languages of the area.

The Kootenai share the Flathead Reservation with the Flathead and Pend d'Oreille Indians. Approximately 1,500 Kootenai Indians presently live on the reservation.

SAY IT RIGHT: A GUIDE TO PRONUNCIATION

When in Montana, you might as well pronounce as the locals do. Don't get caught mispronouncing the following:

- Absaroka: ab-SOR-ka
- Absarokee: ab-SOR-kee
- Charlo: SHAR-lo
- Choteau: SHOW-toe
- creek: CRIK (almost always)
- Ekalaka: EEK-a-lak-a
- Garnet: gar-NET
- Havre: HAV-er
- Helena: HEL-en-a
- Hysham: HI-sham
- Kootenai: KOOT-nee

- Laurin: law-RAY
- Lima: LI-ma
- Makoshika: ma-KOE-shi-ka
- Marias: ma-RI-us
- Meagher: MAR
- Missoula: ma-ZOO-la
- Ronan: ro-NAN
- Rudyard: RUD-yerd
- Spokane: spo-KAN
- Winnett: WIN-et

Pend d'Oreille

These Salish-speaking people are closely related to tribes of the Pacific Coast, but they moved up the Columbia drainages into Montana many thousands of years ago. The Salish tribes were the first to welcome white missionaries to Montana, and St. Ignatius Mission was built in 1854 to minister to the Pend d'Oreille tribe's spiritual needs. The Pend d'Oreille largely retained the culture of Northwest coast Indians, although Plains Indians' influence was evident in some aspects.

Flathead

There is no satisfactory explanation for the term "Flathead," for these Salish-speaking people never practiced head flattening (though other Salish tribes did). The Flathead also differed from their Salish kinsmen by leaving the river valleys of the Columbia drainage and moving onto the plains of central Montana. Here they evolved a culture based largely on the buffalo while maintaining the religious and social traditions of the Northwest coast.

Like other Salish tribes, the Flathead were generally friendly to whites as they entered Montana. The tribe was moved from the Bitterroot Valley and settled on the Flathead Reservation in the Mission Valley.

Crow

The Crow were the first of the contemporary Indian residents to enter Montana from the east, arriving as early as 1600 in response to dislocations farther east. The Crow, or the Absarokee, originally lived in the Great Lakes region, where they lived in earthen lodges and practiced agriculture.

Having arrived first onto the Montana plains, the Crow had the most to lose as other tribes crowded into the state. They became sworn enemies of the Blackfeet and later the Sioux.

Blackfeet

Like other Plains tribes, the Blackfeet originally lived farther east, in the forests north of the Great Lakes. As they drifted westward across the Canadian prairies, the various

Blackfeet tribes evolved into a loose confederation of entities sharing a common language (an Algonquian dialect) and mutual defense of their hunting lands. These groups, later known as the Piegan, the Blood, and the Northern Blackfeet, combined to form the Blackfeet Nation, one of the largest and most feared Indian tribes.

The Piegan ventured farthest south, taking control of much of northern Montana by 1800. The Blackfeet were celebrated horsemen and warriors, and their social order was structured by membership in military societies. Men who were not militarily inclined were treated as women; first reported by French trappers, this cultural practice, called the *berdache,* was later found to be common in other aboriginal societies. Religious practice centered on the ritual Sun Dance and shamanistic powers derived from dreams and visions.

Gros Ventre

Meaning literally "Big Belly," Gros Ventre is a misnomer for a tribe more properly known as the Atsina. The Gros Ventre represent the northernmost tribe of the Arapaho and belong to the Algonquian linguistic family. After moving to the Montana plains from their Minnesota homeland in the late 1700s, they allied with the Blackfeet, sharing in their dominance over the prairies. The Fort Belknap Reservation was established in 1888 for the Gros Ventre and Assiniboin. The Gros Ventre tribe now claims about 2,500 members.

Assiniboin

The Assiniboin are a Siouan-speaking people who historically represented the most northerly of the Yanktonai Sioux in their original homeland north of Lake Superior. They were traditionally allied with the Cree against their common enemy, the Blackfeet. By the 1700s the Assiniboin had crossed into the present-day United States, where they established a territory in the northeastern corner of Montana where the state meets North Dakota. The 2,000-member tribe is today divided onto two reservations, Fort Belknap and Fort Peck.

Sioux

The Sioux, one of the largest Indian nations in North America, divides into three large linguistic groups: the Dakota, the Lakota, and the Nakota. All originally came from Canada and were pushed westward as white settlements displaced other tribes along the eastern seaboard. They arrived on the northern plains comparatively late, around 1800, when they settled in the Dakotas, southern Saskatchewan, and eastern Montana. They were regarded as a noble but fearsome people, skilled in battle and famed hunters of buffalo.

The Yanktonai Sioux settled around Fort Peck, and along with some Assiniboin kinsmen, became residents of that reservation when it was created in 1888. Today almost 10,000 individuals belong to the tribe.

Northern Cheyenne

The Cheyenne are a tribe of Algonquian linguistic ancestry who lived largely agrarian lives in the Minnesota area. Pressures from other tribes forced the Cheyenne westward, and in about a 25-year period they evolved from a people who cultivated corn and other grains and made pottery into a nomadic Plains culture predicated on buffalo hunting. About 1830, after reaching the Black Hills, the tribe divided, with one group moving south to Colorado and the other moving farther westward into traditional Crow territory. Today there are about 5,300 members of the Northern Cheyenne tribe.

Chippewa and Cree

The Chippewa and Cree originally lived in northern Michigan and southern Manitoba. On these northern prairies, the tribes lived close to French trappers and settlers. Intermarriage produced a culture and a people known as Métis. Like so many other native peoples around this time, they moved west in the mid-1700s in response to displacement in the east.

By 1818, when the U.S. border was established, there were estimated to be about

10,000–12,000 Métis people living on the prairies. In 1868 a Métis leader named Louis Riel declared the Métis land a separate province of Canada. His rebellion against English-Canadian authorities failed, and the Chippewa under their chief Rocky Boy along with some of the Métis moved south to Spring Creek, near Lewistown, Montana. In the following years, as the United States evacuated the Métis to Canada and the Canadians deported them back south, they were part of the "landless Indians" (Indians without a reservation) who wandered the West after the United States decided to forego its policy of granting reservations. The Métis, Chippewa, and the Cree were given a part of old Fort Assiniboine as a reservation in 1910.

THE IMMIGRANTS

The establishment of the huge silver and copper mines in western Montana in the 1880s called for a large and stable workforce, supplied mostly by immigrants. The mines demanded workers, and Europe had workers to spare. The population of Montana grew 365 percent from 1880 to 1890, largely as a result of immigration into Butte and Anaconda. Large numbers of Irish, Germans, Slavs, Italians, Finns, and "Cousin Jack" miners from Cornwall poured into Butte to work the mines. These foreign workers settled into separate ethnic neighborhoods, where traditional food, customs, and languages prevailed. Some Jewish immigrants moved to the thriving mining centers and set up retail establishments. In 1910 black settlers in Montana, most of whom lived in mining towns, numbered almost 2,000. Only after the establishment of Air Force bases near Glasgow and Great Falls in the 1960s were there more black residents in the state. Chinese immigrants were also attracted to Butte, where they set up laundries and restaurants. Although Butte's preeminence in Montana has dimmed, the early growth of immigrant populations in the mining communities established Roman Catholicism as the state's dominant religion, and Butte set a

standard of openness to immigrants that is still observed by Montanans.

The railroads brought settlers to the plains of eastern Montana. Ambitious campaigns by the Great Northern and the Milwaukee Road succeeded in luring thousands of farmers to cultivate the dry prairie. Between 1900 and 1910 the number of farms and ranches in Montana doubled, and while many American-born homesteaders settled in Montana during this time, immigrants had an especially strong influence in eastern Montana. By 1910 one quarter of all Montanans were foreign-born. Entire communities of Germans, Russians, and Scandinavians were founded as farms and towns sprung up alongside rail sidings, as did the telltale Lutheran church. Scots and Irish continued to settle the plains as ranchers and herdsmen. Today in northern and central Montana the names in small-town phone books read like similar directories in Norway, Sweden, or Scotland.

Even though droughts and the Great Depression worked to depopulate the Montana plains, the foreign character remains in communities founded by immigrant farmers and ranchers. Fifty thousand foreign-born settlers moved to the state from 1900 to 1920, while 120,000 American-born settlers did so. But during the droughts and bad markets of the 1920s, 10 times more American-born homesteaders than immigrants gave up and moved on. By 1930, people of foreign birth or first-generation Montanans made up 45 percent of the population.

Some foreign settlers moved to Montana expressly to form communities. Mennonite groups settled in Montana during the homesteading years, but many left after the state legislature, urged on by an organization called the Montana Council of Defense, drafted laws during World War I that forbade speaking the German language. Hutterites maintain 22 communities in Montana and currently number more than 2,000 adherents.

War policies have not always driven Montanans from the state. During World

War II, Japanese internees from California were shipped to the state to work in sugar beet fields. Some found Montana to their liking; farming communities along the Yellowstone are still home to Japanese families.

Like other Western states, Montana is now home to a growing population of Hispanics, many of whom work on farms and ranches. Hispanics now make up more than two percent of the state's population.

The Arts and Culture

If there is a Western culture, a lack of snobbery lies at its heart. Even in the literature it shows: A rancher's memoirs share a bookshelf with poems that don't rhyme. Both writers are from Montana, and natives brag on them both. Rural cafés often sell local arts and crafts, whether it's homemade pottery or country scenes painted on old saws—and locals will buy both. Montanans respect people who are creative; rare is the rural community that doesn't have a resident poet, painter, or musician. *L'art naïf* or kitsch? In Montana, as often as not, it's the urge to express that's admired; it's not polite to question the quality of the expression.

From pioneers who kept journals and sent letters back east, to fifth-generation ranchers, to established novelists who have found a home in the state, Montana's literary tradition is a source of pride to Montanans, who generally read a lot and who positively devour the work of regional writers. It's not surprising that Montana should harbor such a dynamic writing community. It's a small step to go from respecting the work of a local rhymester to welcoming a nationally known author to the farm next door.

LITERATURE

Any state that can fill a 1,150-page anthology with its literature is impressive. To have that become a regional best-seller points to a phenomenon. *The Last Best Place* chronicles the literary history of Montana, from Native American stories to modern cowboy poetry. Those who are unfamiliar with Montana's place in the literary firmament will be surprised at the number of writers who have had Montana addresses.

Early Writers

Montana literary history begins with the diaries and memoirs of early settlers and the transliteration of Indian tales. Teddy Blue Abbott trailed cattle up from Texas to Montana during the 1870s and 1880s and wrote *We Pointed Them North.* Andrew Garcia was a novice mountain man when he married a Nez Percé woman who just escaped after Chief Joseph's surrender at Bear Paw. In *Tough Trip through Paradise,* Garcia gives his version of the Nez Percé flight in the 1870s and describes what it was like for him to be an innocent among mountain men and Indians. Frank Bird Linderman got to know Crow chief Plenty Coups and Pretty Shield, a Crow medicine woman, and recorded their stories. *Indian Why Stories* and *How It Came About Stories* are his versions of Indian fireside tales.

Frontier photographer L. A. Huffman brought his camera to early eastern Montana; *Before Barbed Wire* by Mark Brown and W. R. Felton features his photographs and recounts Huffman's life. Evelyn Cameron was an English immigrant whose passion for photographing the early settlement of remote Terry, Montana, resulted in the book *Photographing Montana: 1894–1928* by Donna Lucey. Charlie Russell, whose greatest fame derives from his paintings of frontier Montana, also wrote books. His life straddled the open range and the homesteading eras. His book, *Trails Plowed Under,* recounts this period. Will James had a ranch south of Billings. Books like *Cow Country* were popular adolescent reading during the 1930s.

The Missoula School

The University of Montana at Missoula has

ANNUAL EVENTS

Here is a selective list of some of the most notable annual events in Montana.

JANUARY

- Last weekend – Montana Winter Fair, Lewistown. Just like a state fair, but no displays of fresh prize-winning tomatoes.

FEBRUARY

- Midmonth – Race to the Sky dog sled race, from Helena to Holland Lake and back. This 350-mile race crosses the Rockies, providing mushers with the sport's most mountainous course. Stay at Holland Lodge to watch the excitement.

MARCH

- Early – Rendezvous Cross-Country Ski Race and Winter Festival, West Yellowstone. Become one of the 600-plus skiers of all ages and abilities competing in courses ranging from 5 to 50K.

- Midmonth – C. M. Russell Western Art Auction, Great Falls. This is a huge event in Great Falls that has become a full-fledged arts festival.

- March 17 – St. Patrick's Day Parade, Butte. Experience Irish Montana at its wildest.

APRIL

- Late – International Wildlife Film Festival, Missoula. The whole community gets involved in this highly regarded festival.

MAY

- Third weekend – Miles City Bucking Horse Sale, Miles City. Unvarnished cowboy culture prevails when rodeo representatives shop for the West's wildest horses.

JUNE

- Third weekend – Custer's Last Stand Reenactment, Hardin. The central event of Little Bighorn Days, which also includes an arts festival, a dance, and a book fair.

- Late – Lewis and Clark Festival, Great Falls. Botanical walks, boat trips, bus tours, a cookout, and an intertribal Indian encampment make this a great time to visit Great Falls.

- Last Sunday – American Legion Rodeo, Augusta. This large one-day rodeo packs in a parade, a wild-cow milking, and a full day's worth of rodeo events.

JULY

- July 4 – Northern Cheyenne Powwow, Lame Deer. The Northern Cheyenne hold several powwows each year (including Memorial Day and Labor Day), but this is the big one.

- July 4 – Terry Rodeo, Terry. Local cowboys and cowgirls come in off the range for this rodeo, one of the state's oldest and most authentic, held in a real Old West town.

- July 4 weekend – Arlee Powwow, Arlee. This large gathering includes a parade, much dancing, and ceremonies honoring veterans, as well as gambling that runs the gamut from traditional stick games to video games.

- Midmonth – Yellowstone Boat Float, Livingston to Columbus. Retrace the return route of William Clark and his crew, with overnight stops in Big Timber and Reedpoint.

- Second weekend – North American Indian Days, Browning. Join one of the largest gatherings of U.S. and Canadian tribes for a long weekend of drumming, dancing, and socializing hosted by the Blackfeet Nation.

- Late July or early August – Montana State Fair, Great Falls. A big carnival, live horse racing, a PRCA Rodeo, livestock shows, and enough country music to keep you humming for the rest of your Montana vacation.

AUGUST

- First weekend – Sweet Pea Festival, Bozeman. Food, art, and entertainment take over downtown Bozeman (as if they hadn't already).

- Second week – Festival of Nations, Red Lodge. Since long before multiculturalism was the thing, Red Lodge has celebrated the town's ethnic diversity with this weeklong fair.

- Midmonth – Montana Cowboy Poetry Gathering, Lewistown. Not just poetry but music and storytelling to pass along the old-fashioned ways (sometimes told with a distinctly modern twist).

- Third week – Montana Fair, Billings; Northwestern Montana Fair, Missoula. More variations on the state fair theme.

- Third weekend – Crow Fair, Crow Reservation. This powwow draws about 25,000 participants from across the country.

- Third weekend – Eastern Montana Fair, Miles City. The fun includes rodeos, tractor pulls, a demolition derby, and a carnival.

SEPTEMBER

- Labor Day – Ashland Powwow, Ashland. Drummers and dancers from many tribes gather at this powwow.

- First Saturday – Big-game bow-hunting and game-bird season opens.

- Second weekend – Nordicfest, Libby. Celebrate the area's rich Scandinavian heritage with music, food, and cultural events.

- Third Sunday – Backcountry big-game season opens.

OCTOBER

- Third weekend – Northern International Livestock Exposition, Billings. Prep your prize bull for the NILE show, or just come for the rodeo.

- Fourth Sunday – General big-game season opens. Be sure to dress in blaze-orange before taking a walk in the woods.

NOVEMBER

- November 8 – Anniversary of Montana's statehood (1889).

DECEMBER

- First Saturday – Christmas parade, Bigfork. Bigfork glitters all through December, as the whole town decorates for the holidays.

had a seminal effect on serious writing in the state. In 1919 a writing program was established by Professor H. G. Merriam at the university, only the second such program in the nation. Merriam, who had left Colorado to attend Oxford University in England, returned west determined to promote regional Montana writing. He began the literary journal *Frontier and Midland.* His writing program flourished, soon growing to offer a Master of Fine Arts degree. Students have included A. B. Guthrie Jr., author of *The Big Sky,* and Dorothy Johnson, author of *The Man Who Shot Liberty Valance* and other popular Western stories.

The program has continued to attract many talented students and nationally recognized faculty. Poet Richard Hugo inherited the directorship of the writing program from Leslie Fielder in 1964 and remained until his death in 1982. Hugo had a tremendous influence on the development of Northwest regional literature. His poems speak of disappointment and abandonment in both life and the physical world, sometimes ending with a wry glimmer of hope. Joining Hugo at the U of M at one time or another were Madeline DeFrees, Patricia Goedicke, William Kittredge (who with Annick Smith edited *The Last Best Place*), William Pitt Root, and Tess Gallagher.

Missoula has also attracted writers whose connections with the writing program are more tenuous. Rick DeMarinis (*Under the Wheat*) did a stint as a mathematician before becoming a full-time writer. James Crumley, whose hard-boiled detective novels are frequently placed in the Northwest, still lives in Missoula. Norman Maclean, who wrote *A River Runs Through It,* an idyll to fly-fishing and the spirit, grew up in Missoula. James Welch, who spent his youth on the Blackfeet and Fort Belknap reservations, studied with Hugo. Welch wrote several fine contemporary and historic novels of Indian life, including *Winter in the Blood.* Another Missoulian by way of the Hi-Line is Deirdre McNamer, whose novel *Rima in the Weeds* is set among the missile silos of northern Montana. Malta-

area native Judy Blunt has written *Breaking Clean,* a vivid memoir of growing up female on a traditional cattle ranch. Debra Magpie Earling writes of her upbringing on the Flathead reservation in *Perma Red.*

Natives and Newcomers

Although there are writers scattered across the expanse of Montana, a principality of established authors has grown up around the town of Livingston, north of Yellowstone National Park. Thomas McGuane's novels, including *Keep the Change,* are Westerns filled with modern neuroses. McGuane lives in the area, as has Richard Ford (*Rock Springs*). Ford's *Wildlife* is set in Great Falls, and many of his stories are set in small Montana towns. Richard Brautigan, famous for *Trout Fishing in America,* was also a resident. Jamie Harrison writes Montana-based detective novels (*Going Local, Unfortunate Prairie Occurrence*) from her Livingston home.

In the Internet age, writers can live just about anywhere, and Rick Bass's book *Winter: Notes from Montana* chronicles the author's first winter in remote northwestern Montana. Bass has also written *The Ninemile Wolves,* a passionate book about wolves reestablishing themselves in Montana.

Not all Montana authors are imported. Joseph Kinsey Howard, a journalist and lightning rod for progressive politics in the 1940s, wrote a classic Montana history in *Montana: High, Wide and Handsome.* Ivan Doig's memoirs of his Montana boyhood (*This House of Sky*) and his fictional trilogy about Scottish ranchers in Montana (*Dancing at the Rascal Fair, English Creek,* and *Ride with Me Mariah Montana*) have garnered a wide readership.

Wallace Stegner, although not strictly a Montana writer, spent part of his boyhood in Montana and has written Western novels and memoirs such as *Big Rock Candy Mountain.* Wally McRae, eastern Montana rancher and conservationist, is admired on the cowboy-poet circuit. Another rancher-writer was Spike Van Cleve, who wrote with wit of the changing West in *A Day Late and a Dollar Short.*

To catch the latest-breaking literary movements in Montana, check out *Cutbank* at www.cutbankonline.org.

ART

Montana was visited in its earliest days of settlement by noted artists, who left a rich legacy of landscape and wildlife art. Early artist-explorers Karl Bodmer and John James Audubon passed through Fort Union and up the Missouri; their journals and paintings portray Montana before settlement.

Charlie Russell is the quintessential Montana painter. He knew the West from the inside, having lived the life of a cowhand for many years. A native of St. Louis, Russell came west during the days of the great cattle ranches and lived in the Judith Basin area of central Montana. He began by sketching in bars and around campfires. The lives of the Indians and cowboys that he encountered daily became his subject matter. He often traded his sketches for drinks, and after his death some of the best collections of his works were in bars. His studio in Great Falls is now the Charles M. Russell Memorial Museum. His works are also on display in the Montana Historical Society Museum in Helena.

The regional and Western tradition is still strong in Montana art. Ace Powell of Great Falls inherited the mantle of Charlie Russell and painted fine tableaus of the emerging West. A contemporary master of reproducing the light and shade of the Montana landscape is Russell Chatham. His carefully balanced scenes capture the expanse and intimacy of the Montana countryside. Gary Carter paints wildlife and Western scenes, while Clyde Aspevig concentrates on landscapes.

The Montana arts scene doesn't end with Western-themed painting and sculpture. The universities and the Montana Arts Council foster more experimental artists. In Missoula, Rudy Autio produced nationally recognized ceramic sculpture. Another former U of M professor was Walter Hook, a math professor turned painter. Hook developed a wry syntax of images, including buffalo, kites, and Easter eggs, that recur like visitants across his canvases.

John Buck and Debbie Butterfield are Bozeman-area artists whose work flirts with Western icons. Butterfield sculpts horses out of old signs or commercial media to achieve a haunting dissonance. Buck confounds Western art images, ready-mades, and methods—such as whittling—by incorporating them in aggressively modern constructions.

While the mountains allure writers, the prairies seem to attract—and inspire—visual artists. Far-flung ranches and small towns in eastern Montana harbor conceptual artists. Pat Zentz and Dennis Voss are ranchers who each employ quirky and experimental sculpture and assemblages to convey a sense of Montanan ritual and whimsy. Ted Waddell employs modern expressionistic techniques to paint the cows on his ranch, imbuing them with near-totemic presence. Gary Hornick's installations juxtapose isolation and a rich historicity.

A Missoulian who garnered fame as a poster illustrator is Monte Dolack. His easily recognizable movie and commercial poster paintings are avidly collected. Dolack's Missoula gallery markets his stylish and whimsical fine-art paintings and prints.

Regional Art Centers

Several Montana communities, some of them quite small, have community art centers. These host touring shows of regional art and frequently feature the works of local artists; the gift shop is often a great place to buy that special souvenir. You may be surprised at the sophistication of work turned out by a ranch wife or by a retired railroad worker. Look for regional art centers in Glendive, Miles City, Kalispell, Anaconda, Bigfork, Billings, Colstrip, Great Falls, Hardin, Helena, Lewistown, and Missoula.

Additionally, some towns have developed reputations as visual arts centers, and privately owned galleries proliferate. If you're planning a visual arts tour across Montana, you'll want to check out the private galleries at Bigfork,

Livingston, Bozeman, Big Timber, Missoula, Billings, and Red Lodge.

THEATER

While the most vital theaters in Montana are associated with the universities in Missoula and Bozeman, other community theaters are of note. Billings has two theater venues, and the Missoula Children's Theater has an excellent reputation throughout the Northwest.

Summer-stock theater is especially good in Montana. Bigfork's summer theater recruits many of its actors from the University of Montana. The Fort Peck summer theater also draws heavily from the Montana universities; the theater building is a lovely relic from the CCC days of the 1930s. Virginia City presents summer melodramas in a frontier opera house; West Yellowstone also has a summer family theater. Montana's "newest" summer theater is in Philipsburg—the Opera House Theater, built in 1891 but newly reopened.

Montana State University presents an ambitious Shakespeare in the Parks series. During summers, the troupe tours the entire state, including remote towns in eastern Montana, with its productions.

ESSENTIALS

Getting There

Montana is a long way from just about anywhere, and once you get there, it's a long way between stops. Although Montana has fine airline and bus service, and Amtrak's Empire Builder rolls along Montana's 550-mile border with Canada, the best way to visit the state is with your own vehicle. With so much territory to move around in, you'll want to wander freely.

By Air

There are no international airports in Montana with direct service to foreign destinations, except for regional flights to Alberta. The closest international airports are Seattle in the west, Denver and Salt Lake City to the south, Minneapolis to the east, and Calgary to the north. Billings is the major air hub in Montana and is served by most major western airlines. Missoula, Bozeman, Butte, Helena, Kalispell, and Great Falls are also served by major carriers.

By Train

Amtrak's **Empire Builder,** which travels daily between Chicago and Seattle and Portland, provides rail service to extreme northern Montana. Unfortunately, most of Montana's population and many of its popular tourist destinations are farther to the south (with the exception of

© PAUL LEVY

Glacier National Park). Public transport linking these northern-tier cities to the rest of the state is sketchy, partly because Amtrak has trouble keeping its trains close to their schedule. If you are dependent on public transportation or rental cars, make sure that your Amtrak destination at least offers bus service to other parts of Montana or has vehicles for rent.

By Bus

Greyhound buses (800/231-2222) travel along the interstate system, linking Montana to other regional centers. Buses travel east and west along I-90 and I-94, linking Chicago and Minneapolis to Portland and Seattle. One bus daily travels north and south between Billings and Denver. There is no longer bus service between Salt Lake City and Butte.

By Car

Montana's most traveled roads cross the state east to west. It's no coincidence that these roads parallel early explorer routes; then as now, most travelers come to Montana to get across it as expeditiously as possible. The I-94/I-90 corridor follows the Yellowstone and Clark Fork Rivers and is the most perfunctory route across the state. Dawdlers will prefer to cross the state along more northerly routes. Highway 12 follows the old Milwaukee Road line across central Montana; Highway 2 parallels the Canadian border on Montana's Hi-Line along the old Great Northern rail line. Highway 200 connects the dots between the two. The only major highway cutting north to south is I-15, which links Canada with Great Falls, Helena, and Butte, and extends to Salt Lake City.

Getting Around

There's no question that the best way to see Montana is by automobile. Traveling by public transport is certainly possible, as buses, trains, and planes traverse the state. But the population centers that serve as public transportation hubs are few in number, and who really goes to Montana to see the cities anyway?

By Air

The regional Big Sky Airlines is no longer in operation. There are rumors that Great Lakes Airlines (800/554-5111, www.greatlakesav. com) will pick up Big Sky's former routes. Check the website for confirmation. Another local carrier, Delta-associated SkyWest (800/453-9417), links Billings, Bozeman, Butte, and Helena, with seasonal summer flights to West Yellowstone.

By Train

Amtrak's Empire Builder (800/872-7245) crosses Montana's northern extreme along the old Great Northern rail line. By doing so, it offers service to none of Montana's major population centers. Unless you simply want

to traverse Montana, or have friends or rental cars lined up to ferry you southward (bus links at Whitefish aren't designed to meet the train), Amtrak isn't a very meaningful way to visit the state: You can't get there from here. The good news is that the Empire Builder skirts the southern edge of Glacier National Park and is reckoned to be one of the most scenic Amtrak routes. The independent traveler bent on kicking loose in Montana is best advised to hop off the train at either Spokane, Washington, or Williston, North Dakota, and rent a car.

By Bus

Greyhound buses (800/231-2222) hurtle along I-94 and I-90 and up and down I-15, traveling between Montana's major cities. However, Greyhound offers little service to smaller or remote communities after its pullback in service in 2004. Service along some of these routes, and to some smaller cities off the interstate grid, are served by **Rimrock Trailways** (800/255-7655, www.rimrocktrailways.com); tickets can be booked through Greyhound.

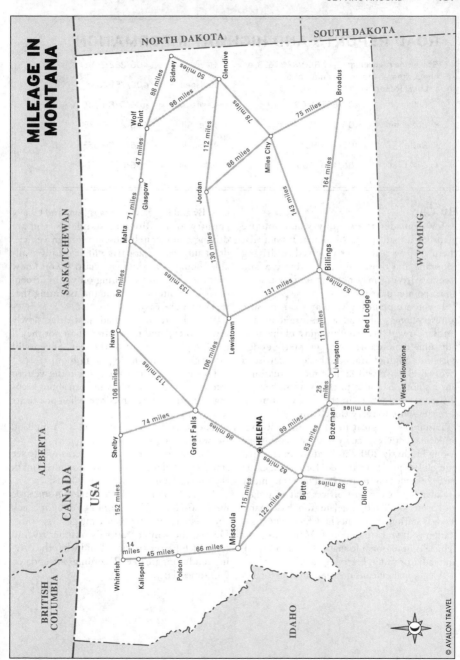

ROAD REPORTS AND HIGHWAY INFORMATION

Statewide recording: 511 or 800/226-7623, or check the website at www.mdt.mt.gov.
  Local Reports:

· Billings	406/657-0209	· Havre	406/262-5551
· Bozeman	406/586-1313	· Kalispell	406/751-2037
· Butte	406/494-9646	· Lewistown	406/538-1358
· Great Falls	406/453-1605	· Miles City	406/233-3638
		· Missoula	406/728-8553
		· Wolf Point	406/653-1692

By Car

A few considerations apply when you are planning a road trip to Montana. It's not that there are any real tricks involved in driving Montana, but those who are used to city and freeway driving may need some reassurance and a pointer or two.

If you are planning to rent a car, be sure to reserve one well in advance. Just about any regular car will serve you fine most of the time, but some remote dirt roads get pretty dodgy without a high-clearance vehicle. Likewise, a two-wheel drive will handle most situations, but it's not a bad idea to throw a tow rope in the trunk, and except in the dead of summer, it makes sense to carry tire chains.

Distances are great in Montana: Fill your tank frequently, especially in eastern Montana. Along Highway 200, hundreds of miles separate gas stations. Plan ahead. Don't assume that every little dot on the map will have gas; many are merely pioneer post offices that mapmakers haven't bothered to delete from base maps. Ask gas station attendants how far the next gas station is, if you are in doubt. Make sure your vehicle is in reasonable shape. Check tires, oil, and radiator water. Carry extra oil and water.

A less apparent consideration involves foreign cars. By and large, Montana is Ford and Chevy country. If, by Montana standards, you are driving a moderately obscure foreign vehicle, don't anticipate that parts will be readily available should a breakdown occur. If you know that the alternator is failing on your Citroën, don't head into rural Montana assuming that repairs will be easy.

If cattle are in the road, just drive slowly toward them, and more often than not they'll grudgingly move out of the way. Sheep will rarely give way in any logical fashion.

Logging trucks rule the roads in the western forests. It's wise not to be stubborn about keeping your piece of the roadbed when one bears down on you.

The speed limit in Montana is 75 mph on freeways, 65 mph on two-lane roads.

The white crosses that you occasionally see standing beside state highways do indeed mark the sites of fatal automobile accidents.

The state **highway information number** is 800/226-7623, TTD 406/444-7696, or check the website at www.mdt.mt.gov/travinfo. During the winter, call this number to find out which passes are closed and what the driving conditions are like. Recordings are updated 2–3 times daily.

Recreation

PUBLIC LANDS
Public lands, state and national forests, and Bureau of Land Management (BLM) land constitute roughly 35 percent of the state, opening much of the state up for recreation and a plethora of other uses.

State Parks
Montana operates more than 40 state parks (406/444-2535, http://fwp.mt.gov) focusing on both recreation and history. Many of the parks include campgrounds, which are open from mid-May to mid-September. Day-use fees for non-Montanans are $2–5 at most state parks, with an additional $12–15 for overnight campers. Some parks feature yurts, tepees, and cabins for rent. The state's parks are diverse, including historic ghost towns, Native American museums, and lakeside campgrounds.

U.S. Forest Service Lands
Much of the public land in Montana's western and southern mountains is administered by the U.S. Forest Service (406/329-3511, www.fs.fed.us/r1). Forest Service ranger stations are good places to get information on camping and recreation. All national forests contain developed hiking trails, and Forest Service roads in winter become de facto cross-country skiing trails. Most national forests also have developed trail systems for mountain bikers and can provide maps highlighting roads and areas best suited for backcountry cycling. Much of this land is also open to hunting in season—usually late September through November. Forest Service maps are good for exploring and for spotting hiking trails and campsites.

Forest Service campgrounds are widespread in western Montana. Fees range from free to $16, depending on the amenities (free campgrounds are those with a pit toilet and no running water—they're usually remote and rarely crowded). The Forest Service also rents out some rustic cabins and fire lookouts, usually for about $20–50 per night. Check the individual national forest's website for cabin descriptions, accessibility, information about what supplies you'll need to bring along, and details about reserving a cabin.

Wilderness Areas
Montana has 17 federally managed wilderness areas, roadless and closed to mechanized use, including mountain bikes. Designated wilderness areas are sometimes more heavily used than remote nonwilderness areas. Stop in at a Forest Service ranger station and ask which local trails they favor. In addition to the wilderness areas that fall under the jurisdiction of the Forest Service, there are several tribal wilderness areas in Montana. Before hiking or fishing on tribal land, be sure you have the necessary permits.

National Parks
Glacier National Park (www.nps.gov/glac) falls entirely within Montana, and its Canadian counterpart, Waterton Lakes National Park (www.watertoninfo.ab.ca), is directly above the border. Although the bulk of Yellowstone National Park (www.nps.gov/yell) is in Wyoming, three of the park's entrances, as well as its northern edge, are in Montana. Entrance fees are $25 for either Glacier or Yellowstone (or $80 for a year-long pass to any national park). This pays for a week's unlimited entrance into the specified park. An extra fee is charged to camp in park campgrounds.

PRIVATE LAND
Even though much of Montana is publicly owned, you sometimes need to cross privately owned land to *reach* public land. This is an issue especially for anglers and hunters, because access to the best streams and hunting grounds is often across private land.

Always ask permission to cross private land, especially when it's fenced and *always* if there is a NO TRESPASSING sign. Don't be surprised if you are asked to pay a small fee to cross private lands, especially in popular fishing areas such as the Madison Valley. In parts of eastern Montana, the state has agreements with private landowners to allow access to private lands for hunting purposes. However, you must have written permission to hunt on these lands and must report in to the landowner.

Most landowners are tolerant of people who ask permission to enter their land, but don't be surprised if permission is not granted. If a pasture is filled with cows and young calves, a rancher probably won't want people trooping through to fly-fish and certainly wouldn't allow someone in to start shooting rifles. Be considerate and polite and you'll usually get the permission you want. You may even make a friendly acquaintance with a real Montanan.

Tribal Lands

Each of Montana's seven Indian reservations is self-governing, and the state does not have authority to regulate fishing, hunting, or other recreational activities on tribal land. In fact, most reservation land is off-limits to all but tribe members. Remember that for many tribes, the land contains sacred sites and possesses a deeper significance to them than it may to you—it's perhaps more than just a cool place to race a mountain bike, in other words. Some tribes are more open to multiuse recreation than others; the Flathead reservation is generally open to nonmembers (as long as they have tribal permits), while the Crow reservation is generally off-limits to the public.

As you would for any privately owned land, always ask permission before trespassing. Tribal permits for hiking or fishing, if necessary, are generally available from most businesses on the reservation. They may be free or they may cost a small fee. When in doubt, call the tribal office to inquire about access and permits.

None of this information is intended to give the impression that reservations are closed to visitors or that tourism isn't welcome. Respectful visitors are welcome at powwows and other cultural and sporting events (Indian rodeos are especially enjoyable). Ask Travel Montana for a brochure on tourism on the state's reservations.

OUTDOOR PURSUITS
Hiking and Backpacking

In a state that's as big as all outdoors, don't be surprised to find that hiking and backpacking are the preferred outdoor activities. Long backpacking trips through national forests and wilderness areas are something of a rite of passage for many Montanans.

The most famous hiking area in the state is **Glacier National Park.** Even more so than Yellowstone, Glacier yields its wonders only to those who get out of the car and hike up its trails. However, in high summer the trails can be very busy and may therefore not deliver the wilderness experience you're looking for. Other areas to consider for longer backpacking trips are the **Bob Marshall Wilderness,** south of Glacier Park; the **Bitterroot Mountains,** south of Missoula; and the **Absaroka-Beartooth Wilderness,** north of Yellowstone.

The national forests are all laced with hiking trails, and the staff at any ranger station can help you put together a hiking trip that suits your interests, time limitations, and endurance.

Cycle Touring and Mountain Biking

There are plenty of opportunities for touring and mountain biking, from Glacier Park to the Pryor Mountains. Missoula is home to the **Adventure Cycling Association** (150 E. Pine, 800/755-2453, www.adventurecycling.org), a touring organization and advocacy group for cyclists. They lead rides across the state and the nation, and can answer questions regarding routes and conditions. Bozeman is another center for biking, especially mountain biking.

Leading local bike shops are usually noted in the text, and their staff members can offer plenty of good advice and route ideas. Many shops carry route maps showing local trails. Most National Forests have developed information and maps for mountain bikers, and ranger stations are another good place to seek advice.

In general, cyclists need to remember two things: Montana is a very big place, and it's a long way between towns, especially in eastern and central Montana. Weather is another consideration. Summer can be a short season, and inclement weather can blow in quickly. Also, much of Montana is windy.

The state Department of Transportation (406/444-9273, www.mdt.mt.gov/travinfo/bikeped) offers information for cyclists. It can provide information on the suitability of specific roads and on road-repair schedules.

Hunting

Hunters flock to Montana in the fall for elk, pronghorn, pheasants, deer, bear, and the occasional mountain lion or bighorn sheep. To hunt for certain animals—including moose, mountain sheep, and mountain goat—hunters need to enter special drawings. Nonresidents also need permits to hunt for antelope. For more information, contact **Montana Department of Fish, Wildlife, and Parks** (406/444-2535, http://fwp.mt.gov). If you'd like to enlist the aid of a hunting guide, check the website for recommendations on established outfitters, or contact the **Montana Guides and Outfitters Association** (406/449-3578, www.montanaoutfitters.org) for a list of licensed outfitters.

Fishing

Montana's streams and rivers are famous for their plentiful but wily trout. Although it's theoretically possible to fish year-round in lakes and large rivers, late June through October are the most popular months for fishing. The state maintains more than 300 fishing-access areas across the state. The basic fee for a fishing license is $18 for adult Montana residents and $60 for a nonresident year-long license (or $15 for a two-day license). A $10 nonresident/$8 resident conservation license is also required.

The list of blue-ribbon fishing streams in Montana is lengthy and includes such well-known (and now crowded) rivers as the Yellowstone, Bighorn, Madison, and Big Hole. However, these are just the famous fisheries; many other rivers and streams provide ample sport and fishing pleasure. Lake fishing is also popular, especially in northwestern Montana, with such bodies as Flathead Lake.

Even arid eastern Montana is a fishing destination, with famed walleye fishing in Fort Peck Reservoir and paddlefishing in the Yellowstone River near Glendive.

You don't have to hire a fishing guide or outfitter to fish in Montana, but if you're new to angling or would like to gain more skill as a fly-fisher, it's a good idea to enlist the aid of an outfitter. Also, access to fishing holes can be a problem, and a local outfitter can remove potential hassles that could otherwise ruin a quick fishing trip to Montana. Each chapter of this book includes the names of reputable fishing guides and fly shops.

Contact the **Montana Department of Fish, Wildlife, and Parks** (406/444-2535, http://fwp.mt.gov) for up-to-date information on licensing and season dates.

Skiing

Whitefish Mountain Resort (formerly Big Mountain), just outside of Whitefish, and Big Sky, some 30 miles south of Bozeman, are Montana's two big destination ski resorts. If you'd rather avoid the development but still can't resist the thrills of downhill, try one of the smaller ski areas outside Libby, Missoula, Bozeman, Anaconda, Darby, Dillon, Neihart, Red Lodge, or Choteau. The ski season generally runs from Thanksgiving through mid-March.

Once the back roads of National Forests are covered with snow, many of them become **cross-country** ski trails. The Forest Service distributes a list of ski trails, and local ranger stations have specific maps for their areas. Trails groomed for both standard cross-country skiing and "freestyle," or "skating," are maintained by lodges, such as the Izaak Walton Inn in Essex, and by individual communities, like the Rendezvous Trails in West Yellowstone. There may be a fee to ski on groomed trails.

For an overview of downhill and cross-country ski areas, contact **Travel Montana** (800/847-4868, www.wintermt.com) and request the *Montana Winter Guide*. This brochure also contains information about **snowmobiling.** Most ski resorts and all larger towns have ski, snowboard, and snowshoe rental facilities.

River Rafting and Floating

Montana's many rivers are popular for white-water rafting and more leisurely float trips. The most famous white-water rivers are the branches of the Flathead near Glacier National Park and the Gallatin and Yellowstone near Yellowstone National Park. These rivers are also popular with kayakers. Other river trips will take you to remote areas of wilderness reached only on multiday float trips. The Wild and Scenic designated portion of the Missouri, downstream from Fort Benton, is a favorite for naturalists and devotees of Lewis and Clark. The Smith River takes anglers through limestone canyons to otherwise unreachable fishing holes.

River trips are offered by many guide services, and boats can be rented in most river towns. For most multiday trips, advance reservations are required; in fact, for popular rivers such as the Smith, you'll need reservations many months in advance. Most white-water guide services offer day and part-day trips that require only a day's advance reservations.

Dependable and experienced guides are listed in the text. For a complete list of guides, contact the **Montana Outfitters and Guides Association** (406/449-3578, www.montanaoutfitters.org). Travel Montana's handy *Travel Planner* also contains a list of licensed outfitters.

Windsurfing hasn't been particularly developed in Montana, but occasionally a sail goes up on Flathead Lake. Strong winds on the Blackfeet Reservation and around Livingston have generated talk, if not actual windsurfing sites.

Horseback Riding and Cattle Drives

Resorts and guest ranches all generally offer horseback riding. Guided trail rides are the norm, although longer pack trips into the mountains are also scheduled. **Cattle drives** remain popular, with more than a dozen Montana ranches offering guests the chance to trail cattle from pasture to pasture or ranch to town. These trips usually involve several days of horseback riding, camping out on the prairie, and eating meals from chuck wagons.

Again, the **Montana Outfitters and Guides Association** (406/449-3578, www.montanaoutfitters.org) is a good place to start. A list of guest and dude ranches, as well as wagon train and cattle drive outfitters, is included in Travel Montana's *Travel Planner*.

Rockhounding and Prospecting

Explore the Treasure State with a pan or a bucket. Prospect for gold near Libby, or buy a bucket of dirt outside Helena or Philipsburg and pick through it in search of sapphires. Hunt for garnets in southwestern Montana, agates along the Yellowstone, and petrified wood in the Gallatin National Forest.

GAMBLING IN MONTANA

Several forms of gambling are legal in Montana, as any visitor to the state will instantly notice—many old-time bars, taverns, clubs, and lounges have all become casinos. Gambling is regulated by the state, which takes 10–15 percent of the proceeds from the various games—and makes about $300 million a year in the process.

While card rooms have always been legal—or at least tolerated—in Montana, electronic gambling has been legalized comparatively recently. Other forms of gambling, such as pari-mutuel and video-link horse racing, calcuttas, and shake-a-day dice games, are legal as well. Montana also participates in three multistate lotteries.

Card Room Games

In the back room of many an old-time bar is a well-burnished green felt table, usually watched over—with hawklike vigilance—by sharp-eyed denizens. At some cue—perhaps the arrival of a newcomer with fresh money, or the advent of a lucky omen—the game begins, often lasting long into the early hours of the morning.

All traditional forms of poker are legal; stud and draw are the favored games. There's a $300 pot limit. To play, you need to buy chips from the house; if you're lucky and win, you cash out your chips from the house. The house will keep its—and the state's—share.

Blackjack, pan, pitch, and other card games

in which the players bet against the house are *not* legal in Montana. Neither are most dice games—including craps—or "beat-the-house" games, such as roulette.

Keno, a hopped-up version of bingo, is legal, both as an electronic game and in its original form—as a barroom diversion. If you've ever wondered what that large checkered game board on the wall of an old bar is, you're probably looking at a lighted keno display.

While it's permissible to watch strangers play poker in the back rooms of bars, remember that there is frequently a lot of money at risk, tempers can be short, and often liquor has flowed liberally. Keep your mouth shut and act reverential. Don't do anything that might break the concentration of the players or that may be interpreted as interaction.

Electronic Games

Video poker is by far the most popular of the various kinds of electronic gambling in Montana. The whirring, ringing, and beeping of the machines have all but eliminated the gentle buzz of conversation in Montana watering holes.

To play video poker, you put a coin—usually a quarter—in the slot. A random five-card hand appears on the screen, and you decide which, if any, of the cards you want to keep. Press the corresponding buttons, then press a different button to receive replacement cards. The machine will let you know if you have any combination of winning cards. Should you win, don't expect a cascade of small change. Winning combinations earn points (which usually equal quarters). You decide whether to use your points to play more hands or to cash them out by contacting the bartender or game-room manager.

Other Legal Gambling

Pari-mutuel **horse racing** is popular at summer fairs. Some bars and clubs offer a more cutting-edge method of betting on horseflesh—video broadcasts of live horse races. You get racing forms, track conditions, lines at the betting booth—everything but the dust and the smell of horse sweat.

A more distinctly Montana form of legal betting is the **calcutta.** Usually held as a charity event, a calcutta involves auctioning off the performance of a sportsman, usually a rodeo contestant or golfer. If the cowboy you "buy" wins his event, then you get a share of his prize money, while the majority of the money raised from the auction goes to the charity.

As in other states, Indians on federal reservations have opened casinos that feature games not otherwise allowed by Montana state law. Under the confusing laws that govern activities on reservations, Native Americans can bypass restrictive state laws by invoking federal laws that recognize reservations as sovereign entities. Nevada-style casinos are present in several locations on Montana reservations.

SPECTATOR SPORTS
Rodeos

Most communities in Montana have rodeos at least once each summer, often on the Fourth of July, during the county fair, or sometimes just whenever enough interested parties come together in one place. "Little Britches" rodeos are held for grade-school children. High-school rodeo clubs are often the largest extracurricular groups in small towns. Intercollegiate rodeo is also popular—and a source of scholarships for Montana students. Bozeman hosts the national finals for intercollegiate rodeo.

Make every attempt to attend *some* rodeo. Rodeos are quintessentially Western but haven't yet become heavily commercialized. Be prepared to get hot and dusty, and be friendly. Summer rodeos are a community's way to visit with friends and family. Dates of rodeos are available from local chambers of commerce or from publications available from regional tourism bureaus.

Rodeos can be confusing to the first-time spectator. **Saddle-bronc riding** involves a cowboy staying on a saddled bucking horse for eight seconds. Similarly, in **bareback bronc riding,** the rider tries to stay aboard a bucking horse for eight seconds, but he has only a "rigging" (a very small seatless leather saddle) for assistance. **Bull riding** pitches an enormous bull, usually a Brahma, against a cowboy, who must ride the bull for eight seconds. The bulls and the horses in these events are strapped around their lower abdomen with a "flank cinch," which annoys the animals into greater bucking fits. In all events, the cowboy must make the ride using only one hand to hang on (using two hands, even briefly, results in disqualification). The cowboys are not judged on the length of their ride. If they make it the necessary eight seconds, the ride is then judged on its particular merits, including amount and quality of spurring (which further annoys the animal, increasing the bucking), the general comportment of the cowboy on the animal, and the fierceness of the animal's bucking.

In **bulldogging,** a steer emerges at full lope from the chute. A cowboy gives chase aboard a galloping horse, jumps from the horse to the steer, and wrestles the steer to the ground. Winners are determined by speed. **Calf roping** begins similarly, but the cowboy must lasso the calf, leap from his horse (while the horse keeps the rope taut), and tie three of the calf's legs to immobilize it for five seconds. Some rodeos also include **team roping,** where one of a pair of cowboys ropes the head and the other the hind legs of a steer.

In most rodeos, the sole cow*girl* event is barrel racing, in which riders zip in a cloverleaf pattern around three barrels. If the horse knocks over a barrel, five seconds are added to the contestant's time.

Other rodeo events include the **grand entry** at the beginning of the rodeo, wherein two young cowgirls "present the colors" (U.S. and state) while galloping around the arena on horseback. Every entrant who has brought a horse to the event immediately joins the flag bearers in the arena for a horseback national anthem.

Clowns are also a part of the rodeo. During the bull-riding event, irate bulls can turn on thrown addled riders and gore them. Clowns draw the bull's attention to themselves by teasing or throwing tractor inner tubes at the bull, while the dazed cowboy makes a safe escape.

Some rodeos also include **novelty events** such as wild-cow milking (first team with any milk at all wins), various kinds of racing, or some children's events such as greased pig contests or wild-sheep riding.

Montana Minor League Baseball

The only other spectator sport in Montana is professional baseball's Pioneer League (www.pioneerleague.com), which has been a crowd-pleaser here since 1939. Most of the players are recent draft picks, and the Pioneer League is their first real baseball job.

The Billings Mustangs (a farm team for the Cincinnati Reds), the Missoula Osprey (associated with the Arizona Diamondbacks), the Helena Brewers (Milwaukee Brewers), and the Great Falls Voyagers (Chicago White Sox) play in the Pioneer League's northern division.

Each team plays 70 games between mid-June and the end of August. Games are taken seriously, and fans often develop a rapport with the young players.

Accommodations and Food

ACCOMMODATIONS
Traditional Lodging

The recent tourism boom in Montana has brought a wide variety of lodging options to the state. Generally speaking, rooms in hotels and motels are rather expensive in the summer season and are often in short supply. Reserve rooms several days in advance, especially if you want a specific type of room or a special hotel. Especially around the national parks, but anywhere on a summer weekend, expect the lodging situation to be tight.

Prices in this guide reflect summer high season rack rates. These prices are usually for the least expensive standard room. Room prices will often change according to the night of the week (weekends may be more expensive). If you're traveling outside high season, expect to find cheaper room rates, especially in tourist areas.

The development of the interstate system has led to clusters of chain motels around the off-ramps on the edges of towns. Better deals on lodgings are often found away from these developments, along the old arterials. Also, don't dismiss staying at old downtown hotels. Some are renovated and reflect the splendor of yore; others, for the more daring, have survived as residential hotels. Chances are you'll have a unique experience.

Guest Ranches and Resorts

High-end resorts have begun to spring up across the state, many with the ambience of a country lodge or guest ranch. More traditional dude and guest ranches and hot-springs resorts, many with a lengthy pedigree, abound. There's scarcely a community in Montana now that does not offer some form of guest ranch accommodation. Some of these can be wonderfully rustic and located in beautiful rural settings, and most offer unlimited horseback riding in addition to other recreational activities. Some small guest ranches enjoy a quiet fame with a long-standing blue-chip (and even royal!) clientele. Hot-springs resorts vary from the full-blown convention-sized facilities, such as Fairmont Hot Springs, to modest mom-and-pop affairs. Some ski resorts like Big Sky and Whitefish Mountain Resort (formerly Big Mountain) have reputations that precede them. They are open year-round for hiking, fishing, and other summer activities.

Other guest ranches and resorts can be much more modest. Your rustic farm vacation might call for you to sleep in the sheep wagon. When you're deciding on a guest ranch vacation, ask plenty of questions on the phone before booking, and make sure that you're comfortable with the accommodations and facilities. The guest ranches and resorts recommended in this guide have each been inspected and represent good values; any of them should guarantee an enjoyable stay.

Another good source for information on guest ranches is the **Montana Dude Ranchers' Association** (1627 W. Main, Ste. 434, Bozeman, MT 59715, www.montanadra.com), which can provide information on its member ranches.

Bed-and-Breakfasts

Bed-and-breakfasts are found across Montana. Many are newly built and luxurious, with swimming pools, trendy New West decor, and hot tubs; others are located in historic homes or buildings and provide a wonderfully evocative insight into the Old West.

If you are among those people leery of B&Bs or have had bad experiences at homestays where it was too much like staying in the back bedroom under Aunt Lulu's watchful eye, rest assured that all of the B&Bs listed in this guide have been personally inspected and are heartily recommended. Another good source for information on quality B&Bs is the **Montana Bed and Breakfast Association** (www.mtbba.com), a self-policing membership organization whose accommodations are inspected and approved according to a rigorous standard of requirements. These standards provide for the highest degree of cleanliness, convenience, and

OUT OF THE WATER CLOSET

Montanans delight in finding alternatives to boring old "men" and "women" on the doors of bathrooms in bars and restaurants. Don't be fooled! A sampling:

- Bulls and Heifers (the Jersey Lily, Ingomar)

- Does and Bucks (Q-Ds, Jordan)

- Eski-Mas and Eski-Pas (Wades, Harlowton)

- Jackeroos and Jilleroos (the Longbranch, Dillon)

- Pistols and Holsters (the Dixon Bar)

- Pointers and Setters, with dog portraits (the Buckhorn Bar, Fort Peck)

comfort for the traveler and are regulated with regular inspections by the association.

Camping and RV Parks

If you're at all inclined toward camping, bring along your gear and head out to the wilds of Montana. Western Montana is especially well-endowed with public campgrounds in national forests and state parks. Tent campers need to plan ahead in other parts of the state if they want formal campsites, because public campgrounds thin out on the prairies. Ask to camp in town parks; the locals will be glad to have their parks appreciated. RV campers will find campgrounds in most towns. Fees in public campgrounds usually range from free to $17; privately owned campgrounds charge $10–30 per night (most have rudimentary facilities for tent campers).

In between a motel and a campground are Forest Service cabins and lookouts, which are rustic accommodations generally with outhouses and without bedding or cooking utensils. They normally rent for $25–50 per night. Contact the USDA Forest Service, Northern Region Office, 200 E. Broadway, Missoula, MT 59802, 406/329-3511, www.fs.fed.us/r1, for a cabin directory.

FOOD

Here's the stereotype, mostly true: Steaks are standard and usually good. Vegetarians manage to make do with the pervasive salad bars. Although the 1990s brought espresso machines to all corners of the state, be prepared for plenty of thin, often bitter coffee laden with sugar and powdered creamer.

There really isn't anything to justify the label "Montana cuisine." Dishes peculiar to the region usually bring changes to established entrées, which is not to say they're bad. Adding huckleberries to every dish does not a cuisine make. However, local beef and fresh Montana trout give even a teenage fry cook a chance for greatness.

Buffalo burgers are simply hamburgers made with ground buffalo meat; promoters claim buffalo is a leaner, more flavorful alternative to beef. Indian tacos load taco ingredients onto fry bread. Rocky Mountain oysters are more often threatened than served; served correctly, lamb or calf testicles are the quintessential offal meat, surprisingly palatable.

But even when restaurant fare seems unimaginative compared to cuisine on the coasts, the general quality of the food is quite good. Home cooking sets the standard, and simple unprepossessing food is often the best.

There are happy exceptions to the rule, however. Chefs have mastered sauces in some pretty out-of-the-way places: Where you least expect it—Chico, Broadus, Essex—you will find that isolated but enterprising cooks have established restaurants with sophisticated dining. The Flathead Valley is accumulating quite a collection of good restaurants; Bigfork can boast of being the culinary capital of the state.

Montanans like to eat out. Cafés and restaurants are social centers, and eating out is a way of combating isolation. The bar is another meeting place, and not just for adults. Entire families meet up at bars, where it's perfectly normal to stick to soft drinks.

Shopping

Montana has no sales tax, and you'll begin to like the idea of provisioning for the holidays while on vacation.

Gifts and Souvenirs

There aren't many places that evoke the Wild West as clearly as Montana, and a gift or souvenir that recalls the Western past makes a good keepsake. Almost every town will have a clothing store and saddlery featuring Western clothes. Pearl snap shirts, tooled leather belts, and other leather goods make nice and functional gifts. If you're wondering why cowboys and cowgirls look so good in their jeans, it's because the pants are Wrangler brand. Look for the Cowboy Cut jeans if you want to squeeze into something that's bound to get attention when you get back home. Likewise, Montana is a good place to buy a pair of cowboy boots. Several saddleries make boots to order; be ready to mortgage your house to pay for them.

Although none of Montana's Indian tribes has a long tradition of commercial arts or crafts, gift shops and galleries now feature the works of native artists. Look for silver or beaded jewelry and leather goods, as well as paintings on hide.

Other local artists and artisans show their works in local craft shops and galleries. Most of the larger towns across Montana—including Sidney, Miles City, Lewistown, Kalispell, Billings, and Glendive—have community art centers that feature the works of local people.

Montana is also a major center for Western art, especially for blue-chip bronze statuary and wildlife art. Bozeman, Livingston, Kalispell, Whitefish, Big Fork, and even such unlikely towns as Wisdom and Big Timber all feature world-class galleries.

Another good gift or souvenir idea is Montana food products. Native fruits and berries make up into delicious jams and jellies. Huckleberry and chokecherry products will make nice remembrances. Local honey is also common and easy to find. Local cherries and wild huckleberries find their way into a wide selection of candies and confections. On the other end of the food scale, dried jerkies and smoked fish are produced by small local companies.

Sporting Goods

Montana is a real mecca of recreation and sports, and several excellent manufacturers and stores have sprung up to serve the market. Again, without a sales tax, Montana may be a tempting place to buy these items.

Almost every little town in western Montana has a fly-fishing shop, complete with hand-tied flies and fancy rods and reels. The R. L. Winston fly rod company in Twin Bridges is especially famous, a place many anglers approach almost with the reverence of religious supplicants on a pilgrimage to a holy site.

Many ski shops turn into mountain bike shops by summer, and vice versa, and you can often get really good prices on skis or bikes if you visit Montana in the right season. Likewise, canoes and kayaks can get pretty cheap at the end of the season, when proprietors need to make room for snowboards.

While it's not a piece of sporting gear that the average reader will use often, nothing says Montana quite like a handmade saddle. The state is home to several famous saddlers, who make saddles to order for professional cowboys, celebrity ranchers, and anyone else capable of paying for them. Expect a handmade saddle to start at around $2,500.

Other Practicalities

CROSSING TO AND FROM CANADA

Of the 15 roads that cross from Montana into Canada, only three are open around the clock. Highways 93 and 15 and Road 16 (in the state's far northeastern corner) have 24-hour ports of entry. U.S. and Canadian citizens should carry their passports to cross the border—even if you can get across the border in one direction with a driver's license and a birth certificate, there's no guarantee that you'll get back across in the other direction. Everyone has stories of stranded travelers caught on the wrong side of the line.

Citizens of any other nation should be prepared to show a passport and the appropriate visas. Citizens of any country may be asked to provide proof that they have sufficient funds for their intended length of stay.

U.S. Customs

Customs allows each person over the age of 21 to bring 34 ounces of liquor and 200 cigarettes into the United States without paying duty. U.S. citizens are allowed to import, duty-free, $400 worth of gifts from abroad, and non–U.S. citizens are allowed to bring in $100 worth. Should you be carrying more than $10,000—in U.S. or foreign cash, traveler's checks, money orders, or the like—you need to declare the excess amount. There is no legal restriction on the amount that may be imported, but undeclared sums in excess of $10,000 may be subject to confiscation.

Canadian Customs

Adults (age varies by province but is generally 19 years) can take 40 ounces of liquor or a case of 24 beers as well as 200 cigarettes, 50 cigars, and 14 ounces of tobacco into Canada. You can bring in gifts totaling up to C$60 in value. Pistols or handguns cannot be taken into Canada, although hunting rifles can be.

TIPS FOR TRAVELERS
Travelers with Disabilities

For the most part, Montana complies with federal and state guidelines for handicap access. State and national parks feature accessible trails when possible, and most modern hotels provide barrier-free lodgings. However, Montana is a rural state, and you may find that facilities are less accessible off the beaten path.

Travel Montana has a TDD line at 406/841-2702.

Women Travelers

Although it's not the expected thing, there's little reason for a woman to feel uneasy about traveling alone around Montana. If you're not up to being outgoing, people will generally leave you alone. But if you get to feeling chatty or flirtatious, you're in real luck. You'll be a curiosity, and men and women alike will sit you down and spin tales, feed you, and make you grin. You do have to look out for weirdos, but they're usually about as much of a threat to the average female traveler as grizzly bears, and easier to deflect. If a place makes you nervous, do the smart thing and leave. On the whole, travel in Montana is exhilarating and ego-boosting for a woman on her own.

Gay and Lesbian Travelers

Like much of the mountain West, Montana is socially conservative, and open displays of affection by gay people won't be found endearing by the majority of natives. While there's no reason to anticipate open discrimination or hostility if you're openly gay, it's good to remember that Matthew Shepard was murdered in neighboring Wyoming—especially in bars, don't assume that everyone is going to think it's cool that you're gay. Don't ask, don't tell is a reasonable rule for gay people traveling in Montana.

That said, both Missoula and Bozeman have active but somewhat underground gay networks, largely because of their large student populations. Montana may seem on the surface more hospitable to lesbians than to gay men—to the untrained eye, there's not a lot of style and fashion differentiation between

MONTANA FASHION

While fashion may not appear to be much of a preoccupation in Montana, even this low-key style has its system. Here are a few clues to understanding the dictates of Montana chic.

In general, fashion is dictated by function. Ranchers dress the way they do because it's effective. Levi's are eschewed in favor of **Wrangler jeans,** for example. One cowboy claimed that Wranglers fit better over boot tops, but a more understandable reason is the seam: On Wrangler jeans, the seam runs down the outside of the leg; the seam running along the *inside* of a pair of Levi's can get pretty uncomfortable for a cowpoke on horseback.

Boots are still mandatory footwear. They provide necessary protection for the feet and calves while riding on horseback, and their high tops are prophylactic against snakebite. Boot-making is still a custom trade in several Montana towns.

Neck scarves are not just colorful accessories: They insulate against cold drafts in winter and dust and chaff the rest of the year.

Cowboy hats are still a popular hedge against the sun and wind: straw for summer and felt for winter. The hegemony of the cowboy hat, though, has been somewhat shaken by the rise of the baseball cap, although no one in Montana would consider calling a head covering by that name. Rather, net caps are known by the brand names they feature – call it a "Cat Cap" or a "King Rope Cap" – and they are both identified and justified within Montana fashion.

The prevalence of **pearl snaps** over buttons is as real as it is, sadly, inexplicable.

As in certain ornithological species, the male's attire is often more engaging than the female's. In marked differentiation from the men's, women's clothing tends to be made of synthetic fibers. It is probably a judgment on Montana couture that women's fashion generally reaches its apex in the menswear department. Women often look their best when they dress in the same clothes as men: jeans, plaid shirts, and boots.

Warning: *Do not try to duplicate Montana fashion.* Most attempts look as staged as they are. Getting yourself up in full Western regalia is probably not going to win you any extra points. While in Montana, just dress comfortably and – especially if you want to win the confidence or friendship of native Montanans – observe a few simple rules:

- Don't wear anything really trendy or goofy. This will put an extra barrier between you and the residents.

- Hot summer weather doesn't necessarily mean shorts for men.

- Shirtlessness is almost taboo.

- Err on the side of comfortable modesty. In Montana, this is considered an element of style.

young lesbians and young straight women out in the backcountry.

PRECAUTIONS

Montana is not a particularly menacing place; however, a few considerations may save the traveler unpleasant experiences.

Animals

Grizzly bears are found in Glacier and Yellowstone National Parks and in smaller populations in wilderness areas in much of the Rockies. When provoked—and it doesn't take much to rile them—grizzlies are vicious. Every year, it seems, someone is mauled by a grizzly, with deaths not infrequent. If you are traveling through grizzly country, check with local rangers for bear updates; areas in Glacier are often closed to hikers because of grizzly problems. Make noise as you hike to forewarn nearby bears; small "bear bells" hooked on packs are common noisemakers. Don't sleep near smelly food, such as bacon; hang food from branches away from tents. If possible, hike in a large group.

Mountain lions are not as aggressive as grizzlies, but as their territory is progressively whittled away, there is more lion-human contact. Mountain lions live in most of the Rocky Mountain region. While human adults are in little danger from mountain lions, small children—especially if unattended—can attract them. Montana newspapers report regularly on mountain lion attacks and sightings of lions stalking people. Again, safety lies in numbers.

Not all threats come from carnivores. **Moose** are great hulking animals given to spontaneous charges if surprised. **Buffalo,** either at Yellowstone Park or on private land, can be short-tempered if provoked. These animals are not vicious, but they are territorial and easily surprised. Be careful.

Rattlesnakes are common over the eastern two-thirds of the state. While a rattlesnake bite is rarely fatal these days, it's no fun either. If you are hiking anywhere in eastern Montana, it is imperative to wear strong boots with high tops. Watch where you step. Be especially careful around rocky promontories: Snakes like to sun themselves on exposed rocks. Rattlesnakes are not aggressive to humans; given their druthers, they will slink away, rattling. If you have never heard a rattlesnake rattle, don't worry that you might mistake it for something else. It is an instinctive human reaction to leap backward and shriek when you hear the rattle. When angered, however, rattlesnakes will coil and strike. If you are bitten, immobilize the affected area and seek immediate medical attention.

Be suspicious of overly friendly small mammals. Rabies is, as elsewhere, a real problem. If you are hiking in the vicinity of stock animals, especially cattle, it is wise to remember that bulls can be threatened by the presence of humans. Give them a wide berth.

Health and Wellness
In Montana, you'll find no unexpected health dangers, and excellent medical attention is readily available. However, in rural parts of the state, doctors and hospitals can be quite far apart, so it's a good idea to begin your journey

in good health and to take no unreasonable risks while traveling the state. The text gives emergency numbers to call should you need medical attention. *Note that in many rural areas the 911 number is* **not** *in operation.*

The greatest risks most travelers will face are related to weather and insect bites. Too much summer sun can lead to sunburn, especially at Montana's higher altitudes. Wear sunscreen. Heat exhaustion can also be a problem if you're struggling up a hot hiking trail in full sun. Be sure to drink plenty of water and slow down if you feel yourself overheating.

If you have insect bite allergies, don't mislead yourself into thinking that Montana's dry climate might be bug-free; it's not. An abundance of fierce insects awaits, and mosquito repellent is definitely recommended. Montana mosquitoes do not carry any diseases, but they can be annoying, and an infected bite can be both unsightly and painful.

Ticks pose some slight risk of diseases such as Rocky Mountain fever and Lyme disease. If practical, wear light-colored clothing so you can spot ticks more easily. When you're hiking through underbrush, wear long-sleeved shirts and long pants tucked into your shoes or boots. Apply an insect repellent containing DEET. Be sure to check your body for ticks after walking in the woods or grassy meadows—and look *everywhere* on your skin—especially in patches of body hair (also be sure to check pets for ticks). If you find a tick with its head imbedded, don't panic. Using tweezers or your fingers, pull gently and steadily on its body until the tick disengages. Do *not* crush the tick, burn it with a match, douse it in alcohol, or any other home remedy, because these actions can cause the tick to regurgitate bacteria into its bite, increasing your chance of infection.

Under no circumstances should you drink unfiltered or untreated water straight from streams, springs, rivers, or lakes. The microscopic parasite **giardia** lives in mountain streams and will happily take up residence in your lower intestinal tract. Giardia enters streams through the fecal remains of animals—especially beavers (which gives the condition its common nickname, "beaver fever")—and is prevalent throughout Montana.

Symptoms of giardia infection include stomach cramps, nausea, a bloated stomach, watery foul-smelling diarrhea, and frequent gas. Giardia can appear several weeks after exposure to the parasite. Symptoms may disappear for a few days and then return, a pattern which may continue. Tinidazole, known as Fasigyn or metronidazole (Flagyl), are the recommended drugs for treatment; both are prescription drugs. Either can be used in a single treatment dose. Antibiotics are not effective as a treatment.

Giardia is a fairly common summer affliction in the region. It has even been known to enter the water supply of entire mountain towns.

Weather

Weather extremes are common in Montana. When outdoors in high temperatures, remember to drink plenty of water. Native Montanans often take salt pills to prevent dehydration. Listen for weather forecasts: Sudden storms can blow in, causing rapid changes in temperature and wind conditions. Certain parts of Montana are known for their windiness: Great Falls ("the Windy City"), Livingston, and Cut Bank each deserve their reputation. If you are driving a high-profile vehicle, listen for wind warnings.

Winter cold is the greatest weather concern. Roads can be treacherous if snow-covered, and incremental melting leaves small, invisible patches of ice on the road. If you travel by automobile in Montana in the winter, make sure you have tire chains, and know how to put them on. Make sure you also have blankets or a sleeping bag, plenty of warm clothing, gloves, a shovel, a flashlight (days aren't long in the winter), and maybe even a paraffin heater. Carrying extra food and water is a good idea. Again, pay attention to weather and road reports, and don't take chances.

MONEY

Almost all Montana banks have ATMs, making it easy to travel without the hassle of traveler's checks. Credit cards are widely—although not universally—accepted.

Foreign Exchange

In short, don't depend on exchanging foreign currency or traveler's checks in Montana. While banks in the larger cities supposedly offer exchange services, the transaction is so out of the ordinary that you may be told to come back another day after they figure out how to do it. Save yourself time and hassle and change your money before getting to Montana. Or just use ATMs to draw money out of your foreign account.

Sales Tax

There is no sales tax or value-added tax (VAT) in Montana. It is one of three American states that do not levy a tax on products at the register (the others are Oregon and New Hampshire). Taxes on property and income, however, are steep.

The frequently dire financial condition of the Montana state government makes the sales tax a tempting revenue enhancer to some politicians, landowners, and advocates of public education. However, voters have repeatedly turned down the sales tax by referendum.

COMMUNICATIONS AND MEDIA

Montana may be remote, but you can use your cellular phone pretty much anywhere in the state. However, in more remote areas, the cell networks are often analog, not digital. Newer digital-only cell phones won't be able to pick up a signal. Most towns have a business with a fax machine you can use. Public libraries usually have computers for public use, including Internet and e-mail connections. Larger towns have business centers with computers, e-mail and Internet connections, and fax machines.

Media

The only national newspapers you can count on finding in Montana are *USA Today* and (to a more limited extent) the *Wall Street Journal.* Regional daily papers include the Billings *Gazette,* the Great Falls *Tribune,* the Butte *Standard,* and the *Missoulian.*

Regional newspapers do a poor job of

reporting national and international news. If you don't want to lose touch with the outside world, your best bet are the various **National Public Radio affiliates** across the state. These public radio stations are indicated in the text, usually under the Information heading. Translator stations carry public radio to pretty remote parts of Montana, so if you are hungry for *Morning Edition* or *All Things Considered,* try scrolling around the bottom end of the FM radio dial.

If you want to read up on Montana on a monthly basis, check out *Montana Magazine,* a high-quality monthly devoted to history, travel, and culture in the state. If you can't find it on your newsstand, contact the magazine for a subscription at P.O. Box 5630, Helena, MT 59604-9930, 888/666-8624, www.montanamagazine.com.

MAPS

The state highway department puts out a free road map that will suffice if you stick to paved roads. Request a copy from Travel Montana, the official Montana travel information source (301 S. Park Ave., Helena, MT 59520-0533, 406/841-2870 or 800/847-4868, www.visitmt.com).

For a more detailed look, the *Montana Atlas and Gazetteer* is a handy book of topographic maps covering the entire state. It's $19.95 and is available at most bookstores in Montana or from De Lorme Mapping (P.O. Box 298, Freeport, ME 04032, 207/865-4171).

National forest maps are invaluable for off-the-beaten-path travel in the western part of the state. Day hikers sticking to established trails will usually be able to navigate nicely with these maps, available at local ranger stations or from the U.S. Forest Service Northern Region Headquarters (P.O. Box 7669, Missoula, MT 59807, 406/329-3511); they're $5.95 from the government, a bit more if you buy them from a bookstore.

Serious backpackers and hunters will want U.S. Geological Survey quadrangle maps. Many sporting-goods stores carry these maps for the more popular areas; they can also be ordered directly from the USGS, Federal Center (P.O. Box 25286, Denver, CO 80225,

303/236-7477). It pays to do a little library research before contacting the USGS; they'll want to know the exact names of the maps you're ordering.

GENERAL INFORMATION AND SERVICES

The **area code** throughout Montana is **406.** The entire state is on mountain time.

Liquor stores are operated by the state and are closed on both Sunday and Monday. However, most bars are also licensed to sell liquor, beer, and wine, so you should have no trouble keeping in alcohol while in Montana. Wine is also for sale in grocery stores.

Most businesses are open from 9 A.M.–6 P.M. Monday–Saturday. In smaller towns, don't count on stores being open on Sunday.

Travel Montana

The state's tourism bureau can answer most questions about travel in Montana. Some of their brochures are invaluable. Especially vital is the *Montana Vacation Planner,* which contains complete listings of all the lodgings, campgrounds, outfitters, resorts, golf courses, ski areas, and pertinent addresses and phone numbers of institutions in the state. (Contact Travel Montana at 301 South Park Ave., Helena, MT 59520-0533, 406/841-2870 or 800/847-4868, www.visitmt.com.)

In addition, Travel Montana has divided the state into six regions. Each local unit also produces brochures about sites, history, and amenities.

Governmental Organizations

The following federal, state, and regional services can provide detailed information on Montana. They will be happy to fill your mailbox with free informational brochures:

- **U.S. Forest Service,** Northern Region, P.O. Box 7669, Missoula, MT 59807, 406/329-3511, www.fs.fed.us/r1.
- **Bureau of Land Management,** 222 N. 32nd Ave., Billings, MT 59101, 406/255-2888, www.mt.blm.gov/bifo.

REGIONAL MONTANA TOURISM INFORMATION

Contact the following regional tourist offices for information about Montana.

- **Russell Country:** 406/761-5036 or 800/527-5348, www.russell.visitmt.com

- **Custer Country:** 406/346-1876 or 800/346-1876, www.custer.visitmt.com

- **Glacier Country:** 406/873-6211 or 800/338-5072, www.glacier.visitmt.com

- **Gold West Country:** 406/846-1943 or 800/879-1159, www.goldwest.visitmt.com

- **Missouri River Country:** 406/653-1319 or 800/653-1319, www.missouririver.visitmt.com

- **Yellowstone Country:** 406/556-8680 or 800/736-5276, www.yellowstone.visitmt.com

---

- **Department of Fish, Wildlife, and Parks,** 1420 6th Ave., Helena, MT 59620, 406/444-2535, http://fwp.mt.gov.

- **Glacier National Park,** West Glacier, MT 59936, 406/888-7800, www.nps.gov/glac.

- **Yellowstone National Park,** Yellowstone National Park, WY 82190, 307/344-7381, www.nps.gov/yell.

- **Montana Historical Society,** 225 N. Roberts, Helena, MT 59620, 406/444-2694, www.his.state.mt.us.

- **Montana Outfitters and Guides Association,** P.O. Box 1248, Helena, MT 59624, 406/449-3578, www.montanaoutfitters.org.

- For **road conditions,** call 800/226-7623.

RESOURCES

Suggested Reading

DESCRIPTION AND TRAVEL

Alwin, John A. *Eastern Montana: A Portrait of the Land and Its People*. Montana Geographic Series, no. 2. Helena: *Montana* magazine, 1982. A broad overview of the people, sights, and regions of eastern Montana, in text and photos.

Federal Writers' Project of the Work Projects Administration for the State of Montana. *Montana: A State Guide Book*. State of Montana: Department of Agriculture, Labor, and Industry, 1939. New York: Hastings House, 1949. Long out of print, but it's worth snaring a copy at a used-book store.

Gildart, R. C., ed. *Glacier Country: Montana's Glacier National Park*. Montana Geographic Series, no. 4. Helena: *Montana* magazine, 1990. An introduction to Glacier Park and its natural history, with ample illustrations and intelligent text.

Gildart, R. C. *Montana's Flathead Country*. Montana Geographic Series, no. 14. Helena: *Montana* magazine, 1986. Colorful histories, a look at the environment, and splendid photos define the area around Flathead Lake.

Gildart, R. C. *Montana's Missouri River*. Montana Geographic Series, no. 8. Helena: *Montana* magazine, 1985. Text and photographs celebrate the Wild and Scenic Missouri.

Meloy, Mark. *Islands on the Prairie: The Mountain Ranges of Eastern Montana*. Montana Geographic Series, no. 13. Helena: *Montana* magazine, 1986. Pictures and text about the often-ignored mountains in eastern Montana.

Mullan, John. *Miners and Travelers' Guide to Oregon, Washington, Idaho, Montana, Wyoming, and Colorado via the Missouri and Columbia Rivers. 1865.* New York: Arno Press, reprinted 1973. One of the earliest travel guides to the region, filled with colorful stories of the opening of the West.

Schneider, Bill. *Montana's Yellowstone River*. Montana Geographic Series, no. 10. Helena: *Montana* magazine, 1985. An enthusiastic portrait of the Yellowstone River, with a strong conservationist cast.

Tirrell, Norma. *Montana*. Oakland, Calif.: Compass American Guides, 1991. An easy-reading and attractive guide that provides a good overview of Montana sights and culture.

HISTORY

Brown, Mark H., and W. R. Felton. *Before Barbed Wire*. New York: Bramhall House, 1956. A commemoration of the life of L. A. Huffman, the frontier photographer who captured on film the era of the Indians and the open range.

Cheney, Roberta Carkeek. *Names on the Face of Montana*. Missoula: Mountain Press, 1983. When you must know how Twodot and Ubet got their names, check this book.

Chesarek, Frank, and Jim Brabeck, eds. *Montana: Two Lane Highway in a Four Lane World*. Missoula: Mountain Press, 1978. A western Montana eighth-grade class created this one-volume history of Montana; now out of print, it may be the single best overview of the colorful history of the state, told with energy and insight.

Connell, Evan S. *Son of the Morning Star*. New York: Harper Collins, 1984. Story of the Battle of Little Bighorn.

Garcia, Andrew. *Tough Trip Through Paradise*. Sausalito, Calif.: Comstock Editions, 1967. Maybe it's true, maybe only half so, but it's a whale of a story about mountain men and Indian life in 1878.

Fritz, Harry, Mary Murphy, and Robert Swartout. *Montana Legacy: Essays on History, People, and Place*. Helena: Montana Historical Society Press, 2002. A lively compendium of essays on Montana history and culture.

Howard, Joseph Kinsey. *Montana: High, Wide, and Handsome*. Lincoln: University of Nebraska Press, 1943. A lively and opinionated history.

Malone, Michael P., and Richard B. Roeder. *Montana: A History of Two Centuries*. Seattle: University of Washington, 1991. Now the accepted text on Montana's history, it is authoritative, rich in vignettes, and almost punchy.

Rinehart, Mary Roberts. *Through Glacier Park in 1915*. Niwot, Colo.: Roberts Rinehart Publishers, 1983. An early account of horsepacking through the park.

Spitzer, Donald E. *Roadside History of Montana*. Missoula: Mountain Press, 1999. Learn the fascinating history of Montana as you motor across the state.

Thompson, Larry. *Montana's Explorers*. Montana Geographic Series, no. 9. Helena: *Montana* magazine, 1985. It's not all explorers; the focus is on naturalists, including Lewis and Clark and Prince Maximilian of Weid.

Vichorek, Daniel N. *Montana's Homestead Era*. Montana Geographic Series, no. 15. Helena: *Montana* magazine, 1987. A mix of reminiscence and history, regarding the huge influx of homesteaders during the early 20th century.

West, Carroll Van. *A Traveler's Companion to Montana History*. Helena: Montana Historical Society Press, 1986. An excellent roadside historical companion.

NATIVE AMERICANS

Bryan Jr., William L. *Montana's Indians*. Montana Geographic Series, no. 11. Helena: *Montana* magazine, 1985. Historical and contemporary sketches.

Eagle/Walking Turtle. *Indian America*. Santa Fe, N.M.: John Muir Press, 1991. Tribal histories and cultural information for visitors.

Ewers, John C. *The Blackfeet: Raiders on the Northwestern Plains*. Norman: University of Oklahoma Press, 1958. An anthropological study of the Blackfeet, this is fascinating reading for nonanthropologists too.

Hungry Wolf, Adolf and Beverly, compilers. *Indian Tribes of the Northern Rockies*. Skookumchuck, B.C.: Good Medicine Books, 1989. Tribal histories from Indian and non-Indian sources.

Lowie, Robert H. *Indians of the Plains*. Lincoln: University of Nebraska Press, 1954. An anthropological look at all the Plains tribes.

Miller, David Humphreys. *Custer's Fall: The Indian Side of the Story*. Lincoln: University of Nebraska Press, 1957. An enthralling retelling of the familiar Custer story based on Indian documentation.

Morgan, R. Kent. *Our Hallowed Ground: Guide to Indian War Battlefield Locations in*

Eastern Montana. Bloomington, Ind.: Authorhouse, 2004. A guide to sites of battles and skirmishes between Native Americans and white forces.

Wilfong, Cheryl. *Following the Nez Percé Trail.* Corvallis: Oregon State University Press, 1990. An absolutely wonderful, well-thought-out, and moving book that will enhance any trip intersecting with the Nez Percé Trail.

LEWIS AND CLARK

Ambrose, Stephen. *Undaunted Courage.* New York: Simon & Schuster, 1996. Scholarly, readable account of the Corps of Discovery, focusing on Lewis.

Cutright, Paul Russell. *Lewis and Clark: Pioneering Naturalists.* Lincoln: University of Nebraska Press, 1969. Lewis and to a lesser extent Clark were the first to write of Montana's flora and fauna. Cutright's narrative draws the reader into the observations of prairie dogs and candlefish.

De Voto, Bernard, ed. *The Journals of Lewis and Clark.* Boston: Houghton Mifflin, 1953. Of the one-volume versions of the journals, this is the best.

Duncan, Dayton. *Out West.* New York: Viking Penguin, 1987. Along the Lewis and Clark Trail in the 1980s.

Lavender, David. *The Way to the Western Sea.* New York: Harper and Row, 1988. One of the West's most noted historians gives the fascinating details of the Lewis and Clark story.

NATURAL SCIENCES AND THE ENVIRONMENT

Alt, David, and Donald W. Hyndman. *Roadside Geology of Montana.* Missoula: Mountain Press, 1986. A comprehensive road-by-road guide to Montana's unique geology. For those willing to read slowly, there's a wealth of information.

Anderson, Bob. *Beartooth Country.* Montana Geographic Series, no. 7. Helena: *Montana* magazine, 1984. An environmentally conscious look at Montana's highest country.

Bass, Rick. *The Ninemile Wolves.* Livingston: Clark City Press, 1992. Passionate book-length essay chronicling wolves' return to northwestern Montana.

Chronic, Halka. *Pages of Stone: Geology of Western National Parks and Monuments, Vol. 1: Rocky Mountains and Western Great Plains.* Seattle: The Mountaineers, 1984. A clearly written and untechnical geology of the West, including Yellowstone and Glacier National Parks.

Dingus, Lowell. *Hell Creek, Montana: America's Key to the Prehistoric Past.* New York: St. Martin's Press, 2004. The story of rich fossil digs in eastern Montana overlain by a tableau of Jordan-area personalities and politics.

Ferguson, Gary. *Montana National Forests.* Billings and Helena: Falcon Press, 1990. A guide to Montana's 10 national forests, amply illustrated.

Fischer, Carol and Hank. *Montana Wildlife Viewing Guide.* Billings and Helena: Falcon Press, 1990. A guide to 113 designated refuges and habitats where Montana wildlife is most easily viewed.

Gildart, Robert C., and Jan Wassink. *Montana Wildlife.* Montana Geographic Series, no. 3. Helena: *Montana* magazine, 1982. An illustrated study of Montana's wildlife heritage and its many ecosystems and species.

Hart, Jeff. *Montana: Native Plants and Early Peoples.* Helena: Montana Historical Society, 1976. Well-illustrated and engagingly written, this is the best book on ceremonial and medicinal plant usage by native Montanans.

Horner, Jack, and James Gorman. *Digging Dinosaurs.* New York: Harper Collins, 1990. Read this before visiting Choteau or the

Museum of the Rockies and you'll be able to keep up with the seven-year-olds.

Kavanagh, James. *Montana Trees and Wildflowers.* Phoenix: Waterford Press, 2005. A pocket-size guide to Montana's flora, good for young naturalists.

Manning, Richard. *Last Stand.* Salt Lake City: Gibbs Smith, 1991. Manning went after the story of logging in Montana and lost his position as the *Missoulian*'s environmental reporter.

McEneaney, Terry. *Birders' Guide to Montana.* Helena: Falcon Press, 1993. Montana's best birding sites and tips on planning a birding trip.

McMillion, Scott. *Mark of the Grizzly.* Helena: Falcon Press, 1998. Well-told stories of grizzly attacks on humans. Dare you to read it in the tent.

McPhee, John. *Rising from the Plains.* New York: Farrar, Straus, Giroux, 1986. OK, so it's about Wyoming. It's still a good read, and the most lucid account of Rocky Mountain geology in print.

Peacock, Andrea. *Libby, Montana: Asbestos and the Deadly Silence of an American Corporation.* Boulder, Colo.: Johnson Books, 2003. A well-researched and very readable account of the public health tragedy in Libby.

Reese, Rick. *Greater Yellowstone.* Montana Geographic Series, no. 6. Helena: *Montana* magazine, 1984. One of the best of this series, with a strong focus on environmental issues.

Schneider, Andrew, and David McCumber. *An Air That Kills.* New York: G. P. Putnam's Sons, 2004. The shocking story of widespread asbestos poisoning in Libby, by the *Seattle Post-Intelligencer* reporter who brought attention to the issue.

Van Bruggen, Theodore. *Wildflowers, Grasses, and Other Plants of the Northern Plains and*

Black Hills. Interior, S.D.: Badlands Natural History Association, 1971. A good guide to the plant life of Montana's arid plains, with photographs.

RECREATION

Bach, Orville. *Hiking the Yellowstone Backcountry.* San Francisco: Sierra Club Books, 1998. Pick a trail and leave the crowded roads of Yellowstone National Park. Also contains backcountry information for mountain bikers, canoeists, and cross-country skiers.

Feldman, Robert, and Montana Hodges. *Rockhounding Montana.* Billings and Helena: Falcon Press, 2006. Feldman breaks the state into over 50 rock-hunting regions, complete with maps.

Fischer, Hank. *Paddling Montana.* Billings and Helena: Falcon Press, 2008. A comprehensive guide to floating 26 Montana rivers.

Fothergill, Chuck, and Bob Sterling. *The Montana Angling Guide.* Woody Creek, Colo.: Stream Stalker, 2002. Comprehensive guide with river maps and fishing tips.

Green, Stewart M. *Back Country Byways.* Billings and Helena: Falcon Press, 1991. A guide to Bureau of Land Management-designated scenic back roads throughout the West.

Henkel, Mark. *The Hunter's Guide to Montana.* Billings and Helena: Falcon Press, 1985. A sensitive guide to hunting in Montana, with a focus on the process of becoming acquainted with wildlife.

Grossenbacher, Brian and Jenny. *Fly-fishing Montana: A No-Nonsense Guide to Top Waters.* Tuscan: No Nonsense Fly Fishing Guidebooks, 2007. A good guide for first-time Montana fly-fishers.

Holt, John. *Knee Deep in Montana's Trout Streams.* Boulder, Colo.: Pruett Publishing Company, 1991. Holt's books (he also authored *Waist Deep in Montana's Lakes* and *Reel Deep in Montana's Rivers*) include frank discussions of environmental and cultural issues affecting Montanans; they're also chock-full of fishing advice.

Holt, John. *Montana Fly Fishing Guide East: East of the Continental Divide.* Guilford, Conn.: Lyons Press, 2002. A guide to top fishing holes in eastern Montana.

Holt, John. *Montana Fly Fishing Guide West: West of the Continental Divide.* Guilford, Conn.: Lyons Press, 2002. A guide to top fishing holes in western Montana.

Kilgore, Gene. *Ranch Vacations.* Berkeley, Calif.: Avalon Travel Publishing, 2005. A comprehensive guide to guest and dude ranches throughout the West.

McCoy, Michael. *Mountain Bike Adventures in the Northern Rockies.* Seattle: The Mountaineers, 1989. Some of the West's best trails for the mountain biker.

Rudner, Ruth. *Bitterroot to Beartooth.* San Francisco: Sierra Club Books, 1985. Indispensable for serious hikers in southwestern Montana, and good environmental reference for casual hikers or readers.

Schneider, Bill and Russ. *Hiking Montana.* Billings and Helena: Falcon Press, 2004. Descriptions and maps of 100 hikes, mostly in western Montana.

Thompson, Curt. *Floating and Recreation on Montana Rivers.* Lakeside, Mont.: Curt Thompson, 1993. Thorough milepost guide to the state's 81 rivers.

Wilderness Adventure Press. *Montana's Best Fishing Waters: 170 Detailed Maps of 34 of the Best Rivers, Streams, and Lakes.* Belgrade, Mont.: Wilderness Adventure Press, 2006. In-depth maps of top Montana fishing holes.

Williams, Rebecca, ed. *Roads and Trails of Waterton-Glacier International Peace Park: The Ruhle Handbook.* Billings and Helena: Falcon Press, 1995. An update of George Ruhle's noteworthy logbook of the park.

LITERATURE

Bass, Rick. *Winter: Notes from Montana.* Boston: Houghton Mifflin Company, 1992. Journals of the author's first winter in far northwestern Montana.

Bevis, William W. *Ten Tough Trips: Montana Writers and the West.* Seattle: University of Washington Press, 1990. One of the first works of literary criticism solely on Montana writers.

Blew, Mary Clearman. *All But the Waltz.* New York: Viking Penguin, 1991. Blew's family came to Montana in 1882. These affecting essays trace their lives in the Judith Basin country. Also look for her collections of short stories *Runaway, Lambing Out, Sister Coyote,* and a memoir, *Balsamroot.*

Cannon, Hal, ed. *Cowboy Poetry: A Gathering.* Salt Lake City: Peregrine Smith, 1985. A historical overview of cowboy poetry.

Cannon, Hal, ed. *New Cowboy Poetry: A Contemporary Gathering.* Salt Lake City: Peregrine Smith, 1990. An anthology of the best of today's cowboy poets.

Crumley, James. *The Last Good Kiss.* New York: Random House, 1978. Follow hard-boiled Montana detectives around the seedy sides of the West in this book—and in *Dancing Bear* and *The Wrong Case.*

Ford, Richard. *Wildlife.* New York: Atlantic Monthly Press, 1990. A Great Falls teenager watches his father go off to fight fires and his mother take up with another man.

Frazier, Ian. *Great Plains.* New York: Farrar, Straus, Giroux, 1989. A wonderful conglomeration of Frazier's rambles across the historical and contemporary plains.

Fromm, Pete. *Indian Creek Chronicles: A Winter in the Bitterroot.* New York: Lyons and Burford, 1993. Good memoir to read by a toasty fireplace. Fromm has also written the novels *How All This Started* and *As Cool As I Am.*

Garcia, Andrew. *Tough Trip Through Paradise.* Sausalito, Calif.: Comstock Editions, 1967. Discovered in 1948, this is the powerfully written chronicle of the 1878 Montana frontier penned by a white man who lived with Native Americans.

Guthrie Jr., A. B. *The Big Sky.* Boston: Houghton Mifflin Company, 1947. Classic, unvarnished tale of a young man living the Western life.

Hugo, Richard. *Making Certain It Goes On.* New York: W. W. Norton, 1984. Hugo's collected poems. For a change of pace, try Hugo's detective novel, *Death and the Good Life,* which hopscotches between the lower Flathead River and Portland, Oregon.

Kittredge, William, ed. *Montana Spaces.* New York: Nick Lyons Books, 1988. Evocative essays by the likes of Thomas McGuane and Gretel Ehrlich with perfect black-and-white photos by John Smart.

Kittredge, William, and Annick Smith, eds. *The Last Best Place.* Helena: Montana Historical Society Press, 1988. This 1,158-page compendium anchors down every Montanan's bedside table. From Native American myths to Paul Zarzyski's modern cowboy poems, it's all here.

Krakel, Dean. *Downriver: A Yellowstone Journey.* San Francisco: Sierra Club Press, 1987. The eclectic chronicle of a float trip down the full length of the Yellowstone River.

Maclean, Norman. *A River Runs Through It.* Chicago: University of Chicago Press, 1976. The classic novella of fly-fishing and two brothers' love and doomed relationship.

McGuane, Thomas. *Keep the Change.* Boston: Houghton Mifflin, 1989. Tough, sensitive guys try to set their lives straight in Deadrock, Montana (which is a lot like Livingston).

McMurtry, Larry. *Lonesome Dove.* New York: Pocket Books, 1985. A masterfully written epic of the last days of the great Texas cattle drives, told from the point of view of faded but wisecracking cowboys. Also from McMurtry, *Buffalo Girls* is an engaging saga of Calamity Jane and her gang.

Raban, Jonathan. *Badlands.* New York: Vintage Books, 1996. Rambling narrative that examines the homesteading movement on the eastern Montana plains.

Stegner, Wallace. *Wolf Willow.* New York: Viking Press, 1962. Stegner spent his youth on a homestead just north of Montana, in Saskatchewan.

Stockton, Bill. *Today I Baled Some Hay to Feed the Sheep the Coyotes Eat.* Billings and Helena: Falcon Press, 1983. Vignettes by a Montana-raised, Paris-educated writer and illustrator on the vicissitudes of sheep ranching.

Van Cleve, Spike. *A Day Late and a Dollar Short.* Kansas City: Lowell Press, 1982. The full-spirited reminiscences of one of Montana's foremost dude ranchers and storytellers.

Welch, James. *The Indian Lawyer.* New York: W. W. Norton, 1990. A Blackfeet lawyer in Helena finds his life suddenly very complicated…it's a page-turner with good insights. Welch's other novels include *Fools Crow, Winter in the Blood,* and *The Death of Jim Loney.*

MAGAZINES

Montana magazine is published in Helena and is a good collage of history, photography, travel information, discussion of current issues, and whatnot. You're warned: It can become addictive reading. Call 800/821-3874 in Montana or 800/654-1105 out of state for subscription information.

Montana Outdoors is published by the Montana Department of Fish, Wildlife, and Parks and contains the latest information on fishing, hunting, and recreation, and of course, great photography. Call 800/678-6668 for subscription information.

ATLAS

Montana Atlas & Gazetteer. Freeport, Maine: DeLorme Mapping Co., 1994. A handy collection of topographic maps covering the entire state.

Internet Resources

www.visitmt.com

The website of **Travel Montana,** the state tourism bureau, with lodging, destinations, events, and much, much more.

http://lewisandclark.state.mt.us

Information on Montana and its many Lewis and Clark sites and celebrations.

www.montanakids.com

Games and resources for kids.

www.wintermt.com

Information on Montana ski areas and winter recreation.

http://fwp.mt.gov

The **Montana Fish, Wildlife, and Parks** site, with information on state parks, wildlife, and recreation.

www.fs.fed.us/r1

The **U.S. Forest Service Region 1** encompasses Montana, and this site provides information on recreation and camping in Montana's public forests.

www.mt.blm.gov

The **U.S. Bureau of Land Management (BLM)** office for Montana provides information on national monuments and hunting on public lands.

www.montanaoutfitters.org

Start here with the **Montana Outfitters and Guides Association** site if you are planning a hunting, fishing, or guided backcountry vacation.

www.montana.com

Links to Montana businesses, publishers, organizations, and Montana legislators.

www.kufm.org

The **Montana Public Radio** site, with information on public radio programming in the state.

www.umt.edu (University of Montana); www.montana.edu (Montana State University)

In addition to enrollment information and links to various departments, you can also reach each university library through these addresses.

www.montanamuseums.org

A listing of contact information for Montana museums from the **Museums Association of Montana.**

www.his.state.mt.us

The state's best museum, the **Montana Historical Society,** also has an excellent online book and gift shop.

http://hotelstravel.com/usmt.html

Listings of all of the major hotels, motels, and B&Bs in Montana.

www.mtbba.com

Comprehensive listing from the **Montana B&B Association** of member bed-and-breakfasts.

www.mdt.mt.gov/travinfo

Check the **Montana Department of Transportation** site for Montana road conditions.

Index

290-291; Missoula 35-37; Musselshell Valley 348-349; Northwestern Montana 43-44, 46, 95-97, 99, 101, 102-103; Paradise Valley 240-242; Polson 66; reading suggestions 477-478; Red Lodge 251-252; Southeastern Montana 274-275; sporting goods stores 467; Swan Valley 74-78; Townsend 199; Troy 96-97; Upper Clark Fork River Valley 154; Upper Missouri Lakes 200-201; Waterton Lakes National Park 136, 138; West Yellowstone 261-263; Whitefish 86-87, 90-91
outfitters: general discussion 462; Bitterroot Valley 54; Blackfoot Valley 80; Broadus 306; Cooke City 255; Dillon 176; Fort Peck 368; Fort Smith 320-321; Gardiner 244; Lone Mountain Ranch 229, 230; Miles City 291; Missouri River 403; Smith River 343; Townsend 199; West Yellowstone 262
Outlaw Trail: 373
Overwhich Falls: 57

P

Pablo National Wildlife Refuge: 63
Pachcephalosaurus: 15, 303
paddlefish: 293, 295, 296
Painted Rocks Lake: 58
paleontology workshops: 15, 415-416
Paradise: 45
Paradise Lake: 102
Paradise Valley: 239-243
parasailing: 368
Paris Gibson Square Museum of Art: 393
park naturalist evening programs: 120-121, 140, 266
passports: 468
pasties: 157
Peet's Hill: 209
Pelican Fishing-Access Site: 247
Pend d'Oreille Tribe: 446
The People's Center: 63
performing arts: 195, 210, 284, 454
Peterson Lake: 53
petrified forests: 267-268
petroglyphs: 285-286
pets, traveling with: 112
Philipsburg: 20, 142, 161-162
Phillips County Museum: 362
Piccadilly Museum of Transportation: 150
Pictograph Cave State Monument: 270, 279-280
pictographs: Augusta 418; Billings 279-280; Gates of the Mountains 201; Great Falls 393;

Kalispell 81; Missouri Headwaters State Park 217-218
Piegan Pass: 132
pigs: 445
pikas: 429
Pine Butte Swamp Preserve: 416
Pintler Lake: 167
Pintler Scenic Route: 158-163
Pioneer Bar: 178
Pioneer Mountains: 168-169
Pioneer Mountain Scenic Byway: 168
Pioneer Park: 280
Pioneer Town: 356, 372
pishkun: see buffalo jumps
Pishkun Reservoir: 416
Plains: 45
plains region: 422-423
planning tips: 10-13; *see also specific place*
plants: general discussion 425-426; Glacier National Park 109; Northwestern Montana 30; Yellowstone National Park 257
Plenty Coups, Chief of the Crows: 310, 342
Plentywood: 373-375
pocket gophers: 427
Polebridge: 117
police departments: *see* emergency services; *specific place*
Polson: 14, 64-67
Polson-Flathead Historical Museum: 65
Pompey's Pillar National Monument: 12, 270, 285-286
Pony: 19, 218-219
Poplar: 371
Poplar Museum: 371
population: 444-449
Porcelain Basin: 265
post offices: Billings 284; East Glacier 130; Helena 198; Missoula 41; *see also specific place*
Potosi Hot Springs: 19
Powder River: 305-306
Powder River Historical Museum: 305
Powell County Museum: 156
Power Block: 192
powwows: Flathead Reservation 62, 68; Missoula 41; Northern Cheyenne Reservation 315
Prairie County Museum: 297
prairie dogs: 245-246, 427
prairies: 337, 425, 427-428
Pray: 19, 242
precipitation: 424
Preston Park: 125-126

Map Index

www.moon.com

DESTINATIONS | ACTIVITIES | BLOGS | MAPS | BOOKS

MOON.COM is all new, and ready to help plan your next trip! Filled with fresh trip ideas and strategies, author interviews, informative blogs, a detailed map library, and descriptions of all the Moon guidebooks, Moon.com is all you need to get out and explore the world—or even places in your own backyard. As always, when you travel with Moon, expect an experience that is uncommon and truly unique.

MAP SYMBOLS

▬▬ Expressway		🝱 Highlight		✗ Airfield		⚲ Golf Course	
▬▬ Primary Road		○ City/Town		✈ Airport		🅿 Parking Area	
▬▬ Secondary Road		◉ State Capital		▲ Mountain		▰ Archaeological Site	
▬▬ Unpaved Road		⊛ National Capital		✦ Unique Natural Feature		⛪ Church	
------ Trail		★ Point of Interest					
·········· Ferry		• Accommodation		⚑ Waterfall		⛽ Gas Station	
▬▬ Railroad		▼ Restaurant/Bar		⚑ Park		🟰 Glacier	
▬▬ Pedestrian Walkway		▪ Other Location		⬛ Trailhead		Mangrove	
⫶⫶⫶ Stairs		⋀ Campground		⛷ Skiing Area		Reef	
						Swamp	

CONVERSION TABLES

$°C = (°F - 32) / 1.8$
$°F = (°C \times 1.8) + 32$
1 inch = 2.54 centimeters (cm)
1 foot = 0.304 meters (m)
1 yard = 0.914 meters
1 mile = 1.6093 kilometers (km)
1 km = 0.6214 miles
1 fathom = 1.8288 m
1 chain = 20.1168 m
1 furlong = 201.168 m
1 acre = 0.4047 hectares
1 sq km = 100 hectares
1 sq mile = 2.59 square km
1 ounce = 28.35 grams
1 pound = 0.4536 kilograms
1 short ton = 0.90718 metric ton
1 short ton = 2,000 pounds
1 long ton = 1.016 metric tons
1 long ton = 2,240 pounds
1 metric ton = 1,000 kilograms
1 quart = 0.94635 liters
1 US gallon = 3.7854 liters
1 Imperial gallon = 4.5459 liters
1 nautical mile = 1.852 km

MOON MONTANA
Avalon Travel
a member of the Perseus Books Group
1700 Fourth Street
Berkeley, CA 94710, USA
www.moon.com

Editor: Tiffany Watson
Series Manager: Kathryn Ettinger
Copy Editor: Christopher Church
Graphics Coordinator: Tabitha Lahr
Production Coordinators: Amber Pirker, Tabitha Lahr
Cover Designer: Tabitha Lahr
Map Editor: Kevin Anglin
Cartographers: Chris Markiewicz, Jon Niemczyk
Indexer: Judy Hunt

ISBN-10: 1-59880-014-0
ISBN-13: 978-1-59880-014-2
ISSN: 1537-579X

Printing History
1st Edition – 1992
7th Edition – March 2009
5 4 3 2 1

Front cover photo: © David Stoecklein/CORBIS

Interior photos: Page 1 beef cattle © Bill McRae; Page 6 Yellowtail Reservoir © Bill McRae; Page 7 Choteau © Bill McRae; Page 8 The Beartooth Highway © Judy Jewell; Page 8 bear © Judy Jewell; Page 9 Miles City © Bill McRae; Page 9 electric engine, Harlowtown © Bill McRae; Page 9 The Graves Hotel © Bill McRae; Page 10 © Paul Levy; Page 11 © Judy Jewell; Page 12 © Bill McRae; Page 13 © Bill McRae; Page 14 © Judy Jewell; Page 16 © Judy Jewell; Page 17 © Judy Jewell; Page 18 © Paul Levy; Page 19 © Judy Jewell; Page 21, Courtesy of the Izaak Walton Inn; Page 23 © Judy Jewell; Page 24 © Judy Jewell

Printed in the United States by RR Donnelley

KEEPING CURRENT

If you have a favorite gem you'd like to see included in the next edition, or see anything that needs updating, clarification, or correction, please drop us a line. Send your comments via email to feedback@moon.com, or use the address above.

ABOUT THE AUTHORS

W. C. McRae

Bill McRae was raised in the badlands of eastern Montana, in a ranching community noted for Old West nonconformity and lawlessness. It's no wonder that he was on the run for most of his university years: from Montana to Scotland, on to France, back to Canada, and then to England. This wayward youth didn't help him much in the job market; over the years he has worked in jobs as varied as bookstore manager, catering chef, tile setter, remodeler, bartender, and bovine artificial inseminator. Nearly all these jobs subsidized him at one time or another while he struggled to establish himself as a writer.

Bill's first travel guide was *Moon Montana,* and of all his books it remains his favorite. He grew up in an immigrant family steeped in the history of Montana – one grandfather of Prussian Jewish extraction helped push the railroad across central Montana, while another emigrated from Scotland to start a sheep ranch in the Big Dry Country. The matriarchy had its own stories of emigration, homesteading, and the Great Depression. This confluence of traditions meant a youth spent listening to family tales. Bill grew up in a household rich with sagas: the early railroad, friendships with Charlie Russell, open-range cowboys, sheepherders, outlaws, and cattle drives. For this son of the West, capturing the essence of Montana's rugged yet courtly spirit was both a challenge and a therapy.

Bill is the co-author of several travel guides, including *Moon Utah* and *Moon Zion & Bryce* (both with Judy Jewell). He has also edited books for National Geographic and Mobil Guides and has written for websites like GORP.com and Expedia.com. In his spare time he earns money by writing polemics for a high-tech PR company. He makes his home in Portland, Oregon, and loves nothing more than setting out on a nice, long road trip with *Cosi fan tutte* playing on the car stereo.